T0300391

Climate Change and Legumes

Global climate change has created unprecedented challenges for human civilization due to its widespread adverse consequences, including a reduction in crop yield and threatening food security across the globe. Among the crop plants, legumes have great potential for ameliorating global warming since they can reduce carbon emissions by lowering reliance on the application of chemical fertilizers, by increasing nitrification and carbon sequestration in soil, and by providing protein-rich diets to both humans and livestock. This book identifies the extent of climate-induced stresses on legume plants and focuses on achieving food security through sustainable agricultural practices.

This book compiles recent research findings and reviews on climate-related problems, the potential of legumes in ameliorating the impacts of climate change, as well as better management of agricultural land and practices for achieving environmental sustainability and food security.

This book will serve as a guideline for scientists, agricultural practitioners, and policymakers working to achieve food security and better management of climate-induced stresses in agricultural interventions. It will also be useful as a reference book for researchers and students of both graduate and postgraduate levels. Furthermore, this book will provide enhanced knowledge about the mechanisms of yield and stress tolerance of legumes as well as developing climate-smart crops and improving cropping systems for a sustainable environment and food security.

Features of the book

- Reviews trends of global climate change and its consequences for food security across the continents
- Identifies the challenges and scopes of cultivating legumes in achieving food security in the context of global climate change
- Focuses on the improvements of legume production through conservation approaches in agricultural practices and modern techniques, including omics-based breeding, biotechnology, genetic engineering, and rhizobium technology
- Discusses the sustainable amelioration options for soils affected by climate-induced stresses
- Cites examples of applications of rhizobium technologies in reducing greenhouse gas emission
- Describes pathways associated with yield, resistance, and tolerance of legumes to climate-induced stresses

Climate Change and Legumes
Stress Mitigation for Sustainability
and Food Security

Edited by
Mohammad Zabed Hossain, Hossain Md Anawar, and
Doongar R. Chaudhary

CRC Press
Taylor & Francis Group
Boca Raton London New York

CRC Press is an imprint of the
Taylor & Francis Group, an **informa** business

First edition published 2023
by CRC Press
6000 Broken Sound Parkway NW, Suite 300, Boca Raton, FL 33487-2742

and by CRC Press
4 Park Square, Milton Park, Abingdon, Oxon, OX14 4RN

CRC Press is an imprint of Taylor & Francis Group, LLC

ISBN: 978-1-032-07984-4 (hbk)
ISBN: 978-1-032-10346-4 (pbk)
ISBN: 978-1-003-21488-5 (ebk)

DOI: 10.1201/9781003214885

Typeset in Times
by MPS Limited, Dehradun

Contents

Preface

Global climate change has created enormous concerns for people of all walks of life. Of the wide-ranging consequences of this global crisis, vulnerability of food security has become an unprecedented challenge in order to feed humans now and the days to come. Although the extent and the magnitude of climate-related problems in crop production have been widely documented, relatively fewer attempts have been made so far for sustainable mitigation and adaptation in this context. Based on our research experiences, we felt the need to produce this book in order to focus on sustainable solutions to this global problem with emphasis on the potentials of legumes in this regard as well as identifying the knowledge gap for future research and development.

We selected a total of 13 chapters from contributors with relevant expertise. These chapters highlight the recent research findings and reviews on the (1) current trends of climate change and their impacts on food security and diversity of genetic resources of legumes, and (2) the potentials of legumes in ameliorating climate-related problems as well as better management of agricultural land and practices for achieving environmental sustainability and food security. The book also discusses technologies for improving legume production through conservation approaches in agricultural practices and modern methods such as omics-based breeding, biotechnology, genetic engineering, and rhizobium technology. Furthermore, the book describes the pathways associated with yield, resistance, and tolerance of legumes to climate-induced stresses, which could be relevant for further development of stress-resistant legume varieties.

We anticipate this book will be useful for researchers, field practitioners and government policymakers working to mitigate the impact of climate change on agriculture and achieve food security. The book will also be used as a reference book for consultants, researchers, and students who are endeavoring to understand the mechanisms of stress tolerance of legumes, develop climate-smart crops, and improve crop production systems for sustainable food security.

We are immensely thankful to the contributors for writing their chapters as per the objectives of this book. Their relentless efforts are highly acknowledged, because without their support it would not be possible to make this piece of book. We are also indebted to the anonymous persons of CRC press who played their role throughout the publication process.

Mohammad Zabed Hossain: Department of Botany, University of Dhaka, Dhaka, Bangladesh

Hossain Md Anawar: School of Chemistry, Physics & Mechanical Engineering, Science and Engineering Faculty, Queensland University of Technology (QUT), Brisbane, Queensland, Australia

Doongar R. Chaudhary: Division of Plant Omics, CSIR-Central Salt and Marine Chemicals Research Institute, G. B. Marg, Bhavnagar, Gujarat, India

Editor Bio

Mohammad Zabed Hossain completed his BSc (Honours) and MSc (with thesis) from the Department of Botany, University of Dhaka, and currently has been serving as professor at the same department. He obtained his PhD from the United Graduate School of Agricultural Sciences (UGAS), Iwate University, Japan, in 2007 and conducted post-doctoral research at Swedish University of Agricultural Sciences (SLU), Uppsala, Sweden during 2009 and 2011. He obtained several awards, including Guest Research Scholarship from Swedish Institute of the Swedish Government for post-doctoral research, Monbukagakusho Scholarship of the Government of Japan for PhD, National Science and Technology Fellowship from the Government of Bangladesh for MSc research, and International Centre for Genetic Engineering and Biotechnology (ICGEB) grant for attending a training program in New Delhi, India. He has more than 20 years of experience in research and teaching on plant ecology, plant molecular ecology, ecosystem ecology, and environmental science. His current research interests focus on adaptation of plants, ecology of invasive plants and plant-microbe interactions in relation to abiotic stresses such as salinity, drought, and heavy metals. He was awarded several research grants from national and international agencies, including International Foundation for Science of Sweden, USAID-AFSI Research Foundation of USA, Ministry of Education, Ministry of Science and Technology, and University Grants Commission of the Government of Bangladesh.

Dr Hossain Md Anawar obtained his MSc and PhD from Nagoya University and Niigata University, respectively, Japan. He recently worked as a research assistant at Science and Engineering Faculty, Queensland University of Technology (QUT), Australia. He has research experience in interdisciplinary fields, including soil and plant nutrition, biogeochemistry, bioremediation, phytoremediation, and soil chemistry. He obtained nationally and internationally competitive scholarships, awards, and research grants in Japan, Spain, Portugal, South Africa, and Botswana. Through his scholarly, innovative, high-quality research works, he has established himself as a nationally and internationally recognized researcher in his field. He published 121 publications in peer-reviewed journals, book chapters, and conference proceedings. Furthermore, he edited three books by Elsevier publisher and CRC press. His papers have a Scopus citation record of 2019 with an H-Index of 24. He has a Google scholar citation record of 3200 with an H-Index of 25. He published research articles in high impactor journals, such as *Agriculture, Pedosphere, Environmental Pollution, Environment International, Chemosphere, Journal of Environmental Management, Science of the Total Environment, Talanta, Applied Geochemistry,* etc. He was editorial board member, associate editor, and guest editor of seven international journals, including *Agriculture* (MDPI) 2020–2021, *Pedosphere* (Elsevier), and *Physics and Chemistry of the Earth* (Elsevier). He was an international expert to review different national project proposals. He reviewed research articles from more than 15 international journals.

Doongar R. Chaudhary was born (1973) in Jodhpur, Rajasthan, India and studied soil science and agricultural chemistry at Rajasthan Agriculture University, Bikaner (campus: Udaipur), Rajasthan. He completed his PhD from ICAR-Indian Agricultural Research Institute, New Delhi in 2002. He started his research career at ICAR-Central Soil Salinity Research Institute, Karnal, Haryana and joined CSIR-Central Salt and Marine Chemicals Research Institute, Bhavnagar (Gujarat) in 2004. He is now working as principal scientist in the Division of Plant Omics. Dr. Chaudhary has been awarded the BOYSCAST (2008–09) fellowship by Department of Science and Technology (GOI) and visited the School of Environment and Natural Resources, Ohio State University for one year. He has also been awarded the Brainpool Fellowship-2015 of Korean Federation of Science and Technology (KOFST) at the School of Civil and Environment Engineering, Yonsei University, Seoul, South Korea for 11 months. He has more than 20 years of research experience in the field of soil fertility, plant nutrition, and soil ecology. His current research interest is rehabilitation of coastal saline soil with halophytes, salt tolerant plant growth promoting rhizobacteria, metagenomics, soil microbial community, nutrient cycling, and biogeochemical processes in the coastal ecosystem. He is involved in the many projects funded by the CSIR, MoES, and SERB.

List of Contributors

Abdul Hameed Baloch
Faculty of Agriculture
Lasbela University of Agriculture, Water
    and Marine Sciences
Pakistan

Aladdin Hamwieh
International Center for Agricultural Research in
    the Dry Areas (ICARDA)
Giza, Egypt

Antonio M. De Ron
Misión Biológica de Galicia (MBG)
Spanish National Research Council (CSIC)
Pontevedra, Spain

Asadullah
Faculty of Agriculture
Lasbela University of Agriculture, Water
    and Marine Sciences
Pakistan

Burcu Yuksel
Kocaeli University
Vocational School of Kocaeli Health Sciences
 Izmit, Kocaeli, Turkey

Celal Yucel
University of Sirnak
 Agriculture Faculty
Field Crops Department
Sirnak, Turkey

Derya Yucel
University of Sirnak
Agriculture Faculty
Field Crops Department
Sirnak, Turkey

Doongar R. Chaudhary
Division of Plant Omics
CSIR-Central Salt and Marine Chemicals
    Research Institute
Bhavnagar, Gujarat, India

Eulogio J. Bedmar
Estación Experimental Zaidín (EEZ)
Spanish National Research Council (CSIC)
Granada, Spain

Filiz Vardar
Marmara University
Sciences and Arts Faculty Department of Biology
Göztepe Istanbul Turkey

Germán Tortosa
Estación Experimental Zaidín (EEZ)
Spanish National Research Council (CSIC)
Granada, Spain

Ghazala Mustafa
Department of Plant Sciences
Quaid-i-Azam University
Islamabad, Pakistan

Gizem Kamçi
University of Sirnak
 Agriculture Faculty
Field Crops Department
Sirnak, Turkey

S Gurumurthy
ICAR-National Institute of Abiotic stress
    Management
Pune, Maharashtra, India

Hossain Md Anawar
School of Chemistry, Physics & Mechanical
    Engineering
Science and Engineering Faculty
Queensland University of Technology (QUT)
Brisbane, Queensland, Australia

James Odra Galla
Department of Crop Science
School of Agricultural Sciences
College of Natural Resources and
    Environmental Studies
University of Juba
Juba, South Sudan

Kalpana Tewari
ICAR-Indian Institute of Pulses Research
Kanpur, Uttar Pradesh, India

Krishnashis Das
ICAR-Indian Institute of Pulses Research
Kanpur, Uttar Pradesh, India

Kusum Sharma
ICAR-Indian Institute of Pulses Research
Kanpur, Uttar Pradesh, India

Kwadwo Ofori
West Africa Centre for Crop Improvement
School of Agriculture
College of Basic and Applied Sciences
University of Ghana
Legon, Ghana

Juan L. Tejada-Hinojoza
Misión Biológica de Galicia (MBG)
Spanish National Research Council (CSIC)
Pontevedra, Spain
and
Faculty of Agronomy
National University San Luis Gonzaga (UNICA)
Ica, Perú

María J. Delgado
Estación Experimental Zaidín (EEZ)
Spanish National Research Council (CSIC)
Granada, Spain

Md. Abul Kashem
Department of Botany
University of Dhaka
Dhaka, Bangladesh

Mohammad Zabed Hossain
Ecology and Environment Laboratory
Department of Botany
University of Dhaka
Dhaka, Bangladesh

Ozlem Aksoy
Kocaeli University
Sciences and Arts Faculty
Department of Biology
Izmit, Kocaeli, Turkey

A. Paula Rodiño
Misión Biológica de Galicia (MBG)
Spanish National Research Council (CSIC)
Pontevedra, Spain

CS Praharaj
ICAR-Indian Institute of Pulses Research
Kanpur, Uttar Pradesh, India

P.S. Basu
ICAR-Indian Institute of Pulses Research
Kanpur, Uttar Pradesh, India

Rafat Sultana
Bihar Agricultural University
Sabour, Bhagalpur, Bihar, India

Setsuko Komatsu
Faculty of Environment and Information Sciences
Fukui University of Technology
Fukui, Japan

Silvestro Kaka Meseka
International Institute of Tropical Agriculture
Oyo Road, Ibadan, Nigeria

SK Chaturvedi
Rani Lakshmi Bai Central Agriculture University
Jhansi, Uttar Pradesh, India

Socorro Mesa
Estación Experimental Zaidín (EEZ)
Spanish National Research Council (CSIC)
Granada, Spain

Surendra K. Meena
ICAR-IIPR, Arid Pulses Research Centre
Bikaner, Rajasthan, India

Syed Rehmat Ullah Shah
Faculty of Agriculture
Lasbela University of Agriculture, Water
and Marine Sciences
Pakistan

Tony Ngalamu
Department of Crop Science, School
of Agricultural Sciences
College of Natural Resources and
Environmental Studies
University of Juba
Juba, South Sudan

Ummed Singh
College of Agriculture (Agriculture University
Jodhpur) Baytu
Barmer, Rajasthan, India

Vaibhav Kumar
ICAR-Indian Institute of Pulses Research
Kanpur, Uttar Pradesh, India

1

Legume Plants in the Context of Global Climate Change: Challenges and Scopes for Environmental Sustainability

M.Z. Hossain[1], Hossain Md Anawar[2], and Doongar R. Chaudhary[3]
[1]*Department of Botany, University of Dhaka, Dhaka, Bangladesh*
[2]*School of Chemistry, Physics & Mechanical Engineering, Science and Engineering Faculty, Queensland University of Technology (QUT), Brisbane, Queensland, Australia*
[3]*Division of Plant Omics, CSIR-Central Salt and Marine Chemicals Research Institute, Bhavnagar, Gujarat, India*

CONTENTS

DOI: 10.1201/9781003214885-1

1.1 Introduction

There is no doubt that the global climate has changed drastically over the past century. An unprecedented increase of approximately 1.0°C of global warming above pre-industrial levels has been reported, and it is predicted that it will increase 1.5°C between 2030 and 2052 if the current rate continues (IPCC, 2013). Such an increase in global warming is causing unusual events that include, but are not limited to, rise of average temperature and sea levels and increase in the frequency of severe weather events (Broomell et al., 2017).

The impacts of global climate change are multifaceted, affecting both biological and ecological systems of the biosphere (Beaugrand, 2012). The consequences of climate change for agriculture are immense since it will alter crop production and humans' coping mechanisms within the agro-ecosystems, change the quantity and quality of the food supply and livestock production systems, alter soil C content, affect fire regimes, and alter livestock metabolism and plant community composition and species distributions, including range contraction and expansion of invasive species (Polley et al., 2013). Further, it will also be a challenge to ensure the quality of food along with quantity if crops like legumes are hampered under future scenarios of the global climate. Therefore, it is important to find sustainable, energy-efficient cultivation in order to reduce the use of fossil fuels as an alternative energy source.

The importance of legumes for well-being has long been understood. Legumes are the major source of essential oils, micronutrients, vegetable proteins, edible fiber, and minerals for both livestock and human consumption; therefore, they are used as a source of food, feed, and fodder in agricultural systems of the tropical, subtropical, and semi-arid regions of the world (Abbo et al., 2009; Raza et al., 2020). These crops are considered to be the second most cultivated crops, covering 14% of the total cultivated land worldwide (Raza et al., 2020). Of this group, grain legumes account for 27% of world crop production, providing 33% of the dietary protein consumed by humans, whereas pasture and forage legumes play a significant role in supplying fodder for livestock (Smýkal et al., 2015). Legumes provide not only the protein-rich food and fodder, but they can also improve soil quality, reducing greenhouse gas emissions, protect the environment, and enhance biodiversity and thus can contribute to achieving environmental sustainability. Therefore, due to its multiple benefits, both demand and production of legumes has increased worldwide over the years (Gowda et al., 2009). However, in spite of its ample potential to achieve socio-economic and environmental sustainability, cultivation of legumes has been facing a number of challenges, including vulnerability to diseases and abiotic stresses (Considine et al., 2017). Moreover, the constraints for cultivation of legumes have been intensified by the anticipated global climate change rendering food security and the potential of sustainability at risk.

Considering the current and future perspectives of agriculture in the context of anticipated climate change, the issue of environmental sustainability becomes the central concern in sustainable development. Due to their potential, legumes can be considered important crops that can play a significant role in achieving sustainability in agriculture by ensuring quality food and fodder, mitigating the risk of emission of greenhouse gases, ensuring soil quality improvement, and promoting biodiversity in mixed cropping systems (Stagnari et al., 2017). Thus, increased demand for food production in order to feed people and achieving environmental sustainability by using biological nitrogen fixation inputs in agriculture highlight the significance of cultivation of legume crops worldwide (Ferguson et al., 2019). Nitrogen deficiency in soil in regions like in the tropics indicates the potential of biological nitrogen fixation by legumes in achieving sustainable fertilization, reducing use of fossil fuels in the production of chemical fertilizers (Hungria and Vargas, 2000). Therefore, it is pertinent to enhance our understanding about the extent of climate-induced effects on growth and yield of legumes in different parts of the world as well as ways to explore the maximum benefits from legumes in attaining sustainable agriculture.

1.2 Global Climate Change: Evidence and Patterns across Continents

1.2.1 Evidence of Global Climate Change

Both observations and data obtained from scientific studies provide substantial evidence that global climate has changed during the past century at an unusual rate. Gradual increase of average global temperature compared to that of the pre-industrial era has been recorded over the past century. Records on temperature data revealed that global mean surface temperature rose 0.85°C over the period starting from 1880 to 2012 (Hartmann et al., 2013). This study also stated that the last three decades (1980–2010) have been the warmest on record, with the longest dataset extending back to 1850. The last three years (2015, 2016, and 2017) were the three warmest years on record for the globe on average (WMO, 2018). Based on substantial reports, it is predicted that global warming will exceed 2°C threshold by the year 2050 (Giorgi and Lionello, 2008). The facts that provide evidence for global climate change include rise of surface, atmospheric, and oceanic temperatures; melting polar ice; thinning snow cover; shrinking sea ice; rising sea levels; acidification of ocean water; and increase in intensity and frequency of rainfall, hurricanes or cyclones, heatwaves, wildfires, and droughts (Overpeck and Udall, 2020).

Climate change results from both natural and man-made causes. The natural causes of climate change include solar output causing fluctuation in the amount of radiation, sunspot activity, orbital changes known as Milankovitch episodes that cause natural warming and cooling due to Wobble, roll and stretch theory, and volcanic activity that releases CO_2 into the atmosphere (Stoffel et al., 2015). On the other hand, human-induced causes of global climate change include burning of fossil fuels, deforestation, overgrazing, dumping of waste in landfills, and agricultural practices that lead to release of nitrogen oxides into the atmosphere (IPCC, 2013).

1.2.2 Continental Patterns of Global Climate Change

Frequency and magnitude of extreme weather events resulting from global warming show spatial variation (IPCC, 2013). Reports demonstrated variation in climate change phenomena among and within continents at both space and time scales (Table 1.1).

1.2.2.1 Climate Change in Asia

Geographic variation in climatic variables has been demonstrated by a number of reports across Asia. The Himalayan highlands significantly influence the regional climate not only of Asia but also of some parts of Europe. Sivakumar and Stefanski (2010) reported a significant warming in this region, including the Tibetan Plateau and arid regions of Asia, with an increase in extreme weather events such as heatwave and intense precipitation. Their data also demonstrated an increased inter-annual variability of daily precipitation in the Asian summer monsoon. Sorg et al. (2012) reported a pronounced glacier shrinkage due to the impacts of climate change in the Tien Shan, also known as the water tower of Central Asia. They observed shifts of seasonal runoff maxima in some rivers, causing water shortfalls. It is anticipated that such climate-driven changes in glacier-fed stream-flow regimes will have direct implications on freshwater supply, irrigation, and hydropower potential in the catchment area.

The middle-eastern countries of Asia are the most serious victims of global change phenomenon. Based on data, it is predicted that the Arab states will face decreased precipitation, a drastic rise in average temperatures, and an increase in seawater intrusion by the year 2030 (UNDP, 2018). Bucchignani et al. (2018) used two simulations with the COSMO-CLM model, respectively, at a spatial resolution of 0.44°C and 0.22°C, over the period 1979–2100 and investigated the projected changes in the future climate conditions for the Middle East over the 21st century. Based on their analysis, climate projections showed a significant warming expected over the whole area considered at the end of the 21st century, along with a reduction in precipitation. These changes are likely to intensify the existing harsh environmental conditions due to extreme dryness in the desert areas.

Jiang et al. (2013) analyzed the trends of climate change of East Asia during the 21st century by using simulating models. Their results showed a rise of surface temperature in China, which was inconsistent with the global average, although the extent of temperature rise was larger in northeastern, western, and central China. Their results also indicated marked inter-annual variations in warming compared with the global average. This study also indicated a remarkable increase in both annual and seasonal precipitation in China in the latter half of the 21st century.

South Asia is another most vulnerable region on Earth to global climate change effects. In a review, Jung (2012) reported changes of mean temperatures from 0.1°C to 0.3°C per decade between 1951 and

TABLE 1.1

Climate Change Phenomena in Different Continents of the World

Continent	Reported climate change phenomena	References
Asia	• Warmer temperature, heat waves, and intense precipitation in the Tibetan Plateau and arid regions • Inter-annual variability of daily precipitation during monsoon • Glacier shrinkage in the Himalayan • Decreased precipitation and warmer temperature • Increased precipitation in China in the latter half of the 21st century • Increased mean temperatures from 0.1°C to 0.3°C per decade between 1951 and 2000, reduced rainfall during 1960–2000, and rise of sea levels by 1–3 mm per year • In South Asia, rise of mean temperatures from 0.1°C to 0.3°C per decade between 1951 and 2000, reduced rainfall during 1960–2000, and rise of sea levels by 1–3 mm per year	Sivakumar and Stefanski (2010) Sorg et al. (2012) UNDP (2018) Jiang et al. (2013) Jung (2012)
Africa	• A general decline in rainfall pattern since the first half of the 19th century • Prolonged droughts and devastating floods • At 2°C–3°C higher temperature, increased precipitation in East Africa and reduced precipitation in Southern Africa • Intense and prolonged droughts	Nicholson (2001) Nkemdirim (2003) James and Washingtonn (2013) Ngaira (2007)
Australia	• Temperature increased over 1°C since 1910 • Extreme weather events increased in number and duration • Number and length of bushfires increased • Rainfall increased in northern Australia and declined in southern Australia	CSIRO (2018)
North America	• Number of warm weather days per year increased • Rainfall intensity increased in conjunction with the hurricane season in October • Northeast will be warmer	Lee and Sheridan (2018) Lu et al. (2015) Polley et al. (2013)
Central and South America	• Increase of temperature from 0.5°C to 3°C during 1901–2012 • Amount, intensity, and duration of precipitation differed between northern and southern South America • Number of extreme warm maximum and minimum temperature events increased, whereas extremely cold temperature events have decreased during the period of 1961–2003	IPCC (2013), Marengo et al. (2014) Aguilar et al. (2007)

2000, reduced rainfall during 1960–2000, and rise of sea levels by 1–3 mm per year. Over the decades, number and intensity of extreme weather events, such as heatwaves, droughts, floods, and tropical cyclones, have increased. For instance, the number of recorded floods and storms has risen dramatically in the Philippines, where the number rose from under 20 between 1960 and 1969 to nearly 120 between 2000 and 2008 (Jung, 2012).

1.2.2.2 Climate Change in Africa

Notable changes in weather events were reported during the last two decades in Africa (Nkemdirim, 2003): the prolonged droughts that happened during 1968–1973, also called Sahelian drought, and the devastating floods that happened in equatorial East Africa in 1997–1998, also known as El Nino flood. These extreme weather events were attributed to the abnormal warming of the eastern Pacific waters. James and Washington (2013) analyzed climate patterns of Africa by using Global Climate Models and showed a small, significant precipitation change at 1°C, then larger anomalies at 2°C, which were strengthened and extended at 3°C and 4°C, including a wet signal in East Africa and dry signals in Southern Africa, the Guinea Coast, and the west of the Sahel. All these data indicate unusual changes in climate in Africa, and such changes will be intensified in the days to come.

Ngaira (2007) analyzed trends of the annual rainfall of semi-arid areas in Kenya and recorded severe droughts every 2–3 years in the 1960s, 1970s, and 1980s. This study also reported prolonged droughts exceeding 5 years during the 1990s toward the 2000s. It also reported that most of equatorial Kenya is becoming drier.

Increased temperatures may exacerbate existing environmental problems, such as coastal flooding due to sea-level rise. It was calculated that ocean expansion could cause a rise in sea level between 20 and 140 cm if the average temperature is increased by 1.5°C to 4.5°C (WMO, 2002) and a rise of 3°C could increase sea level by 80 cm, which is enough to cause floods in huge unprotected coastal lands along both the Eastern and Western Coast of Africa. Warmer sea surface temperature will increase tropical storm frequency and intensity (Nkemdirim, 2003).

1.2.2.3 Climate Change in Europe

Alcamo et al. (2007) reported an increase in temperature by 0.90°C from 1901 to 2005 across Europe. Reports also showed that compared to warming, precipitation was found to be more spatially variable with an increased mean winter precipitation in most of the Atlantic and northern Europe (Tank et al., 2002). On the contrary, trends of precipitation were negative in the eastern Mediterranean region, with no significant changes in the west (Norrant and Douguédroit, 2006).

Giorgi et al. (2004) predicted changes in mean and interannual variability for the 30-year period of 2071–2100 with respect to the period from 1961 to 1990 under forcing from the A2 and B2 IPCC emission scenarios. According to their study, the European region undergoes substantial warming in all seasons, in the range of 1°C–5.5°C, with the warming being 1°C–2°C lower in the B2 than in the A2 scenario. They also reported that the spatial patterns of warming are similar in the two scenarios, with a maximum over Eastern Europe in winter and over western and southern Europe in summer. Different precipitation patterns were also reported with an increase over most of Europe due to increased storm activity and higher atmospheric water vapor loadings, and in summer, a decrease in precipitation over most of western and southern Europe.

1.2.2.4 Climate Change in Australia

The climate of Australia has changed over the years at unprecedented rates. CSIRO (2018) reported several changes in the climatic variables of Australia. An average increase of temperature was noticed over 1°C since 1910 across all seasons. Extreme weather events were also recorded in the recent decades. The mean annual temperature during 2011–2020 was the highest on record, at 0.94°C above average, and 0.33°C warmer than that was during the period from 2001 to 2010. The number and length of bush fire events have increased in recent decades across many parts of Australia, particularly in the southern and eastern Australia. The rainfall pattern has also been altered remarkably, showing an increase across parts of northern Australia, whereas a declined trend was recorded across the southeastern and southwestern parts from April to October.

1.2.2.5 Climate Change in North America

Lee and Sheridan (2018) investigated the trend of climate change in North America during the period from 1979 to 2017. They reported that humid warm weather types were occurring 22 more days per year compared to dry warm weather, which increased by 10 days per year. Their study also showed in the Canadian Archipelago that the warm weather type was occurring 42 more days per year; the cool weather type was occurring 48 fewer times per year; and the desert Southwest US and northern Mexico showed significant increases in dry warm weather types with the increase of 33 to 40 days per year. The study conducted by Polley et al. (2013) also predicted that the Northwest would be warm considerably, but annual precipitation would change little despite a large decrease in summer precipitation.

1.2.2.6 Climate Change in Central and South America

IPCC (2013) provided data that clearly demonstrated the spatial and temporal changes of climatic variables in the South and Central American countries, including Belize, Costa Rica, El Salvador, Guatemala, Honduras, Nicaragua, and Panama, over recent decades. This data showed a gradual increase of temperature from 0.5°C to 3°C, with the more significant increase in tropical regions of South America during the period from 1901 to 2012. During this period of time, a consistent rainfall pattern was also found that showed a gradual increase in South Eastern South America and Northern South America, as well over Northeast Brazil and the Northwest Coast of Peru and Ecuador. This report also demonstrated that reduced rainfall was reported over Northern and Southern Chile, Northern Argentina, and Southern Mexico as well as parts of Central America. Rainfall pattern also have showed some distinct patterns since 1950: although in Central America and the North American Monsoon System rainfall has been increasingly delayed and has become more irregular in space and time, the intensity of rainfall has been increasing during the onset of the season (Marengo et al., 2014; Arias et al., 2012).

Unusual extreme climate events have been recorded in Central and South America over the years (Vincent et al., 2005). In Central America, the number of extreme warm maximum and minimum temperatures has increased, whereas extremely cold temperature events have decreased during the period starting from 1961 to 2003 (Aguilar et al., 2007). During this period, rainfall events were found to be intense, and the contribution of wet and very wet days was enlarged. Vincent et al. (2005) reported significant increasing trends in the percentage of warm nights and decreasing trends in the percentage of cold nights in South America during 1960–2000. Haylock et al. (2006) reported two distinct rainfall patterns: an increased rainfall in Ecuador and northern Peru and the region of southern Brazil, Paraguay, Uruguay, and northern and central Argentina and a decreased rainfall in southern Peru and southern Chile.

1.3 Impact of Climate Change on Crop Production

1.3.1 Impacts on Variety, Species, and Functional Types

Climate is one of the most important factors that determine the geographic distribution of plants (Mather and Yoshioka, 1968). Interactions among adaptation capability of plant species, dispersal barriers and other environmental factors, including climate and soil, influence the distribution of plants. Any alteration in growth and distribution patterns of plants due to climate-induced factors is of utmost importance for both ecological and agricultural aspects. Impacts of climate change on crop production, production systems, vegetation, and ecosystems vary with space and time. Variation in geographical conditions, local environments, ecosystem structure, as well as human population among and within continents will certainly reflect the intensity and severity of the impacts induced by climate change. The ecological consequences of climate change are likely to vary substantially among ecoregions due to the differences in regional antecedent environmental conditions; the rate and magnitude of change in the primary climate change drivers, including elevated carbon dioxide (CO_2), warming and precipitation modification, and non-additive effects among climate drivers (Polley et al., 2013).

Data accumulated over the years indicate that the effects of climate-induced factors on plants vary with both species identity and functional types. Climate change affects crop production by direct (morphology, physiology, phenotype, and productivity), indirect (soil fertility, irrigation, pest, and environmental stresses) and socio-economic effects (food demand, farmer's response, cost, policy, and trade) (Raza et al., 2019). Interspecific differences in the effects of temperature (Fonty et al., 2009), drought, and salinity (Nabila and Hossain, 2017) are well reported. Intervarietal differences in the effects of salinity (Hossain et al., 2018; Hossain et al., 2016a) and drought condition (Hossain et al., 2016b) have been reported. Plant functional types are also reported to vary in their responses to temperature. Although C4 plants are likely to be favored over C3 plants in warm and humid climates, C3 plants are likely to be favored over C4 plants in cool climates (Lara and Andreo, 2011). It is predicted that when global warming is limited to 1.5°C as compared with 2°C, about 50% of the plant species will be lost (Warren et al., 2018).

1.3.2 Trends in Crop Production

Impacts of climate change on crop production have remained a vital concern for its immense relevance to food safety and security, as well as the socio-economic condition of people (Figure 1.1). Lobell et al. (2011) examined the change in climate trends and crop yields for the period starting from 1980 to 2010 and showed that the yields of wheat, maize, and soybeans had declined, whereas that of rice increased in most regions of the world. Simulation results of the study conducted by Qiao et al. (2018) revealed that the climate change had a positive impact on the crop production of wheat, maize, and rice during the period from 1980 to 2010 in the agro-pastoral transitional zone of China. However, some reports predicted that although global crop production may be boosted slightly by global warming in the short term (before 2030), it will ultimately turn negative in the long term (Bruinsma, 2003; IPCC, 2007). This boosting of plant productivity due to climate change has been attributed to the elevated concentration of CO_2 in the atmosphere (Guo et al., 2014). Nevertheless, other changes in environmental factors, such as drought and temperature, influence crop production negatively (Calzadilla et al., 2013). It is estimated that the productivity of the major crops will drop in many countries of the world due to global warming, water shortage, and other environmental impacts/stresses (Raza et al., 2019), and these extremes influence the reproductive phase of plant growth. Direct impacts of climate change are associated with rise in temperatures, indirect impacts due to water availability and changing soil moisture status, intrusion of saline water in agricultural soil (Corwin, 2020), as well as incidence of pest and disease are likely to be felt (Skendžíc et al., 2021). Qiao et al. (2018) also reported that impacts of climate change on crop production may be confounded by other factors, including land-use change.

The impact of climate change on crop production is unlikely to be evenly distributed across regions on Earth. Low latitude countries are expected to suffer more from the agricultural effects of global warming, reflecting their disadvantaged geographic location. In contrast, crop production in high latitude regions will generally benefit from climate change. In a global comprehensive estimate for over 100 countries, Cline (2007) predicted that global agricultural productivity would fall by 15.9% in the 2080s if global warming continues unabated, with developing countries experiencing a disproportionately larger decline of 19.7%. The effects of climate change and increased atmospheric CO_2 levels by 2050 are expected to lead to small increases in European crop productivity (Alcamo et al., 2007). However, if temperature increases greater than approximately 2°C, then it will lead to a decline in the yields of many crops (Easterling et al., 2007). Developing countries in low latitude regions will suffer more because of the greater share of their agriculture to the economies and lower capability to adapt with this altered environment.

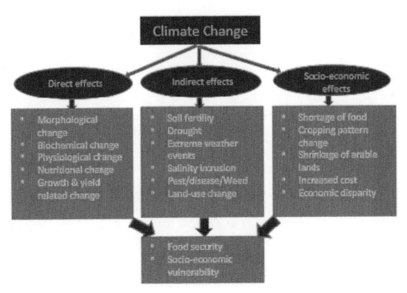

FIGURE 1.1 Impacts of global climate change on food security and socio-economic status.

Increased pest attack and prevalence of diseases for crops suggest immediate actions, including monitoring climate and pest populations and modified integrated pest management strategies to reduce risks. It is also imperative to evaluate climate-induced crop damages in order to formulate innovative technologies and management strategies so that the vulnerability of farms and agriculture can be minimized.

1.4 Legumes and Biological Nitrogen Fixation

1.4.1 Taxonomic Description of Legumes

Fabaceae, with 800 genera and 20,000 species, is the third largest family of flowering plants after Orchidaceae and Asteraceae (Smýkal et al., 2015). This family is classified into three subfamilies, namely Caesalpinioideae, Mimosoideae, and Papilionoideae. Among these three subfamilies, Papilionoideae consists mainly of food and feed crops, such as soybean, chickpea, bean, pea, clover, licorice, lentils, and peanut.

Plants under the family Fabaceae are characterized by the distinct fruit from which the name of the family (legume) has originated. Legume flowers are hermaphroditic and contain both the stamen and pistil, meaning that they are self-fertile. Due to self-fertility, legume populations suffer from less genetic diversity. The flower of the plants of this family usually contains five petals and an ovary with one carpel, cavity, and style. The shape of the legume petals looks like a cup. There is one large petal; the "banner" or "standard" folds over the rest for its protection. In front of the petal, there are two narrower petals called "wings," between which two other petals unite. Therefore, these petals are called the keel. Stamen and pistil remain within the fold. The flower dies after pollination and reveals the growing ovary, which becomes the pod that contains the seeds of the plant. The pod is a one-celled seed container formed by two sealed parts called valves. After maturity is attained, pods split along the seam, which connects the two valves. Legume species vary in thickness, length, curve, and fleshy nature of the pods. Flowers and seeds of legumes show great variation in color, ranging from white to scarlet to blue.

According to their ability to grow in different seasons, legume crops can be divided into two groups, cool-season legumes and warm- or tropical-season legumes, and both of these can be annual and perennial. Cool-season food legumes include broad bean (*Vicia faba*), lentil (*Lens culinaris*), lupin (*Lupinus* spp.), dry pea (*Pisum sativum*), chickpea (*Cicer arietinum*), grass pea (*Lathyrus sativus*), and common vetch (*Vicia sativa*). The other cool season legumes include narrow-leaf clover (*Trifolium angustifolium*), ball clover (*Trifolium incarnatum*), berseem clover (*Trifolium alexandrinum*) and black medic (*Medicago lupulina*), alfalfa (*Medicago sativa*), alsike clover (*Trifolium hybridum*), birdsfoot trefoil (*Lotus corniculatus*), and white clover (*Trifolium repens*). Warm-season food legumes include pigeonpea (*Cajanus cajan*), cowpea (*Vigna unguiculata*), mungbean (*Vigna radiata* var. *radiata*), common bean (*Phaseolus* spp.), and urd bean (*Vigna mungo*), which are mainly grown in hot and humid conditions (Singh and Singh, 2011). The other warm-season legumes include alyce clover (*Alysicarpus vaginalis*), soybeans (*Glycine max*), velvet beans (*Mucuna pruriens*), and Korean lespedeza (*Kummerowia stipulacea*). Moreover, kudzu (*Pueraria montana*) and perennial peanut (*Arachis glabrata*) are warm-season legumes.

The principal grain legumes that are consumed worldwide include common beans (*Phaseolus* spp.), field pea, chickpea, broad bean, pigeon pea, mungbean, cowpea, and lentil (Duc et al., 2015). Grain legumes alone contribute 33% of human protein nutrition (Vance et al., 2000).

1.4.2 Nodulation and Biological Nitrogen Fixation

Legumes have a unique functional trait, which made them able to fix atmospheric nitrogen in stem and root nodules. Nearly 88% of the legume species examined to date are able to form nodules through symbiotic association with a group of bacteria known as *Rhizobia* (de Faria et al., 1989). These nitrogen-fixing bacteria, diazotrophs, are able to fix atmospheric N_2 by using a nitrogenase enzyme system that carries out the metabolically expensive reduction of N_2 to NH_3 (Jochum et al., 2017). Thus, the nitrogenase enzyme complex is the central unit of nitrogen fixation in all known diazotrophic organisms, which remain inside the root or stem-nodules in host legumes. In the presence of nitrogenase enzyme in bacterial cells, one molecule of N_2 is reduced to form two molecules of NH_3, which is then transferred to the host legume plants. This biologically active form can be used by microorganisms and plants for the synthesis of the nitrogenous compounds necessary for their growth. Bacteria, in turn, gain carbon substances as their food from the legume plants.

$$N_2 + 8e^- + 16ATP + 8H^+ \rightarrow 2NH_3 + H_2 + 16ADP + 16P_i \text{ (inorganic phosphate)}$$

The nitrogenase activity is influenced by a number of environmental factors, such as moisture, light intensity, temperature, nutrients, and the ratio between nitrogen and phosphorus (Vitousek et al., 2002). The level of nitrogen fixation depends not only on the function of the nitrogenase enzyme but also on some other factors, such as host plant genotypes, rhizobial strains, compatibility between host legumes and rhizobia, along with other environmental factors, such as soil physico-chemical properties including pH, moisture, N, P, temperature, and salinity (Manchanda and Garg, 2008; Ojiem et al., 2007). Abiotic factors such as elevated temperature, CO_2, drought, and salinity are induced by global climate change and are likely to influence biological nitrogen fixation.

The role of biological nitrogen fixation by legumes is immense since it is directly related to improved diet for humans and livestock, soil fertility, and environmental sustainability. Biological N fixation is a major source of bioavailable nitrogen that represents the most common growth limiting factor for plants on earth. It supports terrestrial primary productivity and plays key roles in mediating changes in global N and carbon cycling (Reis et al., 2020). Given that nitrogen fixation has a profound agronomic, economic, and ecological benefits, the potentials of these functional traits in achieving environmental sustainability in the context of global climate change warrants detailed study.

1.5 Climate-Induced Stresses on Legumes

Climate-induced stresses, such as high temperature, drought, and salinity on yield of crops, are the major constraints in agriculture. These stresses limit the growth and development of plants and hence crop production. Effects of environmental stresses on legume plants are complicated since these plants produce a nodule, a unique structure formed in association with the rhizobial bacteria.

1.5.1 Effects of Drought Stress

Drought is an extreme climatic event that can be the costliest natural hazard and is accelerated by climate change through hydrological processes, making it more intense (Mukherjee et al., 2018). Global warming can lead to moisture deficit in soil through evaporation from the surface of the land. Drought created this way can limit the growth and development of plants, leading to reduced crop production. Although legume crops are commonly grown in arid and semi-arid regions and are tolerant to drought at certain level (Chibarabada et al., 2017), these plants are sensitive to drought stress (Nadeem et al., 2019). Drought induces several devastating effects on plants by disturbing various plant activities, such as the carbon assimilation rate, decreased turgor, increased oxidative damage, and changes in leaf gas exchange, thereby leading to a reduction in yield (Hussain et al., 2018).

Gaur et al. (2015) reported that drought conditions affected reproductive stages of grain legumes by predisposing them to necrotrophic fungi, such as *Rhizoctonia bataticola* that causes dry root rot disease. The most prominent effects of drought include reduced germination, stunted growth, serious damage to the photosynthetic apparatus, decrease in net photosynthesis, and a reduction in nutrient uptake (Nadeem et al., 2019). McDonald and Paulsen (1997) reported the detrimental effects of water deficiency on the growth of common bean (*Phaseolus vulgaris*), cowpea (*Vigna unguiculata*), and field pea (*Pisum sativum*) and also showed that the effects of water deficiency depended on the temperature. Fening et al. (2009) conducted an experiment with *Centrosema pubescens*, *Lablab purpureus*, and *Stylosanthes guianensis* grown separately in pots under greenhouse conditions and treated with moisture stress conditions of 100%, 75%, 50%, and 25% field capacity. They reported significantly reduced plant height, shoot and root dry weights, nodule number per plant, and phosphorus uptake with the increase of moisture deficits and reported interspecific differences. Drought also reduces the nitrogenase activity (acetylene reduction g^{-1}

nodule) and acetylene reduction in the legumes ultimately reduces biological nitrogen fixation (McCulloch et al., 2021) with the mechanisms of C shortage and C metabolism in nodule, oxygen limitation, and feedback regulation by the accumulation of N fixation products (Serraj, 2003).

1.5.2 Effects of Heat Stress

Heat stress can affect grain legumes at different stages; before and after flowering, of the development of plants (Gaur et al., 2015). They reported before flowering effects, such as reduction in germination rate, and increase in the occurrence of abnormal seedlings, early flowering, degeneration of nodules, reduction in membrane stability, photosynthetic activity, and plant biomass, and after flowering effects, such as reduced pollen viability, fertilization, pod set, and seed development, causing substantial loss of yield. Food legumes that are exposed to high-temperature stress during the reproductive stage show flower abortion, pollen and ovule infertility, impaired fertilization, and reduced seed filling, leading to smaller seeds and ultimately poor yields (Sita et al., 2017).

McDonald and Paulsen (1997) studied the effects of high temperature on photosynthesis in common bean (*Phaseolus vulgaris*), cowpea (*Vigna unguiculata*), faba bean (*Vicia faba*), and five cultivars of field pea (*Pisum sativum*) by comparing the responses of all species at 20°C/15°C, 30°C/15°C, or 30°C/25°C day/night conditions. Their results showed a decreased chlorophyll variable fluorescence under high temperature in all species except cowpea, indicating its tolerance. It was also found that day light and night light influenced plants differentially: leaf chlorophyll and most measures of growth were favored by high day temperature but not by high night temperature, and photosynthetic rates were enhanced by high temperatures that increased leaf chlorophyll and nitrogen contents. Their results showed that high temperature affected photosynthesis, growth, and water relations of grain legumes, and sensitivity to the stress differed among species and genotypes.

Bordeleau and Prévost (1994) reported that elevated temperatures could affect biological nitrogen fixation by delaying nodule initiation and development as well as by altering structure and function of nodules in legumes. They also reported that changes in temperature could affect the competitive ability of *Rhizobium* strains, influencing nitrogen fixation. Hungria and Franco (1993) reported that high temperature negatively affected nodulation and nitrogenase activity in common *Phaseolus vulgaris* L. They experimentally demonstrated that nodules formed at high temperatures were ineffective in nitrogen fixation, and such effect was related to thermal shocks under which nitrogenase activity was drastically decreased. Heat stress can cause the degeneration of nodules, affecting nitrogen fixation efficiency in grain legumes (Gaur et al., 2015).

High temperature and drought conditions are major causes responsible for nodulation failure and affect all stages of the symbiosis and limiting rhizobial growth and survival in soil and also contribute to undesirable changes in rhizobia through plasmid deletions, genomic rearrangements, and reduced diversity (Hungria and Vargas, 2000).

1.5.3 Effects of Salinity

Salinity has remained a problem for agriculture since the beginning of the recorded history of human civilization. This problem is associated with the agricultural land under irrigation, particularly in the arid and semi-arid regions of the world, where there is higher rate of evapotranspiration than that of the annual precipitation, causing accumulation of salt in soil. The intrusion of saline water in the coastal region, on the other hand, has become a great concern for cultivation of crops. Severity of salinity through evapotranspiration and intrusion of saline water can be intensified by global warming through enhancing evaporation from the earth's surface and rise of sea level, respectively. Salinity can reduce soil fertility and thus affect the growth and survival of glycophytes drastically (Manchanda and Garg, 2008). Globally, 10% of the total arable land (approximately one billion hectares) is covered with saline and/or sodic soils, and about 25%–30% of irrigated lands are salt-affected (Shahid et al., 2018). As per FAO and ITPS (2015), the area affected by salinity varies among continents (Figure 1.2). The highest salinity affected area is in Asia (193.8 Mha), followed by Africa (122.9 Mha), Central and South America (71.5 Mha), Australia (17.6 Mha), Europe (6.7 Mha), and North America (6.2 Mha).

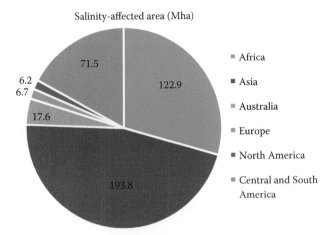

FIGURE 1.2   Continent-wise distribution of salinity affected areas (Mha) in the world.

Manchanda and Garg (2008) also reported that salinity could impose a significant limitation of crop yield due to adverse effects on the growth of the host plant, the root nodule bacteria, symbiotic development, and finally, the nitrogen-fixation capacity. Soil salinity inhibits the water and nutrient uptake, nutrient imbalance, and root growth. Reduction in the growth and development of legumes under salt stress is attributed to the decline in water potential of tissue, which results in closure of stomata, reduction in photosynthesis, a decline in chlorophyll contents, and inhibition in the growth (Nadeem et al., 2019). Responses of plant to salt stress occur through changes at the molecular, biochemical, and physiological levels. Salinity affects the infection process by inhibiting root hair growth and by decreasing the number of nodules produced per plant and the amount of nitrogen fixed per unit weight of nodules. Salinity-induced depressive effects on nodulation, leghemoglobin (Lb) content, and nitrogenase, which were metabolically regulated and operated through the intervention of some key regulatory substances in mung bean (Garg et al., 1988). Nodulation and nitrogen fixation are sensitive to salinity. Thus, in saline soils, the yield of leguminous crops is decreased due to the lack of successful symbiosis.

Salinity has been one of the major causes for the degradation of soil quality of the arable lands. Such degradation of arable land has made agriculture costly and hence put it at risk. It is estimated that land degradation by salinity will not only cause the annual reduction of crop productivity, but it will also cause infrastructure deterioration, employment losses, and associated environmental costs (Abiala et al., 2018). Thus, the actual loss by salt-induced land degradation is higher than expected.

1.6   Benefits of Legumes for Environmental Sustainability

The history of the domestication of legumes by human beings is as old as cereals, which are the staple food of the majority of the people in the world (Abbo et al., 2009). Data on the cultivation date of legumes goes back to prehistoric times (Yadav et al., 2010). Biological nitrogen fixation has fascinated researchers for over a century, and the benefits of cultivating legumes have been recognized for thousands of years (Lindstrom and Mousavi, 2020). Recent concerns for environmental degradation, biodiversity loss, and global climate change have emphasized the importance of exploring the potentials of legumes in mitigating these global crises (Figure 1.3). Because of their ability to fix nitrogen through symbiotic association with rhizobial bacteria, which provides both economic and environmental benefits, legumes can be considered one of the key components of sustainable agriculture.

1.6.1   Role of Legumes in Mitigating Global Warming

Anthropogenic climate change is caused by the three major greenhouse gases CO_2, CH_4, and N_2O that individually contribute the largest to the global warming (Lynch et al., 2021). Legumes have the potential

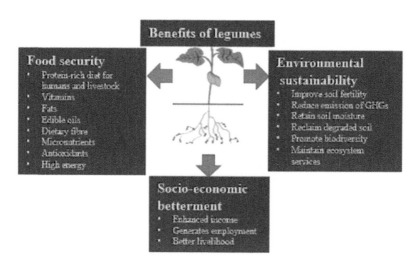

FIGURE 1.3   Beneficial effects of the leguminous crops.

to lower the emission of these greenhouse gases. Since, legumes can fix atmospheric nitrogen in association with symbiotic bacteria, they do not need to depend on the application of nitrogen-fertilizer in the field, whereas other non-legume plants do that in N-limited soils (Stagnari et al., 2017). By minimizing the use of fertilizer N in legume-based cropping systems, it is possible to reduce the use of fossil fuel (CO_2 emissions) in the manufacturing industry, transporting and applying fertilizer N during agricultural activities (Hassen et al., 2017). So, by introducing legumes in the cropping systems, it is possible to reduce dependency on energy and industrially synthesized nitrogen-fertilizers in arable lands. Legume-crop plants can also supply fixed nitrogen to other non-legume crop plants through crop-rotation or co-cultivation practices in cropping systems, which ultimately reduce the requirement of urea fertilizer in the field.

Although the contribution of N_2O to the total atmospheric greenhouse gases is comparatively low (5.5%), the rate of its increase is higher than that of CO_2, indicating its potential active role in global warming (Crutzen et al., 2007). Although agriculture is the main source contributing to the global N_2O (about 50%), it has been releasing to the atmosphere from the cropping and pasture systems mostly through the process of denitrification (Soussana et al., 2010; Rochester, 2003). Such release of N_2O to the atmosphere happens due to the application of nitrogen fertilizer with an estimated rate of about 1.0 kg of N emitted as N_2O from 100 kg of N fertilizer applied to the field. Several studies have demonstrated that legumes release less N_2O gas into the atmosphere than non-leguminous plants. Jeuffroy et al. (2013) demonstrated that peas emitted 69 kg N_2O ha^{-1}, which was lower than that released by winter wheat (368 kg N_2O ha^{-1}) and rape (534 kg N_2O ha^{-1}). Guardia et al. (2016) also compared the emission of N_2O between vetch and barley and found that emission was 2.5 times higher in barley than vetch. Another study conducted by Schwenke et al. (2015) also showed that N_2O emissions from N-fertilized canola (135 g N_2O -N ha^{-1}) was much higher than that from chickpea, faba bean, and field pea, and the values were 166, 166, and 135 g N_2O -N ha^{-1}, respectively. Lötjönen and Ollikainen (2017) demonstrated decrease of nitrogen runoff on an average by 2.6 kg ha^{-1}, with clover-based rotations and 1.2 kg ha^{-1} with pea-based rotations compared with cereal monocultures, indicating the potential of legumes in reducing environmental loads.

However, if fixation of N is higher than the uptake by plants, then the excess amount of N from legumes will result in more nitrate in soil, creating potential risk of increased nitrous oxide (N_2O) emission from the field (Kou-Giesbrecht and Menge, 2019). Nevertheless, emission of N_2O from soil can be minimized by including cereal crops in the cereal-legume intercropping systems because the cereal crop plants will uptake nitrate from soil (Hassen et al., 2017). Introduction of leguminous plants into grass-based forage production systems similarly can reduce the risk of N_2O emission by reducing soil nitrate levels in the intercrop systems. Senbayram et al. (2016) highlights that the effects of legumes in reducing greenhouse gases depends on the management strategy, such as mono-culture or intercropping in the agro-ecosystems. They reported that when faba bean was cultivated as mono cropping, then it caused 3 times higher cumulative N_2O emissions than that of unfertilized wheat (such as 441 g N_2O ha^{-1} vs 152 g N_2O ha^{-1}, respectively), and on the contrary, when faba bean was mixed with wheat intercropping system, cumulative N_2O emissions fluxes were 31% lower than that of N-fertilized wheat. Thus, emission of N_2O will also depend on the identity of species with whom legume species is mixed in the cropping system.

Leguminous plants have the potential to reduce emission of CO_2 gas into the atmosphere. Jensen et al. (2012) reported that CO_2 released during the process of synthesis of N-fertilizer in the industry was derived from fossil fuel energy, whereas that released from the root-nodules of the leguminous plants came from the atmosphere through the photosynthetic activity of the plants, indicating that legumes can reduce the emissions of CO_2 to the atmosphere. Lötjönen and Ollikainen (2017) reported decreased emissions of CO_2 by clover-based and pea-based rotations by 694 kg CO_2-eq ha^{-1} and 307 kg CO_2-eq ha^{-1}, respectively. Bayer et al. (2016) also reported that conservation management practices involving no-till in combination with legume cover crops showed lower emission of CO_2, indicating an effective approach to sustainable low-C footprint food production in subtropical regions. Legumes can play a role in the sequestration of atmospheric carbon (1.42 Mg C ha^{-1} year^{-1}) in soils, can induce the conservation of fossil energy inputs in the system, and can contribute to reducing risks of global warming by releasing up to seven times fewer greenhouse gases per unit area than non-legume crops (Kakraliya et al., 2018). Thus, legumes can contribute to achieving environmental sustainability in agriculture by reducing risks of emissions of greenhouse gases through reducing dependency on chemical fertilizer as well as on use of mechanized cropping practices.

There is substantial evidence that cover cropping with leguminous plants increased soil C sequestration (Kaye and Quemada, 2017; Schipanski et al., 2014; McDaniel et al., 2014). However, Lal (2015) reported significant variability among sites, and the effect of cover cropping on soil C appears to increase with reduced tillage, complex crop rotations, and high N inputs.

1.6.2 Role of Legumes in Improving Soil Fertility

For a long time, leguminous plants have been recognized and valued as "natural soil fertilizers" (Abiala et al., 2018) because these plants can promote nutrient cycling, increase the incorporation of carbon into soil, restore soil nutrients, and minimize erosion; therefore, they can help in the establishment of other plant species (Lange et al., 2015; de Moura et al., 2016).

Legume plants can improve soil fertility by increasing mineral nutrients (e.g., N and P), soil organic carbon (SOC), and humus content availability (Jensen et al., 2012). Legumes increase N availability in the soil through the process of biological nitrogen fixation. Nitrogen fixed thus is used by the host plant as well as the non-legumes grown nearby or in the succeeding season. Legume crops supply 195 Tg N year^{-1} (including actinorhizal species) to the agro-ecosystem through the process of biological nitrogen fixation and contribute to 15% of the N in an intercropped cereal. They thus mitigate the emission of greenhouse gases by reducing the requirement of application of synthetic nitrogenous fertilizers (Kakraliya et al., 2018). Hassen et al. (2017) reported nitrogen fixation by forage legume species and showed that fixation was on average 45 kg N ha^{-1}, and this ranges between 4 and 217 kg N ha^{-1} for herbaceous legumes and 8 and 643 kg N ha^{-1} for fodder tree species. Legumes grown in combination with other crops can increase soil-N availability. Yu et al. (2014) reported that when winter legumes were grown in rice–bean and rice–vetch combination, rice residue N content was enhanced by 9.7%–20.5%, with values ranging from 1.87 to 1.93 g N kg^{-1} soil.

Legumes can increase P availability to plants in soil. These plants take up higher amounts of cations compared to anions, resulting in proton release. Phosphorus deficiency in white lupin stimulated proton release and citrate exudation, an efficient strategy for chemical mobilization of sparingly available P (Neumann et al., 1999). Wang et al. (2012) grew wheat, faba bean, and white lupin in monoculture as well as in a mixture of wheat and legume and found that the less-labile organic P pools (i.e., NaOH extractable P pools and acid-extractable P pools) significantly accumulated in the rhizosphere of legumes. Latati et al. (2016) reported an increased P availability in the rhizosphere soil of cowpea-maize intercropping system, and the availability was associated with the acidification of soil.

Hocking (2001) conducted an experiment with grain legumes, including chickpea, pigeon pea, and white lupin, and showed mobilization of P in soil through the secretion of organic acids such as citrate and malate from the roots. This study also demonstrated interspecific differences in making P available in the soil. Results also showed that white lupin could solubilize more P than other species because of the facilitation of its proteoid roots. Phosphorus released, thus, is beneficial to the crop grown in the next cropping season.

Legumes increase soil organic C by supplying plant biomass into the soil, organic C, and by releasing hydrogen gas as by-product of the biological nitrogen fixation (Stagnari et al., 2017; Wu et al., 2017). Wu et al. (2017) reported that an increase in SOC can occur through increased species diversity during the process of co-cultivation of more than one species in the same field. Another study conducted by Bichel et al. (2016) demonstrated that intercropping of soybean with maize showed more SOC accumulation (23.6 g C kg^{-1}) than that with maize (21.8 g C kg^{-1}). This study also reported that amending the soil only with soybean residue increased about 38.5% of SOC.

Legumes also can exert beneficial effects by producing hydrogen gas as a by-product during the biological nitrogen fixation. This hydrogen gas influences composition of soil microbial communities and hence further favors growth-promoting bacteria associated with plants (Angus et al., 2015). However, the pattern of depletion and accumulation of some macro- and micronutrients may differ between cropping systems e.g., monoculture, mixed culture, and narrow crop rotations as well as among soil management strategies, such as tillage and no-tillage.

1.6.3 Role of Legumes in Soil Moisture Retention

Legumes have the potential to provide beneficial effects by changing the soil moisture in favor of the successive crops. Gan et al. (2016) reported a greater moisture content in soil cultivated with legume crops than with cereal crop, and the reason was attributed to its water use efficiency. It can help the infiltration of water into the deeper soil. Another experiment with mucuna (*Mucuna pruriens*), cowpea (*Vigna unguiculata*), and dolichos (*Lablab purpureus*) cover crops showed a significant increase in soil moisture content where soil moisture content was increased by 49.0%, 25.5%, and 13.6%, respectively, by mucuna, dolichos, and cowpea compared to the control (Mulinge et al., 2017). N-fixing trees have been reported to show greater water use efficiency than non-fixing trees, and these plants are more abundantly found in arid environmental conditions (Adams et al., 2016).

1.6.4 Role of Legumes in Weed, Pest, and Disease Control

When legume is cultivated with crop species other than legume in intercropping and crop rotation systems, they can improve production by reducing prevalence of pests, disease, and weeds (Hassen et al., 2017; Stagnari et al., 2017). Grain legumes are often not susceptible to the same pests and diseases as the main cereal crops; thus, they are helpful as "break crops" in fields when cultivated with wheat-based crop-rotation systems (Zander et al., 2016). Legumes, thus, as break crops contribute in controlling weeds by contrasting their specialization (Seymour et al., 2012; Barbery, 2002). In crop-rotation systems, grain legumes can contribute in controlling pest attacks to the subsequent crop plants, because legumes are not susceptible to the same pests and diseases as the main cereal crops (non-host) and, therefore, become a suitable break crop in wheat-based rotations (Jalli et al., 2021).

Legumes can also play an important role in controlling weed species. As a break crop, grain legumes play a role in controlling weeds by contrasting their specialization and helping to stabilize the agricultural crop weed community composition (Seymour et al., 2012). Naher et al. (2018) carried out an experiment to identify suitable legume crops with maize in maize + legume intercropping systems for better weed suppression, productivity, and economic benefits and reported significant effects of legumes on weed suppression.

1.6.5 Role of Legumes in Reclaiming Degraded Soils

Since legumes can grow on nitrogen-poor soils, they can be efficiently used for improving saline soil fertility and help to reintroduce agriculture to these lands (Manchanda and Garg, 2008). Abiala et al.

(2018) recommended some methods to follow in order to reclaim degraded soils: (a) use of salt-tolerant tree and crop species, (b) improved irrigation and drainage network, (c) testing the quality of water at different times to select a suitable approach for soil treatment, and (d) capacity building for local farmers to follow up the recommended salinity management approaches.

Although legumes have been used over thousands of years as food and fodder, their potential to help in reclaiming salt-degraded soils was proposed only recently. These plants can be used to improve saline soils because they have the potential to remove toxic ions and at the same time to increase N levels in soils (Abiala et al., 2018). Kouas et al. (2010) reported the potential of a pastoral herb *Hedysarum carnosum* to improve the quality of degraded soil since it has the ability to increase Na^+ accumulation in roots and to fix atmospheric nitrogen and hence to enhance soil fertility. Soybean has also been reported as a salt-tolerant crop due to its salt-tolerant status (Butcher et al., 2016; Katerjia et al., 2000; Cao et al., 2018), indicating its ability to restore saline-sodic soils. The use of legume trees has been suggested as the best alternative to overcome soil-N depletion associated with salt-degraded forest soils (Abiala et al., 2018).

Some studies suggested to use tree legumes, such as *Acacia nilotica* and *Leucaena leucophela,* in order to improve degraded saline soil (Dagar, 2018; Bruning and Rozema, 2013). These plants were reported to uptake Na^+ salts at the same time when they were reported to fix atmospheric N, improving the N supply in the soil. Therefore, growing legumes can be considered to be an option for the restoration of salt-degraded soils. A pastoral legume plant was able to increase Na^+ accumulation in the roots and maintain high symbiotic N_2 fixation efficiency and subsequent soil-N content under high salinity (such as 100 mM NaCl) suggesting its potential utilization in the improvement of soil fertility under saline conditions (Kouas et al., 2010).

1.6.6 Role of Legumes in Enhancing Biodiversity and Ecosystem Stability

In crop rotation, different crops are planted sequentially on the same plot. Intercropping is a means of growing two or more crop species on the same plot at the same time. These two practices of crop cultivation have ample potential to achieve sustainable agricultural production. Intercropping is popular for a number of reasons, including better pest control, increased yields with reduced input, insurance against crop damage, reduced pollution, enhanced food or forage yields, enhanced biodiversity, and optimum use of land (Maitra et al., 2021; Lopes et al., 2016; Monti et al., 2016; Smith et al., 2013; Luo et al., 2016). Legumes are considered an important component in intercropping because of their role in biological N fixation and because they provide N to the crop plants grown along with them. Both crop rotation and intercropping encourage crop diversification and reduce the chance of genetic erosion that results from dependency on a single crop for maximum yield and economic benefit. The fungal to bacterial ratio, fungivorous nematode, and arthropod were increased with legume than without legume, which indicated that legumes might enhance the resistance to ecosystem disturbance and positively affected ecosystem functioning (Gao et al., 2017). Legumes increase C and N content of the soil, which increases the microbial populations and activity to a greater extent compared with other crops cultivated with chemical fertilizers (Altieri, 1999). Residues of leguminous crops are a rich source of nitrogen and carbon compounds, which also supply vitamins and more complex substrates, which increases the microbial activities in soil. Nitrogen pools in the soil are increased in the presence of legumes, which are transferred to the other plant functional groups (grasses and herbs) and play a greater role in the ecosystem function (Spehn et al., 2002). Therefore, legumes constitute a key component of biodiversity, influencing the relationship between diversity and ecosystem processes.

1.7 Conclusion and Future Perspectives

Extreme weather events due to global climate change have increased over the years, creating challenges for agriculture across the globe. The severity of climate-indiced stresses varies with time and space. Although the impacts of global climate change are widespread, there are practical difficulties to reverse the current scenarios overnight. However, there are some possible ways to halt and minimize global warming. Legumes have ample potential in achieving sustainable food security as well as in the enhancement of input use efficiency in agriculture. Legumes can contribute to ameliorating global warming through reducing emission of greenhouse gases and achieving environmental sustainability. These plants also have the potential to improve soil fertility and enhance biodiversity in co-cultivation or crop rotation practices. Cultivation of legume can therefore help achieve SDGs (Sustainable Development Goals) as set by the United Nations by the year 2030.

It is also important to identify and preserve natural legume genotypes that are tolerant to environmental stresses to sustain agricultural production. Identification of rhizobial strains tolerant to abiotic stresses, including salinity, drought, and high temperature, is also pertinent for efficient nodulation and biological nitrogen fixation. These strains can be used for further improvement of legume-rhizobial symbiosis for the mitigation of impacts of global climate change on agriculture.

In order to overcome future challenges in agriculture, a combination of molecular techniques such as genome editing technology and conventional plant breeding as well as genetic engineering methods can be helpful to recognize and develop eco-stable varieties with required genotype-environment combinations that may be beneficial in farming under changing climatic circumstances. Enhanced knowledge on omics approaches can help unravel different mechanisms underlying thermotolerance, which is imperative to understand the processes of molecular responses toward a stress condition. Enhanced knowledge about genetics of stress tolerance or resistance and identifying quantitative trait loci (QTLs) linked with DNA markers is relevant to help breeders develop high-yielding, stress-tolerant genotypes.

Use of legumes in agriculture can ensure multiple benefits like enhancement of yield, environmental security, conservation of biodiversity, income generation, as well as production of sustainability and some ecosystem services.

REFERENCES

Abbo, S., Y. Saranga, Z. Peleg, Z. Kerem, S. Lev-Yadun, and A. Gopher. 2009. Reconsidering domestication of legumes versus cereals in the ancient near East. *The Quarterly Review of Biology* 84(1): 29–50.

Abiala, M.A., M. Abdelrahman, D.J. Burritt, and L.-S.P. Tran. 2018. Salt stress tolerance mechanisms and potential applications of legumes for sustainable reclamation of salt-degraded soils. *Land Degradation & Development* 29: 3812–3822.

Adams, M.A., T.L. Turnbull, J.I. Sprent, and N. Buchmann. 2016. Legumes are different: Leaf nitrogen, photosynthesis, and water use efficiency. *Proceedings of the National Academy of Science* 113: 4098–4103.

Aguilar, E., T.C. Peterson, P.R. Obando, R. Frutos et al. 2007. Europe. Climate change 2007: Impacts, adaptation and vulnerability. In *Contribution of working group II to the fourth assessment report of the Intergovernmental Panel on Climate Change*, eds. M.L. Parry, O.F. Canziani, J.P. Palutikof, P.J. van der Linden, and C.E. Hanson, 541–580. Cambridge: Cambridge University Press.

Alcamo, J., Dronin, N., Endejan, M., Golubev, G., and A. Kirilenko. 2007. A new assessment of climate change impacts on food production shortfalls and water availability in Russia. *Global Environmental Change* 17(3–4): 429–444.

Altieri, M.A. 1999. The ecological role of biodiversity in agroecosystems. *Agriculture, Ecosystems and Environment* 74: 19–31.

Angus, J.F., J.A. Kirkegaard, J.R. Hunt, M.H. Ryan, L. Ohlander and M.B. Peoples. 2015. Break crops and rotations for wheat. *Crop Pasture Science* 66: 523–552.

Arias, P.A., Fu, R., and K.C. Mo. 2012. Decadal variation of rainfall seasonality in the North American monsoon region and its potential causes. *Journal of Climate* 25(12): 4258–4274.

Barbery, P. 2002. Weed management in organic agriculture: Are we addressing the right issues. *Weed Research* 42: 177–193.

Bayer, C., J. Gomes, J.A. Zanatta, F.C.B. Vieira, and J. Dieckow. 2016. Mitigating greenhouse gas emissions from a subtropical Ultisol by using long-term no-tillage in combination with legume cover crops. *Soil and Tillage Research* 161: 86–94. doi:10.1016/j.still.2016.03.011

Beaugrand, G. 2012. Unanticipated biological changes and global warming. *Marine Ecology Progress Series* 445: 293–301.

Bichel, A., M. Oelbermann, P. Voroney, and L. Echarte. 2016. Sequestration of native soil organic carbon and residue carbon in complex agroecosystems. *Carbon Management* 7: 1–10.

Bordeleau, L.M., and D. Prévost. 1994. Nodulation and nitrogen fixation in extreme environments. *Plant and Soil* 161: 115–125.

Broomell, S.B., J.-F. Winkles, and P.B. Kane. 2017. The perception of daily temperatures as evidence of global warming. *Weather, Climate and Society* 9: 563–574.

Bruinsma, J. ed. 2003. *World agriculture: Towards 2015/2030 – An FAO perspective.* UK: Earthscan.

Bruning, B., and J. Rozema. 2013. Symbiotic nitrogen fixation in legumes: Perspectives for saline agriculture. *Environmental and Experimental Botany* 92: 134–143. doi:10.1016/j.envexpbot.2012.09.001

Bucchignani, E., P. Mercogliano, H-J. Panitz, and M. Montesarchio. 2018. Climate change projections for the Middle East–North Africa domain with COSMO-CLM at different spatial resolutions. *Advances in Climate Change Research* 9 (1): 66–80.

Butcher, K., Wick, A.F., DeSutter, T., Chatterjee, A., and Harmon, J. 2016. Soil salinity: A threat to global food security. *Agronomy Journal* 108(6): 2189–2200.

Calzadilla, A., K. Rehdanz, R. Betts, P. Falloon, A. Wiltshire, and R.S.J. Tol. 2013. Climate change impacts on global agriculture. *Climatic Change* 120: 357–374.

Cao, D., Y. Li, B. Liu, F. Kong, and L.S.P. Tran. 2018. Adaptive mechanisms of soybean grown on salt-affected soils. *Land Degradation & Development* 29: 1054–1064.

Chibarabada, P.T., Modi, T.A., and T. Mabhandhi. 2017. Expounding the value of grain legumes in the semi and arid tropics. *Sustainability* 960. doi:10.3390/509010060

Cline, W. 2007. *Global warming and agriculture: Impact estimates by country.* Washington, DC: Center for Global Development and Peterson Institute for International Economics.

Considine, M.J., K.H.M. Siddique, and C.H. Foyer. 2017. Nature's pulse power: Legumes, food security and climate change. *Journal of Experimental Botany* 68(8): 1815–1818.

Corwin, D.L. 2020. Climate change impacts on soil salinity in agricultural areas. *European Journal of Soil Science* 72(2): 842–862.

Crutzen, P.J., A.R. Mosier, K.A. Smith, and W. Winiwarter. 2007. N_2O release from agro-biofuel production negates global warming reduction by replacing fossil fuels. *Atmospheric Chemistry and Physics Discussions, European Geosciences Union* 7 (4): 11191–11205.

CSIRO (Commonwealth Scientific and Industrial Research Organisation). 2018. *Australia's changing climate.* Canberra, Australia: CSIRO.

Dagar, J.C. 2018. Utilization of degraded saline habitats and poor-quality waters for livelihood security. *Scholarly Journal of Food and Nutrition* 1(3). SJFN.MS.ID.000115.

de Faria, S.M., G.P. Lewis, J.L. Sprent, and J.M. Sutherland. 1989. Occurrence of nodulation in the leguminosae. *New Phytologists* 111: 607–619.

de Moura, G.G.D., R.D. de Armas, E. Meyer, A.J. Giachini, M.J. Rossi, and C.R.F.S. Soares. 2016. Rhizobia isolated from coal mining areas in the nodulation and growth of leguminous trees. *Revista Brasileira de Ciência do Solo* 40: e0150091. doi:10.1590/18069657rbcs20150091

Duc, G., H. Agrama, S. Bao, J. Berger, V. Bourion, A.M. De Ron, C.L.L. Gowda, A. Mikic, D. Millot, K.B. Singh, A. Tullu, A. Vandenberg, M.C. Vaz Patto, T.D. Warkentin, and X. Zong. 2015. Breeding annual grain legumes for sustainable agriculture: New methods to approach complex traits and target new cultivar ideotypes. *Critical Reviews in Plant Sciences* 34: 381–411. doi:10.1080/07352689.2014.898469

Easterling, W.E., P.K. Aggarwal, P. Batima et al. 2007 Food, fibre and forest products. Climate change 2007: Impacts, adaptation and vulnerability. Contribution of working group II. In *The fourth assessment report of the Intergovernmental Panel on Climate Change*, eds. M.L. Parry, O.F. Canziani, J.P. Palutikof, P.J. van der Linden, and C.E. Hanson, 273–313. Cambridge: Cambridge University Press.

FAO (Food and Agricultural Organization) and ITPS (Intergovernmental Technical Panel on Soils). 2015. Status of the World's Soil Resources (SWSR) – Main report. Food and Agriculture Organization of the United Nations and Intergovernmental Technical Panel on Soils, Rome, Italy. https://www.fao.org/3/i5199e/I5199E.pdf

Fening, J.O., C. Quansah, and A. Sarfo-Kantanka. 2009. Response of three forage legumes to soil moisture stress. *Journal of Science and Technology* 29(3): 24–30.

Ferguson B.J., C. Mens, A.H. Hastwell, M. Zhang, H. Su, C.H. Jones, X. Chu, and P.M. Gresshoff. 2019. Legume nodulation: The host controls the party. *Plant, Cell & Environment* 42: 41–51. doi:10.1111/pce.13348

Fonty, E., C. Sarthou, D. Larpin, and J.-F. Ponge. 2009. A 10-year decrease in plant species richness on a neotropical inselberg: Detrimental effects of global warming? *Global Change Biology* 15: 2360–2374. doi:10.1111/j.1365-2486.2009.01923.x

Gan, Y., C. Hamel, H.R. Kutcher, and Poppy, L. 2016. Lentil enhances agroecosystem productivity with increased residual soil water and nitrogen. *Renewable Agriculture and Food Systems* 32(4): 319–330.

Gao, D., X. Wang, S. Fu, and J. Zhao. 2017. Legume plants enhance the resistance of soil to ecosystem disturbance. *Frontiers in Plant Science* 8: 1295. doi:10.3389/fpls.2017.01295

Garg, N., I.S. Dua, S.K. Sharma, and O.P. Garg. 1988. Nodulation and nitrogen fixing capacity in relation to variable salinity levels in Vigna radiata L. (Mung.). *PU Res Bull (Sci)* 39(III–IV): 187–196.

Gaur, P.M., S. Samineni, L. Krishnamurthy, et al. 2015. High temperature tolerance in grain legumes. *Legume Perspectives* 7: 23–24.

Giorgi, F., X. Bi, and J. Pal. 2004. Mean, interannual variability and trends in a regional climate change experiment over Europe. II: Climate change scenarios (2071–2100). *Climate Dynamics* 23: 839–858.

Giorgi, F., and P. Lionello. 2008. Climate change projections for the Mediterranean region. *Global and Planetary Change* 63: 90–104.

Gowda, C.L.L., P.P. Rao, and S. Bhagavatula. 2009. Global trends in production and trade of major grain legumes. In *International Conference on legumes: Quality improvement, value addition and trade.* Indian Institute of Pulses Research: Indian Society of Pulses Research and Development, Kanpur, India. pp. 282–301.

Guardia, G., A. Tellez-Rio, S. García-Marco, et al. 2016. Effect of tillage and crop (cereal versus legume) on greenhouse gas emissions and Global Warming Potential in a non-irrigated Mediterranean field. *Agriculture, Ecosystem & Environment* 221: 187–197.

Guo, J., R. Feng., Y. Ding, and R. Wang. 2014. Applying carbon dioxide, plant growth-promoting rhizobacterium and EDTA can enhance the phytoremediation efficiency of ryegrass in a soil polluted with zinc, arsenic, cadmium and lead. *Journal of Environmental Management* 141 (1): 1–8.

Hartmann, D.L., A.M.G.K. Tank, M. Rusticucci et al. 2013. Observations: Atmosphere and surface. In *Climate change 2013: The physical science basis (contribution of working group I to the fifth assessment report of the Intergovernmental Panel on Climate Change),* eds. T.F. Stocker, D. Qin, G.-K. Plattner, M. Tignor, S.K. Allen, J. Boschung, A. Nauels, Y. Xia, V. Bex, and P.M. Midgley, 159–254. Cambridge, UK and New York: Cambridge University Press. doi:10.1017/CBO9781107415324.008

Hassen, A., D.G. Talore, E.H. Tesfamariam, M.A. Friend, and T.D.E. Mpanza. 2017. Potential use of forage-legume intercropping technologies to adapt to climate-change impacts on mixed crop-livestock systems in Africa: A review. *Regional Environmental Change* 17: 1713–1724.

Haylock, M.R., T. Peterson, L.M. Alves, et al. 2006. Trends in total and extreme South American rainfall in 1960–2000 and links with sea surface temperature. *Journal of Climate Change* 19: 1490–1512.

Hocking, P.J. 2001. Organic acids exuded from roots in phosphorus uptake and aluminum tolerance of plants in acid soils. *Advances in Agronomy* 74: 63–97.

Hossain, M.Z., M.M. Hasan, J. Ferdous, and S. Hoque. 2016a. Growth responses of lentil (*Lens culinaris* Medik.) varieties to the properties of selected soils in Bangladesh. *Mol* 16: 18–29.

Hossain, M.Z., I.U. Rasel, and R. Samad. 2016b. Soil moisture effects on the growth of lentil (*Lens culinaris* Medik.) varieties in Bangladesh. *Mol* 16: 30–40.

Hossain, M.Z., M.M. Hasan, and M.A. Kashem. 2018. Intervarietal variation in salt tolerance of lentil (*Lens culinaris* Medik.) in pot experiments. *Bangladesh Journal of Botany* 47(3): 405–412.

Hungria, M., and A.A. Franco. 1993. Effects of high temperature on nodulation and nitrogen fixation by *Phaseolus vulgaris* L. *Plant and Soil* 149: 95–102.

Hungria, M., and M.A.T. Vargas. 2000. Environmental factors affecting N_2 fixation in grain legumes in the tropics, with an emphasis on Brazil. *Field Crops Research* 65(2–3): 151–164.

Hussain, M., S. Farooq, W. Hasan, et al. 2018. Drought stress in sunflower: Physiological effects and its management through breeding and agronomic alternatives. *Agricultural Water Management* 201(31): 152–166.

IPCC (The Intergovernmental Panel on Climate Change). 2007. *Climate change 2007: Impacts, adaptation and vulnerability—Contribution of work group II to the fourth assessment report of the Intergovernmental Panel on Climate Change.* Cambridge: Cambridge University Press.

IPCC (The Intergovernmental Panel on Climate Change). 2013. Summary for policymakers. In *Climate change 2013: The physical science basis. Contribution of working group I to the fifth assessment report of the Intergovernmental Panel on Climate Change,* eds. T.F. Stocker, D. Qin, G.-K. Plattner, M. Tignor, S.K. Allen, J. Boschung, A. Nauels, Y. Xia, V. Bex, and P.M. Midgley, Cambridge, UK and New York: Cambridge University Press, pp. 3–29.

Jalli, M., E. Huusela, H. Jalli, et al. 2021. Effects of crop rotation on spring wheat yield and pest occurrence in different tillage systems: A multi-year experiment in Finnish growing conditions. *Frontiers in Sustainable Food Systems* 5. doi: 10.3389/fsufs.2021.647335

James, R., and R. Washington. 2013. Changes in African temperature and precipitation associated with degrees of global warming. *Climatic Change* 117: 859–872.

Jensen, E.S., M.B. Peoples, R.M. Boddey, et al. 2012. Legumes for mitigation of climate change and the provision of feedstock for biofuels and biorefineries. *Agronomy for Sustainable Development* 32: 329–364. doi.org/10.1007/s13593-011-0056-7

Jeuffroy, M.H., E. Baranger, B. Carrouée, E.D. Chezelles, M. Gosme, and C. Hénault. 2013. Nitrous oxide emissions from crop rotations including wheat, oilseed rape and dry peas. *Biogeosciences* 10: 1787–1797.

Jiang, D-B, H-J. Wang, and X-M. Lang. 2013. East Asian climate change trend under global warming background. *Chinese Journal of Geophysics* 47: 675-681. doi.org/10.1002/cjg2.3536

Jochum, T., A. Fastnacht, S.E. Trumbore, J. Popp and T. Frosch. 2017. Direct Raman spectroscopic measurements of biological nitrogen fixation under natural conditions: An analytical approach for studying nitrogenase activity. *Analytical Chemistry* 89: 1117–1122.

Jung, T.Y. 2012. Review of the economics of climate change on Southeast Asia. In *Climate Change in Asia and the Pacific How Can Countries Adapt?* eds. V. Anbumozhi, M. Breiling, S. Pathmarajah, and V.R. Reddy, 9–6. Asian Development Bank Institute: SAGE Publications India Pvt Ltd, New Delhi.

Kakraliya, S.K., U. Singh, A. Bohra, et al. 2018. Nitrogen and legumes: A meta-analysis. In *Legumes for soil health and sustainable management*, eds. R. Meena, A. Das, G. Yadav, and R. Lal, Singapore: Singapore.

Katerjia, N., J.W. van Hoorn, A. Hamdy, and M. Mastrorilli. 2000. Salt tolerance classification of crops according to soil salinity and to water stress day index. *Agricultural Water Management* 43: 99–109. doi: 10.1016/S0378-3774(99)00048-7

Kaye, J.P., and Quemada, M. 2017. Using cover crops to mitigate and adapt to climate change. A review. *Agronomy for Sustainable Development* 37(4). doi: 10.1007/s13593-016-0410-x

Kouas, S., T. Slatni, I. Ben Salah, and C. Abdelly. 2010. Eco-physiological responses and symbiotic nitrogen fixation capacity of salt-exposed *Hedysarum carnosum* plants. *African Journal of Biotechnology* 9: 462–7469. doi: 10.5897/AJB10.211

Kou-Giesbrecht, S., and D. Menge. 2019. Nitrogen-fixing trees could exacerbate climate change under elevated nitrogen deposition. *Nature Communications* 10: 1493. doi: 10.1038/s41467-019-09424-2

Lal, R. 2015. Soil carbon sequestration and aggregation by cover cropping. *Journal of Soil and Water Conservation* 70: 329–339. doi: 10.2489/jswc.70.6.329

Lange, M., N. Eisenhauer, C.A. Sierra, et al. 2015. Plant diversity increases soil microbial activity and soil carbon storage. *Nature Communications* 6: 6707. doi: 10.1038/ncomms7707

Lara, M.V., and C.S. Andreo. 2011. C4 plants adaptation to high levels of CO_2 and to drought environments. In *Abiotic stress in plants –Mechanisms and adaptations*, A. Shanker (ed), ISBN: 978-953-307-394-1, InTech, Available from: http://www.intechopen.com/books/abiotic-stress-in-plantsmechanisms-and-adaptations/c4-plants-adaptation-to-high-levels-of-co2-and-to-drought-environments

Latati, M., A. Bargaz, B. Belarbi, M. Lazali, S. Benlahrech, and S. Tellah. 2016. The intercropping common bean with maize improves the rhizobial efficiency, resource use and grain yield under low phosphorus availability. *European Journal of Agronomy* 72: 80–90.

Lee, C.C., and S.C. Sheridan. 2018. Trends in weather type frequencies across North America. *Climate and Atmospheric Science* 1: 41.

Lindstrom, K., and S.A. Mousavi. 2020. Effectiveness of nitrogen fixation in rhizobia. *Microbial Biotechnology* 13(5): 1314–1335.

Lobell, D.B., W. Schlenker, and J. Costa-Roberts. 2011. Climate trends and global crop production since 1980. *Science* 333(6042): 616–620.

Lopes, T., S. Hatt, Q. Xu, J. Chen, Y. Liu, and F. Francis. 2016. Wheat (*Triticum aestivum* L.)-based intercropping systems for biological pest control: A review. *Pest Management Science* 72: 2193–2202.

Lötjönen, Sanna, and M. Ollikainen. 2017. Does crop rotation with legumes provide an efficient means to reduce nutrient loads and GHG emissions? *Review of Agricultural, Food and Environmental Studies* 98: 283–312.

Lu, H., R.B. Bryant, A.R. Buda, A.S. Collick, G.J. Folmar, and P.J.A. Kleinman. 2015. Long-term trends in climate and hydrology in an agricultural, headwater watershed of Central Pennsylvania, USA J hydrology. *Reg Stud* 4: 713–731. doi: 10.1016/j.ejrh.2015.10.004

Luo, S., L. Yu, Y. Liu, et al. 2016. Effects of reduced nitrogen input on productivity and N_2O emissions in a sugarcane/soybean intercropping system. *European Journal of Agronomy* 81: 78–85.

Lynch, J., M. Cain, D. Frame, and R. Pierrehumbert. 2021. Agriculture's contribution to climate change and role in mitigation is distinct from predominantly fossil CO_2-emitting sectors. *Frontiers in Sustainable Food Systems* 4: 518039. doi:10.3389/fsufs.2020.518039

Maitra, S., A. Hossain, M. Brestic, M. Skalicky, P. Ondrisik, H. Gitari, K. Brahmachari, T. Shankar, P. Bhadra, J.B. Palai, J. Jena, U. Bhattacharya, S.K. Duvvada, S. Lalichetti, and M. Sairam (2021). Intercropping—A low input agricultural strategy for food and environmental security. *Agronomy* 11: 343. doi:10.3390/agronomy11020343

Manchanda, G., and N. Garg. 2008. Salinity and its effects on the functional biology of legumes. *Acta Physiologiae Plantarum* 30: 595–618.

Marengo, J.A., Chou, S.C., Torres, R.R., Giarolla, A., Alves, L.M., and A. Lyra. 2014. Climate change in Central and South America: Recent trends, future projections, and impacts on regional agriculture. CCAFS Working Paper no. 73. Copenhagen, Denmark: CGIAR Research Program on Climate Change, Agriculture and Food Security (CCAFS). https://hdl.handle.net/10568/41912

Mather, J.R., and G.A. Yoshioka. 1968. The role of climate in the distribution of vegetation. *Annals of the Association of American Geographers* 58(1): 29–41.

McCulloch, L.A., D. Piotto, and S. Porder. 2021. Drought and soil nutrients effects on symbiotic nitrogen fixation in seedlings from eight Neotropical legume species. *Biotropica* 53: 703–713. 10.1111/btp.12911

McDonald, G.K., and G.M. Paulsen. 1997. High temperature effects on photosynthesis and water relations of grain legumes. *Plant and Soil* 196: 47–58.

McDaniel, M., L. Tiemann, and A.S. Grandy. 2014. Does agricultural crop diversity enhance soil microbial biomass and organic matter dynamics? A meta-analysis. *Ecological Applications* 24: 560–570. doi:10.1890/13-0616.1

Monti, M., A. Pellicanò, C. Santonoceto, G. Preiti, and A. Pristeri. 2016. Yield components and nitrogen use in cereal-pea intercrops in Mediterranean environment. *Field Crop Research* 196: 379–388.

Mukherjee, S., A. Mishra, and K.E. Trenberth. 2018. Climate change and drought: A perspective on drought indices. *Current Climate Change Reports* 4: 145–163.

Mulinge, J., H.M. Saha, L. Mounde., and L.A. Wasilwa. 2017. Effect of legume cover crops on soil moisture and orange root distribution. *International Journal of Plant and Soil Science* 16(4): 1–11.

Nabila, M., and M.Z. Hossain. 2017. Ecophysiological responses of crop plants under different functional types to salt stress. *Mol* 17: 55–65.

Nadeem, M., J. Li, M. Yahya, et al. 2019. Research progress and perspective on drought stress in legumes: A review. *International Journal of Molecular Sciences* 20: 2541.

Naher, Q., S.M.R. Karim, and M. Begum. 2018. Performance of legumes on weed suppression with hybrid maize intercropping. *Bangladesh Agronomic Journal* 21(2): 33–44.

Neumann, G., A. Massonneau, E. Martinoia, and V. Römheld. 1999. Physiological adaptations to phosphorus deficiency during proteoid root development in white lupin. *Planta* 208: 373–382. doi:10.1007/s004250050572

Ngaira, J.K.W. 2007. Impact of climate change on agriculture in Africa by 2030. *Scientific Research and Essays* 2(7): 238–243

Nicholson, S.E. 2001. Climatic and environmental change in Africa during the last two centuries. *Climate Research* 17: 123–144. doi:10.3354/cr017123

Nkemdirim, L.C. 2003. *Climates in transition: Commission on climatology.* Washington DC: Minateman Press.

Norrant, C., and A. Douguédroit. 2006. Monthly and daily precipitation trends in the Mediterranean. *Theoretical and Applied Climatology* 83: 89–106.

Ojiem, J.O., B. Vanlauwe, N. De Ridder, and K.E. Giller. 2007. Niche-based assessment of contributions of legumes to the nitrogen economy of Western Kenya smallholder farms. *Plant and Soil* 292: 119–135. doi:10.1007/s11104-007-9207-7

Overpeck, J.T., and B. Udall. 2020. Climate change and the aridification of North America. *Proceedings of the National Academy of Sciences* 117(22): 11856–11858.

Polley, H.W., D.D. Briske, J.A. Morgan, K. Wolter, D.W. Bailey, and J.R. Brown. 2013. Climate change and North American rangelands: trends, projections, and implications. *Rangeland Ecology & Management* 66(5): 493–511.

Qiao, J., Y.U. Deyong, Q. Wang, and Liu Y. 2018. Diverse effects of crop distribution and climate change on crop production in the agro-pastoral transitional zone of China. *Frontiers of Earth Science* 12(2): 408–419.

Raza, A., A. Razzaq, S.S. Mehmood, et al. 2019. Impact of climate change on crops adaptation and strategies to tackle its outcome: A review. *Plants* 8: 34. doi:10.3390/plants8020034

Raza, A., N. Zahra, M.B. Hafeez, et al. 2020. Nitrogen fixation of legumes: Biology and physiology. In *The plant family Fabaceae*, eds. M. Hasanuzzaman, S. Araújo, and S. Gill, Singapore: Springer, pp 43–74. doi:10.1007/978-981-15-4752-2_3

Reis, C.R.G., F.S. Pacheco, S.C. Reed, et al. 2020. Biological nitrogen fixation across major biomes in Latin America: Patterns and global change effects. *Science of The Total Environment* 746, 1 December 2020, 140998.

Rochester, I.J. 2003. Estimating nitrous oxide emissions from flood irrigated alkaline grey clays. *Australian Journal of Soil Research* 41: 197–206.

Schipanski, M., M. Barbercheck, M.R. Douglas, et al. 2014. A conceptual framework for evaluating ecosystem services provided by cover crops in agroecosystems. *Agricultural Systems* 125: 12–22. doi: 10.1016/j.agsy.2013.11.004

Schwenke, G.D., D.F. Herridge, C. Scheer, D.W. Rowlings, B.M. Haigh, and K.G. McMullen. 2015. Soil N_2O emissions under N_2-fixing legumes and N-fertilised canola: A reappraisal of emissions factor calculations. *Agriculture, Ecosystem & Environment* 202: 232–242.

Senbayram, M., C. Wenthe, A. Lingner, et al. 2016. Legume-based mixed intercropping systems may lower agricultural born N_2O emissions. *Energy, Sustainability and Society* 6: 2. doi:10.1186/s13705-015-0067-3

Serraj, R. 2003. Effects of drought stress on legume symbiotic nitrogen fixation: Physiological mechanisms. *Indian Journal of Experimental Biology* 41: 1136–1141. PMID: 15242280.

Seymour, M., J.A. Kirkegaard, M.B. Peoples, P.F. White, and R.J. French. 2012. Break-crop benefits to wheat in Western Australia-insights from over three decades of research. *Crop and Pasture Science* 63: 1–16.

Shahid, S.A., Zaman, M., and L. Heng. 2018. Soil Salinity: Historical perspectives and a world overview of the problem. In *Guideline for salinity assessment, mitigation and adaptation using nuclear and related techniques*, eds. Zaman, M. et al., Springer, Cham. pp. 43–53. doi:10.1007/978-3-319-96190-3_2

Singh, D.P., and B.B. Singh. 2011. Breeding for tolerance to abiotic stresses in mungbean. *Journal of Food Legumes* 24(2): 83–90.

Sita, K., A. Sehgal, B. HanumanthaRao, et al. 2017. Food legumes and rising temperatures: Effects, adaptive functional mechanisms specific to reproductive growth stage and strategies to improve heat tolerance. *Frontiers in Plant Science* 8: 1658. doi:10.3389/fpls.2017.01658

Sivakumar, M.V.K., and R. Stefanski. 2010. Climate change in South Asia. In *Climate change and food security in South Asia*, eds. R. Lal, M.V.K. Sivakumar, S.M.A. Faiz, A.H.M.M. Rahman, and K.R. Islam, Springer, Dordrecht, pp. 13–30.

Skendžíc, S., M. Zovko, I.P. Živkovíc, V. Lešíc, and D. Lemíc. 2021. The impact of climate change on agricultural insect pests. *Insects* 12: 440. doi:10.3390/insects12050440

Smith, J., B.D. Pearce, M. Wolfe, and S. Martin. 2013. Reconciling productivity with protection of the environment: Is temperate agroforestry the answer? *Renewable Agriculture and Food Systems* 28: 80–92.

Smýkal, P., Coyne, C.J., Ambrose, M.J., et al. 2015. Legume crops phylogeny and genetic diversity for science and breeding. *Critical Reviews in Plant Sciences* 34(1–3): 43–104. doi: 10.1080/07352689. 2014.897904

Sorg, A., T. Bolch, M. Stoffel, O. Solomina, and M. Beniston. 2012. Climate change impacts on glaciers and runoff in Tien Shan (Central Asia). *Nature Climate Change* 2: 725–731.

Soussana, J.F., T. Tallec, and V. Blanfort. 2010. Mitigating the greenhouse gas balance of ruminant production systems through carbon sequestration in grasslands. *Animal* 4: 334–350.

Spehn, E.M., M. Scherer-Lorenzen, B. Schmid, et al. 2002. The role of legumes as a component of biodiversity in a cross-European study of grassland biomass nitrogen. *Oikos* 98: 205–218. doi:10.1034/j. 1600-0706.2002.980203.x

Stagnari, F., A. Maggio, A. Galieni, and M. Pisante. 2017. Multiple benefits of legumes for agriculture sustainability: An overview. *Chemical and Biological Technologies in Agriculture* 4: 2. doi:10.1186/ s40538-016-0085-1

Stoffel, M., M. Khodri., C. Corona., et al. 2015. Estimates of volcanic-induced cooling in the Northern Hemisphere over the past 1,500 years. *Nature Geoscience* 8: 784–788.

Tank, A.M.G.K., J.B. Wijngaard, and G.P. Konnen. 2002. Daily dataset of 20th-century surface air temperature and precipitation series for the European climate assessment. *International Journal of Climatology* 22: 1441–1453.

UNDP (United Nations Development Programme) 2018. *Climate change adaptation in the Arab states best practices and lessons learned.* Bangkok: UNDP.

Vance, C.P., P.H. Graham, and D.U. Allan. 2000. Biological nitrogen fixation: Phosphorus- a critical future need. In *Nitrogen fixation: From molecules to crop productivity*, eds. F.O. Pedrosa, M. Hungria, M.G. Yates, and W.E. Newton, 506–514, Dordrecht, The Netherlands: Kluwer Academic Publishers.

Vincent, L.A., T.C. Peterson, V.R. Barros, et al. 2005. Observed trends in indices of daily temperature extremes in South America 1960–2000. *Journal of Climate* 18 (23): 5011–5023

Vitousek, P.M., K. Cassman, C. Cleveland, et al. 2002. *Biogeochemistry* 57: 1–45.

Wang, Y., P. Marschner, and F. Zhang. 2012. Phosphorus pools and other soil properties in the rhizosphere of wheat and legumes growing in three soils in monoculture or as a mixture of wheat and legume. *Plant and Soil* 354: 283–298.

Warren, R., J. Price, E. Graham, N. Forstenhaeusler, and J. van der Wal. 2018. The projected effect on insects, vertebrates, and plants of limiting global warming to 1.5°C rather than 2°C. *Science* 360: 791–795.

WMO (World Meteorological Organization). 2002. Iintroduction to climate change: Lecture notes for meteorologigsts: WMO-No. 926.

WMO (World Meteorological Organization). 2018. WMO Statement on the state of the global climate in 2017; WMO-No. 1212.

Wu, G-L., Y. Liu, F-P. Tian, and Z-H. Shi. 2017. Legumes functional group promotes soil organic carbon and nitrogen storage by increasing plant diversity. *Land Degradation & Development* 28: 1336–1344.

Yadav, S.S., D.L. McNeil, R. Redden, and Patil, S.A. 2010. *Climate change and management of cool-season grain legume crops.* Springer, Dordrecht.

Yu, Y., L. Xue, and L. Yang. 2014. Winter legumes in rice crop rotations reduces nitrogen loss, and improves rice yield and soil nitrogen supply. *Agronomy for Sustainable Development* 34: 633–640.

Zander, P., T.S. Amjath-Babu, S. Preissel, et al. 2016. Grain legume decline and potential recovery in European agriculture: A review. *Agronomy for Sustainable Development* 36: 26. doi: 10.1007/s13593-016-0365-y

2

Diversity in Legume Genetic Resources for Adaptation to Climate Stress

Burcu Yuksel[1] and Ozlem Aksoy[2]
[1]*Kocaeli University, Vocational School of Kocaeli Health Services, Izmit, Kocaeli, TURKEY*
[2]*Kocaeli University, Sciences and Arts Faculty, Department of Biology, Izmit, Kocaeli, TURKEY*

CONTENTS

2.1 Introduction

Heat stress caused by global warming has become a serious concern for agricultural production across the world (Sun et al., 2019). The reason for this is that transient or persistent elevated temperature brings about a series of morphological-physiological, biochemical, and genetic alterations in plants, which may influence plant growth and improvement, leading to a serious decrease in agricultural and economic efficiency (Bita and Gerats, 2013; Mathur et al., 2014; Mickelbart et al., 2015). By developing heat-tolerant crop varieties using numerous approaches, the negative impacts of heat stress on the plant can be alleviated or prevented. Therefore, it is essential to understand better plants' physiological reactions to heat, temperature tolerance, and potential strategies to mitigate the heat stress problem in agriculture.

A thorough understanding of plant heat-stress tolerance includes potential genetic strategies for improving heat tolerance, traditional and contemporary molecular breeding protocols, and transgenic approaches (Wahid et al., 2007). By using conventional breeding protocols, tolerant plants against heat can be acquired. These plant varieties can be enhanced by identifying genes that have known effects on plant heat-stress tolerance. Heat resistance, avoiding damage caused by heat stress, is an active process in which plant metabolism is structured and functionally oriented (Hasanuzzaman et al., 2013; Sah et al., 2016; Hasanuzzaman et al., 2017; Ohama et al., 2017). Although plants' biochemical and molecular perspectives to heat tolerance are comparatively understood, more inquisition is required to modulate heat tolerance by crop plants. Identifying and mapping genes (or QTLs) that specifically provide heat tolerance will make it easier to grow heat-tolerant crops and will be useful in cloning and characterizing key genetic factors that can be helpful for plant genetic studies (Acuña-Galindo et al., 2015; Bhusal

DOI: 10.1201/9781003214885-2

et al., 2017; Sukumaran et al., 2018). This chapter focuses on the diversity of legume genetic resources for adaptation to climate-related stresses due to global warming.

2.2 Implications for Plants' Response to Climate Change

Throughout the plant ontogeny, the increased expression of various heat shock proteins, other stress-related proteins, and the production of reactive oxygen species (ROS) against heat stress generate basic plant reactions (Kotak et al., 2007; Hasanuzzaman et al., 2013). Numerous mechanisms, including preservation of membrane determination, removal of ROS, generation of antioxidants, aggregation and regulation of osmoprotectants, induction of mitogen-activated protein kinase (MAPK), and calcium-dependent protein kinase (CDPK), are maintained by plants to handle heat stress. CDPK cascades, chaperone signalling, and transcriptional activation are the most important of these mechanisms (Qu et al., 2013). Furthermore, the development of the plants under temperature stress is encouraged by all these mechanisms, which are regulated at the molecular and physiological levels. (Figure 2.1).

Although the temperature threshold level varies significantly at different stages of development, it is a factor that affects the growth of the plant. For example, during the seed germination stage, depending on the plant variety and the density of heat stress, high heat can slow down or stop germination completely. Besides photosynthesis, respiration, osmotic pressure, and membrane stability can be badly affected by heat stress in the subsequent stages. Furthermore, heat stress can alter hormone rates and primary plus secondary metabolites (Wahid and Close, 2007; Prasad et al., 2008). Plants have anatomical, biochemical, cytological, and genetic response systems to these stresses. Anatomical responses of plants to high heat stress include closure and shortening of stomata due to water loss, observation of an increase in stomatal and thylakoids densities, and formation of large xylem vessels in both root and shoot structures (Krishnan et al., 2011). Also, the increase in the number of mesophyll cells and polymorphic leaves creates an increase in the permeability of the plasma membrane in response to water loss stress (Lipiec et al., 2013). Generally, plants tend to keep tissue water status constant. However, excessive heat stress severely disrupts

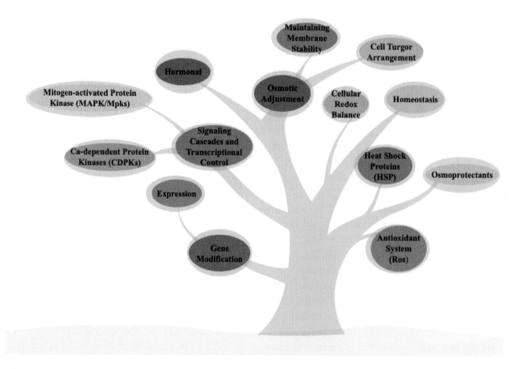

FIGURE 2.1   Various mechanisms of plants to cope with the heat stress condition.

this trend (Farooq et al., 2011). At high night temperatures, the leaf water potential and its components are kept in optimal conditions by root hydraulic conductivity (Farooq et al., 2009). In addition, plants release various sugars and sugar alcohols (polyols), osmolytes such as proline, tertiary and quaternary ammonium composites, tertiary sulfonium composites, plus especially under high temperature, glycine betaine (GB) (Rizhsky et al., 2004; Wahid and Close, 2007; Wassmann et al., 2009).

High temperatures cause sunburn in leaves, branches, and stems; leaf aging; slowing of shoot and root growth; damage and deterioration of fruit color; and decreased yield (Vollenweider and Gunthardt-Goerg, 2005; Wahid and Close, 2007; Hemantaranjan et al., 2014). Also, the temperature that the organism cannot tolerate causes the development of pollen and anther to deteriorate, damages fertilization, and causes a decrease in seed production (Fahad et al., 2017). One of the damages it can cause at the molecular level is changes in thylakoids' organization. With these changes, the structure of chloroplasts changes, and a significant decrease in photosynthesis is observed (Kaushal et al., 2016). Also, high temperatures may cause losses in chloroplasts, granas, and degradation in mitochondria crystals (Zhang et al., 2005). Zhang et al. (2005) also reported that such changes lead to impairments in the formation of photosystem-II and reduced photosynthesis formation. The effects of high temperatures on the growth and function of some plants are shown in Table 2.1. Therefore, high temperatures significantly affect crop production. For all these reasons, it is important to know the responses and processes of the plant against heat stress during the development stages in order to determine the heat tolerance potential of the crop. With genetic approaches, the heat tolerance of the crop can be increased, and the production losses can be reduced by increasing the plants' capacity to resist heat stress.

TABLE 2.1

Effects of Elevated Temperature on the Growth and Function of Plants

Sl. No.	Plant Responses	Plants Species Name	References
1	Damage to photosystem-II, degradation in mitochondria crystals, losses in chloroplasts, losses in granas	*Vitis vinifera* L.	Zhang et al., 2005
2	Damage to thylakoids' organization	Barley Pima cotton *Vicia faba* L	Kaushal et al., 2016
3	Damage to fertilization	*Phaseolus vulgaris* L *Arachis hypogea* L *Lycopersicum esculentum* Mill.	Fahad et al., 2017
4	Damage to the development of pollen and anther	*Saccharum officinarum* L	Fahad et al., 2017
5	Slowing of shoot and root growth, leaf aging, deterioration of fruit color	*Melampsora sp.* *Cladosporium sp.* *Populus tremula* *Pinus cembra* *Picea abies* *Pinus mugo* *Pinus sylvestris*	Vollenweider and Gunthardt-Goerg, 2005
6	Decline of leaf photosynthesis	*Hordeum vulgare*	Wahid and Close, 2007
7	Chloroplast changes, decrease in photosynthesis	*Hordeum vulgare* *Pima cotton* *Lolium perenne*	Kaushal et al., 2016
8	Inhibition of Rubisco activase	*Gossypium hirsutum* L.	Hemantaranjan et al., 2014
9	Reduction in photosynthetic function and sucrose synthesis, chlorophyll disruption, damage in the cell membrane	Lentil *(Lens culinaris Medik. ssp. Culinaris)*	Bhandari et al., 2016

(Continued)

TABLE 2.1 (Continued*)*

Effects of Elevated Temperature on the Growth and Function of Plants

Sl. No.	Plant Responses	Plants Species Name	References
10	Arrested photosynthetic activity, impeded nitrogen fixation	Pea *(Pisum sativum* L)	Georgieva and Lichtenthaler, 1999; Michiels et al., 1994
11	Impeded nitrogen fixation	Common bean *(Phaseolus vulgaris* L)	Piha and Munns, 1987
12	Inhibited nitrogen fixation	Chickpea *(Cicer arietinum* L.)	Rodrigues et al., 2006
13	Reduction of plant productivity	Faba bean *(Vicia faba* L.),	Bishop et al., 2016
14	Nitrogen-fixing bacterial infection, impeded nitrogen fixation	Cowpea *(Vigna unguiculata* (L.) Walp.)	Rainbird et al., 1983; Michiels et al., 1994
15	Negatively affected symbiotic bacterial infection, restricted biological nitrogen fixation	Groundnut *(Arachis hypogaea* L.)	Kishinevsky et al., 1992; Michiels et al., 1994
16	Limited biomass production	Mung bean *(Vigna radiata* (L.) Wilczek)	Kaur et al., 2015
17	Reduction in photosynthetic rate, stomatal devastated, restricted biological nitrogen fixation, reduced isoflavone content, storage proteins and carbohydrates affected, negatively affected tocopherol content	Soybean *(Glycine max* L. Merr.)	Djanaguiraman et al., 2011; Michiels et al., 1994; Chennupati et al., 2011; Chennupati et al., 2012

2.3 Legume Genetic Resources

The Leguminosae (Fabaceae) family is the third-largest family with 750 genera and 20,000 species, including herbs, shrubs, and trees, although most of them are herbaceous of the order Fabales. Some legume species are used as human food, such as beans, broad beans, chickpeas, soy, lentils, and peas. Species such as pseudo acacia, wild locust, acacia, and rosemary have a woody structure (Turland and Jarvis, 1997). Grain legumes are the basic protein resource that provides improved nutrition to the people of numerous developing countries. Legume germplasm constitutes 15% of 7.4 million specimens preserved in the world. These genetic resources have been studied mostly in terms of morpho-agronomic features. Local varieties and protection of wild species is extremely important (Upadhyaya et al., 2011). Approximately, 1.1 million legume germplasm are present in different gene banks worldwide (Sharma et al., 2013).

The first phylogenetic studies of legumes started with the plastid *rbcL* gene (Doyle, 1995; Kass and Wink, 1997), followed by the analysis of the more variable *matK* gene (Wojciechowski et al., 2004). The aim of the gene banks was to protect genetic substance, fundamentally gene aggregations, so that these genetic substances may be used in the future (Fowler and Hodgkin, 2004), usually as seed or qua cells or tissues of plant material (Tanksley and McCouch, 1997) to avoid fluctuations in environmental conditions before discussions about climate change started. The samples are stored in gene banks at low temperatures to stop the cells' chemical and biological activities and prevent them from degrading.

Specimens are frozen with liquid nitrogen at −196°C by some gene banks. In the frosting process, the other liquids, like glycerin, change places with the water inside the cells. This liquid minimizes the possibility of ice crystals forming in the cell and prevents ice crystals from damaging the cell wall. Later, biologists remove the glycerin or used liquid from the cell during melting, thus allowing the cell to take in the water again.

2.4 Preservation of Seeds in Medium- and Long-Term Collections

The *ex-situ* seed storage method is the most economical and commonly used conservation method. Active collections are kept in conditions that maintain vitality above 65% for approximately 20 years. The longevity can be increased when different storage conditions, such as temperature, humidity, and pest removal, are applied (IPGRI, 1996). For long-term seed storage, basic collections can be maintained for more than 50 years, usually at −20°C (FAO / IPGRI, 1994). An important issue to be considered in *ex situ* conservation is monitoring the viability of the stored materials at certain time intervals and controlling their regeneration if necessary (Breese, 1989). Botanical gardens are an *ex-situ* way for seed collection and conservation. They can help to cope with climate change. The number of legume species was decreased as the climatic conditions change. However, fortunately, preservation policies are consolidated, and their contribution to critically endangered species recovery programs is enhanced by several botanical gardens (Smýkal et al., 2015).

Local varieties are produced in small areas, using little input, in marginal lands where commercial varieties are not grown. Local varieties with wide genetic variation are important genetic resources because they contain genes related to resistance to stress conditions, diseases, and pests as well as many desired quality traits. Therefore, preserving genetic diversity in local varieties is extremely important (Tan, 2009). Important progress has been made in the use of genetic resources. High-yielding varieties with good adaptability have been brought to the economy, and added value has been created. It is thought that by carrying out more detailed studies with new technological developments, it will be possible to develop materials that are more resistant to adverse climate (temperature, drought) changes, disease agents, and pest populations that will occur with the effect of global warming we will encounter in the coming years (Ozpinar et al., 2017).

2.5 Legume Production Sustainability and Climate Change

Climate change is closely connected to food production and its security. Regardless of how it occurs, climate change, which also can be in the form of drought, flood, typhoon, or soil acidification, affects all stages of food generation and eventually food efficiency and farmers. Unless urgent and sustainable measures are taken, climate change will continue to pressure agricultural ecosystems, especially vulnerable regions and populations. Scientists studying climate change estimated that the increasing atmospheric CO_2 concentrations and global temperatures would have a serious effect on modified rainfall patterns and would increase the frequency of extreme weather events within the next 100 years (Andrews and Hodge, 2010).

Beans, peas, and chickpeas constitute a large part (67.5%) of the total legume production in the world (Parca et al., 2018). Significant increases were observed in lentil, cowpea, and lupine production during 1996–2000. At the same time, 31.6% of world legume production is from beans, and peas placed in the second position by contributing 20.6% (Zając et al., 2013). The rate of chickpea production is 15.3%, whereas that of lentils is 5.2%. Important countries in the world for bean production are India, Brazil, China, the United States, Myanmar, Mexico, and Indonesia (68.9% of world production).

On the other hand, Australia, Canada, China, France, Germany, India, Russia, Ukraine, the United Kingdom, and the United States are pioneers for pea production (85.1% of the world production) (Gul and Isık, 2002). The top legume producer countries in the world are Bangladesh, India, and Pakistan. Australia, Canada, France, Turkey, and the United States export the bulk of the legumes they produce. Researchers estimated that South Asia's population would be approximately 700 million, and the need for cool-season grain legumes will increase by 30% until the year 2035. Climate change will give results such as increased production in developed countries at mid and high-mid latitudes but decreased production in developing countries in the tropics and sub-tropics (Andrews and Hodge, 2010; Foyer et al., 2016).

Crop development strategies such as the micropropagation of stress-tolerant varieties of legumes, the use of adaptation strategies, crop substitution methods, and changes in sowing date may be used to cope with the consequences of climate change on cool-season grain legumes (Andrews and Hodge, 2010). *Lathyrus sativus* and *Vicia ervilia*, mainly used in animal feeding, have an important role as essential plants in the world's regions with marginal climatic and environmental conditions (Deikman et al., 2012; Araujo et al., 2015). These plants are seen as an assurance in terms of food safety with their tolerance to drought and salinity stress conditions, and they have begun to attract researchers' attention.

The common expectations of producers and consumers are high-yielding new varieties that do not contain harmful substances. It should be considered as a priority to control the genetic material existing in the natural flora without erosion and to implement the improvement projects in which these materials are included. The introduction of legumes in agricultural production can play an important role in increasing resistance to climate change. Legume products have a wide range of genetic variability from which advanced species can be obtained and grown. This variety is an especially significant feature because it allows for the development of more climate-resistant diversities. Climate experts suggest that heat stress will be the most important threat to bean production in the coming decades. Therefore, improved legumes are critical, especially for granular agricultural production systems.

2.6 The Effect of Climate Change on Product Yield and Genetic Approaches

It is necessary to have knowledge about the distribution and extent of genetic variation in order to use sources effectively in plant breeding processes. For this, the genetic variety of adaptive characteristics, mutation information, phenotypic influence, genetic variants, plus their interactions with the environment must be known (Doebley et al., 2006). Abundant food has been provided to humanity by domesticating plants with genetic variation (Diamond, 2002). Nevertheless, when they are compared to their wilder ancestors, domesticated crops have decreased genetic variety due to the climate crises and the increase in population (Gepts, 2010; Mousavi-Derazmahalleh et al., 2019). While lower sequence variation was observed in the domesticated species, its effect on the symbiotic life of the plant was negative (Kim et al., 2014). Changes in genetic variation in plants are important for crop expansion, cultivation, and future agriculture. Comprehension of all presumptive variances that lead to adaptation is a must to completely comprehend adaptive evolution. Accordingly, when it is focused on the role of genomics to produce climate-smart legumes, we must also consider genetic variations where phenotypic changes occur.

Drought and temperature rise is presently the most common in legumes and yield-limiting abiotic stress in many crops (Vadez et al., 2012). Therefore, studies have focused on the adaptation part of plants in the Legume family against heat stress. Epigenetic mechanisms include DNA methylation, modification of histones, and processes of expressing RNAs that do not alter DNA sequences but can affect the gene (Springer and Schmitz, 2017). Hereditary DNA methylation has been shown to increase drought tolerance in *Arabidopsis thaliana* (Zhang et al., 2013). In another study, it was found that flowering increased due to the overexpression of the photoperiodic regulator with the help of methylated genes in the circulation of cotton (Song et al., 2017). Although these studies are suitable for identifying excellent examples of epigenetic potential, it is unknown whether the genomics and epigenomics of new sources of variation applied in crop breeding are integrated into other species. Addressing this gap leads to significant advances in the breeding of ready-to-eat crops, including legumes.

The CRISPR / Cas9 model was applied in legume plants. An optimized version of the targeted gene mutation in soybeans was obtained from the CRISPR / Cas9 platform. It was found to alter both *Glycine max* and *Medicago truncatula* root somatic cells (Michno et al., 2015). It was also determined that an optimized agrobacterium interrupted the MtPDS gene, which was included in carotenoid biosynthesis in *Medicago truncatula* (Meng et al., 2017). Adding to the accessibility of high-quality reference genomes, these samples make CRISPR studies a popular choice for genome editing of legume models. By way of quantitative trait locus (QTL) mapping and genome-wide association studies (GWAS), identifying resistant genetic sources, suitable natural variations, and the transfer of these natural variations to elite varieties is possible (Takeda and Matsuoka, 2008; Varshney et al., 2016).

2.7 Conclusions and Perspectives

Heat stress has become a serious problem for crop production worldwide, affecting plants' growth, development, and productivity. Therefore, the mechanisms underlying plant response and adaptation to heat and the improvement of high-temperature tolerance should be better comprehended for agricultural products. The physiological, genetic, and molecular reactions of plants against high temperature have densely been the subject of studies in recent years. Molecular genetic approaches that reveal response and tolerance mechanisms will help develop crop varieties that can tolerate abiotic stresses. We believe that the cultivation of stress-tolerant legume varieties, which are important in human and animal nutrition, using genomic tools, will be significantly beneficial both in dealing with the climate crisis and the problem of hunger.

REFERENCES

Acuña-Galindo, M.A., R.E. Mason, N.K. Subramanian, and D.B. Hays. 2015. Meta-analysis of wheat QTL regions associated with adaptation to drought and heat stress. *Crop Science* 55: 477–492.

Andrews, M. and S. Hodge. 2010. Climate change, a challenge for cool-season grain legume crop production. In *Climate change and management of cool-season grain legume crops*. Yadav S. S. and Redden R. Eds. (pp. 1–9). Springer, Dordrecht.

Araujo, S.S., S. Beebe, M. Crespi, B. Delbreil, E.M. Gonzalez, V. Gruber, et al. 2015. Abiotic stress responses in legumes: Strategies used to cope with environmental challenges. *Critical Reviews in Plant Sciences* 34: 237–280.

Bhandari, K., K.H.M. Siddique, N.C. Turner, J. Kaur, S. Singh, S. Agrawal, et al. 2016. Heat stress at reproductive stage disrupts leaf carbohydrate metabolism, impairs reproductive function, and severely reduces seed yield in Lentil. *Journal of Crop Improvement* 30: 118–151.

Bhusal, N., A.K. Serial, P. Sharma, and S. Sareen. 2017. Mapping QTLs for grain yield components in wheat under heat stress. *PLoS One* 12: e0189594.

Bishop, J., S.G. Potts, and H.E. Jones. 2016. Susceptibility of faba bean (*Vicia faba* L.) to heat stress during floral development and anthesis. *Journal of Agronomy and Crop Science* 202: 508–517.

Bita, C. and T. Gerats. 2013. Plant tolerance to high temperature in a changing environment: Scientific fundamentals and production of heat stress-tolerant crops. *Frontiers in Plant Science* 4: 273.

Breese, E.L. 1989. Regeneration and multiplication of germplasm resources in seed genebanks: The scientific background. *International Board of Plant Genetic Resources*, Rome.

Chennupati, P., P. Seguin, R. Chamoun, and S. Jabaji. 2012. Effects of high-temperature stress on soybean isoflavone concentration and expression of key genes involved in isoflavone synthesis. *Journal of Agriculture and Food Chemistry* 60: 12421–12427.

Chennupati, P., P. Seguin, and W. Liu. 2011. Effects of high temperature stress at different development stages on soybean isoflavone and tocopherol concentrations. *Journal of Agriculture and Food Chemistry* 28: 13081–13088.

Deikman, J., M. Petracek, and J.E. Heard. 2012. Drought tolerance through biotechnology: Improving translation from the laboratory to farmers' fields. *Current Opinion in Biotechnology* 23: 243–250.

Diamond, J. 2002. Evolution, consequences and future of plant and animal domestication. *Nature* 418: 700–707.

Djanaguiraman, M., P.V.V. Prasad, D.L. Boyle, and W.T. Schapaugh. 2011. High temperature stress and soybean leaves: *Leaf Anatomy and Photosynthesis Crop Science* 5: 2125–2131.

Doebley, J.F., B.S. Gaut, and B.D. Smith. 2006. The molecular genetics of crop domestication. *Cell* 127: 1309–1321.

Doyle, J.J. 1995. DNA data and legume phylogeny: A progress report. In *Advances in legume systematics.* pp. 11–30. Part 7: Phylogeny. Crisp, M. and Doyle, J.J., Eds., Royal Botanic Gardens, Kew.

FAO/IPGRI 1994. Genebank standards. Food and Agricultural Organization of the United Nations, International Plant Genetic Resources Institute, Rome.

Fahad, S., A.A. Bajwa, U. Nazir, S.A. Anjum, A. Farooq, A. Zohaib, and J. Huang. 2017. Crop production under drought and heat stress: Plant responses and management options. *Frontiers in Plant Science* 8: 1147.

Farooq, M., H. Bramley, J.A. Palta, and K.H. Siddique. 2011. Heat stress in wheat during reproductive and grain-filling phases. *Critical Reviews in Plant Sciences* 30: 491–507.

Farooq, M., A. Wahid, N. Kobayashi, D.B. Fujita, and S.M.A. Basra. 2009. Plant drought stress: Effects, mechanisms and management. In *Sustainable Agriculture* 153–188. Lichtfouse, E., Navarrete, M., Debaeke, P., Véronique, S., and Alberola, C., Eds., Springer, Dordrecht.

Fowler, C., and T. Hodgkin. 2004. Plant genetic resources for food and agriculture: Assessing global availability. *Annual Review of Environment and Resources* 29: 143–179.

Foyer, C.H., H.M. Lam, H.T. Nguyen, K.H. Siddique, R.K. Varshney, T.D. Colmer, et al. 2016. Neglecting legumes has compromised human health and sustainable food production. *Nature Plants* 2: 1–10.

Georgieva, K., and H. Lichtenthaler. 1999. Photosynthetic activity and acclimation ability of pea plants to low and high temperature treatment as studied by means of chlorophyll fluorescence. *Journal of Plant Physiology* 155: 416–423.

Gepts, P. 2010. Crop domestication as a long!term selection experiment. *Plant Breeding Reviews* 24: 1–44.

Gul, M., and H. Isık. 2002. Dünyada ve Türkiye'de Baklagil Üretim ve Dış Ticaretindeki Gelişmeler. *MKU Ziraat Fakültesi Dergisi* 7: 59–72.

Hasanuzzaman, M., K. Nahar, M. Alam, R. Roychowdhury, and M. Fujita. 2013. Physiological, biochemical, and molecular mechanisms of heat stress tolerance in plants. *International Journal of Molecular Sciences* 14: 9643–9684.

Hasanuzzaman, M., K. Nahar, T.I. Anee, and M. Fujita. 2017. Glutathione in plants: Biosynthesis and physiological role in environmental stress tolerance. *Physiology and Molecular Biology of Plants* 23: 249–268.

Hemantaranjan, A., A.N. Bhanu, M.N. Singh, D.K. Yadav, P.K. Patel, R. Singh, and D. Katiyar. 2014. Heat stress responses and thermotolerance. *Advances in Plants & Agriculture Research* 1: 1–10.

IPGRI 1996. Report of the internally commissioned external review of the CGIAR Genebank operations. International Plant Genetic Resources Institute, Rome.

Kass, E., and M. Wink. 1997. Molecular phylogeny and phylogeography of *Lupinus* (Leguminosae) inferred from nucleotide sequences of the *rbcL* gene and ITS regions of rDNA. *Plant Systematics and Evolution* 208: 139–167.

Kaur, R., T.S. Bains, H. Bindumadhava, and H. Nayyar. 2015. Responses of mungbean (*Vigna radiata* L.) genotypes to heat stress: Effects on reproductive biology, leaf function and yield traits. *Scientia Horticulturae* 197: 527–541.

Kaushal, N., K. Bhandari, K.H. Siddique, and H. Nayyar. 2016. Food crops face rising temperatures: An overview of responses, adaptive mechanisms, and approaches to improve heat tolerance. *Cogent Food & Agriculture* 2: 1134380.

Kim, D.H., M. Kashyap, A. Rathore, R.R. Das, S. Parupalli, H. Upadhyaya, et al. 2014. Phylogenetic diversity of Mesorhizobium in chickpea. *Journal of Biosciences* 39: 513–517.

Kishinevsky, B.D., D. Sen, and R.W. Weaver. 1992. Effect of high root temperature on Bradyrhizobium-peanut symbiosis. *Plant and Soil* 143: 275–282.

Kotak, S., J. Larkindale, U. Lee, P. von Koskull-Döring, E. Vierling, and K.D. Scharf. 2007. Complexity of the heat stress response in plants. *Current Opinion in Plant Biology* 10: 310–316.

Krishnan, P., B. Ramakrishnan, K.R. Reddy, and V.R. Reddy. 2011. High-temperature effects on rice growth, yield, and grain quality. *Advances in Agronomy* 111: 87–206.

Lipiec, J., C. Doussan, A. Nosalewicz, and K. Kondracka. 2013. Effect of drought and heat stresses on plant growth and yield: A review. *International Agrophysics* 27: 463–477.

Mathur, S., D. Agrawal, and A. Jajoo. 2014. Photosynthesis: Response to high temperature stress. *Journal of Photochemistry and Photobiology B: Biology* 137: 116–126.

Meng, Y., Y. Hou, H. Wang, R. Ji, B. Liu, J. Wen, et al. 2017. Targeted mutagenesis by CRISPR/Cas9 system in the model legume Medicago truncatula. *Plant Cell Reports* 36: 371–374.

Michiels, J., C. Verreth, and J. Vanderleyden. 1994. Effects of temperature stress on bean-nodulating Rhizobium strains. *Applied and Environment Microbiology* 60: 1206–1212.

Michno, J.M., X. Wang, J. Liu, S.J. Curtin, T.J. Kono, and R.M. Stupar. 2015. CRISPR/Cas mutagenesis of soybean and Medicago truncatula using a new web tool and a modified Cas9 enzyme. *GM Crops and Food* 6: 243–252.

Mickelbart, M.V., P.M. Hasegawa, and J. Bailey-Serres. 2015. Genetic mechanisms of abiotic stress tolerance that translate to crop yield stability. *Nature Reviews Genetics* 16: 237–251.

Mittler, R., A. Finka, and P. Goloubinoff. 2012. How do plants feel the heat?. *Trends in Biochemical Sciences* 37: 118–125.

Mousavi-Derazmahalleh, M., P.E. Bayer, J.K. Hane, B. Valliyodan, H.T. Nguyen, M.N. Nelson, and D. Edwards. 2019. Adapting legume crops to climate change using genomic approaches. *Plant, Cell and Environment, 42*: 6–19.

Ohama, N., H. Sato, K. Shinozaki, and K. Yamaguchi-Shinozaki. 2017. Transcriptional regulatory network of plant heat stress response. *Trends in Plant Science* 22: 53–65.

Ozpınar, H., F.N. İnal, E. Ay, A.A. Acar, and C.O. Sabancı. 2017. Türkiye Yem Bitkileri Genetik Kaynakları. *Anadolu, Journal of AARI* 27: 51–55.

Parca, F., Y.O., Koca, and A. Unay. 2018. Nutritional and antinutritional factors of some pulses seed and their effects on human health. *International Journal of Secondary Metabolite* 5 (4) 331–342.

Piha, M.I., and D.N. Munns. 1987. Sensitivity of the common bean (*Phaseolus vulgaris* L.) symbiosis to high soil temperature. *Plant and Soil* 98: 183–194.

Prasad, P.V.V., S.A. Staggenborg, and Z. Ristic. 2008. Impacts of drought and/or heat stress on physiological, developmental, growth, and yield processes of crop plants. In *Response of crops to limited water: Understanding and modeling water stress effects on plant growth processes*. Ahuja, L.R., Reddy, V.R., Saseendran, S.A., and Yu, Q., Vol. 1, pp. 301–355.

Qu, A.L., V.F. Ding, Q. Jiang, and C. Zhu. 2013. Molecular mechanisms of the plant heat stress response. *Biochemical and Biophysical Research Communications* 432: 203–207.

Rainbird, R.M., C.A. Atkins, and J.S. Pate. 1983. Effect of temperature on nitrogenase functioning in cowpea nodules. *Plant Physiology* 73: 392–394.

Rizhsky, L., H. Liang, J. Shuman, V. Shulaev, S. Davletova, and R. Mittler. 2004. When defense pathways collide. The response of Arabidopsis to a combination of drought and heat stress. *Plant Physiology* 134: 1683–1696.

Rodrigues, C.S., M. Laranjo, and S. Oliveira. 2006. Effect of heat and pH stress in the growth of chickpea Mesorhizobia. *Current Microbiology* 53: 1–7.

Sah, S.K., K.R. Reddy, and J. Li. 2016. Abscisic acid and abiotic stress tolerance in crop plants. *Frontiers in Plant Science* 7: 571.

Sharma, S., H.D. Upadhyaya, R.K. Varshney, and C.L.L. Gowda. 2013. Pre-breeding for diversification of primary gene pool and genetic enhancement of grain legumes. *Frontiers in Plant Science* 4: 309.

Smýkal, P., C.J. Coyne, M.J. Ambrose, N. Maxted, H. Schaefer, M.W. Blair, et al. 2015. Legume crops phylogeny and genetic diversity for science and breeding. *Critical Reviews in Plant Sciences 34*: 43–104.

Song, Q., T. Zhang, D.M. Stelly, and Z.J. Chen. 2017. Epigenomic and functional analyses reveal roles of epialleles in the loss of photoperiod sensitivity during domestication of allotetraploid cottons. *Genome Biology* 18: 99.

Springer, N.M., and R.J. Schmitz. 2017. Exploiting induced and natural epigenetic variation for crop improvement. *Nature Reviews Genetics* 18: 563–575.

Sukumaran, S., M.P. Reynolds, and C. Sansaloni. 2018. Genome-wide association analyses identify QTL hotspots for yield and component traits in durum wheat grown under yield potential, drought, and heat stress environments. *Frontiers in Plant Science* 9: 81.

Sun, Q., C. Miao, M. Hanel, A.G. Borthwick, Q. Duan, D. Ji, et al. 2019. Global heat stress on health, wildfires, and agricultural crops under different levels of climate warming. *Environment International* 128: 125–136.

Tan, A. 2009. Türkiye Geçit Bölgesi Genetik Çeşitliliğinin In situ (Çitçi Şartlarında) Muhafazası olanakları. *Anadolu, Journal of AARI* 19: 1–12.

Takeda, S., and M. Matsuoka. 2008. Genetic approaches to crop improvement: Responding to environmental and population changes. Nature Reviews. *Genetics* 9: 444–457.

Tanksley, S.D., and S.R. McCouch. 1997. Seed banks and molecular maps: Unlocking genetic potential from the wild. *Science* 277: 1063–1066.

Turland, N.J., and C.E. Jarvis. 1997. Typification of Linnaean specific and varietal names in the Leguminosae (Fabaceae). *Taxon* 46(3): 457–485.

Upadhyaya, H.D., S.L. Dwivedi, M. Ambrose, N. Ellis, J. Berger, P. Smýkal, et al. 2011. Legume genetic resources: Management, diversity assessment, and utilisation in crop improvement. *Euphytica* 180: 27–47.

Vadez, V., J.D. Berger, T. Warkentin, S. Asseng, P. Ratnakumar, K.P.C. Rao, et al. 2012. Adaptation of grain legumes to climate change: A review. *Agronomy for Sustainable Development* 32: 31–44.

Varshney, R.K., V.K. Singh, J.M. Hickey, X. Xun, D.F. Marshall, J. Wang, et al. 2016. Analytical and decision support tools for genomics-assisted breeding. *Trends in Plant Science* 21: 354–363.

Vollenweider, P., and M.S. Gunthardt-Goerg. 2005. Diagnosis of abiotic and biotic stress factors using the visible symptoms in foliage. *Environmental Pollution* 137: 455–465.

Wahid, A., and T.J. Close. 2007. Expression of dehydrins under heat stress and their relationship with water relations of sugarcane leaves. *Biologia Plantarum* 51: 104–109.

Wahid, A., S. Gelani, M. Ashraf, and M.R. Foolad. 2007. Heat tolerance in plants: An overview. *Environmental and Experimental Botany* 61: 199–223.

Wassmann, R., S.V.K. Jagadish, S. Heuer, A. Ismail, E. Redona, R. Serraj, and K. Sumfleth. 2009. Climate change affecting rice production: The physiological and agronomic basis for possible adaptation strategies. *Advances in Agronomy* 101: 59–122.

Wojciechowski, M.F., M. Lavin, and M.J. Sanderson. 2004. A phylogeny of legumes (Leguminosae) based on analysis of the plastid *matK* gene resolves many well-supported subclades within the family. *American Journal of Botany* 91: 1846–1862.

Zając, T., A. Klimek-Kopyra, A. Oleksy, and A. Lenart 2013. Vertical distribution of Pea (Pisum sativum L.) seed yield depending on the applied bacterial inoculants. *Journal of Agricultural Science* 5(1): 260–268.

Zhang, J.-H., W.-D. Huang, Y.-P. Liu, and Q.-H. Pan. 2005. Effects of temperature acclimation pretreatment on the ultrastructure of mesophyll cells in young grape plants (*Vitis vinif*era L. cv. Jingxiu) under cross-temperature stresses. *Journal of Integrative Plant Biology* 47: 959–970.

Zhang, Y.Y., M. Fischer, V. Colot, and O. Bossdorf. 2013. Epigenetic variation creates potential for the evolution of plant phenotypic plasticity. *New Phytologist* 197: 314–322.

3

Diversity and Distribution of Legumes in Pakistan

Syed Rehmat Ullah Shah, Asadullah, and Abdul Hameed Baloch
Faculty of Agriculture, Lasbela University of Agriculture, Water and Marine Sciences, Pakistan

CONTENTS

3.1 Introduction

Legumes play a central role in the food system, both for human and animal consumption, as a source of plant proteins and have increasing importance in improving humans' health. Besides serving as important sources of oil, fiber, and protein-rich food and feed, legumes have a great role in the sustainable agro-ecosystem by supplying nitrogen (N) via their unique ability to fix atmospheric N_2 in symbiosis with the soil bacteria, called rhizobia, increasing soil carbon content and stimulating the productivity of crops (Wani Ladha 1995). Their ability to fix atmospheric nitrogen and mitigate greenhouse gases makes them potentially suitable for inclusion in low-input cropping systems and in the diversification of crops in agro-ecosystems. Based on a few major cultivated species and their use as fodder, legumes break the cycles of pests and diseases and contribute to balance the deficit in plant protein production around the world, including Pakistan (Stagnari et al., 2017). However, the role of legumes has rarely been considered in the context of their potential to contribute to the mitigation of climate change by reducing fossil fuel use or by providing feedstock for the emerging bio-based economies where fossil sources of energy and industrial raw materials can be replaced in part by sustainable and renewable biomass resources (Jensen et al., 2012).

Unfortunately, legume diversity in Pakistan has declined drastically over the past few decades. Many native species have become extinct, including some species that were once widespread and common. It is assumed that this decline is largely due to the massive increase in population, which is continuously increasing at an alarming rate, followed by deforestation, deterioration of rangelands by over-grazing, soil erosion, as well as depletion of the major water resources (Wiseman and Hopkins, 2000). An

DOI: 10.1201/9781003214885-3

TABLE 3.1

Phytogeographical Regions of Pakistan

S. No.	Region	Major Included Areas in Pakistan
1	Saharo-Sindian	Plain area of Khyber Pakhtunkhwa (KPK) province, central and southern Punjab, Sindh and southern Balochistan
2	Irano-turanian i. Western subregion ii. Eastern subregion (Central Asiatic)	North of Balochistan and Wasiristan of KPK Northern areas of Gilgit and Chiral
3	Sino-Japanese	Kashmir, partial areas of Swat, Hazara, Dir, Chitral Astor, Naltar and Bagrot valleys
4	Indian	Sub-Himalayan region and eastern and western regions of river Jhelum

extensive survey in Pakistan has not been carried out yet, and more specific studies are required to focus on the conservation of legumes.

3.2 Geographic Distribution of Plants

Phytogeographically, Pakistan partially covers four major regions (Table 3.1) that represent its natural phyto-diversity. These include the Saharo-Sindian region, Irano-turanian region with two subregions divided into Western and Eastern regions, Sino-Japanese region, and Indian region (Nasir and Rafiq, 1995). All these regions cover different parts of the provinces of Pakistan. Boundaries for these areas do not limit the distribution of plants. Some flora may overlap among the regions. In the Saharo-Sindian region, the mean daily maximum temperature in summer ranges from 41°C to 46°C and sometimes 50°C or above in Sindh and Punjab. Mean annual rainfall in this region is 140–347 mm (Nasir and Rafiq, 1995).

Irano-turanian is considered to be a large floristic region, which is further divided into two sub-regions with different climatic conditions. The Western subregion includes the northern areas of Balochistan and Khyber Pakhtunkhwa (KPK), where the average temperature varies between −15°C in winter and 40°C in summer in various areas of this region. The average rainfall is between 200 and 250 mm annually. On the other hand, the Eastern subregion includes the mountains of Central Asia and Tibet, where the average temperature remains as low as −40°C during winter and rises up to 0°C in summer. Mean annual rainfall in this region is 120–500 mm with subhumid conditions. In Pakistan, the Sino-Japanese region lies between approximately 32° and 35° 5' north, which includes Kashmir and a major portion of the present KPK, where the average temperature is 11°C. Mean annual rainfall is around 2,853 mm, which accounts for 112.3 inches per year. Similarly, the Indian region lies mainly in the north from 29°5'–32° N and about 73° E, which comprises the northeast Punjab (including foothills of sub-Himalayan tracks). The average temperature varies between 9°C in winter and 18°C in summer in various areas of this region, with a mean annual rainfall of around 535 mm.

3.3 Distribution of Legumes in Pakistan

Leguminous plants grow throughout the world, but their greatest diversity is found in the tropics. Legumes are well distributed in Pakistan, as they are grown on 1.6 million ha; that is, 1.9% of the total cultivated land of Pakistan. Almost all of this land is in two northern provinces, Punjab and KPK, and is concentrated in the Thal and Potohar divisions (Punjab) and in the Malakand (KPK). Some edible legumes, such as Lathyrus and chickpea, are also grown as irrigated crops in the Sindh province

(Aslam et al., 1995). Some legumes are indigenous, whereas others are introduced and have become widely naturalized (Kirkbride, 1986).

Ecologically, Pakistan has many promising zones for growing all types of food legumes. Moreover, in Pakistan medicinal legumes are distributed in 25 genera and all three subfamilies of Fabaceae. Legume species growing under natural growth conditions were surveyed for their nodulating ability from various parts of Pakistan. Legumes form a prominent and widespread part of the flora of Pakistan, where 107 genera have been reported by Ali and Qaiser (1986), of which 68 genera have one or more native species. A total of 539 legume species are reported to occur in Pakistan, of which 426 are native (Kirkbride, 1986).

An ethnobotanical survey of indigenous and exotic plants was carried out in different parts of the Balochistan province of Pakistan (Hameed, 2015). This study was composed of an exhaustive distribution and collection of medicinal and economically important plants. The study identified that medicinal plants play a crucial role in the daily life of the Baloch people, who use different parts of these plants for multiple purposes, such as a cure for ailments, as fodder, for tanning leather, and for firewood. Similarly, another team from the Pakistan Forestry Institute, Peshawar carried out an ethnobotanical study in northern areas of Pakistan (Rasool, 1998). This study identified economically valuable trees that can be collected from the wild and medicinal plants that can be grown commercially on common or agricultural land. Several species are no longer found in the area, including *Taxus baccata*, the source of the anti-cancer agent Taxol. There is potential for cultivating medicinal plants as an income-generating activity (Athar & Ahmad, 2004; Athar & Siddiqi, 2004).

3.4 Genetic Diversity

Fabaceae (Leguminosae), with 800 genera and 20,000 species, is the third largest family of flowering plants, after Orchidaceae and Asteraceae (Lewis et al., 2005). Members of Fabaceae are characterized by their distinct fruit, termed "legume," which gives the family its original name. It is an extremely diverse family with worldwide distribution, encompassing a broad range of life forms, from arctic alpine herbs and temperate or tropical perennial shrubs to annual xerophytes and equatorial giant trees. Some legumes are considered weeds of cereal crops, whereas others are major grain crops; these latter species are known as grain legumes, or pulses, and are grouped together with two pasture and forage legumes. Fabaceae includes many economically important and versatile species, with the majority providing grains and pulses. Among the grain legumes are some of humanity's earliest crop plants, including soybean and mungbean in East Asia; faba bean, lentil, chickpea, and pea in the Fertile Crescent of the Near East; and the common bean or lupin in Central and South America. Legumes' symbiosis with nitrogen-fixing bacteria not only provides added value in agriculture but also plays an important role in natural ecosystems.

3.5 Taxonomy, Distribution, and Uses of Legumes in Pakistan

Legumes are amazing natural resources. These plants do not just benefit soil in restoring their fertility, but also provide wood for home building, packaging that keeps food fresh during shipment, and natural products like cellulose that are found in everything from the instant soup that we eat to the fabrics that we wear. These plants are everlasting, easily available, and centuries old, tested sources for healing various ailments (Athar & Siddiqi, 2004; Athar & Nasir, 2005).

Currently, based on morphological characters, the following three major groups are recognized and regarded as subfamilies: the papilionoid legumes, Papilionoideae (or family Fabaceae/Papilionaceae with 28 tribes and 13,800 species); the mimosoid legumes, Mimosoideae (sometimes regarded as family Mimosaceae with four tribes and 3,270 species); and the caesalpinioid legumes, Caesalpinoideae (or family Caesalpiniaceae with four tribes and 2,250 species) (Lewis et al., 2005). A brief description of these subfamilies is given below:

3.5.1 Papilionoideae

Pilionoideae is a monophyletic group, according to all recent phylogenetic analyses, making it by far the largest subfamily with 476 genera and about 14,000 species. The flower structure of this subfamily is highly variable; however, the butterfly-like (papilionoid) flower is almost universal in this subfamily. Smykal et al. (2015) stated that the largest group of papilionoids is Hologalegina, with nearly 4,000 species in 75 genera, including the large galegoid tribes (Galegeae, Fabeae, Trifolieae, Genisteae, etc.), united by the loss of one copy of the chloroplast inverted repeat (IR), often referred to as the IR loss clade. Of great economic and scientific interest are the Fabeae and Trifolieae, which together comprise 11 genera and nearly 800 species (Smykal et al., 2015). Furthermore, this subfamily has a number of species under different genera in Pakistan, illustrated in Figure 3.1.

When cultivated grain legumes, or pulses, are considered, the Papilionoideae can be divided into the following four clades (1) Phaseoloids (*Glycine* Willd., *Phaseolus* L., *Cajanus* L., and *Vigna* Savi), (2) Galegoids (*Pisum* L., *Lens* Mill., *Lathyrus* L., *Vicia* L., *Medicago* L., and *Cicer* L.), (3) Genistoids (*Lupinus* L.) and (4) Dalbergoids (*Arachis* L. and *Stylosanthes* Sw.) (Lewis et al., 2005). Phaseoloids are pan-tropical and often referred to as "warm season," "tropical," or "millettioid" clade. By contrast, Galegoids are often referred to as "cool-season," "temperate," or "Hologalegina" legume crops, since they are mainly distributed in temperate regions of the world, such as Europe and the Mediterranean. In addition to this, Pakistan plays a diverse role in the availability of a different genera of legumes that lies under this specific subfamily, which are presented in Table 3.2 (Hameed, 2015; Pakistan Plant Database, nd and Wikimedia Foundation, nd).

3.5.2 Mimosoideae

Plant species that belong to Mimosoideae (sometimes regarded as the family Mimosaceae with four tribes and 3,270 species) are mostly woody trees and shrubs. Many are valuable for timber (*Acacia* spp. Mill., *Albizia* Benth.), medicines (*Leucaena leucocephala* L., *Mimosa pudica* L., *Albizia lebbeck* (L.) Benth., *Prosopis juliflora* L.), green manuring (Mimosa pudica L., *Mimosa hamata* Willd.), forage (*Acacia jacquemontii* Benth., *Acacia modesta* Wall., *Mimosa hamata* Willd.), insecticides (*Derris*

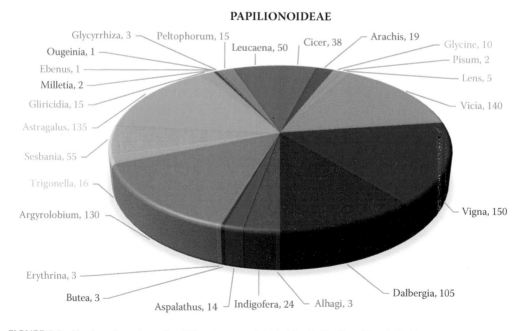

FIGURE 3.1 Number of species under different genera of the subfamily Papilionoideae in Pakistan.

TABLE 3.2

Distribution of Subfamily Papilionoideae in Various Regions of Pakistan

Scientific name	English name	Local name	Plant part	Distribution	Uses
Cicer arietinum L.	Chickpea	Channa	Seeds, leaves	Rain-fed areas of Pakistan	Vitamins such as riboflavin, niacin, thiamin, folate, and the vitamin A precursor β-carotene.
Arachis hypogaea L.	Groundnut	Mong phalli	Seeds	Punjab	Rich in potassium, calcium, phosphorus, and B vitamins
Glycine max L.	Soybean	Soya bean	Seeds	KPK	Source of food, protein, and oil,
Pisum sativum L.	Pea	Mattar	Seeds	KPK, Punjab, Sindh	Vitamins C and E, zinc, and other antioxidants
Lens esculenta, L culinaris (L.)	Lentil	Masoor	Seeds	Temperate regions	Lower cholesterol and protect against diabetes and colon cancer
Vicia faba L.	Horse bean	Faba bean	Seeds	Northern Pakistan	Fiber, nutrients, protein source
Vigna radiata L.	Mungbean	Mung	Seeds	Punjab	Antioxidants, nutrients, protein source
Dalbergia sisso (Roxb).	Sisso	Shisham	Woods, leaves	Punjab, Sindh, KPK	Stimulant, gonorrhea, astringent
Alhagi maurorum Medic.	Camel thorn bush	Shinz, Shuthar khar	Leaves, flowers	Karachi (Sindh), Southern Balochistan	Forage, blood coagulant, piles
Butea monosperma (Lam.) Taub.	Bengal kino	Dhak	Leaves, seeds, bark, flowers gum	(Rawalpindi) Punjab and KPK	Anti-pyretic, appetizer, aphrodisiac, blood purifier
Argyrolobium roseum Jaub. & Spach.	Cambess	Mashnamot	Leaves	Khuzdar (Balochistan)	Forage
Erythrina variegata L.	Variegated coral tree	Pangar	Leaves, seeds, bark	Roadside tree	Source of betaine, choline, hyaphorin
Gliricidia sepium (Jacq).	Madre tree	Lal tali	Leaves, root	Karachi (Sindh), Islamabad	Fever, pain, kidney ailments, gonorrhea
Milletia pinnata L.	Pongam	Karanja	Flowers	Karachi (Sindh), Punjab	Used for diabetes
Ougeinia oojeinensis (Roxb).	Sandan	Sandan	Bark	Punjab, Mirpur	Febrifuge, diarrhea, dysentery
Ebenus stellata Boiss.	Ebenus	Chukipith	Stem, leaves	Quetta, Khuzdar (Balochistan)	Forage, firewood, medication
Glycyrrhiza triphylla Fisch & Mey.	Liquorice	Khwashdar	Leaves, flowers	Balochistan	Cough, sore throat, fever
Peltophorum pterocarpum (DC).	Cropperpod tree	Peela Gulmohar	Bark	Roadside (Punjab)	Astringent, afterpain at childbirth
Sesbania grandiflora (L). Pers.	Sesbania	Bansa	Root, flowers, leaves	Karachi (Sindh), Punjab	Rheumatism, phlegm, diabetes, suppuration
Trigonella polycerata Linn.	Fenugreek	Shirona	Leaves	Kalat, Jhalawan (Balochistan)	Forage

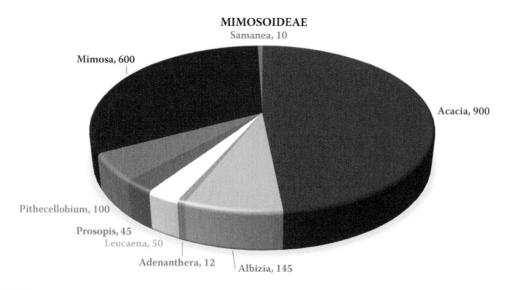

FIGURE 3.2   Number of species under different genera of the subfamily Mimosoideae in Pakistan.

elliptica (Wall.) Benth), *Albizia procera* (Roxb.) Benth.), and tannins (*Acacia jacquemontii* Benth., *Acacia dealbata* Link., *A. decurrens* Desv.). Hameed (2015) stated in his book that members of this subfamily also take part in treating human disorders such as diarrhea, migraines, headaches, indigestion, flu, fever, and eye infections. This subfamily has a number of species under different genera in Pakistan, as illustrated in Figure 3.2. Furthermore, the taxonomic position with multiple uses of various species of legume plants is given in Table 3.3 (Hameed, 2015; Pakistan Plant Database, nd and Wikimedia Foundation, nd).

3.5.3 Caesalpinoideae

Members of the Caesalpinoideae (or family Caesalpiniaceae with four tribes and 2,250 species) are found in three categories of plant habit: herbs, shrubs, and trees (except vines). Many of them are valuable for medicines (*Saraca indica* L., *Cassia obtusifolia, C. alata* (L.) Roxb., *Senna occidentalis* (L.) Link.), food (*Tamarindus indicus* L., *Ceratonia siliqua* L., *Leucaena esculenta* Sesse & Moc.), and animal fodder (*Bauhinia* spp. L.) (Smykal et al., 2015). In addition to this, this category of legumes can cure human diseases i.e., diarrhea, dysentery, headache, malaria, and skin diseases. Plants grown for ornamental purposes are also in this subfamily i.e., *Parkinsonia aculeata* L., *Senna alata* (L.) Roxb, and *Cassia fistula* L (Hameed, 2015). This subfamily has a number of species under different genera in Pakistan, as illustrated in Figure 3.3. Furthermore, Pakistan has a major part in the diverse genera of legumes that lies under this specific subfamily (Table 3.4) (Hameed, 2015; Pakistan Plant Database, nd and Wikimedia Foundation, nd).

3.6 Status of Legume Genebank

The Plant Genetic Resources Program (PGRP) of PARC/NARC has undertaken more than 10 expeditions on collecting food legume plants in different agro-ecological regions of the country in collaboration with national coordinated commodity programmes and International Agricultural Research Centres (IARC). The genebank maintains around 5,000 accessions of food legumes (Table 3.5). The major crops, i.e., chickpea, lentil, mungbean, and lobia, have been intensively collected with high genetic diversity from different areas of Pakistan. Details of these accessions are given below (Ahmed, Z., 2007):

TABLE 3.3

Distribution and Uses of the Different Species of the Subfamily Mimosoideae in Various Regions of Pakistan

Scientific name	English name	Local name	Plant part	Distribution	Uses
Acacia nilotica (L.) Delile	Gum arabic	Kikar	Flowers, root, bark, leaves	All over Pakistan	Cure for jaundice, palpitation, blood dysentery
Acacia jacquemontii Benth.	Jacq gum	Chigrid, Babul	Leaves, bark, branches	Balochistan	Fodder purposes, tanning leather, abortion
Acacia farnesiana (L.f.) Wild.	Sweet acacia	Kabuli kikar	Leaves, flowers	(Karachi) Sindh, Punjab	Tuberculosis, fever, eye and throat infections
Acacia modesta Wall.,	Gum tree	Phulai, Phulab	Gum, leaves	Nasirabad, Sibi (Balochistan)	Forage, firewood, medication
Acacia senegal L.	Gum arabic acacia	Khor	Gum, bark	Karachi (Sindh), Balochistan	Inflammations, intestinal mucosa
Albizia chinesis (Osbeck) Merr.	Albiz	Ohi	Bark	Punjab	Scabies and skin diseases
Acacia catechu (L.f.) Wild.	Black cutch	Khair, Katha	Root, bark	KPK, Punjab	Astringent, rheumatism
Albizia julibrissin Durazz.	Silk tree	Ghulabi siris	Flowers	Outer Himalayan zone	Mild constipation, boils, swelling
Adenanthera pavonina L.	Bead tree	Barighumchi	Bark, leaves	Karachi (Sindh)	Migraines, headaches, tonsillitis, diarrhea
Leucaena leucocephala L.	Ipil-Ipil	Ipil-Ipil	Root, bark, leaves	KPK, Punjab, Sindh	Fever, typhoid, digestive track ailments
Prosopis cineraria L.	Mesquite	Jhnad	Flowers	Punjab, Sindh, Balochistan	Miscarriage
Pithecellobium dulce (Roxb.) Benth.	Black bead	Jungle jaleebi	Root, leaves, seeds	Sindh, Balochistan	Dysentery, indigestion, venereal lesions and pain, hemoptysis
Albizia lebbeck (L.) Benth.	Lebbek tree	Siris, Shrin	Fruit, leaves	Sindh, Punjab, KPK	Anxiety, nervousness, dysentery
Albizia procera (Roxb.) Benth.	Lebbek tree	Sufaid-siris	Leaves	Karachi (Sindh), Mirpur, Hassanabdal	Poultice on ulcers, insecticides
Samanea saman (Jacq.) Merr.	Lebbek tree	Siris	Flowers	Karachi (Sindh)	Mild constipation, boils, swelling
Mimosa pudica L.	Moimosa	Chui Mui, Lajwanti	Leaves, flower, fruit	Nasirabad (Balochistan)	Medicinal, green manure, fodder

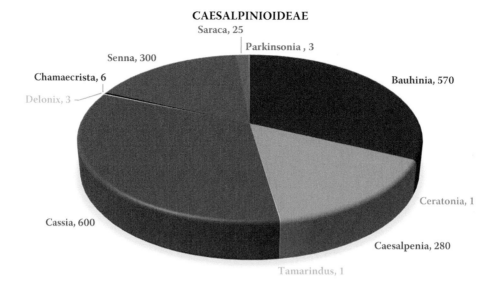

CAESALPINIOIDEAE

FIGURE 3.3   Number of species under different genera of the subfamily Caesalpinioideae in Pakistan.

TABLE 3.4

Distribution of Subfamily Caesalpinioideae in Various Regions of Pakistan

Scientific name	English name	Local name	Plant part	Distribution	Uses
Bauhinia purpurea L.	Purple bauhinia	Kaliar	Flowers, stem bark	Rawalpindi, KPK	Purgative, indigestion, body pain, fever
Bauhinia semla L.	Bauhinia	Kandla	Stem bark, leaves	Rawalpindi, Hazara	Diarrhea, dysentery, headaches, malaria
Caesalpenia bonduc (L.) Roxb.	Grey nicker bean	Fevernut	Leaves, seeds	Gardens of Pakistan	Fever, asthma, mental distress
Caesalpenia pulcherrima (L.) Sw.	Paradise flower	Gul-e-mohur	Flowers, root	Gardens of Pakistan	Asthma, bronchitis, as anti-pyretic and expectorant
Delonix regia (Bojerex Hook.) Raf.	Peacock flower	Gulmohar	Leaves, flower	Karachi, Hyderabad (Sindh), Lahore (Punjab)	Constipation, anthelmintic
Bauhinia variegata L.	Mountain ebnoy	Kachnar	Flowers	Sindh, Punjab, Nasirabad (Balochistan)	Aperient
Chamaecrista absus L.	Cassia	Chasku	Seeds	KPK, Punjab	Cure for skin diseases
Ceratonia siliqua L.	Carob	Kharnub	Seed husk, pods	KPK, Punjab, Islamabad	Astringent, purgative
Tamarindus indica L.	Tamarind	Imli	Leaves, flower, fruit	Karachi (Sindh), Jehlum (Punjab)	Throat infection, constipation, affect appetite
Cassia fistula L.	Golden shower	Amaltus	Flowers	Nasirabad, Lasbela (Balochistan)	Diarrhea, dysentery, headache, malaria
Cassia occidentalis Linn.	Cassia	Kosandi, Howar	Leaves, seeds, roots	Bolan Pass, Nasirabad (Balochistan)	Cure for sore eyes, antibacterial drugs
Cassia obtusifolia L.	Cassia	Kaspind, chakunda	Leaves, flowers	Balochistan	Emodin source for medication

TABLE 3.4 (Continued)

Distribution of Subfamily Caesalpinioideae in Various Regions of Pakistan

Scientific name	English name	Local name	Plant part	Distribution	Uses
Senna italica Mill.	Kasordhi	Senna	Pods, seeds	Punjab and Sindh	Stomachache, malaria, constipation
Senna alexandrina Mill.	Indian senna	Sennahindi	Stem, pods, leaves	Punjab and Sindh	Expectorant, laxative, antidysentric
Cassia senna L.	Casca	Sona, Senna-i-makki	Dried leaves	Lasbela, Makran (Balochistan)	Skin ailment, blood purifier
Saraca indica L.	Ashok tree	Ashok	Stem bark	Gardens of Punjab and Sindh	Astringent, scorpion-sting
Parkinsonia aculeata L.	Parku	Baboor	Flowers	Lasbela, (Balochistan)	Medicine, ornamental

TABLE 3.5

Status of Legumes at Genebank (PGRP)

S. No.	Food legumes	Accessions
1	Chickpea (*Cicer arietinum* L.)	2243
2	Chickpea (wild cicer)	90
3	Lentil (*Lens culinaris* L.)/its wild relatives	808
4	Mungbean (*Vigna radiata* L.)	643
5	Mashbean (*Vigna mungo* L.)	799
6	Cowpea (*Vigna unguiculata* L.)	212
7	Lobia (*Phaseolus vulgaris* L.)	109
8	*Vicia* species	172
9	Moth (*Vigna acontifolia* L.)	66
10	Matri (*Lathyrus* species)	148
11	Groundnut (*Arachis hypogaea* L.)	754
12	Soybean (*Glycine max* L.)	133

3.7 Conclusion

Pakistan has great diversity in legumes, which is mainly a reflection of its diverse climate and the topography of its four major phytogeographical regions. All three major legume subfamilies, Mimosoideae, Papilionoideae, and Caesalpinoideae, represent the diversity of legumes in Pakistan. Papilionaceae is the major subfamily containing 13,800 species in Pakistan. These plants contribute as fodder crops, weeds, medicinal plants, and forest species. However, legume diversity has been dwindling over the years. Therefore, appropriate measures should be taken for conservation and management of legumes.

REFERENCES

Ahmed, Z. 2007. *Country report on plant genetic resources for food and agriculture.* Pakistan Agricultural Research Council. P27.

Ali, S.I., and M. Qaiser, 1986. A phytogeographical analysis of the phanerogams of Pakistan and Kashmir. *Proceedings of the Royal Society of Edinburgh, Section B: Biological Sciences,* 89, 89–101.

Aslam, M., S.N. Khokhar, I.A. Mahmood, T. Sultan, and S. Ahmed, 1995. *Pakistan agricultural research council: Annual report,* 1994–95. Pakistan Agricultural Research Council, Islamabad.

Athar, M., and Z. Ahmad, 2004. Taxonomy, distribution, and medicinal uses of legume trees of Pakistan. *SIDA, Contributions to Botany*, 21(2), 951–962.

Athar, M., and S.M. Nasir, 2005. Taxonomic perspective of plant species yielding vegetable oils used in cosmetics and skin care products. *African Journal of Biotechnology*, 4(1), 36–44.

Athar, M., and M.A. Siddiqi, 2004. Reflections on the taxonomy and distribution of medicinal flowers of Pakistan. *SIDA, Contributions to Botany*, 21(1), 357–368.

Hameed, B. 2015. *Balochistan Ethnobotany: An exhaustive collection of medicinal and economically important plants from Balochistan*. Lasbela University of Agriculture, Water and Marine Sciences, Pakistan.

Jensen, E.S., M.B. Peoples, R.M. Boddey, P.M. Gresshoff, H. Hauggaard-Nielsen, B.J. Alves, and M.J. Morrison, 2012. Legumes for mitigation of climate change and the provision of feedstock for biofuels and biorefineries. *A Review. Agronomy for Sustainable Development*, 32(2), 329–364.

Kirkbride, J.H. 1986. Phylogeny and classification of Pakistani legumes. *Pakistan Journal of Botany*, 18, 287–299.

Lewis, G., B. Schrire, B. Mackinder, and M. Lock, 2005. *Legumes of the world*. Royal Botanic Gardens, Kew, UK.

Nasir, J.J., and R.A. Rafiq, 1995. *Wild flowers of Pakistan*, Oxford University Press, London.

Pakistan Plant Database. http://legacy.tropicos.org/Project/Pakistan

Rasool, G. 1998. *Medicinal plants of northern areas of Pakistan: Saving the plants that save us*. Pakistan Forest Institute, Peshawar, Pakistan.

Smykal, P., C.J. Coyne, M.J. Ambrose, N. Maxted, H. Schaefer, M.W. Blair, and R.K. Varshney, 2015. Legume crops phylogeny and genetic diversity for science and breeding. *Critical Reviews in Plant Sciences*, 34(1–3), 43–104.

Stagnari, F., A. Maggio, A. Galieni, and M. Pisante, 2017. Multiple benefits of legumes for agriculture sustainability: An overview. *Chemical and Biological Technologies in Agriculture*, 4, 2.

Wani, S.P., Rupela, O.P., and Lee, K.K. 1995. Sustainable agriculture in the semi-arid tropics through biological nitrogen fixation in grain legumes. In: Ladha J.K., Peoples M.B. (eds.), *Management of biological nitrogen fixation for the development of more productive and sustainable agricultural systems. Developments in plant and soil sciences*, vol. 65. (pp. 29–49). Springer, Dordrecht. 10.1007/978-94-011-0053-3_2

Wikimedia Foundation. http://en.wikipedia.org/wiki (Accessed September 4th 2021).

Wiseman, R., and L. Hopkins, 2000. *Sowing the seeds for sustainability: Agriculture, biodiversity, economic and society*. Proceeding of the Eighth Interactive session held at the Second IUCN World Conservation Congress, Amman, Jordan, 11–21.

4

Legume Inoculants Using Rhizobia Strains Effective to Reduce Nitrous Oxide Emissions

Eulogio J. Bedmar[1], María J. Delgado[1], Socorro Mesa[1], Germán Tortosa[1], A. Paula Rodiño[2], Juan L. Tejada-Hinojoza[2,3], and Antonio M. De Ron[2]

[1]*Estación Experimental Zaidín (EEZ), Spanish National Research Council (CSIC), Granada, Spain*
[2]*Misión Biológica de Galicia (MBG), Spanish National Research Council (CSIC), Pontevedra, Spain*
[3]*Faculty of Agronomy, National University San Luis Gonzaga (UNICA), Ica, Perú*

CONTENTS

4.1 Introduction

4.1.1 Biological Fixation of Atmospheric Nitrogen

Nitrogen (N) is an essential element of all forms of life since it is a component of key compounds such as proteins, nucleic acids, hormones, etc. It is also the fourth most abundant element in biomass after carbon (C), hydrogen (H_2), and oxygen (O_2). Although it is the most abundant element in the atmosphere, of

N-CYCLE

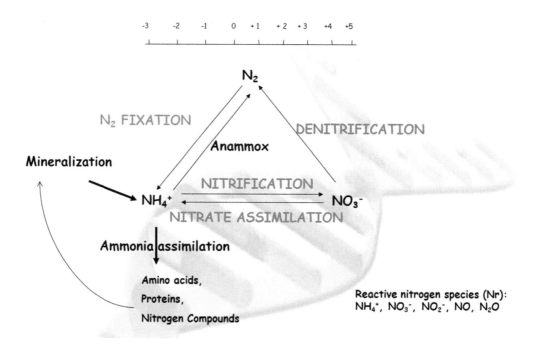

FIGURE 4.1   Schematic representation of the N cycle.

which it makes up 80%, its chemical state makes it biologically inert for most living beings. Hence, with the exception of water, N is the most common limiting nutrient in agricultural practice.

The N cycle (Figure 4.1) in nature begins with the reduction of molecular nitrogen (N_2) to ammonium (NH_4^+), a reaction catalyzed exclusively by diazotrophic bacteria containing the enzyme nitrogenase, the only enzyme capable of breaking the covalent triple bond of N_2 (Good and Dixon, 2021). Through this process, in short, N_2 passes from an inert to a biologically active form (NH_4^+) that can already be used by microorganisms and plants for the synthesis of the nitrogenous compounds necessary for their growth.

4.1.2   Nitrous Oxide

Nitrous oxide (N_2O) is a colorless, water-soluble, sweet-tasting gas also known as laughing gas. It has analgesic and anesthetic properties, is relatively inert at room temperature, and is hardly toxic to microorganisms that can tolerate millimolar concentrations of the gas. It is also used in the automotive industry for its ability to increase the oxygen available for combustion, with a consequent increase in power.

N_2O is a potent greenhouse gas (GHG) that, along with carbon dioxide (CO_2), methane (CH_4), and some chlorofluorocarbon compounds (CFCs), is implicated in global climate change. N_2O has a warming capacity 296 times greater than that of CO_2, and is responsible for 6% of current global warming (Erisman et al., 2011, 2015; Intergovernmental Panel on Climate Change, IPCC, 2019). The long residence time of N_2O in the atmosphere, with a minimum lifetime of about 120–150 years, makes possible its transport to the stratosphere, where it is transformed by photolysis into nitric oxide (NO), which, in turn, removes ozone (O_3) to produce nitrogen dioxide (NO_2) that reacts with water to give rise to nitric acid (HNO_3).

The HNO_3 dissolved in water falls to earth in the form of acid rain, which contaminates soil, water, and sediment. It also affects vegetation, causing significant damage in forested areas. Because of its corrosive nature, acid rain has a negative impact on buildings and infrastructure. It can dissolve calcium carbonate ($CaCO_3$), causing the deterioration of monuments and buildings made of marble or limestone. In addition, the protons (H^+) that come from acid rain can drag some ions from the soil, such as Fe, Ca, Al, Pb, Zn, etc., and, as a consequence, produce impoverishment in essential nutrients for plant growth. Nitrates and sulphates, together with cations leached from soils, contribute to the eutrophication of rivers, lakes, reservoirs, and coastal regions, which deteriorate their natural environmental conditions and decrease their utilization (Erisman et al., 2015).

4.1.3 Sources of Nitrous Oxide Emissions

Most of the N_2O produced takes place during the N cycle by the processes of nitrification and denitrification, which are described below. It should be noted that the N cycle is eminently biological since the microorganisms are responsible for carrying out the oxidation-reduction reactions of the cycle and for maintaining the balance between the reduced and oxidized forms of N (Daims et al., 2015; Kuypers et al., 2018; Wu et al., 2020).

4.1.3.1 Nitrification

Although some ammonium is volatilized to the atmosphere as ammonia (NH_3), it can also be oxidized to nitrate by nitrification (Figure 4.1). First, ammonium is oxidized to nitrite via the formation of hydroxylamine (NH_2OH) catalyzed by a hydroxylamine oxidoreductase (Hao), a reaction that gives rise to the formation of N_2O. Hao is a multi-heme enzyme encoded by a highly conserved gene cluster in the bacteria in which it has been analyzed. The genomes of ammonium-oxidizing bacteria encode about 10 Hao-like enzymes, making the study of these proteins difficult.

A second step during nitrification is nitrite oxidation, a main biochemical pathway producing nitrate. The reaction is catalyzed by nitrite oxidoreductase (Nxr), a molybdoenzyme containing Fe and S in its molecule. Two phylogenetically distinct enzymes have been described, both associated with the cell membrane and composed of the subunits NxrA, which contains the active center, and NxrB and NxrC, which channel nitrite-derived electrons to NxrA. The *nxrA*, *nxrB*, and *nxrC* genes encode, respectively, each of the three subunits that make up the nitrite-oxidizing enzymes and are widely distributed in nature.

In addition to nitrification, the oxidation of ammonium with nitrite as an electron acceptor under anoxic conditions results in the formation of N_2 as the final product, a process referred to as anammox (ANaerobic AMmonia OXidation).

Classically, the oxidation of NH_4^+ and NO_2^- during nitrification has been considered to be carried out by different groups of prokaryotes. While NH_4^+ oxidizing microorganisms are included in the genera *Nitrosomonas, Nitrosospira, Nitrosolobus*, and *Nitrosococcus* of the Bacteria domain, and *Nitrososphaera, Nitrosotalea*, and *Nitrosoarchaeum* of the Archaea domain, *Nitrobacter, Nitrospina, Nitrococcus*, and *Nitrospira* are the main genera involved in nitrite oxidation. Interestingly, *Nitrospira* was found to carry out the complete oxidation of NH_4^+ to NO_3^-, a process now known as comammox (COMplete AMMonia OXidation).

4.1.3.2 Denitrification

This is the process by which nitrate is reduced to N_2, which returns back to the atmosphere, thus closing the N cycle. From a biochemical point of view, denitrification is an alternative form of respiration whereby, under O_2-limiting conditions, nitrate, and its derived nitrogen oxides (NOx), act as a final electron acceptor in a transport chain until the formation of N_2 (Zumft, 1997). These reactions are catalyzed by the sequential activity of the enzymes nitrate reductase (Nar/Nap), nitrite reductase NirS/ NirK), nitric oxide reductase (cNOr, qNor), and nitrous oxide reductase (Nos), respectively. The reduction of NOx is coupled to ATP formation for cell growth.

Most denitrifying microorganisms do not possess, or do not express, all of the denitrification genes (Jones et al., 2008; Zilli et al., 2020). When the enzyme nitrous oxide reductase is absent, N_2O accumulates and can be released to the atmosphere. It is a paradox that denitrification, being the only biological process to remove nitrates, is also a source of emission of such a potent greenhouse gas.

Although denitrification was long considered to be restricted to prokaryotes, it is now known that several species of fungi and yeasts are capable of denitrification. In fungi, the enzymes involved are nitrite reductase and cytochrome P450nor, which acts in the manner of nitric oxide reductase (Shoun and Fushinobu, 2017).

Compared to bacteria, the O_2 demand threshold by denitrifying fungal communities is higher, so they emit more N_2O in ecosystems where O_2 is not strictly limiting. In contrast, bacteria dominate fungi under strict O_2 limiting conditions. In addition, fungi exhibit wider pH ranges for optimal growth, and they predominate at acidic pH, whereas bacteria predominate at neutral and alkaline pH. However, the actual role of fungi in N_2O production remains largely unknown (Maeda et al., 2015).

In most denitrifying species, the expression of denitrification genes is tightly regulated by the availability of a NOx and the limitation of intracellular O_2 levels. However, the exact level of oxygen limitation required for such expression can differ widely between organisms. Likewise, denitrifying activity may persist in the presence of O_2 in environments that have changed from anoxic to aerobic.

4.2 Agriculture and Nitrous Oxide

In pre-industrial times, for decades, soil fertility was maintained by the use of manures, plant residues, and the use of legumes to supply the N demands for needs of crops. However, the demand to feed a growing population favored the massive use of synthetic nitrogen fertilizers. In fact, estimations show that more than a quarter of the world's current population has been fed by the use of these fertilizers to increase crop yields; therefore, the benefits that they represent for the livelihood of the population on a global scale are undeniable (Erisman et al., 2015).

Until the industrial synthesis of urea, ammonium, and nitrate, biological N_2 fixation and denitrification possessed similar yields of about 110 tons of NH_4^+ produced from fixed N_2 and 108 tons of NO_3^- removed as N_2O or N_2 by denitrification. Although denitrifying activity has not increased significantly, the total amount of N produced is close to 240–260 Tg N/year due to 125–150 Tg N/year from synthetic N fertilization. Other inorganic and organic nitrogen compounds, such as livestock slurry, urban solid and liquid wastes, industrial activities, etc., can contribute up to an annual total close to 345 Tg N/year (Gruber and Galloway, 2008; Fowler et al., 2015).

Once in the soil, nitrogenous compounds, whether organic or synthetic, are converted to nitrate, and N_2 by the nitrification and denitrification processes, respectively; thus, N_2O can be formed. The global emission of natural N_2O has been quantified at 10–12 Tg N/yr, of which about 5.3 Tg N/yr is considered to be of anthropogenic origin due to agricultural practices (Syakila and Kroeze, 2011). Of this, atmospheric N_2O concentration has progressively increased from 277.2 ppb in 1900 to 287.7 in 1950, 299.1 in 1975, 316.02 in 2000, and 374.74 in December 2020 (https://www.n2olevels.org), an increase that has been linked to N applied as fertilizer.

The contribution of each agricultural sector to global GHG emissions, expressed in units of CO_2 equivalent, can be found in the FAO archives (FAOSTAT, http://www.fao.org/faostat/es/#home), which provides free access to information on food and agriculture for more than 245 countries and 35 regions, from 1961 to the present year. Among them, information on global and country-specific N_2O emissions can be found.

4.3 Nitrogen Use Efficiency

It is significant that the amount of N recovered from crops per unit of N applied to the soil (Nitrogen Use Efficiency; NUE) is extremely low due to the processes of volatilization, leaching, soil erosion, nitrification, denitrification, etc. These events cause the loss of most of the N applied to the soil so that its recovery in crops does not exceed 50% (Smil, 2011). On the other hand, the fact that the excess N produced due to anthropic activity cannot be eliminated by denitrification ultimately results in the pollution of soils, surface and groundwater, seas and oceans, and sediments, in addition to causing erosion, soil loss, loss of biodiversity, and damage to animal and human health. This fact is particularly serious in countries or regions with high agricultural and livestock productivity and variable rainfall, where long periods of drought can occur, making it necessary to use water for human, animal, and agricultural consumption. Hence, there is a need to optimize the quantity and improve the efficiency of N use, both organic and synthetic, applied during agricultural practices.

The world population is expected to approach 10 billion by 2050 (WPP, 2019), putting enormous pressure on agricultural land that must provide food for a growing population. It is at this crossroads, on the one hand, the existence in the environment of excess N and, on the other, the need to produce food for an increasing number of inhabitants on the planet, that efforts must be made to develop programs and practices that seek to dispense, or reduce as much as possible, the use of synthetic fertilizers, to improve NUE, and to implement environmentally friendly agricultural activities. These are the basis for the conservation of ecosystems at the local, regional, and global levels, and for the sustainable development of agriculture.

4.4 The Legumes

With more than 19,500 species and 770 genera, legumes or pulses (family Fabaceae or Leguminosae) constitute, after the families Asteraceae and Orchidaceae, the third most abundant angiosperm plants in number of species (Sprent et al., 2017; LPWG, 2017). Legumes played an important role in the early development of agriculture, were domesticated along with grasses, and today occupy diverse aquatic and terrestrial environments in nearly every biome on Earth, even the most extreme habitats (Lewis et al., 2005). The *matK* gene encodes a maturase intron enzyme that splices plant plastid group II introns and is used for plant species delineation. An analysis based on the *matK* sequences of 698 of the 765 currently recognized genera groups legumes into six subfamilies: Caesalpinioideae DC, CerciDoideae LPWG, Detarioideae Burmeist, Dialioideae LPWG, Duparquetioideae LPWG, and Papilionoideae DC; in this classification, the subfamily Mimosoideae is included in the Caesalpinioideae pending classification (LPWG, 2017).

Currently second only to cereals, legumes are an important source of food for a large part of the world's population, providing protein, carbohydrates, minerals, vitamins, oil, fiber, and other compounds with nutraceutical value and health-promoting properties. Legumes also play a key role as fodder and green manure, and they are used for their wood, resins, tannins, oils, and medicines, as well as in the horticultural trade. The recognition of the nutritional benefits of legumes, their importance in food security, sustainable agriculture, and in mitigating biodiversity loss and climate change was recognized by the United Nations General Assembly, which designated 2016 as the International Year of Pulses.

4.5 The Rhizobia

Rhizobia are Gram-negative bacteria well known for their ability to establish atmospheric N_2-fixing symbiotic associations with leguminous plants. From pioneering experiments conducted in 1888, Hellriegel and Wilfarth demonstrated the existence of "assimilation" of atmospheric nitrogen by bacteria associated with legume roots. Beijerinck, in the same year, isolated and classified them as *Bacillus radicicola*, and Frank, in 1889, reclassified them as *Rhizobium leguminosarum*.

Until 2001, it was believed that rhizobia belonged to the class Alphaproteobacteria and were included in the genera *Rhizobium, Ensifer* (formerly *Sinorhizobium*), *Allorhizobium, Pararhizobium, Neorhizobium,* and *Shinella* of the family Rhizobiaceae of the order Rhizobiales. In that, and subsequent years, the existence of other bacterial families containing species that do not belong to the Rhizobiaceae but are capable of nodulating legumes was demonstrated, among them the Phyllobacteriaceae (genera *Mesorhizobium, Aminobacter, Phyllobacterium*), Brucellaceae (genus *Ochrobactrum*), Methylobacteriaceae (genera *Methylobacterium* and *Microvirga*), Bradyrhizobiaceae (genus *Bradyrhizobium*), Hyphomicrobiaceae (genus *Devosia*), and Xanthobacteraceae (genus *Azorhizobium*), all included in the Alphaproteobacteria class of the phylum Bacteria. Also in 2001, two parallel reports suggested that legume nodulation may not be restricted to Alphaproteobacteria. Moulin et al. (2001) described two *Burkholderia* strains isolated from nodules of *Aspalathus carnosa* and *Machaerium lunatum*, and Chen et al. (2001) isolated bacteria of the genus *Cupriavidus* (formerly *Ralstonia*) from nodules of *Mimosa*, which showed the ability of Betaproteobacteria to nodulate legumes. These bacteria are included in the family Burkholderiaceae containing the genera *Burkholderia* (currently comprising genera *Paraburkholderia*, *Cupriavidus*, and *Trinickia*) (Estrada de los Santos et al., 2018; de Lajudie et al., 2019).

In a broad sense, despite their membership in various classes, orders, families, genera, and species, all those bacteria that establish N_2-fixing symbioses with legumes are known by the generic name of rhizobia.

4.6 The Rhizobia-Legume Symbiosis

A symbiotic association is established between rhizobia and legumes, resulting in the fixation (reduction) of N_2. To initiate symbiosis, the bacteria migrate toward plant roots, attach, and subsequently enter them to form a specialized organ, the nodule, where N_2 fixation takes place (Oldroyd and Downie, 2008; Oldroyd et al., 2011, 2013; Andrews and Andrews, 2017; Wheatley and Poole, 2018).

Inside the nodule, rhizobia infect plant cells and become enclosed in vesicles called symbiosomes (Roth and Stacey, 1989; Martin et al., 2017; Coba de la Peña et al., 2018). Within the symbiosomes, the bacteria differentiate into bacteroids, specialized cells that synthesize nitrogenase, the enzyme needed to reduce N_2 to ammonium (Good and Dixon, 2021). The NH_4^+ formed is excreted into the cytosol of surrounding plant cells and used for the synthesis of amides (glutamine and asparagine) or ureides (allantoin and allantoic acid) that are formed in nodules of indeterminate or determinate type, respectively, and exported to the rest of the plant, where they are used for the synthesis of nitrogenous compounds (Udvardi and Poole, 2013; Poole et al., 2018).

Although many soil bacteria are diazotrophs and can reduce N_2, the NH_4^+ produced is used exclusively for cell growth. Only when cell death of these microorganisms occurs does the N released to the soil become available to plants, and then animals, for consumption. In the case of legumes, the NH_4^+ that is produced is directly available to the plant for growth and development. Hence, these plants survive in arid, infertile soils with little or no N content. When they die, much of the N assimilated by the plant returns to the soil, where the next crop can take advantage of it. This explains why legumes are plants that fertilize the soil where they are grown and used as green manure, as well as their ancestral use in crop rotation and in revegetation and reforestation programs (Rodiño et al., 2011). Also, because legumes can diminish addition of synthetic N to soils, they are considered a sustainable N source for plants, as well as an alternative to chemical fertilizers in order to improve soil fertility and biodiversity.

Legume crops have been described to reduce nitrate leaching and N_2O emissions by 22% and 33%, respectively, compared to non-legume crops (Reckling et al., 2016). This demonstrates that these crops are more environmentally friendly than those treated with nitrogen fertilizers. Furthermore, diazotrophic-bacteria-based inoculants are applied on an area close to 60 million ha every year in Brazil and Argentina together, a biofertilization system that, in terms of N-fertilizer equivalents, represents economical savings corresponding to the cost of 12 Tg of mineral-N per year (Hungría and Mendes, 2015).

4.7 Nitrous Oxide Emission by Legume Nodules

Although genes involved in denitrification are widespread in prokaryotes of the domains Bacteria and Archaea, microorganisms capable of carrying out complete denitrification, i.e. the reduction of nitrate/nitrite to N_2, are scarce. Most denitrifiers only perform partial or incomplete denitrification, which is due to the fact that they do not possess in their genome, or do not express, the set of genes necessary for the synthesis and activity of each of the denitrifying enzymes they encode. Denitrification, understood as the ability of a microorganism to use nitrate as a source of N for the formation of nitrogenous compounds and, simultaneously, as a final electron acceptor for ATP synthesis under O_2-limiting conditions, is not frequent in rhizobia. Here, we review the current status of denitrification genes and N_2O emissions in rhizobia, both free-living and symbiotic conditions (Figure 4.2).

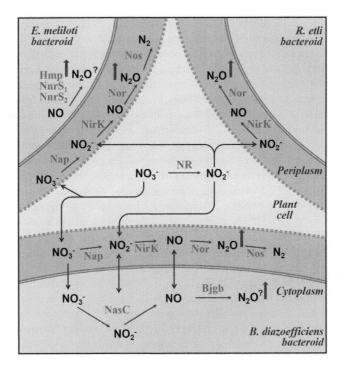

FIGURE 4.2 Sources of N_2O in *B. diazoefficiens*, *E. meliloti*, and *R. etli* root nodules. Green color represents the cytosol of the plant cells. The periplasm of the bacteroids is shown in orange color. The enzymes involved in denitrification are: NapA, periplasmic nitrate reductase; NirK, nitrite reductase; NorC, nitric oxide reductase; and NosZ, nitrous oxide reductase. Other enzymes involved in N_2O production are: Hmp, *E. meliloti* flavohemoglobin; NnrS1 and NnrS2, *E. meliloti* enzymes suggested to contribute to nitrosative-stress tolerance; NR, assimilatory nitrate reductase; Bjgb, *B. diazoefficiens* single domain hemoglobin. Question marks denote mechanisms still unknown.

4.7.1 Nitrous Oxide Emission by Nodules of Soybean (*Glycine max*)

Soybean (*Glycine max* L., Merr.) is an oils and protein crop that has aroused great interest worldwide due to its multiple uses, derived from its high protein content and oil quality. On average, dry grain contains 40% protein and 20% oil. The main by-products of soybean are flour and oil. The flour is mainly destined for the elaboration of balanced foods for animal consumption. The oil is used in food, cosmetics, soaps, and biofuels. It is a herbaceous, annual, spring-summer plant, whose vegetative cycle ranges from three to seven months. Soybean comes from another wild species, *Glycine ussuriensis*. Its center of origin is located in the Far East (China, Japan, Indochina), as evidenced by the almost unlimited number of varieties existing in those countries.

Soybean is the most cultivated legume in the world, estimated to contribute over 75% of the biologically fixed N_2 by crop legumes, and around 20–30% of the total fixed together by crops and planted pastures worldwide (Herridge et al., 2008). In rhizobia-related denitrification studies, *Bradyrhizobium diazoefficiens* [former name *B. japonicum* until reclassification by Delamuta et al. (2013)], is a model soybean endosymbiont in which the reduction of nitrate to N_2 is carried out by the sequential activity of the enzymes nitrate reductase (Nap), nitrite reductase (Cu-Nir), nitric oxide reductase (cNor), and nitrous oxide reductase (Nos) encoded by the *napEDABC*, *nirK*, *norCBQD*, and *nosRZDFYLX* genes, respectively (Bedmar et al., 2005; Bueno et al., 2012; Sánchez and Minamisawa 2019; Salas et al., 2021). Accordingly, in *B. diazoefficiens* the complete denitrification pathway is composed of the following partial reactions:

$$2\ NO_3^- + 4\,e^- \rightarrow 2\ NO_2^- + 2\,e^- \rightarrow 2NO + 2\,e^- \rightarrow N_2O + 2\,e^- \rightarrow N_2$$

Denitrification by *B. diazoefficiens* is not limited to free-living cells, but it also happens in legume nodules. That bacteroids can denitrify was demonstrated by histochemical detection of denitrification gene expression in nodules of nitrate-grown soybean plants inoculated with *B. diazoefficiens* strains containing transcriptional fusions of the *nirK*, *norC,* and *nosZ* genes with the *lacZ* reporter gene (Mesa et al., 2004). Previously, the presence of denitrification activity in bacteroids had been shown following a) the detection of the reduction of NO_3^- to N_2O by *B. diazoefficiens* isolated from nodules of *G. max* and by *B. lupini* (formerly *R. lupini*) isolated from nodules of *Lotus pedunculatus*, and b) the reduction of NO_3^- to N_2 by bacteroids of *E. meliloti* (formerly *R. meliloti*) from nodules of *Medicago sativa* (O'Hara et al., 1983). Using gas chromatography, linear correlations between nitrate concentration and N_2O emissions were found in nodules of soybeans treated with nitrate and inoculated with *B. diazoefficiens* USDA110 (Hirayama et al., 2011; Tortosa et al., 2015). The denitrification origin of the N_2O produced was confirmed when inoculation was done with a strain deficient in the *napA* gene, which resulted in the interruption of NO_3^- reduction and, consequently, in negligible N_2O production by the nodules (Tortosa et al., 2015). These experiments demonstrated that *B. diazoefficiens* bacteroids convert NO_3^- to N_2O by denitrification and that nitrous oxide reductase (NosZ) is a key enzyme playing a major role in the reduction of N_2O to N_2 in the soybean nodules (Figure 4.2).

In addition to denitrification, production of N_2O has also been attributed to the NasC-Bjgb proteins in the cytosol of *B. diazoefficiens* bacteroids (Figure 4.2). NasC is an assimilatory nitrate reductase that produces NO from nitrate, and Bjgb is a putative single-domain hemoglobin coordinated with NasC to produce N_2O (Figure 4.2). Current research, however, suggests that the main role of the NasC-Bjgb system is NO detoxification (Salas et al., 2021 and references therein), preventing increases in the intracellular NO concentration and maintaining an efficient symbiosis.

The observations made in nodules coincide with those obtained in free-living denitrifying bacteria, whether rhizobia or not, making NosZ the only enzyme capable of reducing N_2O emission to the atmosphere. Analysis, however, of several *B. diazoefficiens* strains has shown that the *napA*, *nirK*, and *norC* genes are most frequently present, whereas the *nosZ* gene seems to be less common (Sameshima-Saito et al., 2006). Out of 250 bradyrhizobial strains isolated from Argentinian soils cultivated with soybean, only 41 were considered as probable denitrifiers (Fernández et al., 2008), and other *Bradyrhizobium* strains used for soybean inoculation do not harbor all the denitrification genes (Obando et al., 2019).

In silico analyses of 14 available genome sequences of the most commonly used strains in Brazil and Argentina present in commercial inoculant products recommended for soybean, cowpea, and common bean inoculation showed the presence of different denitrification genes (Zilli et al., 2020). Thus, while the *B. diazoefficiens* strains CPAC 7 and USDA 110 have the complete set of genes for denitrification, some of them were not found in the strains CPAC 15 and E109 of *B. japonicum* and BR 3267 of *B. yuanmingense*, including the *nosZ* gene. The strains SEMIA 587 and BR 29 of *B. elkanii* also lack most of the denitrification genes, and no genes related to denitrification were found in *B. pachyrhizi* strain BR 3262.

4.7.2 Nitrous Oxide Emission by Nodules of Alfalfa (*Medicago sativa*)

Originally from Asia Minor and Southern Caucasus, alfalfa was introduced by the Persians in Greece, and from there it passed to Italy in the 4th century BC. The great diffusion of alfalfa was carried out by the Arabs through North Africa, further it reached Spain, from where it spread throughout Europe. Alfalfa is a perennial, lively, and erect plant widely distributed in countries with a temperate climate. It is a natural source of protein, fiber, vitamins, and minerals, reasons why it is mainly used for intensive livestock farming, as a cover crop, and in rotation with cereals.

E. meliloti is the main microsymbiont of alfalfa (*Medicago sativa*) and other medic legumes such as *Melilotus* and *Trigonella*. Located in the symbiotic pSymA megaplasmid, it also contains the *napA*, *nirK*, *norC*, and *nosZ* genes responsible for complete denitrification (Torres et al., 2014) (Figure 4.2). In contrast to *B. diazoefficiens*, *E. meliloti* 1021 does not grow when cultured under anoxic (<0.5% O_2) conditions, though it does grow when cultivated with nitrate as the final electron acceptor in microoxia (~2% O_2) (Torres et al., 2014). The inability to grow under anoxic conditions is recovered in strains that overexpress the enzyme Nap, which indicates that a limitation of its expression is responsible for the absence of growth when the cells grow under anoxic conditions with nitrate (Torres et al., 2018). In addition, monitoring the O_2 consumption and NOx production during the transition from an oxic to hypoxic conditions with a robotized system, *E. meliloti* strain 1021 was able to reduce N_2O supplied externally to N_2, thus showing its potential to act as a sink of N_2O (Bueno et al., 2015). The occurrence of N_2O production by nodules of alfalfa formed by *E. meliloti* strain L5-30 was reported by Casella et al. (1984) after growing the plants in NO_3^--enriched agar medium. The *E. meliloti* L5-30 Nap and NirK denitrification enzymes are involved in NO production by alfalfa root nodules (Cam et al., 2012; Horchani et al., 2011), but their potential involvement on N_2O emissions needs to be investigated.

In addition to Nor, the main enzyme involved in N_2O production, a flavohemoglobin (Hmp), and the NnrS1 and NnrS2 proteins have been reported to produce N_2O from NO as a mechanism for NO detoxification (Figure 4.2).

4.7.3 Nitrous Oxide Emission by Nodules of Common Beans (*Phaseolus vulgaris*)

P. vulgaris L. (common bean) is an herbaceous legume native to Central and South America that is currently cultivated in countries on all continents by small farmers and large producers, with both green pods and dried seeds being marketed. This legume is among the three most important legume crops worldwide along with soybean and peanut (*Arachis hypogaea*). *P. vulgaris* grows in different soil-climatic conditions, and there are varieties with contrasting ripening times and seeds with a wide variety of sizes, shapes, and colors (De Ron et al., 2015). *P. vulgaris* is the most cultivated species of the genus worldwide, although other species such as *P. coccineus*, *P. dumosus,* and *P. lunatus* are also cultivated, mainly in American countries.

Europe is considered a secondary center of diversification of beans from both Andean and Mesoamerican origin, with gene pools of both present on this continent. A high proportion of bean germplasm is derived from hybridization of these two gene pools, with hybrids being frequent in Central Europe and the Iberian Peninsula (Santalla et al., 2002; Angioi et al., 2010). In Europe, a large area is cultivated whose productivity reached 1,500,000 tons in 2018, including dry and green beans, most of them belonging to the species *P. vulgaris* (https://fao.org/faostat/en/#data/QC), of which 156,000 tons were produced in Spain (www.mapa.gob.es).

Because of their economic importance, special attention has been paid to the study of bean micro-symbionts, of which up to 20 rhizobial species, including alpha- and beta-Proteobacteria, have been described. Despite the wide range of rhizobia with which the bean establishes N_2-fixing symbioses, it is considered a poor plant with respect to N_2-fixing capacity compared to other grain legumes, a problem attributed to the inefficiency of the rhizobia that nodulate it.

Although the first studies on rhizobia nodulating *P. vulgaris* were carried out in France, the two main gateways of entry of this legume into Europe were Spain and Portugal (De Ron et al., 2016). In Spain, common beans form nodules mainly by the symbiovar phaseoli of *R. etli* and *R. leguminosarum* species (Shamseldin and Velázquez, 2020).

In addition to Alphaproteobacteria, *P. vulgaris* can be nodulated by species of the genus *Burkholderia* of the Betaproteobacteria. The ability to fix N_2 by free-living *Burkholderia* was discovered during studies with *B. vietnamiensis* (Gillis et al., 1995), an ability that was subsequently observed in other species. More than 15 *Burkholderia* species have been described that effectively nodulate legumes, of which the genus *Mimosa* is the most abundant. *Burkholderia* has also been isolated from bean nodules in Morocco (Talbi et al., 2010), Mexico (Martínez-Aguilar et al., 2013), and Brazil (Dall'Agnol et al., 2017).

Burkholderia species inhabit very diverse ecological niches and have been isolated from soil, plants, insects, industrial settings, hospital environments, and infected humans (Coenye and Vandamme 2003; Eberl and Vandamme 2016). Some *Burkholderia* strains have attracted considerable interest for the possibility of their use in agriculture, industry, bioremediation of recalcitrant xenobiotics, biocontrol, and plant growth promotion (PGPR, from Plant Growth Promoting Rhizobacteria) (Eberl and Vandamme 2016).

Of the rhizobia nodulating common beans, *R. etli* strain CFN42 only possesses the *nir* and *nor* genes (Gómez-Hernández et al., 2010) (Figure 4.2), and no denitrification genes were found in the genome of *R. tropici* strain CIAT 899 (Zilli et al., 2020). *Rhizobium freirei* strain PRF 81 was isolated from nodules of *P. vulgaris* by Dall'Agnol et al. (2013) and has been shown to contain the *narG*, *narH*, *narJ*, and *narI*, but it lacks the catalytic subunits of the remaining reductases (Zilli et al., 2020). The presence of denitrifying genes in members of *Burkholderia* has been shown only in *B. denitrificans* (Lee et al., 2012) and *B. thailandensis* (Vitale et al., 2020), but N_2O emission by nodules has not been reported.

N_2O emission by nodulated common beans was obtained in plants inoculated with the strain CFN42 and treated with 2 or 4 mM KNO_3 (Hidalgo-García et al., 2017). More information on the extent of N_2O emissions by nodules of *P. vulgaris* is missing, and scientific knowledge on denitrification properties in other *P. vulgaris*-nodulating rhizobia is unknown.

4.7.4 N_2O Emission by Other Rhizobia

R. sullae (formerly *R. hedysari*) forms nodules in *Hedysarum coronarium* (sulla). Studies on denitrification using the strain HCNT1, *in planta*, in free-living bacteria, and in bacteroids *ex planta* showed that nitrite reductase is the only denitrification-related enzyme, that is induced when grown in low oxygen conditions, and that, unlike other rhizobia, the strain HCNT1 does not couple nitrate or nitrite reduction with energy conservation (Squartini et al., 2002 and references therein). Regarding N_2O emission by nodules, Casella et al. (1984) reported that nodules formed by *R. sullae* strains RH19-R14 and CC1337 evolved N_2O when the plants grew in the presence of 12 mM NO_3^-.

Formation of N_2O from nodules of *Pisum sativum* was detected after inoculation with the strain LPR1 of R. *leguminosarum,* and rates of emission grew at increasing rates of nitrate present in the medium (Casella et al., 1984).

In our knowledge, to date, strains of *B. diazoefficiens* and *E. meliloti* are the only rhizobia in which the presence of the complete set of the denitrification genes has been reported. Because denitrification in nodules is the major pathway for N_2O generation, other mechanisms have been proposed to participate in formation of the gas (Figure 4.2).

4.7.5 Measuring N_2O Production by Nodules

The probable existence of denitrification by free-living cells can be observed by measuring increases in optical density/protein content of the cultures growing in the presence of nitrate under microoxic/anoxic conditions. During denitrification, in the absence of nitrous oxide reductase activity, N_2O accumulates, and its presence is usually recorded by gas chromatography using a thermal ionization detector or the more sensitive electron capture detector. Accordingly, N_2O production was detected when a *B. diazoefficiens nosZ* mutant was grown under oxygen-limited conditions in the presence of nitrate (Velasco et al., 2004). Oxygen concentrations in the nodule interior are at nanomolar levels (Layzell et al., 1993; Rutten and Poole 2019). In these conditions, the terminal oxidase cbb_3, whose affinity for O_2 is very high, is the enzyme responsible for the production of the ATP necessary to maintain the nitrogenase activity of the bacteroids, and thus the reduction of N_2 to NH_4^+ (Preisig et al., 1996; Kopat et al., 2017).

Denitrification was shown to occur in soybean nodules of plants treated with 4 mM nitrate without affecting nodulation and nitrogen fixation (Mesa et al., 2004; Sánchez et al., 2011; Hirayama et al., 2011; Tortosa et al., 2015). Using this model system, N_2O production by nodules of soybean plants inoculated with the wild type *B. diazoefficiens* USDA110 was detected, and significant increases were recorded when the plants were nodulated by mutant strains lacking the *nosZ* gene (Hirayama et al., 2011; Tortosa et al., 2015).

Often, N_2O emissions by legume nodules formed by wild-type rhizobial strains are very low, making its detection difficult. During studies on denitrification, Tortosa et al (2015) found that waterlogging produced a 150- and a 830-fold induction of the N_2O emission rates by soybeans inoculated with the wild-type (*nosZ*-containing) *B. diazoefficiens* strain USDA110 or by its *nosZ* mutant derivative, respectively. These results show that flooding is an environmental factor involved in the increase of N_2O emissions by nodulated legumes due to denitrification by their cognate rhizobial species. Since the effect of flooding on N_2O emission could be more likely due to the decrease in the O_2 concentration of the rooting medium (Akiyama et al., 2013), it is possible that other abiotic stresses such as salinity, drought, and others resulting in the reduction of O_2 diffusion also increase N_2O emissions by nodules. Nevertheless waterlogging did not favor N_2O production by nodules of *P, vulgaris* inoculated with *R. etli* CFN42, more likely due to the high sensitivity of the *P. vulgaris*-*R. etli* CFN42 symbiosis to flooding (Hidalgo-García et al., 2017).

Direct detection of N_2O production by nodulated legumes under field conditions is difficult to assess owing to the presence of rhizobial and non-rhizobial denitrifiers in the soil where the plants grow. For soybean, increased N_2O fluxes were detected at later stages of growth when increases in mineral N in soil after mineralization of senesced aerial and below-ground plant material were found (Yang and Cai 2005). In fact, an input of about 30 kg/ha of senesced leaves was estimated a few weeks before harvesting (Zotarelli et al., 2012). A study by Morais (2012) comparing N_2O emissions by soil planted with *Canavalia ensiformis* and *Sorghum bicolor* after incorporation to the soil of the plant biomass showed that N_2O fluxes from the area cultivated with the legume emitted 1.8 and 2.2 times more N_2O than those from the control and sorghum-cultivated sites, respectively. This could be explained assuming that the residues with the lowest C/N ratio lead to higher N_2O emissions (Baggs et al., 2000), and that there is no interference due to the combination of the soil N plus the residue N content (Chen et al., 2013).

In addition to above-ground plant residues, nodule decomposition has been shown to be a source of N_2O in soils cultivated with soybeans. [15]N tracer experiments demonstrated that emission of N_2O from the soybean rhizosphere was mainly derived from the N_2 fixed in the nodules (Inaba et al., 2012) and that the gas was emitted at the late growth period by decomposed nodules (Uchida and Akiyama, 2013). These results clearly show that the biological fixation of N_2 is an indirect source for N_2O during nodule degeneration (Sánchez and Minamisawa 2019). Denitrifiers, others than rhizobia, also play a role in denitrification in the soybean rhizosphere. Inaba et al. (2012) used *B. diazoefficiens* USDA and its *nosZ*-defective strain to show that during nodule degradation *Bradyrhizobium* was responsible for about 41% of the total N_2O produced, and that other rhizosphere microorganisms accounted for the remaining 59%. Thus, the soybean rhizosphere is a hotspot for N_2O production (Sánchez and Minamisawa, 2019).

4.7.6 Perspectives and Strategies to Mitigate N_2O Production by Nodules

That legumes enrich the soils where they grow with nutrients, especially N, and promote soil fertility and crop rotation has been known since ancient times. The industrial synthesis of urea, ammonium, and nitrate reduced the use of legumes as an agricultural practice which, in turn, led to the pollution of waters and sediments by nitrates and of the atmosphere by the greenhouse gas nitrous oxide.

Contribution of N_2O release into the atmosphere by legume crops is not well known and needs further research on a global scale. However, considering the vast tracts of land surface cultivated with legumes, it is clear that they represent a huge source of N_2O production.

NirK and NosZ are metalloenzymes that contain Cu in their active centers, so this element is essential for their biosynthesis and function and, accordingly, a key component in the design of strategic plans aimed at decreasing N_2O emission. However, Cu is a metallic pollutant, so its use should be directed to the increase of its bioavailability, not to the increase of its concentration.

Addition of Cu to urban soils inhibited soil denitrification function and decreased the abundance of denitrifiers (Li et al., 2019). Moreover, Tortosa et al. (2021) found that Cu added to nitrate-treated soybean plants inoculated with *B. diazoefficiens* USDA110 decreased N_2O production by nodules until a Cu concentration was reached that significantly affected nodulation, plant physiology, and symbiotic N_2 fixation. Interestingly, under conditions of excess Cu, the activity of the Nap and Nir enzymes decreased and that of the Nos enzyme increased.

Other mitigation strategies are related to biotic and abiotic factors that affect N_2O production by bulk and rhizosphere soil where the plants grow. Soil pH and temperature, soil moisture and O_2 availability, the soil C content and the C/N ratio of applied substrates among the abiotic, and the abundance of bacterial and archaeal nitrifiers, bacterial and fungal denitrifiers, and the influence of the plant have to be considered (Sanz-Cobeña et al., 2017). Nevertheless, the extent to which these factors can affect N_2O production by leguminous nodules is not known.

Plants have been shown to produce and emit N_2O into the atmosphere. Although for a long time it was believed that plants were a conduit to transport the N_2O produced by the soil-inhabiting microorganisms, evidence accumulates to support that the gas is formed within the plant. Once incorporated into the cytosol of the plant cells, nitrate can be reduced to nitrite, which is transported to the interior of the mitochondria, where it is metabolized to yield nitric oxide. Within the mitochondria, nitric oxide is then reduced to N_2O by a reduced form of the enzyme cytochrome c oxidase (Timilsina et al., 2020). These reactions, however, occur only when the plants are subjected to hypoxic or anoxic conditions. The reduction of NO to N_2O under those conditions could be a mechanism to protect the mitochondria integrity from the toxicity of NO accumulation. If one considers that nitrate is a common nutrient in the soil solution, and that diverse environmental factors can produce hypoxia and anoxia during the life cycle of the plants, then a significant global biogenic source of N_2O can be formed in the mitochondria.

Among the options to mitigate N_2O emissions by legumes is obtaining rhizobial inoculants with high nitrous oxide reductase activity. Itakura et al. (2013) first showed that inoculation of soybeans with a *B. diazoefficiens* strain overexpressing the *nosZ* gene retained higher nitrous oxide reductase activity in free-living and symbiotic conditions. During the corresponding farm-scale study, the same authors also showed that inoculation of soybeans with the *nosZ* overexpressing strain reduced by 54% the N_2O emissions produced at postharvest. Similar effect, however, was not observed when soybean plants grew in a soil of different texture, which indicates that some factors in the soybean rhizosphere reduced the potential N_2O mitigation ability of the overexpressing *nosZ* strain. It has also been shown that inoculation of soybean with enriched cultures of indigenous *nosZ*-containing *B. diazoefficiens* strains reduced N_2O emissions; accordingly, it would be expected that inoculation with mixed rhizobial cultures is more competitive and adaptable to changing environmental conditions than inoculation with a single strain (Akiyama et al., 2016).

Information on N_2O production by rhizobial endosymbionts is scarce, limited to a few plant-bacteria associations. Under field conditions, leguminous roots can be nodulated by different rhizobial strains differing in denitrification activity, as well as in N_2 fixation efficiency. The search for rhizobial cells with null or diminished N_2O production should be considered a priority for inoculation of legumes under field conditions. It should also be considered that mitigation of N_2O emission may be due not only to the presence of the nitrous oxide reductase enzyme but also to that of any other reductases whose activity prevents the formation of the gas.

Using a robotized system, *E. meliloti* was shown to grow through anaerobic respiration of N_2O to N_2. This, together with the finding that the pH and the C source affected the activity of the nitrous oxide reductase enzyme, points to the idea that a better understanding of the mechanisms and factors regulating N_2O consumption and production would improve our knowledge on N_2O mitigation (Bueno et al., 2015).

Acknowledgments

This work has been supported by grants from MINECO AGL2017-85676-R, Junta de Andalucía P18-RT-1401, and Ministerio de Ciencia e Innovación PID2020-114330GB-100 and PID2021-1240070B-100 awarded to the Nitrogen Metabolism Research Group of Estación Experimental del Zaidín-CSIC, and from Xunta de Galicia IN607A2021/03 and CSIC-202040E190 awarded to the Biology of Agrosystemns Research Group of Misión Biológica de Galicia-CSIC. The authors thank J. Cabrera and A. Jiménez-Leiva for preparation of the figures.

REFERENCES

Akiyama, H., Y. Hoshino, M. Itakura et al. 2016. Mitigation of soil N_2O emission by inoculation with a mixed culture of indigenous *Bradyrhizobium diazoefficiens*. *Science Report* 6:32869. 10.1038/srep32869

Akiyama, H., S. Morimoto, M. Hayatsu et al. 2013. Nitrification, ammonia-oxidizing communities, and N_2O and CH_4 fluxes in an imperfectly drained agricultural field fertilized with coated urea with and without dicyandiamide. *Biology and Fertility of Soils* 49:213–223. 10.1007/s00374-012-0713-2

Andrews, M., and M.E. Andrews. 2017. Specificity in legume-rhizobia symbioses. *International Journal of Molecular Sciences* 18:705. 10.3390/ijms18040705

Angioi, S.A., D. Rau, Attene G. et al., 2010. Beans in Europe: Origin and structure of the European landraces of *Phaseolus vulgaris* L. *Theoretical and Applied Genetics* 121:829–843. 10.1007/s00122-010-1353-2

Baggs, E.M., R.M. Rees, K.A. Smith, and A.J.A. Vinten. 2000. Nitrous oxide emission from soils after incorporating crop residues. *Soil Use Management* 16:82–87. 10.1111/j.1475-2743.2000.tb00179.x

Bedmar, E.J., E.F. Robles, and M.J. Delgado. 2005. The complete denitrification pathway of the symbiotic, nitrogen-fixing bacterium *Bradyrhizobium japonicum. Biochemical Society Transactions* 33:145–148. 10.1042/BST0330141

Bueno, E., D. Mania, A. Frostegard, E.J. Bedmar, L.R. Bakken, and M.J. Delgado. 2015. Anoxic growth of *Ensifer meliloti* 1021 by N_2O-reduction, a potential mitigation strategy. *Frontiers in Microbiolgy* 6:537. 10.3389/fmicb.2015.00537

Bueno, E., S. Mesa, E.J. Bedmar, D.J. Richardson, and M.J. Delgado. 2012. Bacterial adaptation of respiration from oxic to microoxic and anoxic conditions: Redox control. *Antioxidant and Redox Signaling (ARS)* 16:819–852. 10.1089/ars.2011.4051

Cam, Y., O. Pierre, E. Boncompagni, D. Hérouart, E. Meilhoc, and C. Bruand. 2012. Nitric oxide (NO): A key player in the senescence of *Medicago truncatula* root nodules. *New Phytology* 196:548–560. 10.1111/j.1469-8137.2012.04282.x

Casella, S., C. Leporini, and P.M. Nuti. 1984. Nitrous oxide production by nitrogen-fixing, fast-growing rhizobia. *Microbial Ecology* 10:107–114. 10.1007/BF02011418

Chen, W.M., S. Laevens, T.M. Lee, T. Coenye, P. de Vos, M. Mergeay, and P. Vandamme. 2001. *Ralstonia taiwanensis* spp. nov. isolated from root nodules of *Mimosa* species and sputum of a cystic fibrosis patient. *International Journal of Systematic and Evolutionary Microbiology* 51:1729–1735. 10.1099/00207713-51-5-1729

Chen, H., X., Li, F. Hu, and W. Shi. 2013. Soil nitrous oxide emissions following crop residue addition: A meta-analysis. *Global Change Biology* 19:2956–2964. 10.1111/gcb.12274

Coba de la Peña, T., E. Fedorova, J.J. Pueyo, and M. Lucas. 2018. The symbiosome: Legume and rhizobia co-evolution toward a nitrogen-fixing organelle? *Frontiers in Plant Science* 8:2229. 10.3389/fpls.2017.02229

Coenye, T., and P. Vandamme. 2003. Diversity and significance of *Burkholderia* species occupying diverse ecological niches. *Environmental Microbiology* 5:719–729. 10.1046/j.1462-2920.2003.00471.x

Dall'Agnol, R.F., C. Bournaud, S. Miana de Faria, et al., 2017. Genetic diversity of symbiotic *Paraburkholderia* species isolated from nodules of *Mimosa pudica* (L.) and *Phaseolus vulgaris* (L.) grown in soils of the Brazilian Atlantic Forest (Mata Atlantica). *FEMS Microbiology Ecology* 93:2017. fix027. 10.1093/femsec/fix027

Dall'Agnol, R.F., R.A. Ribeiro, E. Ormeño-Orrillo et al., 2013. *Rhizobium* freirei sp. nov., a symbiont of *Phaseolus vulgaris* that is very effective at fixing nitrogen. *International Journal of Systematic and Evolutionary Microbiology* 63:41674173. 10.1099/ijs.0.052928-0

Daims, H., E.V. Lebedeva, P. Pjevac, et al., 2015. Complete nitrification by *Nitrospira* bacteria. *Nature* 528:504–509. 10.1038/nature16461

De Lajudie P., M.J. Andrews, J. Ardley, et al., 2019. Minimal standards for the description of new genera and species of rhizobia and agrobacteria. *Intermational Journal of Systematic and. Evolutionary Microbiology* 69:1852–1863. 10.1099/ijsem.0.003426

Delamuta, J.R.M., R.A. Ribeiro, E. Ormeño-Orrillo, I.S. Melo, E. Martínez-Romero, and M.A. Hungria. 2013. Polyphasic evidence supporting the reclassification of *Bradyrhizobium japonicum* group Ia strains as *Bradyrhizobium diazoefficiens* sp. nov. *International Journal of Systematic and Evolutionary Microbiology* 63:3342–3351. 10.1099/ijs.0.049130-0

De Ron, A.M., A.M. González, A.P. Rodiño, M. Santalla, L. Godoy, and R. Papa. 2016. History of the common bean crop: Its evolution beyond its areas of origin and domestication. *Arbor* 192(779):a317. 10.3989/arbor.2016.779n30

De Ron, A.M., R. Papa, E. Bitocchi, et al., 2015. Common bean. In *Grain legumes, Handbook of plant breeding*, ed. A. M. De Ron. Springer, New York, USA. p. 438. ISBN 978-1-4939-2796-8.

Eberl, L., and P. Vandamme. 2016. Members of the genus *Burkholderia*: Good and bad guys. *F1000 Research* 5:1007. 10.12688/f1000research.8221.1

Erisman, J.W., J.N. Galloway, N.B. Dise, et al., 2015. Nitrogen: Too much of a vital resource. *Science in brief*. WWF Netherlands, Zeist, The Netherlands. ISBN 978-90-74595-22-3.

Erisman, J.W., J.N. Galloway, S. Seitzinger, A. Bleeker, and K. Butterbach-Bahl. 2011. Reactive nitrogen in the environment and its effect on climate change. *Current Opinions in Environmental Sustainability* 3:281–290. 10.1016/j.cosust.2011.08.012

Estrada de los Santos, P., M. Palmer, B. Chávez-Ramírez, et al. 2018. Whole genome analyses suggest that *Burkholderia sensu lato* contains two additional novel genera (*Mycetohabitans* gen. nov., and *Trinickia* gen. nov.): Implications for the evolution of diazotrophy and nodulation in the Burkholderiaceae. *Genes* (Basel) 1;9(8):389. 10.3390/genes9080389

Fernández, L.A., E. Perotti,, M.A. Sagardoy, and. A. Gómez. 2008. Denitrification activity of *Bradyrhizobium* sp. isolated from Argentine soybean cultivated soils. *World Journal of Microbial Biotechnology* 24:2577–2585. 10.1007/s11274-008-9828-x

Fowler, D., C.E. Steadman, D. Stevenson, et al., 2015. Effects of global change during the 21st century on the nitrogen cycle. *Atmosphere Chemical Physics* 15:13849–13893. 10.5194/acp-15-13849-2015

Gillis, M., T.V. Van, R. Bardin, et al., 1995. Polyphasic taxonomy in the genus *Burkholderia* leading to an emended description of the genus and proposition of *Burkholderia vietnamiensis* sp. nov. for N_2-fixing isolates from rice in Vietnam. *Intermational Journal of Systematic and. Evolutionary Microbiology* 45:274–289. 10.1099/00207713-45-2-274

Gómez-Hernández, N., A. Reyes-González, C. Sánchez, Y. Mora, Delgado. M.J., and L. Girard. 2010. Regulation and symbiotic role of *nirK* and *norC* expression in *Rhizobium etli*. *Moleular Plant-Microbe Interactions* 24:233–245. 10.1094/MPMI-07-10-0173

Good, A.G., and R. Dixon. 2021. The nitrogen fixation dream: The challenges and the future. In *Nitrogen cycle: Ecology, biotechnological applications and environmental impact*s, ed. J. Gonzalez-Lopez and A. Gonzalez-Martinez, pp. 22–33, CRC Press Boca Raton. 10.1002/9780470400531.eorms0040

Gruber, N., and J.N. Galloway. 2008. An earth-system perspective of the global nitrogen cycle. *Nature* 451:293–296. 10.1038/nature06592

Herridge, D.F., M.B. Peoples, and R.M. Boddey. 2008. Global inputs of biological nitrogen fixation in agricultural systems. *Plant and Soil* 311:1–18. 10.1007/s11104-008-9668-3

Hidalgo-García, A., G. Tortosa, E.J. Bedmar, and M.J. Delgado. 2017. Efecto del nitrato y el encharcamiento en la emisión del gas invernadero N_2O por la simbiosis *Phaseolus vulgaris-Rhizobium etli*. In *Actas de la Asociación Española de Leguminosas (AEL7)*, ed. A. Clemente and A.M. De Ron, pp. 51–61, Editorial Atrio S.L. ISBN: 978-84-15275-61-9.

Hirayama, J., S. Eda, H. Mitsui, and K. Minamisawa. 2011. Nitrate-dependent N_2O emission from intact soybean nodules via denitrification by *Bradyrhizobium japonicum* bacteroids. *Applied and Environmental Microbiology* 77:8787–8790. 10.1128/AEM.06262-11.ien

Horchani, F., Prevot, M., Boscari, A., et al., 2011. Both plant and bacterial nitrate reductases contribute to nitric oxide production in *Medicago truncatula* nitrogen-fixing nodules. *Plant Physiology* 155:1023–1036. 10.1104/pp.110.166140

Hungria, M., and I.C. Mendes. 2015. Nitrogen fixation with soybean: The perfect symbiosis? In *Biological nitrogen fixation*, ed. F.J. de Bruijn, pp. 1009–1024, John Wiley and Sons, New Jersey. 10.1002/978111 9053095.ch99

Inaba, S., F. Ikenishi, M. Itakura, et al., 2012. N_2O emission from degraded soybean nodules depends on denitrification by *Bradyrhizobium japonicum* and other microbes in the rhizosphere. *Microbes and Environment* 27:470–476. 10.1264/jsme2.me12100

IPCC, 2019. N_2O emissions from managed soils and CO_2 emissions from lime and urea application. Refinement to the 2006 IPCC In *Guidelines for National Greenhouse Gas Inventories* prepared by the National Greenhouse Gas Inventories Programme IGES, Hayama, Japan.

Itakura, M., Uchida, Y., Akiyama, H., et al., 2013. Mitigation of nitrous oxide emissions from soils by *Bradyrhizobium japonicum* inoculation. *Nature Climate Change* 3:208–212. 10.1038/nclimate1734

Jones, C., B. Stres, M. Rosenquist, and S. Hallin. 2008. Phylogenetic analysis of nitrite, nitric oxide, and nitrous oxide respiratory enzymes reveal a complex evolutionary history for denitrification. *Molecular Biology and Evolution* 25:1955–1966. 10.1093/molbev/msn146

Kopat, V.V., E.R. Chirak, A.K. Kimeklis, et al., 2017. Evolution of *fixNOQP* genes encoding cytochrome oxidase with high affinity to oxygen in rhizobia and related bacteria. *Russian Journal of Genetics* 53:1022e7954. 10.1134/S1022795417070067

Kuypers, M.M.M., H.K. Marchant, and B. Kartal. 2018. The microbial nitrogen-cycling network. *Nature Review Microbiology* 16:263–276. 10.1038/nrmicro.2018.9

Layzell, D.B., L. Diaz del Castillo, S. Hunt, M. Kuzma, O. van Cauwenberghe, and I. Oresnik. 1993. The regulation of oxygen and its role in regulating nodule netabolism. In *New horizons in nitrogen fixation*.

Current plant science and biotechnology in agriculture, vol. 17, ed. R. Palacios, J. Mora, and W.E. Newton. pp. 393–398. Springer, Dordrecht. 10.1007/978-94-017-2416-6_39

Lee, C.M., H.Y. Weon, S.H. Yoon, S.J. Kim, B.S. Koo, and S.W. Kwon. 2012. *Burkholderia denitrificans* sp. nov., isolated from the soil of Dokdo Island, Korea. *Journal of Microbiology* 50:855–859. 10.1007/s12275-012-1554-2

Lewis, G.P., B. Schrire, B. Mackinder, and M. Loyck. 2005. *Legumes of the world*. Royal Botanic Gardens, Kew, UK. ISBN 1 900347 80 6.

Li, S., X. Yang, D. Buchner, H. Wang, H. Xu, S.B. Haderlein, and Y. Zhu. 2019. Increased copper levels inhibit denitrification in urban soils. *Earth and Environmental Science Transactions of the Royal Society of Edinburgh* 109:421–427. 10.1017/S1755691018000592

LPWG, 2017 (The Legume Phylogeny Working Group). A new subfamily classification of the Leguminosae based on a taxonomically comprehensive phylogeny. *Taxon* 66:44–77.

Maeda, K., A. Spor, V. Edel-Hermann, et al., 2015. N_2O production, a widespread trait in fungi. *Science Reports* 5:9697. 10.1038/srep09697

Martin, F.M., S. Uroz, and D.G. Barker. 2017. Ancestral alliances: Plant mutualistic symbioses with fungi and bacteria. *Science* 356(6340):1e9. 10.1126/science.aad4501

Martínez-Aguilar, L., C. Salazar-Salazar, R.D. Méndez, et al., 2013. *Burkholderia caballeronis* sp. nov., a nitrogen fixing species isolated from tomato (*Lycopersicon esculentum*) with the ability to effectively nodulate *Phaseolus vulgaris*. *Antonie van Leeuwenhoek* 104:1063–1071. 10.1007/s10482-013-0028-9

Mesa, S., J.D. Alché, E.J. Bedmar and M.J. Delgado. 2004. Expression of *nir*, *nor* and *nos* denitrification genes from *Bradyrhizobium japonicum* in soybean root nodules. *Physiologia Plantarum* 120:205–211. 10.1111/j.0031-9317.2004.0211.x

Morais, R.F. 2012. Manejo da adubação nitrogenada e emissão de gases de efeito estufa em capim-elefante parabioenergia. PhD. *Thesis. Universidade Federal Rural do Rio de Janeiro*, Seropédica, RJ, Brazil. Cited in Zilli et al., (2020).

Moulin, L., A. Munive, B. Dreyfus, and C. Boivin-Masson. 2001. Nodulation of legumes by members of the β-subclass of Proteobacteria. *Nature* 411:948–950. 10.1038/35082070

Obando, M., D. Correa-Galeote, J. Gualpa, A. Hidalgo-Garcia, J.D. Alché, E.J. Bedmar, and F. Cassán. 2019. Analysis of the denitrification pathway and greenhouse gases emissions in *Bradyrhizobium* sp. strains used as biofertilizers in South America. *Journal of Applied Microbiology* 127:739–749. 10.1111/jam.14233

O'Hara, G.W., R.M. Daniel, and K.W. Steele. 1983. Effect of oxygen on the synthesis, activity and breakdown of the rhizobium denitrification system. *Microbiology* 129:2405–2412. 10.1099/00221287-129-8-2405.

Oldroyd, G.E.D. 2013. Speak, friend, and enter: Signaling systems that promote beneficial symbiotic associations in plants. *Nature Review Microbiology* 11:252–263. 10.1038/nrmicro2990

Oldroyd, G.E.D., and A.J. Downie. 2008. Coordinating nodule morphogenesis with rhizobial infection in legumes. *Annual Review Plant Biology* 59:519e546. 10.1146/annurev.arplant.59.0326J.07.092839

Oldroyd, G.E.D., J.D. Murray, P.S. Poole, and A.J. Downie. 2011. The rules of engagement in the legume-rhizobial symbiosis. *Annual Review Genetics* 45:119e144. 10.1146/annurev-genet-110410-132549

Poole, P., V. Ramachandran, and J. Terpolilli. 2018. Rhizobia: From saprophytes to endosymbionts. *Nature Reviews/Microbiology* 15:291–303. 10.1038/nrmicro.2017.171

Preisig, O., R. Zufferey, L. Thöny-Meyer, C.A. Appleby, and H. Hennecke. 1996. A high-affinity *cbb₃*-type cytochrome oxidase terminates the symbiosis-specific respiratory chain of *Bradyrhizobium japonicum*. *Journal of Bacteriology* 178:1532e1538. 10.1128/jb.178.6.1532-1538.1996

Reckling, M., J.M. Hecker, G. Bergkvist, et al., 2016. A cropping system assessment framework-evaluating effects of introducing legumes into crop rotations. *European Journal of Agronomy* 76:186–197. 10.1016/j.eja.2015.11.005

Rodiño, A.P., M. de la Fuente, A.M. De Ron, M.J. Lema, J.J. Drevon, and M. Santalla. 2011. Variation for nodulation and plant yield of common bean genotypes and environmental effects on the genotype expression. *Plant and Soil* 346:349–361. http://hdl.handle.net/10261/66024.

Roth, L.E., and G. Stacey. 1989. Bacterium release into host-cells of nitrogen-fixing soybean nodules–the symbiosome membrane comes from 3 sources. *European Journal of Cell Biology* 49:13–23. PMID: 2759097.

Rutten, P.J., and P.S. Poole. 2019. Oxygen regulatory mechanisms of nitrogen fixation in rhizobia. *Advances in Microbial Physiology* 75. 10.1016/bs.ampbs.2019.08.001

Salas, A., J.J. Cabrera, A. Jiménez-Leiva, S. Mesa, E.J. Bedmar, D.J. Richardson, A.J. Gates, and M.J. Delgado. 2021. Bacterial nitric oxide metabolism: Recent insights in Rhizobia. *Advances in Microbial Physiology* 78:259–315. 10.1016/bs.ampbs.2021.05.001

Sameshima-Saito, R., K. Chiba, and K. Minamisawa. 2006. Correlation of denitrifying capability with the existence of *nap*, *nir*, *nor* and *nos* genes in diverse strains of soybean bradyrhizobia. *Microbes and Environment* 21:174–184. 10.1264/jsme2.21.174

Sánchez, C., E.J. Bedmar, M.J. Delgado, G. Tortosa, and M.J. Delgado. 2011. Involvement of *Bradyrhizobium japonicum* denitrification in symbiotic nitrogen fixation by soybean plants subjected to flooding. *Soil Biology and Biochemistry* 43:212–217. 10.1016/j.soilbio.2010.09.020

Sánchez, C. and K. Minamisawa. 2019. Nitrogen cycling in soybean rhizosphere: Sources and sinks of nitrous Oxide (N$_2$O). *Frontiers in Microbiology* 10:1943. 10.3389/fmicb.2019.01943

Santalla, M., A.P. Rodiño, and A.M. De Ron. 2002. Allozyme evidence supporting Southwestern Europe as a secondary center of genetic diversity for common bean. *Theoretical and Applied Genetics* 104:934–944. 10.1007/s00122-001-0844-6

Sanz-Cobeña, A., L. Lassaletta, E. Aguilera, et al., 2017. Strategies for greenhouse gas emissions mitigation in Mediterranean agriculture: A review. *Agriculture, Ecosystems and Environment* 238:5–24. 10.1016/j.agee.2016.09.038

Shamseldin, A., and E. Velázquez. 2020. The promiscuity of *Phaseolus vulgaris* L. (common bean) for nodulation with rhizobia: A review. *World Journal of Microbiology and Biotechnology* 36:63. 10.1007/s11274-020-02839-w

Shoun, H., and S. Fushinobu. 2017. Denitrification in fungi. In *Metalloenzymes in denitrification: Applications and environmental impacts*, ed. J.M. Moura., J.G. Pauleta, and L.B. Maia, pp. 331–348. Royal Society of Chemistry, UK. ISNN. 2045-547X.

Smil, V. 2011. Nitrogen cycle and world food production. *World Agriculture* 2:9–13.

Sprent, J., J. Ardley, and E.J. James. 2017. Biogeography of nodulated legumes and their nitrogen fixing symbionts. *New Phytology* 215:40–56. 10.1111/nph.14474

Squartini, A., P. Struffi, D. Heidi, et al., 2002. *Rhizobium sullae* sp. nov. (formerly '*Rhizobium hedysari*'), the root-nodule microsymbiont of *Hedysarum coronarium* L. *International Journal of Systematic and Evolutionary Microbiology* 52:1267–1276. 10.1099/00207713-52-4-1267

Syakila, A., and C. Kroeze. 2011. The global nitrous oxide budget revisited. *Greenhouse Gas Measurement and Management* 1:17–26. 10.3763/ghgmm.2010.0007

Talbi, C., M.J. Delgado, L. Girard, A. Ramírez-Trujillo, J. Caballero-Mellado, and E.J. Bedmar. 2010. *Burkholderia phymatum* capable of nodulating *Phaseolus vulgaris* are present in Moroccan soils. *Applied an Environmental Microbiology* 76:4587–4591. 10.1128/AEM.02886-09

Timilsina, A., C. Zhang, B. Pandey, B.F. Bizimana, W. Dong, and C. Hu. 2020. Potential pathway of nitrous oxide formation in plants. *Frontiers in Plant Sciences* 11:1177. 10.3389/fpls.2020.01177

Torres, M.J., S. Ávila, E.J. Bedmar, and M.J. Delgado. 2018. Overexpression of the periplasmic nitrate reductase supports anaerobic growth by *Ensifer meliloti*. *FEMS Microbiology Letters* 365(7). 10.1093/femsle/fny041

Torres, M.J., M.I. Rubia, T. Coba de la Peña, J.J. Pueyo, E.J. Bedmar, and M.J. Delgado. 2014. Genetic basis for denitrification in *Ensifer meliloti*. *BMC Microbiology* 14:142. 10.1186/1471-2180-14-142

Tortosa, G., A. Hidalgo, A. Salas, E.J. Bedmar, S. Mesa, and M.J. Delgado. 2015. Nitrate and flooding induce N$_2$O emissions from soybean nodules. *Symbiosis* 67:125–133. 10.1007/s13199-015-0341-3

Tortosa, G., S. Parejo, J.J. Cabrera, E.J. Bedmar, and S. Mesa. 2021. Oxidative stress produced by Paraquat reduces nitrogen fixation in soybean-*Bradyrhizobium diazoefficiens* symbiosis by decreasing nodule functionality. *Nitrogen* 2:30–40. 10.3390/nitrogen2010003

Uchida, Y., and H. Akiyama. 2013. Mitigation of postharvest nitrous oxide emissions from soybean ecosystems: A review. *Soil Sciences of Plant Nutrition* 59:477–487. 10.1080/00380768.2013.805433

Udvardi, M., and P.S. Poole. 2013. Transport and metabolism in legume-rhizobia symbioses. *Annual Review Plant Biology* 64:781–805. 10.1146/annurev-arplant-050312-120235

Velasco, L., S. Mesa, C.A. Xu, M.J. Delgado, and E.J. Bedmar. 2004. Molecular characterization of *nosRZDFYLX* genes coding for denitrifying nitrous oxide reductase of *Bradyrhizobium japonicum*. *Antonie van Leuwenhoek* 85:229–235. 10.1023/B:ANTO.0000020156.42470.db

Vitale, A., S. Paszti, K. Takahashi, M. Toyofuku, G. Pessi, and L. Eberl. 2020. Mapping of the denitrification pathway in *Burkholderia thailandensis* by genome-wide mutant profiling. *Journal of Bacteriology* 202:e00304-20. 10.1128/JB.00304-20

Wheatley, R.M., and P.S. Poole. 2018. Mechanisms of bacterial attachment to roots. *FEMS Microbiology Reviews* 42:448e461. 10.1093/femsre/fuy014

WPP, 2019. *United Nations, Department of Economic and Social Affairs, Population Division. World Population Prospects 2019: Highlights* (ST/ESA/SER.A/423).

Wu, G., T. Zhang, M. Gu, A. Chen, and Q. Yin. 2020. Review of characteristics of anammox bacteria and strategies for anammox start-up for sustainable wastewater resource management. *Water Science Technology* 82:1742–1757. 10.2166/wst.2020.443

Yang, L., and Z. Cai. 2005. The effect of growing soybean (*Glycine max*, L.) on N_2O emission from soil. *Soil Biology and Biochemistry* 37:1205–1209. 10.1016/j.soilbio.2004.08.027

Zilli, J.E., B.J.R. Alves, L.F.M. Rouws, et al., 2020. The importance of denitrification performed by nitrogen-fixing bacteria used as inoculants in South America. *Plant and Soil* 451:5–24. 10.1007/s11104-019-04187-7

Zotarelli, L., N.P. Zatorre, R.M. Moddey, R.S. Urquiaga, C.P. Jantalia, J.C. Franchini, and B.J.R. Alves. 2012. Influence of no-tillage and frequency of a green manure legume in crop rotations for balancing N outputs and preserving soil organic C stocks. *Field Crop Research* 132:185–195. 10.1016/j.fcr.2011.12.013

Zumft, W.G. 1997. Cell biology and molecular basis of denitrification. *Microbiology and Molecular Biology Reviews* 61:533–616. 10.1128/mmbr.61.4.533-616.1997

5

Proteomics: Aim at Stress Mitigation in Soybean under Flooding

Ghazala Mustafa[1] and Setsuko Komatsu[2]
[1]Department of Plant Sciences, Quaid-i-Azam University, Islamabad, Pakistan
[2]Faculty of Environment and Information Sciences, Fukui University of Technology, Fukui, Japan

CONTENTS

5.1 Introduction

Climatic conditions around the world are rapidly changing and cause an imbalance in the environment (Eigenbrod et al., 2015). Environmental variations are responsible for changes in precipitation patterns, which lead to reduction in crop development and production (Easterling et al., 2007). Flooding is the most serious abiotic stress, which induces growth retardation, yield reduction, and death of crops (Normile, 2008). Flooding causes complete or partial submergence stress, which has a deteriorative effect on seed germination, vegetative, and reproductive development of plants. Flooding induces oxygen-deficient conditions that adversely alter the growth stages of the plant's life cycle (Zhong et al., 2020a). Low oxygen conditions alter the plant metabolism from aerobic respiration to anaerobic fermentative pathways that is responsible for impairment of plant development (Christianson et al., 2009; Xu et al., 2014). These findings clearly indicate that plant growth and development are badly impaired by reduced oxygen during long-term exposure of flooding stress.

Soybean is an important agricultural crop because of its rich protein and vegetable oil content. Soybean is highly intolerant to flooding stress, which is a vital constraint in its production worldwide (VanToai et al., 2010). Soybean growth is severely declined by flooding stress, which causes a reduction in crop yield (Githiri et al., 2006). At the seedling stage, flooding causes destruction of the root system and cotyledons due to excessive imbibition of water (Nakayama et al., 2004). Flooding reduces root elongation and hypocotyl pigmentation (Hashiguchi et al., 2009). Soybean experiences oxygen deficiency under flooding stress, which tends to cause a metabolic shift from aerobic to anaerobic pathways to fulfill energy demands under unfavorable conditions (Voesenek et al., 2006). Flooding induces alcoholic fermentation, and various types of fermentative bypass happen depending on which metabolic products are accumulated inside the cell, causing poisoning (Liao and Lin, 2001). These studies explained that flooding induced severe damage at the early growth stage of soybean via alteration of different metabolic processes.

Efficacy and advancement of the new proteomic technologies improved the number of proteins identified in a single study. Proteomic analyses were done to understand the flood-response strategy in soybean. In soybean, proteomic studies have been performed at different developmental stages, organs, and organelles (Wang and Komatsu, 2020). These studies reported a glut of different biological pathways, including glycolysis, fermentation, hormone regulation, signal transduction, programmed cell death, electron transport chain, calcium/gibberellic acid/abscisic acid signaling, and cell wall loosening (Komatsu et al., 2012). Flooding stress also induces changes in the subcellular proteomics (Komatsu and Hashiguchi, 2018), and protein post-translational modifications of soybean (Hashiguchi and Komatsu, 2016). Flooding responsive mechanisms of soybean have been comprehensively studied using different proteomic strategies; however, mitigation strategies to understand the flooding-tolerant mechanism still need further investigation.

In this chapter, the soybean response mechanism with the help of proteomic studies is explained in detail. Furthermore, different mitigation strategies, including the application of plant-derived smoke, abscisic acid, nanoparticles, and calcium, are described. The molecular mechanism of the mode of action of these chemicals is comprehensively discussed in soybean under flooding stress. Lastly, the tolerant mechanism of soybean with the help of developed transgenic and mutant lines is elaborated.

5.2 Proteomics for Flooding Response Mechanism in Soybean

Plant proteomics is a fascinating strategy with the potential to address the major issues with respect to crop production, ecological sustainability, and environmental pollution (Gemperline et al., 2016). Proteomics helps to find out crude proteins produced/altered under flooding stress. These proteins are utilized by the plants for sustaining various physiological and biochemical processes during the stress caused by the waterlogged condition. Proteomic procedures are used to scrutinize the molecular mechanisms of soybean due to its economic importance and role in agriculture.

At the early growth stages of soybean, carbohydrate metabolism and calcium signaling related proteins were regulated as a response under flooding stress (Yin et al., 2014; Nakamura et al., 2012). Long-term exposure to flooding stress induced root cell death and declined synthesis of the cell wall as well as protein metabolism (Komatsu et al., 2013a; Khatoon et al., 2012). During recovery from the flooding stage, proteins related to secondary metabolism, glycolysis, and cell reorganization helped soybean to recover from stress by regulating the energy calamity and reactive oxygen species (Salavati et al., 2012; Khan et al., 2015). The soybean root undergoes an imbalance of the carbon-nitrogen ratio as evident by the accumulation of metabolites used in the tricarboxylic acid cycle and accumulated gamma-aminobutyric acid (Nakamura et al., 2012; Komatsu et al., 2011b). Various studies were carried out to understand the flooding response mechanism using the proteomic technique (Wang and Komatsu, 2018; Komatsu et al., 2015; Yin and Komatsu, 2017). By using identified proteins from these studies, a schematic illustration of the soybean response mechanism under flooding stress is explained in Figure 5.1.

Plant responses to environmental stimuli are regulated by post-translational modifications, which are involved in controlling protein localization, its activity, and protein-protein interactions (Hashiguchi and Komatsu, 2016). Flooding changes the manifestation of phosphorylated proteins engaged in energy production and cell structure/protein folding with the help of the dephosphorylated protein profile (Nanjo et al., 2010, 2012). Glycosylation and ubiquitination play a critical function in protein degradation and synthesis during flooding stress. During a 2-day flooding stress, the formation of glycoproteins inhibited (Wang and Komatsu, 2016) and ubiquitin mediated protein degradation initiated (Yin and Komatsu, 2017). Under flooding stress, the response generated by *S*-nitrosylation proteins enhanced

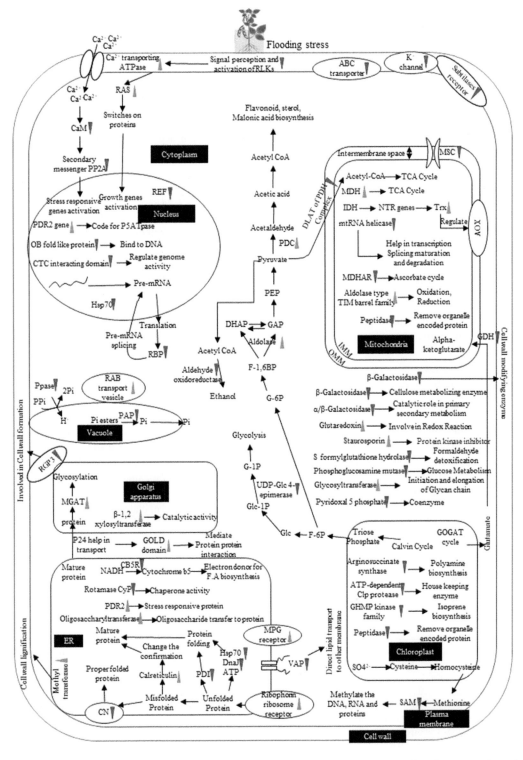

(caption on next page)

cellular pathways like glycolysis and fermentation. The activated and deactivated forms of sugar degrading enzymes played a triggering response during the course of *S*-nitrosylation (Hashiguchi and Komatsu, 2018). All these findings indicate that the initial response to flooding is protein phosphorylation, which is involved in stress-responsive RNA processing and protein synthesis.

Subcellular compartmentalization is vital for control of plant growth and development. Subcellular proteomics reveals the localized cellular responses and highlights the possible interactions between subcellular compartments during the processes of plant development and stress response. In soybean plasma membrane, flooding-induced proteins related to the antioxidative system, stress, and signaling played roles in protecting the cell from oxidative damage, protein degradation, and ion homeostasis (Komatsu et al., 2009). In flooded soybean, the cell wall lignification was reduced due to reduction in the reactive oxygen species and the jasmonate biosynthesis pathway (Komatsu et al., 2010). In soybean root tip, nuclear proteins related to poly-ADP-ribosylation were enhanced, whereas RNA metabolism related proteins were declined under flooding stress (Oh et al., 2014a). At initial stages of flooding stress, protein translation drops due to suppression of pre-ribosome biogenesis and mRNA metabolism related protein in the soybean nucleus (Yin et al., 2016). In the mitochondria of flooded soybean, the electron transport chain was damaged, and ATP was decreased, which led to oxidative damage (Kamal and Komatsu, 2015) and eventually, cell damage (Komatsu et al., 2011a). Flooding stress negatively affected protein synthesis and glycosylation in the endoplasmic reticulum of flooded soybean (Komatsu et al., 2012). In soybean endoplasmic reticulum, protein synthesis was hindered due to the calnexin/calreticulin cycle that led to reduced accumulation of glycoproteins under flooding stress (Wang and Komatsu, 2016). Subcellular proteomic of soybean under flooding stress provides more comprehensive understanding of the molecular functions and the coordination between different organelles under stress.

5.3 Proteomics of Soybean with Application of Chemicals for Flooding Tolerance

Plant breeding, conventional genetic engineering, and marker-assisted selection techniques are successful methods for developing flood-tolerant crops (Ahmed et al., 2013). Artificial methods to induce mutations cause huge genetic variations, which make it possible to select the best suitable lines for stressed conditions (Liu et al., 2020). Apart from these traditional methods for germplasm screening and mutations, various new strategies are applied to enhance soybean growth under flood conditions or to lessen the harmful impacts of flooding stress on soybean. These strategies include application of chemicals like nanoparticles, calcium, abscisic acid, plant-derived smoke, and radiations. Application of these strategies as a mitigation tool for flooding tolerance in soybean are summarized in Table 5.1.

5.3.1 Plant-Derived Smoke Treatment

Smoke results from incinerating plant materials. Smoke is a combination of different biologically active compounds that have potential applications in the agriculture sector (Kulkarni et al., 2011). Plant-derived

FIGURE 5.1 Flooding response mechanism in soybean. Upregulated and downregulated proteins are highlighted with orange and red color, respectively. Flooding induces a rapid and transient change in gene expression of proteins associated with major changes in plant responses. Under flooding stress, a major number of proteins belonging to chloroplast, mitochondria, and endoplasmic reticulum were decreased. Abbreviations are as follow: CaM, Calmodulin; CN, Calnexin; DHAP, Dihydroxyacetone phosphate; DLAT, Dihydrolipoamide acetyltransferase long form protein; F-6-P, Fructose 6-phosphate; F-1,6BP, F-1,6-Bisphosphate, G-1P, Glucose 1-phosphate; GAP, Glyceraldehyde phosphate; GDH, Glutamate dehydrogenase; Glc-1P, Galactose 1-phosphate; Glc, Galactose; HSF70, Heat shock protein 70; IDH, isocitrate dehydrogenase; IMM, Inner mitochondrial membrane; MDH, Malate dehydrogenase MGAT, α-1,3 mannosyl glycoprotein β 1,2 N-acetylglucosaminyl transferase putative; MPG, Membrane associated progesterone binding protein MSC, Mitochondrial substrate carrier protein; OMM, outer mitochondrial membrane; PDC, Pyruvate decarboxylase; PDI, Protein disulphide isomerase; PDR2, Phosphate deficiency response 2; PEP, Phosphoenolpyruvate; PP2A, Protein phosphatase 2A; RBP, RNA binding protein; REF, Rubber elongation factor protein; RGP3, Reversibly glycosylated polypeptide 3; SAM, S adenosyl L methionine; Trx, Thioredoxin; UDP-Glc 4-epimerase, UDP-Galactose 4-epimerase; VAP, VAMP associated protein.

TABLE 5.1

Proteomics of Soybean with Application of Chemicals for Flooding Tolerance

Application	Value of Treatment	Organ/Stage of Application	Major Findings	Ref.
Plant-derived smoke	2000 ppm smoke solution for 2 days	Root/hypocotyl 2-day-old seedlings	Increased: sucrose synthase, isoamylase, 6-phosphofructokinase 1, O-fucosyltransferase family protein Decreased: peptidyl-prolyl cis-trans isomerase, Bowman-Birk proteinase isoinhibitor D-II	Li et al., 2018
	2000 ppm smoke solution for 2 days	Root/hypocotyl 2-day-old seedlings	Increased: pathogenesis-related proteins, arginase, polyadenylate-binding protein Decreased: GTP-binding protein SAR1, glutamine synthase, argininosuccinate synthase, histone H3	Zhong et al., 2020a
	2000 ppm smoke solution for 2 days	Root/cotyledons/ 4-day-old seedlings	Increased: mitochondrial electron transport chain, ATP synthesis (Glyma10g41330) and mitochondrial HSO70, H+ ATPase, ascorbate peroxidase Decreased: proteins decreased under flooding stress	Otori et al., 2021
Abscisic acid	10 μM ABA for 2 days	2-day-old seedlings/ roots	Increased: secondary metabolism, cell wall and minor Cho metabolism related proteins, glyceraldehyde-3-phosphate dehydrogenase, alcohol dehydrogenase and pyruvate decarboxylase, histone deacetylase and U2 small nuclear ribonucleoprotein Decreased: urease, formate dehydrogenase, pyrimidine 2, GTP-binding family protein including development, fermentation, and cell wall proteins	Komatsu et al., 2013b
	10 μM ABA	2-day-old roots and cotyledon	Increased: uricase/nodulin 35, aluminum-induced protein with YGL/LRDR motifs, enolase, and polygalacturonase-inhibiting protein Decreased: cell wall, tricarboxylic acid cycle, oxidative pentose phosphate, photorespiration, and ROS scavenging system	Yin et al., 2016
Nano-particles	50 ppm Al_2O_3 (30–60nm)	Roots	Increased: HAD superfamily subfamily IIIB acid phosphatase, cell wall-related proteins, NmrA, Actin 11, Actin 7, Actin Decreased: fermentation and glycolysis-related proteins glyceraldehyde-3-phosphate dehydrogenase, Lipoxygenase 1, Oleosin family protein	Mustafa et al., 2015a

(Continued)

TABLE 5.1 (Continued)

Proteomics of Soybean with Application of Chemicals for Flooding Tolerance

Application	Value of Treatment	Organ/Stage of Application	Major Findings	Ref.
	2 ppm AgNPs 15 nm for 4 days	Roots/cotyledons	Increased: aspartyl protease family protein and expansin-like B1 Decreased: beta-ketoacyl reductase, glyoxalase II 3, Rmlc-like cupin superfamily protein, sucrose synthase, pyruvate decarboxylase 2 and alcohol dehydrogenase 1	Mustafa et al., 2015b
	5 ppm Ag-NPs 2,15, 50–80 nm)	2-day-old seedlings	Increased: beta ketoacyl reductase 1, amino acid synthesis and related proteins, cytochrome P450 family 93 subfamily D polypeptide 1 Decreased: protein synthesis, expansin	Mustafa et al., 2016
	50 ppm Al_2O_3 (5, 135 or 30–60 nm) for 3 days	Root mitochondria	Increased: ascorbate glutathione pathway (5nm) and ribosomal proteins Decreased: glycolysis related, amino acid metabolism, ascorbate glutathione pathway (135 and 30–60nm NPs)	Mustafa and Komatsu, 2016
	50 ppm Al_2O_3 NPs 30–60 nm for 10 days	Roots/hypocotyl	Increased: protein synthesis, stress, signaling, nitrogen metabolism, and lipid metabolism related proteins, ribosomal proteins, expansin like B1, polygalacturonase inhibiting proteins, and invertase/pectin methylesterase inhibitor, S-adenosyl-1-methionine dependent methyltransferases Decreased: fermentation-related proteins, polygalacturonase-inhibiting protein, Concanavalin A like lectin protein kinase family protein, enolase	Yasmeen et al., 2016
	5 ppm Ag NP (15 nm) + organic/inorganic chemicals for 2 days	4-day-old seedlings	Increased: protein degradation and synthesis, calnexin/calreticulin and glycoproteins, methyltransferases, aldo-ket-red-domain-containing transport protein and ubiquitin conjugating protein Decreased: MLO-like protein	Hashimoto et al., 2020
	10 ppm Biologically synthesized AgNP (16 nm) Chemically synthesized AgNP (15 nm)	4-day-old seedlings/roots	Increased: peroxidases increased under CS Decreased: protein-degradation related proteins	Mustafa et al., 2020
Calcium	50 mM $CaCl_2$ for 2 days	2-day-old soybean seedlings 4-day-old roots	Increased: ribosomal proteins, HSP 70, glycine cleavage T protein family, enolase, calcium-dependent phosphotriesterase superfamily proteins, Cupin family proteins, Kunitz family trypsin, and protease inhibitor protein Decreased: DNA synthesis, cell wall, and protein degradation/synthesis/posttranslational modification, Thymidylate synthase 2 and hexokinases	Oh et al., 2014b

	Treatment	Tissue	Protein changes	Reference
	1 mM CaCl$_2$ for 24 h	3-day-old root tips	Increased: pyruvate decarboxylase, 2-Oxoglutarate dehydrogenase, enolase and pyruvate kinase, pyruvate decarboxylase. Decreased: calnexin/HSPs, 2-oxoglutarate dehydrogenase, isocitrate dehydrogenase	Wang and Komatsu, 2017
	5, 10, 50, 100 mM CaCl$_2$ for 3 days	Radicle	Decreased: late embryogenesis abundant, dehydrin, gibberellic acid, abscisic acid	Wang et al., 2021a
Millimeter wave	10 mW for 0, 10, 20, 40, and 80 min	Root and hypocotyl	Increased: UDP-sugar pyrophosphorylase 1, expansin, citrate synthase, metallothionein-II protein, glutamate dehydrogenase, 60S ribosomal protein, mitochondrial-processing peptidase subunit. Decreased: phospho-2-dehydro-3-deoxyheptonate aldolase, mitochondrial fission 1 protein, seed maturation protein PM25, 3-hydroxybutyryl-CoA epimerase, cytochrome c oxidase subunit 6a, guanine nucleotide-binding protein subunit	Zhong et al., 2020b
Melatonin	10, 50, or 100 µM for 2 days	Root tip	Increased: eukaryotic aspartyl protease family protein. Decreased: eukaryotic translation initiation factor 5A, 13-hydroxylupanine O-tigloyltransferase	Wang et al., 2021b

smoke is successfully involved in breaking seed dormancy, hastening seed germination, and enhancing seedling vigor that ultimately improves plant growth (Bose et al., 2020; Khatoon et al., 2020). Under salt stress, plant-derived smoke acted as a growth regulator and lessened the harmful effects by regulating the physiological and biochemical characteristics of rice (Jamil et al., 2014). In rice, deleterious effects of lead stress were mitigated by the application of plant-derived smoke, and growth improved (Akhtar et al., 2017). Plant-derived smoke has tremendous potential that might be used for stress mitigation in different crop plants, including soybean.

During recovery from flooding stress, plant-derived smoke boosts soybean growth by regulating the balance of sucrose/starch metabolism and glycolysis. Cell wall related proteins were accumulated, which acts as an important factor for recovery of soybean from flooding stress (Li et al., 2018). In soybean, plant-derived smoke improved seedling growth through ornithine synthesis and ubiquitin proteasome pathways under flooding stress. Plant-derived smoke impeded the ubiquitin proteasome pathway, causing the loss of root tip that ultimately promoted the accumulation of metabolites, leading to accelerated growth under the recovery stage (Zhong et al., 2020a). In another study, plant-derived smoke enhanced soybean root growth through reactive oxygen species scavenging and energy production under flooding stress. Plant-derived smoke elevated the ascorbate/glutathione cycle, which led to improved tolerance against flooding stress (Otori et al., 2021). Plant-derived smoke has the potential of flooding stress mitigation in soybean, which might be exploited further to develop a stress-tolerant soybean.

5.3.2 Abscisic Acid Treatment

Abscisic acid is an important phytohormone involved in multiple physiological mechanisms of plant growth and development (Dong et al., 2015). Internal abscisic acid levels are controlled by biosynthesis, transport, catabolism, and signal transduction pathways. Endogenous levels of abscisic acid are vital for regulating the abscisic acid dependent signaling pathways during plant growth in response to climatic variations. Plants use abscisic acid-dependent and abscisic acid-independent signaling pathways to display a response toward osmotic stress (Yoshida et al., 2014). The abscisic acid signaling pathway acts as a central regulator of the plant's response toward abiotic stresses through alteration in gene expression and various adaptive physiological processes (Danquah et al., 2014). Abscisic acid balances the growth and adaptation to abiotic stress and ensures the plant's survival through crosstalk with brassinosteroid (Wang et al., 2020). These studies indicate that abscisic acid has a crucial function in plant acclimation under abiotic stress conditions through regulation of physiological and cellular processes.

Flooding induces low oxygen conditions, which leads to anoxic tissue along with the accumulation of carbon dioxide and ethylene hormone in plants (Pedersen et al., 2017). Accumulation of ethylene facilitates the plant in flooding acclimation via sugar, reactive oxygen species, nitric oxide, and ethylene response factors (Sasidharan and Voesenek, 2015). Accumulated ethylene inhibited the abscisic acid biosynthesis pathway and induced the petiole elongation in *Rumex palustris*, thus highlighting the interaction mechanism between ethylene and abscisic acid (Benschop et al., 2005). Exogenous application of abscisic acid enhanced the tolerance of maize against anoxic conditions via synthesis of new proteins and increased alcohol dehydrogenase activity (Hwang and Vantoai, 1991). Under flooding stress, internal abscisic acid content was less in tolerant soybean as compared to the susceptible line (Kim et al., 2015). Aerenchyma cells were well developed in tolerant soybean as compared to the susceptible line. Proteomic analysis of exogenous application of abscisic acid, under flooding stress, revealed that abscisic acid induced flooding tolerance through regulation of energy conservation, glycolysis, and cell division (Komatsu et al., 2013b). These findings suggested that abscisic acid might hinder the aerenchyma formation and conserve the energy through glycolysis to impart tolerance in soybean under flooding stress.

5.3.3 Nanoparticle Treatment

Advancements in the nanotechnology field led to its utilization in different sectors, including agriculture, as favorable agents for fertilizers, pesticides, plant growth, and sustainable crop production (Khot et al., 2012). Nanoparticles were considered to have genotoxic effects on plants, thereby limiting plant growth and development (Ghosh et al., 2019). Along with the toxic effects, engineered nanoparticles are key players in the agriculture sector as plant growth regulators and fertilizers (Landa, 2021). Potential harmful and positive impacts of nanoparticles are evaluated on different crop plants (Hossain et al., 2020). Growing evidence suggests that nanoparticles have the potential to alleviate the damaging effects of salt stress in crop plants (Zulfiqar and Ashraf, 2021). Therefore, stress mitigative impacts of nanoparticles might be exploited on other crops, including soybean.

In soybean, different nanoparticles are used for the mitigation strategies against flooding stress. Silver nanoparticles reduced the harmful effects of flooding stress by regulating the detoxification of cytotoxic by-products. Moreover, silver nanoparticle-treated soybean experienced less oxygen-deprivation stress and helped the metabolic transfer from fermentative pathways to regular cellular processes (Mustafa et al., 2015a). Among different sizes of silver nanoparticles, 15 nm enhanced soybean seedling growth under flooding stress by regulating the proteins related to amino acid synthesis and wax formation (Mustafa et al., 2016). Positive alleviation of flooding stress effects was further enhanced by the supplementation of nicotinic acid and potassium nitrate via regulation of protein quality control for mis-folded proteins in the endoplasmic reticulum (Hashimoto et al., 2020). In a comparative study, biosynthesized silver nanoparticles promoted soybean growth, through protein degradation related proteins and ATP contents, compared to chemically synthesized silver nanoparticles (Mustafa et al., 2020). Silver nanoparticles might act as potential flooding stress mitigators for soybean.

Aluminum oxide nanoparticles are progressively being used as dynamic stuff and as elements of agricultural products, such as pesticides and fertilizers (Navrotsky, 2004; Vernikov et al., 2009; Stadler et al., 2010). Aluminum oxide nanoparticles controlled metabolism for energy production and cell death to enhance the growth of flooded soybean. Proteins related to protein synthesis/degradation, glycolysis, and lipid metabolism predominantly responded to aluminum oxide nanoparticles under flooding stress (Mustafa et al., 2015b). Size-dependent effects of aluminum oxide nanoparticles depicted that 30–60 nm nanoparticles enhanced soybean growth under flooding stress through energy metabolism. On the other hand, 135 nm aluminum oxide nanoparticles increased mitochondrial membrane permeability, indicating membrane leakage that ultimately led to cell death (Mustafa and Komatsu, 2016). During soybean recovery from flooding stress, aluminum oxide nanoparticles regulated the protein synthesis, development, and transport related proteins that helped the plant to recover from drastic impacts of flooding stress (Yasmeen et al., 2016). Bringing together all these findings, the results indicate that nanoparticle application enhanced soybean survival under flooding stress, mainly by adjusting energy metabolism, mitochondrial function, and lipid oxidation.

5.3.4 Calcium Application

Calcium, as an important plant nutrient, controls the cell wall and membrane structures and regulates plant growth and development (Hepler, 2005). Calcium helps to protect cell membrane integrity, reduces membrane permeability, and prevents ionic leakage under stressed conditions (Lin et al., 2008). Artificial application of calcium improved plant biomass and tolerance against drought stress (Xu et al., 2013). Mitochondrial oxidative phosphorylation was well-adjusted via calcium-dependent mitochondrial carriers (Stael et al., 2011). Exogenous application of calcium might be used as a strategy to improve plant growth and stress tolerance.

In soybean, calcium-boosted proteins related to the cell wall, hormones, protein synthesis/degradation, and DNA synthesis declined under flooding stress (Oh et al., 2014b). Moreover, exogenous calcium application in soybean regulated radicle protrusion by increasing the seed's sensitivity to gibberellic acid and abscisic acid. Calcium controlled the abundance of late embryogenesis proteins to regulate the radicle protrusion (Wang et al., 2021a). Flooding and drought stresses elevated the levels of cytosolic calcium that disturbed the protein folding process in the endoplasmic reticulum (Wang and Komatsu, 2016). In the endoplasmic reticulum, calcium channels and cell membrane calcium-ATPase were blocked, which reduced the levels of cytosolic calcium in soybean on exposure to flooding and drought stresses (Wang and Komatsu, 2017). Calcium effectively uplifted the flooding and drought stress from soybean seedlings by regulating the endoplasmic reticulum associated protein folding and degradation (Wang and Komatsu, 2017). These studies highlighted the importance of calcium in regulation of flooding stress tolerance in soybean.

5.3.5 Other Applications

In soybean, various applications are used to enhance tolerance against flooding stress. Melatonin is a natural derivative of tryptophan that is found in animals and plants. Application of melatonin in plants improves growth and imparts tolerance against stress conditions (Wang et al., 2018; Shi et al., 2015). In maize, melatonin application improved germination and protected against oxidative damage (Cao et al., 2019). In flooded soybean, melatonin application enhanced the lignification of the root tip that was damaged under flooding stress. Melatonin ameliorated the harmful impacts of flooding stress by reducing cell degradation and enhancing the intercellular spaces in soybean (Wang et al., 2021b). These results suggested that melatonin might help in reducing the harmful effects of flooding stress on soybean.

Millimeter wave radiations are environmentally friendly because of their long wavelength, and they are less dangerous for human beings (Mignone and Barnes, 2011). These millimeter waves can cause variable effects on living organisms. Millimeter waves are reported to induce enzyme synthesis, cell division, vital activity, and biomass growth of microorganisms (Usatii et al., 2010). Millimeter wave treated wheat plants grow better and produce more yield compared to untreated ones (Betskii et al., 2007). Based on these studies, millimeter waves have the potential to provide positive impacts on plants. Millimeter waves regulate the expression profiles of endoplasmic reticulum chaperons and stress sensitive genes (Zhadobov et al., 2007; Nicolaz et al., 2009). Zhong et al. (2020b) reported that millimeter waves improved soybean growth under flooding stress. Glycolysis and ascorbate/glutathione pathway related proteins remain unaffected; however, millimeter waves helped soybean plants to reverse the oxidative damage caused due to oxidative stress. Synthesis of sugars, especially trehalose, was activated in millimeter wave treated soybean. Millimeter wave treatment facilitated the soybean to recover from flooding stress by regulating oxidative stress and energy production.

5.4 Proteomics Using Generated Flood-Tolerant Soybean Lines/Varieties

Flooding stress causes severe damage to soybean growth and yield. Various studies have been performed to identify flooding-tolerant varieties of soybean. In order to determine the flooding-tolerant mechanisms, comparative proteomic analysis is an effective technique compared to germplasm screening (Figure 5.2). Therefore, proteomic studies are carried out with the tolerant varieties, mutant, and transgenic lines to get a more comprehensive understanding of flooding tolerance in soybean (Table 5.2).

5.4.1 Soybean Varieties with Flooding Tolerance

Comprehensive evaluation of flooding tolerance from 730 varieties indicated that soybean varieties from India, South America, and Southeast Asia are extremely tolerant compared to other localities (Hou and Thseng, 1991). From Asian varieties, Jangbaegkong, Danbaegkong, Sowonkongkong, Socheong2, and Suwon269 were reported to be flooding tolerant among 192 investigated varieties (Koo et al., 2014). Out of 722 soybean genotypes, five breeding lines were developed with high-yield and flood-tolerance characters using conventional breeding (Wu et al., 2017). Flooding-tolerant varieties have enhanced adventitious root formation compared to sensitive varieties. Varietal analysis of 21 soybean varieties showed that VND2, Nam Vang, and ATF15-1 varieties are more tolerant toward flooding stress under field and green house conditions. Plant height of these three varieties was increased under flooding stress, indicating the potentially new germplasm for genetic improvement of flooding-tolerant soybean (VanToai et al., 2010). Genetic improvement might be used as an efficient technique to develop flooding-tolerant soybean varieties/lines.

The flooding-tolerant index, consisting of plant survival rate, lack of obvious damage, development of lateral root, and post-flooding radicle elongation level, divided 128 soybean varieties into tolerant, moderately tolerant, and sensitive groups (Nanjo et al., 2014). Comparative proteomic analysis of these three groups revealed that RNA binding/processing and flooding stress indicator proteins have strong linkage with the tolerance mechanism. Four QTLs are responsible for maintaining the genetic origin of flooding tolerance in soybean varieties (Sayama et al., 2009). Transcriptomic and proteomic analyses of

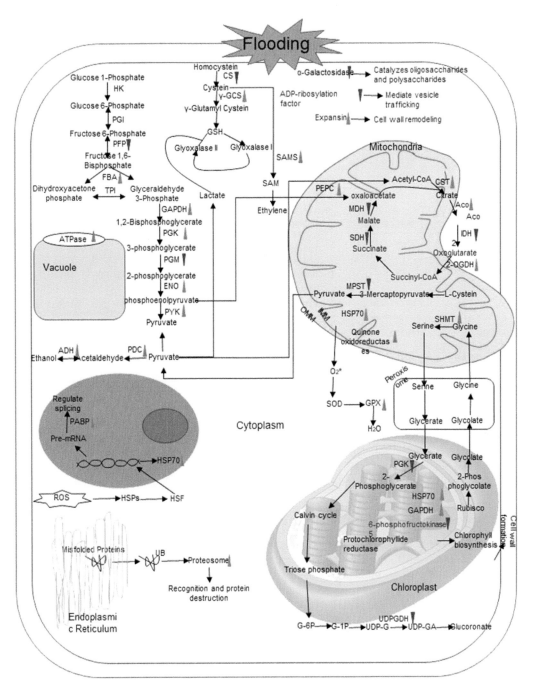

FIGURE 5.2 Flooding-tolerant mechanism in soybean. Upregulated and downregulated proteins are highlighted with orange and red color, respectively. Abbreviations are as follow: 2-OGDH, 2-Oxoglutarate dehydrogenase; Aco, Aconitase; ADH, Alcohol dehydrogenase; CS, Cystein synthetase; CST, Citrate synthetase; ENO, Enolase; FBA, Fructose 1,6-Bisphosphate Aldolase; G 6-P, Glucose 6-phosphate; G-1P, Glucose 1-phosphate; GAPDH, Glyceraldehyde-3-phosphate dehydrogenase; GPX, Glutathione peroxidase; GSH, Glutamyl Cystein; HK, Hexokinase; HSF, Heat shock factor; HSP70, Heat shock protein 70; IDH, Isocitrate dehydrogenase; MDH, Malate dehydrogenase; MPST, 3-mercaptopyruvate sulfurtransferase; PABP, Polypyrimidine tract-binding protein; PDC, Pyruvate decarboxylase; PEPC, phosphoenolpyruvate carboxylase; PFP, fructose-6-phosphate 1-phosphotransferase; PGI, Glucose 6-Phosphate Isomerase; PGK, Phosphoglycerate kinase; PGK, Phosphoglycerate kinase; PGM, phosphoglycerate mutase; PYK, phosphoenolpyruvate Kinase; SAM, S-adenosylmethionine; SAMS, S-adenosylmethionine synthase; SDH, Succinate dehydrogenase; SHMT, Serine hydroxymethyltransferase; TPI, Triose phosphate isomerase; UDP-G, UDP Glucose UDP-GA, UDP glucuronic acid; UDPGDH, UDP glucuronic acid dehydrogenase; γ-GCS, Gamma-glutamyl Cystein synthetase.

TABLE 5.2

Proteomics Using Generated Flood-Tolerant Soybean Lines/Varieties

Experimental materials	Organ/stage of application	Major findings	Ref.
Cultivar	Radicle	Increased: flooding stress indicator proteins Decreased: cell organization, vesicle transport and glycolysis related proteins	Nanjo et al., 2014
Mutant	Root	Increased: proteasome subunit beta type-6, ADH1, pyruvate decarboxylase isozymes 1 and 2, elongation factor protein Decreased: ADH activity was only decreased after 2 days of stress in mutant type	Komatsu et al., 2013a
	2-day-old root and cotyledon	Increased: cell wall, tricarboxylic acid cycle, oxidative pentose phosphate, photorespiration, and reactive oxygen species scavenging system along with protein synthesis-related proteins, including NAC and chaperonin 20 Decreased: RmlC-like cupin, RNA-binding (RRM/RBD/RNP motifs) and glycine-rich protein 2B	Yin et al., 2016
	Root including hypocotyl	Increased: phosphofructokinase, fructose, *hexokinase 1* Decreased: sucrose	Wang et al., 2017
Transgenic alcohol dehydrogenase transgene	Seedling	Increased: overexpression of *GmAdh2,* glycolysis, and alcohol fermentation	Tougou et al., 2012

flooding tolerant cultivar, Qihuang 34, depicted the enrichment of glycolysis to fulfill the increased energy demands of soybean under oxygen deficient conditions. Moreover, lignin biosynthesis was suppressed that caused the softening of plant tissues under long-term stress conditions (Lin et al., 2019). These studies suggest that tolerant lines are the best materials to understand the molecular basis of flooding tolerance that might be used further to improve soybean growth under unfavorable conditions.

5.4.2 Mutant Soybean with Flooding Tolerance

Internode elongation or stunted growth is an adaptive strategy of flood-tolerant rice under flooding stress (Nagai et al., 2010). Pea seeds follow the quiescence strategy to preserve energy and the escape mechanism of immediate germination by using the energy generated from protein metabolism (Zaman et al., 2019). A flooding-tolerant soybean mutant was developed using gamma radiations, and the most tolerant mutant was selected based on tolerance screening (Komatsu et al., 2013a). In the mutant line, cell wall loosening proteins did not increase compared to the wild type; therefore, the root tip was unspoiled, which allowed for rapid growth during post-flooding recovery (Komatsu et al., 2013a). As an alternate strategy, plants tend to shift the aerobic pathway toward anaerobic metabolism. Proteomic analysis of the mutant line depicted an increase in fermentation-related proteins, which confers flooding tolerance in soybean (Komatsu et al., 2013a). These studies suggested that the balanced regulation of glycolysis and fermentation is the key stone to confer tolerance in soybean under flooding stress.

Comparative transcriptomic analysis of flooding-tolerant mutant and abscisic acid-treated soybean reported that the expression pattern of the genes related to RNA regulation and protein metabolism were altered during flooding stress (Yin et al., 2017). Upregulation of the transcript levels of *glucose-6-phosphate isomerase, cytochrome P450 77A1, matrix metalloproteinase,* and *ATPase family AAA domain containing protein 1* were reported in soybean under flooding stress contrary to no change in flooding-tolerant mutant and abscisic acid-treated soybean (Yin et al., 2017). Under flooding stress, the lignification of root tissue was enhanced in the soybean mutant. Protein synthesis and RNA regulation related proteins played an important role in activating flooding tolerance (Yin et al., 2016). Cell wall integrity and balance in glycolysis is critical for attaining tolerance in soybean under flooding stress. At the metabolomic level, fructose was found to be a critical metabolite regulated through hexokinase and phosphofructokinase to impart flooding tolerance in soybean (Wang et al., 2017). Furthermore, metabolites involved in carbohydrate/organic acid and proteins related to glycolysis/tricarboxylic acid cycle were unified. Integration of transcriptomics, proteomics, and metabolomics highlighted the regulation of glycolysis in soybean under flooding stress that might be involved in bestowing tolerance against flooding stress.

5.4.3 Transgenic Soybean Overexpressed Flood-Response Gene

In soybean, overexpression of FvC5SD, which is C-5 sterol desaturase gene, induced tolerance against drought stress by decreasing the accumulation of reactive oxygen species and decreasing enzyme activities (Zhang et al., 2019). Drought response element binding protein of soybean imparted drought tolerance in wheat varieties through regulation of osmotic adjustments and photosynthetic activity (Zhou et al., 2020). Transgenic soybean with the peroxidase gene *GsPRX9* imparts tolerance against salt stress. Overexpression of *GsPRX9* enhanced the root fresh weight/length and peroxidases/superoxide dismutase activities, whereas it decreased the hydrogen peroxide contents. Therefore, the antioxidant response mechanism was improved that induced tolerance in soybean (Jin et al., 2019). Transgenics with enhanced antioxidant defense system might help in soybean tolerance toward flooding stress.

In soybean, *AtXTH31* overexpression imparts flooding tolerance by increasing germination rate and seedling length compared to the wild type (Song et al., 2018). Transcript profiling of the *XTH* gene family was performed in soybean. Ethylene controlled the transcript levels of 23 *GmXTH*, highlighting the role of ethylene in the *GmXTH*-mediated cell wall renovation in soybean under flooding stress (Song et al., 2018). Under flooding stress, *GmAdh2* was specifically identified in roots (Komatsu et al., 2011b). Soybean growth damaged by flooding stress was reverted in the *GmAdh2* transgenic line. Furthermore, the alcohol dehydrogenase activity was increased in the transgenic line. *GmAdh2* regulated the glycolysis and alcohol fermentation pathways and improved the germination of soybean under flooding stress (Tougou et al., 2012). These studies suggest that regulation of energy production through alcoholic fermentation and root adaptability might be critical alterations for tolerance in soybean under flooding stress.

5.5 Conclusion and Future Prospective

Soybean is an important legume crop and highly susceptible to flooding stress. Proteomics technique could be used as an effective tool to understand the molecular mechanisms to get an insight into the plant response and tolerance strategies. This information is further used to develop stress-tolerant lines. This chapter provides a detailed overview of the different mitigation strategies that are effectively used for flooding stress tolerance in soybean. Application of different chemicals and their impacts at the protein level are discussed. Possible regulation of molecular pathways provides us information regarding key factors that are crucial for soybean improvement. Under flooding stress, proteins associated with tricarboxylic acid cycle, glycolysis, and fermentation markedly increased in tolerant soybean (Figure 5.2). Soybean under flooding stress experienced metabolic shift from aerobic toward anaerobic pathways. *GmAdh2* overexpressed in transgenic soybean along with increased accumulation of alcohol dehydrogenase in mutant soybean. Flooding stress reduced the production of ATP and tricarboxylic acid cycle, which were regained in flooding-tolerant lines. Under flooding stress, misfolded proteins accumulate due to inhibition of calnexin cycle, which led to protein degradation. However, calnexin cycle was enhanced in flood-tolerant lines, which ensures the proper folding of protein and maintains protein homeostasis (Figure 5.2). In the future, more studies are required focusing on the subcellular and post-translational modification levels coupled with bioinformatics technology to get a more precise and comprehensive overview of flooding tolerance mechanisms.

REFERENCES

Ahmed, F., M.Y. Rafii, M.R. Ismail et al. 2013. Waterlogging tolerance of crops: Breeding, mechanism of tolerance, molecular approaches, and future prospects. *Biomed Res. Int.* 2013:963525.

Akhtar, N., S. Khan, I. Malook, S.U. Rehman, and M. Jamil. 2017. Pb-induced changes in roots of two cultivated rice cultivars grown in lead-contaminated soil mediated by smoke. *Environ. Sci. Pollut. Res.* 24:21298–21310.

Benschop, J.J., M.B. Jackson, K. Gühl et al. 2005. Contrasting interactions between ethylene and abscisic acid in Rumex species differing in submergence tolerance. *Plant J.* 44(5):756–768.

Betskii, O., N. Lebedeva, A. Tambiev, N. Kirikova, and V. Slavin. 2007. Millimeter waves in the newest agricultural biotechnologies. *Journal of Science and Engineering* 23:236–252.

Bose, U., A. Juhász, J.A. Broadbent, S. Komatsu, and M.L. Colgrave 2020. Multi-omics strategies for decoding smoke-assisted germination pathways and seed vigour. *Int. J. Mol. Sci.* 21(20):7512.

Cao, Q., G. Li, Z. Cui et al. 2019. Seed priming with melatonin improves the seed germination of waxy maize under chilling stress via promoting the antioxidant system and starch metabolism. *Sci. Rep.* 9(1):15044.

Christianson, J.A., I.W. Wilson, D.J. Llewellyn, and E.S. Dennis. 2009. The low-oxygen-induced NAC domain transcription factor ANAC102 affects viability of Arabidopsis seeds following low-oxygen treatment. *Plant Physiology* 149:1724–1738.

Danquah, A., A. de Zelicourt, J. Colcombet, and H. Hirt. 2014. The role of ABA and MAPK signaling pathways in plant abiotic stress responses. *Biotechnol. Adv.* 32(1):40–52.

Dong, T., Y. Park, and I. Hwang. 2015. Abscisic acid: Biosynthesis, inactivation, homoeostasis and signalling. *Essays Biochem.* 58:29–48.

Easterling, W.E., P.K. Aggarwal, P. Batima et al. (Eds.) 2007. Climate change 2007: Impacts, adaptation and vulnerability. *Contribution of working group II to the fourth assessment report of the Intergovernmental Panel on Climate Change*; Cambridge University Press: Cambridge, UK, 273–313.

Eigenbrod, F., P. Gonzalez, J. Dash, and I. Steyl. 2015. Vulnerability of ecosystems to climate change moderated by habitat intactness. *Global Change Biology* 21:275–286.

Gemperline, E., C. Keller, and L. Li. 2016. Mass spectrometry in plant-omics. *Anal. Chem.* 88:3422–3434.

Ghosh, M., I. Ghosh, L. Godderis, P. Hoet, and A. Mukherjee. 2019. Genotoxicity of engineered nanoparticles in higher plants. *Mutat Res.* 842:132–145.

Githiri, S.M., S. Watanabe, K. Harada, and R. Takahashi. 2006. QTL analysis of flooding tolerance in soybean at an early vegetative growth stage. *Plant Breeding* 125:613–618.

Hashiguchi, A., and S. Komatsu. 2016. Impact of post-translational modifications of crop proteins under abiotic stress. *Proteomes* 4(4):42.

Hashiguchi, A., and S. Komatsu. 2018. Early changes in *S*-nitrosoproteome in soybean seedling under flooding stress. *Plant Mol. Biol. Rep.* 36:822–831.

Hashiguchi, A., K. Sakata, and S. Komatsu. 2009. Proteome analysis of early-stage soybean seedlings under flooding stress. *J. Proteome Res.* 8:2058–2069.

Hashimoto, T., G. Mustafa, T. Nishiuchi, and S. Komatsu. 2020. Comparative analysis of the effect of inorganic and organic chemicals with silver nanoparticles on soybean under flooding stress. *Int. J. Mol. Sci.* 21(4):1300.

Hepler, P.K. 2005. Calcium: A central regulator of plant growth and development. *Plant Cell* 17:2142–2155.

Hossain, Z., F. Yasmeen, and S. Komatsu. 2020. Nanoparticles: Synthesis, morphophysiological effects, and proteomic responses of crop plants. *Int. J. Mol. Sci.* 21(9):3056.

Hou, F.F., and F.S. Thseng. 1991. Studies on the flooding tolerance of soybean seed: Varietal differences. *Euphytica* 57:169–173.

Hwang, S.Y., and T.T. Vantoai. 1991. Abscisic acid induces anaerobiosis tolerance in corn. *Plant Physiol.* 97(2):593–597.

Jamil, M., M. Kanwal, M.M. Aslam et al. 2014. Effect of plant-derived smoke priming on physiological and biochemical characteristics of rice under salt stress condition. *Aust. J. Crop. Sci.* 8:159–170.

Jin, T., Y. Sun, R. Zhao, Z. Shan, J. Gai, and Y. Li. 2019. Overexpression of peroxidase gene gsprx9 confers salt tolerance in soybean. *Int. J. Mol. Sci.* 20(15):3745.

Kamal, A.H., and S. Komatsu. 2015. Involvement of reactive oxygen species and mitochondrial proteins in biophoton emission in roots of soybean plants under flooding stress. *J Proteome Res.* 14(5):2219–2236.

Khan, M.N., K. Sakata, and S. Komatsu. 2015. Proteomic analysis of soybean hypocotyl during recovery after flooding stress. *J. Proteomics* 121:15–27.

Khatoon, A., S. Rehman, M.W. Oh, S.H. Woo, and S. Komatsu. 2012. Analysis of response mechanism in soybean under low oxygen and flooding stresses using gel-base proteomics technique. *Mol. Biol. Rep.* 39:10581–10594.

Khatoon, A., S.U. Rehman, M.M. Aslam, M. Jamil, and S. Komatsu. 2020. Plant-derived smoke affects biochemical mechanism on plant growth and seed germination. *Int. J. Mol. Sci.* 21(20):7760.

Khot, L.R., S. Sankaran, J.M. Maja, R. Ehsani, and E.W. Schuster. 2012. Applications of nanomaterials in agricultural production and crop protection: A review. *Crop. Prot.* 35:64–70.

Kim, Y.H., S.J. Hwang, M. Waqas et al. 2015. Comparative analysis of endogenous hormones level in two soybean (*Glycine max* L.) lines differing in waterlogging tolerance. *Front Plant Sci.* 6:714.

Komatsu, S., T. Deschamps, S. Hiraga et al. 2011b. Characterization of a novel flooding stress-responsive alcohol dehydrogenase expressed in soybean roots. *Plant Mol. Biol.* 77:309–322.

Komatsu, S., C. Han, Y. Nanjo et al. 2013b. Label-free quantitative proteomic analysis of abscisic acid effect in early-stage soybean under flooding. *J Proteome Res.* 12(11):4769–4784.

Komatsu, S., and A. Hashiguchi. 2018. Subcellular proteomics: Application to elucidation of flooding-response mechanisms in soybean. *Proteomes* 6(1):13.

Komatsu, S., S. Hiraga, and Y. Yanagawa. 2012. Proteomics techniques for the development of flood tolerant crops. *J. Proteome Res.* 11(1):68–78.

Komatsu, S., Y. Kobayashi, K. Nishizawa, Y. Nanjo, and K. Furukawa. 2010. Comparative proteomics analysis of differentially expressed proteins in soybean cell wall during flooding stress. *Amino Acids* 39:1435–1449.

Komatsu, S., R. Kuji, Y. Nanjo, S. Hiraga, and K. Furukawa. 2012. Comprehensive analysis of endoplasmic reticulum-enriched fraction in root tips of soybean under flooding stress using proteomics techniques. *J. Proteomics* 77:531–560.

Komatsu, S., Y. Nanjo, and M. Nishimura. 2013a. Proteomic analysis of the flooding tolerance mechanism in mutant soybean. *J. Proteomics* 79:231–250.

Komatsu, S., M. Tougou, and Y. Nanjo. 2015. Proteomic techniques and management of flooding tolerance in soybean. *J. Proteome Res.* 14:3768–3778.

Komatsu, S., T. Wada, Y. Abaléa et al. 2009. Analysis of plasma membrane proteome in soybean and application to flooding stress response. *J Proteome Res.* 8:4487–4499.

Komatsu, S., A. Yamamoto, T. Nakamura et al. 2011a. Comprehensive analysis of mitochondria in roots and hypocotyls of soybean under flooding stress using proteomics and metabolomics techniques. *J. Proteome Res.* 10:3993–4004.

Koo, S.C., H.T. Kim, B.K. Kang et al. 2014. Screening of flooding tolerance in soybean germplasm collection. *Korean J. Breed. Sci.* 46(2):129–135.

Kulkarni, M.G., M.E. Light, and J. van Staden. 2011. Plant-derived smoke: Old technology with possibilities for economic applications in agriculture and horticulture. *S. Afr. J. Bot.* 77:972–979.

Landa, P. 2021. Positive effects of metallic nanoparticles on plants: Overview of involved mechanisms. *Plant Physiol Biochem.* 161:12–24.

Li, X., S.U. Rehman, H. Yamaguchi et al. 2018. Proteomic analysis of the effect of plant-derived smoke on soybean during recovery from flooding stress. *J Proteomics.* 181:238–248.

Liao, C.T., and C.H. Lin. 2001. Physiological adaptation of crop plants to flooding stress. *Proceedings of the National Science Council Republic of China, Part B, Life Sciences* 25:148–157.

Lin, K.H., Y.K. Chiou, S.Y. Hwang, L.F.O. Chen, and H.F. Lo. 2008. Calcium chloride enhances the anti-oxidative system of sweet potato (*Ipomoea batatas*) under flooding stress. *Ann. Appl. Biol.* 152:157–168.

Lin, Y., W. Li, Y. Zhang et al. 2019. Identification of genes/proteins related to submergence tolerance by transcriptome and proteome analyses in soybean. *Scientific Reports* 9(1):14688.

Liu, S., M. Zhang, F. Feng, and Z. Tian. 2020. Toward a 'green revolution' for soybean. *Mol. Plant* 13:688–697.

Mignone, C., and R. Barnes. 2011. More than meets the eye: The electromagnetic spectrum. *Science School* 20:51–59.

Mustafa, G., M. Hasan, H. Yamaguchi, K. Hitachi, K. Tsuchida, and S. Komatsu. 2020. A comparative proteomic analysis of engineered and bio synthesized silver nanoparticles on soybean seedlings. *J. Proteomics.* 224:103833.

Mustafa, G., and S. Komatsu. 2016. Insights into the response of soybean mitochondrial proteins to various sizes of aluminium oxide nanoparticles under flooding stress. *J. Proteome Res.* 15:4464–4475.

Mustafa, G., K. Sakata, Z. Hossain, and S. Komatsu. 2015a. Proteomic study on the effects of silver nano-particles on soybean under flooding stress. *J. Proteomics.* 122:100–118.

Mustafa, G., K. Sakata, and S. Komatsu. 2015b. Proteomic analysis of flooded soybean root exposed to aluminum oxide nanoparticles. *J. Proteomics.* 128:280–297.

Mustafa, G., K. Sakata, and S. Komatsu. 2016. Proteomic analysis of soybean root exposed to varying sizes of silver nanoparticles under flooding stress. *J. Proteomics.* 148:113–125.

Nagai, K., Y. Hattori, and M. Ashikari. 2010. Stunt or elongate? Two opposite strategies by which rice adapts to floods. *J. Plant Res.* 123:303–309.

Nakamura, T., R. Yamamoto, S. Hiraga et al. 2012. Evaluation of metabolite alteration under flooding stress in soybeans. *JARQ Jpn. Agric. Res. Q.* 46:237–248.

Nakayama, N., S. Hashmoto, S. Shimada et al. 2004. The effect of flooding stress at the germination stage on the growth of soybean in relation to initial seed moisture content. *Journal of Crop Sciences*, 73:323–329.

Nanjo, Y., H. Jang, H.S. Kim, S. Hiraga, S.H. Woo, and S. Komatsu. 2014. Analyses of flooding tolerance of soybean varieties at emergence and varietal differences in their proteomes. *Phytochemistry*, 106:25–36.

Nanjo, Y., L. Skultety, Y. Ashraf, and S. Komatsu. 2010. Comparative proteomic analysis of early-stage soybean seedlings responses to flooding by using gel and gel-free techniques. *J. Proteome Res.* 9:3989–4002.

Nanjo, Y., L. Skultety, L. Uváčková, K. Klubicová, M. Hajduch, and S. Komatsu. 2012. Mass spectrometry-based analysis of proteomic changes in the root tips of flooded soybean seedlings. *J. Proteome Res.* 11:372–385.

Navrotsky, A. 2004. Energetic clues to pathways to biomineralization: Precursors, clusters, and nanoparticles. *Proc. Natl. Acad. Sci. USA.* 101(33):12096–12101.

Nicolaz, C.N., M. Zhadobov, F. Desmots et al. 2009. Study of narrow band millimeter-wave potential interactions with endoplasmic reticulum stress sensor genes. *Bioelectromagnetics* 30(5):365–373.

Normile, D. 2008. Agricultural research. Reinventing rice to feed the world. *Science* 321: 330–333.

Oh, M.W., Y. Nanjo, and S. Komatsu. 2014a. Identification of nuclear proteins in soybean under flooding stress using proteomic technique. *Protein Pept Lett.* 21(5):458–467.

Oh, M., Y. Nanjo, and S. Komatsu. 2014b. Gel-free proteomic analysis of soybean root proteins affected by calcium under flooding stress. *Front Plant Sci.* 5:559.

Otori, M., Y. Murashita, S. ur Rehman, and S. Komatsu. 2021. Proteomic study to understand promotive effects of plant-derived smoke on soybean (*Glycine max* L.) root growth under flooding stress. *Plant Mol. Biol. Rep.* 39:24–33.

Pedersen, O., P. Perata, and L.A.C.J. Voesenek. 2017. Flooding and low oxygen responses in plants. *Funct Plant Biol.* 44(9):iii–vi.

Salavati, A., A. Khatoon, Y. Nanjo, and S. Komatsu. 2012. Analysis of proteomic changes in roots of soybean seedlings during recovery after flooding. *J. Proteomics.* 75:878–893.

Sasidharan, R., and L.A. Voesenek. 2015. Ethylene-mediated acclimations to flooding stress. *Plant Physiol.* 169(1):3–12.

Sayama, T., T. Nakazaki, G. Ishikawa et al. 2009. QTL analysis of seed-flooding tolerance in soybean (*Glycine max* [L.] Merr.). *Plant Sciences* 176(4):514–521.

Shi, H., X. Wang, D.X. Tan, R.J. Reiter, and Z. Chan. 2015. Comparative physiological and proteomic analyses reveal the actions of melatonin in the reduction of oxidative stress in Bermuda grass (*Cynodon dactylon* (L). Pers.). *J Pineal Res.* 59(1):120–131.

Song, L., B. Valliyodan, S. Prince, J. Wan, and H.T. Nguyen. 2018. Characterization of the XTH gene family: New insight to the roles in soybean flooding tolerance. *Int. J. Mol. Sci.* 19:2705.

Stadler, T., M. Buteler, and D.K. Weaver. 2010. Novel use of nanostructured alumina as an insecticide. *Pest Manag. Sci.* 66(6):577–579.

Stael, S., A.G. Rocha, A.J. Robinson, P. Kmiecik, U.C. Vothknecht, and M. Teige 2011. Arabidopsis calcium-binding mitochondrial carrier proteins as potential facilitators of mitochondrial ATP-import and plastid SAM-import. *FEBS Lett.* 585(24):3935–3940.

Tougou, M., A. Hashiguchi, K. Yukawa et al. 2012. Responses to flooding stress in soybean seedlings with the alcohol dehydrogenase transgene. *Plant Biotechnol.* 29:301–305.

Usatii, A., E. Molodoi, A. Rotaru, and T. Moldoveanu. 2010. The influence of low intensity millimeter waves on the multiplication and biosynthetic activity of *Saccharomyces carlsbergensis* CNMN-Y-15 yeast. Did you mean: The Annals of Oradea University. *Biology Fascicle* 17:208–212.

VanToai, T.T., T.T.C. Hoa, T.N.H. Nguyen, T.H. Nguyen, G. Shannon, and A.R. Mohammed. 2010. Flooding tolerance of soybean [*Glycine max* (L.) Merr.] germplasm from southeast Asia under field and screen-house environments. *Open Agr. J.* 4:38–46.

Vernikov, V.M., E.A. Arianova, I.V. Gmoshinskiĭ, S.A. Khotimchenko, and V.A. Tutel'ian 2009. Nanotechnology in food production: Advances and problems. *Vopr Pitan.* 78(2):4–17.

Voesenek, L.A., T.D. Colmer, R. Pierik, F.F. Millenaar, and A.J. Peeters. 2006. How plants cope with complete submergence. *New Phytologist* 170:213–226.

Wang, Q., F. Yu, and Q. Xie. 2020. Balancing growth and adaptation to stress: Crosstalk between brassinosteroid and abscisic acid signaling. *Plant Cell Environ.* 43(10):2325–2335.

Wang, X., H. Hu, F. Li, B. Yang, and S. Komatsu, S. Zhou. 2021a. Quantitative proteomics reveals dual effects of calcium on radicle protrusion in soybean. *J Proteomics.* 230:103999.

Wang, X., and S. Komatsu. 2016. Gel-free/label-free proteomic analysis of endoplasmic reticulum proteins in soybean root tips under flooding and drought stresses. *J Proteome Res.* 15(7):2211–2227.

Wang, X., and S. Komatsu. 2017. Proteomic analysis of calcium effects on soybean root tip under flooding and drought stresses. *Plant Cell Physiol.* 58(8):1405–1420.

Wang, X., and S. Komatsu. 2018. Proteomic approaches to uncover the flooding and drought stress response mechanisms in soybean. *J. Proteomics.* 172:201–215.

Wang, X., and S. Komatsu. 2020. Review: Proteomic techniques for the development of flood-tolerant soybean. *Int. J. Mol. Sci.* 21(20):7497.

Wang, X., F. Li, Z. Chen, B. Yang, S. Komatsu, and S. Zhou. 2021b. Proteomic analysis reveals the effects of melatonin on soybean root tips under flooding stress. *J Proteomics.* 232:104064.

Wang, X., W. Zhu, A. Hashiguchi, M. Nishimura, J. Tian, and S. Komatsu. 2017. Metabolic profiles of flooding-tolerant mechanism in early-stage soybean responding to initial stress. *Plant Mol. Biol.* 94:669–685.

Wang, Y., R.J. Reiter, and Z. Chan. 2018. Phytomelatonin: A universal abiotic stress regulator. *J Exp. Bot.* 69(5):963–974.

Wu, C., A. Zeng, P. Chen et al. 2017. Evaluation and development of flood-tolerant soybean cultivars. *Plant Breeding* 136:913–923.

Xu, C., X. Li, and L. Zhang. 2013. The effect of calcium chloride on growth, photosynthesis, and antioxidant responses of *Zoysia japonica* under drought conditions. *PLoS One* 8(7):68214.

Xu, X., H. Wang, X. Qi, X. Qiang, and X. Chen. 2014. Waterlogging-induced increase in fermentation and related gene expression in the root of cucumber (*Cucumis sativus* L.). *Scientia Horticulturae* 179:388–395.

Yasmeen, F., N.I. Raja, G. Mustafa, K. Sakata, and S. Komatsu. 2016. Quantitative proteomic analysis of post-flooding recovery in soybean root exposed to aluminum oxide nanoparticles. *J. Proteomics.* 143:136–150.

Yin, X., S. Hiraga, M. Hajika, M. Nishimura, and S. Komatsu. 2017. Transcriptomic analysis reveals the flooding tolerant mechanism in flooding tolerant line and abscisic acid treated soybean. *Plant Mol. Biol.* 93(4-5):479–496.

Yin X., and S. Komatsu. 2017. Comprehensive analysis of response and tolerant mechanisms in early-stage soybean at initial-flooding stress. *J. Proteomics.* 169:225–232.

Yin, X., M. Nishimura, M. Hajika, and S. Komatsu. 2016. Quantitative proteomics reveals the flooding-tolerance mechanism in mutant and abscisic acid-treated soybean. *J Proteome Res.* 15(6):2008–2025.

Yin, X., K. Sakata, Y. Nanjo, and S. Komatsu. 2014. Analysis of initial changes in the proteins of soybean root tip under flooding stress using gel-free and gel-based proteomic techniques. *J. Proteomics.* 106:1–16.

Yoshida, T., J. Mogami, and K. Yamaguchi-Shinozaki. 2014. ABA-dependent and ABA-independent signaling in response to osmotic stress in plants. *Curr. Opin. Plant Biol.* 21:133–139.

Zaman, M.S.U., A.I. Malik, W. Erskine, and P. Kaur. 2019. Changes in gene expression during germination reveal pea genotypes with either "quiescence" or "escape" mechanisms of waterlogging tolerance. *Plant Cell Environ.* 42(1):245–258.

Zhadobov, M., R. Sauleau, L. Le Coq et al. 2007. Low-power millimeterwave radiations do not alter stress-sensitive gene expression of chaperone proteins. *Bioelectromagnetics* 28:188–196.

Zhang, L., T. Li, Y. Wang, Y. Zhang, and Y.S. Dong. 2019. FvC5SD overexpression enhances drought tolerance in soybean by reactive oxygen species scavenging and modulating stress-responsive gene expression. *Plant Cell Rep.* 38(9):1039–1051.

Zhong, Z., T. Furuya, K. Ueno et al. 2020b. Proteomic analysis of irradiation with millimeter waves on soybean growth under flooding conditions. *Int. J. Mol. Sci.* 21(2):486.

Zhong, Z., T. Kobayashi, W. Zhu et al. 2020a. Plant-derived smoke enhances plant growth through ornithine-synthesis pathway and ubiquitin-proteasome pathway in soybean. *J Proteomics.* 221:103781.

Zhou, Y., M. Chen, J. Guo et al. 2020. Overexpression of soybean DREB1 enhances drought stress tolerance of transgenic wheat in the field. *J. Exp. Bot.* 71(6):1842–1857.

Zulfiqar, F., and M. Ashraf. 2021. Nanoparticles potentially mediate salt stress tolerance in plants. *Plant Physiol. Biochem.* 160:257–268.

6

Impact of High Temperature Stress and Its Alleviation in Fabaceae

Burcu Yuksel[1] and Filiz Vardar[2]
[1]*Kocaeli University, Vocational School of Kocaeli Health Sciences, Izmit, Kocaeli, TURKEY*
[2]*Marmara University, Sciences and Arts Faculty, Department of Biology, Göztepe Istanbul, TURKEY*

CONTENTS

6.1 Introduction

With the age of technology, the acceleration of migration from the rural areas to the cities in the world, the increase in population density in the cities, uncontrolled industrialization, rapid destruction of the natural environment, unconscious consumption of resources on the earth, unplanned urbanization, and increase in fossil fuel consumption have disrupted the ecological balance, and environmental problems are also increasing (Popp et al., 2010). Among these multifaceted problems, environmental problems are becoming the most serious concerns because they are not only threats human's lives but also to biodiversity. Global warming is one of the most alarming problems that threatens human existence on earth by altering current adaptation strategies, including agricultural practices (Yuksel et al., 2018). Global warming is causing problems associated with large-scale economic loss and environmental degradation. Among the environmental problems, threats to growth and yield of crop plants is of great concern for human civilization. According to the World Health Organization (WHO, 2018), expenses that directly harm health in areas such as agriculture, water, and sanitation will likely cost between 2 and 4 billion USD/year by 2030. Global atmospheric temperature is projected to increase by 0.2°C in the coming ten years, resulting in temperatures 1.8–4.0°C higher than the current level by 2100 (Solomon, 2007). Although ever-increasing ambient temperature is regarded as one of the most harmful stresses, it significantly affects living systems as a whole.

It is anticipated that global warming will deepen the problems of drought because of increased evaporation and reduced rainfall, which will be caused by increased CO_2 levels due to greenhouse gases. The impacts of global warming will affect different parts of the world where chickpeas and lentils are commonly grown. Due to such changes in climatic conditions, yield and production of these legumes and field crops will be dramatically altered in different parts of the world. Many of the developing countries will encounter significant loss of legume production, which serve enhanced nutrition to the poor people in these areas (Yadav et al., 2010). Considering such problems, it is important to develop an efficient agricultural production system and resistant high-yielding varieties as well as use diverse crop varieties to cope with the harsh environmental conditions. This chapter presents a comprehensive review of the effects of elevated temperature on legume crops as well as the molecular approaches to reduce risks on those crops.

6.2 Heat Stress and Its General Effects on Plants

High temperature (HT) stress is a major environmental stress that limits plant growth, metabolism, and productivity worldwide (Hasanuzzaman et al., 2013a). Because plants cannot move toward favorable environments from unfavorable ones, their growth and development processes are significantly impacted if they are under HT stress, and being in this situation is often fatal (Peng et al., 2004; Costello et al., 2009; Yamori et al., 2014). HT is a potential source of danger, particularly for crop production (Table 6.1), and keeping high yields of crop plants in HT conditions is among the significant goals of many agricultural planning schemes (Das and Roychoudhury, 2014). Plants' responses to HT stress vary according to the degree, duration, and plant species (Hasanuzzaman et al., 2013a). Plants have some cytological, biochemical, and genetic mechanisms to deal with HT states. With HT stress, ion transporters, proteins, osmoprotectants, antioxidants, and genetic aspects related to signal cascades and transcriptional control are triggered to balance the biochemical and physiological changes caused by stress (Hildebrandt et al., 2015; Liu et al., 2015; Mathur et al., 2014). Preventing the plant from HT significantly improves its survival, its ability to generate signals, gene expression, metabolite synthesis, and tolerance to initiate appropriate physiological and biochemical changes (Budak et al.2015; Ohama et al., 2017).

HT stress also contributes to the emergence of the extremely reactive oxygen species (ROS) that leads to oxidative stress (Hasanuzzaman et al., 2013b). This species regulates homeostatic mechanisms by protecting cell turgor with physical changes in the plant body, metabolic signals, osmotic adjustment, and adjusting cellular redox balance with the antioxidant system. Thus, it can tolerate heat stress to some extent (Akula and Ravishankar, 2011; Krasensky and Jonak, 2012). Also, at the molecular level, adaptation to HT stress is achieved by creating changes in the expression of genes responsible for the expression of osmoprotectants, detoxifying enzymes, and regulatory proteins (Shinozaki & Yamaguchi-Shinozaki, 2007; Atkinson and Urwin, 2012; Singh et al., 2016).

The development of new HT-tolerant crop varieties is a major challenge for plant scientists (Mittler et al., 2012; Huang et al., 2014). The negative impact of heat stress can be reduced by using improved heat-tolerant crop plants by means of numerous molecular methods. Plants show dynamic responses to HT due to other environmental factors, but it is still incomprehensible to confirm the properties that make plants HT tolerant (Fahad et al., 2017). Researchers are trying to explore their responses and also how plants can be managed in HT conditions. The aim is to develop transgenic plants with omic techniques and manipulation of target genes with molecular approaches that have been widely studied recently (Singh et al., 2016). By investigating molecular processes and developing stress-tolerant varieties, growing agriculturally important crop plants exposed to HT can be established. For this purpose, physiological, biochemical events, and molecular reactions observed in plants as a reaction to HT stress can be improved by transgenic approaches.

6.3 Production Loss in Legumes due to Heat Stress

Dry peas (*Pisum sativum*), chickpeas (*Cicer arietinum*), broad beans (*Vicia faba*), lentils (*Lens culinaris*), lupine (*Lupinus spp.*), grass peas (*Lathyrus sativus*), and common vetch (*Vicia sativa*) are among more than 100 legumes that can grow in all countries across the continents (except Antarctica). Although legumes are among the oldest crops, data on the cultivation date goes back to prehistoric times (Yadav et al., 2010). Their ability to grow in dry and harsh environments and their high nutritious value has an important place in millions of people's daily food intake. Trade with legumes is more than $ 1,200 million per year (Yadav et al., 2010). These crops are regarded as modern-age products due to having few requirements for input during cultivation, being environmentally friendly to the cropping

TABLE 6.1

Effects of Elevated Temperature on Some of the Species of Fabaceae and Poaceae

Family	Species	Harmful Temperature Day/Night	Morphological, Physiological, and Molecular Effects	Yield	Genes Associated with Temperature Control	References
Fabaceae	Soybean (*Glycine max*)	>36°C/24°C	• Decreased nitrogen fixation • Increase in ascorbate precursors and various antioxidant metabolites • Molecular changes in sugar and nitrogen metabolism	• Reproductive stage decrease • Reductions in pod number • Reduced yield components and seed yield • Decrease in germination (50%) of seeds	• HSF AP2/EREB MAD-box, WRKYs	Puteh et al. (2013); Chebrolu et al. (2016); Das et al. (2017); Valdés-López et al. (2016).
Fabaceae	Peanut (*Arachis hypogaea* L.)	>34°C/22°C	• Reduction in photosynthesis, seed number, seed yield, and total dry weight • Elongated root, decreased stomatal density • High chlorophyll content • Increased specific leaf area • Increased photosynthesis • Increase in proline amounts	• Decrease in reproductive stage • Reductions in pod number • Reduced seed germination	• AtDREB2A AtHB7 AtABF3 AhRbx1 AhHSP70 AhDIP AhLea4	Clifford et al. (2000); Ketring (1991). Kambiranda et al. (2011); Pruthvi et al. (2014).
Fabaceae	Chickpea (*Cicer arietinum* L.)	>34°C/19°C	• Decrease in photosynthesis • Inhibition of sucrose metabolism in leaves • Disruption of sucrose metabolism in developing seeds	• Low germination rates and lower seed viability in seeds • Pollen sterility • Heavy flower drop or pod abortion • Reduced pod set • Poor pollen germination, tube growth, and fertilization • Formation of small and shrivelled seeds	• CarHsfA2 A6a A6c B2a	Kaushal et al. (2013); Chakrabarti et al. (2013); Samarah et al. (2009); Upadhyaya et al. (2011); Devasirvatham et al. (2013); Chidambaranathan et al. (2018).
Fabaceae	Common bean (*Phaseolus vulgaris* L.)	>30°C/20°C	• High respiration • Low photosynthesis • Closed stomata • High leaf temperature	• Reduced pod development • Anthers to maturity of individual pods decreased • Limited and shallow root system during flowering • Flower development significantly decreased fruit set • The lowest pod set	• ClpB/HSP100 VuNCED1	Seidel et al. (2016); Rainey et al. (2005); Reynolds-Henne et al. (2010); Ahmed et al. (1992).
Fabaceae	Cowpea (*Vigna unguiculata* L.)	>33°C/22°C	• Electrolyte leakage • Membrane thermostability deterioration • Dehydrin protein formation • Reduced overall carbohydrate content, especially peduncle sugars • Decrease in photosynthetic rates	• Inanimate and anther separation • Endothelial formation in anthers • Demonstrated floral development • Premature deformation of the tapetal layer and absence of endothelial growth • Low pollen viability • Low anther dehiscence • Low pod set • Damage to floral buds	• ClpB/HSP100	Warrag & Hall (1984); Hall (2004); Ahmed et al. (1993).

(Continued)

TABLE 6.1 (Continued)

Effects of Elevated Temperature on Some of the Species of Fabaceae and Poaceae

Family	Species	Harmful Temperature Day/Night	Morphological, Physiological, and Molecular Effects	Yield	Genes Associated with Temperature Control	References
Fabaceae	Faba bean (*Vicia faba* L.)	>32°C/22°C	• Decreased photochemical efficiency • Reduction in sucrose synthesis, chlorophyll disruption • High leaf temperature	• Reduced pod number • Loss of pollen viability • Reduced plant productivity • Yield lost at lower nodes • Reduced floral development and anthesis • Gametophyte damage and consequent failure of fertilization	• VfHsp17.9-CII • sHsp17.9 • ClpB/HSP100	Bishop et al. (2016a); Bishop et al. (2016b); Lake et al. (2019); Kumar et al. (2012).
Fabaceae	Lentil (*Lens culinaris* M.)	>32°C/23°C	• Reduction in photosynthetic function • Decreased sucrose synthesis and chlorophyll disruption • Damage in cell membrane • Increased damage to membranes, chlorosis • Decreased photochemical efficiency • Adverse effects on albumins and globulins	• Decreased vegetative bio-mass, flower number, and pod setting • Pollen sterility	• DN68776_c2_g • DN19596_c0_g • DN81013_c1_g8 • DN57816_c0_g • DN41180_c0_g • DN60393_c0_g4	Bhandari et al. (2016); Kaushal et al. (2013); Sita et al. (2018); Singh et al. (2019a).
Fabaceae	Pea (*Pisum sativum* L.)	>35°C/18°C	• Drastically reduced nitrogen fixation • Decreased photochemical efficiency • Decreased sucrose synthesis, chlorophyll disruption • High leaf temperature	• Reduced seed yield • Anther indehiscence • Ovary abortion • Expediting the crop lifecycle and decreasing pod and seed amount • Most devastating impact on younger reproductive development (flowers and pods grow at a later time) • Seed abortion in all ovule positions within pods	• HsfA1d • GOR2 • GOR1,	Gonzalez et al. (2001); Jiang et al. (2020); Jiang (2016); Shah et al. (2020); Stevens et al. (1997).
Fabaceae	Common Bean (*Phaseolus vulgaris* L.)	>34°C/24°C	• Elevated photosynthesis • Reduction in seed quantity, seed production, and total dry weight • Greater leaf photosynthetic rates • Enhanced biomass accumulation • Distribution pattern of the rough endoplasmic reticulum (RER) in the tapetum • ER structure and blocked function in the tapetum	• Reproductive stage decrease • Reductions in pod number • Structural abnormalities in the microspore • Degenerative changes in the tapetum • Decreased pollen maturation • Decreased pollen growth and damaged female performance in most flowers • Stigma and closer to the peduncle	• MED23, • MED25, • HSFB1, • HSP40, • HSP20 • MED25, • MBD9, • PAP • GAE6 • AUX_IAA	Prasad et al. (2002); Hatfield et al. (2011); Porch and Jahn (2001); Suzuki et al. (2001); Monterroso and Wien (1990); López-Hernández and Cortés (2019)
Poaceae	Wheat (*Triticum aestivum*)	>35°C/18°C	• Loss of growing leaf area • Reduction in green leaf time period • Reduced nucellus development • Abnormal embryo sacs	• Male sterility and damaged female sexual function • Poor germination and lower plant population • Decreased number of grains per ear at maturity • No pollen tube reached the ovary • Pollen tubes showed abnormal growth	• HsfA3 • MYB, • MADS • WRKY • AN1 • OsFKBP20 • DREB2B • DREB6A • annexin1 • CDPK	Khalil et al. (2009); Saini et al. (1983); Hossain et al. (2013); Qin et al. (2008).

Family	Crop	Temperature	Effects	Genes	References
Poaceae	Rice (*Oryza sativa*)	>35°C/25°C	• Expanded photosynthesis and amount of seeds • Increased yield and total dry weight of seed • Panicle extrusion, flowering period, and the number of anthesing spikelets • Reduction in growth and development and tube length of pollens, reduced number of pollens on stigma • Decreased fertility	• OsGSK1 • TT1 • HSP70 • OsEnS45, OsHSP74.8 • OsHSP70	Lu et al. (2009); Krishnan et al. (2011); Jagadish et al. (2014); Matsui and Omasa (2002); Das et al. (2014); Wahab et al. (2020).
Poaceae	Barley (*Hordeum vulgare*)	>30°C/25°C	• Little cytoplasm • Little starch accumulation • Reduced nucellus development • Development of short anthers • 21% and 40% yield reductions • Decline in grain weight • Seed abortion in all ovule positions within pods	• ADP-ribosylation factor 1 • HSP90	Sakata et al. (2000); Abiko et al. (2005); Fahad et al. (2017); Rapacz et al. (2012).
Poaceae	Maise (*Zea mays*)	>38°C/22°C	• Affects morphological shapes • Decreased green leaf duration • Stigma and closer to the peduncle • 21% and 40% yield reductions • Fewer leaves • Reduced number of cobs and rows	• OsMYB55 • ZmVPP1	Casaretto et al. (2016); Tiwari and Yadav (2019)
Poaceae	Oat (*Avena sativa*)	>35°C/25°C	• Decreased photochemical efficiency • Decreased sucrose synthesis • High leaf temperature • Poor germination, lower plant population • Decreased pollen maturation	• hva1 • bar • EF-Tu • eEF1A	Warchol et al. (2019); Chen et al. (2016); Maqbool et al. (2002); Djukić et al. (2019).

system, and having a very high share in the market. Changes in global temperature and increased CO_2 levels can probably shake our agricultural efficiency and can also pose a risk to food safety and security worldwide. As a result, it is important to understand the plant's response to temperature stress because it is urgent to preserve future crops (Mickelbart et al., 2015). Legumes, like other plants, are exposed to extreme environmental conditions. Legumes, especially in tropical savannas, are exposed to scorching temperatures and high harmful UV radiation levels. These extreme conditions are more felt by crop farmers whose crops are badly affected after a long period of drought (Lal et al., 2018). It was found that damage of genetic materials and meiotic abnormalities increased in some legumes due to uncontrolled expansion of agricultural areas, increased use of chemicals, spread of heavy metals to the environment, and contamination with pharmaceutical or industrial wastes (Fuchs et al., 2018). Exposure to these factors causes ovaries and embryo development to be stopped or slowed down by hormones responsible for seed and fruit development due to environmental stress, especially in flowering plants. Overall yield in legumes is associated with these irreversible changes and the aging process of fruits and seeds. These anatomical changes may negatively affect the yield of legumes by affecting the total dry matter content, amount of leaf area, photosynthetic area, respiratory rate, CO_2 metabolism, and water retention potential of the leaf (Freitas et al., 2017).

Andrews and Hodge (2010) evaluated how anticipated climate change would impact the yield of legume crops in large production fields and concluded that the probability of falling in the Indian subcontinent is high. Concerning existing major exporting countries, Canada, the USA, and France would increase yields, and a decreased yield is observed with climate change in Australia and Turkey. As a result, if climate change results in declining pea, lentil, and chickpea yields in the Indian sub-continent in the following five decades, Canada, France, and the USA can be among countries to suffer from this decline with their increasing need for these legumes (Yadav et al., 2010). Understanding the approaches to maintain high yields of crop plants exposed to HT stress is important in agriculture. Therefore, the productivity and sustainability of the legume crop system also need to be studied in detail. All stakeholders should be concerned about maintaining the environmental quality, sustaining soil fertility, and paying attention to yield quality and quantity.

6.4 Comparison of the Family Fabaceae with Poaceae against Heat Stress

Plant growth and development involve numerous biochemical and physiological changes depending on temperature. A plant's response to HT varies according to the degree and duration of HT that the plant has been exposed to and the type of plant (Hasanuzzaman et al., 2013b). Plants have morphological, biochemical, and genetic mechanisms to cope with the HT states they are exposed to. Plant survival under HT stress depends on sensing the HT stimulus, generating and transmitting the signal, and initiating suitable physiological and biochemical modifications. HT caused gene expression, and metabolite synthesis dramatically advances tolerance as well. The morphological, physiological, and molecular effects of legumes resulting from HT stress have been compared with some species of the family Poaceae (Table 6.1).

HT action begins from seed germination to flowering, as the different phases of the plant's life cycle depend on the temperature in the environment. Seed germination and seed viability are harmed by HT. This leads to thermal damage or loss of the seed, burning of leaves and stems in plants, leaf fall, and aging, inhibition of shoot and root viability or reduced flower number, pollen tube growth and pollen infertility, and fruit damage, causing catastrophic losses in crop yield by causing various physiological changes (Bita and Gerats, 2013; Hemantaranjan et al., 2014). The potential implications of this are that climate change is expected to have disproportionately large impacts on food security, so action needs to be taken in this regard.

6.5 Alleviation of Heat Stress

Heat stress is one of the crucial abiotic stress factors causing adverse effects on plant growth and development. It is a global concern due to reduced crop productivity. Plants as sessile organisms evolve different strategies to manage the detrimental effects of heat stress. Therefore, clarifying the molecular mechanisms of the heat-stress responses and tolerance are essential for ensuring the supply of food today and in the future (Lobell and Field, 2007; Nazar et al., 2017).

Plants trigger to upregulate their antioxidant system, induce several heat-inducible genes, synthesize heat-shock proteins, and accumulate proline to overcome heat stress and generate thermo-tolerance (Christou et al., 2014; Alayafi, 2019). In this manner, the plant preserves cellular homeostasis and fixes the injuries for plant survival under elevated temperature (Hemantaranjan et al., 2014; Alayafi, 2019). Overcoming the adverse effects of heat stress is interconnected with complex signalling pathways in plants (Rasmussen et al., 2013). It has been reported that exogenous applications of osmoprotectants, plant growth regulators (PGRs), and nutrients have beneficial effects on plant growth and development under HT conditions (Figure 6.1). PGRs such as auxin, GA (gibberellic acid), CKs (cytokinins), ABA (abscisic acid), ethylene, JA (jasmonic acid), SA (salicylic acid), BRs (brassinosteroids), and PAs (polyamines) play a significant role in perception and response to environmental stresses as well as heat stress (Table 6.2). PGRs also play a critical role in ameliorating heat stress by regulating/mediating plant growth, development, and stress response processes. They act synergistically or antagonistically to control plant metabolism and provoke plant defence by inducing gene expression (Song et al., 2013; Lubovská et al., 2014; Nazar et al., 2017).

Reports showed that under abiotic stress conditions, auxin-mediated regulation of growth and development depends on transport, biosynthesis, fusion, recognition, and signalling of auxin (Korver et al., 2018). Studies on *Arabidopsis* revealed that heat stress induced auxin on the expression of *MsCPK3* and *YUCCA*, which are involved in phytohormone and auxin biosynthesis, respectively (Sakata et al., 2010; Nazar et al., 2017). ABA has a crucial role in combining environmental stress signals and controlling stress responses (Tuteja, 2007). It has been confirmed that ABA reduces oxidative stress in *Arabidopsis* during heat stress (Larkindale and Knight, 2002). In addition, ABA

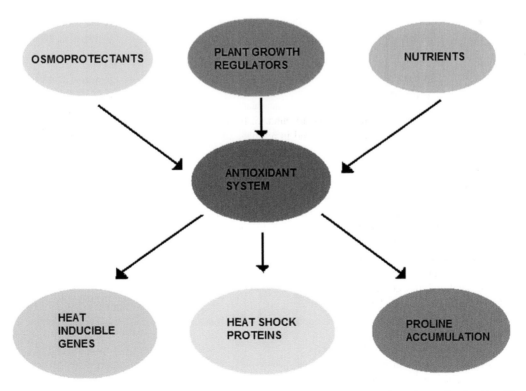

FIGURE 6.1 General mechanisms of osmoprotectants, plant growth regulators, and nutrients that are involved in mitigation of heat stress.

TABLE 6.2

Heat Stress Related Plant Growth Regulators (PGRs) and Their Functions in Different Plant Species

PGRs	Heat stress related functions	Plant species	References
Auxin	Expression of *MsCPK3* and *YUCCA* genes	*Arabidopsis*	• Sakata et al., 2010 • Nazar et al., 2017
Abscisic acid	Reduces oxidative stress	*Arabidopsis*	• Larkindale and Knight, 2002
	Accumulation of osmoprotectants	*C. arietinum*	• Kumar et al., 2012
Ethylene	Enhanced heat-shock protein synthesis and upregulation of *the APX1* gene	*Arabidopsis*	• Wu et al., 1994
Cytokinins	Modulate and enhance antioxidant enzymes and upregulation of heat-shock proteins	In most plant species	• Xu and Huang, 2009 • Lubovská et al., 2014
	Increase photosynthetic capacity and leaf longevity	*Arabidopsis*	• Xu et al., 2010
Gibberellic acids	Modulate SA biosynthesis and signal heat-shock protein accumulation	*Arabidopsis*	• Alonso-Ramírez et al., 2009
	Amylase activity	*P. vulgaris*	• Mansoor and Naqvi, 2013
Salicylic acid	Induces plant tolerance	*S. tuberosum* *B. juncea* *L. esculentum* *P. vulgaris* *Arabidopsis* *T. aestivum*	• Larkindale and Knight, 2002 • Khan et al., 2013
	Reduces electrolyte leakage and H_2O_2 accumulation	*C. sativus*	• Shi et al., 2006
	Enhances the activity of antioxidants and heat-shock protein 21	*V. vinifera*	• Wang and Li, 2006 • Wang et al., 2010
	Increases proline activity	*T. aestivum*	• Khan et al., 2013
Brassinosteroids	Enhance the synthesis of heat-shock proteins	*B. juncea*	• Dhaubhadel et al., 1999
	Increase the carboxylation efficiency and antioxidant system	*L. esculentum*	• Ogweno et al., 2008
	Stimulate H_2O_2 accumulation	*C. sativus*	• Xia et al., 2009
	Enhance photosynthetic pigment content and photochemical activity	*C. melo*	• Zhang et al., 2013
	Enhance stomatal conductance and quantum efficiency of photosystem II	*S. melongena*	• Wu et al., 2014
	Enhance pollen germination and seed setting	*O. sativa*	• Thussagunpanit et al., 2013
Jasmonic Acid	Enhances total phenolics	*R. ellipticus*	• Ghasemnezhad and Javaherdashti, 2008
	Stimulates photosystem II activity and stomatal control	*Arabidopsis*	• Heckatorn et al., 1998; • Munemasa et al., 2011
Polyamines	Enhance the antioxidant system and reduce electrolyte leakage	*C. sativus*	• Asthir and Deep, 2011
	Activate antioxidant enzymes and the expression of stress-related genes	Trifoliate orange seedlings	• Fu et al., 2014
	Activate the glyoxalase system	*O. sativa*	• Mostafa et al., 2014 • Tang et al., 2018
	Alleviate plasma membrane integrity	*G. max*	• Amooaghaie and Moghym, 2011
	Enhance expression of heat-shock protein-related genes	*Arabidopsis*	• Sagor et al., 2013
	Recover root and hypocotyls	*P. vulgaris*	• Basra et al., 1997
	Increase tolerance by sustaining steadiness in the cell membrane, accumulating antioxidant enzyme activities, developing PSII, and gene expression	*F. arundinacea*	• Zhang et al., 2017

facilitates the accumulation of osmoprotectants in *Cicer arietinum* (Kumar et al., 2012). Li et al. (2014a) also reported that a combination of indole acetic acid (IAA) and ABA stimulates the signal transduction pathway and monitors the development and quality of *Poa pratensis* under heat-stress conditions. Zimmerli et al. (2008) remarked that β-aminobutyric acid (a nonprotein amino acid) stimulated acquired thermo-tolerance in *Arabidopsis*, probably via induced ABA pathway.

Ethylene basically has an important role in ripening, abscission, and senescence in plants. It also triggers the antioxidative defence system, culminating in reduced oxidative stress. So, ethylene initiates recovery in the growth and photosynthetic efficiency of plants (Srivastava, 2012). In *Arabidopsis*, ethylene enhanced heat-shock protein synthesis and upregulated *the APX1* (cytosolic ascorbate peroxidase) gene during heat stress (Wu et al., 1994).

The phytohormones, such as cytokinins (CKs), which regulate cell division, fundamentally have diverse functions in response to environmental stresses (Cortleven et al., 2019). Both ethylene and CKs have been observed to transmit the signal of heat stress and alleviate its injurious effects in plants (Suzuki et al., 2008; Li et al., 2011; Nazar et al., 2017). Several studies revealed that CKs modulate and enhance the activities of antioxidant enzymes and upregulation of heat-shock proteins in different plant species (Xu and Huang, 2009; Lubovská et al., 2014). Moreover, CKs increase photosynthetic capacity and leaf longevity in *Arabidopsis* under heat-stress conditions (Xu et al., 2010).

GA induces shoot elongation basically; however, it has been suggested that it also modulates salicylic acid (SA) biosynthesis and signalling and heat-shock protein accumulation under heat stress in *Arabidopsis* (Alonso-Ramírez et al., 2009). Mansoor and Naqvi (2013) observed that application of GA induced amylase activity in *Phaseolus vulgaris*.

SA, which is one of the plant growth regulators, acts as a stress signalling molecule and induces plant-tolerance to abiotic stresses. It has been found that SA protects *Solanum tuberosum*, *Brassica juncea*, *Lycopersicon esculentum*, *P. vulgaris*, *Arabidopsis*, and *Triticum aestivum* against heat stress (Larkindale and Knight, 2002; Khan et al., 2013). Shi et al. (2006) indicated that SA reduces electrolyte leakage and H_2O_2 accumulation in *Cucumis sativus*. It also enhances the activity of antioxidants and heat-shock protein 21 in *Vitis vinifera* (Wang and Li, 2006; Wang et al., 2010). Besides, SA also increased the proline activity in *T. aestivum* (Khan et al., 2013). Overall, the results are evidenced that SA induces thermo-tolerance, even in rice pollen grain (Feng et al., 2018).

BRs have diverse roles in plant growth and development. Moreover, they alleviate the adverse effects of abiotic stress by regulating plant responses (Srivastava, 2012). Dhaubhadel et al. (1999) revealed that BRs enhanced the synthesis of heat-shock proteins in *B. juncea* during heat stress. BRs also increase the carboxylation efficiency and antioxidant system in *L. esculentum* (Ogweno et al., 2008). In *C. sativus*, BRs stimulate H_2O_2 accumulation to overcome heat stress (Xia et al., 2009). In addition, they enhance photosynthetic pigment content and photochemical activity in *Cucumis melo* (Zhang et al., 2013). Wu et al. (2014) also reported that BRs enhance stomatal conductance and quantum efficiency of photosystem II in *Solanum melongena*. Detailed morphological studies revealed BRs enhance pollen germination and seed setting in *Oryza sativa* under heat stress (Thussagunpanit et al., 2013).

Jasmonic acid (JA) is one of the essential plant signalling molecules closely associated with the generation of plant tolerance against abiotic stress. Under heat stress, JA enhances total phenolics in raspberry during heat stress (Ghasemnezhad and Javaherdashti, 2008). Furthermore, it stimulates photosystem II activity and stomatal control in *Arabidopsis* (Heckatorn et al., 1998; Munemasa et al., 2011).

Polyamines (PAs) regulate various cellular processes and abiotic stress tolerance as signalling molecules. As described by Asthir and Deep (2011), PAs enhance the antioxidant system and reduce electrolyte leakage in the *C. sativus* under heat stress. Similarly, PAs activate antioxidant enzymes and the expression of stress-related genes in trifoliate orange seedlings (Fu et al., 2014). Besides the antioxidant system, they also activate the glyoxalase system in *O. sativa* (Mostafa et al., 2014; Tang et al., 2018). In addition, PAs alleviate plasma membrane integrity in *Glycine max* and enhance expression of heat-shock protein-related genes in *Arabidopsis* under heat-stress conditions (Amooaghaie and Moghym, 2011; Sagor et al., 2013). Moreover, PAs recover root and hypocotyls in *P. vulgaris* after heat stress (Basra et al., 1997). Zhang et al. (2017) indicated that spermidine, which is one of the PAs, increases the tolerance to HT of *Festuca arundinacea* by sustaining the steadiness in cell membrane, accumulating antioxidant enzyme activities, developing PSII, and gene expression.

Cavusoglu and Kabar (2007) applied different PGRs separately or combined to alleviate heat stress during seed germination in radish. According to their results, BRs, PAs, and triacontanol (a natural PGR found in epicuticular waxes) are reported as effective as GA and CKs in ameliorating the effects of heat stress.

Nitric oxide (NO) is a key signalling molecule in mediating various plant responses and attracting the attention of plant scientists due to its role in resistance to plant stress conditions such as heat stress (Parankusam et al., 2017). Song et al. (2006) reported that NO generates thermo-tolerance by activating the antioxidant system during heat stress in *Phragmites communis*. In addition, it manages the thermo-tolerance by ABA induction (Song et al., 2008). A higher amount of NO was also seen in tobacco leaf cells and alfalfa under heat-stress conditions (Gould et al., 2003). As evidenced by Piterková et al. (2013), it regulates heat-shock protein 70 production in *L. esculentum*. It has been determined that NO enhances the expression of stress-related genes, heat-shock protein 26, rubisco activity, and carotenoid in *O. sativa* (Uchida et al., 2002; Song et al., 2013). Photosystem II recovery is also monitored in *F. arundinaceae* (Chen et al., 2013).

Ascorbate is a key regulator of reactive oxygen species in plants under stress conditions (Foyer and Noctor, 2011). In a detailed study by Alayafi et al. (2019), ascorbic acid alleviated heat-stress effects in *L. esculentum* by reducing oxidative stress and increasing endogenous ascorbic acid, proline, and photosynthetic pigments. Similarly, Hu et al. (2016) exogenously applied citric acid to alleviate the hostile effects of heat stress in tall fescue (*Lolium arundinaceum*). According to their results, citric acid reduced electrolyte leakage and lipid peroxidation and enhanced chlorophyll content, photochemical efficiency, and antioxidant enzyme activity during heat stress.

Ali et al. (2020) also proposed that the detrimental effects of heat stress may be alleviated by the application of chitosan in *C. sativus*. Chitosan is a natural conditioner that is an alternative to chemicals obtained from the chitin, and it is preferred against biotic and abiotic stresses (Kurtuluş and Vardar, 2021). The researchers revealed that chitosan spray at 200 ppm exhibited the ultimate potential to ameliorate the effect of heat stress in cucumber.

Waraich et al. (2012) suggested that for amelioration of the adverse effects of heat stress, plant nutrients may also be beneficial. Better plant nutrition can effectively alleviate the detrimental effects of temperature by several biochemical and physiological mechanisms as well as in various types of abiotic stress. The application of macronutrients may decrease the toxicity of reactive oxygen species by stimulating the antioxidant system in the plants. Macro elements like K (potassium) and Ca (calcium) recover water absorption, which promotes stomatal regulation and enhances stress tolerance by sustaining the common plant temperature. In addition, these elements also regulate osmotic potential. The microelements such as B, Mn and Se may ameliorate the adverse effects of HT by stimulating biochemical and physiological processes in plants. It has been known that Se application enhances antioxidant enzyme activity in cucumber and reduces lipid peroxidation in membranes (Balal et al., 2016). In support of this, Se may stimulate tolerance to temperature stress. Sarwar et al. (2019) alleviated the detrimental effect of heat stress in *Gossypium hirsitum* through foliar spray of some nutrients K, Zn, and B. Whereas the adverse effects of HT were modified due to the nutrient application, Zn was the most effective element in comparison to K and B. Zn increased the antioxidant capacity, chlorophyll content, photosynthetic rate, stomatal conductance, water potential, seed coat weight, and yield. Ali et al. (2021) applied sulfur to mitigate heat stress, and it enhanced proline, N, P, and K in tomato under stress conditions. Similar results were reported to NaHS as hydrogen sulphide (HS) donor; it also mitigates the heat stress-inducing antioxidant defence system in wheat (Yang et al., 2016) and strawberry (Christou et al., 2014).

On the other hand, some pioneer studies suggest that some microorganisms may be beneficial to overcome environmental stresses (Rajkumar et al., 2017; Keswani et al., 2019). Shin et al. (2019) revealed that two *Bacillus* strains promote plant growth and mitigate heat and drought stress in cabbage. Moreover, CO_2 enrichment in *L. esculentum*, glycine betaine in *Hordeum vulgare,* and unicanozole in *Brassica napus* are also effective in stimulating thermo-tolerance (Zhou and Leul, 1999; Wahid and Shabbir, 2005; Li et al., 2014b).

6.6 Conclusion

Factors such as increased drought due to rising temperatures, increased evaporation and altering precipitation, and elevated CO_2 levels because of greenhouse gases are predicted to significantly affect the agricultural production and crop productivity in different ecosystems and agroecological zones. Heat stress especially is one of the important abiotic stresses for plants. There are several breeding or transgenic studies that have successful results in triggering thermo-tolerance; however, these approaches do not apply to the agronomic field conditions and are very costly. For that reason, exogenously applied chemicals are more practical and successful. Several reports revealed that PGRs, nutrients, and organic acids play a critical role in stimulating thermo-tolerance in different plant species. This chapter provides a comprehensive overview on the effects of HT on legumes, which are considered crops of the age with very high trade shares, are economically favorable, are eco-friendly, and have high nutritional value.

However, although studies on *Arabidopsis*, *Lycopersicon esculentum* and some other species of Poaceae are available available studies on Fabaceae are rare. Therefore, more research is required to determine the proper chemical application on leguminous plants for stimulating heat-stress tolerance.

REFERENCES

Abiko, M., K. Akibayashi, T. Sakata, et al. 2005. High-temperature induction of male sterility during barley (*Hordeum vulgare* L.) anther development is mediated by transcriptional inhibition. *Sexual Plant Reproduction 182*:91–100.

Ahmed, F.E., A.E. Hall, and D.A. DeMason. 1992. Heat injury during floral development in cowpea (*Vigna unguiculata*, Fabaceae). *American Journal of Botany 79*:784–791.

Ahmed, F.E., A.E. Hall, and M.A. Madore. 1993. Interactive effects of high temperature and elevated carbon dioxide concentration on cowpea [*Vigna unguiculata* (L.) *Walp.*]. *Plant, Cell & Environment 16*:835–842.

Akula, R. and G.A. Ravishankar. 2011. Influence of abiotic stress signals on secondary metabolites in plants. *Plant Signaling & Behavior 6*:1720–1731.

Alayafi, A.A.M. 2019. Exogenous ascorbic acid induces systemic heat stress tolerance in tomato seedlings: transcriptional regulation mechanism. *Environmental Science and Pollution Research 27*:19186–19199.

Ali, M., C.M. Ayyub, Z. Hussain, R. Hussain, and S. Rashid. 2020. Optimisation of chitosan level to alleviate the drastic effects of heat stress in cucumber (*Cucumis sativus* L.). *Journal of Pure and Applied Agriculture 5*:30–38.

Ali, M.M., S.M. Waleed, S. Gull, et al. 2021. Alleviation of heat stress in tomato by exogenous application of sulfur. *Horticulturae 7*:21–33.

Alonso-Ramírez, A., D. Rodriguez, D. Reyes, et al. 2009. Evidence for a role of gibberellins in salicylic acid modulated early plant responses to abiotic stress in Arabidopsis seeds. *Plant Physiology 150*:1335–1444.

Amooaghaie, R. and Moghym, S. 2011. Effect of polyamines on thermotolerance and membrane stability of soybean seedling. *Afr J Biotechnol 47*:9673–9679.

Andrews, M., and S. Hodge. 2010. Climate change, a challenge for crop production. *Climate change and management of cool season grain legume crops*. Springer, Heidelberg/New York.

Asthir, B., and A. Deep. 2011. Thermotolerance and antioxidant response induced by putrescine and heat acclimation in wheat seedlings. *Seed Sci Biotechnol 5*:42–46.

Atkinson, N.J., and P.E. Urwin. 2012. The interaction of plant biotic and abiotic stresses: From genes to the field. *Journal of Experimental Botany 63*:3523–3543.

Balal, R.M., M.A. Shahid, M.M. Javaid, et al. 2016. The role of selenium in amelioration of heat-induced oxidative damage in cucumber under high temperature stress. *Acta Physiol Plant 38*:158.

Basra, R.K., A.S. Basra, C.P. Malik, and I.S. Grover. 1997. Are polyamines involved in the heat-shock protection of mung bean seedlings?. *Bot Bull Acad Sin 38*:165–169.

Bhandari, K., K.H. Siddique, N.C. Turner, et al. 2016. Heat stress at the reproductive stage disrupts leaf carbohydrate metabolism, impairs reproductive function, and severely reduces seed yield in lentils. *Journal of Crop Improvement 30*:118–151.

Bishop, J., S.G. Potts, and H.E. Jones. 2016a. Susceptibility of faba bean (*Vicia faba L.*) to heat stress during floral development and anthesis. *Journal of Agronomy and Crop Science 202*:508–517.

Bishop, J., H.E. Jones, M. Lukac, and S.G. Potts. 2016b. Insect pollination reduces yield loss following heat stress in faba bean (*Vicia faba* L.). *Agriculture, Ecosystems & Environment* 220:89–96.

Bita, C., and T. Gerats. 2013. Plant tolerance to high temperature in a changing environment: Scientific fundamentals and production of heat stress-tolerant crops. *Frontiers in Plant Science* 4:273.

Budak, H., B. Hussain, Z. Khan, N.Z. Ozturk, and N. Ullah. 2015. From genetics to functional genomics: improvement in drought signaling and tolerance in wheat. *Frontiers in Plant Science* 6:1012.

Casaretto, J.A., A. El-kereamy, B. Zeng, S.M. Stiegelmeyer, X. Chen, Y.M. Bi, and S.J. Rothstein. 2016. Expression of OsMYB55 in maise activates stress-responsive genes and enhances heat and drought tolerance. *BMC Genomics* 17:312.

Cavusoglu, K., and K. Kabar. 2007. Comparative effects of some plant growth regulators on the germination of barley and radish seeds under high temperature stress. *Eur Asia J Bio Sci* 1:1–10.

Chakrabarti, B., S.D. Singh, V. Kumar, R.C. Harit, and S. Misra. 2013. Growth and yield response of wheat and chickpea crops under high temperature. *Indian J. Plant Physiol* 18:7–14.

Chebrolu, K.K., F.B. Fritschi, S. Ye, H.B. Krishnan, J.R. Smith, and J.D. Gillman. 2016. Impact of heat stress during seed development on soybean seed metabolome. *Metabolomics* 12:28.

Chen, K., L. Chen, J. Fan, and J. Fu. 2013. Alleviation of heat damage to photosystem II by nitric oxide in tall fescue. *Photosynth Res* 116:21–31.

Chen, L., Q. Chen, L. Kong, F. Xia, H. Yan, Y. Zhu, and P. Mao. 2016. Proteomic and physiological analysis of the response of oat (*Avena sativa*) seeds to heat stress under different moisture conditions. *Frontiers in Plant Science* 7:896.

Chidambaranathan, P., P.T.K. Jagannadham, V. Satheesh, et al. 2018. Genome-wide analysis identifies chickpea (Cicer arietinum) heat stress transcription factors (Hsfs) responsive to heat stress at the pod development stage. *Journal of Plant Research* 131:525–542.

Christou, A., P. Filippou, G.A. Manganaris, and V. Fotopoulos. 2014. Sodium hydrosulfide induces systemic thermotolerance to strawberry plants through transcriptional regulation of heat shock proteins and aquaporin. *BMC Plant Biology* 14:42.

Clifford, S.C., I.M. Stronach, C.R. Black, P.R. Singleton-Jones, S.N. Azam-Ali, N.and N. Crout. 2000. Effects of elevated CO2, drought and temperature on the water relations and gas exchange of groundnut (*Arachis hypogaea*) stands grown in controlled environment glasshouses. *Physiologia Plantarum* 1:78–88.

Cortleven, A., J.E. Leuendorf, M. Frank, D. Pezzetta, S. Bolt, and T. Schmülling. 2019. Cytokinin action in response to abiotic and biotic stress in plants. *Plant Cell and Environment* 42:998–1018.

Costello, A., M. Abbas, A. Allen, S. Ball, S. Bell, R. Bellamy, and C. Patterson. 2009. Managing the health effects of climate change: Lancet and University College London Institute for Global Health Commission. *The Lancet* 373:1693–1733.

Das, A., P.J. Rushton, and J.S. Rohila. 2017. Metabolomic profiling of soybeans (*Glycine max L.*) reveals the importance of sugar and nitrogen metabolism under drought and heat stress. *Plants* 6:21.

Das, K., and A. Roychoudhury. 2014. Reactive oxygen species (ROS) and response of antioxidants as ROS-scavengers during environmental stress in plants. *Frontiers in Environmental Science* 2:53.

Das, S., P. Krishnan, M. Nayak, and B. Ramakrishnan. 2014. High temperature stress effects on pollens of rice (*Oryza sativa* L.) genotypes. *Environmental and Experimental Botany* 101:36–46.

Devasirvatham, V., P.M. Gaur, N. Mallikarjuna, T.N. Raju, R.M. Trethowan, and D.K. Tan. 2013. Reproductive biology of chickpea response to heat stress in the field is associated with the performance in controlled environments. *Field Crops Research* 142:9–19.

Dhaubhadel, S., S. Chaudhary, K.F. Dobinson, and P. Krishna. 1999. Treatment with 24-epibrassinolide, a brassinosteroid, increases the basic thermotolerance of Brassica napus and tomato seedlings. *Plant Mol Biol* 40:333–342.

Djukić, N., D. Knežević, D. Pantelić, D. Živančev, A. Torbica, and S. Marković. 2019. Expression of protein synthesis elongation factors in winter wheat and oat in response to heat stress. *Journal of Plant Physiology* 240:153015.

Fahad, S., A.A. Bajwa, U. Nazir, et al. 2017. Crop production under drought and heat stress: Plant responses and management options. *Frontiers in Plant Science*, 8:1147.

Feng, B., C. Zhang, T. Chen, et al. 2018. Salicylic acid reverses pollen abortion of rice caused by heat stress. *BMC Plant Biology* 18:245.

Foyer, C.H., and G. Noctor. 2011. Ascorbate and Glutathione: The heart of the Redox Hub. *Plant Physiology* 155:2–18.

Freitas, R., J.L.D. Dombroski, F.C.L.D. Freitas, N.W. Nogueira, and J.R.D.S. Pinto. 2017. Physiological responses of cowpea under water stress and rewatering in no-tillage and conventional tillage systems. *Revista Caatinga, 30*(3): 559–567.

Fu, X.J., F. Xing, N.Q. Wang, et al. 2014. Exogenous spermine pretreatment confers tolerance to combined high-temperature and drought stress in vitro in trifoliate orange seedlings via modulation of antioxidative capacity and expression of stress-related genes. *Biotechnol Biotechnol Equip* 28:192–198.

Fuchs, K., L. Hörtnagl, N. Buchmann, W. Eugster, V. Snow, and L. Merbold. 2018. Management matters: Testing a mitigation strategy for nitrous oxide emissions using legumes on intensively managed grassland. *Biogeosciences, 15*(18):5519–5543.

Ghasemnezhad, M., and M. Javaherdashti. 2008. Effect of methyl jasmonate treatment on antioxidant capacity, internal quality and postharvest life of raspberry fruit. *J Environ Sci* 6:73–78.

Gonzalez, A., L. Galvez, M. Royuela, P. Aparicio-Tejo, and C. Arrese-Igor. 2001. Insights into the regulation of nitrogen fixation in pea nodules: Lessons from drought, abscisic acid and increased assimilate availability. A*gronomie 21*:607–613.

Gould, K.S., O. Lamotte, A. Klinguer, A. Pugin, and D. Wendehenne. 2003. Nitric oxide production in tobacco leaf cells: A generalised stress response. *Plant Cell Environ* 26:1851–1862.

Hall, A.E. 2004. Breeding for adaptation to drought and heat in cowpea. *European Journal of Agronomy 21*:447–454.

Hasanuzzaman, M., K. Nahar, M. Alam, R. Roychowdhury, and M. Fujita. 2013a. Physiological, biochemical, and molecular mechanisms of heat stress tolerance in plants. *International Journal of Molecular Sciences 14*:9643–9684.

Hasanuzzaman, M., K. Nahar, and M. Fujita. 2013b. Extreme temperature responses, oxidative stress and antioxidant defense in plants. In *Abiotic stress – Plant responses and applications in agriculture*, Vol. 6, 169–205. InTechOpen. 10.5772/54833

Hatfield, J.L., K.J. Boote, B.A. Kimball, et al. 2011. Climate impacts on agriculture: Implications for crop production. *Agronomy Journal 103*:351–370.

Heckatorn, S., C. Downs, T. Sharkey, and J. Coleman. 1998. The small methionine rich heat-shock protein protects PSII electron transport during heat stress. *Plant Physiology 116*:439–444.

Hemantaranjan, A., A.N. Bhanu, M.N. Singh, et al. 2014. Heat stress responses and thermotolerance. *Adv. Plants Agric. Res. 1*:1–10.

Hildebrandt, T.M., A.N. Nesi, W.L. Araújo, and H.P. Braun. 2015. Amino acid catabolism in plants. *Molecular Plant* 8:1563–1579.

Hossain, A., M.A.Z. Sarker, M. Saifuzzaman, J.A. Teixeira da Silva, M.V. Lozovskaya, and M.M. Akhter. 2013. Evaluation of growth, yield, relative performance and heat susceptibility of eight wheat (*Triticum aestivum* L.) genotypes grown under heat stress. *International Journal of Plant Production* 7:615–636.

Hu, L., Z. Zhang, Z. Xiang, and Z. Yang, Z. 2016. Exogenous application of citric acid ameliorates the adverse effect of heat stress in tall Fescue (*Lolium arundinaceum*). *Frontiers In Plant Science* 7:179.

Huang, B., M. DaCosta, and Y. Jiang. 2014. Research advances in mechanisms of turfgrass tolerance to abiotic stresses: From physiology to molecular biology. *Critical Reviews in Plant Sciences 33*:141–189.

Jagadish, K.S.V., P. Craufurd, W. Shi, and R. Oane. 2014. A phenotypic marker for quantifying heat stress impact during microsporogenesis in rice (*Oryza sativa* L.). *Functional Plant Biology 41*:48–55.

Jiang, Y. 2016. *Effect of heat stress on pollen development and seed set in field pea (Pisum sativum L.)* (Doctoral dissertation, University of Saskatchewan).

Jiang, Y., D.L. Lindsay, A.R. Davis, et al. 2020. Impact of heat stress on pod-based yield components in field pea (*Pisum sativum L.*). *Journal of Agronomy and Crop Science* 206:76–89.

Kambiranda, D.M., H.K. Vasanthaiah, R. Katam, A. Ananga, S.M. Basha, and K. Naik. 2011. Impact of drought stress on peanut (*Arachis hypogaea* L.) productivity and food safety. *Plants and environment*, eds. K.H. Hemanth, H.K. Vasanthaiah, and D.M. Kambiranda, 249–272. InTech.

Kaushal, N., R. Awasthi, K. Gupta, P. Gaur, K.H. Siddique, and H. Nayyar. 2013. Heat-stress-induced reproductive failures in chickpea (*Cicer arietinum*) are associated with impaired sucrose metabolism in leaves and anthers. *Funct. Plant Biol. 40*:1334–1349.

Keswani, C., H. Dilnashin, H. Birla, and S.P. Singh. 2019. Unravelling efficient applications of agriculturally important microorganisms for alleviation of induced inter-cellular oxidative stress in crops. *Acta Agriculturae Slovenica 114*:121–130.

Ketring, D.L. 1991. Physiology of oil seeds: IX. Effects of water deficit on peanut seed quality. *Crop Science* *31*:459–463.

Khalil, S.I., H.M.S. El-Bassiouny, R.A. Hassanein, and H.A. Mostafa. 2009. Antioxidant defense system in heat-shocked wheat plants previously treated with arginine or putrescine. *Aust. J. Basic Appl. Sci. 3*:1517–1526.

Khan, M.I.R., N. Iqbal, A. Masood, T.S. Per, and N.A. Khan. 2013. Salicylic acid alleviates adverse effects of heat stress on photosynthesis through changes in proline production and ethylene formation. *Plant Signal Behav. 8*:26374.

Korver, R.A., I.T. Koevoets, and C. Testerink. 2018. Out of shape during stress: A key role for Auxin. Trends in *Plant Science 23*:783–793.

Krasensky, J., and C. Jonak. 2012. Drought, salt, and temperature stress-induced metabolic rearrangements and regulatory networks. *Journal of Experimental Botany 63*(4):1593–1608.

Krishnan, P.B., K. Ramakrishnan, R. Raja, and V.R. Reddy. 2011. High-temperature effects on rice growth, yield, and grain quality. *Advances in Agronomy 111*:87–206.

Kumar, S., N. Kaushal, H. Nayyar, and P. Gaur. 2012. Abscisic acid induces heat tolerance in chickpea (*Cicer arietinum* L.) seedlings by facilitated accumulation of osmoprotectants. *Acta Physiol Plant 34*:1651–1658.

Kurtuluş, G., and F. Vardar. 2021. The effects of chitosan application against aluminum toxicity in wheat (*Triticum aestivum* L.) roots. *Annali di Botanica 11*:121–134.

Lake, L., D.E. Godoy-Kutchartt, D.F. Calderini, A. Verrell, and V.O. Sadras. 2019. Yield determination and the critical period of faba bean (*Vicia faba* L.). *Field Crops Research 241*:107575.

Lal, M.A., R. Kathpalia, R. Sisodia, and R. Shakya. 2018. Biotic stress. In *Plant physiology, development and metabolism*. pp. 1029–1095. Springer, Singapore.

Larkindale, J., and M.R. Knight. 2002. Protection against heat stress-induced oxidative damage in Arabidopsis involves calcium, abscisic acid, ethylene, and salicylic acid. *Plant Physiology 128*:682–695.

Li, F., D. Zhan, L. Xu, L. Han, and X. Zhang. 2014a. Antioxidant and hormone responses to heat stress in two Kentucky bluegrass cultivars contrasting in heat tolerance. *J Amer Soc Hortic Sci 139*:587–596.

Li, S., Q. Fu, L. Chen, W. Huang, and D. Yu. 2011. *Arabidopsis thaliana* WRKY25, WRKY26, and WRKY33 coordinate induction of plant thermotolerance. *Planta 233*:1237–1252.

Li, X., G.J. Ahammed, Y.Q. Zhang, et al. 2014b. Carbon dioxide enrichment alleviates heat stress by improving cellular redox homeostasis through an ABA-independent process in tomato plants. *Plant Biology 17*:81–89.

Liu, J., L. Feng, J. Li, and Z. He. 2015. Genetic and epigenetic control of plant heat responses. *Frontiers in Plant Science 6*:267.

Lobell, D.B., and C.B. Field. 2007. Global-scale climate–crop yield relationships and the impacts of recent warming. *Environ Res Lett 2*:014002.

López-Hernández, F., and A.J. Cortés. 2019. Last-generation genome–environment associations reveal the genetic basis of heat tolerance in common bean (*Phaseolus vulgaris* L.). *Frontiers in Genetics 10*:954.

Lu, J., R. Zhang, X.F. Zong, S.G. Wang, and G.H. He. 2009. Effect of salicylic acid on heat resistance of rice seedling under heat stress. *Chin. J. Eco-Agric., 17*:1168–1171.

Lubovská, Z., J. Dobrá, and W.H.N. Storchová. 2014. Cytokinin oxidase/dehydrogenase overexpression modifies antioxidant defense against heat, drought and their combination in Nicotiana tabacum plants. *J Plant Physiol 171*:1625–1633.

Mansoor, S., and F.N. Naqvi. 2013. Isoamylase profile of mung bean seedlings treated with high temperature and gibberellic acid. *Afr J Biotechnol 12*:1495–1499.

Maqbool, S., H. Zhong, Y. El-Maghraby, et al. 2002. Competence of oat (*Avena sativa* L.) shoot apical meristems for integrative transformation, inherited expression, and osmotic tolerance of transgenic lines containing hva1. *Theoretical and Applied Genetics 105*:201–208.

Mathur, S., D. Agrawal, and A. Jajoo. 2014. Photosynthesis: response to high temperature stress. *Journal of Photochemistry and Photobiology B: Biology 137*:116–126.

Matsui, T. and K. Omasa. 2002. Rice (*Oryza sativa* L.) cultivars tolerant to high temperature at flowering: Anther characteristics. *Annals of Botany 89*:683–687.

Mickelbart, M.V., P.M. Hasegawa, and J. Bailey-Serres. 2015. Genetic mechanisms of abiotic stress tolerance that translate to crop yield stability. *Nat. Rev. Genet. 16*:237–251.

Mittler, R., A. Finka, and P. Goloubinoff. 2012. How do plants feel the heat?. *Trends in Biochemical Sciences 37*:118–125.

Monterroso, V.A., and H.C. Wien. 1990. Flower and pod abscission due to heat stress in beans. *Journal of the American Society for Horticultural Science 115*:631–634.

Mostafa, M.G., N. Yoshida, and M. Fujita. 2014. Spermidine pretreatment enhances heat tolerance in rice seedlings through modulating antioxidative and glyoxalase systems. *Plant Growth Regul 73*:31–44.

Munemasa, S., M.A. Hossain, Y. Nakamura, I.C. Mori, and Y. Murata. 2011. The Arabidopsis calcium-dependent protein kinase, CPK6, functions as a positive regulator of methyl jasmonate signaling in guard cells. *Plant Physiol 155*:553–561.

Nazar, R., N. Iqbal, and N.A. Khan. 2017. *Salicylic acid: A multifaced Hormone*. *Springer Nature*, Singapore.

Ogweno, J.O., X.S. Song, K. Shi, et al. 2008. Brassinosteroids alleviate heat-induced inhibition of photosynthesis by increasing carboxylation efficiency and enhancing antioxidant systems in Lycopersicon esculentum. *J Plant Growth Regul 27*:49–57.

Ohama, N., H. Sato, K. Shinozaki, and K. Yamaguchi-Shinozaki. 2017. Transcriptional regulatory network of plant heat stress response. *Trends in Plant Science 22*:53–65.

Parankusam, S., S.S. Adimulam, P. Bhatnagar-Mathur, and K.K. Sharma. 2017. Nitric oxide (NO) in plant heat stress tolerance: Current knowledge and perspectives. *Frontiers in Plant Science 8*:1582.

Peng, S., J. Huang, J.E. Sheehy, et al. 2004. Rice yields decline with higher night temperature from global warming. *Proceedings of the National Academy of Sciences 101*:9971–9975.

Piterková, J., L. Luhová, B. Mieslerová, A. Lebeda, and M. Petrivalsky. 2013. Nitric oxide and reactive oxygen species regulate the accumulation of heat shock proteins in tomato leaves in response to heat shock and pathogen infection. *Plant Sci 207*:57–65.

Popp, D., R.G. Newell, and A.B. Jaffe. 2010. Energy, the environment, and technological change. *Handbook of the Economics of Innovation 2*:873–937.

Porch, T.G., and M. Jahn. 2001. Effects of high-temperature stress on microsporogenesis in heat-sensitive and heat-tolerant genotypes of Phaseolus vulgaris. *Plant, Cell & Environment 24*:723–731.

Prasad, P.V., K.J. Boote, L.H. Allen Jr, and J.M. Thomas. 2002. Effects of elevated temperature and carbon dioxide on seed-set and yield of kidney bean (*Phaseolus vulgaris* L.). *Global Change Biology 8*:710–721.

Pruthvi, V., R. Narasimhan, and K.N. Nataraja. 2014. Simultaneous expression of abiotic stress-responsive transcription factors, AtDREB2A, AtHB7 and AtABF3 improves salinity and drought tolerance in peanut (*Arachis hypogaea* L.). *PLoS One 9*:111152.

Puteh, A.B., M. ThuZar, M.M.A. Mondal, A.P.B. Abdullah, and M.R.A. Halim. 2013. Soybean [*Glycine max* (L.) Merrill] seed yield response to high temperature stress during reproductive growth stages. *Australian Journal of Crop Science 7*:1472.

Qin, D., H. Wu, H. Peng, et al. 2008. Heat stress-responsive transcriptome analysis in heat susceptible and tolerant wheat (*Triticum aestivum* L.) by using Wheat Genome Array. *BMC Genomics 9*:1–19.

Rainey, K.M., and P.D. Griffiths. 2005. Inheritance of heat tolerance during reproductive development in snap bean (*Phaseolus vulgaris* L.). *J. Am. Soc. Hortic. Sci. 130*:700—706.

Rajkumar, M., L.B. Bruno, and J.R. Banu. 2017. Alleviation of environmental stress in plants: The role of beneficial *Pseudomonas* spp. *Critical Reviews in Environmental Science and Technology 47*(6): 372–407.

Rapacz, M., A. Stępień, and K. Skorupa. 2012. Internal standards for quantitative RT-PCR studies of gene expression under drought treatment in barley (*Hordeum vulgare* L.): The effects of developmental stage and leafage. *Acta Physiologiae Plantarum 34*:1723–1733.

Rasmussen, S., P. Barah, M.C. Suarez-Rodriguez, et al. 2013. Transcriptome responses to combinations of stresses in Arabidopsis. *Plant Physiology 161*:1783–1794.

Reynolds-Henne, C.E., A. Langenegger, J. Mani, N. Schenk, A. Zumsteg, and U. Feller. 2010. Interactions between temperature, drought and stomatal opening in legumes. *Environmental and Experimental Botany 68*:37–43.

Sagor, G.H.M., T. Berberich, Y. Takahashi, M. Niitsu, and T. Kusano. 2013. The polyamine spermine protects Arabidopsis from heat stress-induced damage by increasing expression of heat shock-related genes. *Transgenic Res. 22*:595–605.

Saini, H.S., M. Sedgley, and D. Aspinall. 1983. Effect of heat stress during floral development on pollen tube growth and ovary anatomy in wheat (*Triticum aestivum* L.). *Functional Plant Biology 10*(2): 137–144.

Sakata, T., T. Oshino, S. Miura, et al. 2010. Auxins reverse plant male sterility caused by high temperatures. *Proc Natl Acad Sci USA 107*:8569–8574.

Sakata, T., H. Takahashi, L. Nishiyama, and A. Higashitani. 2000. Effects of high temperature on the development of pollen mother cells and microspores in barley *Hordeum vulgare* L. *Journal of Plant Research 113*:395.

Samarah, N.H., N. Haddad, and A. Alqudah. 2009. Yield potential evaluation in chickpea genotypes under late terminal drought in relation to the length of reproductive stage. *Ital. J. Agron. 3*:111–117.

Sarwar, M., M.F. Saleem, N. Ullah, et al. 2019. Role of mineral nutrition in alleviation of heat stress in cotton plants grown in glasshouse and field conditions. *Scientific Reports 9*:13022.

Seidel, S.J., S. Rachmilevitch, N. Schütze, and N. Lazarovitch. 2016. Modelling the impact of drought and heat stress on common bean with two different photosynthesis model approaches. *Environmental Modelling & Software 81*:111–121.

Shah, Z., A. Iqbal, F.U. Khan, H.U. Khan, F. Durrani, and M.Z. Ahmad. 2020. Genetic manipulation of pea (Pisum sativum L.) with Arabidopsis's heat shock factor HsfA1d improves ROS scavenging system to confront thermal stress. *Genetic Resources and Crop Evolution 67*:2119–2127.

Shi, Q., Z. Bao, Z. Zhu, Q..Ying, and Q. Qian. 2006. Effects of different treatments of salicylic acid on heat tolerance, chlorophyll fluorescence, and antioxidant enzyme activity in seedlings of *Cucumis Sativa* L. *Plant Growth Regul 48*:127–135.

Shin, D.J., S.J. Yoo, J.K. Hong, H.Y. Weon, J. Song, and M.K. Sang. 2019. Effect of Bacillus aryabhattai H26-2 and B. siamensis H30-3 on growth promotion and alleviation of heat and drought stresses in Chinese Cabbage. *Plant Pathol. J. 35*:178–187.

Shinozaki, K., and K. Yamaguchi-Shinozaki. 2007. Gene networks involved in drought stress response and tolerance. *Journal of Experimental Botany 58*:221–227.

Singh, A., R. Kukreti, L. Saso, and S. Kukreti. 2019a. Oxidative stress: A key modulator in neurodegenerative diseases. *Molecules 24*:1583.

Singh, D., C.K. Singh, J. Taunk, V. Jadon, M. Pal, and K. Gaikwad. 2019b. Genome-wide transcriptome analysis reveals the vital role of heat-responsive genes in regulatory mechanisms of lentil (*Lens culinaris* Medikus). *Scientific Reports 9*:1–19.

Singh, S., P. Parihar, R. Singh, V.P. Singh, and S.M. Prasad. 2016. Heavy metal tolerance in plants: Role of transcriptomics, proteomics, metabolomics, and economics. *Frontiers in Plant Science 6*:1143.

Sita, K., A. Sehgal, K. Bhandari, J. Kumar, S. Kumar, and S. Singh. 2018. Impact of heat stress during seed filling on seed quality and seed yield in lentil (*Lens culinaris* Medikus) genotypes. *J. Sci. Food Agric. 98*:5134–5141.

Solomon, S. 2007. The physical science basis: Contribution of working group I to the fourth assessment report of the Intergovernmental Panel on Climate Change. Intergovernmental Panel on Climate Change (IPCC), *Climate Change 2007*:996.

Song, L., W. Ding, J. Shen, Z. Zhang, Y. Bi, and L. Zhang. 2008. Nitric oxide mediates abscisic acid-induced thermotolerance in the calluses from two ecotypes of reed under heat stress. *Plant Sci 175*:826–832.

Song, L., W. Ding, M.G. Zhao, B.T. Sun, and L.X. Zhang. 2006. Nitric oxide protects against oxidative stress under heat stress in the calluses from two ecotypes of reed. *Plant Sci 171*:449–458.

Song, L., L. Yue, H. Zhao, and M. Hou. 2013. Protection effect of nitric oxide on photosynthesis in rice under heat stress. *Acta Physiol Plant 35*:3323–3333.

Srivastava, S., A.D. Pathak, P.S. Gupta, and A.K. Shrivastava. 2012. Hydrogen peroxide-scavenging enzymes impart tolerance to high temperature-induced oxidative stress in sugarcane. *J Environ Biol 33*:657–661.

Stevens, R.G., G.P. Creissen, and P.M. Mullineaux. 1997. Cloning and characterisation of a cytosolic glutathione reductase cDNA from pea (*Pisum sativum* L.) and its expression in response to stress. *Plant Molecular Biology 35*:641–654.

Suzuki, K., H. Takeda, T. Tsukaguchi, and Y. Egawa. 2001. Ultrastructural study on degeneration of tapetum in anther of snap bean (*Phaseolus vulgaris* L.) under heat stress. *Sexual Plant Reproduction 13*:293–299.

Suzuki, N., S. Bajad, J. Shuman, V. Shulaev, and R. Mittler. 2008. The transcriptional co-activator MBF1c is a key regulator of thermotolerance in Arabidopsis thaliana. *J Biol Chem 283*:9269–9275

Tang, S., H. Zhang, L. Li, et al. 2018. Exogenous spermidine enhances the photosynthetic and antioxidant capacity of rice under heat stress during early grain-filling period. *Functional Plant Biology 45*:911–921.

Thussagunpanit, J., K. Jutamanee, L. Kaveeta, W. Chai-arree, P. Pankean, and A. Suksamrarn. 2013. Effects of a brassinosteroid and an ecdysone analogue on pollen germination of rice under heat stress. *J Pestic Sci 38*:105–111.

Tiwari, Y.K., and S.K. Yadav. 2019. High temperature stress tolerance in maise (*Zea mays* L.): physiological and molecular mechanisms. *Journal of Plant Biology 62*:93–102.

Tuteja, N. 2007. Abscisic Acid and Abiotic Stress Signaling *Plant Signaling & Behavior 2*(3):135–138.

Uchida, A., A.T. Jagendorf, T. Hibino, T. Takabe, and T. Takabe. 2002. Effects of hydrogen peroxide and nitric oxide on both salt and heat stress tolerance in rice. *Plant Sci 163*:515–523.

Upadhyaya, H.D., N. Dronavalli, C.L.L. Gowda, and S. Singh. 2011. Identification and evaluation of chickpea germplasm for tolerance to heat stress. *Crop Science 51*:2079–2094.

Valdés-López, O., J. Batek, N. Gomez-Hernandez, et al. 2016. Soybean roots grown under heat stress show global changes in their transcriptional and proteomic profiles. *Frontiers in Plant Science 7*:517.

Wahab, M.M.S., S. Akkareddy, P. Shanthi, and P. Latha. 2020. Identification of differentially expressed genes under heat stress conditions in rice (*Oryza sativa L.*). *Molecular Biology Reports 47*:1935–1948.

Wahid, A., and A. Shabbir. 2005. Induction of heat stress tolerance in barley seedlings by pre-sowing seed treatment with glycine betaine. *Plant Growth Regulation 46*:133–141.

Wang, L.J., L. Fan, W. Loescher, et al. 2010. Salicylic acid alleviates decreases in photosynthesis under heat stress and accelerates recovery in grapevine leaves. *BMC Plant Biol 10*:34.

Wang, L.J., and S.H. Li. 2006. Salicylic acid-induced heat or cold tolerance in relation to Ca2+ homeostasis and antioxidant systems in young grape plants. *Plant Sci 170*:685–694.

Waraich, E.A., R. Ahmad, A. Halim, and T. Aziz. 2012. Alleviation of temperature stress by nutrient management in crop plants: A review. *Journal of Soil Science and Plant Nutrition 12*:221–244.

Warchoł, M., L. Czyczyło-Mysza, I. Marcińska, et al. 2019. Factors inducing regeneration response in oat (*Avena sativa L.*) anther culture. *In Vitro Cellular & Developmental Biology-Plant 55*:595–604.

Warrag, M.O.A., and A.E. Hall. 1984. Reproductive responses of cowpea (*Vigna unguiculata L.*) to heat stress. II. Responses to night air temperature. *Field Crops Research 8*:17–33.

WHO. 2018. Climate change and health. Available at: http://www.who.int/en/news-room/fact-sheets/detail/climate-change-and-health

Wu, S.H., C. Wong, J. Chen, and B.C. Lin. 1994. Isolation of a cDNA encoding a 70 kDa heat shock cognate protein expressed in the vegetative tissue of Arabidopsis. *Plant Mol Biol 25*:577–583.

Wu, X., X. Yao, J. Chen, Z. Zhu, H. Zhang, and D. Zha. 2014. Brassinosteroids protect photosynthesis and antioxidant system of eggplant seedlings from high-temperature stress. *Acta Physiol Plant 36*:251–261.

Xia, X.J., Y.J. Wang, Y.H. Zhou, et al. 2009. Reactive oxygen species are involved in brassinosteroid-induced stress tolerance in cucumber. *Plant Physiol 150*:801–814.

Xu, Y., T. Gianfagna, and B. Huang. 2010. Proteomic changes associated with expression of a gene (ipt) controlling cytokinin synthesis for improving heat tolerance in a perennial grass species. *J Exp Bot 61*:3273–3289.

Xu, Y., and B. Huang. 2009. Effects of foliar-applied ethylene inhibitor and synthetic cytokinin on creeping bentgrass to enhance heat tolerance. *Crop Sci 49*:1876–1884.

Yadav, S.S., D.L. McNeil, R. Redden, and S.A. Patil. 2010. *Climate change and management of cool-season grain legume crops*. Springer Science & Business Media.

Yamori, W., K. Hikosaka, and D.A. Way. 2014. Temperature response of photosynthesis in C 3, C 4, and CAM plants: Ttemperature acclimation and temperature adaptation. *Photosynthesis Research 119*:101–117.

Yang, M., B. Qın, X. Ma, et al. 2016. Foliar application of sodium hydrosulfide (NaHS), a hydrogen sulfide (H2S) donor, can protect seedlings against heat stress in wheat (*Triticum aestivum L.*). *Journal of Integrative Agriculture, 15*:2745–2758.

Yuksel,, B., S. Mert, and S.Y. Arsal. 2018. The impact of global warming on human health. *International Marmara Science and Social Sciences Congress 1079–1081*.

Zhang, L., T. Hu, E. Amombo, G. Wang, Y. Xie, and J. Fu. 2017. The alleviation of heat damage to photosystem II and enzymatic antioxidants by Exogenous Spermidine in tall Fescue. *Front. Plant Sci. 8*:1747.

Zhang, Y.P., X.H. Zhu, H.D. Ding, S.J. Yang, and Y.Y. Chen. 2013. Foliar application of 24-epibrassinolide alleviates high-temperature induced inhibition of photosynthesis in seedlings of two melon cultivars. *Photosynthetica 51*:341–349.

Zhou, W., and M. Leul. 1999. Uniconazole-induced tolerance of rape plants to heat stress in relation to changes in hormonal levels, enzyme activities and lipid peroxidation. *Plant Growth Regulation 27*:99–104.

Zimmerli, L., B.H. Hou, C.H. Tsai, G. Jakab, B. Mauch-Mani, and S. Somerville. 2008. The xenobiotic β-aminobutyric acid enhances Arabidopsis thermotolerance. *Plant J 53*:144–156.

7

Genetic Improvement for Development of a Climate Resilient Food Legume Crops: Relevance of cowpea breeding approach in improvement of food legume crops for future

Tony Ngalamu[1], James Odra Galla[1], Kwadwo Ofori[2], and Silvestro Kaka Meseka[3]
[1]*Department of Crop Science, School of Agricultural Sciences, College of Natural Resources and Environmental Studies, University of Juba, P.O. Box 82, Juba, South Sudan*
[2]*West Africa Centre for Crop Improvement, School of Agriculture, College of Basic and Applied Sciences, University of Ghana, PMB 30, Legon, Ghana*
[3]*International Institute of Tropical Agriculture, PMB 5320, Oyo Road, Ibadan, Nigeria*

CONTENTS

DOI: 10.1201/9781003214885-7

7.1 Introduction

The world population at present stands at 7.6 billion. The United Nations Department of Economic and Social Affairs estimates that the earth's human population will surpass 9.1 billion by the year 2050 (UNDESA, 2013). At this point or even before, it is believed that challenges of climate change combined with increased demand from population and economic growth will create global food shortage, resulting in hunger, and the number of people living below the poverty line will increase. This necessitates finding sustainable and eco-friendly technological agricultural approaches to improve crop yields with nutritional value. The literature on legume improvement is vast; as such, this chapter covers only the essential legume improvement tools required in development of resistant and tolerant legume crops for food and nutrition security. Food legumes ranked second among the most valued food sources after cereals. Despite the notable accomplishment in breeding food legumes, there is a gap that requires more population development activities and continuous legume improvement in order to meet the increasing global food demand.

Several legume production constraints have been documented; however, some biotic and abiotic stresses were noted to have more effect on legume productivity at a global scale. Thus, there is a need to study the genetics of legume food crops and genomics as well as their biology to establish facts about the genes or quantitative trait loci (QTLs) that influence yield of food legume crops and set the foundation for the legume breeding program. Use of molecular tools has made crop improvement accomplishable within a short period of time with relatively pocket-friendly prices. Henceforth, legume improvement programme deploying genomic approaches in identifying and targeting of specific genes, such as genes responsible for enhancing yield, conditioning tolerance to abiotic stresses, and improving level of resistance to biotic stresses, would be appropriate.

7.2 The Importance of Legumes in Meeting Food and Nutrition Security

The Food and Agriculture Organization of the United Nations reported that globally grain and forage legume crops are grown on approximately 180 million hectares, or 12% to 15% of the available arable land (Table 7.1).

The production of legume crops accounts for over 27% of global production, whereas both forage and food legumes contribute roughly 33% of the dietary protein nitrogen (N) needs of humans (Vance et al., 2000). However, under subsistence cropping systems, the contribution of legume protein N in the diet of the farming communities could be twice the projected 33%. Preference and ranking of legume crops vary from one region to the other. Thus, globally, rank order follows this trend: bean (*Phaseolus vulgaris*), pea (*Pisum sativum*), chickpea (*Cicer arietinum*), broad bean (*Vicia faba*), pigeon pea (*Cajanus cajan*), cowpea (*Vigna unguiculata*), and lentil (*Lens culinaris*). Based on the report by National Academy of Science (1994), this set of legume crops constitutes the primary dietary food legumes. Two legume crops, soybean (*Glycine max*) and groundnuts (*Arachis hypogaea*), solely provide more than 35% of the globally processed vegetable oil (Graham and Vance, 2003), and these two food legume crops are also rich sources of dietary protein required in both the poultry and pork industries. The potential of food legume crops could not be denied since there is high market demand in Europe, Asia, and humanitarian interventions in Africa. The evidence of high demand for food legumes is shown by the increment in soybean production in Brazil, resulting in high rate of forest depletion (Lima et al., 2011). However, food, nutritional, and soil benefits of legume crops are much higher compared to cereals (Figure 7.1).

TABLE 7.1

Depiction of Area Under Various Crop Production Systems

Crop	Production Mt $\times 10^6$	Area harvested ha $\times 10^6$
Grain legumes	275	160
Forage legumes	605	20
Wheat (*Triticum aestivum*)	583	214
Rice (*Oryza sativa*)	590	152
Maize (*Zea mays*)	609	138
Barley (*Hordeum vulgare*)	141	54
Potatoes (*Solanum tuberosum*)	308	19
Cassava (*Manihot esculenta* Crantz.)	179	20
Total	**3,320**	**777**

Source: Food and Agriculture Organization of the United Nations (FAO) database (http://apps.fao.org/page/collections).

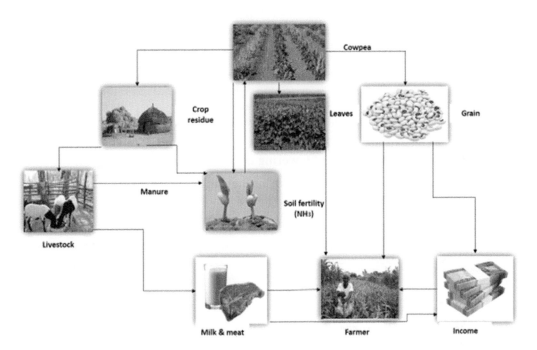

FIGURE 7.1   Benefits of food legume crops to the soil, animals, and humans.

Crop failure is one of the important attributes to world agricultural losses reflected in low productivity and crops of less nutritional value as a result of a phenomenon known as climate change. This phenomenon is caused by global warming resulting in re-occurrence of severe weather events, such as heavy rains in some areas and drought in others. The implication of this phenomenon is that approximately more than two billion people may suffer from malnutrition problems due to hunger/famine resulting from intake of poor-quality food with insufficient essential micronutrients and prevailing disguised hunger (Campbell et al., 2014). Based on the World Health Organization's standards, deficiency in core micronutrients such as, zinc (Zn), iron (Fe), and selenium (Se) negatively influences human health. For instance, deficiency of Zn is manifested in the inappropriate physical growth, healing of wounds, and poor skeletal development; in addition, deficiency of Zn is associated with augmented risk of infection. Anemia and fatigue arise as a result of Fe deficiency, in addition to compromised immune system. Incidences of reduced male fertility, impaired immune system, high chance of infections retarding mental development, and hypothyroidism are all associated with Se deficiency (Khan et al., 2019). In order to achieve the desired food and nutrition security status in the face of climate change, there is a need to improve food legumes that are resilient to vagaries of climate change. This can be realized using climate-smart agriculture, an approach that aims to deploy tolerant and resistant legume crop varieties to avert effects and hazards of climate change, approaches that should be environmentally friendly (Campbell et al., 2014).

7.3 Performance of Food Legumes under Drought and Heat Stress

Several researchers have documented the adverse effects of drought and heat stress on the reproductive phase of food legume crops, a phase more sensitive to both drought and heat stress. Reports indicated that co-occurrence of these two stresses results in a number of abnormalities: (i) impaired micro-sporogenesis and mega-sporogenesis (Young et al., 2004), (ii) loss of viability of pollen grains (Kafizadeh et al., 2008), (iii) poor quality of pollen grain resulting in undesirable germination (Porch and Jahn, 2001), (iv) underdeveloped pollen tube (Pressman et al., 2006; Kafizadeh et al., 2008), (v) inability of stigma to produce pollen due to loss of stigma receptivity (Jagadish et al., 2007), (x) non-functional status of ovule (Gross and Kigel, 1994), (xi) impaired fertilization (Dupuis and Dumas, 1990), (xii) limited embryogenesis (Zinn et al., 2010), and (xiii) reduction in the number of ovule and high rate of ovule abortion (Whittle et al., 2009), leading to poor seed setting (Young et al., 2004). In addition, drought and heat stress acting together were found to be a development accelerator during the reproductive phase of the plant. Thus, the cycle of this phase is shortened and the yield compromised (Boote et al., 2005). However, the responsiveness of food legume crops at reproductive stages such as flowering and pod filling to drought and heat stresses varies (Sung et al., 2003).

7.3.1 Drought and Heat Stress at Flowering and Pod Formation of Legumes

Food legume crops respond alike when subjected to stress treatments. For instance, in a faba bean experiment, genotypes were stressed by withholding water at floral initiation, the number of days to 50% flowering, and when half of the genotypes were podding (Agbicodo et al., 2009). In addition, the levels of photosynthesis, stomatal conductance, leaf water potential, and leaf extension were measured as well. A well-watered set of similar treatment was also included as control. The experiment revealed that early developmental stage of podding was the most sensitive to drought stress and heat stress, thus resulting into 50% reduction in harvest index and seed yields.

7.4 Environmental Resources Utilization by Legumes

7.4.1 Soil Environment

Most food legume crops thrive well in broad types of soil with varied nutrient status and pH ranging from 5.5 to 6.5. However, in the case of legume crops like cowpea, well-drained sandy loams and sandy soils were reported to be the best (Davies and Zhang, 1991). Cowpea flourishes largely under humid conditions. Some genotypes have been reported to be tolerant to heat and water deficit; however, they are sensitive to frost. When soil temperature is above 1.9°C, legume seeds germinate rapidly, whereas lower temperatures were observed to allow slow germination. This is evident when legumes are grown under well-watered and water-stressed conditions or two irrigation regimes (Davies and Zhang, 1991).

7.4.2 Water Use of Legumes

Severe vegetative-stage drought stress is recurrent in the sahelian zone of sub-Saharan Africa (SSA). Consequently, crops that use less water should increasingly become important as one of the strategies to increase food production under such conditions of recurrent drought stress. Research on water use of grain legumes indicated that legumes generally use less water than cereal, tuber, and root crops (Chibarabada et al., 2017). When the growth performance of two food legumes, cowpea (*Vigna unguiculata*) and peanut (*Arachis hypogaea*), and a cereal, pearl millet (*Pennisetum glaucum*), were compared, cowpea was observed to continue to stay green for a long period of time and equally to produce appreciable yield, even though the crops were grown in the same fields under similar condition (Singh and Matsui, 2002).

Water use efficiency (WUE) of crop legumes is usually greater than that of non-legume crops (Chibarabada et al., 2017). Unfortunately, plant breeders seem not to use this knowledge in their breeding program to greatly enhance the WUE of the current agricultural crops.

Thus, WUE is the ratio between assimilation and transpiration:

$$WUE = (P_a - P_i)/(1.6 * (VP_i - VP_a))$$

Where P_a is the partial pressure of CO_2 in the air; P_i partial pressure of CO_2 inside the leaf; VP_i water vapor pressure inside the leaf; and VP_a is water vapor pressure in the air. The term $P_a - P_i$ is the assimilation, and $1.6 * (VP_i - VP_a)$, the transpiration.

WUE is considered at highest point when P_i is low; this reduces plant growth when the air is humid (VP_a high), as well as when air temperatures are low (as in the highlands), and when other factors such as lack of nutrients or leaf diseases and pests are not reducing growth. Genetic variations for WUE in field crops do exist. Thus, WUE could be measured using the ratio of stable C isotopes, C^{13}/C^{12} (Δ) in the plant, which is proportional to P_i/P_a in C_3 plants, itself a reflection of the ratio of assimilatory capacity to stomatal conductance, and hence negatively associated with WUE (Hall et al., 1994). The same general relationship holds for C_4 plants, but the level of discrimination of the isotopes is much lower. Hence, WUE of legume crops can be used by breeders to breed food legumes resilient to climate.

Delayed leaf senescence (DLS), a morphological feature in legumes, could be a trait for development of climate-resilient legume food crops. DLS ensures that the duration of leaf area is extended, thus extending the period of photosynthetic efficiency of the canopy, which might indicate a certain level of drought tolerance at the reproductive stage in erect legume genotypes. Flowering in some cowpea varieties starts at approximately 35 days after planting and producing a yield of 2.0 t/ha of grain in two months. An additional 1.0 t/ha of cowpea grain could be obtained 100 days from planting. This is ascribed to the ability of the legume plant to produce a second flush of pods (Belko et al., 2013).

7.4.3 Effect of Photoperiod

Photoperiod or length of the day has little or no direct effect on leaf appearance of food legumes such as cowpea (Ishiyaku et al., 2005); its effect on other aspects of vegetative growth, branching, and internode elongation have not been reported. In contrast, photoperiod can have a great effect on reproductive development, although some genotypes are unresponsive (Ellis et al., 1994). Cowpea responds to photoperiod in a quantitative way of short-day plants (SDP). Singh and Ntare (1985) reported that longer photoperiodic duration than the critical value did not affect flowering. Thus, day neutral legume genotypes are extensively desired in a breeding program. In contrast, several scientists (Craufurd et al., 1997; Ishiyaku et al., 2005) observed that long photoperiod during reproductive growth reduces flowering and pod production and eventually grain yield in some varieties of cowpea. Craufurd et al. (1997) reported that the neutrality of some legumes to photoperiod with respect to the onset of flowering could then be markedly sensitive with pod production, although it's logical to assume that long days affect legume post-flowering growth and development.

7.5 Consequences of Drought and Heat Stress on Productivity of Legumes

The consequences of drought and heat stress on productivity of food legume crops are expected to worsen. Postel (2000) reported that with the projected rapid expansion of water-stressed areas of the

TABLE 7.2

Effects of Heat Stress on the Development of Various Tissues in Some Legume Crops

Legumes	Heat stress	Impacts on seed setting	References
Chickpea	[a]34/19°C	Reduced number of anther locule, anther epidermis wall thickening, ovule and ovary abnormality	Devasirvatham et al. (2012a, 2013)
	40/25°C 32/20°C	Diminished stigma receptivity, impeded pollen germination, obstruction of pollen tube elongation	Kumar et al. (2013); Kaushal et al. (2011)
Pea	27,30,33,36°C	Pollen germination, pollen tube length, pod length, seed number per pod	Jiang et al. (2015)
Cowpea	33°C	Embryo abortion, anther indehiscence	Warrag and Hall (1984); Ahmed et al. (1992)
Soybean	[a]38/28°C	Thicker exine wall and disintegrated tapetum layer	Djanaguiraman et al. (2012, 2013) Tan et al. (2011)
		Decreased leaf P_n and stomatal conductance (gs); increased thicknesses of the palisade and spongy layers; damaged plasma membrane, chloroplast membrane, and thylakoid membranes; distorted mitochondrial membranes, cristae, and matrix	
Common bean	32/27°C	Lower pollen viability, impaired female performance and pollen germination rate, anther indehiscence	Konsens et al. (1991); Ormrod et al. (1967); Gross and Kigel (1994)
Groundnut	33–48°C	Pollen sterility, retarded pollen tube growth	Prasad et al. (2001)
Lupin	33/28°C	Ovule abortion	Downes and Gladstones (1984)
Lentil	35/20°C >32/20°C	Pod abortion, reduced flower number, shortened flowering period, reduced pollen viability, pollen germination, stigmatic function, ovular viability, pollen tube elongation	Bhandari et al. (2016) Sita et al. (2017a)

Adapted from Liu et al., 2019;
Note
[a]   *Day temperature/Night temperature.*

world from 28–30 countries to 50 countries entails that the livelihood of 3 billion people will be threatened by the year 2030. Liu et al. (2019) reported the effect of heat stress on some male and female tissues of legume food crops and the repercussions on seed setting (Table 7.2). As such, there is a crucial need to introgress genes of drought and heat tolerance in food legume crops; it was established that when drought and heat concurrently and frequently occur, soil salinity also develops as a factor of concern. Thus, improving genotypes with a desirable level of salinity tolerance is an additional breeding objective in those drought-prone areas. Hence, the ideal legume type in the tropics should be tolerant to drought, heat, and salinity.

It is important to develop combiners with desirable root architecture and reduced leaf area with epicuticular waxy coating in order to minimize water loss. Lessons learned from development of food legume crops, such as cowpea, could be deployed in the selection of less tolerant food legumes. For instance, beans could be selected for early maturity and efficiency in the partitioning of assimilates to reproductive structures, including phenotypic plasticity (Afshari et al., 2013).

7.6 Mechanisms of Drought and Heat Stress Tolerance

The ability to withstand drought and heat stress should reflect a balance amid the three mechanisms of escape (avoidance), dehydration avoidance, and tolerance while at the same time supporting appreciable productivity (Agbicodo, 2009). It should be remembered that in the tropics and subtropics drought and heat stress occur together. Hence, Levitt (1972) has for many years recognized avoidance and tolerance as the main mechanisms for heat resistance in plants in general.

7.6.1 Escape (Drought Avoidance)

Escape may be defined as the preparedness of field crops to accomplish their lifespan ahead of the occurrence of severe water deficit. In other words, drought escapers are drought avoiders that mature rapidly before the onset of drought (Agbicodo et al., 2009). Persistent drought incidences in legume-producing areas have resulted into alteration of the planting date of early maturing materials. Legume varieties that are early maturing tend to best escape terminal drought and heat, albeit they are exposed to intermittent drought and heat stress at the vegetative stage; the yield is severely affected. According to Fatokun et al. (2012), intermittent drought and heat stress impedes yield by 50% to 67% in cowpea.

7.6.2 Dehydration and Heat Avoidance

Dehydration avoidance is a measure of an extent to which plant water turgidity status is kept during drought stress. Plants that avoid dehydration may also be called dehydration post-ponders. Heat avoidance, on the other hand, maybe defined as adaptation by plants that effectively reduces the radiation energy build-up in the leaves. Drought-tolerant field crops could maintain leaf turgor through adjustment of osmotic pressure, thereby increasing rate of water uptake and lessening the rate of water loss by stomatal control. The incidence of drought stress during the vegetative phase of crop development was observed to have little effect on grain production when successive conditions at the sites are favorable to encourage recovery. Nevertheless, acute water deficit and heat during floral initiation and the flowering phase can result in almost comprehensive detachment of formed flowers and immature pods, leading to 100% yield loss (Agbicodo et al., 2009).

7.6.3 Tolerance to Drought and Heat (Dehydration Tolerators)

Plants generally may tolerate drought and heat using one or combination of the following adaptations:

7.6.3.1 Morphological Adaptation

Adaptations such as extensive and deep rooting system, leaf rolling, production of epicuticular wax, and orientation of leaves parallel to the incident radiation and high leaf reflectivity enable the plant to avoid dehydration and heat during drought (Odra, 1985). Drought tolerance of legumes by morphological adaptation encompasses adjustment at the tissue, molecular, physiological, and whole plant system. Intrinsic single or combination of changes in legumes determine its ability to withstand moisture stress conditions.

7.6.3.2 Physiological Adaptation

An understanding of the science of physiological adaptation that triggers plants' response to water and heat stress at the physiological level and their adaptive features for responsiveness, tolerance, and resistance entitles and sound knowledge of how those stresses affect plants' performance is important (Campbell et al., 2014). Stomatal control and osmatic adjustment (solute accumulation) are the two physiological mechanisms that enable legume food crops to be resilient in the face of climate change. Odra (1985) reported that these mechanisms do not act independently of each other, in that turgor potentials of the leaf cells are partially or fully maintained by osmatic adjustment during water stress; as a result of this, stomata may also remain open. In the case of heat tolerance, adaptation at whole plant level appears to be related to thermal stability of the chloroplast component and enzymes involved in photosynthesis (Bjorkman et al., 1980).

7.6.3.3 Molecular and Biochemical Adaptation

Understanding gene signalling adaptation to drought and heat stress at the molecular and biochemical level and how this process influences tolerance to drought and resistance to heat stress could lead to development of varieties suitable to withstand such stressors. Yang et al. (2010) found that drought and heat stresses trigger the expression of many genes responsible for bio-chemical metabolism, including key enzymes, transcription factors, hormones, amino acids, and carbohydrates. The most triggered are phytohormone, abscisic acid (ABA), proline, tryptophan, late embryogenesis abundant (LEA) proteins, trehalose, raffinose, mannitol, glycine-betaine, and superoxide dismutase (Nguyen and Blum, 2004). Gosal et al. (2009) found that several hundred genes are either induced or repressed during drought stress. These biomolecules are involved in dehydration avoidance or dehydration tolerance events such as osmotic adjustment, membrane stabilization, anti-oxidation, scavenging of reactive oxygen species (ROS), and gene regulation (Ashraf, 2010; Yang et al., 2010). Gene(s) linked with drought tolerance have enhanced our understanding of this complex phenomenon. Knowing the genetics of drought tolerance and identifying quantitative trait loci (QTLs) linked with DNA markers help breeders to develop high-yielding drought-tolerant genotypes (Khan et al., 2010).

7.7 Breeding Approaches for Combating Drought and Heat Stress

Several legume breeders have established key challenges in improvement of drought- and heat-tolerant crops (Blum, 2011). These challenges are: timing (growth stages), genetic diversity, intensity of drought and heat stress, low heritability and quantitative/polygenic nature of drought and heat responsive traits, epistatic QTL interactions, genotype and environment interaction, and concomitant occurrences of biotic and abiotic factors. Genetics of drought and heat tolerance/sensitivity is complex, with the associated traits being complex and polygenic, making the task of developing drought- and heat-tolerant genotypes difficult. However, the current high-throughput technologies to carry out precise phenotyping, dissection of the plant genome through transcriptomics, proteomics, metabolomics, genotyping, and SNP (Single Nucleotide Polymorphism) chip assay, and bioinformatics software bring optimism to identify drought- and heat-tolerant food legume crops. Therefore, recent technologies such as high-throughput phenotyping, next generation sequencing (NGS), and genetic engineering should be utilized for drought-tolerance improvement in wheat (Mwadzingeni et al., 2015), which can be used to breed drought-tolerant legume varieties.

7.7.1 Physiological Breeding Approach

Breeders can opt to focus on high yield under optimum conditions, to focus on high yield under actual drought conditions, or to improve drought tolerance in high-yielding genotypes (Danquah and Blay, 1999). Breeding for drought and heat tolerance entails two approaches: conventional and molecular approaches. As water deficit levels rise, the interaction between genotype and water-deficit diverse plant traits that influence yield is affected. As a result, the pathway involved in the interaction could be explored significantly in the development of the drought-tolerant population. Nevertheless, this approach is variedly not optimal because of the polygenic nature of the yield, high influence of genotype × environment interaction, and low heritability (Babu et al., 2003).

Cattivelli et al. (2008) confirmed that having in-depth knowledge of the physiological and molecular basis of drought tolerance in the field crop of interest may aid the breeder in identifying the core traits that influence yield. Thus, this window of opportunity will be a huge asset to the traditional breeding program, and it will accelerate the pace of crop improvement. Undoubtedly, with the advancement in molecular biology platforms, the ability to locate and sequence genes of interest is enhanced. Efficient utilization of the molecular tool in the introgression of quantitative trait loci (QTL) and even selection or genetic transformation of hard-to-introgress desired quantitative trait loci strongly depends on plant breeders' sound thoughtful insight on the yield-determining physiological procedures (Araus et al., 2002). When screening for drought tolerance, there is a need to investigate many traits, and they can be measured at different levels: physiological, biochemical, and morphological (Hamidou et al., 2007). Several screening tests and methods are used to estimate drought tolerance and water-use efficiency. The most common ones are wooden boxes, pots, hydroponic, and field screenings (Singh et al., 1999; Ogbonnaya et al., 2003). Regularly measured traits under drought conditions are the leaf area index, chlorophyll stability index, relative water content, leaf water potentials, carbon isotope discrimination, and root/shoot ratio (Singh et al., 1999). Evidently, developing drought- and heat-tolerant genotypes could be through classical breeding approaches. Relying on water-use efficiency of the genotypes is the most common and early plant responsiveness to drought stress conditions. Genotypes exhibit considerable variations for water-use efficiency, thus validating that it is a gene-linked trait. Taiz and Zeiger (2002) observed that drought-tolerant genotypes have reduced transpiration through reduction of the leaf area or restriction of the stomatal opening or both and concurrently without much effect on the biomass production (Taiz and Zeiger, 2002).

Costa et al. (1997) reported that genotypes that are unable to reduce water loss and adjust their organ size or maintain biomass production under water-limited conditions are susceptible. They have considerably reduced water-use efficiency. Condon et al. (2004) pronounced key procedures to be considered in water-use efficiency hybridization in crops. These three processes are: (i) enhancing level of available water uptake, (ii) boosting production of biomass per unit of water transpired, and (iii) dividing of biomass produced in the harvested product.

7.7.2 DNA Marker-Assisted Selection

The whole plant crop genomes are involved in population development when using conventional breeding and then identification and selection of outstanding recombinants from amid many segregating populations. This traditional approach is cumbersome and time consuming, demanding several crosses, generations, and cautious field evaluation. Occurrence of tight linkage of unwanted traits with the wanted loci makes the process hard for a breeder to accomplish a wished breeding outcome. The advent of molecular biology resulted in the development of advanced technologies, such as numerous molecular breeding strategies and types of molecular markers that offer opportunities to geneticists and breeders to overcome many of the difficulties encountered when utilizing conventional breeding approach.

Khan et al. (2010) reported that field crop adaptation to drought stress is a multiplex trait governed by several genes or QTLs of small effects. Several researchers embrace the fact that breeding for drought tolerance necessitates amalgamation of both traditional and molecular approaches (Chaves et al., 2003; Blum, 2011).

Efforts to develop drought-tolerant genotypes in the past were obstructed by the polygenic nature of the traits as well as lack of in-depth knowledge of the physiological mechanisms influencing yield in water-deficit conditions (Passioura, 2002). The molecular approach or genomics offered an exceptional opportunity for examination of quantitative traits into their single genetic determinants (QTLs), which consequently laid the foundation of genetic engineering (Salvi and Tuberosa, 2005) and marker-assisted selection (Morgante and Salamini, 2003). Use of molecular markers in plant breeding for drought tolerance can be divided into three core categories:

a. Characterization of germplasm finger printing.
b. Recognition and characterization of genome regions (QTLs) associated in the expression of the desired trait, and
c. Accelerated crop improvement via marker-assisted selection (MAS) approach.

From advancement in the molecular biology have emerged new scientific disciplines such as plant functional genomics. This discipline focuses on the study of gene functions. As a result, substantial progress has been made in area of sequencing plant genomes, including sequencing of approximately 620 Mbp cowpea genomes. The other advents in plant breeding molecular approaches are detection of genome-wide SNP by means of genotype by sequencing (GBS), genetic diversity analysis of a worldwide germplasm, using genome-wide association (GWAS), and SNP markers linked to morpho-agronomic trait identification, ability to withstand biotic incidences, as well as tolerance to abiotic stress. When breeding for seed quality in cowpea, marker-assisted and genome-wide selection are the best tools a breeder can rely on for selection. Selection of some agronomic traits such as plant growth habit, dry pod coloration, pod placement, mature seed pattern, color of seed coat, eye pattern color, flower color, seed protein, and sugar contents are possible through GWAS (genome-wide association selection). Muchero et al. (2013) reported that SNP markers are also being identified for these agronomic traits: grain (seed) yield, 100-seed weight, and seed size. In addition, SNPs could be used to identify traits associated with biotic and abiotic (disease and pest) resistance/tolerance to cowpea wilt (*Fusarium oxysporum* f. sp. tracheiphilum), cowpea mosaic virus (CPMV), bacterial blight (*Xanthomonas axonopodis* pv. vignicola), cowpea aphid *Aphis craccivora*), iron deficiency chlorosis (IDC), and low phosphorus uptake efficiency.

7.8 Legume Floral Traits and Early Maturity

The most critical stage influencing the yield of cowpea is flowering. The onset of drought stress was found to influence pod setting, its number per plant, as well as number of seeds per locule (Singh et al., 1997). Hall and Patel (1985) reported that erect cowpea genotypes that flower in 30 days after planting in the tropics have proved useful in some dry environments. This is attributed to the capability of genotypes to escape drought stress. Subsequently, these types of genotypes may be more sensitive to midseason drought (intermittent) than medium cycle spreading genotypes. Occurrence of drought stress at floral bud formation or flowering usually results in floral abortion or barrenness. Reduction in assimilate flux below some threshold level to the developing pods that is deemed necessary for growth and optimal grain filling is one of the major causes of abortion or barrenness (Martinez et al., 2003). However, in cowpea, when the flowering stage coincides with drought stress, seed yield is reduced by 100% (Agbicodo et al., 2009).

7.8.1 Genetics of Early Maturity in Food Legume Crops

Xu et al. (2009) reported that, early maturing food legume crops such as cowpea produce pods that mature in about 55 days, and this pattern of maturity is essential in addressing the hunger gap period in sub-Saharan African countries. Ojomo (1971) studied the inheritance of flowering in cowpea, by crossing an exotic early flowering genotypes to local late flowering genotypes, and found that flowering date was governed by two major gene pairs; early flowering being dominant over late flowering. Ishiyaku et al. (2005) reported that earliness is under polygenic control with additives × additive (I), additive × dominance (j), dominance × dominance.

The genetics of earliness heritability is estimated using a simple statistical method that measures variance (phenotypic) among the F_2 population developed from the hybridization process between two sets of districted parental lines. Thus, the overall phenotypic variance among the F_2 population is made up of both the genotypic and environmental variances (Xu et al., 2009). Furthermore, they explained that an estimated mean of the phenotypic variance among plants of the parental lines could be used to compute environmental variance. In addition, they stated that the difference between the phenotypic variance and environmental variance of the F_2 individuals was the genetic variance.

Estimated heritability may be defined as the ratio of the genetic variance to the total phenotypic variance. It is worth mention that this type of analysis has narrow inference space simply because it solely depends on the genetic differences between two selected inbred lines. Hence, making this type of heritability is not suitable and cannot be generalized to other populations (Lynch and Walsh, 1998). The most used computation method is the method that estimates broad-sense heritability with large inference space. This way of estimating heritability does not need any hybridization procedure. It can be carried out by analyzing multiple lines for traits of performance using simple analysis of variance (Singh and Chaudhary, 1985).

7.8.2 Genetics of Drought and Heat Tolerance in Food Legumes

As a breeder, having fair knowledge of genes controlling traits of interest is essential, and it's applicable to any crop improvement program (Table 7.3). Hinkossa et al. (2013) reported that having information

TABLE 7.3

Chromosomal Distribution of Genes Controlling Tolerance to Abiotic Stresses (*Adapted from* Richard and Wang, 2020)

Plant Species	Genes	Stress	Mechanisms	Chromosome	Chromosome Arm			Reference
					Distal	proximal	Total	
Soybean (*Glycine max*)	calmodulin binding transcription activator gene (*GmCAMTA*)	Drought	Calmodulin-binding Ca-CaM-CAMTA-mediated stress regulatory mechanisms	8 out of 20 (5, 7, 8, 9, 11, 15, 17, 18)	10	5	15	Noman et al. (2019)
Cotton (*Gossypium hirsutum*)	nodule inception-like protein (*GhNLP*) genes	Nitrogen deficiency	Promoters of NLP genes interact with stress-associated transcription factors and are targeted by many miRNAs	All 26	91	14	105	Magwanga et al. (2019)
Cucumber (*Cucumis sativus* L.)	GAGA-binding BASIC PENTACYSTEINE (BPC) transcription factor genes (*CsBPCs*)	Salt, drought, cold, heat, ABA, SA, JA, ETH, 2,4-D, GA	Germination, growth and development, as well as responses to abiotic stresses and plant hormones	3 of 7 (2, 5, 7)	3	1	4	Li et al. (2019)
Carnation (*Dianthus caryophyllus*)	Heat shock transcription factors (Hsfs)	Heat, drought, cold, salt, ABA, SA	Promoters included various cis-acting elements that were related to stress, hormones, as well as development processes, controlling reactive oxygen species homeostasis, and ABA-mediated stress signaling	17 scaffolds	10	7	17	Li et al. (2019)
Cotton (*Gossypium hirsutum*)	Histone Acetyltransferase (HAT) Gene family	Salt, drought, cold, heavy metal, DNA damage, ABA, NAA	Affects cotton growth, fiber development, and stress adaptation by regulation of chromatin structure, activates the gene transcription implicated in various cellular processes	8 of 26 (A-5,6,8,11 and D-5,6,10,11)	16	2	18	Imran et al. (2019)
Chinese kale (*Brassica oleracea*)	Multi-protein bridging factor (MBF) 1c (*BocMBF1c*)	Heat stress: cellular response to hypoxia, ethylene-activated signaling pathway, positive regulation of transcription, DNA-templated response to abscisic acid heat, and water deprivation	BocMBF1c contains three heat shock elements (HSEs) and helix-turn-helix (HTH) domains, regulating ABRFs, SA, trehalose, and ET thermal resistance-related pathways by binding with CTAGA, including DREB2A	not presented; ortholog on chromosome 3 of *Arabidopsis thaliana*[*]	-; 0	-; 1*	-; 1*	Zou et al. (2019)
Soybean (*Glycine max*)	Pentatricopeptide-repeat (PPR) proteins DYW subgroup genes; *GmPPR4*	Drought and salt	Delayed leaf rolling; higher content of proline (Pro); and lower contents of H_2O_2, O_2, and malondialdehyde (MDA); increased transcripts of several drought-inducible genes	all 20 chromosomes; *GmPPR4* is on chromosome 1 distal end	143	36	179	Su et al. (2019)
Arabidopsis thaliana	Stress-Responsive NAC Transcription Factor (*LlNAC2*) of tiger lily	Cold, drought, salt stresses, and abscisic acid (ABA)	DREB1/ZFHD4/CBF-COR interaction and ABA signaling pathways	1S (in *Arabidopsis*)	1	0	1	Yong et al. (2019)

(Continued)

TABLE 7.3 (Continued)

Chromosomal Distribution of Genes Controlling Tolerance to Abiotic Stresses *(Adapted from Richard and Wang, 2020)*

Plant Species	Genes	Stress	Mechanisms	Chromosome	Distal	proximal	Total	Reference
Arabidopsis thaliana	MYB-related homolog (*LlMYB3*) of tiger lily	Cold, drought, and salt stresses, ABA treatment	LlCHS2 and anthocyanin biosynthesis pathway	5L (in *Arabidopsis*)	1	0	1	Yong et al. (2019)
Soybean (*Glycine max*)	four QTLs for resistance to high-intensity UV-B irradiation (UVBR12-1, 6-1, 10-1, and 14-1)	UV-B irradiation (high light, heat, dehydration)	Possibly, actin-binding spectrin like protein interacting with membrane phosphoinositides in cellular signaling for defense	12, 6, 10, and 14	2	2	4	Yoon et al. (2019)
Woodland Strawberry (*Fragaria vesca*)	Gibberellin-Insensitive (GAI), Repressor of GAI-3 (RGA) and SCARECROW (SCR) protein (*FveGRAS*) genes	Cold, heat, and GA3 treatments	Stolon formation, fruit ripening, and abiotic stresses	All 7	25	10	35	Chen et al. (2019)
Arabidopsis thaliana	N-MYC Downregulated Like Proteins (NDL1, NDL2, NDL3) interacting with ANN1, SLT1, OAS-TL, ARS27A, RGS1, AGB1 genes	Heat, cold, dehydration, DNA damage, reducing agent, increased intracellular calcium, metal ions like cadmium, nickel and cobalt, hormones	N-MYC Downregulated Like Proteins (NDLs) interacting with G-Proteins in signal transduction in response to drought, heat, salinity, and light intensity	All 5	5	4	9	Katiyar and Mudgil, 2019
Soybean (*Glycine max*)	calmodulin binding transcription activator gene (*GmCAMTA*)	Drought	Calmodulin-binding Ca-CaM-CAMTA-mediated stress regulatory mechanisms	8 out of 20 (5, 7, 8, 9, 11, 15, 17, 18)	10	5	15	Noman et al. (2019)
Cotton (*Gossypium hirsutum*)	nodule inception-like protein (*GhNLP*) genes	Nitrogen deficiency	Promoters of NLP genes interact with stress-associated transcription factors and are targeted by many miRNAs	All 26	91	14	105	Magwanga et al. (2019)
Cucumber (*Cucumis sativus* L.)	GAGA-binding BASIC PENTACYSTEINE (BPC) transcription factor genes (*CsBPCs*)	Salt, drought, cold, heat, ABA, SA, JA, ETH, 2,4-D, GA	Germination, growth and development, as well as responses to abiotic stresses and plant hormones	3 of 7 (2, 5, 7)	3	1	4	Li et al. (2019)
Carnation (*Dianthus caryophyllus*)	Heat shock transcription factors (Hsfs)	Heat, drought, cold, salt, ABA, SA	Promoters Yangincluded various cis-acting elements that were related to stress, hormones, as well as development processes, controlling reactive oxygen species homeostasis, and ABA-mediated stress signaling	17 scaffolds	10	7	17	Li et al. (2019)
Cotton (*Gossypium hirsutum*)	Histone Acetyltransferase (HAT) Gene family	Salt, drought, cold, heavy metal, DNA damage, ABA, NAA	Affects cotton growth, fiber development, and stress adaptation by regulation of chromatin structure, activates the gene transcription implicated in various cellular processes	8 of 26 (A-5,6,8,11 and D-5,6,10,11)	16	2	18	Imran et al. (2019)

Species	Gene/protein	Stress/treatment	Findings	Genomic distribution				Reference
Chinese kale (*Brassica oleracea*)	multi-protein bridging factor (MBF) 1c (*BocMBF1c*)	Heat stress: cellular response to hypoxia, ethylene-activated signaling pathway, positive regulation of transcription, DNA-templated response to abscisic acid heat, and water deprivation	BocMBF1c contains three heat shock elements (HSEs) and helix-turn-helix (HTH) domains, regulating ABRFs, SA, trehalose, and ET thermal resistance-related pathways by binding with CTAGA, including *DREB2A*[*]	not presented; ortholog on chromosome 3 of *Arabidopsis thaliana*[*]	-; 0	-; 1 [*]	-; 1 [*]	Zou et al. (2019)
Soybean (*Glycine max*)	Pentatricopeptide-repeat (PPR) proteins DYW subgroup genes; *GmPPR4*	Drought and salt	Delayed leaf rolling; higher content of proline (Pro); and lower contents of H_2O_2, O_2, and malondialdehyde (MDA); increased transcripts of several drought-inducible genes	all 20 chromosomes; *GmPPR4* is on chromosome 1 distal end	143	36	179	Su et al. (2019)
Oilseed rape (*Brassica napus*)	Fructose-1,6-bisphosphate aldolase (FBA) gene family (*BnaFBA*)	Salt, heat, drought, *Sclerotinia sclerotiorum* infection, and strigolactones (SLs) treatments	Processes of glycolysis, gluconeogenesis, and Calvin cycle; Various cis-acting regulatory elements existed within the promoter regions of *BnaFBA* genes	19 on 15 *B. napus* chromosomes; 3 others to 2 random chromosomes (two on the An chromosomes and one on the Cn chromosome)	7	15	22	Zhao et al. (2019)
Soybean (*Glycine max*)	Calcium-dependent protein kinases (CDPKs) genes; *GmCDPK3*[*]	Drought and salt	Increased proline (Pro) and chlorophyll contents and decreased malondialdehyde (MDA) content	12 of 20 (1 to 6, 10, 11, 14, 16, 18, 19)	14; 1 [*]	3	17	Wang et al. (2019a)
Radish (*Raphanus sativus*)	Lipoxygenases (LOXs) gene family *RsLOX*	Abiotic (drought, salinity, heat, and cold) and biotic (*Plasmodiophora brassicae* infection) stress conditions	Three tandem-clustered RsLOX genes are involved in response to various environmental stresses via the jasmonic acid pathway	5 of 9 (2, 5, 7, 8, 9)	5	6	11	Wang et al. (2019b)

Int. J. Mol. Sci. 2020, 21, 1820; doi:10.3390/ijms21051820

about the effect and magnitude of gene action governing traits of interest must be well understood and determined. Traits such as drought tolerance and yield are polygenic. They are controlled by numerous genes and affected by environmental factors that are not transmissible from parents to offspring. It is, therefore, necessary to determine the genetic factors conditioning these traits in order to establish an efficient breeding program.

Singh and Chaudhary (1985) reported that there are three types of gene effects: additive, dominance, and epistatic. Dominance and epistatic constitute the non-additive part. The dominance gene effect can either be ambidirectional, a condition where numerous genes impact phenotype, or unidirectional, dominance in one direction or positive and negative dominance at different gene loci (Kearsey and Pooni, 1996). Interaction of alleles at different loci is known as epistasis. There are two concepts about epistatic gene action. Thus, it's important for both plant breeders and biostatisticians to distinguish between the concepts of statistical epistasis and physiological epistasis. Physiological epistasis is referred to as the effect of interactions between loci on the phenotype of an individual. This type of epistasis is a property of genotypes, and its values are independent of gene frequency. Moreover, statistical epistasis is the genetic variance within a population that can be attributed to interactions among loci. This type of epistasis is a population-level phenomenon and unlike previous epistasis; this latter epistasis changes as gene frequencies change. At some gene frequencies, there may be physiological epistasis, but no statistical epistasis. The other scenario is, if there is statistical epistasis, there must also be physiological epistasis (Goodnight, 1995).

The effects of additive genes are reflected in the extent to which offspring are likely to have resemblance to their parents, as reflected in narrow–sense heritability (Derera, 2005). Estimation of relative proportion of additive genetic effects (or general combining ability of a line, GCA) and non–additive genetic effects (or specific combining ability of a population, SCA) controlling the drought adaptive traits and their interactions with the environment is useful for designing a breeding program and assembling germplasm for population advancement (Shahi and Singh, 1985). Thus, generated information about GCA and SCA of parental lines is statistically helpful and aids in the interpretation of the genetic basis of the underlying inheritance pattern of the trait of interest. It estimates the mean performance of generations in the series of hybrid combination (GCA) and the contribution of a line to hybrid performance in a cross with a specific line in relation to its contribution in crosses with an array of other lines (SCA). Several researchers, such as Acquaah (2012) and Alidu et al. (2013), reported a significant GCA effect for cowpea grain yield under drought stress condition, suggesting that yield under drought can be improved by exploiting the multitude of additive gene effects. Ayo-Vaughan et al. (2013) in a separate study on combining ability for pod and seed traits in cowpea reported that additive gene effects significantly controlled the number of pods per plant, pod length, the number of seeds per pod, and 100-seed weight.

As a notable feature in self–pollinating crops such as cowpea, accurate identification of parental combinations required for generation of superior pure lines for farmers to adopt is very crucial to the success of the breeding program. Several studies have been dedicated to developing and evaluating methods of envisaging cross potential in early generations (Thurling and Ratinam, 1987). Several scientists (Khan et al., 2010; Acquaah, 2012; Nduwumuremyi et al., 2013) reported that proper choice of mating designs and selection of suitable parental lines are imperative to rewarding crop improvement schemes depending on a number of factors, such as objectives of the study, cost, time, space, and other biological limitations.

Singh and Chaudhary (1985) define mating design as a procedure of producing progenies on which further selection will be carried out. Theoretically and practically, plant breeders and geneticists use diverse types of mating designs and activities for targeted purposes. The outstanding importance of mating designs are: (1) provision of data on the gene controlling trait being studied; (2) population development to be used as the basis for selection and advancement of progenies into prospective varieties; (3) estimation of genetic gain; and (4) provision of data required for evaluation of the parental lines used in the improvement program (Acquaah, 2012; Nduwumuremyi et al., 2013). Thus, combining ability is the capacity of an individual to transmit superior traits to its progenies. Hence, it is the gene governing the trait of interest to be improved. GCA is referred to as the average performance of a genotype in a series of hybrid combinations and is attributed to additive gene action. Whereas SCA is defined as cases in which certain hybrid combinations are better or poorer than expected based on the mean performance of the parental lines. The estimation of general combining ability for a genotype is governed by the mating design, but essentially, it is the deviance of the progeny average from the mean of the parental lines evaluated (Acquaah, 2012). As a matter of fact, there is limited information on the combining ability of lines that have been previously used in the cowpea breeding program in the International Institute of Tropical Agriculture (IITA) for the development of drought-tolerant lines and Centro Internacional de Agricultura Tropical (CIAT) working of heat-tolerant grain legumes. Richard and Wang (2020) reported the number of genes conferring drought tolerance in different crops and presented their functions and mechanisms (Table 7.3). This has resulted in the tremendously slow phase of developing improved and drought-tolerant cowpea genotypes (Agbicodo et al., 2009).

7.9 Seed Traits and Grain Quality

Globally, drought and temperature stress (heat and cold) in the era of climate change are the most common abiotic stresses affecting production of food legumes (Toker and Mutlu, 2011). The negative effects of drought and temperature stress vary from one region to the other, depending on timing, duration, and intensity (Serraj et al., 2004; Hall, 2012). It is known that the key objective of any legume crop improvement targets yield; thus, plant breeders address this by breeding varieties that are early maturing and drought and heat tolerant with acceptable grain quality; resistant to some important diseases and pests; and have significant high grain yields (Ehlers and Hall, 1996). Grain yield is the primary trait of interest, although several secondary traits contribute to final yields. Contribution of various seed traits varies significantly; therefore, identification of traits with their level of contribution into seed yield might help breeders in selection of high-yielding cowpea varieties. A breeding program aimed at increasing yield under stress conditions should consider the correlation between yield and yield components through estimation of genotypic and phenotypic relationships. Arun et al. (2018) summarized Table 7.4 the adaptive traits that could be used by legume breeders for development of abiotic tolerant and resistant food legume varieties. These associations could help in formulation of selection indices that aid in crop improvement programs.

TABLE 7.4

Adaptive Traits Related to Abiotic Stresses in Legume Crops (*Adapted from* Arun et al., 2018)

Stress	Trait	Crop
Drought	High water use efficiency	Alfalfa, faba bean
	Vigorous root growth	Alfalfa, chickpea
	Osmolyte accumulation/osmotic adjustment/turgor maintenance	Alfalfa, faba bean
	Accumulation of antioxidants	Alfalfa
	Increased leaf cuticular wax	Alfalfa
	Early flowering/maturity	Chickpea, common bean, cowpea, faba bean, lentil
	Low leaf conductance/stomatal regulation/transpiration	Faba bean
	Delayed leaf senescence	Alfalfa
	Changed leaf orientation	Soybean
	Reduced canopy temperature	Chickpea, faba bean, soybean
	Relative water content	Faba bean
Salinity	Accumulation of osmolytes/osmotic adjustment/turgor maintenance	Field pea
Flooding	High stomatal conductance	Lentil
	Large air-spaces and aerenchyma in roots	Lentil, field pea, soybean

(Continued)

TABLE 7.4 (Continued)

Adaptive Traits Related to Abiotic Stresses in Legume Crops (*Adapted from* Arun et al., 2018)

Stress	Trait	Crop
Heat	Increased pollen germination under stress	Field pea
	Reduced canopy temperature	Chickpea
	Accumulation of leaf cuticular wax	Field pea
	Early flowering/maturity	Lentil, field pea, chickpea
	Indeterminate growth habit	Field pea, chickpea
Cold	Presence of dehydrin protein	Cowpea
	Increased osmoprotectants	Faba bean
	Increased fatty acid desaturation of membrane lipids	Faba bean
	Maintenance of photosynthesis	Field pea

7.10 Breeding for Resistance to Bacterial, Fungal, and Viral Diseases

Development of genotypes with a high level of resistance to bacterial and fungal diseases has been the focus of most food legume improvement programs per country for years. The success in developing varieties resistant to bacterial and fungal diseases depends on the availability of good sources of resistance, an accurate disease scoring method, and the mode of resistance inheritance. Backcrossing is desired if the gene conditioning resistance to the disease is conferred by single genes. However, introgression of quantitative resistance governed by several minor genes/QTLs is challenging. For instance, with monogenic resistances individuals carrying the gene are easily identified in breeding populations, whereas quantitative polygenic traits, which are usually highly influenced by environment and genotype, cannot be easily identified using phenotype. As a result, most of the available resistant food legume varieties are developed through introgression of major genes, although some successes have been obtained in some polygenic resistances (Rubiales et al., 2015). For instance, resistance against bacterial wilt incited by *Ralstonia solanacearum* is considered essential in groundnut (Jiang et al., 2007). Although available resistant cultivars have relatively low yields with poor resistance or tolerance to other constraints, such as foliar diseases and drought, there is prospect for exploitation of these sources of resistance to breed for bacterial wilt resistance (Jiang et al., 2013). Resistance to *R. solanacearum* in *M. truncatula* is governed by major QTL located on chromosome 5 (Vailleau et al., 2007). Comparison of parental line sequences revealed 15 candidate genes with sequence polymorphisms, but no evidence of differential gene expression upon infection.

   Resistance to pea seed-borne mosaic virus has been reported in pea, and several recessive resistance genes have been identified (Hagedorn and Gritton, 1973; Khetarpal et al., 1990). Molecular markers associated with the resistance gene are now available (Gao et al., 2004). Resistances to pea enation mosaic virus, white lupin mosaic virus, and bean yellow mosaic virus have also been reported (Provvidenti and Hampton, 1993; Yu et al., 1995, 1996). Resistances to bean yellow mosaic virus and bean leaf roll virus have been identified in faba bean (Gadh and Bernier, 1984; Bond et al., 1994; Kumari and Makkouk, 2003).

7.11 Breeding for Resistance to Nematodes

Nematodes severely impede food legume production globally. Thus, developing a legume population with the level of resistance against nematode is promising. However, the breakdown of the resistance normally occurs when other pathogens exist in the same field. In chickpea, Sasser and Freckman (1987) reported that globally, the loss of productivity due to plant parasitic nematodes was estimated to be 14%. However, important effective integrated control of plant-parasitic nematodes in cropping systems are:

(a) correct diagnosis of the nematode species, (b) effective rotations with non-hosts or fallow periods, and (c) use of tolerant and resistant crop genotypes (Thompson et al., 2000). Accurate diagnosis of nematode species requires extensive knowledge of nematode taxonomy and/or application of molecular diagnostic tools. Options for crop rotations are restricted in fields that are infested with nematode species with wide host ranges (Greco, 1987). Application of nematicides is avoided due to environmental and economic reasons. The most effective and sustainable long-term strategy to overcome constraints to chickpea production caused by plant-parasitic nematodes is the use of resistant cultivars. Resistance is the ability of a plant to reduce nematode reproduction such that no nematode reproduction occurs in a highly resistant plant, a low level of reproduction occurs in a moderately resistant plant, and unhindered nematode reproduction occurs in a susceptible plant (Roberts et al., 2005). Tolerance is a separately measured trait that characterizes the ability of a plant to grow and yield well even when infested with nematodes (Trudgill, 1991). Growing resistant genotypes have the advantage of preventing nematode reproduction and reducing yield losses in the current crop. Moreover, after growing resistant cultivars, nematode populations residual in the soil to damage subsequent crops are less than after susceptible cultivars, thus benefiting the whole farming system. Advances in chickpea genomic resources resulting from the advent of next generation sequencing (NGS) technology, has the potential to greatly assist molecular breeding approaches to improve resistance to plant-parasitic nematodes and thereby help in achieving the yield potential of chickpea (Thudi et al., 2012). Recent reviews highlight the application of gene-editing technologies to control plant-parasitic nematodes (Leonetti et al., 2018) and improvements in chickpea genetic transformation technologies (Amer et al., 2019).

7.12 Breeding for Resistance to Insect Pests and Parasitic Weeds

The genetic control of resistance to insect pests ranges from monogenic and oligogenic, precisely for insects such as *Callosobruchus chinensis* and *Callosobruchus maculatus* in mungbean (Redden et al., 1983; Chen et al., 2007; and Somta et al., 2007), to polygenic level of resistance in *Pisum fulvum* accessions to pea weevil (*Bruchus pisorum*) Somta et al., 2007, and Somta et al., 2008). The presence of α-amylase variants of polypeptide inhibitors in seeds of haricot bean were found to be linked with arcelin and inherited as single co-dominant gene (Suzuki et al., 1995). It was found that mostly additive and dominant genes condition insect pest resistance in many legume crops (Somta et al., 2006; Somta et al., 2007 and Somta et al., 2008). However, in some instances, cytoplasmic gene effects are also found to influence resistance to insect pests (Redden et al., 1983 and Somta et al., 2006; Somta et al., 2007). Based on that, it is evidently clear that, different breeding methods may be deployed to tackle different improvement objectives. For instance, when seed resistance is under cytoplasmic gene effects, then the backcross method is more relevant for introgression of the cytoplasm gene from the donor parent into the receipt parent denoted as the female (Singh, 2002). In such a case, allowances for one more generation is also required in order to test the preceding generation; third generation F_3 seeds from F_2 plants are required to test F_2 segregation.

The major sources of genetic variation for improving resistance against insect pests, like many other biotic stresses, include assembly of germplasm from local sources, introduction and acquisition of germplasm from exotic sources, and recombinants resulting from crossings of selected parents of all sources. These basic selection methods—mass, bulk, pedigree and backcross methods, and/or their modifications—may be applied depending on the mode of inheritance and the number of genes controlling resistance under a given condition.

Breeding for resistance to parasitic weeds is among the major crop improvement programs as a result of change in climate. For instance, cowpea production in the Sahelian zone of SSA is prone to parasitic weed infestation. Thus, one of the improvement mandates is to develop cowpea varieties with resistance to *Striga gesnerioides* and *Alectra vogueli*. Some resistant cowpea were identified and released to farmers (Singh et al., 1993). Li and Timko (2009) found a gene-for-gene interaction has been demonstrated in *S. gesnerioides* cowpea interaction, and molecular markers associated with race-specific resistance genes have been identified; several sequence-confirmed amplified regions (SCARs) have also been developed (Li and Timko, 2009).

REFERENCES

Acquaah, G. 2012. Principles of plant genetics and breeding. Second Edition. John Wiley and Sons, LTD., Publication.

Afshari, M., F. Shekari, R. Azimkhani, H. Habibiand, and M.H. Fotokian. 2013. Effects of foliar application of salicylic acid on growth and physiological aattributes of cowpea under water stress conditions. *Iran Agricultural Research*, 32(1): 55–69.

Agbicodo, E.M. 2009. Genetic analysis of abiotic and biotic resistance in cowpea [(Vigna unquiculata L) Walp.] PhD Thesis. ISBN 9789085854777.

Agbicodo, E.M., C.A. Fatokun, S. Muranaka, R.G.F. Visser, and C.G. Linden van der. 2009. Breeding drought tolerant cowpea: Constraints, accomplishments, and future prospects. *Euphytica*, 167: 353–370.

Ahmed, F.E., A.E. Hall, and D.A. DeMason, 1992. Heat injury during floral development in cowpea (*Vigna unguiculata, Fabaceae*). *American Journal of Botany*, 79: 784–791. doi: 10.1002/j.1537-2197.1992.tb13655.x

Alidu, M.S., R. Akromah, and I.D.K. Atokple. 2013. Genetic analysis of vegetative-stage drought tolerance in cowpea. *Greener Journal of Agricultural Sciences*, 3(6): 476–491.

Amer, A., G. Mohamed, V. Pantaleo, P. Leonetti, and M.S. Hanafy. 2019. In vitro regeneration through organogenesis in Egyptian chickpea. *Plant Bio-systems*, 835–842. doi: 10.1080/11263504.2018.1549616

Araus, J.L. 2002. Plant breeding and drought in C3 cereals: What should we breed for? *Annals of Botany*, 89(7): 925–940.

Arun, S.K.S., K. Udhaya, J. Yunfei, A.D. Ketema, and Y.G. Linda. 2018. Physiology based approaches for breeding of next-generation food legumes. Plants, 7(3): 1–20. doi: 10.3390/plants7030072. www.mdpi.com/journal/plants

Ashraf, M. 2010. Inducing drought tolerance in plants: Recent advances. *Biotechnology Advances*, 28: 169–183.

Ayo-Vaughan, M.A., O.J. Ariyo, I.O. Daniel, and C.O. Alake. 2013. Combining ability and genetic components for pod and seed traits in cowpea lines. *Italian Journal of Agronomy*, 8(2): 73–78.

Babu, R.C., B.D. Nguyen, V.P. Chamarerk, P. Shanmugasundaram, P. Chezhian, S.K. Jeyaprakash, A. Ganesh, S. Palchamy, S. Sadasivam, S. Sarkarung, L.J. Wade, and H.T. Nguyen. 2003. Genetic analysis of drought resistance in rice by molecular markers. *Crop Science*, 43: 1457–1469.

Belko, N., M. Zaman-Allah, N.N. Diop, N. Cisse, G. Zombre, J.D. Ehlers, and V. Vadez. 2013. Restriction of transpiration rate under high vapour pressure deficit and non-limiting water conditions is important for terminal drought tolerance in cowpea. *Plant Biology*, 15: 304–316.

Bhandari, K., K.H.M. Siddique, N.C. Turner, J. Kaur, S. Singh, S.K. Agrawal, et al. 2016. Heat stress at reproductive stage disrupts leaf carbohydrate metabolism, impairs reproductive function, and severely reduces seed yield in lentil. *Journal of Crop Improvement*, 30: 118–151. doi: 10.1080/15427528.2015.1134744

Bjorkman, O., M.R. Badger, and P.A. Armond. 1980. Response and adaptation of photosynthesis to high temperatures, in Adaptation of plants to water and high temperature stress, eds N.C. Turner and P.J. Kramer (New York: John Wiley and Sons), 233–253.

Blum, A. 2011. Plant breeding for water limited environments. New York: Springer-Verlag, 252.

Bond, D.A., G.J. Jellis, G.G. Rowland, J. Le Guen, L.D. Robertson, S.A. Khalil, and L. Li-Juan. 1994. Present status and future strategy in breeding faba beans (*Vicia faba* L.) for resistance to biotic and abiotic stresses. *Euphytica*, 73: 151–166.

Boote, K.J., L.H. Allen, P.V.V. Prasad, J.T. Baker, R.W. Gesch, A.M. Snyder, D. Pan, and J.M.G. Thomas. 2005. Elevated temperature and CO_2 impacts on pollination, reproductive growth, and yield of several globally important crops. *Journal of Agro Meteorology*, 60: 469–474.

Chaves, M.M., J.P. Maroco, and J.S. Pereira. 2003. Understanding plant responses to drought from genes to the whole plant. *Functional Plant Biology*, 30: 239–264.

Chen, H.M., C.A. Liv, C.G. Kuo, C.M. Chien, H.C. Sun, C.C. Huang, Y.C. Lin, and H.M. Ku. 2007. Development of molecular marker for a bruchid (*Callosobruchus chinensis*) resistance gene in mungbean. *Euphytica*, 157: 113–122.

Chibarabada, P.T., T.A. Modi, and T. Mabhandhi. 2017. Expounding the value of grain legumes in the semi and arid tropics. *Sustainability*, 9: 1–25. doi: 10.3390/509010060

Campbell, B.M., P. Thornton, R. Zougmoré, P. van Asten, and L. Lipper. 2014. Sustainable intensification: What is its role in climate smart agriculture? *Current Opinion Environmental Sustain*ability, 8: 39–43.

Cattivelli, L., F. Rizza, F.W. Badeck, E. Mazzucotelli, A.M. Mastrangelo, E. Francia, C. Mare, A. Tondelli, and A.M. Stanca. 2008. Drought tolerance improvement in crop plants: An integrative view from breeding to genomics. *Field Crop Research*, 105: 1–14.

Chen, H., H.H. Li, X.Q. Lu, L.Z. Chen, J. Liu, and H. Wu. 2019. Identification and expression analysis of GRAS transcription factors to elucidate candidate genes related to stolons, fruit ripening and abiotic stresses in woodland strawberry (*Fragaria vesca*). *International Journal of Molecular Sciences*, 20, 45–93.

Condon, A.G., R.A. Richards, G.J. Rebetzke, and G.D. Farquhar. 2004. Breeding for high water-use efficiency. *Journal of Experimental Botany*, 55: 2447–2460.

Costa, L.D., G.D. Vedove, G. Gianquinto, R. Giovanardi, and A. Peressotti. 1997. Yield, water use efficiency and nitrogen uptake in potato: Influence of drought stress. *Potato Research*, 40: 19–34.

Craufurd, P.Q., M. Subedi, and R.J. Summerfield. 1997. Leaf appearance in cowpea: Effects of temperature and photoperiod. *Crop Science*, 37(131): 167–171.

Danquah, E., and E. Blay. 1999. Breeding for stress tolerance: Drought as a case study. Ghana. *Journal of Agricultural Science*, 32: 229–236.

Davies, W.J., and J. Zhang. 1991. Root signals and the regulation of growth and development of plants in drying soil. *Annual Review of Plant Physiology and Plant Molecular Biology*, 42: 55–76.

Derera, J. 2005. Genetic effects and associations between grain yield potential, stress tolerance and yield stability in Southern African Maize (*Zea mays* L.). Base Germplasm. A PhD Thesis in Plant Breeding (unpublished), African Centre for Crop Improvement (ACCI), School of Biochemistry, Genetics, Microbiology and Plant Pathology, Faculty of Science and Agriculture, University of KwaZulu-Natal, Republic of South Africa.

Devasirvatham, V., D.K.Y. Tan, P.M. Gaur, T.N. Raju, and R.M. Trethowan. 2012a. High temperature tolerance in chickpea and its implications for plant improvement. *Crop Pasture Science*, 63, 419–428. doi: 10.1071/CP11218

Djanaguiraman, M., P.V.V. Prasad, D.L. Boyle, and W.T. Schapaugh. 2012. Soybean pollen anatomy, viability and pod set under high temperature stress. *Journal of Agronomy and Crop Science*, 199: 171–177. doi: 10.1111/jac.12005

Devasirvatham, V., P.M. Gaur, N. Mallikarjuna, T.N. Raju, R.M. Trethowan, and D.K. Tan. 2013. Reproductive biology of chickpea response to heat stress in the field is associated with the erformance in controlled environments. *Field Crop Research*, 142: 9–19. doi: 10.1016/j.fcr.2012.11.011

Djanaguiraman, M., P.V.V. Prasad, and W.T. Schapaugh. 2013. High day or night time temperature alters leaf assimilation, reproductive success, and phosphatidic acid of pollen grain in soybean [Glycine max (L.) Merr.]. *Crop Science*, 53: 1594–1604. doi: 10.2135/cropsci2012.07.0441

Downes, R.W., and J.S. Gladstones. 1984. Physiology of growth and seed production in *Lupinus angustifolius* L. I. Effects on pod and seed set of controlled short duration high temperatures at flwering. *Crop Pasture Science*, 35: 493–499.

Dupuis, I., and C. Dumas. 1990. Influence of temperature stress on in vitro fertilization and heat shock protein synthesis in maize (*Zea mays* L.) reproductive tissues. *Plant Physiology*, 94: 665–670.

Ehlers, J.O., and A.E. Hall. 1996. Genotypic classification of cowpea based on responses to heat and photoperiod. *Crop Science*, 36: 673–679.

Ellis, R.H., R.J. Lawn, R.J. Summerfield, A. Qi, E.H. Robert, P.M. Chay, J.B. Brouwer, J.L. Rose, S.J. Yeates, and S. Sandover. 1994. Towards the reliable prediction of time to flowering in six annual crops. IV. Cultivated and wild mung bean. *Experimental Agriculture*, 30: 31–41.

Fatokun, C.A., O. Boukar, and S. Muranaka. 2012. Evaluation of cowpea (*Vigna unguiculata* (L.) Walp.) germplasm lines for tolerance to drought. *Plant Genetic Resources: Characterisation and Utilisation*, 10(3): 171–176.

Gadh, I.P.S., and C.C. Bernier. 1984. Resistance in faba bean (*Vicia faba*) to bean yellow mosaic virus. *Plant Disease*, 68: 109–111.

Gao, Z., S. Eyers, C. Thomas, N. Ellis, and A. Maule. 2004. Identification of markers tightly linked to sbm recessive genes for resistance to pea seed-borne mosaic virus. *Theoretical Applied Genetics*, 109: 488–494.

Goodnight, C.J. 1995. Epistasis and the increase in additive genetic variance: Implications for phase 1 of wright's shifting-balance process. *Evolution International Journal of Organic Evolution*, 49(3): 502–511.

Gosal, S.S., S.H. Wani, and M.S. Kang. 2009. Biotechnology and drought tolerance. *Journal of Crop Improvement*, 23(1): 19–54.

Graham, P.H., and C.P. Vance. 2003. Legumes: Importance and constraints to greater use. *Plant Physiology*, 131: 872–877. doi: 10.1104/pp.017004

Greco, N. 1987. Nematodes and their control in chickpea, in The Chickpea, eds M.C. Saxena and K.B. Singh (Wallingford: CAB International), 271–281.

Gross, Y., and J. Kigel. 1994. Differential sensitivity to high temperature stress in the reproductive development of common bean (*Phaseolus vulgaris* L.). *Field Crops Research*, 36: 201–212.

Hagedorn, D.J., and E.T. Gritton. 1973. Inheritance of resistance to the pea seed-borne mosaic virus. *Phytopathology*, 63: 1130–1133.

Hall, A.E., and P.N. Patel. 1985. Breeding for resistant to drought and heat, in Cowpea research production and utilization, eds S.R. Singh and K.O. Rachie (New York, USA: John Wiley and Sons), 137–151.

Hall, A.E., S. Thiaw, and D.R. Krieg. 1994. Consistency of genotypic ranking for carbon isotope discrimination by cowpea grown in tropical and sub-tropical zones. *Field Crops Research*, 36: 125–131.

Hall, A.E. 2012. Heat stress, in Plant stress physiology, ed S. Shabala (Wallingford, UK: CAB International), 118–131.

Hamidou, F., G. Zombre, D. Diouf, N.N. Diop, S. Guinko, and S. Braconnier. 2007. Physiological, biochemical and agro-morphological responses of five cowpea (*Vigna unguiculata* L.) Walp.), genotypes to water deficit under glasshouse conditions. *Biotechnology, Agronomy, Society and Environment*, 11: 225–234.

Hinkossa, A., S. Gebeyehu, and H. Zeleke. 2013. Generation mean analysis and heritability of drought resistance in common bean (Phaseolus vulgaris L.). *African Journal of Agricultural Research*, 8 (15): 1319–1329.

Imran, M., S. Shafiq, M.A. Farooq, M.K. Naeem, E. Widemann, A. Bakhsh, K.B. Jensen, and R.R.C. Wang. 2019. Comparative genome-wide analysis and expression profiling of histone acetyltransferase (HAT) gene family in response to hormonal applications, metal and abiotic stresses in cotton. *International Journal of Molecular Sciences*, 20: 5311.

Ishiyaku, M.F., B.B. Singh, and P.Q. Craufurd. 2005. Inheritance of time to flowering in cowpea (*Vigna unguiculata* (L.) Walp). *Euphytica*, 142(3): 291–300.

Jagadish, S.V.K., P.Q. Craufurd, and T.R. Wheeler. 2007. High temperature stress and spikelet fertility in rice (*Oryza sativa* L.). *Journal of Experimental Botany*, 58: 1627–1635.

Jiang, Y., R. Lahlali, C. Karunakaran, S. Kumar, A.R. Davis, and R.A. Bueckert. 2015. Seed set, pollen morphology and pollen surface composition response to heat stress in field pea. *Plant Cell Environment*, 38: 2387–2397. doi: 10.1111/pce.12589

Jiang, H., B. Liao, X. Ren, Y. Lei, E. Mace, T. Fu, and J.H. Crouch. 2007. Comparative assessment of genetic diversity of peanut (*Arachis hypogaea* L.) genotypes with various levels of resistance to bacterial wilt through SSR and AFLP analyses. *Journal of Genetics and Genomics*, 34: 544–554.

Jiang, H., X. Ren, Y. Chen, L. Huang, X. Zhou, J. Huang, L. Froenicke, J. Yu, B. Guo, and B. Liao. 2013. Phenotypic evaluation of the Chinese mini-mini core collection of peanut (*Arachis hypogaea* L.) and assessment for resistance to bacterial wilt disease caused by *Ralstonia solanacearum*. *Plant Genetic Research*, 11: 77–83.

Kafizadeh, N., J. Carapetian, and K.M. Kalantari. 2008. Effects of heat stress on pollen viability and pollen tube growth in pepper. *Research Journal of Biological Sciences*, 3: 1159–1162.

Katiyar, A., and Y. Mudgil. 2019. Arabidopsis NDL-AGB1 modules play role in abiotic stress and hormonal responses along with their specific functions. *International Journal of Molecular Sciences*, 20: 4736.

Kaushal, N., K. Gupta, K. Bhandhari, S. Kumar, P. Thkur, and H. Nayyar. 2011. Proline induces heat tolerance in chickpea (*Cicer arietinum* L.) plants by protecting vital enzymes of carbon and antioxidative metabolism. *Physiology and Molecular Biology of Plants*, 17: 203–213. doi: 10.1007/s12298-011-0078-2

Kearsey, M.J., and H.S. Pooni. 1996. The genetical analysis of quantitative traits. London: Chapman and Hall.

Khan, H.R., J.G. Paull, K.H.M. Siddique, and F.L. Stoddard. 2010. Faba bean breeding for drought affected environments: A physiological and agronomic perspective. *Field Crops Research*, 115: 279–286.

Khan, A., J. Singh, V.K. Upadhayay, A.V. Singh, and S. Shah. 2019. Microbial bio-fortification: A green technology through plant growth promoting microorganisms, in Sustainable green technologies for environmental management. Singapore: Springer.

Khetarpal, R.K., Y. Maury, R. Cousin, A. Burghofer, and A. Varma. 1990. Studies on resistance of pea to pea seed borne mosaic virus pathotypes. *Annals of Applied Biology*, 116: 297–304.

Konsens, I., M. Ofi, and J. Kigel. 1991. The effect of temperature on theproduction and abscission of flowers and pods in snap bean (*Phaseolus vulgaris* L). *Annals of Botany*, 67: 391–399. doi: 10.1093/oxfordjournals.aob.a088173

Kumari, S.G., and K.M. Makkouk. 2003. Differentiation among bean leaf roll virus susceptible and resistant lentil and faba bean genotypes on the basis of virus movement and multiplication. *Journal of Phytopathology*, 151: 19–25.

Kumar, S., P. Thkur, N. Kaushal, J.A. Malik, P. Gaur, and H. Nayyar. 2013. Effect of varying high temperatures during reproductive growth on reproductive function, oxidative stress and seed yield in chickpea genotypes differing in heat sensitivity. *Archive of Agronomy and Soil Science*, 59: 823–843. doi: 10.1080/03650340.2012.683424

Li, W., X.L. Wan, J.Y. Yu, K.L. Wang, and J. Zhang. 2019. Genome-wide identification, classification, and expression analysis of the Hsf gene family in carnation (*Dianthus caryophyllus*). *International Journal of Molecular Sciences*, 20: 5233.

Leonetti, P., G.P. Accotto, M.S. Hanafy, and V. Pantaleo. 2018. Viruses and phytoparasitic nematodes of (C arietinum L): Biotechnological approaches in interaction studies and for sustainable control. *Frontiers Plant Science*, 9: 319. doi: 10.3389/fpls.2018.00319

Levitt, J. 1972. Responses of plants to environmental stresses. New York, NY: Academic Press, 698.

Li, J., and M.P. Timko. 2009. Gene for gene resistance in striga-cowpea association. *Science*, 325(5944): 1094. doi: 10.1126/Science.1174754

Lima, M., M. Skutsch, and G. de Medeiros Costa. 2011. Deforestation and the social impacts of soy for biodiesel: Prospectives of farmers in the South Brazilian Amazon. *Ecology and Society*, 16(4): 4. doi: 10.5751/ES-04366-160404

Liu, Y., J. Li, Y. Zhu, A. Jones, R.J. Rose, and Y. Song. 2019. Heat stress in legume seed setting: Effects, causes, and future prospects. *Frontiers*Plant *Science*, 10: 938. doi: 10.3389/fpls.2019.00938

Lynch, M., and B. Walsh. 1998. Genetic and analysis of quantitative traits. Sunderland, Mass: Sinauer Associates.

Magwanga, R.O., J.N. Kirungu, P. Lu, X.Y. Cai, Z.L. Zhou, Y.C. Xu, Y.Q. Hou, S.G. Agong, K.B. Wang, and F. Liu. 2019. Map-based functional analysis of the GhNLP genes reveals their roles in enhancing tolerance to N-deficiency in cotton. *International Journal of Molecular Sciences*, 20: 49–53.

Martinez, C., E. Pons, G. Prats, and J. Leon. 2003. Salicylic acid regulates flowering time and links defense responses and reproductive development. *Plant Journal*, 36: 209–217.

Morgante, M., and F. Salamini. 2003. From plant genomics to breeding practice. *Current Opinion in Biotechnology*, 14(2): 214–219.

Muchero, W., P.A. Roberts, N.N. Diop, I. Drabo, and N. Cisse. 2013. Genetic architecture of delayed senescence, biomass, and grain yield under drought stress in cowpea. *Plos One*, 8(7): 1–10.

Mwadzingeni, L.H., H. Shimelis, E. Dube, M.D. Laing, and T.J. Tsilo. 2015. Breeding wheat for drought tolerance: Progress and technologies. *Journal of Integrative Agriculture*, 15(5): 1–13. doi: 10.1016/52 095-3119(15)61102-9

National Academy of Science. 1994. Biological nitrogen fixation. Washington, DC: National Academy Press.

Nduwumuremyi, A., P. Tongoona, and S. Habimana. 2013. Mating designs: Helpful tool for quantitative plant breeding analysis. *Journal of Plant Breeding and Genetics*, 1: 117–129.

Nguyen, H., and A. Blum. 2004. Physiology and biotechnology integration for plant breeding. Henry, T. Nguyen, Abraham, Blum (Eds), Marcel Dekker Inc. New York-Basel, 270 Madison Avenue New York, N.Y. 10016 USA, ISBN 0-8247-4802-6. doi: 10.1201/9780203022030. Chapter 16.

Noman, M., A. Jameel, W.D. Qiang, N. Ahmad, W.C. Liu, F.W. Wang, and H.Y. Li. 2019. Overexpression of GmCAMTA12 enhanced drought tolerance in arabidopsis and soybean. *International Journal of Molecular Sciences*, 20: 48–49.

Odra, J. 1985. Physiological investigation of drought and heat resistance in sorghum (*sorghum bicolor* (L) Moench). Thesis submitted to Department of Agricultural Biology, University of Newcastle Upon Tyne, UK.

Ogbonnaya, C.I., B. Sarr, C. Brou, O. Diouf, N.N. Diop, and H. Roy-Macauley. 2003. Selection of cowpea genotypes in hydroponics, pots, and field for drought tolerance. *Crop Science*, 43: 1114–1120.

Ojomo, O.A. 1971. Inheritance of flowering date in cowpea (Vigna uniquiculata L Walp). *Tropical Agriculture (Trinidad)*, 48: 277–282.

Ormrod, D.P., C.J. Woolley, G.W. Eaton, and E.H. Stobbe. 1967. Effect of temperature on embryo sac development in (Phaseolus vulgaris L). *Canadian Journal of Botany*, 45: 948–950. doi: 10.1139/b67-097

Prasad, P.V.V., P.Q. Craufurd, V.G. Kakani, T.R. Wheeler, and K.J. Boote. 2001. Influence of high temperature during pre- and post-anthesis stages of floral development on fruit set and pollen germination in peanut. *Functional Plant Biology*, 28: 233–240. doi: 10.1071/PP00127

Passioura, J.B. 2002. Review: Environmental biology and crop improvement. *Functional Plant Biology*, 29: 537–546.

Pressman, E., l.D. Hare, E. Zamski, R. Shaked, L. Althan, K. Rosenfeld, and N. Firon. 2006. The effect of high temperatures on the expression and activity of sucrose cleaving enzymes during tomato (Lycopersicon esculentum) anther development. *Journal of Horticultural Science and Biotechnology*, 81: 341–348.

Porch, T.G., and M. Jahn. 2001. Effects of high-temperature stress on microsporogenesis in heat sensitive and heat-tolerant genotypes of *Phaseolus vulgaris*. *Plant, Cell and Environment*, 24: 723–731.

Provvidenti, R., and R.O. Hampton. 1993. Inheritance of resistance to white lupin mosaic virus in common pea. *Horticultural Science*, 28: 836–837.

Postel, S.L. 2000. Entering an era of water scarcity. *Ecological Applications*, 10: 941–948.

Redden, R.J., P. Dobie, and A.M.R. Gatehouse. 1983. The inheritance of seed resistance to *Callosobruchus rnaculatus* F. in cowpea (*Vigna unguiculata* L. Walp.). I. Analyses of parental, F_1, F_2, F_3 and backcross seed generations. *Australian Journal of Agricultural Research*, 34: 681–695.

Richard, R., and C. Wang. 2020. Chromosomal distribution of genes conferring tolerance to abiotic stresses versus that of genes controlling resistance to biotic stresses in plants. *International Journal of Molecular Sciences*, 21: 1820. doi: 10.3390/ijms21051820

Roberts, P.A., W.C. Mathews, and J.D. Ehlers. 2005. Nematode resistant cowpea cover crops in tomato production systems. *Agronomy Journal*, 97: 1626–1635.

Rubiales, D., S. Fondevilla, W. Chen, L. Gentzbittel, T.J.V. Higgins, M.A. Castillejo, K.B. Singh, and N. Rispail. 2015. Achievements and challenges in legume breeding for pest and disease resistance. *Critical Reviews in Plant Sciences*, 34: 195–236.

Salvi, S., and R. Tuberosa. 2005. To clone or not to clone plant QTLs: Present and future challenges. *Trends Plant Science*, 10: 297–304.

Sasser, J.N., and D.W. Freckman. 1987. A world perspective on nematology: The role of the society, in Vistas on nematology, eds J.A. Veech and D.W. Dickson (Hyattsville, MD: Society of Nematologists), 7–14.

Serraj, R., L. Krishnamurthy, J. Kashiwagi, J. Kumar, S. Chandra, and J.H. Crouch. 2004. Variation in root traits of chickpea (*Cicer arietinum* L.) grown under terminal drought. *Field Crops Research*, 88: 115–127.

Shahi, J.P., and I.S. Singh. 1985. Estimation of genetic variability for grain yield and its components in a random mating population of maize. *Crop Improvement*, 12: 126–129.

Singh, R.K., and B.D. Chaudhary. 1985. Biometrical methods in quantitative genetic analysis. New Delhi: Kalyani Publisher.

Singh, B.B., and B.R. Ntare. 1985. Development of improved cowpea varieties in Africa, in Cowpea research, production and utilization, eds S.R. Singh, and K.O. Rachie (NY: John Wiley and Sons Ltd), 105–115.

Singh, B.B., D.R.M. Raj, K.E. Dashiell, and L.E.N. Jackai. 1997. Advances in Cowpea Research Co-publication of International Institue of Tropical Agriculture (IITA) and Japan International Research Center for Agricultural Sciences (JIRCAS), Ibadan, Nigeria, Sayce Publishing, Devon, UK, 1–390.

Singh, B.B., A.M. Emechebe, and I.D.K. Atokple. 1993. Inheritance of *Alectra* resistance in cowpea genotype B301. *Crop Science*, 33: 70–72.

Singh, B.B., Y. Mai-kodomi, and T. Terao. 1999. A simple screening method for drought tolerance in cowpea. *Indian Journal of Genetics*, 59: 211–220.

Singh, B.D. 2002. Plant breeding: Principles and methods. New Delhi, India: Kalyani Publishers.

Singh, B.B., and T. Matsui. 2002. Cowpea varieties for drought tolerance, in Challenges and opportunities for enhancing sustainable cowpea production, eds C.A. Fatokun, S.A. Tarawali, B.B. Singh, P.M. Kormawa, and M. Tamo' (Ibadan: IITA), 287–300.

Sita, K., A. Sehgal, J. Kumar, S. Kumar, S. Singh, K.H. Siddique., et al. 2017a. Identification of high-temperature tolerant lentil (*Lens culinaris* Medik.) genotypes through leaf and pollen traits. *FrontiersPlant Science*, 8: 744. doi: 10.3389/fpls.2017.00744

Somta, P., C. Ammaranan, P.A.C. Ooi, and P. Srinives. 2007. Inheritance of seed resistance of bruchids in cultivated mungbean (*Vigna radiate* L. Wilezek). *Euphytica*, 155: 47–55.

Somta, P., A. Kaga, N. Tomooka, T. Isemura, D.A. Vaughan, and P. Srivines. 2008. Mapping of quantitative trait loci for a new source of resistance to bruchids in the wild species *Vigna nepalensis* Tateishi & Maxted (*Vigna subgenus* Ceratotropis). *TAG* Theoretical Applie*d Genetics*, 117: 621–628.

Somta, P., N.S. Talekar, and P. Srinives. 2006. Characterization of *Callosobruchus chinensis* (L.) resistance in *vigna umbellata* (Thunb.). *Journal of Stored Products Research*, 42: 313–327.

Su, H.G., B. Li, X.Y. Song, J. Ma, J. Chen, Y.B. Zhou, M. Chen, D.H. Min, Z.S. Xu, and Y.Z. Ma. 2019. Genome-wide analysis of the DYW subgroup PPR gene family and identification of GmPPR4 responses to drought stress. *International Journal of Molecular Sciences*, 20: 56–67.

Sung, D.Y., F. Kaplan, K.J. Lee, and C.L. Guy. 2003. Acquired tolerance to temperature extremes. *Trends in Plant Science*, 8: 179–187.

Suzuki, K., M. Ishimoto, M. Iwanaga, F. Kikuchi, and K. Kitamura. 1995. Inheritance of seed α-amylase inhibitor in the common bean and genetic relationship to arcelin. *Theoretical Applied Genetics*, 90: 762–766.

Taiz, L., and E. Zeiger. 2002. Plant Physiology, Third edition, Publisher: Sinauer Associates; Language: English ISBN: 0878938230.

Tan, W., Q.W. Meng, M. Brestic, K. Olsovska, and X. Yang. 2011. Photosynthesis is improved by exogenous calcium in heat-stressed tobacco plants. *Journal of Plant Physiology*, 168: 2063–2071.

Thompson, J.P., N. Greco, R. Eastwood, S.B. Sharma, and M. Scurrah. 2000. Integrated control of nematodes of cool season food legumes, in Linking research and marketing opportunities for pulses in the 21st century, 3rd edn, ed. R. Knight (Dordrecht: Kluwer Academic Publishers), 491–506. doi: 10.1007/978-94-011-4385-1_45

Thudi, M., Y. Li, S.A. Jackson, G.D. May, and R.K. Varshney. 2012. Current state-of-art of sequencing technologies for plant genomics research. Brief. *Functional Genomics*, 11: 3–11. doi: 10.1093/bfgp/elr045

Thurling, N., and M. Ratinam. 1987. Evaluation of parent selection methods for yield improvement of cowpea (*Vigna unquiculata* L Walp). *Euphytica*, 36: 913–926.

Toker, C., and N. Mutlu. 2011. Breeding for abiotic stress, in Biology and breeding of food legumes, eds A. Pratap, and J. Kumar (Wallingford, UK: CAB International), 35–48.

Trudgill, D.L. 1991. Resistance to and tolerance of plant parasitic nematodes in plants. *Annual Review of Phytopathology*, 29: 167–192. doi: 10.1146/annurev.py.29.090191.001123

UNDESA. World Population Prospects: The 2012 Revision, United Nations Department of Economic and Social Affairs, New York. 2013. Available online: https://population.un.org/wpp/Publications/Files/WPP2012_HIGHLIGHTS.pdf

Vailleau, F., E. Sartorel, M.F. Jardinaud, F. Chardon, S. Genin, T. Huguet, L. Gentzbittel, and M. Petitprez. 2007. Characterization of the interaction between the bacterial wilt pathogen *Ralstonia solanacearum* and the model legume plant Medicago truncatula. *Molecular Plant-Microbe Interactions*, 20: 159–167.

Vance, C.P., P.H. Graham, and D.L. Allan. 2000. Biological nitrogen fixation. Phosphorus: A critical future need, in Nitrogen fixation: From molecules to crop productivity, eds F.O. Pedrosa, M. Hungria, M.G. Yates, and W.E. Newton (Dordrecht, The Netherlands: Kluwer Academic Publishers), 506–514.

Wang, D., Y.X. Liu, Q. Yu, S.P. Zhao, J.Y. Zhao, J.N. Ru, X.Y. Cao, Z.W. Fang, J. Chen, Y.B. Zhou, et al. 2019a. Functional analysis of the soybean GmCDPK3 gene responding to drought and salt stresses. *International Journal of Molecular Sciences*, 20: 59–69.

Wang, J.L., T.H. Hu, W.L. Wang, H.J. Hu, Q.Z. Wei, X.C. Wei, and C.L. Bao. 2019b. Bioinformatics analysis of the lipoxygenase gene family in radish (*Raphanus sativus*) and functional characterization in response to abiotic and biotic stresses. *International Journal of Molecular Sciences*, 20: 60–95.

Warrag, M.O.A., and A.E. Hall. 1984. Reproductive responses of cowpea (*Vigna unguiculata* (L.) Walp.) to heat stress. I. Responses to soil and day air temperatures. *Field Crop Research*, 8: 3–16.

Whittle, C.A., S.P. Otto, M.O. Johnston, and J.E. Krochko. 2009. Adaptive epigenetic memory of ancestral temperature regime in Arabidopsis thaliana. *Botany*, 87: 650–657.

Xu, F., W. Guo, W. Xu, Y. Wei, and R. Wang. 2009. Leaf morphology correlates with water and light availability: What consequences for simple and compound leaves. National Natural Science Foundation of China and Chinese Academy of Sciences. *Progress in Natural Science*, 19(12): 1789–1798.

Young, L.W., R.W. Wilen, and P.C. Bonham-Smith. 2004. High temperature stress of Brassica napus during flowering reduces micro- and mega gametophyte fertility, induces fruit abortion, and disrupts seed production. *Journal of Experimental Botany*, 55: 485–495.

Yang, S., B. Vanderbeld, J. Wan, and Y. Huang. 2010. Narrowing down the targets: Towards successful genetic engineering of drought-tolerant crops. *Molecular Plant*, 3: 469–490.

Yong, Y.B., Y. Zhang, and Y.M. Lyu. 2019. A MYB-related transcription factor from *Lilium lancifolium L.* (LlMYB3) is involved in anthocyanin biosynthesis pathway and enhances multiple abiotic stress tolerance in Arabidopsis thaliana. *International Journal of Molecular Sciences*, 20: 3195.

Yoon, M.Y., M.Y. Kim, J. Ha, T. Lee, K.D. Kim, and S.H. Lee. 2019. QTL analysis of resistance to high-intensity UV-B irradiation in soybean (*Glycine max [L.] Merr.*). *International Journal of Molecular Sciences*, 20: 3287.

Yu, J., W.K. Gu, R. Provvidenti, and N.F. Weeden. 1995. Identifying and mapping two DNA markers linked to the gene conferring resistance to pea enation mosaic virus. *Journal of the American Society Horticultural Science*, 120: 730–733.

Yu, J., W.K. Gu, N.F. Weeden, and R. Provvidenti. 1996. Developement ASAP marker for resistance to bean yellow mosaic virus in *Pisum sativum. Pisum Genet*, 28: 31–32.

Zhao, W. , H. Liu , L. Zhang , Z. Hu , J. Liu , W. Hua , and J. Liu. 2019. Genome-wide identification and characterization of FBA gene family in polyploid crop *Brassica napus. International Journal of Molecular Sciences*, 20(22): 5749. doi: 10.3390/ijms20225749

Zinn, K.E., M. Tunc-Ozdemir, and J.F. Harper. 2010. Temperature stress and plant sexual reproduction: Uncovering the weakest links. *Journal of Experimental Botany*, 61(7): 1959–1968.

Zou, L.F., B.W. Yu, X.L. Ma, B.H. Cao, G.J. Chen, C.M. Chen, and J.J. Lei. 2019. Cloning and expression analysis of the BocMBF1c gene involved in heat tolerance in Chinese kale. *International Journal of Molecular Sciences*, 20: 5637.

8

Innovations in Agronomic Management for Adaptation to Climate Change in Legume Cultivation

Derya Yucel[1], Celal Yucel[1], Gizem Kamçi[1], and Aladdin Hamwieh[2]
[1]*University of Sirnak, Agriculture Faculty, Field Crops Department, Sirnak-TURKEY*
[2]*International Center for Agricultural Research in the Dry Areas (ICARDA), Giza, Egypt*

CONTENTS

8.1 Introduction

Legumes rank among humanity's most important agricultural food crops. They are grown in almost every climatic region and on a wide range of soil types. Although edible legume crops and pulses are primarily grown for human consumption, there is, in addition, substantial demand for them as forages. Pulses are edible dry seeds of plants consumed in the form of whole seed, split-grain, dehulled split-grain, and flour. Of these, the major ones, in terms of global production and consumption quantities, are the common bean, chickpea, dry pea, lentil, cowpea, mung bean, faba bean, and pigeon pea. In addition, there are a large number of minor pulses that are grown and consumed in different parts of the world, such as Lathyrus, winged bean, and kersting's groundnut.

Grain legumes are important in the human diet for providing protein, energy in the form of starch or oil, dietary fiber, micro- and macronutrients, vitamins, and numerous bioactive phytochemicals (Strohle et al., 2006), such as flavonoids and other antioxidants (Scalbert et al., 2005), essential amino acids, and nutrients (Rebello et al., 2014). Current nutritional guides such as *The Eatwell Guide* in the United Kingdom (Public Health England, 2016) and the Finnish National Nutrition Council (VRN, 2014) suggest decreased consumption of animal protein and increased use of vegetable protein, particularly

DOI: 10.1201/9781003214885-8

from legumes, because of the significant positive effects on human health when animal proteins are replaced by plant protein, including lowering cholesterol (Harland and Haffner, 2008). Frequent intake of legumes has been associated with a reduction in the risk of cardiovascular diseases as well as prevention of some cancers, diabetes, digestive tract diseases, and obesity (Duranti, 2006; Campos- Vega et al., 2010). In addition to their high protein content, forage legumes have the advantage of high voluntary intake and animal production when feed supply is non-limiting (Phelan et al., 2015).

Pulses, like other plants of the Fabaceae family, have root nodules that absorb inert nitrogen from soil air and convert it into biologically useful ammonia, a process referred to as biological nitrogen fixation. Consequently, the pulse crops do not need any additional nitrogen as fertilizer, and because of the release of excess nitrogen in the soil, the requirement of fossil fuel-based chemical nitrogen fertilization in crops that follow in the cropping cycle is also reduced. They have also been found to increase soil carbon (C) and N content, improve the resistance of soil to erosion, and reduce the incidence of certain soil pathogens (Bagayoko et al., 2000; Sainju et al., 2005). When used as manure in conservation agriculture, legumes can enhance soil porosity and reduce bulk density (Sultani et al., 2007).

In this chapter, we demonstrate the importance of focusing on legume crop production and encourage organic agriculture to be applied in the fields. We also outline its contribution in crop rotation, inter-cropping, soil tillage, and zero-tillage technologies. Furthermore, in this chapter, we try to introduce the readers to the new plant breeding and genetic approaches, as well as the importance of biodiversity in our eco-friendly cultivation. It is necessary to transfer the new updated knowledge and technologies to farmers. This transfer must be faster and wider to meet the global demands and challenges made by climate change.

8.2 Climate Change

The world population is expected to be 10 billion in 2050 (FAO, 2020). In order to meet the nutritional needs of this growing population, food production should be increased by 70% and efficiency should be increased by 60% (Tripathi et al., 2019). The growing human population and changing environment have raised significant concern for global food security, with the current improvement rate of several important crops inadequate to meet future demand. In addition, in recent years, with the effect of global climate change, insufficient or irregular rainfall, extreme weather events, shifting growing seasons, and increased global warming, drought- and stress-tolerant breeding studies in legumes are needed, as well as the development of effective selection techniques to distinguish potential conditions of genotypes. It is necessary to have information about genetic diversity in drought tolerance. It is an important strategy to investigate the effects of drought and temperature stress factors, especially caused by global climate change, on the development of legume varieties. This knowledge is expected to add a new dimension to the improvement of breeding research in this scientifically important area.

Climatic conditions are a primary determinant of agronomic crop productivity. Besides, plant metabolic processes are controlled by weather variables like maximum and minimum temperature, solar radiation, carbon dioxide concentration, and availability of water (Wang et al., 2008; Farooq et al., 2015). Climate change over the past few decades has been fairly rapid in many agricultural regions around the world. The climate will continue to change in the future, and it raises many questions related to global agricultural security, including changes in rates of human population growth, income growth and distribution, dietary preferences, disease incidence, increased demand for land and water resources, and rates of improvement in agricultural productivity (Lobell and Gourdji, 2012). Climate change, the multiple effects of the COVID-19 pandemic, population growth/food security, and competition for land and water resources have come together to push more people into hunger and poverty. World demand for legumes is expected to grow in the foreseeable future, not only in developing countries but also in developed nations. Promoting legume cultivation could therefore emerge as an effective approach to achieving the Millennium Development Goals of reducing poverty and hunger, improving health, and maintaining environmental sustainability (Abate et al., 2012). Adapting to climate change entails taking the right measures to reduce the negative effects of climate change (or exploit the positive ones) by making the appropriate adjustments and changes. Adaptation has three possible objectives: to reduce exposure to the risk of damage; to develop the capacity to cope with unavoidable damages, and to take advantage of new opportunities. This chapter discusses agronomic management strategies employed to reduce the negative effects of climate change in legume cultivation in the world.

Although agriculture is one of the main sectors responsible for the increase in CO_2 concentration in the atmosphere, this effect could be considerably mitigated through the use of proper cover crops and soil management (Delgado et al., 2011). Crop rotations with lower N inputs may favor ECO_2 and decrease C assimilation by soil microbial biomass (Marquez et al., 2000). Conversely, crop residues with high N content and low C/N are more readily decomposed by microorganisms due to lower straw recalcitrance, resulting in a fast loss of CO_2 to the atmosphere (Zhou et al., 2016). Many studies have been carried out in the world to reduce the effects of climate change on agricultural production and especially on the production of legumes (Table 8.1).

TABLE 8.1

Effects of Agronomic Practices on Environmental Sustainability

	Agronomic practice	Merits/demerits	References
1	Breeding	Emphasizes productivity	Paulsen, 1994; Ishag et al., 1996; Bray, 2000; Setimela et al., 2005; Gaur et al., 2007; Yücel Özveren et al., 2012; Yücel et al., 2012; 2013; Samineni et al., 2019; Idrissi, 2020
2	Improving genetic variability	Expands biodiversity/reduces adverse impact of climate change	Kashiwagi et al., 2005; Ahmed et al., 2008; Arbaoui et al., 2008; Keneni et al., 2010; Link et al., 2010; Krishnamurthy et al., 2010; Upadhyaya et al., 2012; Krishnamurthy et al., 2013; Landry et al., 2015; Ali et al., 2016; Purushothaman et al., 2016; Sabaghpour et al., 2006
3	Genetic engineering	Gene transformation and genome editing technology/biosafetly issue	Lobell et al., 2005; Mantri et al., 2007; Thudi et al., 2014;Trevaskis, 2015; Korres et al., 2016; Ortiz, 2018; Garg et al., 2016
4	Improving water productivity	Reduces water usage/too much usage of water leads to wastage and can affect the soil	Leport et al., 1998; Davies et al., 1999; Fang et al., 2010
5	Agricultural soil and crop practices (i.e. Raisedbed)	Minimum soil tillage and intercropping will increase the water retention capability of the soil and biomass yield	Marquez et al., 2000; Kögel-Knabner, 2002; Liu et al., 2006; Dhima et al., 2007; Carbone et al., 2011; Conceição et al., 2013;Yücel et al., 2014; Brito et al., 2015; Alhameid et al., 2017; Yücel et al., 2018a, 2018b; Hobley et al., 2018; Maiga et al., 2019; Aydemir, 2019; Iqbal et al., 2019; Ortas and Yucel, 2020; Yucel et al., 2020
6	Planting date	Minimizes exposure to climatic stresses and maximizes productivity	Bilalis et al., 2003; Guilioni et al., 2003; Pellissier et al., 2007; Roy et al., 2009; Saleh et al., 2012; Prasad et al., 2012; Ouji and Mouelhi, 2017; Cubero, 2017; Shunmugam et al., 2018; Richards et al., 2020
7	Plant density	Uses optimum plant density in order to obtain maximum yield per unit area	Dantuma and Thompson, 1983; Turk et al., 2003; López-Bellido et al., 2005; Vanderpuye, 2010; Saleem et al., 2012; Fernandes et al., 2015; Silva et al., 2017; Kamara et al., 2018; Boakye et al., 2019; Samadi and Peighambari, 2000; Souza et al., 2020
8	Mechanized agriculture	Uses mechanical weed control methods and mechanical harvest of legumes	Anil et al., 1998; Baird et al., 2009
9	Genetic sources	Source of novel traits	Croser et al., 2003; Berger et al., 2012; Sharma et al., 2013; Gorim and Vandenberg, 2017; Singh et al., 2020

8.3 Plant Breeding and Genetic Approaches

Throughout evolution, plants have developed appropriate strategies to survive and reproduce even under unfavorable conditions. However, breeding studies have focused on the productivity of plants rather than their viability. Thus, while high-yielding varieties of plants became widespread, their productivity became increasingly important. The negative effects of biotic and abiotic stress factors on vegetative production in recent years led scientists to take new measures to reduce the negative effects of possible climate change (Yücel et al., 2012; 2013).

Drought stress as abiotic stress is exacerbated by the continued increase in the world population and the decrease in limited water resources used in crop production. Due to the climate changes that have occurred in recent years because of insufficient or irregular rainfall, the water needs of agricultural products cannot be met as required, and significant product losses occur as a result. For this reason, more efficient use of water by plants and the development of drought-tolerant varieties are among the most important research topics in the world. It is expected that drought will affect every product group and will mostly affect the production of legumes negatively. High temperature is considered to be another abiotic stress factor limiting the productivity of many important agricultural plants (Paulsen, 1994; Ishag and Mohamed, 1996). In arid and semi-arid regions where soil surface temperatures exceed 50°C, high soil temperature significantly decreases plant populations (Setimela et al., 2005). Increasing temperature inhibits different stages of plant development (Ishag and Mohamed, 1996) especially fertilization. The ability of a genotype to survive at high temperatures may vary depending on the species or variety of the plant, the plant development stage, the sensitivity of the cell types, and the degree and duration of the high temperature (Bray, 2000; Yücel, 2012). Plant breeding and genetics provide dynamic mechanisms for the adaptation of legume cropping systems to heat stress. The combination of molecular (including genome editing technology) and conventional plant breeding and genetic methods can be helpful to recognize and develop eco-stable varieties with required genotype-environment combinations that will be beneficial in farming under changing climatic circumstances (Lobell et al., 2005; Trevaskis, 2015; Korres et al., 2016; Ortiz, 2018).

Conventional breeding has produced several high-yielding legume genotypes without exploiting its potential yield owing to a number of constraints. Among these, abiotic stresses, including drought, salinity, waterlogging, high temperature, and chilling, frequently limit growth and productivity. The development of new varieties adapted to a wide range of environmental conditions is the main aim of legume breeding programs with a crucial goal of improving competitiveness. Breeding for tolerance of any of the abiotic stresses is a complex phenomenon for which the genetic complexity of these abiotic stresses and lack of proper screening techniques, phenotyping techniques, and genotype-by-environment interaction have further jeopardized the breeding program in legumes. Therefore, scientists have to understand the knowledge gap involving the physiological, biochemical, and molecular complex networks of abiotic stress mechanisms.

Pure line breeding is a resource-intensive activity that takes 10 years or more to develop a new cultivar. Among the legume crops, rapid generation turnover has been demonstrated in a few species. In chickpea (*Cicer arietinum* L.), Gaur et al. (2007) demonstrated that three seed-to-seed generations can be achieved within a year. Increasing the response to selection in plant breeding programs by reducing the time required to complete a generation of inbreeding can significantly shorten the time to release a cultivar. Recently, speed breeding strategies that manage temperature, increase the photoperiod to 22 h/day, and use micronutrients showed a significant reduction in time to inbreeding in several crops (González-Barrios et al., 2020). For example, plant breeders at ICARDA have developed the protocol of speed breeding for each of bread/durum wheat, barley, chickpea, and lentil. By scaling up this technology, we expect positive impacts to increase genetic gain in the near future.

Besides, changes in climate could also destroy predator-prey relationships, which could become one of the reasons for loss of biodiversity. Thus, in order to preserve biodiversity and reduce the adverse impact of climatic change on productivity and quality of crops, there is a need to develop new varieties that are tolerant to high temperature, moisture stress, salinity, and climate-proofing through conventional and non-conventional breeding techniques and various biotechnological approaches.

The adverse effect leads to the development of a small, short-stemmed crop with few branches and pods, as in the case of some legume crops (Sita et al., 2017). Many researchers revealed that there was great genetic variability for abiotic stress tolerance in legume crops. Significant progress in breeding for abiotic stress, such as heat, drought, waterlogging, and frost, was made, and several faba bean cultivars were improved for different growing areas (Arbaoui et al., 2008; Keneni et al., 2010; Link et al., 2010; Landry et al., 2015; Ali et al., 2016).

Numerous studies have been conducted on the abiotic stresses on chickpea, including early maturity; root traits; carbon isotope discrimination; shoot biomass (Kashiwagi et al., 2005; Krishnamurthy et al., 2010; Upadhyaya et al., 2012; Krishnamurthy et al., 2013; Purushothaman et al., 2016); and morphological (Sabaghpour et al., 2006; Ahmed et al., 2008), physiological (Turner et al., 2007; Rahbarian et al., 2011), biochemical (Gunes et al., 2006; Mafakheri et al., 2010), and molecular traits (Mantri et al., 2007; Thudi et al., 2014; Garg et al., 2016) to understand the tolerance mechanism and select to the most tolerant chickpea varieties. Previous studies have shown that during abiotic stress, seed yield decreases significantly compared with irrigated plants, due to flower and pod abortion; reduced pod production; and reduced seed size, pollen viability, and stigma/style function in different legume varieties (Leport et al., 1998; Davies et al., 1999; Fang et al., 2010; Fang et al., 2010). Concerning tolerance to abiotic stress conditions, it is important to know the stress mechanism as well as implement the appropriate breeding program. The objective of breeding programs is to shorten the breeding cycle and release more resilient high-yielding chickpea varieties for targeted environments through the application of a range of technologies in controlled and field conditions. Speed breeding, accommodating up to seven generations per year, is now widely applied, and with this process, seven generations per year can be obtained in legumes (Samineni et al., 2019; Idrissi, 2020)

8.4 Planting Date – A Factor for Crop Production

Crop plants have a range of avoidance or tolerance strategies in order to survive abiotic constraints (Shunmugam et al., 2018). Early phenology is a common crop strategy of escaping late-season stresses and facilitates adaptation to short-season environments. The plant growth duration must suit or complement a production environment and/or farming enterprise. The most important adaptive criterion in legume crops is appropriate phenology that minimizes exposure to climatic stresses and maximizes productivity under climate change. Given that most Mediterranean and semi-arid legume crops are indeterminate and therefore capable of continuing vegetative growth after the onset of reproduction, the key phenological stage is the onset of flowering. The final seed number and final seed weight depend on plant growth rate during the flowering period and the seed filling period, respectively (Guilioni et al., 2003; Pellissier et al., 2007). Thus, high temperature and water deficit indirectly affect seed number and seed weight. Moreover, severe heat stress can cause the abortion of flowers, resulting in a significant reduction of seed number (Guilioni et al., 1997). Besides, in the areas where legume cultivation is carried out, the flowering and podding periods of the plants come to the hot and dry periods. This situation intensifies the yield reduction. However, modifying the crop calendar can take advantage of better earlier season moisture conditions and prolonged growing seasons, making more effective use of rainfall and stored soil moisture and helping minimize drought risk periods during grain filling. Also, changing planting time to avoid the harmful influences of high temperature at anthesis and during pollination and fertilization has been suggested as an adaptation tactic for climate warming. For example, earlier sowing of winter and spring legume crops and delayed sowing of summer and autumn legumes to escape hot and dry periods in growing seasons, is one useful adaptation to climate uncertainty. Therefore, the optimum sowing date has been adjusted according to optimum temperature conditions, resulting in substantial yield increases by escaping temperature stress during the grain-filling phase. However, the indeterminate growth pattern of most legumes provides plasticity to environmental stresses by allowing the development of additional flowers and then seeds under favorable growing conditions. Experiments conducted in India and Australia on chickpea showed that early sowing (mid-April) generally delayed flowering, extending the crop's vegetative period, and the progressive delay in sowing resulted in shorter vegetative and podding growth phases, which affected the seed yield. As a result of this research, it could be concluded that environmental factors (such as temperature, moisture availability, and day length) are the main drivers of phenological development in chickpea. Using a range of sowing dates across diverse sites and years is a practical way of testing for adaptability in new regions, by matching the performance of these varieties to the long-term average climatic conditions (Prasad et al., 2012; Richards et al., 2020). Another experiment carried out in India and Australia on lentil showed that delay in sowing of lentil lines from November to February reduced some morphological traits as well as grain yield/ha by 66% (Roy et al., 2009; Ouji and Mouelhi, 2017,). Using the future climate data, Saleh et al. (2012) reported that pods and seeds yield will be reduced, and the negative impact could be minimized when the sowing date of dry bean was delayed from September 10th to October 10th. Pods and seed yield will be reduced from −3.2% to −14.2% for pods and from −4.4% to −13.4% for seeds (with adaptation) in the years 2025 to 2100 in the new sowing dates. Besides, Faba bean is usually planted in autumn, in areas of Europe characterized by mild winter climatic conditions (Bilalis et al., 2003). In cooler agro-climatic zones, sowing is postponed until the end of winter or early spring to prevent frost damage (Sallam et al., 2015). In some areas of the Mediterranean Basin, the earliest varieties can be sown at the end of summer, with the aim of harvesting them by the end of autumn (Cubero, 2017).

8.5 Plant Population

As with all product, the ultimate goal in legumes is to obtain the highest yield per unit area. Considering that legumes are grown widely in arid and semi-arid regions and are generally grown in soils defined as inefficient, optimum plant density should be provided in order to obtain maximum yield per unit area. With high plant density, plants are not able to use enough of the soil moisture. Also, competing with each other to make more use of light will slow down the vegetative growth of plants. In this case, the amount of photosynthesis will decrease in the plants that have not shown sufficient vegetative development, and this situation may lead to a direct decrease in yield. In contrast, low plant density may allow weeds to grow more aggressively limit possible crop yield. Plants grown at lower plant density are usually shorter and branchy, which increases losses during combined harvest. In a study with chickpea in Canada, a plant population density of 55 plants m^{-2} produced a 23% to 49% seed yield above that of the recommended plant population density of 44 plants m^2 (Vanderpuye, 2010).

Plant density is the first yield component to be established at the early crop cycle; it is largely dictated and controlled by the farmer himself, and finally, it is largely unaffected by environmental change (Dantuma and Thompson, 1983). However, other yield components, such as the number and weight of pods and seeds per plant and 100-seed weight, which are established at a later stage, are significantly affected by environmental conditions. Furthermore, the contribution efficiency of these components in the final seed yield is also associated with the number of plants per unit area (López-Bellido et al., 2005).

In beans, the potential yield could be impaired in conditions of water stress due to the lag in the processes of transpiration and absorption as a result of the low water availability (Fernandes et al., 2015; Silva et al., 2017) Beyond the use of water deficit, another option to increase yield is the planting density technique. The increase in planting density should be carefully chosen so that intraspecific competition does not happen and it results in the best use of available resources for grain's growth and yield. As a result of the field experiment in Brazil, 30 plants per m^2 planting densities were more efficient in water use (Souza et al., 2020). Some studies have been carried out in beans, in a range of 100,000 to 400,000 plants ha^{-1}, to verify the best plant density for beans (Kamara et al., 2018; Boakye et al., 2019). Research to investigate the effect of various sowing rates on seed yield of lentil in Pakistan concluded that a seed rate of 40–45 kg ha^{-1} for small to medium grain-size lentil varieties should be used by farmers to increase yield (Saleem et al., 2012). Besides, Turk et al. (2003) reported that high yields (1817 kg ha^{-1}) in lentil were obtained for high plant density (120 plants m^2) in Jordan. Samadi and Peighambari (2000) in Karaj, Iran found that for lentil cv. Ziba optimum sowing time was December, and the best seed rate was 60–165 kg ha^{-1}. On the other hand, Baird et al. (2009) reported that weed biomass decreased with increasing seeding rate by up to 68%. Field pea reached a maximum economic return at a seeding rate of 200 seeds m^2 and an actual plant density of 120 plants/m^2. Organic farmers should increase the seeding rate of field pea to increase returns and provide better weed suppression.

8.6 Biodiversity for Agricultural Sustainability

Biodiversity plays an important role in combating climate change. Due to the increasing concentration of greenhouse gases, global warming, and climate changes, irregular rainfall distribution, drought, floods, and natural disasters are expected to cause significant problems in food production. It is necessary to increase agricultural production in order to meet the food deficit. Agricultural production can only be made by increasing the production per unit area due to the high level of arable agricultural areas and the decrease in the possibilities to increase them. The use of intensive chemical inputs and energy to increase the production per unit area has negative effects on the environment and healthy food production. By increasing the price of food costs, the problem of insufficient and unhealthy nutrition arises. Reducing the effects of possible climate changes on agricultural production, increasing the sustainability of agricultural ecosystems, and producing healthy and sufficient food will be less harmful to the environment and increase biodiversity.

Wild relatives are native and adapted, through evolution, to the environmental conditions experienced at the crop's centers of origin. This makes them potential genetic sources of abiotic stress tolerance through exploiting the mechanisms and strategies they use to survive adverse conditions at the areas of origin. Therefore, to attain further breakthrough for enhancing genetic gains, new target traits are needed to be identified and introgressed into the cultivated gene pool for widening the genetic base of cultigens. Crop wild relatives (CWRs) are an invaluable reservoir of productivity enhancement-related characters with the resilience to climate change and farming system, and they are a source of novel traits (Maxted, 2008; Lane, 2007). Several studies showed that within *Cicer arietinum*, among the wild relatives, *C. bijugum*, *C. chorassanicum, C. cuneatum, C. echinospermum, C. judaicum, C. pinnatifidum, C. reticulatum,* and *C. yamashitae* seem to have tolerance to abiotic stresses and are readily crossable with the cultivated chickpea, with the others often producing infertile hybrids (Croser et al., 2003; Berger et al., 2012; Sharma et al., 2013,). The importance of wild relatives has also been observed in other pulse crops, for example in lentils, where incorporation of favorable traits such as reduced transpiration rates and deeper rooting systems into modern varieties enables lentil to escape, avoid, or tolerate drought conditions (Gorim et al., 2017). Identification of the most promising genotypes carrying resistance against major biotic stresses could be utilized in the cultivated or susceptible varieties of lentil for enhancing genetic gains. The lentil genetic material consisting of *Lens orientalis, L. odemensis, L. tomentosus, L. nigricans, L. ervoides, L. lamottei,* and *L. culinaris* (cultivated) was evaluated under multi-location and multi-season performance for target characters viz. earliness, pod number, seed yield, and biotic stress under field and controlled screening conditions. The study has identified some trait-specific accessions, which could also be taken into consideration while planning distant hybridization in lentil (Singh et al., 2020).

8.7 Choice of Crop – A Vital Issue for Eco-friendly Cultivation

The current agricultural practice is monoculture (the cultivation of the same crops in the same field one after the other). In regions where the wheat-corn crop-growing system is effective and where there are no different crops (such as legumes), there are structural deteriorations in the soil, lack of organic matter, and consequently a decrease in yield. The producer uses more fertilizer than the plant needs in order to get more product per unit area. Fertilizers given outside the need of the plant are washed in various ways (irrigation water and rainfall) and cause pollution of groundwaters, and in advanced stages, groundwater, rivers, and seas. Although this affects biodiversity in the environment, it also causes residues in the product. In addition, the monoculture production system causes the use of more chemicals to reduce crop losses by increasing the population of diseases, pests, and weeds. Excessive chemical application can cause residues in the environment and the product. In order to reduce these negative effects, the development of production systems where different products are grown will benefit in terms of soil and environmental quality. Since legumes have a deep root system, they will help improve the soil structure if grown with wheat. In addition, in a symbiotic partnership within the root nodule, legumes supply nutrients to rhizobia that fix N_2 gas from the atmosphere into reduced forms that are supplied to the legume. These symbiotic associations have been estimated to fix ~80% of the biologically fixed N_2 in agricultural areas. This issue increases the importance of legumes in the crop rotation system. In this way, without the need for additional fertilization or with less fertilization, both the input cost will be reduced and healthier products will be obtained with an environmentally friendly approach model. With the effect of climate change, insufficient precipitation or changes in the precipitation regime, and the increase in temperature, evapotranspiration becomes high. In this case, it is important to include legumes in the crop rotation according to the climate demand in order to make the best use of the water in the soil. Growing different crops on behalf of each other will reduce the production risk with the effect of climate change (chickpeas and lentils for the winter period; soybean, peanuts, and beans for the summer period).

8.8 Crop Rotation and Cover Crops

Crop rotation and reduced tillage were the most important factors affecting soil fertility, soil texture, soil physical and chemical characteristics, and water status. Rotation experiments showed that combining cereal with legume can reduce the nitrate level in the soil, and that sweet corn with faba bean reduces salt accumulation. Legume-wheat and quinoa-wheat rotations have a beneficial effect on soil fertility and sustainability. The crops influence soil nitrogen and EC besides changes in soil structure (Parikh et al., 2012). Further, crop rotations will play an important role in improving weed control, minimizing disease risk, and increasing nutrient availability. The introduction of drought and salt-tolerant crop species such as quinoa and amaranth may result in more resilient crop rotations and high-value cash crop products.

Mono-cropping is the main productivity constraint in the dry regions, and this system is affected by multiple abiotic stresses and is further aggravated by climate changes. The effect of the introduction of legumes in the crop rotation was compared to wheat monocropping, and the results revealed a positive impact of crop rotation over monocropping on biomass and soil organic matter. An example of a rotation experiment design is illustrated from Turkey in Table 8.2.

One of the cropping systems will be existing wheat-corn or wheat-cotton rotation based on local climate and land suitability. The proposed crop rotation will be an extended integration of existing crops with cover crop mix between planting seasons or during fellow periods.

Cover crop mixes (berseem clover, common vetch, field pea, radish, triticale, phacelia) will be grown for nitrogen, as mulch to reduce evapotranspiration and control weeds, and to alleviate soil compaction. Forage soybean-corn or soy-sorghum mixtures will be grown as silage or energy feedstock. Another sample for crop rotation is given in Figure 8.1.

Considering the existing mono-cropping systems, three food legume crops (chickpea, faba bean, and lentil) and two new crops (quinoa and amaranth) showed potential to integrate and improve overall agricultural productivity and soil quality. These results are expected to help extension workers and farmers with making informed decisions in selecting appropriate food legume and new crops for developing site-specific crop rotations. However, new crops must add value to the existing farming

TABLE 8.2

Crop Rotation Design from Turkey

Crop*	Planting	Harvest	Duration
Wheat (main crop)	December	June	1st/2nd year
Forage soybean/sorghum	June	October/November	2nd year
Cover crops mix	November	April	2nd/3rd year
Cotton (main crop)	April	October	3rd year
Cover crop mix	October	February/May	3rd/4th year
Corn (main crop)	March/May	November	4th year

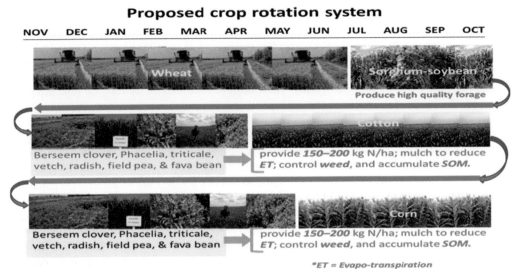

FIGURE 8.1   Crop rotation system.

systems in competition with established cropping systems in an economically viable crop rotation. Emission (E) CO_2 also depends on the crop rotations used in the agricultural system, which are affected by the quality of crop residue left on the soil and the amount of easily mineralizable C (Kögel-Knabner, 2002). Crop rotations with lower N inputs may favor emission CO_2 (ECO_2) and decrease C assimilation by soil microbial biomass (Marquez et al., 2000). A number of institutional and market barriers as well as "support schemes" are likely to have an impact on the market as well as the field level for new crops. Long-term cropping studies under no-till have resulted in increased soil organic carbon (SOC) and total N with increased crop rotation.

8.9 Intercropping

Intercropping is one of the common agricultural practices used in low-input farming systems worldwide (Aydemir, 2019; Iqbal et al., 2019). Intercropping systems, especially those employing cereal crops with legumes, have several major advantages, such as higher biomass yield and better land use management efficiency (Dhima et al., 2007, Yucel et al., 2020).

The benefits of intercropping are increased yield and forage quality (Yücel et al., 2018a, 2018b), N contributions from legumes, higher yield stability, and reduced incidence of pests, weeds, and diseases (Anil et al., 1998). The use of annual legumes in cereal cropping systems can improve sustainability by biological N fixation, reduced weed competition, and increased soil organic matter (Izaurralde et al., 1993).

8.10 Cover Crops

Cover crops are important components of sustainable agricultural systems. Growing cover crops in the agricultural production system will be an important agricultural production model in order to improve the soil quality and store organic carbon. Cover crops are defined as plants left on the soil surface and growing different plants together in the period between the two main crops. It provides important benefits in the protection of soil, the environment, and water in agricultural ecosystems. Cover crops in the soil increase organic matter and contribute to increasing the quality of the soil, the passage of water to the soil, and consequently more water retention in the soil, balancing the soil temperature due to its role as mulch, preventing the evaporation of water, and preventing soil erosion that may occur on the soil surface by wind and water. In addition, the use of root-root legumes increases the biological breakdown of soil compaction and the density and microbial activities of soil microorganisms. Weed control makes a significant contribution to environmental quality by reducing the density of harvests and pests, especially nematodes, providing a suitable habitat for beneficial predator insects, reducing the density of greenhouse gases by storing more C in the soil, and preventing excessive nitrogen use as legumes bring those into the soil biologically. These positive contributions increase the functionality of ecosystems due to the decrease in inputs, such as labor and energy, in agricultural production. They improve the structure and water-holding capacity of the soil and thus increase the effectiveness of applied N fertilizer. Legume cover crops such as hairy vetch and crimson clover fix nitrogen and contribute to the nitrogen requirements of subsequent crops. Nitrogen (N) is the most important nutrient essential for plant growth. Generally, agricultural soils are deficient in N; therefore, chemical fertilizers and manure or biosolids as a source of N are routinely applied for growing crops.

Since carbon (C) and nitrogen (N) are stoichiometrically linked together in soil organic matter (SOM) to provide ecosystem services, one of the highly debated issues is the terrestrial C sequestration to improve or maintain soil quality in response to progressive N limitations (PNL). Cover crop residues left on the soil surface can decrease the soil temperature and retain soil moisture and eventually ECO_2 (Carbone et al., 2011; Brito et al., 2015).

Management practices based on the integration of holistic approaches of continuous no-till (NT) with cover crops in the rotation have been suggested to improve soil quality. Conventional tillage (CT) is linked to the degradation of soil aggregate stability and hence, depleting SOM content. In contrast, NT is expected to improve soil aggregate stability by C and N accumulation (Yücel et al., 2014). Ortas and Yucel (2020) reported that the mycorrhizal inoculum significantly influenced the cover crops' growth and biomass production under sterilized soils than that of non-sterile soils. Generally, in sterile and mycorrhizal conditions, plants grow better and have high total C fixation. Their results suggested that cover crops in single or mixed stands with mycorrhizal inoculations are expected to provide a significantly greater amount of biomass, which would contribute to soil organic matter and nutrient recycling for crop production. The indigenous AM fungus populations in intercropped and cover cropped fields reduced the need for chemical fertilization, especially P inputs (Elbon and Whalen, 2015). Cover crops influence the soil quality by supporting microbial diversity, providing organic matter, and recycling organically bound nutrients for plant growth as well. Cover crops fix atmospheric CO_2 and subsequently translate it into SOM via biological metabolism and chemical polymerism. According to Wagger et al. (1998), the cover crops are the most important choice to determine the dynamics of carbon and nitrogen in agricultural systems. In relation to the species of cover crops, Lal (2004) considered that the association of crop rotation system with NTS may increase the SOM and decrease the loss of carbon. Legumes as cover crops often contribute to the soil N fertility through biological N fixation (Barea et al., 2011). Mahama et al. (2016) reported that including legumes in the cropping systems has the potential to improve the N availability and crop yield with a substantial reduction in chemical N fertilization.

8.11 Soil Tillage

Excessive and traditional plowing, especially moldboard plowing parallel to the slope, has reportedly accelerated evaporation and wind erosion, as well as loss of biodiversity and soil organic matter content. Likewise, routine burning of crop residues not only increased CO_2 emission, but also increased evaporation, salinity, and soil erosion with an accelerated loss of biodiversity and soil organic matter content and degradation of soil quality.

Frequent inefficient irrigation, extensive plowing and crop residue burning, the dominance of the mono-cropping system, and excessive fertilization and reactive chemical use under naturally dry conditions results in accelerated loss of soil moisture by evapotranspiration (ET) and frequent droughts, severe wind erosion, secondary soil salinization (directly by upward movement of dissolved salts and indirectly by salt-tolerant weed plant uptake and surface deposition), dominance of drought and salt-tolerant weeds (e.g., velvet leaf, prickly pears, and *Salicornia* sp.), and imbalanced soil with reduced agroecosystem services.

Tillage, which is the first ring of agricultural production, is traditionally carried out deeply and by overturning with a plow. This processing technique leads to more evaporation in the soil, to the transport of soil by wind erosion, and to the loss of biological diversity and soil organic matter content. Zero or reduced tillage practices, which are a new agricultural application model against traditional tillage methods with high energy inputs, primarily reduce the deterioration of soil structure, reduce energy requirements, control soil erosion, increase soil organic matter, and reduce water evaporation and water losses on the soil surface to have a significantly positive effect on crop productivity in semi-arid areas to make ecosystems sustainable. Tillage was mechanized and done generally with disc harrow that opens the soil, increases soil evaporation, and reduces soil biological activity and fertility

Important results with no-tillage, including the use of cover crops and crop rotation, have been observed in research, mainly by growers who have obtained higher stability and higher productivity in soybean, maize, sorghum, beans and horticulture crops, perennial crops, etc., thus proving the efficiency of these systems toward sustainability (Calegari, 2020).

Crop residues with high N content and low C/N are more readily decomposed by microorganisms due to the lower straw recalcitrance, resulting in a fast loss of CO_2 to the atmosphere (Zhou et al., 2016). Tillage practices have a major effect on the distribution of C and N, as well as the rates of organic matter decomposition and N mineralization. Proper adoption of crop rotation can increase or maintain the quantity and quality of soil organic matter, and improve soil chemical and physical properties (Liu et al., 2006). Long-term cropping studies under no-till have resulted in increased SOC and total N with increased crop rotation diversity (Alhameid et al., 2017; Maiga et al., 2019), Cropping systems that incorporate legumes under no-till have also resulted in increased SOC (Conceição et al., 2013; Hobley et al., 2018).

Improvements in crop production may arise from several strategies, such as early sowing enabled by minimum tillage, increased use of organic manure, and efficient weed control. A range of crop and management strategies might be combined for a specific target environment in order to optimize crop productivity. These combinations can then be used as a guide to future decision support systems for crop production.

8.12 Fertilizing and Irrigation

It is necessary to develop new approaches to increase the fertility of the soil, which is of immense importance in agricultural production. Zeolite based on calcium clinoptilolite, which increases efficiency by affecting water-use efficiency, as well as physical, chemical, and microbial activities of the soil, and increases the efficiency of nitrogen and phosphorus, has recently been evaluated as a new approach in agricultural production. These approaches contribute to the protection of the environment, increase the water-holding capacity of the soil, and enable the soil to use nutrient cycles more effectively. The porous structure of zeolites controls the moisture in the soil. Water kept in a porous environment can be used when the plant needs it, and excessive irrigation practices are avoided. Zeolite can also be considered as a fertilization technique in terms of nitrogen retention, storage, and slow release. Storing the fertilizer in the pores with water will provide the plant with enough water and nitrogen as it is needed during the growing season. Considering this aspect, zeolite application will decrease nitrate accumulation in products and increase efficiency with the effective use of nitrogen. At the same time, the nitrogen stuck in the pores will wash off and prevent the groundwater from contamination. Soil-zeolite-N dynamics vary according to the physical-chemical structure of the soil, N fertilizer application, and crop management. Zeolite application is seen as a tool in order to reduce the negative effects of nitrogen fertilization on the environment and to increase fertilizer efficiency. Developing production models in crop production is an important agricultural strategy in terms of soil, environment, yield, and quality.

8.13 Conclusions

Legumes rank among humanity's most important agricultural food crops. They are grown in almost every climatic region and on a wide range of soil types. Thus, legume agriculture tends to be concentrated in marginal areas of low rainfall without irrigation, or as a dry season rotation crop after cereals grown in the rainy (monsoon) season. Legumes are important in human and animal feed for providing protein, micro- and macronutrients, vitamins, and essential amino acids. Within farming systems, legumes broadly constitute a valuable break crop that is important for weed control and prevention of soil and stubble-borne diseases through disrupting inoculum build-up. Also, legumes fix atmospheric nitrogen and therefore improve soil fertility by retaining the residual nitrogen in the soil.

Climatic changes due to temperature, water availability variation, and increases in CO_2 have become a major concern to agricultural development. At the same time, the world population is expected to be 10 billion in 2050. As a result, humanity is facing a major challenge in producing enough food for an additional three billion people, i.e., about 50% more, within the next 30 year. World demand for legumes is expected to grow in the foreseeable future, not only in developing countries, but also in the developed nations given the trend toward healthy dieting.

Climate changes certainly put pressure on productivity of field crops in general, and legume crops in particular, as legumes are more sensitive to such fluctuations and changes. Thus, it is essential internationally to make strategic decisions and implement approaches to combat and mitigate the challenges of climate change as early as possible.

There are many agronomic approaches for stress management. Some of them include making land management changes; making an informed choice of crops and varieties to be grown; and manipulating planting date, planting method, and sowing depth. Other options include changes to plant population, use of cover crops, alterations in intercropping, improved weed control, modifications to fertilizer application, interlinking and networking of national and international organizations, and implementation of integrated crop production and management technologies.

Especially in light of the effects on climate change, we should emphasize the possible troubled scenarios in arid and semi-arid zones, which can worsen in the near future. The requirements for strategies useful to alleviate the deficiencies of insufficient agricultural production could be based on a multidisciplinary global approach.

REFERENCES

Abate, T., A.D. Alene, D. Bergvinson, B. Shiferaw, S. Silim, A. Orr, and S. Asfaw. 2012. *Tropical grain legumes in Africa and South Asia: Knowledge and opportunities.* Nairobi: Kenya International Crops Research Institute for the Semi-Arid Tropics.

Ahmed, A., K.M. Khalafallah, Tawfik, A. Zinab, and Abd. El-Gawad 2008. Tolerance of seven faba bean varieties to drought and salt stresses. *Res. J. Agric. Biol. Sci* 4(2): 175–186.

Alhameid, A., M. Ibrahim, S. Kumar, P. Sexton, and T.E. Schumacher. 2017. Soil organic carbon changes impacted by crop rotation diversity under no-till farming in South Dakota, USA. *SSSA* 81: 868–877. 10.2136/sssaj2016.04.0121

Ali, M., G.C. Welna, A. Sallam, R. Martsch, C. Balko, B. Gebser, and W. Link. 2016. Association analyses to genetically improve drought and freezing tolerance of faba bean (L.). *CropScience* 56(3): 1036–1048. 10.2135/cropsci2015.08.0503

Anil, L., J. Park, R.H. Phippsand, and F.A. Miller. 1998. Temperature intercropping of cereals for forage: A review of the potential for growth and utilization with particular reference to the UK. *GrassForageScience* 53: 301–317.

Arbaoui, M., C. Balko, and W. Link. 2008. Study of faba bean (Vicia faba L.) winter-hardiness and development of screening methods. *Field Crop Res* 106(1): 60–67.

Aydemir, K.S. 2019. Maize and soybean intercropping under different seed rates of soybean under ecological condition of Bilecik, Turkey. *Int. J. Environ. Sci. Technol* 16: 5163–5170.

Bagayoko, M., A. Buerkert, G. Lung, A. Bationo, and V. Römheld. 2000. Cereal/legume rotation effects on cereal growth in Sudano-Sahelian West Africa: Soil mineral nitrogen, mycorrhizae and nematodes. *Plant Soil* 218: 103–116.

Baird, J.M., F.L. Walley, and S.J. Shirtliffe. 2009. Optimal seeding rate for organic production of field pea in the northern great plains. *Can. J. Plant Sci* 89: 455–464.

Barea, J.M., J. Palenzuela, P. Cornejo, I. Sanchez-Castro, C. NavarroFernandez, A. Lopez-Garcia, B. Estrada, R. Azcon, N. Ferrol, and C. Azcon-Aguilar. 2011. Ecological and functional roles of mycorrhizas in semi-arid ecosystems of Southeast Spain. *J. Arid. Environ. Dec* 75: 1292–1301.

Berger, J.D., S. Kumar, H. Nayyar, K.A. Street, J.S. Sandhu, J.M. Henzell, J. Kaure, and, H.C. Clarke. 2012. Temperature-stratified screening of chickpea (*Cicer arietinum* L.) genetic resource collections reveals very limited reproductive chilling tolerance compared to its annual wild relatives. *Field Crop Res* 126:119–129. 10.1016/j.fcr.2011.09.020.

Bilalis, D., N. Sidiras, G. Economou, and C. Vakali. 2003. Effect of different levels of wheat straw soil surface coverage on weed flora in *Vicia faba* crops. *J. Agron. Crop Sci* 189: 233–241. 10.1046/j.1439-037X.2003.00029.x

Boakye, B.A., and G. Wilson. 2019. Effect of cowpea (Vigna unguiculata) variety and plant spacing on grain and fodder yield, Asian. *J. Adv. Agric. Res* 10(1):1–9.

Bray, E.A. 2000. Responses to abiotic stresses, in Biochemistry and molecular biology of plants, eds. Buchanan, B., W. Gruissem, and R. Jones, (Rockville: American Society of Plant Physiologists), 1158–1203.

Brito, L.F., M.V. Azenha, E.R. Janusckiewicz, A.S. Cardoso, E.S. Morgado, E.B. Malheiros, R.A. Reis, and A.C. Ruggier. 2015. Seasonal fluctuation of soil carbon dioxide emission in differently managed pastures. *Agron. J* 107: 957–962.

Calegari, A. 2020. Crop Rotation and Cover Crop on No-Tillage. II Congresso Mundial sobre Agricultura Conservacionista. https://www.researchgate.net/publication/341039462 (accessed February 06, 2021).

Campos-Vega, R., and G.O. Loarca-Pina. 2010. Minor components of pulses and their potential impact on human health. *Food Res. Int* 43: 461–482.

Carbone, M.S., C.J. Still, A.R. Ambrose, T.E. Dawson, A.P. Williams, C.M. Boot, S.M. Schaeffer, and J.P. Schimel. 2011. Seasonal and episodic moisture controls on plant and microbial contributions to soil respiration. *Oecologia* 167: 265–278.

Conceição, P.C., J. Dieckow, and C. Bayer. 2013. Combined role of no-tillage and cropping systems in soil carbon stocks and stabilization. *Soil Tillage Res* 129: 40–47. 10.1016/j.still.2013.01.006

Croser J.S., F. Ahmad, H.J. Clarke, and K.H.M. Siddique. 2003. Utilisation of wild Cicer in chickpea improvement progress, constraints, and prospects. *Aust. J. Agric. Res* 54(5): 429–444. PubMed/NCBI Google Scholar

Cubero, J.I. 2017. Leguminosas hortícolas: Guisantes, judías y habas hortícolas, in Cultivos hortícolas al aire libre, eds. Maroto J.V. and C. Baxauli (Almería: Cajamar Caja Rural), 703–741.

Dantuma, G., and R. Thompson. 1983. Whole-crop physiology and yield components, in The faba bean (*Vicia faba* L.), eds. Hebblethwaite P.D., (London: Butterworths Publisher), 143–158.

Davies, S.L., N.C. Turner, K.H.M. Siddique, J.A. Plummer, and L. Leport. 1999. Seed growth of desi and Kabuli chickpea (Cicer arietinum L.) in a short-season Mediterranean-type environment. *Aust. J. Exp. Agr* 39: 181–188.

Delgado, J.A., P.M. Groffman, M.A. Nearing, T. Goddard, D. Reicosky, R. Lal, N.R. Kitchen, C.W. Rice, D. Towery, and P. Salon. 2011. Conservation practices to mitigate and adapt to climate change. *J. Soil Water Conserv* 66: 118A–129A.

Dhima, K.V., A.S. Lithourgidis, I.B. Vasilakoglou, and C.A. Dordas. 2007. Competition indices of common vetch and cereal intercrops in two seeding ratio. *Field Crops Res* 100: 249–256.

Duranti, M. 2006. Grain legume proteins and nutraceutical properties. *Fitoterapia* 77: 67–82. PMID: 16406359.

Elbon, A., and J.K. Whalen. 2015. Phosphorus supply to vegetable crops from arbuscular mycorrhizal fungi: A review. *Biol. Agric. Hortic* 31: 73–90.

Fang, X., N.C. Turner, G. Yan, F. Li, and K.H. Siddique. 2010. Flower numbers, pod production, pollen viability, and pistil function are reduced and flower and pod abortion increased in chickpea (*Cicer arietinum* L.) under terminal drought. *J. Exp. Bot* 61(2): 335–345.

FAO, IFAD, UNICEF, WFP and WHO. 2020. The State of Food Security and Nutrition in the World 2020. Transforming food systems for affordable healthy diets. Rome, FAO. 10.4060/ca9692en2020

Farooq, M., M. Hussain, A. Wakeel, and K.H.M. Siddique. 2015. Salt stress in maize: Effects, resistance mechanisms, and management. A review. *Agron. Sustain. Dev* 35: 461–481. 10.1007/s13593-015-0287-0

Fernandes, F.B.P., C.F. De Lacerda, E.M. De Andrade, A.L.R. Neves, C.H.C. De Sousa. 2015. Efeito de manejos do solo no déficit hídrico, trocas gasosas e rendimento do feijão-de-corda no semiárido. *Revista Ciência Agronômica* 46: 506–515.

Garg, R., R. Shankar, B. Thakkar, H. Kudapa, L. Krishnamurthy, N. Mantri, R.K. Varshney, S. Bhatia, and M. Jain. 2016. Transcriptome analyses reveal genotype- and developmental stage-specific molecular responses to drought and salinity stresses in chickpea. *Sci. Rep* 13(6): 19228.

Gaur, P.M., S. Srinivasan, C.L.L. Gowda, and B.V. Rao. 2007. Rapid generation advancement in chickpea. *SAT eJ* 3: 1.

González-Barrios, P., M. Bhatta, M.P. HalleySandro, and L. Gutiérrez. 2020. Speed breeding and early panicle harvest accelerates oat (*Avena sativa* L.) breeding cycles. *Crop Sci* 61: 320–330.

Gorim, L.Y., and A. Vandenberg. 2017. Evaluation of wild lentil species as genetic resources to improve drought tolerance in cultivated lentil. *Front. Plant Sci* 8: 1129. PubMed/NCBI Google Scholar

Guilioni, L., J. Wéry, and J. Lecoeur. 2003. High temperature and water deficit may reduce seed number in field pea purely by decreasing plant growth rate. *Funct. Plant Biol* 30: 1151–1164.

Guilioni, L., J. Wéry, and F. Tardieu. 1997. Heat stress-induced abortion of buds and flowers in pea: Is sensitivity linked to organ age or torelations between reproductive organs. *Ann. Bot* 80: 159–168.

Gunes, A., N. Cicek, A. Inal, M. Alpaslan, F. Eraslan, E. Guneri, and T. Guzelordu. 2006. Genotypic response of chickpea (Cicer arietinum L.) cultivars to drought stress implemented at pre-and post-anthesis stages and its relations with nutrient uptake and efficiency. *Plant Soil Environ* 52: 368–376.

Harland, J.I., and T.A. Haffner. 2008. Systematic review, meta-analysis and regression of randomised controlled trials reporting an association between an intake of circa 25 g soya protein per day and blood cholesterol. *Atherosclerosis* 200: 13–27.

Hobley, E.U., B. Honermeier, A. Don, M.I. Gocke, W. Amelung, and I. Kögel-Knabner. 2018. Decoupling of subsoil carbon and nitrogen dynamics after long-term crop rotation and fertilization. *Agr. Ecosyst Environ* 265: 363–373. 10.1016/j.agee.2018.06.021

Idrissi, O. 2020. Application of extended photoperiod in lentil: Towards accelerated genetic gain in breeding for rapid improved variety development. *Mor. J. Agri. Sci* 1(1): 14–19.

Iqbal, M.A., A. Hamid, T. Ahmad, M.H. Siddiqui, I. Hussain, S. Ali, A. Ali, and Z. Ahmad. 2019. Forage sorghum-legumes intercropping: Effect on growth, yields, nutritional quality and economic returns. *Bragantia* 78(1): 82–95. 10.1590/1678-4499.2017363

Ishag, H.M., and A.B. Mohamed. 1996. Write the sur. *Field Crops Res* 46: 169–176.

Izaurralde, R.C., N.G. Juma, W.B. McGill, D.S. Chanasyk, S. Pawluk, and M.J. Dudas. 1993. Performance of conventional and alternative cropping systems in cryoboreal subhumid central Alberta. *JAS* 120(01): 33–42.

Kamara, A.Y., L.O. Omoigui, N. Kamai, S.U. Ewansiha, and H.A. Ajeigbe. 2018. Improving cultivation of cowpea in West Africa, in Achieving sustainable cultivation of grain legumes volume 2: Improving cultivation of particular grain legumes, eds. Sivasankar S., D. Bergvinson, P.M. Gaur, S.K. Agrawal, S. Beebe, and M. Tamò, (Sawston, UK: Burleigh Dodds Science Publishing), 1–18. ISBN 978-1-78676-140-8.

Kashiwagi, J., L. Krishnamurthy, H.D. Upadhyaya, H.S. Krishna Chandra, V. Vadez, and R. Serraj. 2005. Genetic variability of drought-avoidance root traits in the mini-core germplasm collection of chickpea (Cicer arietinum L.). *Euphytica* 146: 213–222. 10.1007/s10681-005-9007-1

Keneni, A., F. Assefa, and P.C. Prabu. 2010. Characterization of acid and salt tolerant rhizobial strains isolated from faba bean fields of Wollo, Northern Ethiopia. *JAST* 12: 365–376.

Kögel-Knabner, I. 2002. The macromolecular organic composition of plant and microbial residues as inputs to soil organic matter. *Soil Biol. Biochem* 4: 139–162.

Korres, N.E., K.J. Norsworthy, P. Tehranchian, K.T. Gitsopoulos, A.D. Loka, M.D. Oosterhuis, D.R. Gealy, S.R. Moss, R.N. Burgos, R.M. Miller, and M. Palhano. 2016. Cultivars to face climate change effects on crops and weeds: A review. *Agron. Sustain. Dev.* 36: 12. 10.1007/s13593-016-0350-5

Krishnamurthy L., J. Kashiwagi, P.M. Gaur, H.D. Upadhyaya, and V. Vadez. 2010. Sources of tolerance to terminal drought in the chickpea (Cicer arietinum L.) minicore germplasm. *Field Crops Res* 119: 322–330. 10.1016/j.fcr.2010.08.002

Krishnamurthy L., J. Kashiwagi, S. Tobita, O. Ito, H.D. Upadhyaya, C.L.L. Gowda, M.P. Gaur, M.S. Sheshshayee, S. Singh, V. Vadez, and K.R. Varshney. 2013. Variation in carbon isotope discrimination and its relationship with harvest index in the reference collection of chickpea germplasm. *Funct Plant Biol* 14: 1350–1361. 10.1071/FP13088

Lal, R. 2004. Soil carbon sequestration to mitigate climate change. *Geoderma* 123(1): 1–22.

Landry, E.J., J.E. Lafferty, C.J. Coyne, W.L. Pan, and J. Hu. 2015. Registration of four winter-hardy faba bean germplasm lines for use in winter pulse and cover crop development. *J. Plant Regist* 9(3): 367–370. 10.3198/jpr2014.12.0087crg

Lane, A., and A. Jarvis. 2007. Changes in climate will modify the geography of crop suitability: Agricultural biodiversity can help with adaptation. Climate proofing innovation for poverty reduction and food security. Patancheru: ICRISAT.

Leport, L., N.C. Turner, R.J. French, D. Tennant, B.D. Thomson, and K.H.M. Siddique. 1998. Water relations, gas exchange and growth of cool-season grain legumes in a Mediterranean-type environment. *Eur. J. Agron* 9: 295–303.

Link, W., C. Balko, and F.L. Stoddard. 2010. Winter hardiness in faba bean: Physiology and breeding. *Field Crop Res* 115(3): 287–296. 10.1016/j.fcr.2008.08.004

Liu, X., S.J. Herbert, A.M.X. HashemiZhang, and G. Ding. 2006. Effects of agricultural management on soil organic matter and carbon transformation – A review. *Plant Soil Environ* 52(12): 531–543.

Lobell, D.B., and S.M. Gourdji. 2012. The influence of climate change on global crop productivity. *Plant Physiology* 160: 1686–1697.

Lobell, D.B., J.I. Ortiz-Monasterio, G.P. Asner, P.A. Matson, R.L. Naylor, and W.P. Falcon. 2005. Analysis of wheat yield and climatic trends in Mexico. *Field Crops Res* 94: 250–256. 10.1016/j.fcr.2005.01.007

López-Bellido, F.J., L. López-Bellido, and R.J. LópezBellido. 2005. Competition, growth and yield of faba bean (*Vicia faba* L.). *Eur. J. Agron* 23: 359–378.

Mafakheri A., A. Siosemardeh, B. Bahramnejad, P.C. Struik, and Y. Sohrabi. 2010. Effect of drought stress on yield, proline and chlorophyll contents in three chickpea cultivars. *Aust. J. Crop Sci* 4: 580–585.

Mahama, G.Y., P.V.V. Prasad, K.L. Roozeboom, J.B. Nippert, and C.W. Rice. 2016. Cover crops, fertilizer nitrogen rates, and economic return of grain sorghum. *Agron J* 108: 1–16.

Maiga, A., A. Alhameid, S. Singh, A. Polat, J. Singh, S. Kumar, and S. Osborne. 2019. Response of soil organic carbon, aggregate stability, carbon and nitrogen fractions to 15 and 24 years of no-till diversified crop rotations. *Soil Res* 57: 149–157. 10.1071/SR18068

Mantri N.L., R. Ford, T.E. Coram, and E.C. Pang 2007. Transcriptional profiling of chickpea genes differentially regulated in response to high-salinity, cold and drought. *BMC Genomics* 8: 303.

Marquez, T.C.L.L.S.M., C.A. Vasconcellos, I. Pereira Filho, G.E. França, and J.C. Cruz. 2000. Evolved carbon dioxide and nitrogen mineralization in a dark-red latosol with different managements. *Pesqui Agropecu Bras* 30: 581–589 (in Portuguese, with abstract in English).

Maxted, N., B.V. Ford, S.P. Kell, J.M. Iriondo, and M.E. Dulloo. 2008. Crop wild relative conservation and use. Wallingford, UK: CABI publishing.

Ortas, İ., and C. Yucel. 2020. Do mycorrhizae influence cover crop biomass production? Acta Agriculturae Scandinavica. Section B — *Soil Plant Sci* 70(8): 657–666. 10.1080/09064710.2020.1833975

Ortiz, R. 2018. Role of plant breeding to sustain food security under climate change, in Food security and climate change, eds. Yadav S.S., R.J. Redden, J.L. Hatfield, A.W. Ebert, and Danny Hunter, (John Wiley & Sons Ltd), 145–158.

Ouji, A., and M. Mouelhi. 2017. Influence of sowing dates on yield and yield components of lentil under semi-arid region of Tunisia. *Agri. BioTech* 38(2): 2077–2082.

Parikh, S.J., and James, B.R. 2012. Soil: The foundation of agriculture. ed. Parikh, S. J. *Nature Education Knowledge* 3(10): 2.

Paulsen, G.M. 1994. High temperature responses of crop plants, in Physiology and determination of crop yield, ed. Boote E. (Madison: ASA, CSSA, and SSSA), 365–389.

Pellissier, V., N.G. Munier-Jolain, and A. Larmure. 2007. High temperatures applied during seed filling of pea (*Pisum sativum* L.) affect seed growth and nitrogen partitioning within plant. in 6th European Conference on Grain Legumes. Lisbonne. Portugal. 12–16 November 2007.

Phelan, P., A.P. Moloney, E.J. McGeough, J. Humphreys, J. Bertilsson, E.G. Riordan, and P. O'Kiely. 2015. Forage legumes for grazing and conserving in ruminant production systems. *Critical Rev. Plant Sci* 34: 281–326.

Prasad, D., A.S. Bangarwa, S. Kumar, and A. Ram. 2012. Effect of sowing dates and plant population on chickpea (Cicer arietinum) genotypes. *Indian J. Agr* 57(2): 206–208.

Public Health England 2016. The Eatwell Guide. Department of Health in association with the Welsh Assembly Government, the Scottish Government and the Food Standards Agency in Northern Ireland, London.

Purushothaman, R., L. Krishnamurthy, H.D. Upadhyaya, V. Vadez, and R.K. Varshney. 2016. Shoot traits and their relevance in terminal drought tolerance of chickpea (*Cicer arietinum* L.). *Field Crop Res* 197: 10–27. 10.1016/j.fcr.2016.07.016

Rahbarian, R., R.K. Nejad, A. Ganjeali, A. Bagheri, and F. Najafi. 2011. Drought stress effects on photosynthesis, chlorophyll fluorescence and water relations in tolerant and susceptible chickpea (Cicer arietinum L.) genotypes. *Acta Biol. Cracoviensia Ser. Botanica* 53: 47–56. 10.2478/v10182-011-0007-2

Rebello, C.J., F.L. Greenway, and J.W. Finley. 2014. A review of the nutritional value of legumes and their effects on obesity and its related co-morbidities. *Obes. Rev* 15(5): 392–407. 10.1111/obr.12144

Richards, M.F., A.L. Preston, T. Napier, L. Jenkins, and L. Maphosa. 2020. Sowing date affects the timing and duration of key chickpea (*Cicer arietinum* L.) growth phases. *Plants* 9: 1257. 10.3390/plants9101257

Roy, T.S., T. Nishizawa, M.S. Islam, M.A. Razzaque, and M. Hasanuzzaman. 2009. Potentiality of small seedling tuber derived from true potato seed (*Solanumtuberosum* L.) and its economic return as affected by progeny and clump planting. *IJAEB* 2(4): 385–392.

Sabaghpour S.H., A.A. Mahmodi, A. Saeed, M. Kamel, and R.S. Malhotra. 2006. Study on chickpea drought tolerance lines under dryland condition of Iran. *Indian J. Crop Sci* 1: 70–73.

Sainju U.M., W.F. Whitehead, and B.P. Singh. 2005. Biculture legume–cereal cover crops for enhanced biomass yield and carbon and nitrogen. *Agron J* 97: 1403–1412.

Saleem, A., M.A. Zahid, H.I. Javed, M. Ansar, A. Ali, R. Saleem, and N. Saleem. 2012. Effect of seeding rate on lentil (*Lens culinaris* medik) seed yield under rainfed conditions. *Pakistan J. Agric. Res* 25: 3.

Saleh, S.M., S.M. Abou-Shleel, and A.F. Abou-Hadid. 2012. Prediction and adaptation of dry bean yield under climate change conditions. *Res. J. Agric. Biol. Sci* 8(2): 147–153.

Sallam, A., R. Martsch, and Y.S. Moursi. 2015. Genetic variation in morpho-physiological traits associated with frost tolerance in faba bean (*Vicia faba* L.). *Euphytica* 205: 395–408. 10.1007/s10681-015-1395-2

Samadi, B.Y., and S.A. Peighambari. 2000. Effect of sowing dates and seed rate on agronomic characteristics of lentil (Lens culinaris) in Karaj. *Iranian J. Agric. Sci* 31(4): 667–675.

Samineni S., M. Sen, S.B. Sajja, and P.M. Gaur. 2019. Rapid generation advance (RGA) in chickpea to produce up to seven generations per year and enable speed breeding. *Crop J* 8(1): 164–169.

Scalbert, A., C. Manach, C. Morand, C. Remesy, and L. Jimenez. 2005. Dietary polyphenols and the prevention of diseases. *Critical Rev. Food Sci* 45: 287–306.

Setimela, P.S. 2005. Screening sorghum seedlings for heat tolerance using a laboratory method. *Eur. J. Agron.* 23: 103–107.

Sharma, S., H.D. Upadhyaya, R.K. Varshney, C.L.L. Gowda. 2013. Pre-breeding for diversification of primary gene pool and genetic enhancement of grain legumes. *Front Plant Sci* 4: 309. PubMed/NCBI Google Scholar

Shunmugam, A.S.K., U. Kannan, Y. Jiang, K.A. Daba, and L.Y. Gorim. 2018. Physiology based approaches for breeding of next-generation food legumes. *Plants* 7: 72.

Silva, D.M.R., J.D. Santos, R.N. Costa, A.D.S. Lima, S.A. Santos, and L.D.S. Santos Silva. 2017. Resposta do feijoeiro alâminas de água aplicada em relação à evapotranspiração da cultura. *AGROTEC* 38: 71.

Singh, M., S. Kumar, A.K. Basandrai, D. Basandrai, N. Malhotra, R.D. Saxena, D. Gupta, A. Sarker, and K. Singh. 2020. Evaluation and identification of wild lentil accessions for enhancing genetic gains of cultivated varieties. *PLoS ONE* 15(3): e0229554. 10.1371/journal.pone.0229554

Sita, K., A. Sehgal, B. HanumanthaRao, R.M. Nair, P.V. Vara Prasad, S. Kumar, and H. Nayyar. 2017. Food legumes and rising temperatures: Effects, adaptive functional mechanisms specific to reproductive growth stage and strategies to improve heat tolerance. *Front. Recent Dev. Plant Sci* 8: 1658. 10.3389/fpls.2017.01658

Souza, S.A., V.J. Higino, F.B.D.S. Diego, G.H.D. Silva, and C.C. Aleman. 2020. Impact of irrigation frequency and planting density on bean's morpho-physiological and productive traits. *Water* 12: 2468. 10.3390/w12092468

Strohle, A., A. Waldmann, M. Wolters, and A. Hahn. 2006. Vegetarian nutrition: Preventive potential and possible risks part 1: Plant foods. *Wien Klin Wochenschr* 118: 580–593.

Sultani, M.I., M.A. Gill, M.M. Anwar, and M. Athar. 2007. Evaluation of soil physical properties as influenced by various green manuring legumes and phosphorus fertilization under rain fed conditions. *Int. J. Environ. Sci. Technol* 4(1): 109–118.

Thudi, M., H.D. Upadhyaya, A. Rathore, P.M. Gaur, L. Krishnamurthy, M. Roorkiwal, S.N. Nayak, S.K. Chaturvedi, P.S. Basu, N.V. Gangarao, A. Fikre, P. Kimurto, P.C. Sharma, M.S. Sheshashayee, S. Tobita, J. Kashiwagi, O. Ito, A. Killian, and R.K. Varshney. 2014. Genetic dissection of drought and heat tolerance in chickpea through genome-wide and candidate gene-based association mapping approaches. *PLoS One* 9(5): 96758.

Trevaskis, B. 2015. Wheat gene for all seasons. *Proc. Natl. Acad. Sci* 112: 11991–11992. 10.1073/pnas.15163 98112

Tripathi, A.D., R. Mishra, K.K. Maurya, R.B. Singh, and D.W. Wilson. 2019. Estimates for world population and global food availability for global health, in The role of functional food security in global health, eds. Singh R.B., R.R. Watson, and T. Takahashi (Cambridge: Academic Press), 3–24.

Turk, M.A., A.M. Tawaha, and M.K.J. El-Shatnawi. 2003. Response of lentil (*Lens culinaris* Medik) to plant density, sowing date, phosphorus fertilization and ethephon application in the absence of moisture stress. *J. Agron. Crop Sci* 189: 1–6.

Turner, N.C., S. Abbo, J.D. Berger, S.K. Chaturvedi, R.J. French, C. Ludwig, D.M. Mannur, S.J. Singh, and H.S. Yadava. 2007. Osmotic adjustment in chickpea (Cicer arietinum L.) results in no yield benefit under terminal drought. *J. Exp. Bot* 58(2): 187–194.

Upadhyaya, H.D., J. Kashiwagi, R.K. Varshney, P.M. Gaur, K.B. Saxena, L. Krishnamurthy, C.L. Gowda, R.P. Pundir, S.K. Chaturvedi, and P.S. Basu. 2012. Singh IP Phenotyping chickpeas and pigeonpeas for adaptation to drought. *Front Physiol* 3: 179.

Valtion Ravitsemusneuvottelukunta (VRN) 2014, Nutrition Recommendations Available at: http://www.ravitsemusneuvottelukunta.fi/portal/en/nutrition+recommendations/ (accessed March 30 2016).

Vanderpuye, A.W. 2010. Canopy architecture and plant density effect in short-season chickpea (*Cicer arietinum* L.), Phd Thesis, University of Saskatchewan, Saskatoon, Canada. http://hdl.handle.net/10388/etd-09122010-182808

Wagger, M.G., M.L. Cabrera, and N.N. Ranells. 1998. Nitrogen and carbon cycling in relation to cover crop residue quality. *Soil Water Conserv* 53(3): 214–218.

Wang, H.L., Y. Gan, R.Y. Wang, J.Y. Niu, H. Zhao, Q.G. Yang, and G.C. Li. 2008. Phenological trends in winter wheat and spring cotton in response to climate changes in northwest China. *Agric. For. Meteorol* 148: 1242–1251. 10.1016/j.agrformet.2008.03.003

Yücel, D. 2012. The effect of different priming treatments and germination temperatures on germination performance of lentil (*Lens culinaris Medik*) seeds. *ARPN J. Agri. Bio Sci* 7(12): 977–998.

Yücel Özveren, D., A. Ton, and A.E. Anlarsal. 2012. Determining the Yield and Yield Components of Some Winter Chickpea (*Cicer arietinum* L.) Genotypes in Mediterranean Climate Conditions. Inter. Symposium for Agriculture and FoodXXXVII Faculty-Economy MeetingIV Macedonian Symposium for Viticulture and Wine Production VII Simposium for Vegetable and Flower Production, December, 12–14 Skopje.

Yucel, C., M. Avcı, M. Kızılsimsek, and R. Hatipoğlu. 2020. Yield and quality of silage from soybean-maize intercropping. *Fresenius Environ Bull* 29(2): 874–883.

Yücel, C., M. Avcı, H. Yucel, U. Sevilmiş, and R. Hatipoğlu. 2018b. Effects of seed mixture ratio and harvest time on forage yield and silage quality of intercropped berseem clover with triticale. *Fresenius Environ. Bull* 27(8): 5312–5322.

Yücel, C., D. Yücel, İ. Ortaş, and K.R. Islam. 2013. İklim Değişikliklerinin Tarım Üzerine Olası Etkileri, Alınması Düşünülen Tarımsal Önlemler. Türkiye X. Tarla Bitkileri Kongresi, 10-13 Eylül 2013 Konya.

Yücel, C., İ. İnal, D. Yucel, and R. Hatipoğlu. 2018a. Effects of mixture ratio and cutting time on forage yield and silage quality of intercropped Berseem clover and Italian ryegrass Legume Research. *Fresenius Environ. Bull* 41(5): 1–8.

Yücel, C., D. Yücel, I. Ortaş, and K.R. Islam. 2014. Management systems impact on soil aggregate protected carbon and nitrogen sequestration. Balkan Agriculture Congress 08–11 September 2014 (Oral Presentation) Edirne-TURKEY (Oral Presentation) 206-206.

Zhou, G., J. Zhang, C. Zhang, C. Feng, L. Chen, Z. Yu, X. Xin, and B. Zhao. 2016. Effects of changes in straw chemical properties and alkaline soils on bacterial communities engaged in straw decomposition at different temperature. *Sci. Rep* 6: 22186.

9

Sustainable Amelioration Options and Strategies for Salinity-Impacted Agricultural Soils

Hossain Md Anawar[1] and Mohammad Zabed Hossain[2]
[1]Ariban AgriEnviro Engineering Ltd., Mirpur-1, Dhaka, Bangladesh
[2]Department of Botany, University of Dhaka, Dhaka, Bangladesh

CONTENTS

9.1 Introduction

Salinity significantly affects the productivity of crop plants (Shrivastava and Kumar, 2015). Increased salinity negatively affects plants by influencing germination, growth, reproduction, and physiological processes, including photosynthesis, respiration, transpiration, membrane properties, nutrient balance, enzymatic activity, metabolic activities, cellular homeostasis, hormone regulation, and production of reactive oxygen species. In severe stress, it leads to plant death (Mahajan and Tuteja, 2005; Hasanuzzaman et al., 2012; Khan et al., 2014). Although the average record yield of most of the important crops ranges between 20% and 50%, for the rest, most of the losses occur due to drought and high soil salinity, indicating the severity of the problem globally. The total salt-affected area in the world is 831 million ha, which includes 397 and 434 million ha of saline and sodic soils, respectively (FAO, 2000). More than 45 million ha of irrigated land are affected by salt, which account for 20% of total land, and 1.5 million ha of land are taken out of production each year owing to high salinity levels (Pitman and Läuchli, 2002; Munns and Tester, 2008). If this trend of increased salinity continues in such a way, 50% of cultivable lands will be lost by the middle of the 21st century (Mahajan and Tuteja, 2005). Simple extrapolation suggests that the global annual cost of salt-induced land degradation in irrigated areas could be US$ 27.3 billion because of lost crop production (Qadir et al., 2014). Moreover, the anticipated global climate change has created enormous concerns about the extent of salinity problems through sea-level rise. Given the salt-affected lands as a valuable resource, it can be cost-effective to invest in sustainable land management and effective remediation of salt-affected lands in countries confronting salt-induced land degradation (Qadir et al., 2014).

A wide range of adaptations and mitigation strategies are required to cope with the impacts of salinity. The various ways for remediation and proper utilization of saline soils include soil amendment, agronomic practices, use of salt-tolerant crop varieties, and phytoremediation. Salinity and sodicity of agricultural soils cause nutrient deficiency and ion toxicity in crop plants. Therefore, the remediation of saline and sodic soils can potentially improve the fertility of sodic soils. However, fertilizer application and improvement of soil organic matter are essential to increase yields to match the potential yield predictable from climate (Naidu and Rengasamy, 1993). Salinity stress can be reduced or removed by proper management of resources and improvement of crops breeds. However, such strategies are long drawn and cost intensive, so there is a need to develop simple and low-cost biological methods for the management of salinity stress, which can be used on a short-term basis (Shrivastava and Kumar, 2015). Thus, methods for efficient remediation and amelioration for salt-affected soils vary with the nature and extent of the severity of the problem. Therefore, enhanced knowledge about the mechanisms of various methods for mitigation and amelioration of salinity as well as about the advantages and disadvantages of these methods are relevant to tackle salinity-induced problems in agricultural soils.

9.2 Strategies for Mitigating Salt Stress

Most of the salinity-affected cropping lands are reported to be found in the high agricultural activity areas of Asia and Australia (Ondrasek et al., 2011). The excessive concentration (EC) and ratios (e.g. ESP, SAR) among particular salts (Na, Cl, Ca, Mg) and pH conditions should be monitored and managed for reclamation of salt-affected soils in crop production. Such salt-affected soils can be categorized into: (i) saline (ECe > 4 dS/m, ESP < 15 and pH <8.5), (ii) saline-sodic (ECe > 4 dS/m, ESP > 15 and pH <8.5), and (iii) sodic (ECe >4 dS/m, ESP >15 and pH >8.5), each requiring specific approaches for reclamation (Horney et al., 2005) and sustainable land management practices, which are usually costly and difficult to implement, and may even result in further degradation. A broader strategy is required to ensure identification and effective removal of barriers to the adoption of sustainable land management, including perverse subsidies. Adopting the strategies to reverse land degradation by salinity would need several years. Therefore, short-term salinity management strategies could provide an alternative for effective remediation of salinity-affected soils. Some researchers reported that costless removal of salinity would augment annual profits by A$187 million, and sodicity by A$1034·6 million in Australia. Two main approaches are adopted for sustainable agricultural management of salt-affected soils (Ondrasek et al., 2011): a prevention process to avoid further salinization and remediation management (i.e. reclamation of existing salinized land/water), but these processes usually overlap (Biggs et al., 2010). Several important parameters should be considered in the selection of the most appropriate management strategies or approaches: (i) the characteristics of soil

TABLE 9.1

Principles, Advantages, and Disadvantages of Various Methods Used for Mitigation and Amelioration of Salinity and Sodicity in Soil

Basic principle	Methods	Advantages/Disadvantages
Biological	1. Use of salt-tolerant variety and transgenic	1. Environmentally friendly 2. Use of salt-tolerant variety is effective in poor-quality irrigation water 3. Traditional breeding method for the development of salt-tolerant variety is time-consuming 4. Does not remove salts from soil 5. Development of stress-tolerant crop varieties by genetic engineering is expensive 6. Lack of knowledge about the fundamental mechanisms of stress tolerance in plants
	1. Microorganisms	1. Cost effective 2. Environmentally friendly 3. Rapid
	2. Phytoremediation	1. Environmentally friendly 2. Economically feasible 3. Time-consuming 4. Process is limited to soil depth associated with the rooting zone
Inorganic fertilizers amendments	1. Application of lime	1. Not environmentally friendly 2. Economically not feasible
	2. Application of gypsum	1. Not environmentally friendly 2. Cost-intensive
	3. Application of Zn-fertilizer	1. Not environmentally friendly 2. Cost-intensive
	4. Integrated plant nutrient supplies	1. Economically feasible 2. Prior knowledge on soil nutrient status is required
Organic amendments	1. Biochar and compost	1. Environmentally friendly 2. Renewable 3. Economically feasible
	2. Peat	1. Environmentally friendly 2. Non-renewable
	3. Furfural residues	1. Environmentally friendly 2. Renewable
Cropping system	1. Cropping system adaptation	1. Environmentally friendly 2. Economically feasible
	2. Irrigation	1. Environmentally friendly 2. Economically feasible

chemistry (i.e. salt type and concentrations, acidity, alkalinity), (ii) groundwater hydrology (e.g. watertable fluctuation), (iii) climate conditions (precipitation, evapotranspiration), and (iv) plant species selection.

The various methods used for mitigation and amelioration of salt-affected soils have their own advantages and disadvantages (Table 9.1). Based on the basic mechanism of mitigation and amelioration, these methods could be grouped into agronomic practices, biological amendments, chemical amendments, and organic amendments described as follows:

9.2.1 Agronomic Practices

The extent of salinity can be reduced by various agronomic practices, including opportunity cropping. Opportunity cropping assumes implementation of conservation tillage systems to restrict losses of soil moisture; prevent soil erosion; and reduce soil compaction, disturbance, and energy consumption, i.e. conserve plant-available water and OM. Under such land management, at least 30% of the crop residues may remain on the soil surface. Besides these, opportunity cropping offers some other measures, such as double cropping (consociation of cereals and forages), selection of crop species (e.g. perennial deep rotted, more salt-tolerant), presence of pasture and tree species (for windbreaks, controlling groundwater level), and so forth. Lucerne, as a relatively salt-tolerant and deep-rooted legume/perennial pasture, can very effectively control groundwater recharge and dewater in the soil profile within the first 18 months of establishment (Powell, 2004).

9.2.1.1 Irrigation

Proper selection of modern irrigation systems (e.g. drippers vs. micro sprinklers) and mulch cropping approaches may significantly reduce negative ecological consequences (e.g. yield/vegetative growth declining, mortality of cultured crop, increased EC created by use of saline water for irrigation [ECw up to 7 dS/m] [Romic et al., 2008]). Thus, establishing adequate drainage and/or ensuring sufficient volume of good-quality (low-salinity) water for irrigation and salt leaching from the root zone may be an appropriate strategy for at least partially reclaiming saline soils.

Salinization can be restricted by leaching of salt from root zone and changed farm management practices (Shrivastava and Kumar, 2015). Partial root zone drying methodology, and drip or micro-jet irrigation can provide efficient use of water and better irrigation in agriculture. The cultivation of deep-rooted perennial plants can reduce the amount of water passing beyond the roots and reduce the spread of dry land salinity. These plant roots prevent rising water tables and the movement of salt to the soil surface (Manchanda and Garg, 2008). Proper timing of irrigation can help to avoid low levels of soil water that cause increased salinity. Frequent water applications maintain low matric water stress and keep the salts moving through and away from the root mass.

9.2.1.2 Crop Rotation

Farming systems can be changed to diversified approaches that include perennial plants in rotation with annual crops (phase farming), in mixed plantings (alley farming, intercropping), or in site-specific plantings (precision farming) (Munns et al., 2002) if the cost and availability of good water quality or water resource is sustainable.

9.2.1.3 Use of Grafting

Grafting is a widely used technique in horticulture for asexual propagation and may also be helpful in withstanding deleterious salinity effects (e.g. Cl toxicity) in crops. It was well documented that certain rootstock-scion combinations can reduce uptake and root-shoot translocation/accumulation of dissolved salts (Na^+ and/or Cl^-) in mango (Schmutz and Ludders, 1999), citrus (reviewed by Storey and Walker, 1999), and grapevines (Stevens and Walker, 2002).

9.2.1.4 Use of Priming Techniques

Several attempts have been made to improve salt tolerance by hydropriming, pre-sowing chilling treatment (Basra et al., 2005), halopriming (Kamboh et al., 2000), and ascorbate priming (Borsani et al., 2001; Afzal et al., 2006). Priming can augment the activity of free radicals, which can scavenge enzymes and reduce the salt stress-induced damages in plants. Seed priming (osmoconditioning) with salinized (NaCl) solution prior to sowing is one of possible methods for improving salt tolerance in a wide range of relatively salt-sensitive crops (e.g. tomato, muskmelon, cucumber) (e.g. Sivritepe et al., 2003, 2005). Cuartero and Fernández-Muñoz (1999) conducted a detailed literature review, which suggested priming in 1 M NaCl for 36 hours in the case of direct sowing, and for seedlings, conditioning in moderately saline solution or by withholding water for 20–24 hours, although specific duration and concentrations should be adapted to a particular crop (Ondrasek et al., 2011).

9.2.2 Biological Methods

9.2.2.1 Use of Salt-Tolerant Crops and Transgenics

Using salt-tolerant crops is one of the most important strategies to solve the problem of salinity (Shrivastava and Kumar, 2015). Salt tolerance in crops will allow the more effective use of poor-quality irrigation water. Enhanced salt tolerance in crop plants may be achieved via traditional and molecular breeding and transgenic approaches (Ondrasek et al., 2011). In addition, cell and tissue culture techniques are used to identify somaclonal variants and screen germplasm for salt tolerance in vitro (Arzani, 2008).

Some proteins respond to salt stress in plants and can directly regulate the levels of osmolytes and control ion homeostasis. Osmolytes, such as mannitol, fructans, proline, and glycinebetaine, are also active in scavenging reactive oxygen species. Genetic engineering of these osmolytes resulted in increasing salt tolerance (Harinasuth et al., 1996; Sahi et al., 2006; Zhu, 2001). Conventional techniques and more recently genetic breeding program are applied to enhance the salt tolerance of crops. However, fundamental mechanisms of stress tolerance in plants are not completely understood.

9.2.2.2 Remediation by Using Microorganisms

Plant-associated microorganisms can play an important role in conferring resistance to abiotic stresses. These organisms could include rhizoplane, rhizosphere, and endophytic bacteria and symbiotic fungi, which operate through a variety of mechanisms like triggering osmotic response, providing growth hormones and nutrients, acting as biocontrol agents, and inducing novel genes in plants (Shrivastava and Kumar, 2015). Microbial inoculation to alleviate stresses in plants could be a more cost-effective, environmentally friendly option that could be available in a shorter time frame.

Some studies reported that the utilization of plant growth promoting bacteria (PGPB) can alleviate salinity stress to plants (Yao et al., 2010). Inoculations with AM (arbuscular mycorrhizal) fungi improved plant growth under salt stress (Cho et al., 2006). Kohler et al. (2006) demonstrated the beneficial effect of PGPR, *Pseudomonas mendocina* strains on stabilization of soil aggregate. Kohler et al. (2009) investigated the influence of inoculation with a PGPR, *P. mendocina*, alone or in combination with an AM fungus, *Glomus intraradices*, or *G. mosseae* on growth and nutrient uptake and other physiological activities of *Lactuca sativa* under salt stress.

Plants treated with Exo-poly saccharides (EPS) producing bacteria showed higher resistance to water and salinity stress due to improved soil structure (Sandhya et al., 2009). EPS can also bind to cations, including Na^+, thus making it unavailable to plants under saline conditions. Chen et al. (2007) reported correlation of proline accumulation with drought and salt tolerance in plants. Increased production of proline, along with decreased electrolyte leakage, maintenance of relative water content of leaves, and selective uptake of K ions resulted in salt tolerance in *Zea mays* co-inoculated with *Rhizobium* and *Pseudomonas* (Bano and Fatima, 2009). Tank and Saraf (2010) showed that PGPRs, which are able to solubilize phosphate and produce phytohormones and siderophores in salt conditions, promote growth of tomato plants under 2% NaCl stress.

9.2.2.3 Phytoremediation of Salt-Affected Soil

Use of salt-tolerant crops does not remove the salt; hence, halophytes that have the capacity to accumulate and exclude the salt can be an effective way to remove salt from the soil (Ashraf et al., 2005, 2010; Rabhi et al., 2008, 2009; Stuart et al., 2012). Several halophyte species, including grasses, shrubs, and trees, can remove the salt from different kinds of salt-affected problematic soils through salt exclusion, excretion, or accumulation by their morphological, anatomical, and physiological adaptation in their organelle level and cellular level. Halophytes planted to reduce salinity can meet some basic needs of people in salt-affected areas as well.

Halophytes can effectively improve saline soil as they are well adjusted in a salt environment because of their diversified adaptation mechanisms, including ion compartmentalization, osmotic adjustment, succulence, ion transport and uptake, antioxidant systems, maintenance of redox status, and salt inclusion or excretion (Lokhande and Suprasanna, 2012). There are diversified species of halophytes suited to grow in different saline regions throughout the world. So, these plants can be grown in land and water containing high salt concentration; can be substituted for conventional crops; can be a good source of food, fuel, fodder, fiber, essential oils, and medicine (Lokhande and Suprasanna, 2012); and can be used from the reclamation of salt-affected soils (de Villiers et al., 1995; Gul et al., 2000; Jithesh et al., 2006). *Salicornia bigelovii*, an oilseed halophyte, for example, yields $2\,t\,ha^{-1}$ of seed containing 28% oil and 31% protein, which is similar to soybean yield and seed quality (Glenn et al., 1999). As the reclamation of salt-affected soils is not completely feasible, and is not always cost-effective, researchers are searching for biosaline agriculture; thus, it is necessary to obtain a better understanding of how naturally adapted plants (halophytes) handle salts. On the other hand, given their high potential, halophytes can be applied for desalination and restoration of saline soils and phytoremediation as well. However, more research is needed to study the utilization of halophytes to remove excess salinity added by irrigation.

9.2.3 Amendments by Inorganic Fertilizers

Application of inorganic fertilizers, lime, gypsum, etc. to pedosphere with excessive concentration of salts has multiple beneficial roles. As an example, cation exchange of Ca for Na (e.g. with Ca-based amendments) i.e. the addition of an electrolyte, such as Ca (also Mg) helps to maintain micro-aggregate integrity in the soil profile. The surface and/or deep treatment by applied lime or gypsum, with or without deep-ripping to 25–30 cm ameliorated subsoil constraints, such as subsurface compaction, acidity, and/or subsoil sodicity or salinity on canola yields in southern NSW; and canola was surprisingly tolerant to most subsoil constraints (Swan et al., 2010). Supplementary application of Ca may result in many benefits (e.g. reduced accumulation of Na and improved K and Ca uptake, dry matter production, yield) for crops grown under saline conditions (Cuartero and Fernández-Muñoz, 1999). The Maize (*Zea mays* L.) plants showed substantial reduction in some parameters (e.g. germination, early growth, biomass, total nitrogen, nitrate reductase activity, photosynthetic function, leaf area, chlorophyll contents) due to imposition of salinity and sodicity in root medium (Khan et al., 2014). The use of additional K brought about an enhancement in these parameters.

9.2.3.1 Application of Lime

Application of lime ($CaCO_3$) provides an electrolyte source for ensuring sufficient Ca-for-Na replacement, whereas in naturally $CaCO_3$-sufficient soils, H_2SO_4 application (or its precursor, elemental S) in reaction with carbonates ultimately produces gypsum i.e. exchangeable Ca (e.g. Horney et al., 2005). However, the low solubility of lime in neutral and alkaline soils prevents Ca release to participate in exchange reactions. Lime application to an acid sodic soil will address both the acidity and sodicity. Application of lime to a neutral or alkaline sodic soil will have little or no effect (Menzies et al., 2015). Some of the adverse soil structural aspects of sodicity may be addressed by increasing the organic matter content of soils -the organic matter acting to bind soil aggregates, sustaining soil structure. Although it is not an easy task, farmers usually try to increase the organic matter content of their soils due to its different beneficial effects.

9.2.3.2 Amelioration by Gypsum Addition

The most common ameliorant applied to sodic soils to correct soil structural problems is gypsum (Menzies et al., 2015). It promotes flocculation through both mechanisms; increasing soil solution ionic strength and supplying divalent Ca ions to displace Na from exchange sites. The first of these effects (increased ionic strength) is immediate and can be achieved by relatively low rates of gypsum application, but the effect is short lived (especially if the application rate is low). The use of gypsum can effectively improve soil surface conditions at sowing, provide better soil tilth, and reduce crusting.

The use of gypsum ($CaSO_4 \cdot 2H_2O$) provides Ca (Ca^{2+}) in saline soils, which reduces a high percentage of the exchangeable Na^+ in soils and reduces Na^+ from the cations exchange sites, resulting in its reduced uptake by plants (Mahmoodabadi et al., 2013; Bello et al., 2021). This exchange of Ca^{2+} for

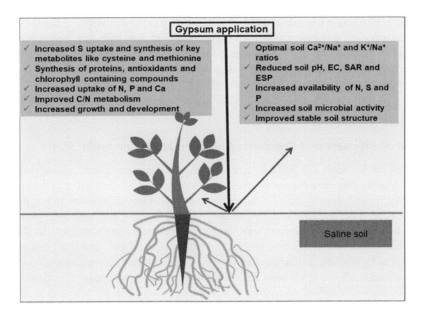

FIGURE 9.1 The effects of gypsum at the soil–plant interface in salinity-affected soil (From Bello et al., 2021, creative commons license).

Na$^+$ in the soil colloids improves soil stabilization and permeability (Equation (1)). However, the gypsum should be thoroughly mixed with the soil followed by adequate water application to remove the displaced Na$^+$ from the rhizosphere and increase more Ca$^+$ availability and uptake by plants (Figure 9.1). Ca supplementation enhances the hydraulic conductivity and leaf surface area, resulting in increased crop tolerance to salinity stress (Bello et al., 2021). Furthermore, Ca^{2+} performs a few more beneficial effects: the activation of salt signalling pathways, such as the SOS pathway and a quick response against salt stress; maintaining cell membrane integrity and selectivity; preventing excessive accumulation of Na$^+$ and Cl$^-$; increasing the K$^+$/Na$^+$ ratio in salinity-stressed plants; and reversing the negative impact of salinity on P uptake.

$$\text{Soil colloids} - Na^+ + CaSO_4 \cdot 2H_2O = \text{Soil colloids} - Ca^{2+} + Na_2SO_4 + 2H_2O$$

9.2.3.3 By Using Zinc-Fertilizers

Application of Zn fertilizer may be beneficial in a saline/sodic environment. It was confirmed that ZnSO$_4$ may improve salt tolerance in cereals and results in several other important benefits, such as crop micronutrient enrichment (e.g. by 90% for Zn) and reduced uptake/phytoaccumulation of toxic elements (e.g. by >100% for Cd) (Khoshgoftar et al., 2004). However, Zn fertilization is not always suitable due to its ecological/economic consequences, whereas cropping of Zn-efficient species/genotypes on such Zn-deficient soils is one possible approach, which can reduce land degradation and minimize the use of fertilizers (Khoshgoftar et al., 2004; Rengel and Graham, 1995).

9.2.3.4 Integrated Plant Nutrient Supplies

The nutrient availability in soil and uptake by plants are influenced by the high concentrations of salts, especially salinity and sodicity. The crop responses to applied nutrients demonstrate great variations in saline and sodic soils, because they have different chemical composition, precipitation-dissolution reactions, adsorption-desorption kinetics, and transformation of nutrients. The high concentrations of CaCO$_3$ and poor air-relations affect the solubility and availability of nutrients in sodic soils. In saline soils, the solubilities of these cations do not decrease, and they remain in available forms. The degree of salinity also influences crop response to fertilizer. The integrated plant nutrient supplies can alleviate the adverse effects of salinity and sodicity, whereas crop residues are available at the farm level. The multiple/diverse nutrient sources can be applied to maintain crop yields and reclaim the soil. In short, special plant nutrient management strategies are needed for salt-affected soils.

9.2.4 Organic Amendments

9.2.4.1 Use of Biochars and Composts to Remediate Saline-Sodic Soil

The application of biochars and organic amendments is more sustainable, cost-effective, and environmentally friendly than more expensive inorganic amendments to reclaim salt-affected soils. The study of Chaganti (2015) and Solaiman et al. (2020) showed that soil aggregate stability and hydraulic conductivity improvements were greatest with composts. Biochars increase soil aggregate stability and soil hydraulic conductivity relative to untreated soils. Organic amendments significantly increased Na^+ leaching, with corresponding decreases in leaching times. Cumulative losses of Ca^{2+} and Mg^{2+} were greatest from composts followed by biochars, indicating their potential to contribute divalent cations. Both biochars and composts significantly affect soil pH and CEC. Biochars and composts improve significantly the physio-chemical and biological factors of soils, resulting in improved crop yields (Solaiman et al., 2020).

High alkalinity and/or salinity decreases microbial activity and hence the rate of N mineralization. Thus, it necessitates higher rates of N fertilizers (Rashid, 2006). Also, due to the adverse effects of salinity and sodicity on transformations of soil and applied fertilizer N, crops respond to much higher levels of N in these soils compared with normal soils. Green manuring can improve fertilizer N use efficiency by crops.

9.2.4.2 Use of Peat

Peat is generated partly by the decomposition process of plants that slowly accumulates in pond and lake bottoms and swamp areas. Sedge peat and sphagnum peat moss are the most common types of peat used for soil remediation, and the former is a fine-textured and more decomposed type of peat. Sedge peat can hold water and nutrients 10 to 15 times its own weight when fully saturated, yet still can hold 40% air and can reduce salinity effects (Wang et al., 2014). Peat has high soil CEC and pH buffering capacity owing to its great soil-specific surface and chelation capacity, and it can be used to ameliorate salt-affected soils.

9.2.4.3 Furfural Residues

Furfural residue is the by-product of furfural production and is mainly obtained from corn cobs by acid catalysis at high temperature. Because the cellulose and lignin in corn cobs are relatively stable, furfural residue is enriched in cellulose and lignin. Furfural residue has proved to be useful for amendment of salt-affected soil (Wang et al., 2014).

9.2.5 Effects of Bio-organic Amendments on Saline Soils

There are different types of organic materials, such as organic compost, straw, organic manure, green manure, humic substances, and biochar. The use of these organic materials with saline soils may improve soil quality and health as well as microbial populations for increased crop production. Bio-organic amendments, which include the integrated use of beneficial microbes and organic sources of nutrients in the agricultural crop production, have a high potential to improve both soil and crop productivity through increased soil organic matter, essential nutrients (especially, N and P) and water availability, stable soil structure, and increased microbial activity (Bello and Yusuf, 2021). The beneficial microbes or bio-fertilizers, especially plant growth-promoting (PGP) microorganisms, arbuscular mycorrhizal fungi (AMF), cellulose-decomposing bacteria, P-solubilizing bacteria, and N-fixing bacteria improve the

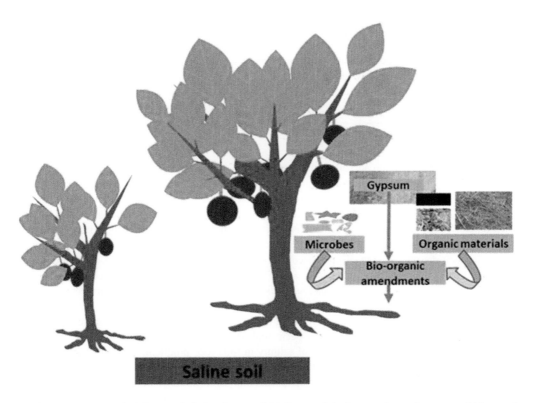

FIGURE 9.2 A hypothetical diagram depicting the potential influence of the integrated use of gypsum and bio-organic amendments on crop production (From Bello et al., 2021, creative commons license).

tolerance of crops to salinity stress (Mbarki et al., 2017). For example, *Trichoderma harzianum* significantly improved soil fertility, biodiversity, and yield of tomato under salinity stress conditions.

9.2.6 Combined Use of Gypsum and Bio-organic Amendments

Although there are many amendments, $CaSO_4 \cdot 2H_2O$ and bio-organic amendments are continuously recognized to be more effective to improve the biological, physical, and chemical properties of saline soils for increased food production. Given the significant positive effects of the beneficial microbes and organic materials in soil fertility improvement, their integration with gypsum application has the potential to have a remarkable effect on the amelioration of saline soils (Figure 9.2).

A soil column study demonstrated that the combined application of gypsum and organic compost (rice straw and hyacinth) significantly reduced the salinity and sodicity levels of a saline-sodic soil compared to the control or the use of either gypsum or compost alone (Abdel-Fattah, 2012). The use of gypsum and compost together showed the highest yield of onion in a saline-sodic soil by causing a reduction in EC, ESP, pH, and SAR (Kitila et al., 2020).

9.3 Global Climate Change and Salinity: A Case Study of Reclamation and Adaptations

Increased sea level rise as a consequence of global climate change has increased salinity problems in the agriculture of coastal areas in countries like Bangladesh. Reduced flow of freshwater from upstream has intensified the salinity problem in Bangladesh. The crop cultivation pattern has become challenging in these salt-affected areas. Farmers try to handle the salinity problem at their own level through applying lime, gypsum, etc. in the southwest region of Bangladesh, where climate change and sea level rise has exacerbated the salinity problem (Haider and Hossain, 2013). They cultivate crops in relatively less affected land. They adopt the policy of diversification for crop production on these agricultural lands. They also emphasize the need for more active government participation for solving the salinity problem (e.g. installing a good drainage system). Farmers also emphasize maintaining the groundwater at a level where re-salinization can be maintained to a minimum level for sustainable reclamation.

9.4 Conclusion

Soil salinization is a widespread soil degradation process, exacerbated by a mismatch between water demands for irrigation in food production and the amount of quality (nonsaline) water. The problem is increasing rapidly throughout the world. More than half a billion hectares of land are not being properly used for crop production. Both an economically and ecologically sustainable solution is needed to tackle this problem. Some important factors, which enhance the beneficial effects of different soil amendments in salt-affected soils, are as follows: (i) uniform soil incorporation (mixing), (ii) adequate soil water content for their dissolution, and (iii) presence of a certain microbial population (e.g. sulphuric bacteria for S oxidation). However, more sustainable and effective techniques need to be developed and applied to improve saline soils so that farmers can use these lands for highly productive and meaningful land-use systems to meet the current challenges of global food security.

Different land, crop, and/or water management approaches (e.g. conservation tillage, crop selection/ rotation, groundwater level control) have been applied to fight against salinity problems in agro-ecosystems and reduce the adverse effects of salinity in food/feed production. Although salt resistance in plants is multigenic and thus complex, breeding and transgenic approaches to improve salinity resistance could contribute to enhancing crop production over millions of ha of salt-affected areas worldwide. In addition, crop adaptability to saline conditions should be improved. Despite the importance of salinity in shaping the composition of coastal plant communities, our knowledge about how different species respond physiologically to variable salinities is limited. We have limited understanding about the physiological/biochemical mechanisms underlying halophytes under variable salinities. Hence, physiological and molecular studies to reveal the underlying mechanisms of these processes are important. In addition, discovering the induction of signaling cascades leading to profound changes in specific gene expression is also considered an important salt-stress adaptation.

Molecular knowledge of response and tolerance mechanisms will pave the way for engineered plants that can tolerate salt stress and could be the basis for production of crops, which can result in economic yield under salt-stress conditions. However, it is necessary to find plants with the ability to remove the maximum quantity of salts by producing higher biomass with some economic importance. They are mainly selected for phytoremediation, and the selected plant species should tolerate high salt concentration. The forthcoming challenge for using halophytes to remediate soil salinity is to develop a plant with diverse salt-accumulating capacity in a cost-effective way. Identification of novel genes with high biomass yield characteristics and the subsequent development of transgenic plants with superior remediation features would be crucial for such research.

REFERENCES

Abdel-Fattah, M.K.. 2012. Role of gypsum and compost in reclaiming saline-sodic soils. *J. Agric. Vet. Sci* 1: 30–38.

Afzal, I., S.M.A. Basara, M. Faooq, and A. Nawaz. 2006. Alleviation of salinity stress in spring wheat by hormonal priming with ABA, salicylic acid and ascorbic acid. *Int. J. Agric. Biol* 8: 23–28.

Ashraf, M.Y., M. Ashraf, and G. Sarwar. 2005. Physiological approaches to improving plant salt tolerance, in *Crops: Growth, Quality and Biotechnology*, R. Dris (Ed.), pp. 1206–1227, WFL Publisher, Helsinki, Finland.

Ashraf, M.Y., M. Ashraf, K. Mahmood, J. Akhter, F. Hussain, and M. Arshad. (2010). Phytoremediation of saline soils for sustainable agricultural productivity, in *Plant Adaptation and Phytoremediation*, M. Ashraf, M. Ozturk, and M.S.A. Ahmad (Eds.), pp. 335–3355, Springer, Berlin, Germany.

Arzani, A. 2008. Improving salinity tolerance in crop plants: A biotechnological view. *In Vitro Cellular Developmental Biology-Plant* 44(5): 373–383.

Bano, A., and M. Fatima. 2009. Salt tolerance in *Zea mays* (L.) following inoculation with *Rhizobium* and Pseudomonas. *Biol. Fertility Soils* 45: 405–413.

Basra, S.M.A., I. Afzal, S. Anwar, M. Shafique, A. Haq, and K. Majeed. 2005. Effect of different seed invigoration techniques on wheat (Triticum aestivum L.) seeds sown under saline and non-saline conditions. *J. Seed Technol* 28: 135–141.

Bello, S.K., and A.A. Yusuf. 2021. Phosphorus influences the performance of mycorrhiza and organic manure in maize production. *J. Plant Nutr.* 44: 679–691.

Bello, S.K., A.H. Alayafi, S.G. AL-Solaimani, and K.A.M. Abo-Elyousr. 2021. Mitigating soil salinity stress with gypsum and bio-organic amendments: A review. *Agronomy* 11: 1735.

Biggs, R., F.R. Westley, and S.R. Carpenter. 2010. Navigating the back loop: Fostering social innovation and transformation in ecosystem management. *Ecol. Soc* 15(2): 9.

Borsani, O., V. Valpuesta, and M.A. Botella. 2001. Evidence for a role of salicylic acid in the oxidative damage generated by NaCl and osmotic stress in Arabidopsis seedlings. *Plant Physiol* 126: 1024–1030.

Chaganti, V.N., D.M. Crohn, and J. Simunek. 2015. Leaching and reclamation of a biochar and compost amended saline–sodic soil with moderate SAR reclaimed water. *Agricultural Water Management* 158: 255–265.

Chen, M., H. Wei, J. Cao, R. Liu, Y. Wang, and C. Zheng. 2007. Expression of Bacillus subtilis proAB genes and reduction of feedback inhibition of proline synthesis increases proline production and confers osmotolerance in transgenic *Arabdopsis*. *J. Biochem. Mol. Biol* 40(3): 396–403.

Cho, K., H. Toler, J. Lee, B. Owenley, J.C. Stutz, J.L. Moore, and R.M. Auge. 2006. Mycorrhizal symbiosis and response of sorghum plants to combined drought and salinity stresses. *J. Plant Physiol* 163: 517–528.

Cuartero, J., and R. Fernández-Muñoz. 1999. Tomato and salinity. *Scientia Horticulturae* 78(1–4): 83–125.

de Villiers A.J., M.W. van Rooyen, G.K. Theron, and A.S. Claassens. 1995. Removal of sodium and chloride from a saline soil by Mesembryanthemum barklyi. *J. Arid Environ* 29: 325–330.

FAO. 2000. Global Network on Integrated Soil Management for Sustain-Able Use of Salt-Affected Soils, Rome, Italy. http://www.fao.org/ag/agl/agll/spush

Gul, B., D.J. Weber, and M.A. Khan. 2000. Effect of salinity and planting density on physiological responses of Allenrolfea occidentalis. *Western North American Naturalist* 60(2): 188–197.

Glenn, E.P., J.J. Brown, and E. Blumwald. 1999. Salt tolerance and crop potential of halophytes. *Critical Rev. Plant Sci* 18(2): 227–255.

Haider, M.Z., and M.Z. Hossain. 2013. Impact of salinity on livelihood strategies of farmers. *J. Soil Sci. Plant Nutrition* 13(2): 417–431.

Harinasuth, P., K. Tsutsui, T. Takabe, M. Nomura, T. Takabe, and S. Kishitani. 1996. Exogenous glycinebetaine accumulation and increased salt-tolerance in rice seedlings. *Biosci. Biotech. Biocem* 60(2): 366–368.

Hasanuzzaman, M., M.A. Hossain, J.A.T. da Silva, and M. Fujita. 2012. Plant responses and tolerance to abiotic oxidative stress: Antioxidant defense is a key factor, in *Crop Stress and Its Management: Perspectives and Strategies*, V. Bandi, A.K. Shanker, C. Shanker, and M. Mandapaka (Eds.), pp. 261–316, Springer, Berlin, Germany.

Horney, R.D., B. Taylor, D.S. Munk, B.A. Roberts, S.M. Lesch, and E. Richard. 2005. Development of practical site-specific management methods for reclaiming salt affected soil. *Comput. Electron. Agriculture* 46: 379–397.

Jithesh, M.N., S.R. Prashanth, K.R. Sivaprakash, and A.K. Parida. 2006. Antioxidative response mechanisms in halophytes: Their role in stress defence. *J. Genetics* 85(3): 237–254.

Kamboh, M.A., Y. Oki, and T. Adachi. 2000. Effect of pre-sowing seed treatments on germination and early seedling growth of wheat varieties under saline conditions. *Soil Sci. Plant Nutr.* 46: 249–255.

Khan, N.A., M.I.R. Khan, M. Asgher, M. Fatma, A. Masood, and S. Syeed. 2014. Salinity tolerance in plants: Revisiting the role of sulfur metabolites. *J. Plant Biochem. Physiol* 2: 120.

Khoshgoftar, A.H., H. Shariatmadari, N. Karimian, M. Kalbasi, S.E.A.T.M. van der Zee, and D.R. Parker. 2004. Salinity and Zn application effects on phytoavailability of Cd and Zn. *Soil Sci. Soc. Am. J* 68: 1885–1889.

Kitila, K., A. Chala, and M. Workina. 2020. Effect of gypsum and compost application in reclaiming sodic soils at small scale irrigation farm in Bora District of East Shewa Zone, Oromia, Ethiopia. *Agriways* 08: 28–44.

Kohler, J., F. Caravaca, L. Carrasco, and A. Roldan. 2006. Contribution of *Pseudomonas mendocina* and *Glomus intraradices* to aggregates stabilization and promotion of biological properties in rhizosphere soil of lettuce plants under field conditions. *Soil Use Manage* 22: 298–304.

Kohler, J., J.A. Hernandez, F. Caravaca, and A. Roldan. 2009. Induction of antioxidant enzymes is involved in the greater effectiveness of a PGPR versus AM fungi with respect to increasing the tolerance of lettuce to severe salt stress. *Environ. Exp. Bot.* 65: 245–252.

Lokhande, V.H., and P. Suprasanna. 2012. Prospects of halophytes in understanding and managing abiotic stress tolerance, in *Environmental Adaptations and Stress Tolerance of Plants in the Era of Climate Change*, P. Ahmad and M.N.V. Prasad (Eds.), pp. 29–56, Springer, New York, NY, USA.

Mahajan, S., and N. Tuteja. 2005. Cold, salinity and drought stresses: An overview. *Archives Biochem. Biophys* 444(2): 139–158.

Mahmoodabadi, M., N. Yazdanpanah, L.R. Sinobas, E. Pazira, and A. Neshat. 2013. Reclamation of calcareous saline sodic soil with different amendments (I): Redistribution of soluble cations within the soil profile. *Agric. Water Manag* 120: 30–38.

Manchanda, G., and N. Garg. 2008. Salinity and its effects on the functional biology of legumes. *Acta Physiol. Plant* 30: 595–618.

Mbarki, S., A. Cerda, M. Brestic, R. Mahendra, C. Abdelly, and J.A. Pascual. 2017. Vineyard compost supplemented with *Trichoderma Harzianum* T78 improve saline soil quality. *Land Degrad. Dev* 28: 1028–1037.

Menzies, N., Bell M., and Kopittke P.. 2015. Soil Sodicity chemistry physics and amelioration. GRDC updated papers, 25.02.

Munns, R. 2002. Comparative physiology of salt and water stress. *Plant Cell Environ* 25: 239–250.

Munns, R., and M. Tester. 2008. Mechanisms of salinity tolerance. *Annu. Rev. Plant Biol* 59: 651–681.

Naidu R. , and P. Rengasamy. 1993. Ion interactions and constraints to plant nutrition in Australian sodic soils. *Aust. J. Soil Res* 31: 801–819.

Ondrasek, G., Z. Rengel, and S. Veres. 2011. Soil Salinisation and Salt Stress in Crop Production, Abiotic Stress in Plants - Mechanisms and Adaptations, Prof. Arun Shanker (Ed.), ISBN: 978-953-307-394-1.

Pitman, M.G., and A. Läuchli. 2002. Global impact of salinity and agricultural ecosystem, in *Salinity: Environment—Plants—Molecules*, A. Läuchli and U. Lüttge (Eds.), pp. 3–20, Kluwer Academic, Dodrecht, The Netherlands.

Powell, J.. 2004. *Dryland salinity: On-farm decisions and catchment outcomes. A guide for leading producers and advisors*. Land and Water Australia, Canberra

Qadir, M., E. Quillérou, V. Nangia, G. Murtaza, M. Singh, R.J. Thomas, and A.D. Noble. 2014. Economics of salt-induced land degradation and restoration. *Nat. Resour. Forum* 38(4): 282–295.

Rabhi, M., C. Hafsi, A. Lakhdar, S. Hajji, B. Zouhaier, and M.H. Hamrouni. 2009. Evaluation of the capacity of three halophytes to desalinize their rhizosphere as grown on saline soils under nonleaching conditions. *African J. Ecol* 47(4): 463–468.

Rabhi, M., O. Talbi, A. Atia, A. Chedly, and A. Smaoui. 2008. Selection of halophyte that could be used in the bio reclamation of salt affected soils in arid and semi-arid regions. In *Biosaline Agriculture and High Salinity Tolerance*, pp. 242–246.

Rengel, Z., and R.D. Graham. 1995. Wheat genotypes differ in Zn deficiency when grown in cheated buffer. *Growth. Plant Soil* 176: 307–316.

Rashid, A.. 2006. Salinity and associated nutrient constraints in Indian subcontinent. In 18th World Congress of Soil Science, July 9–15, 2006, Philadelphia, Pennsylvania, USA.

Romic, D., G. Ondrasek, M. Romic, B. Josip, M. Vranjes, and D. Pestosic. 2008. Salinity and irrigation method affect crop yield and soil quality in watermelon (Citrullus lanatus L.) growing. *Irrig. Drainage* 57: 463–469.

Sandhya V., Z. Ali Sk., M. Grover, G. Reddy, and B. Venkateswarlu. 2009. Alleviation of drought stress effects in sunflower seedlings by exopolysaccharides producing *Pseudomonas putida* strain. *Biol. Fertility Soil* 46: 17–26.

Sahi, C., A. Singh, E. Blumwald, and A. Grover. 2006. Beyond osmolytes and transporters: Novel plant salt-stress tolerance-related genes from transcriptional profiling data. *Physiologia Plantarum* 127(1): 1–9.

Schmutz, U., and P. Ludders. 1999. Effect of NaCl salinity on growth, leaf gas exchange and mineral composition of grafted mango rootstocks (var. '13-1' and 'Turpentine'). *Gartenbauwissenschaf* 64: 60–64.

Solaiman, Z.M., M.I. Shafi, E. Beamont, and H.M. Anawar. 2020. Poultry litter biochar increases mycorrhizal colonisation, soil fertility and cucumber yield in a fertigation system on sandy soil. *Agriculture* 10: 480.

Swan, B.K., C.J. Ehrhardt, K.M. Reifel, L.I. Moreno, and D.L. Valentine. 2010. Archaeal and bacterial communities respond differently to environmental gradients in anoxic sediments of a California hypersaline lake, the Salton Sea. *Appl. Environ. Microbiol* 76: 757–768.

Stevens, R.M., and R.R. Walker. 2002. Response of grapevines to irrigation-induced saline-sodic soil conditions. *Australian J. Exp. Agriculture* 42: 323–331.

Storey, R., and R.R. Walker. 1999. Citrus and salinity. *Sci. Hortic* 78: 39–81.

Sivritepe, HÖ, N. Sivritepe, A. Eriş, and E. Turhan 2005. The effects of NaCl pre-treatments on salt tolerance of melons grown under long-term salinity. *Scientia Horticulturae* 106(4): 568–581.

Sivritepe, N., H.O. Sivritepe, and A. Eris. 2003. The effects of NaCl priming on salt tolerance in melon seedlings grown under saline conditions. *Scientia Horticulturae* 97(3–4): 229–237.

Shrivastava, P., and R. Kumar. 2015. Soil salinity: A serious environmental issue and plant growth promoting bacteria as one of the tools for its alleviation. *Saudi J. Biol. Sci* 22(2): 123–131.

Stuart, J.R., M. Tester, R.A. Gaxiola, and T.J. Flowers. 2012. Plants of saline environments. In *Access Science*. http://www.accessscience.com

Tank, N., and M. Saraf. 2010. Salinity-resistant plant growth promoting rhizobacteria ameliorates sodium chloride stress on tomato plants. *J. Plant Interact* 5: 51–58.

Wang, L., X. Sun, S. Li, T. Zhang, W. Zhang, and P. Zhai. 2014. Application of organic amendments to a coastal saline soil in North China: Effects on soil physical and chemical properties and tree growth. *Plos One* 9 (2): e89185.

Yao, L., Z. Wu, Y. Zheng, I. Kaleem, and C. Li. 2010. Growth promotion and protection against salt stress by *Pseudomonas putida* Rs-198 on cotton. *Eur. J. Soil Biol* 46: 49–54.

Yensen, N.P. 2008. Halophyte uses for the twenty-first century, in *Ecophysiology of High Salinity Tolerant Plants*, M.A. Khan and D.J. Weber (Eds.), pp. 367–396.

Zhu, J.-K. 2001. Plant salt tolerance. *Trends Plant Sci* 6: 66–71.

Zhu, J.-K. 2000. Genetic analysis of plant salt tolerance using Arabidopsis. *Plant Physiol* 124: 941–948.

10

Microbial Populations and Soil Fertility in the Coastal Lands of India

Doongar R. Chaudhary
CSIR-Central Salt and Marine Chemicals Research Institute, Bhavnagar, Gujarat, India

CONTENTS

10.1 Introduction

Soil salinity occurs mainly in arid and semi-arid regions that result from natural and anthropogenic-induced actions and is a major global issue due to adverse influence on productivity and sustainability of agriculture. As a result of soil salinization, soil structure degrades that is more prone to wind and water erosion, soil compaction, and crust formation on the surface; soil fertility and productivity decreases; uptake of nutrients is impaired; soil microbial diversity reduces; and groundwater quality is affected. Soil salinization is a global problem and is increasing with time. Around 932 million ha are salt-affected in the world, of which 351 mha and 581 mha area are under saline and sodic soils, respectively (Sparks, 2003). As per the estimation of FAO (2008), more than 1,100 million ha of land area of the world is affected by salinity and sodicity, of which about 60% are saline, 26% sodic, and the remaining 14% saline-sodic. Salt-affected areas are found in all continents; however, the most affected regions are the Middle East, Australia, North Africa, and Eurasia (FAO, 2008). Saline soil in coastal areas has a high salt content because of the intrusion of seawater and is distributed in a long narrow belt along the seashore. Global coastal soil salinity was estimated to be approximately 230 million ha; this estimate was based on the trends observed in China and India (Cao et al., 2013; Li et al., 2014). The distribution of coastal saline soil is in four regions: (1) the seaboard of Central Asia and North Africa, including the Black Sea, Caspian Sea, and Mediterranean Sea; (2) Australia, including the seaboard of Australia and the land of Tasmania; (3) the seaboard of East and Southeast Asia, including the Bohai Sea, Yellow Sea, East China Sea, Vietnam, and Thailand; and (4) the seaboard of the Gulf of Mexico, including South America, eastern Mexico, and Cuba (Li et al., 2014). The remaining regions are

DOI: 10.1201/9781003214885-10

mainly located in some large river estuaries, such as the Congo River, Ganges River, Mekong River, and Indus River (Li et al., 2014).

Coastal lands are intermediate zones (transition areas) between the mainland and sea, and they exist in dynamic equilibrium between both (Bandyopadhyay et al., 2011). The coastal area of India is distributed from Rann of Kutch (Gujarat) to Malabar Coast (Kerala) on the western coast and to Coromandel coast (Tamil Nadu) to Sunder Banns (West Bengal) on the eastern coast (Figure 10.1). Besides this, the coastal tract also includes the two island territories (Andaman and Nicobar, and Lakshadweep) (Central Water Commission, 2017). The coastal length of India is 7517 km, which is distributed in nine states and four union territories. The coastal zone of India exhibits a tropical climate and experiences constant high temperatures. In the coastal regions, salinization causes changes in the chemical composition of natural water resources; deterioration of the quality of the water supply to households, agriculture, and the industrial sector; loss of biodiversity; loss of soil quality and fertility; loss of soil productivity; and health problems, thus hindering the economic development of the region. Soil salinization has substantial implications on socio-economic aspects of the society, including a decline in agricultural productivity, low income for farmers, change of livelihood, and related social constraints. The coastal regions of India are frequently encountered with climatic disasters like cyclones (recently Tauktae, Yaas, Nisarga etc.), storms, tsunamis, or other climatic disturbances, which cause severe loss of lives

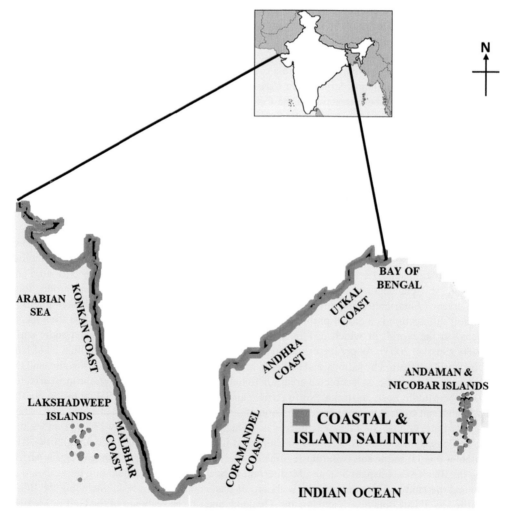

FIGURE 10.1   Distribution of coastal soil salinity in India (not to scale).

and property for coastal peoples. Saline seawater enters into the agricultural field and freshwater bodies (ponds, water resources etc.) and turns them very saline and unproductive (Bandyopadhyay et al., 2011). The coastal ecosystem of India has a wide variety of climatic and topographical conditions; it is fragile in nature and prone to the ill effects of anthropogenic activities. Most of the farmers of the coastal region of India are small to marginal and living below the poverty line. Apart from the reduction in the net cultivable area by soil salinization, it has very serious consequences for crop productivity and soil quality, the choice of cultivable crops, biodiversity, water quality, supply of water for human consumption and industrial use, infrastructure development, and livelihood security of the public (Kumar and Sharma, 2020). A continuous increase in acreage of salinization is a national as well as an international threat to food security and sustainable development. A paradigm shift is needed in the policies for food production for food grain security to meet the requirement of the burgeoning population. Simultaneously, attempts need to be made for agricultural area expansion and increased crop productivity. Restoration of highly saline degraded lands with alternative crops like halophyte needs to be attempted for potential application for agriculture and industries.

10.2 Land Degradation by Salinity

Land degradation may be defined as any form of deterioration that affects the natural potential of land productivity, biological richness, and resilience (Bandyopadhyay et al., 2011) (Figure 10.2). Coastal soils are degraded due to salt accumulation, drainage congestion, drought, soil acidity etc. but predominantly due to soil and water salinity. Soil salinity is measured with soil saturation extract or soil: water suspension. Salt-containing water is able to conduct electricity (EC, electrical conductivity) and is usually measured in Micro Siemens per centimeter ($\mu S\ cm^{-1}$) or Desi Siemens per meter ($dS\ m^{-1}$). Saline soils are defined as the soil having pH <8.5, exchangeable sodium percent (ESP) <15, and electrical conductivity of saturation extract (ECe) > 4 $dS\ m^{-1}$, with preponderance of chloride (Cl^{-1}) and sulfate (SO_4^{2-}) of sodium (Na^+), potassium (K^+), calcium (Ca^{2+}), and magnesium (Mg^{2+}). The salinity status of coastal soils varied from ECe 0.5 (rainy season) to 50 $dS\ m^{-1}$ (summer season), which contains dominant salt as NaCl followed by Na_2SO_4. Saline soil is also called white alkali or solonchak soils because of the appearance of white color due to the white crust of salts on the surface of the soil; these

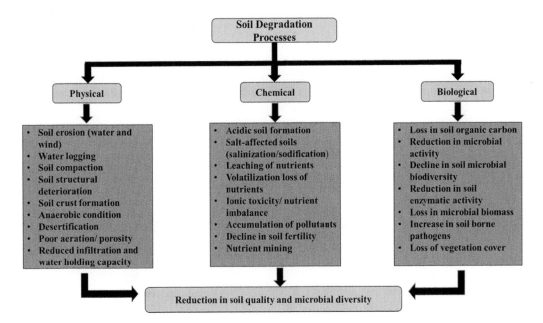

FIGURE 10.2 Different soil degradation processes.

soils have good permeability for water and air and contain an appreciable amount of salt, which adversely affects the growth of most crop plants. Generally, coastal soils are free from sodicity except in a few patches at the south and west coast (Das, 2014).

The upward capillary movement of the saline shallow groundwater table and its evaporation during the post-monsoon season accumulates the salt on the surface of the soil. Evaporation rates are high in arid and semi-arid regions compared to rainfall that favors the accumulation of salt on the soil surface. Soil salinization may be caused due to natural as well as anthropogenic reasons. During soil-forming processes and weathering of rocks and minerals containing a higher amount of salt, salts are released and transported through surface/groundwater, which accumulates at low-laying areas (Kumar and Sharma, 2020). The marine and lacustrine deposits (fossil salt deposits) can be dissolved in water storage and transmission, causing salinization. Seawater ingress, salt-laden winds, and rains carry the salt in sufficient quantities to cause soil salinization in the coastal area. Coastal areas are also prone to progressive salinity due to the cyclone, storms, tidal surges, and flooding (Kumar and Sharma, 2020). Another reason for natural salinization is upstream rivers, which bring and deposit the salt in plains. Among the anthropogenic reasons for soil salinization are changes in land use and clearance of vegetation, presence of an impermeable/less permeable layer in subsoil (which intercepts percolation), indiscriminate and improper use of irrigation water and brackish water with poor drainage, raising the water table, overexploitation of groundwater, seepages from irrigation canals, injudicious of agrochemical (fertilizers and soil amendments), use of untreated sewage sludge, and industrial effluents.

10.3 Distribution and Occurrence of Coastal Land in India

For assessment of salt-affected soils in the coastal areas, visible, infrared, and thermal bands of remote sensing were integrated with ground-truthing and physico-chemical characteristics of soils; digitized maps were prepared using a geographical information system (GIS) for better management of salt-affected soils (Mandal et al., 2018). The distribution of salt-affected soils in the west coast of India (located near the Arabian Sea and Indian Ocean) covers Gujarat (Katch, Surendranagar, Junagadh, Bhavnagar, Jamnagar, Bharuch, Rajkot, Amreli, Kheda, Surat, and Valsad), Maharashtra (Thane and Rayagadh), and Kerala (Kottayam, Alleppy, Thrissur, Malappuram, and Ernakulum). The east coast of India (situated near the Bay of Bengal and the Indian Ocean) covers Tamil Nadu (Ramanathapuram, Cuddalore, and Pudukottai), Andhra Pradesh (Nellore, Krishna, Prakasam, East Godavari, Chittoor, Guntur, Srikakulam, West Godavari, and Vishakhapatnam), Orissa (Kendrapara, Bhadrak, Puri, Baleshwar, Jagatsighapur, Ganjam, and Khordha), West Bengal (24-Parganas (S & N), Medinipur (E & W) and Howrah) and Andaman and Nicobar Islands (south and middle Andaman, North Andaman and Mayabunder, Car Nicobar and Nancowry, and Little and Great Nicobar). In the coastal region of India, the total area under salt-affected soils is 2.5 mha (Table 10.1; Mandal et al., 2018), which contributes around

TABLE 10.1

Distribution of salt-affected soils in the coastal region of India

State/union territory	Total area (ha)
West Bengal	441,272
Orrisa	147,138
Andhra Pradesh	191,016
Tamil Nadu	319,217
Kerala	20,000
Maharashtra	51,381
Gujarat	1,254,345
Andaman and Nicobar islands	51,381
Total	**2,501,369**

37% of the total salt-affected area. Among the coastal salt-affected areas, Gujarat state alone contributes 50% of the coastal saline area.

The coastal salt-affected soil is occurring mainly in the deltas of rivers such as Krishna, Godavari, Cauvery, Mahanadi, and Ganga in the eastern coast and numerous creeks, estuaries, and deltas in the western coast. The topography of these soils is nearly level to gentle sloping with an elevation of <10m above mean sea level. These soils are distributed in the alluvial and black soil regions. These soils are derived from the inland alluvial materials or marine deposits of basalt and highly weathered lateritic materials. Soil consists of a higher amount of salt, waterlogging, inadequate drainage, and subsoil water with very high salinity. There is also a localized problem of acid saline soils in Kerala. The soil acidity is due to the sulfate released from the oxidation of pyrite and jarosite parent materials. Mangroves and halophytic vegetations are very common in the tidal region, with frequent inundation of seawater. The arable crops are not possible in the intertidal zone, where frequent inundation of seawater creates a very high salinity.

10.4 Crop Production Constraints in Coastal Soils

Soil salinity affects all developmental stages of plants, including germination, vegetative growth, and reproductive. In coastal areas, soil salinity and saline groundwaters are the major limiting factor for plant growth, and these factors also contribute to the distribution of plants in the natural habitat. Coastal soils vary from alluvial to lateritic, coarse sand to clay in texture, non-saline to highly saline, alkaline to highly acidic, well-drained to poorly drained, low to high organic matter content, and deficiency as well as the toxicity of some nutrient elements (Maji and Lama, 2016). The presence of a high amount of soluble salts in the soil increases the osmotic potential of soil solution, which hampers water (osmotic stress) and nutrient uptake by plants and consequently affects the normal growth and development of plants (Kumar and Sharma, 2020; Mahajan et al., 2020)

The osmotic stress is created due to the low osmotic potential of soil solution water in saline soils, which badly affects the water as well as nutrient absorption by plants. Plants encounter nutrient stress due to toxicity (Na^+, Cl^-, B) as well as deficiency (N, Ca, K, P, Fe, Zn) in the saline soils, which create nutrient imbalance in the plant. The deficiencies of phosphorus (P), potassium (K), and calcium (Ca) are very common in acid-saline soils and coarse-textured soils (Maji and Lama, 2016). Acid sulfate soils occur in the low-lying areas of Kerala, Sundarbans of W. B., and Andaman and Nicobar Islands, which contain toxic amounts of soluble Fe and Al (Maji and Lama, 2016). Higher salt concentrations significantly inhibit seed germination and seedling growth due to the combined effects of high osmotic potential and ion toxicity (Safdar et al., 2019). The growth and yield of crops is directly related to the photosynthesis and photosynthetic activities that are suppressed by salinity (Netondo et al., 2004). The decrease in the photosynthetic rate of the plant due to salinity is attributed to many factors like dehydration of cell membranes (reduction in the permeability to CO_2), reduction in photosynthetic pigments, the toxicity of Na^+ and Cl^- ions (Cl^- inhibit the NO_3^- uptake by plant), translocation of assimilates, closing of stomata (due to water stress or reduced availability of CO_2 for carboxylation reactions), changes in chloroplast activity, reduced efficiency of RuBPCase, enhanced senescence, or changes in enzyme activity (Netondo et al., 2004; Parida and Das, 2005; Safdar et al., 2019; Iyengar and Reddy, 1996).

Soil salinity significantly reduces phosphorus uptake by plants because phosphate ions precipitate with Ca^{2+} ions. The enhanced Na^+ absorption in sodic soils reduces K^+ absorption, which adversely affects the enzymatic activities involved in metabolic processes like photosynthesis and protein synthesis (Hauser and Horie, 2010), which is detrimental for plant growth. Reduced leaf area, chlorophyll content, and stomatal conductance in salt-affected soils also affect photosynthesis (Netondo et al., 2004).

10.5 Effect of Soil Salinity on Plants

A high concentration of salt in the soil solution reduces the uptake of water, which is known as the osmotic or water-deficit effect of salts in the soil. All soils contain some amount of salt, but the harmful effect of salt occurs on the plant when the amount of salt is high enough to suppress the growth and development of the plants. Symptoms of soil salinity on the plants are resemble similar to the water stress/deficient/drought condition and induce wilting. Soil salinity affects plant growth by increasing soil osmotic pressure, interference with plant nutrition, ionic toxicity and nutrient imbalance. As a consequence of these effects of soil salinity stress, caused by its hyperosmotic effect, secondary stresses, such as oxidative damage, often occur (Zhu, 2001). High concentrations of salts in the soil can significantly impede seed germination and seedling growth due to the combined effects of high osmotic pressure and specific ion toxicity (Na^+ and Cl^-), which adversely affect the functioning and metabolism of plants that ultimately reduce the productivity (Zhao et al., 2020). Plants with prolonged exposure to very high salinity receive severe injury and tissue death. Plants vary in their response to salinity; salt-tolerant plants are better able to adjust internally to soil salinity compared to salt-sensitive plants. Further, salinity tolerance of the plants depends on the climate, soil condition, cultural practice, and varietal selection. For example, during cool weather, transpirational loss of water is less. The salt injury will be less compared to warm and dry weather.

Soil salinity affects the plant by reducing photosynthesis through decreased CO_2 availability (reduction in diffusion), reduction in chlorophyll contents, decreased stomatal and mesophyll conductance to CO_2, reduction in leaf area expansion and light harvesting, overall limiting the growth of plants (Flexas et al., 2007; Delfine et al., 1999; Di Martino et al., 1999; Delfine et al., 1998; Alvino et al., 2000). Soil salinity imposes ionic imbalance/ionic stress/ion toxicity in the plant, which is associated with disproportionate accumulation of Na^+ and Cl^- in the cells. The cytotoxicity of Na^+ affects the plant in two ways; first, Na^+ has a high charge-to-mass ratio (compared to K^+), which disrupts water structure and lower down hydrophobic interactions within proteins (Jones and Pollard, 1983), and second, Na^+ inhibits enzyme activity involved in the primary metabolism (Calvin cycle, phenylpropanoid pathway, glycolysis, polyamine, and starch synthesis), either directly through binding with inhibitory sites or indirectly through displacing K^+ from activation sites (Serrano, 1996; Zhao et al., 2020). High soil Na^+ content negatively affects intracellular K^+ influx because most cells retain high K^+ and low Na^+ concentration in the cytosol accomplished by the coordinated regulation of different transporters for proton, potassium, calcium, and sodium (Mahajan and Tuteja, 2005). The harmful effects of Cl^- on plant growth may not be due to the toxicity but may be due to the Cl^- induced deficiency of key plant essential nutrients (such as nitrogen and sulfur) because uptake of NO_3^- and SO_4^{2-} is mediated by the same (non-selective) anion transporters as Cl^- in the plants; therefore, Cl^- interferes with the uptake and metabolism of plant nutrients (Bazihizina et al., 2019; Zhao et al., 2020). Visual symptoms of salt injury are wilting of plants, yellowed leaves (chlorosis), inhibited/stunted growth, leaf tip burning, necrosis of leaves, and scorching of leaves.

10.6 Salt Tolerance in Halophytes

Most crop or plant species are highly sensitive to salinity and are called glycophytes, whereas those plants whose growth is enhanced by salt are said to be halophyte and complete their life cycle in high salt concentration (Breckle, 1995). Halophytes are extremophiles that are found in salt marshes and other salty environments like saline depressions, inland deserts, and rocky coasts or sand dunes. Halophytes are valuable natural bio-resources and have potential economic value (Figure 10.3). Halophytes possess special anatomical, morphological, and physiological mechanisms that help the plants to withstand saline conditions (Waisel, 1972; Hasanuzzaman et al., 2014). Halophytes are well adjusted to salinity with their different types of adaptation mechanisms, such as ion compartmentalization, succulence, osmotic adjustment, regulative ion transport and uptake, production of osmolytes, maintenance of energetic and redox status, and salt excretion or inclusion (Lokhande and Suprasanna, 2012). They have developed many adaptive characters that help them grow and complete the life cycle under high soil salinity (Flowers and Colmer, 2008). Based on the different salt adaptation mechanisms, halophytes have been classified into three categories: salt excluding, salt excreting, and salt accumulating.

Salt-excluding plants possess a special type of root system that works based on an ultrafiltration mechanism. The roots of halophytes exclude the salt from water at the root surface through filtration (Kim et al., 2016). The salt overly sensitive (*SOS*) gene is mainly expressed in the root cell membrane and may play an important function in the Na^+ extrusion (Munns, 2005; Sreeshan et al., 2014). The *SOS* pathway is

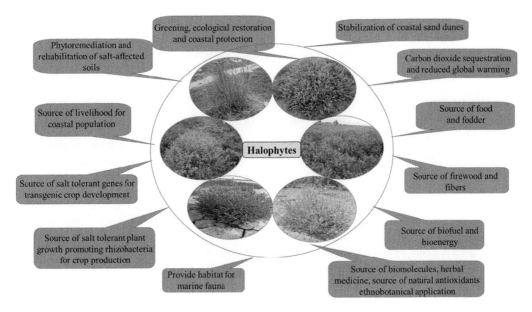

FIGURE 10.3 Potential utilization of halophytes.

activated by Ca^{2+} ions, and Ca^{2+} ions significantly provide salt tolerance to plants under salinity stress (Mahajan and Tuteja, 2005). The presence of high salt concentration in the soil environment causes increased cytosolic Ca^{2+} concentration, which is released from the apoplast and intracellular compartments (Knight et al., 1997). The increment of Ca^{2+} in the cytoplasm recruits stress signal transduction pathway (*SOS* pathway), which leads to providing salt tolerance. The *SOS* pathway causes exclusion of extra Na^+ out of the cell with the help of plasma membrane Na^+/H^+ (*SOS1*) antiport and supports the maintenance of homeostasis of cellular ions. There are three proteins - *SOS1, SOS2,* and *SOS3* - that work in a coordinated manner in the *SOS* pathway for reducing the salinity effects (Mahajan and Tuteja, 2005). Salt excluder halophytes include *Avicennia marina, Ceriops candolleana,* and *Rhizophora mucronata* (Drennan and Pammenter, 1982; Waisel, 1972; Waisel et al., 1986; Hasanuzzaman et al., 2014).

Salt-excreting plants regulate internal salt concentration by removing salt with the help of specialized structures like bladders or glands located on their leaves, for example: *Avicennia sp., Aeluropus lagopoides, Acanthus ilicifolius,* and *Aeluropus littoralis* (Waisel, 1972; Barhoumi et al., 2007; Hasanuzzaman et al., 2014; Sanadhya et al., 2015). Salt glands are characteristic of exo-recretohalophytes, which release salt periodically. Salt is thought to be transported into the salt gland through both the plasmodesmata and the regions that are not covered by the cuticle (Zhao et al., 2020). The salt bladder is characteristic of endo-recretohalophytes, which deposit the salt in the bladder and after accumulation of salt to a threshold amount, the bladder ruptures and releases the salt into the outer environment; examples: quinoa, *Atriplex* species.

Salt accumulating halophytes accumulate a very high amount of salt to maintain water status inside the cell. Halophytes have evolved with the mechanism of osmotic adjustment through vacuolar storage of salts (mainly NaCl) and organic molecule accumulation in the cytosol. The mechanism of Na^+ and Cl^- entry in halophyte cells is not fully known but might involve different types of ion channels, transporters, and pinocytosis (Hasanuzzaman et al., 2014). The Na^+/H^+ antiporters are required for the uptake of Na^+ ions into the vacuoles (Munns and Tester, 2008). It is also reported that halophyte plants often possess large vacuoles, which makes them efficient for the accumulation of salt in the cells (Hajibagheri et al., 1984; Dracup and Greenway, 1985). Although the amount of salt accumulated in shoots is not the same for all halophytes, this depends on the adaptive strategies occupied by different species of halophytes for salt tolerance. The salt-accumulating succulent halophytes are *Sonneratia alba, Limnitzera racemosa, Salvadora persica, Suaeda nudiflora, Sesuvium portulacastrum, Pentatropis siansh, Suaeda maritima, Salicornia brachiata, Salicornia persica,* and *Halimocnemis pilifera* (Ravindran et al., 2007;

Hasanuzzaman et al., 2014; Rathore et al., 2016; Mangalassery et al., 2017). Halophyte succulence is an important adaptive strategy that accumulates excessive NaCl and preserves water. This characteristic mostly occurs in the dicot halophytes belonging to the *Chenopodioideae* and *Salicornioideae* family (Zhao et al., 2020).

10.7 Soil Fertility of the Coastal Soils of India

Most of the coastal saline soils of India are deficient in nitrogen due to decreased use of nitrogenous fertilizers and reduced mineralization of soil organic nitrogen due to salinity, resulting in the slow release of native soil nitrogen to the plant (Das, 2014). Loss of nutrients by run-off and leaching during heavy rain is a common phenomenon in coastal lands. Phosphorus deficiency is also quite common in coastal acid sulfate or acid saline soils. However, in some saline soils, available phosphorus is found in the range of medium to higher availability. Available potassium in the coastal soil ranges from the medium to higher category of availability.

The organic carbon, available nitrogen, and phosphate in the soils from coastal villages of Digha, West Bengal, varied from 0.61% to 0.93%, 11.2 to 29.5 mg kg^{-1} and 230.8–503.09 mg kg^{-1}, respectively (Azmi and Chatterjee, 2016). Mitran et al. (2014) studied the soil fertility constraints of villages of Sundarbans and revealed that these soils are poor in available N and medium in available P and Zn, but the native supply of available K, S, and micronutrients is very pronounced. Further, they concluded that nitrogen-based fertilization supplemented with organic inputs should be used for optimum growth and yield of crops.

The coastal soils of Gujarat were low in NH$_4^+$-N and NO$_3^-$-N (2.55–6.29 and 0.92–2.27 mg kg^{-1}, respectively), medium to high in available P content (8.06–20.23 mg kg^{-1}), and higher in available K (1921–2489 mg kg^{-1}) (Rathore et al., 2016). It was revealed that the coastal soils (200 samples analyzed) of Jamnagar, Gujarat, were low in available N (85%), P (50.0%), and S (50.5%), whereas about one-third of these soils were low in available K (Shirgire et al., 2018). Another study of coastal Gir Somnath, Gujarat, indicated (180 soil samples analyzed) that soils were deficient with respect to available N and P, whereas medium in available S and high in available K status (Polara and Chauhan, 2015).

Soil nutrients of five soil series of the eastern coastal part of Odisha showed that these rice soils suffer from different nutrient deficiencies (N, P, and Zn) and toxicities (Fe, Mn, and Cu) at the root zone (Srinivasan et al., 2022). Results of soils from the East and South-Eastern Coastal Plain Agroclimatic zone of Odisha revealed that available nitrogen content varies from low (87.5 kg ha^{-1}) to medium (337. 5 kg ha^{-1}), available phosphorous low to very high (12.4 to 293.6 kg ha^{-1}), available potassium low to very high (73.9 to 510.7 kg ha^{-1}), and available soil sulfur deficient to sufficient (0.97 to 76.4 mg kg^{-1}) (Behera et al., 2016a). Barik et al. (2017) reported that available nitrogen, phosphorus, and potassium contents ranged from 87.5 to 187.5 kg ha^{-1}, 3.38 to 259.2 kg ha^{-1}, and 59.1 to 446.0 kg ha^{-1}, respectively, in the soils from Puri, Odisha. The available N varied from 85 to 259 kg ha^{-1}, available P from 10.7 to 57.1 kg ha^{-1}, and available K from 57 to 438 kg ha^{-1} in the different horticultural land-use systems in the Odisha coastal plain (Srinivasan et al., 2017), and researchers recommended better treatment or management for maintaining sustainable productivity.

Results of 383 geo-referenced soil samples collected from North Goa District in the Western Ghats revealed that soils were found to be highly acidic with low available N and P, and medium exchangeable K, with widespread Zn, Cu, and Fe deficiency (Verma et al., 2018). In the coastal saline soils of Goa, India, exchangeable K, and Ca+Mg varied from 0.14 to 1.81 meq 100 g^{-1} and 1.39 to 7.51 meq 100 g^{-1}, respectively (Mahajan et al., 2016). In another study at coastal soils of Goa, it was observed that these soil were found low, low to medium, and medium to high with respect to soil available N, P, and K, respectively, whereas soils were sufficient in micronutrients (Mahajan et al., 2015). The mean values of organic carbon, available P, and K were 19.8, 24.7, and 270 mg kg^{-1}, respectively, observed in the oil palm (*Elaeis guineensis* Jacq.) plantations of the west coastal area of India, and researchers suggested that the yield of oil palm can be improved by the application of proper quantity and kind of fertilizers (Behera et al., 2016b).

Soils from the coastal agro-ecosystem of Karnataka showed a deficiency of N, P, K, and Zn (Mathews et al., 2009), and the study emphasized soil test-based, site-specific nutrient recommendations. More than 60% of soil samples were low in N, P, and K; >80% of samples were low in exchangeable Ca, Mg, and available S content in the Western Ghats and Coastal area in Karnataka (Sidharam et al., 2017). An assessment of available nutrient status on a pilot scale (Mirjan village) under coastal agro-ecosystem of Karnataka (India) showed that the available nitrogen content of the soils was generally low to medium, the majority of the study area had low P status, whereas the majority of the area was low in available K (Dasog et al., 2006). Soils from coastal soils of the Guntur district in Andhra Pradesh showed that soils were low in available nitrogen (28 to 247 kg ha^{-1}), medium to high in available P (6.60 to 90.10 kg ha^{-1}), and high in available K (241 to 2016 kg ha^{-1}) (Tantuja, 2020). The carbon, nitrogen, phosphorus, and potassium content ranged from 0.4 % to 2.44%, 90 to 125 kg ha^{-1}, 7.5 to 12.5 kg ha^{-1}, and 863 to 1575 kg ha^{-1}, respectively, in the Pichavaram mangrove forest (Bharathkumar et al., 2008).

10.8 Soil Microbial Community Structure in Coastal Soil

Soil microorganisms play a vital role in the decomposition of organic matter, release and transformation of nutrients, nutrient (C, N, P, S etc.) cycling, and biogeochemical processes in the soil. The soil is a complex and heterogeneous environment that consists of a bigger reservoir of microbial diversity. Studies on the diversity of microbes is limited because we cannot isolate/culture all of them; however, hardly 1% of microorganisms in the soil could be cultured with classic laboratory techniques (Stefanis et al., 2013). The soil microbial community structure and composition are significantly influenced by environmental factors, such as soil salinity, soil moisture, soil pH, nutrients availability, soil air, redox potential, soil depth, organic matter, and texture. The soil heterogeneity influences the composition and structure of the microbial population because soil affects the organic carbon/energy and nutrient availability. Soils with higher organic matter and nutrient load had more microbial diversity. Seasons also play an important role in shaping the microbial community composition due to changes in nutrient availability. The principal methods for extraction and identification of soil microbial populations are the microscope, as well as biochemical and molecular techniques. Under microscopic methods, microbes are cultured in the laboratory with different media and identified under fluorescence microscopy (microbial cells are labeled with a fluoresce marker), or electron microscopy (scanning electron microscopy and transmission electron microscopy). Plate counts (culture-dependent method, cultured in liquid or solid medium), community-level phylogenetic profile (CLPP, sole carbon source utilization pattern), fatty acid methyl ester (FAME), and phospholipids fatty acid analyses (PLFA) are used as biochemical methods. Much advancement has occurred in the recent past in the molecular techniques for the identification of microbes. The advantage of the molecular technique is the identification of microbes based on the gene characteristics and size of the nucleic acid sequence (Stefanis et al., 2013). Fluorescent in situ hybridization, PCR techniques, hybridization techniques, sequencing techniques, array technology, and next-generation sequencing are molecular methods used for the identification of microbes.

Microbial life in the hypersaline environments (coastal salinity) is primarily dominated by bacteria and archaea with eukaryotes (protists and fungi). Generally, halophilic archaea use a salt-in strategy and accumulate KCl molecules equal to NaCl in their environment, whereas bacteria and eukaryotes primarily use a salt-out strategy, exclude salts from the cytoplasm, and either accumulate or synthesize compatible solutes (DasSarma and DasSarma, 2015). Some halophiles used combinations of one or more adaptive mechanisms under a saline environment.

10.8.1 Plant-Microbe Interaction in the Coastal Ecosystem

Vegetations of the coastal ecosystem significantly influence the soil microbial community through interaction with the surrounding soil environment. Different types of signal molecules are released by sediment microorganisms and are recognized by plants that give signals to release chemical molecules called root exudates (Chaparro et al., 2012). The amount and types of root exuded compounds vary among different plant species and change according to received signals from the surrounding environment and plant stage, type of soil, and other abiotic and biotic factors (Rovira, 1969; De-la-Pena et al., 2010; Tang et al., 1995; Flores et al., 1999). The root exudates include sugars, ions, flavonoids, amino acids, aliphatic acids, enzymes, mucilage, proteins, and many types of carbon-containing primary and secondary metabolites (Bais et al., 2006; Badri et al., 2009; Sharma et al., 2019). All these chemical compounds form a unique microenvironment at the rhizosphere site, which attracts microorganisms in the soil (Bais et al., 2006). These microorganisms are the key players in nutrient cycling and organic residue decomposition, which provides nutrients to the plant (Nielsen and Winding, 2002). In addition, microbes improve the physical structure of the soil by the release of polysaccharides and other cellular debris, which act as cementing agents for soil aggregates and result in the improvement of water-holding capacity and infiltration rate, and reduce crusting, erodibility, and soil compaction (Elliott et al., 1996; Nielsen and Winding, 2002).

Rhizospheric microbes utilize root exudates as carbon and a nutrient source that enhances the microbial activity in the rhizosphere and ultimately provide nutrients to the plant by decomposition and the mineralization process compared to bulk soil (Collignon et al., 2011; Koranda et al., 2011). Similarly, the activities of soil enzymes are found to be higher in the rhizosphere than bulk soils because the microbial activities are induced by enzymes and exudates released by roots (Zhang et al., 2012). It is also observed that rhizospheric soils have a higher abundance of Gram-negative bacteria because they mainly grow on plant labile carbon, whereas Gram-positive bacteria may be higher in root-free soils (Bird et al., 2011; Chaudhary et al., 2012; Chaudhary et al., 2015). Rathore et al. (2017) observed variations in soil microbial community composition and enzyme activities in four perennial halophytes (*Aeluropus lagopoides, Suaeda nudiflora, Arthrocnemum indicum,* and *Heleochloa setulosa*) covered and control (without vegetation) soils and reported higher abundances of Gram-negative, Gram-positive, and total bacteria halophyte covered soil compared to the control soils. They showed that perennial halophytes significantly improved soil microbial activities and played a vital role in healthy ecosystem functioning. In another study, the abundance of Gram-negative and fungi were higher in rhizospheric than bulk sediments of halophytes (Chaudhary et al., 2017). These findings suggested the positive contribution of halophytes in improving the quality of coastal saline soils.

Mangroves are typically tropical and subtropical coastal ecosystems of the inter-tidal zone and dynamic ecotones. Sulfate-reducing bacteria (*Desulfovibrio, Desulfotomaculum, Desulfosarcina, Desulfococcus* spp.), the primary decomposers, and N_2 fixing bacteria (*Azotobacter, Rhizobium* spp.) that recycle nitrogen in anoxic mangrove sediments were dominant (Chandrika et al., 1990). The bacterial diversity in the Bhitarkanika mangrove soil showed the predominance of bacterial genera, such as *Bacillus, Pseudomonas, Desulfotomaculum, Desulfovibrio, Desulfomonas, Methylococcus, Vibrio, Micrococcus, Klebsiella* and *Azotobacter* (Mishra et al., 2012)

Fluctuation in soil salinity with the season is a typical characteristic of coastal soils. In a study carried out at the salt-affected soils of the coastal region of Bay of Bengal, India showed that ECe of soil in the summer season was about five times higher than that of monsoon season, and microbial biomass C, basal soil respiration, and fluorescein diacetate hydrolyzing activity were lowest during the summer season, which indicated a negative influence of soil salinity (Tripathi et al., 2006). Shannon-Wiener and Simpson Index of the soils from coastal villages of Digha, West Bengal ranged from 1.56 to 1.88 and 3.85–5.73, respectively (Azmi and Chatterjee, 2016). In the coastal saline soils of Goa, India, soil microbial and enzyme activities were adversely affected by salinity under low pH conditions and increased salinity reduced the microbial biomass carbon and basal respiration rate and increased the metabolic quotient (Mahajan et al., 2016). Based on the metagenomics analysis, dominance of *Alphaproteobacteria* and *Gammaproteobacteria* (*Pseudomonas, Halorhodospira, Ectothiorhodospira, Bradyrhizobium, Agrobacterium, Amorphomonas*) was observed as nitrogen fixers in coastal–saline soil ecosystems of Gujarat (Yousuf et al., 2014)

The seasonal and spatial fluctuation of the culturable microbial population was determined in the sediment of the Sunderban mangrove forest. It was observed that cellulose-degrading bacteria were found to be maximum during post-monsoon, whereas the fungal population was found to be maximum during pre-monsoon, and the decreasing order abundances of microbes were nitrifying bacteria, phosphorous solubilizing bacteria, free-living nitrogen-fixing bacteria, and sulfur-reducing bacteria (Das et al., 2012). In another study at a mangrove system in Kerala, India, bacteria from the phylum *Proteobacteria* were the major taxon (Imchen et al., 2017). In analysis of 16S rRNA sequences, members belonging to the phylum *Firmicutes* dominated the Pichavaram mangrove forest (Bharathkumar et al., 2008). Using 16S rRNA gene pyrosequencing of sediments from coastal mangrove of Sundarbans, *Proteobacteria* were the most dominant phyla with the predominance of *Deltaproteobacteria*, *Alphaproteobacteria*, and *Gammaproteobacteria* (Basak et al., 2015). The molecular phylogeny study revealed the dominance of *Actinobacteria, Firmicutes,* and *Proteobacteria* along with archaeal members of *Halobacteraceae* in the coastal saline-alkaline soil (Keshri et al., 2013). Sequencing and analysis of 16S rDNA from concentrator and crystallizer ponds of solar salterns revealed the presence of members affiliated with actinobacterial genera: *Streptomyces, Micromonospora, Nocardia, Nocardiopsis, Saccharopolyspora,* and *Nonomuraea* (Jose and Jebakumar, 2012). The intertidal mangrove forest of Bhitarkanika, India, showed that *Actinobacteria* were more abundant in the monsoon, whereas γ-*Proteobacteria* demonstrated higher abundance in summer (Behera et al., 2019).

The quantitative real-time PCR approach has been used by Keshri et al. (2013) to estimate phylogenetic (16S rRNA) and functional genes (*cbbL, nifH, amoA* and *apsA*) abundance in saline-alkaline soil samples collected from the coastal region of Gujarat, India. They found significantly higher bacterial abundance over archaeal and *cbbL* abundance over *nifH* gene and found a higher copy number of 16S rRNA, *cbbL,* and *nifH* genes in non-saline soil than saline soils (Keshri et al., 2015). They suggested that the reduction in gene abundance in saline soils was due to the extra stress on the microbial community imposed by higher sodicity and salinity decreased the utilization of carbon resources (Keshri et al., 2015).

10.8.2 Salt-Tolerant Plant Growth-Promoting Rhizobacteria (PGPR)

Development of salt tolerance in plants is from plant breeding, genetic engineering, genetic transformation, and use of PGPR; however, microbial inoculations in soil that are used to reduce salinity stress are a good option as they are economical, sustainable, and non-hazardous to nature. These PGPRs are an important remedy to alleviate salinity stress, as PGPR not only promotes the growth of plants but also helps plants with imparting salt tolerance (Figure 10.4). These PGPR help the plant in many ways with growth improvement under salinity stress, such as improvement in water absorption, enhancing nutrient uptake (biological N_2, solubilization of phosphorus and potassium, chelation of iron and zinc by siderophores), production of phytohormones (indole acetic acid, gibberellins, and cytokinins), increased expression of SOS genes and transporters, accumulation of osmolytes (proline, glutamate, glycine betaine, soluble sugars, choline, o-sulfate, and polyols), increases in antioxidant enzyme activities in the plant tissues (superoxide dismutase, peroxidase, catalase, ascorbate peroxidase, monodehydroascorbate reductase, dehydroascorbate reductase and glutathione reductase), production of secondary compounds (exopolysaccharides), and increases in non-enzymatic antioxidant activity in plant tissues (ascorbate, glutathione, tocopherol, carotenoids and polyphenols) (Abd El-Azeem et al., 2012; Hanin et al., 2016; Santos et al., 2018; Gill and Tuteja, 2010; Jogawat, 2019; Etesami and Beattie, 2018; Arora, 2020).

Several species of halotolerant soil bacteria, such as *Brachybacterium saurashtrense sp. nov., Pseudomonas* sp., *Klebsiella, Agrobacterium, Bacillus endophyticus, Bacillus tequilensis, Planococcus rifietoensis, Variovorax paradoxus, Arthrobacter agilis, Bacillus safensis, Bacillus pumilus, Kocuria rosea, Enterobacter aerogenes, Aeromonas veronii, Arthrobacter pascens, Arthrobacter, Azospirillum, Alcaligenes, Burkholderia, Enterobactor, Flavobacterium,* and *Rhizobium,* have been isolated from soil growing with halophytes that had PGPR properties (1-aminocyclopropane-1-carboxylate deaminase activity, indole-3-acetic acid, phosphate and zinc solubilizing activities, biological N-fixation) and significantly stimulated the growth of the host plant and ameliorated salt stress in the crop plant (Egamberdiyeva, 2005; Saghafi et al., 2019; Sharma et al., 2016; Zhao et al., 2016; Jha et al., 2012; Mukhtar et al., 2020; Ullah and Bano, 2015).

Salinity stress

PGPR imparting salinity tolerance

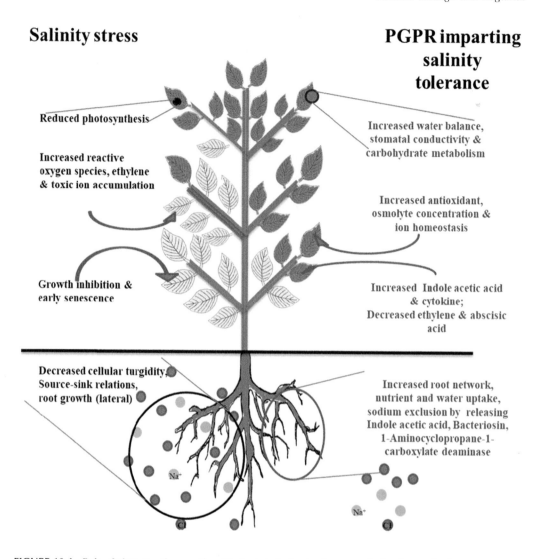

Reduced photosynthesis

Increased reactive oxygen species, ethylene & toxic ion accumulation

Growth inhibition & early senescence

Decreased cellular turgidity, Source-sink relations, root growth (lateral)

Increased water balance, stomatal conductivity & carbohydrate metabolism

Increased antioxidant, osmolyte concentration & ion homeostasis

Increased Indole acetic acid & cytokine; Decreased ethylene & abscisic acid

Increased root network, nutrient and water uptake, sodium exclusion by releasing Indole acetic acid, Bacteriosin, 1-Aminocyclopropane-1-carboxylate deaminase

FIGURE 10.4   Role of plant growth-promoting rhizobacteria in the development of salt tolerance in plants.

10.9 Conclusions

India has a very long coastline, distributed in nine states and four union territories, with tropical climates, and it experiences constant high temperatures. The problem of coastal saline soils occurs in varying degrees due to the lack of drainage systems, overdraft of groundwater, ingress of saline sea water, and injudicious use of natural resources, which results in changes in chemical composition of natural water resources, deterioration of quality of water, loss of biodiversity, loss of soil quality and fertility, and loss of soil productivity. Soil salinization has substantial implications on socioeconomic aspects of the society, including a decline in agricultural productivity, low income for farmers, change of livelihood, and related social constraints. A paradigm shift is needed in the policies for food production for food grain security for the burgeoning population, and attempts need to be made for agricultural area expansion and increases in crop productivity. Restoration of highly saline-degraded lands with alternative crops like halophyte needs to be attempted for potential application for agriculture and industries. Halophytes are extremophiles, which are distributed on the salt marshes and other salty environments like saline depressions, inland deserts, and rocky coasts or sand dunes. Halophytes are valuable natural bio-resources and have potential economic value for the livelihood of the coastal population. Halophytes possess special anatomical, morphological, and physiological mechanisms to withstand saline conditions. Most of the coastal saline soils of India are deficient in nitrogen and phosphorus due to lesser use of fertilizers and reduced mineralization of soil organic matter due to salinity loss of nutrients by run-off and leaching during heavy rain. Chemical fertilization supplemented with organic inputs should be used for optimum growth and yield of crops for maintaining sustainable productivity. Microorganisms of coastal soils are the key players in nutrient cycling and organic residue decomposition; further, microbes also improve soil quality. Salt-tolerant plant growth-promoting microbial inoculations in soil are used to reduce salinity stress in the plant and are a good option as they are economical, sustainable, and non-hazardous to nature. These PGPR help the plant in many ways for growth improvement under salinity stress, such as improvement in water absorption, enhancement of nutrient uptake, production of phytohormones, increased expression of salt-sensitive genes and transporters, accumulation of osmolytes, increased antioxidant enzyme activities, production of secondary compounds, and increased non-enzymatic antioxidant activity in plant tissues.

Acknowledgments

The financial support received from the Council of Scientific and Industrial Research (CSIR), Govt. of India, New Delhi [MPL0049(1); Biostimulants] and SERB, New Delhi [GAP2125; CRG/2020/000542] are thankfully acknowledged. Help received from Mr. Shrikant D. Khandare is gratefully acknowledged. CSIR-CSMCRI Communication No: 185/2021.

REFERENCES

Abd El-Azeem, S., E. Mohmmed, J.K. Sung, and Y.S. Ok. 2012. Alleviation of salt stress in eggplant (*Solanum melongena* L.) by plant-growth-promoting rhizobacteria. *Communications in Soil Science and Plant Analysis* 43:1303–1315. 10.1080/00103624.2012.666305

Alvino, A., R. D'Andria, S. Delfine, A. Lavini, and P. Zanetti. 2000. Effect of water and salinity stress on radiation absorption and efficiency in sunflower. *Italian Journal of Agronomy* 4:53–60.

Arora, N.K., T. Fatima, J. Mishra, et al. 2020. Halo-tolerant plant growth promoting rhizobacteria for improving productivity and remediation of saline soils. *Journal of Advanced Research* 26:69–82. 10.1016/j.jare.2020.07.003

Azmi, S.A., and S. Chatterjee. 2016. Population dynamics of soil bacteria in some areas of Midnapore coastal belt, West Bengal, India. *3 Biotech*, 6:37. 10.1007/s13205-015-0361-y

Badri, D.V., T.L. Weir, D. van der Lelie, and J.M. Vivanco. 2009. Rhizosphere chemical dialogues: plant-microbe interactions. *Current Opinion in Biotechnology* 20:642–650. 10.1016/j.copbio.2009.09.014

Bais, H.P., T.L. Weir, L.G. Perry, S. Gilroy, and J.M. Vivanco. 2006. The role of root exudates in rhizosphere interactions with plants and other organisms. *Annual Review of Plant Biology*, 57:233–266. 10.1146/annurev.arplant.57.032905.105159

Bandyopadhyay, B.K., D. Burman, and S. Mandal. 2011. Improving agricultural productivity in degraded coastal land of India – experiences gained and lessons learned. *Journal of the Indian Society of Coastal Agricultural Research* 29:1–9.

Barhoumi, Z., W. Djebali, A. Smaoui, W. Chaïbi, and C. Abdelly. 2007. Contribution of NaCl excretion to salt resistance of *Aeluropus littoralis* (Willd) Parl. *Journal of Plant Physiology* 164:842–850. 10.1016/j.jplph.2006.05.008

Barik, R.A., S.U. Saren, A.N. Mishra, and B.P. Acharya. 2017. Soil fertility status of some villages in Astaranga bock of Puri District of East and South Eastern Coastal Plain Agro Climatic Zone of Odisha. *Annals of Plant and Soil Research* 19:408–412.

Basak, P., N.S. Majumder, S. Nag, et al. 2015. Spatiotemporal analysis of bacterial diversity in sediments of Sundarbans using parallel 16S rRNA gene tag sequencing. *Microbial Ecology* 69:500–511. 10.1007/s00248-014-0498-y

Bazihizina, N., T.D. Colmer, T.A. Cuin, S. Mancuso, and S. Shabala. 2019. Friend or foe? Chloride patterning in halophytes. *Trends Plant Science* 24:142–151. 10.1016/j.tplants.2018.11.003

Behera, P., M. Mohapatra, J.Y. Kim, T.K. Adhya, A.K. Pattnaik, and G. Rastogi. 2019. Spatial and temporal heterogeneity in the structure and function of sediment bacterial communities of a tropical mangrove forest. *Environmental Science and Pollution Research* 26:3893–3908. 10.1007/s11356-018-3927-5

Behera, S., A. Mishra, B.P. Acharya, S. Saren, and J. Mishra. 2016a. Soil fertility status of some villages under east and south eastern coastal plain agroclimatic zone of Odisha. *Journal of the Indian Society of Coastal Agricultural Research* 34:63–67.

Behera, S.K., K. Suresh, B.N. Rao, et al. 2016b. Spatial variability of some soil properties varies in oil palm (*Elaeis guineensis* Jacq.) plantations of west coastal area of India. *Solid Earth* 7:979–993. 10.5194/se-7-979-2016

Bharathkumar, S., N. Ramesh Kumar, D. Paul, V.R. Prabavathy, and S. Nair. 2008. Characterization of the predominant bacterial population of different mangrove rhizosphere soils using 16S rRNA gene-based single-strand conformation polymorphism (SSCP). *World Journal of Microbiology and Biotechnology* 24:387–394. 10.1007/s11274-007-9487-3.

Bird, J.A., D.J. Herman, and M.K. Firestone. 2011. Rhizosphere priming of soil organic matter by bacterial groups in a grassland soil. *Soil Biology and Biochemistry* 43:718–725. 10.1016/j.soilbio.2010.08.010

Breckle, S.W. 1995. How do halophytes overcome salinity? In *Biology of Salt Tolerant Plants*, ed. M.A. Khan, and I.A. Ungar, 199–213. Department of Botany, University of Karachi, Pakistan.

Cao, L., J. Song, X. Li, H. Yuan, N. Li, and L. Duan. 2013. Research progresses in carbon budget and carbon cycle of the coastal salt marshes in China. *Acta Ecologica Sinica* 33:5141–5152. (In Chinese).

Central Water Commission. 2017. *A Report on Problems of Salination of Land in Coastal Areas of India and Suitable Protection Measures*. Hydrological Studies Organization, Central Water Commission, New Delhi.

Chandrika, V., P.V.R. Nair, and L.R. Khambhadkar. 1990. Distribution of phototrophic thionic bacteria in the anaerobic and micro-aerophilic strata of mangrove ecosystem of Cochin. *Journal of the Marine Biological Association India* 32:77–84.

Chaparro, J.M., A.M. Sheflin, D.K. Manter, and J.M. Vivanco. 2012. Manipulating the soil microbiome to increase soil health and plant fertility. *Biology and Fertility of Soils* 48:489–499. 10.1007/s00374-012-0691-4

Chaudhary, D.R., R.K. Gautam, B. Yousuf, A. Mishra, and B. Jha, 2015. Nutrients, microbial community structure and functional gene abundance of rhizosphere and bulk soils of halophytes. *Applied Soil Ecology* 91:16–26. 10.1016/j.apsoil.2015.02.003

Chaudhary, D.R., A.P. Rathore, R. Kumar, and B. Jha, 2017. Spatial and halophyte-associated microbial communities in intertidal coastal region of India. *International Journal of Phytoremediation* 19:478–489. 10.1080/15226514.2016.1244168

Chaudhary, D.R., J. Saxena, N. Lorenz, L.K. Dick, and R.P. Dick. 2012. Microbial profiles of rhizosphere and bulk soil microbial communities of biofuel crops switchgrass (*Panicum virgatum* L.) and jatropha (*Jatropha curcas* L.). *Applied and Environmental Soil Science* 2012. 10.1155/2012/906864

Collignon, C., C. Calvaruso, and M.P. Turpault. 2011. Temporal dynamics of exchangeable K, Ca and Mg in acidic bulk soil and rhizosphere under Norway spruce (*Picea abies* Karst.) and beech (*Fagus sylvatica* L.) stands. *Plant and Soil* 349:355–366. 10.1007/s11104-011-0881-0

Das, M. 2014. Soil management intervention in cyclone affected coastal areas. In *Management of Cyclone Disaster in Agriculture Sector in Coastal Areas*, ed. A. Kumar, P.S. Brahmanand, and A.K. Nayak, 57–66. Directorate of Water Management, Bhubaneswar, India.

Das, S., M. De, R. Ray, C. Chowdhury, T.K. Jana, and T.K. De. 2012. Microbial ecosystem in Sunderban mangrove forest sediment, North-East coast of bay of Bengal, India. *Geomicrobiology Journal* 29:656–666. 10.1080/01490451.2011.605988

Dasog, G.S., P.L. Patil, V. Mini, et al. 2006. Assessment of changes in soil fertility status over seasons by GIS technique in coastal agro-ecosystem of Karnataka, India. In AFITA 2006: the Fifth International Conference of the Asian Federation for Information Technology in Agriculture, Indian Institute of Science Campus, India.

DasSarma, S., and P. DasSarma. 2015. Halophiles and their enzymes: negativity put to good use. *Current Opinion in Microbiology* 25:120–126. 10.1016/j.mib.2015.05.009

De-la-Pena, C., D.V. Badri, Z. Lei, et al. 2010. Root secretion of defense-related proteins is development-dependent and correlated with flowering time. *Journal of Biological Chemistry* 285:30654–30665. 10.1 074/jbc.M110.119040

Delfine, S., A. Alvino, M. Zacchini, and F. Loreto. 1998. Consequences of salt stress on conductance to CO_2 diffusion, Rubisco characteristics and anatomy of spinach leaves. *Functional Plant Biology* 25:395–402. 10.1071/PP97161

Delfine, S., A. Alvino, M.C. Villani, and F. Loreto. 1999. Restrictions to carbon dioxide conductance and photosynthesis in spinach leaves recovering from salt stress. *Plant Physiology* 119:1101–1106. 10.11 04/pp.119.3.1101

Di Martino, C., S. Delfine, A. Alvino, and F. Loret. 1999. Photorespiration rate in spinach leaves under moderate NaCl stress. *Photosynthetica* 36:233–242. 10.1023/A:1007099627285

Dracup, M.N.H., and H. Greenway. 1985. A procedure for isolating vacuoles from leaves of the halophyte *Suaeda maritima*. *Plant, Cell and Environment* 8:149–154. 10.1111/j.1365-3040.1985.tb01222.x

Drennan, P., and N.W. Pammenter. 1982. Physiology of salt excretion in the mangrove *Avicennia marina* (Forsk.) Vierh. *New Phytologist* 91:597–606.

Egamberdiyeva, D. 2005. Plant-growth-promoting rhizobacteria isolated from a Calcisol in a semi-arid region of Uzbekistan: biochemical characterization and effectiveness. *Journal of Plant Nutrition and Soil Science* 168:94–99. 10.1002/jpln.200321283

Elliott, L.F., J.M. Lynch, and R.I. Papendick. 1996. The microbial component of soil quality. In *Soil Biochemistry* ed. G. Stotzky, and J.M. Bollag, 1–21. Marcel Dekker Inc., New York.

Etesami, H., and G.A. Beattie. 2018. Mining halophytes for plant growth-promoting halotolerant bacteria to enhance the salinity tolerance of non-halophytic crops. *Frontiers in Microbiology* 9:148. 10.3389/fmicb.2018.00148

FAO. 2008. Harmonized World Soil Database (version 1.0), FAO, Rome, Italy and IIASA, Laxenburg, Austria.

Flexas, J., A. Diaz-Espejo, J. Galmés, R. Kaldenhoff, H. Medrano, and M. Ribas-Carbo. 2007. Rapid variations of mesophyll conductance in response to changes in CO_2 concentration around leaves. *Plant Cell Environment* 30:1284–1298. 10.1111/j.1365-3040.2007.01700.x.

Flores, H.E., J.M. Vivanco, and V.M. Loyola-Vargas. 1999. 'Radicle' biochemistry: the biology of root-specific metabolism. *Trends in Plant Science* 4:220–226. 10.1016/s1360-1385(99)01411-9

Flowers, T.J., and T.D. Colmer. 2008. Salinity tolerance in halophytes. *New Phytologist* 179:945–963. 10.1111/j.1469-8137.2008.02531.x

Gill, S., and N. Tuteja. 2010. Reactive oxygen species and antioxidant machinery in abiotic stress tolerance in crop plants. *Plant Physiology and Biochemistry* 48:909–930. 10.1016/j.plaphy.2010.08.016

Hajibagheri, M.A., J.L. Hall, and T.J. Flowers. 1984. Stereological analysis of leaf cells of the halophyte *Suaeda maritima* (L.) Dum. *Journal of Experimental Botany* 35:1547–1557. 10.1093/jxb/35.10.1547

Hanin, M., C. Ebel, M. Ngom, L. Laplaze, and K. Masmoudi. 2016. New insights on plant salt tolerance mechanisms and their potential use for breeding. *Frontier in Plant Science* 7:1–17. 10.3389/fpls.2016.01787

Hasanuzzaman, M., K. Nahar, M. Alam, et al. 2014. Potential use of halophytes to remediate saline soils. *BioMed Research International* 2014. 10.1155/2014/589341

Hauser, F., and T. Horie. 2010. A conserved primary salt tolerance mechanism mediated by HKT transporters: a mechanism for sodium exclusion and maintenance of high K^+/Na^+ ratio in leaves during salinity stress. *Plant Cell and Environment* 33:552–565. 10.1111/j.1365-3040.2009.02056.x

Imchen, M., R. Kumavath, D. Barh, et al. 2017. Searching for signatures across microbial communities: metagenomic analysis of soil samples from mangrove and other ecosystems. *Scientific Reports* 7:1–13. 10.1038/s41598-017-09254-6

Iyengar, E.R.R., and M.P. Reddy. 1996. Photosynthesis in highly salt-tolerant plants. In *Handbook of Photosynthesis*, ed.M. Pesserkali, 897–909. Marshal Dekar, Baten Rose, USA.

Jha, B., I. Gontia, and A. Hartmann. 2012. The roots of the halophyte *Salicornia brachiata* are a source of new halotolerant diazotrophic bacteria with plant growth-promoting potential. *Plant and Soil* 356:265–277. 10.1007/s11104-011-0877-9

Jogawat, A. 2019. Osmolytes and their role in abiotic stress tolerance in plants. In *Molecular Plant Abiotic Stress: Biology and Biotechnology*, ed. A. Roychoudhury, and D.K. Tripathi, 91–104. John Wiley and Sons Ltd., Hoboken.

Jones, R.G.W., and A. Pollard. 1983. Proteins, enzymes and inorganic ions. In *Encyclopedia of Plant Physiology*, ed. A. Lauchli, and A. Pirson, 528–562. Springer, Berlin.

Jose, P.A., and S.R.D. Jebakumar. 2012. Phylogenetic diversity of actinomycetes cultured from coastal multipond solar saltern in Tuticorin, India. *Aquatic Biosystems* 8:23. 10.1186/2046-9063-8-23

Keshri, J., A. Mishra, and B. Jha. 2013. Microbial population index and community structure in saline-alkaline soil using gene targeted metagenomics. *Microbiological Research* 168:165–173. 10.1016/j.micres.2012.09.005

Keshri, J., B. Yousuf, A. Mishra, and B. Jha. 2015. The abundance of functional genes, *cbbL, nifH, amoA* and *apsA*, and bacterial community structure of intertidal soil from Arabian Sea. *Microbiological Research* 175:57–66. 10.1016/j.micres.2015.02.007

Kim, K., E. Seo, S.K. Chang, T.J. Park, and S.J. Lee. 2016. Novel water filtration of saline water in the outermost layer of mangrove roots. *Scientific Reports* 6:20426. 10.1038/srep20426

Knight, H., A.J. Trewavas, and M.R. Knight. 1997. Calcium signalling in *Arabidopsis thaliana* responding to drought and salinity. *The Plant Journal* 12:1067–1078. 10.1046/j.1365-313x.1997.12051067.x

Koranda, M., J. Schnecker, C. Kaiser, et al. 2011. Microbial processes and community composition in the rhizosphere of European beech-the influence of plant C exudates. *Soil Biology and Biochemistry* 43:551–558. 10.1016/j.soilbio.2010.11.022

Kumar, P., and P.K. Sharma. 2020. Soil salinity and food security in India. *Frontiers in Sustainable Food Systems* 4:533781. 10.3389/fsufs.2020.533781

Li, J., L. Pu, M. Zhu, J. Zhang, P. Li, X. Dai, Y. Xu, and L. Liu. 2014. Evolution of soil properties following reclamation in coastal areas: a review. *Geoderma* 226:130–139. 10.1016/j.geoderma.2014.02.003

Lokhande, V.H., and P. Suprasanna. 2012. Prospects of halophytes in understanding and managing abiotic stress tolerance. In *Environmental Adaptations and Stress Tolerance of Plants in the Era of Climate Change*, ed. P. Ahmad, and M.N.V. Prasad, 29–56. Springer, New York.

Mahajan, G., B. Das, S. Morajkar, et al. 2020. Soil quality assessment of coastal salt-affected acid soils of India. *Environmental Science and Pollution Research* 27:26221–26238. 10.1007/s11356-020-09010-w

Mahajan, G.R., B.L. Manjunath, A.M. Latare, R. D'Souza, S. Vishwakarma, and N.P. Singh. 2016. Microbial and enzyme activities and carbon stock in unique coastal acid saline soils of Goa. *Proceedings of the National Academy of Sciences, India Section B: Biological Sciences* 86:961–971. 10.1007/s40011-015-0552-7.

Mahajan, G.R., B.L. Manjunath, A.M. Latare, R. D'souza, S. Vishwakarma, and N.P. Singh. 2015. Fertility status of the unique coastal acid saline soils of Goa. *Journal of the Indian Society of Soil Science* 63:232–237. 10.5958/0974-0228.2015.00031.6

Mahajan, S., and N. Tuteja. 2005. Cold, salinity and drought stresses: an overview. *Archives of Biochemistry and Biophysics* 444:139–158. 10.1016/j.abb.2005.10.018

Maji, B., and T.D. Lama. 2016. Improving productivity of vulnerable coastal soils under changing climate. *SATSA Mukhapatra-Annual Technical Issue* 20:46–52.

Mandal, A.K., G.P. Obi Reddy, T. Ravisankar, and R.K. Yadav. 2018. Computerized database of salt-affected soils for coastal region of India. *Journal of Soil Salinity and Water Quality* 10:1–13.

Mangalassery, S., D. Dayal, A. Kumar, et al. 2017. Pattern of salt accumulation and its impact on salinity tolerance in two halophyte grasses in extreme saline desert in India. *Indian Journal of Experimental Biology* 55:542–548.

Mathews, D.V., P.L. Patil, and G.S. Dasog. 2009. Identification of soil fertility constraints of a pilot site in coastal agro ecosystem of Karnataka by geographic information systems technique. *Karnataka Journal of Agricultural Sciences* 22:77–80. 10.13140/2.1.3595.3282

Mishra, R.R., M.R. Swain, T.K. Danga, and H. Thatoi. 2012. Diversity and seasonal fluctuation of pre-dominant microbial communities in Bhitarkanika, a tropical mangrove ecosystem in India. *Revista de Biología Tropical* 60:909–924.

Mitran, T., P.K. Mani, N. Basak, B. Mandal, and S.K. Mukhopadhyay. 2014. Soil fertility constraint assessment using spatial nutrient map at three selected villages of coastal Sundarbans. *Journal of Soil Salinity and Water Quality* 6:1–8.

Mukhtar, S., M. Zareen, Z. Khaliq, S. Mehnaz, and K.A. Malik. 2020. Phylogenetic analysis of halophyte-associated rhizobacteria and effect of halotolerant and halophilic phosphate-solubilizing biofertilizers on maize growth under salinity stress conditions. *Journal of Applied Microbiology* 128:556–573. 10.1111/jam.14497

Munns, R. 2005. Genes and salt tolerance: bringing them together. *New Phytologist* 167:645–663. 10.1111/j.1469-8137.2005.01487.x

Munns, R., and M. Tester. 2008. Mechanisms of salinity tolerance. *Annual Review of Plant Biology* 59:651–681. 10.1146/annurev.arplant.59.032607.092911

Netondo, G.W., J.C. Onyango, and E. Beck. 2004. Sorghum and salinity: II. Gas exchange and chlorophyll fluorescence of sorghum under salt stress. *Crop Science* 44:806–811. 10.2135/cropsci2004.8060

Nielsen, M.N., and A. Winding. 2002. Microorganisms as Indicators of Soil Health. Technical Report No. 388. National Environmental Research Institute, Denmark. https://www2.dmu.dk/1_viden/2_Publikationer/3_fagrapporter/rapporter/FR388.pdf (accessed 22.09.2021).

Parida A., and A. Das. 2005. Salt tolerance and salinity effects on plants: a review. *Ecotoxicology and Environmental Safety* 60:324–349. 10.1016/j.ecoenv.2004.06.010

Polara, J.V., and R.B. Chauhan. 2015. Fertility status of irrigated soils of coastal Gir Somnath district of Gujarat. *Asian Journal of Soil Science* 10:263–265. 10.15740/HAS/AJSS/10.2/263-265

Rathore, A.P., D.R. Chaudhary, and B. Jha. 2016. Biomass production, nutrient cycling, and carbon fixation by *Salicornia brachiata* Roxb: a promising halophyte for coastal saline soil rehabilitation. *International Journal of Phytoremediation* 18:801–811. 10.1080/15226514.2016.1146228

Rathore, A.P., D.R. Chaudhary, and B. Jha. 2017. Seasonal patterns of microbial community structure and enzyme activities in coastal saline soils of perennial halophytes. *Land Degradation and Development* 28:1779–1790. 10.1002/ldr.2710

Ravindran, K.C., K. Venkatesan, V. Balakrishnan, K.P. Chellappan, and T. Balasubramanian. 2007. Restoration of saline land by halophytes for Indian soils. *Soil Biology and Biochemistry* 39:2661–2664. 10.1016/j.soilbio.2007.02.005

Rovira, A.D. 1969. Plant root exudates. *The Botanical Review* 35:35–57. 10.1007/BF02859887

Safdar, H., A. Amin, Y. Shafiq, A., et al. 2019. A review: impact of salinity on plant growth. *Nature and Science* 17:34–40. 10.7537/marsnsj170119.06

Saghafi, D., M. Ghorbanpour, H.S. Ajirloo, and B.A. Lajayer. 2019. Enhancement of growth and salt tolerance in *Brassica napus* L. seedlings by halotolerant Rhizobium strains containing ACC-deaminase activity. *Plant Physiology Reports* 24:225–235. 10.1007/s40502-019-00444-0.

Sanadhya, P., P. Agarwal, and P.K. Agarwal. 2015. Ion homeostasis in a salt-secreting halophytic grass. *AoB Plants*, 7:plv055. 10.1093/aobpla/plv055

Santos, A., J. da Silveira, A. Bonifacio, A. Rodrigues, and M. Figueiredo. 2018. Antioxidant response of cowpea co-inoculated with plant growth-promoting bacteria under salt stress. *Brazilian Journal of Microbiology* 49, 513–521. 10.1016/j.bjm.2017.12.003

Serrano, R. 1996. Salt tolerance in plants and microorganisms: toxicity targets and defense responses. *International Review of Cytology* 165:1–52. 10.1016/s0074-7696(08)62219-6

Sharma, S., C. Chen, S. Navathe, R. Chand, and S.P. Pandey. 2019. A halotolerant growth promoting rhizobacteria triggers induced systemic resistance in plants and defends against fungal infection. *Scientific Reports* 9:4054. 10.1038/s41598-019-40930-x

Sharma, S., J. Kulkarni, and B. Jha. 2016. Halotolerant rhizobacteria promote growth and enhance salinity tolerance in peanut. *Frontiers in Microbiology* 7:1600. 10.3389/fmicb.2016.01600

Shirgire, S.T., S.G. Savalia, and N.B. Misal. 2018. Assessment of available macro and micronutrient status of coastal Jamnagar district in Saurashtra region of Gujarat. *Journal of the Indian Society of Soil Science* 66:182–187. 10.5958/0974-0228.2018.00023.3

Sidharam, P., K.A. Kumar, and C.A. Srinivasamurthy. 2017. Soil fertility status and nutrient index for primary nutrients in Western Ghats and Coastal Karnataka under different agro-ecological systems. *Asian Journal of Soil Science* 12:314–319. 10.15740/HAS/AJSS/12.2/314-319

Sparks, D.L. 2003. *Environmental Soil Chemistry*, Elsevier Academic Press, UK, p. 352.

Sreeshan, A., S.P. Meera, and A. Augustine 2014. A review on transporters in salt tolerant mangroves. *Trees* 28:957–960. 10.1007/s00468-014-1034-x

Srinivasan, R., D.C. Nayak, R. Gobinath, S.N. Kumar, D.N. Rao, and S.K. Singh. 2022. Consequential rice crop response to resultant soil properties in a toposequence in eastern coastal plain of Odisha, India. *Modeling Earth Systems and Environment* 8:2135–2150. 10.1007/s40808-021-01216-2

Srinivasan, R., S.K. Singh, D.C. Nayak, and S. Dharumarajan. 2017. Assessment of soil properties and nutrients status in three horticultural land use system of coastal Odisha, India. *International Journal of Bio-resource and Stress Management* 8:33–40. 10.23910/IJBSM/2017.8.1.1697

Stefanis, C., A. Alexopoulos, C. Voidarou, S. Vavias, and E. Bezirtzoglou. 2013. Principal methods for isolation and identification of soil microbial communities. *Folia Microbiologica* 58:61–68. 10.1007/s12223-012-0179-5

Tang, C.S., W.F. Cai, K. Kohl, and R.K. Nishimoto. 1995. Plant stress and allelopathy. In *Allelopathy: Organisms, Processes, and Applications*, ed. K.M. Inderjit, and F.A. Einhellig, 582, 142–157. ACS Symposium Series, American Chemical Society, Washington. 10.1021/bk-1995-0582.ch011

Tantuja, N. 2020. Nutrient status of some coastal soils of Guntur district, Andhra Pradesh. *Journal of the Indian Society of Coastal Agricultural Research* 38:70–75.

Tripathi, S., S. Kumari, A. Chakraborty, A. Gupta, K. Chakrabarti, and B.K. Bandyapadhyay. 2006. Microbial biomass and its activities in salt-affected coastal soils. *Biology and Fertility of Soils* 42:273–277. 10.1007/s00374-005-0037-6

Ullah, S., and A. Bano. 2015. Isolation of plant-growth-promoting rhizobacteria from rhizospheric soil of halophytes and their impact on maize (*Zea mays* L.) under induced soil salinity. *Canadian Journal of Microbiology* 61:307–313. 10.1139/cjm-2014-0668

Verma, R.R., B.L. Manjunath, N.P. Singh, et al. 2018. Soil mapping and delineation of management zones in the Western Ghats of coastal India. *Land Degradation and Development* 29:4313–4322. 10.1002/ldr.3183

Waisel, Y. 1972. Biology of Halophytes. Academic Press, New York. 10.1016/B978-0-12-730850-0.X5001-6

Waisel, Y., A. Eshel, and M. Agami. 1986. Salt balance of leaves of the mangrove *Avicennia marina*. *Physiologia Plantarum* 67:67–72. 10.1111/j.1399-3054.1986.tb01264.x

Yousuf, B., R. Kumar, A. Mishra, and B. Jha. 2014. Differential distribution and abundance of diazotrophic bacterial communities across different soil niches using a gene-targeted clone library approach. *FEMS Microbiology Letters* 360:117–125. 10.1111/1574-6968.12593

Zhang, C., G. Liu, S. Xue, and C. Zhang. 2012. Rhizosphere soil microbial properties on abandoned croplands in the Loess Plateau, China during vegetation succession. *European Journal of Soil Biology* 50:127–136. 10.1016/j.ejsobi.2012.01.002

Zhao, C., H. Zhang, C. Song, J.K. Zhu, and S. Shabala. 2020. Mechanisms of plant responses and adaptation to soil salinity. *The Innovation* 1:100017. 10.1016/j.xinn.2020.100017

Zhao, S., N. Zhou, Z.Y. Zhao, K. Zhang, G.H. Wu, and C.Y. Tian. 2016. Isolation of endophytic plant growth-promoting bacteria associated with the halophyte *Salicornia europaea* and evaluation of their promoting activity under salt stress. *Current Microbiology* 73:574–581. 10.1007/s00284-016-1096-7

Zhu, J.K. 2001. Plant salt tolerance. *Trends Plant Science* 6:66–71. 10.1016/s1360-1385(00)01838-0

11

Strategic Solutions and Futuristic Challenges for the Cultivation of Food Legumes in India

CS Praharaj[1], Ummed Singh[2], and Rafat Sultana[3]
[1]ICAR-Indian Institute of Pulses Research, Kanpur, Uttar Pradesh, India
[2]College of Agriculture (Agriculture University, Jodhpur), Baytu, Barmer, Rajasthan, India
[3]Bihar Agricultural University, Sabour, Bhagalpur, Bihar, India

CONTENTS

11.1 Introduction

India is the world's largest producer of pulses, with 25.72 million tons during 2020–2021 (DES, 2021). In India, over a dozen pulse crops are grown, including chickpea, pigeonpea, lentil, mungbean, urdbean, cowpea, mothbean, and fieldpea. The productivity of the pulses, however, continues to remain under 1 ton/ha as these are generally grown as rainfed crops under poor management conditions that are dependent on various kinds of biotic and abiotic stresses. Moreover, nutritional hungry and thirsty soils, unfavorable weather, low availability of quality seeds, socioeconomic factors, poor postharvest handling/storage, and inadequate market support are the major constraints in realizing the potential of productivity gains in these pulses. In spite of these factors, pulse crops have witnessed several technological breakthroughs that have

DOI: 10.1201/9781003214885-11

not only helped its spread in new niches but also made impressive productive gains. Further, remarkable gains in production and productivity have been realized following the introduction of new varieties, as well as improved agro-technologies and their adoption (IIPR, 2020).

Water use in agriculture is at the core of issues related to water and food security. Agriculture accounts for, on average, 70% of all water withdrawals globally, and an even higher share of "consumptive water use" due to the evapotranspiration requirements of crops. Worldwide, over 330 million hectares are equipped for irrigation. Irrigated agriculture represents 20% of the total cultivated land, but contributes 40% of the total food produced worldwide (TWB, 2021). Further, competition for water resources is expected to increase in the future, with particular pressure on agriculture. Due to population growth, urbanization, industrialization, and climate change, improved water use efficiency will need to be matched by reallocation of as much as 25% to 40% of water in water-stressed regions, from lower to higher productivity and employment activities (TWB, 2021). In most cases, this reallocation is expected to come from agriculture, due to its high share of water use. Therefore, availability of adequate quantity and quality of water are key factors for achieving higher productivity levels. In addition, judicious use of irrigation water, implementation of precision technologies, and farmers' friendly water policies have the potential to enhance water productivity and profitability. Investments in conservation of water, improved techniques to ensure its timely supply, development of water-efficient technologies, and improving its allocation for efficient use are some of the imperatives that the country needs to augment. Poor irrigation efficiency of conventional irrigation systems has not only reduced the anticipated outcome of investments made toward water resource development, but also has resulted in environmental problems, like waterlogging and soil salinity, thereby affecting crop yields. Under the scenario of reduced water availability, low water productivity, increasing drought frequency, erratic monsoon behavior, and uncertainties associated with changing climate, precision irrigation associated with principles of conservation agriculture (tillage, residue retention, cropping sequence, and now control of weeds) plays a crucial role (Rani et al., 2020). Therefore, committed national and international efforts are needed to implement technologies that are appropriate for different farming systems to reduce both water and energy use, while improving crop yield and quality.

Pulses are usually grown under rainfed conditions all over India during both rainy months (pigeonpea, mungbean, urdbean, and cowpea) and the winter (chickpea, lentil, fieldpea, and rajmash). Among the pulses grown during rainy months, pigeonpea *(Cajanus cajan* L. Millsp) is primarily grown as a rainfed crop under diverse cropping systems, including inter/mixed cropping. Although medium duration cultivars are prevalent in the rainfed South and Central Zone, early and long-duration genotypes are more prevalent in the North Zone. The crop productivity also does vary with the length of the growing season and its life cycle (duration of crop). For example, pigeonpea in India had a very low yield with a low compound production growth rate of 0.8% between 1950 and 2004, which is due to various biotic and abiotic stresses (Ahlawat et al., 2005). However, the factors largely responsible for its average low productivity (800 kg/ha) in the Indian subcontinent is mainly attributed to the abiotic stresses related to microclimate, such as moisture and nutrient availability (that includes climate change).

Pulses are the important vegetable protein sources of Indian food. As per FAO, every person requires 50 g of pulses daily. Both *Kharif* and *Rabi* pulses play a major role in Indian food grain production. The split grains of these pulses are called *dal* and are an excellent source of high-quality protein, essential amino and fatty acids, fiber, minerals, and vitamins. These crops have an inherent role in improving soil fertility through biological N fixation by their root nodules, thereby enhancing soil nitrogen status, long-term soil fertility, and sustainability of the cropping systems. Thus, a majority of N need of these pulses is met from symbiotic nitrogen fixation from air, and the rest is left behind in the form of residual nitrogen and organic matter for the use of subsequent crops in rotation. The input needs of these pulses are also meager, and in respect to water, is about one-fifth of the requirement of cereals (Table 11.1). They are mostly grown as rainfed crops all over India (87%). Pulses are mainly valued for their importance in nutritional security, soil amelioration, and sustainable crop production (IIPR, 2020).

Excess soil moisture or waterlogging during monsoon season create unfavorable conditions for crop growth, including reduced aeration, hampered nodulation, reduced nutrient uptake, and favorable environment for blight and seedling rot, resulting in reduced crop stand and poor yield. Thus, the effect of suitable land configuration, such as ridge and raised planting, has a role in maintenance of optimum

TABLE 11.1

Water Requirements of Major Food Crops (Praharaj et al., 2016)

Crops	Duration (days)	Water requirements (cm)
Rice	100	95–100
Ragi	105	45–50
Pulses (short duration)	70	20–25
Pulses (long duration)	150–250	30–50
Maize	100	40–45
Cotton	165	60–75
Groundnut	105	60–65
Sugarcane	300	225–250

plant population and crop productivity vis-à-vis flat planting/broadcasting. On the other hand, moisture stress in the post-monsoon period adversely affects the development of reproductive organs, leading to depressed yields. Thus, soil moisture-related limitation is the major constraint to higher productivity of pulses in the Indian subtropics. Similarly, in the absence of moisture, availability of nutrients is another constraint limiting productivity of these crops.

Improved agro-technologies on water use have been a boon to profitable pulses cultivation. These include precision water management strategies. For optimum water management in pulses, normally 1-2 irrigation at critical stages, such as branching and/or pod development, prove highly productive (Table 11.2) in most of winter pulse crops on light textured soils in comparison to other food crops. Irrigation should be avoided during the active flowering period; otherwise, flower shedding and reversion to vegetative growth may occur. In chickpea and pigeonpea, two irrigations *viz.,* one each at branching and pod formation, are optimum in central India. In NWPZ and NEPZ, response to irrigation is generally low due to adequate winter rains and high relative humidity. On micro-irrigation, drip-fertigation at branching and pod development with N & K at one-quarter of the recommended dose (of 20:20 kg/ha) at 5 splits in the above stage (along with ½ of N & K + full P at sowing) gives higher yield and returns in long-duration pigeonpea (Praharaj et al., 2016). Besides pigeonpea, the micro-irrigation benefits have also been extended to other pulses viz., mungbean, chickpea, lentil, fieldpea, and rajmash.

Thus, following acute moisture stress, one or two need-based irrigations directly applied to its root zone through appropriate water-saving technology is required and shown to elevate crop performance. Thus, a need is arisen to apply life-saving/supplementary irrigation as per crop demand right in place/time/quantity in case deficit rainfall occurs during the most critical phase in its growth cycle. In this context, micro-irrigation has become the fastest growing segment of the irrigation industry worldwide and has the potential to increase the quality of food supply through improved water fertilizer efficiency. With the involvement of government machineries and farmers' cooperatives, it has become reality, even for most favored crops (MFC) that are rainfed like pulses as well as remunerative fruits and vegetables

TABLE 11.2

Critical Stages of Irrigation in Pulses (Praharaj et al., 2016)

Crop	Critical stages
Chickpea and lentil	Branching and pod development
Dwarf fieldpea	Branching, flowering, and pod development
Mungbean and urdbean (summer)	Growth, flowering, and pod development
Mungbean and urdbean (rainy season)	Flowering and pod development
Pigeonpea	Flowering and pod development
Rajmash	Growth, flowering, and pod development

(CSE, 2021). This further enables better management of precious water through a community sharing approach through cooperatives and village welfare schemes.

Water resource conservation with appropriate agro-techs (referred to as RCT) involving new crop production technologies are usually associated with reduction in tillage operations/mechanical operations, appropriate crop (or animal) husbandry with suitable crop(s) or cropping/farming systems, and more biomass (crop) or residue retention on the soil surface. These play a key role in sustainability of crop production systems. Conservation agriculture (CA), through its key components articulated with fortification through adequate soil cover, least soil traffic, and appropriate cropping systems, proves to be a giant leap toward sufficiency in agricultural production (Page et al., 2020). In India, judicious use of water as a natural resource - the most precious one - needs to be conserved, recycled, and channelized through cultivation of water-efficient crops/enterprises for the livelihood security of teeming millions. One good example highlighting water as the most critical input for productivity enhancement is supplementary irrigation(s) that could prove wonderful in realizing higher resource use efficiency (RUE), especially in grain legumes or pulses. In this paper, an attempt is made to discuss how grain legumes could play a pivotal role in upscaling water productivity and crop sustainability.

CA has put forth a management decision in water use strategically in order to conserve and preserve our natural resources against soil deterioration and its environmental repercussions. Appropriate major technological interventions in today's agriculture are those that are strategically adopted so as to fit in the ecosystem or agricultural production system for its overall improvement over space and time. Here comes the role of resource conservation with appropriate conservation tillage that characterizes the development of new crop production technologies that are normally associated with some degree of tillage reductions, minimum mechanical operations, and more crop residue retention on the soil surface. Conserving natural resources, however, removes the emphasis from the tillage component and addresses an enhanced concept of the complete agricultural system as CA refers to the gamut of practice or technological interventions (RCT) with three basic principles of minimum disturbance of soil through practices like zero or no tillage, keeping soil surfaces covered by leaving crop residues on them, adopting diversified crop rotation measures, and growing crops that have a symbolic correlation to each other. Thus, CA - with its aim at providing permanent soil cover, minimum soil disturbance, and crop rotations (adequate weed control) - is now considered the *EXPRESS WAY* to sustainable agriculture (Jat et al., 2012).

Water being the critical input for productivity enhancement, there is a need for its optimum and judicious use (through supplementary irrigation) for realizing higher input use efficiency through various technological options available. These should be in synchrony with the above basic principles of resource conservation. In this paper, an attempt is made to discuss the novel strategies for upscaling water productivity and sustainability through grain legumes with an implication of bringing together all the stakeholders to share information/experiences and to encourage interaction for future research and development efforts in fulfilling the mandates of Sustainable Developmental Goals (SDGs) for realizing production sustainability through conservation agriculture. The key technological interventions include some of the strategically important components of CA.

Several technology adoptions are largely influenced by externalities. To cite an example, say in drip-fertigation, a serious problem associated with the system is salt encrustation and clogging of lateral pipes in the case of salt water. While ranking the reasons for non-adoption of drip irrigation by Garetts ranking technique, salt encrustation and clogging of conveyance pipes ranked first, followed by high initial cost, delay in incentives amount disbursement, and finally undulated terrain nature (Palanisamy and Palanisamy, 2000). To meet the high initial cost and to popularize this water-saving method, the Government has extended incentives for varying categories of farmers at present up to 50% of the drip irrigation system cost.

11.2 Challenges Identified for the Cultivation of Legumes

Managing agro-inputs with the help of modern tools/techniques is most crucial so as to enhance crop productivity through improved input use efficiency. Specific agro-techniques such as supplemental irrigation at critical stages of crop growth, efficient application of water and nutrients through micro-irrigation, fertigation at optimum times, timely planting, and efficient planting systems play a significant role in increasing pulses productivity (Praharaj et al., 2017; 2018). Because water is a key input for sustained pulses production, its efficient management through optimum water-saving measures, such as micro-irrigation, has a greater role in an agrarian and developing economy like India. In addition, as its share for agricultural use is gradually diminishing every day, there is a need to use it judiciously, sensibly, and based on need, which is possible only through application of water-saving technology.

One of the approaches for effective on-farm management of allocated precious water is the use of drip-irrigation and fertigation through which a measured quantity of water is applied along with fertilizer at the root zone, ensuring direct benefit to plants. In India, since pulses are mostly grown under rainfed agro-ecology; moisture stress is commonly encountered during monsoon break and the post-monsoon period. It is observed that deficit rain occurs once in 4-5 years (Table 11.3). Moreover, scanty rainfall not only limits crop growth and development, but also puts on hold its potential productivity. Therefore, in the event of acute moisture stress, one or two irrigations directly applied to its root zone is shown to elevate crop performance. Thus, the importance of one or two lifesaving irrigations, especially at critical stages, makes sense. Hence, under the existing condition of agro-ecology, micro-irrigation technology meant for quick and immediate distribution of water delivered near the root zone, accompanied with dissolved fertilizer(s), is a boon for both appropriate utilization of precious input (water and nutrient) and their increased utilization efficiency. Micro-irrigation, such as drip and sprinklers, is having an additional advantage of reduced conveyance losses and ease of portability within the field and near the crop, thus making it user friendly (Ramamurthy et al., 2009).

In addition, precision irrigation system has proved its superiority over the other conventional system of irrigation, especially in remunerative fruit and vegetable crops, owing to precise and direct application of water in root zones (Bahadur and Singh, 2005). It is relatively unadopted and uncommon for field grown food crops, such as pulses. Although benefits of micro-irrigation, such as drip and sprinkler are aplenty like, improved water and nutrient use efficiency (due to no loss of nutrient or water through deep percolation or leaching), increased plant growth and development, higher yield and improved quality, and its flexibility in scheduling water application, because of narrow row spacing and higher population per unit area in the case of pulses, its adoption is inadequate and not popular. Unlike that of cereals and oilseed, which require frequent irrigation, pulses are mostly grown under rainfed condition; therefore, the application of precision or other micro-irrigation in the case of pulses, such as pigeonpea, is still remote and thus, a need is felt to strengthen it in the case of pulses so as to realize higher farm output and input use efficiency.

Similarly, the plant population and plant arrangement can have a pronounced effect on development, growth, and yield of crop. Plant rectangularity (arrangement of plants in unit area) could have direct bearing on final productivity of the crop since it decides the number of plants per unit area and per plant productivity through influencing leaf area and canopy photosynthesis in the field crops. In the majority of the pulses, population dynamics have a greater role to play as a minimum threshold number of plants are required to be maintained for yielding a stable optimum productivity. This is more critical and challenging in the presence of both abiotic and biotic stress that the crop faces during its completion of

TABLE 11.3

Deficient Monsoon Years (% of Normal) in India Between 1982 and 2009[*]

Years	June	July	Aug	Sep	Net less
1982	−16.8	−23.1	8.9	−32.2	−14.5
1986	10.8	−14.2	−12.7	−31.2	−12.7
1987	−21.6	−28.8	−3.7	−25.1	−19.4
2002	9.4	−54.2	−1.7	−12.9	−19.2
2004	−0.8	−19.9	−4.3	−30.0	−13.8
2009	−47.2	−4.3	−26.5	−20.2	−21.8

Source: Hindustan Times, Lucknow June 03, 2013 (p. 3).
Note
[*] falls between 96% and 104% of 890 mm (50 years average) is considered normal rainfall for India.

life cycle. Despite best efforts, population maintenance is more troublesome during the rainy months, where a number of uncontrolled factors, such as waterlogging, weed menace, and seedling blight, do play a role in minimizing the final plant stand in pulses grown during this time. In addition, pulses being grown under the upland condition, both excess and deficit in moisture availability, cause plant mortality and reduction in the plant population and seed yield. Therefore, standard practice (rainfed grown crop) should be refined for an effective and efficient on-farm scheduling of life-saving irrigation.

11.3 Desired Strategic Solution

11.3.1 Resource Use Efficient Technologies

There is a need for evaluating existing CA technologies for developing efficient water management strategies for their farm-level impact in India. CA technologies, such as precision land levelling, no-till systems, furrow irrigated raised bed (FIRB) planting systems, crop diversification, and residue management, have shown tremendous potential for efficient water-use efficiency (WUE) for sustainable farming systems (Praharaj et al., 2016; Singh et al., 2016). Unevenness of the soil surface influences farming operations, the drudgery involved, energy use, aeration, crop stand, and productivity, mainly through nutrient-water interactions. The general practices of land levelling used by farmers in India are either through use of plankers drawn by draft animals and small tractors or by iron scrappers/levelling boards drawn by four-wheel tractors (as in Indo-Gangetic Plains of India, known as IGP), and they are not perfect (less input use efficiencies and low yield at the cost of more water).

Here, laser land levelling is useful, especially in intensively cultivated, irrigated farming through achieving a better crop stand while saving irrigation water with improved input use efficiencies. As a result, zero-till seed drill performed better on a well-levelled field compared to an unleveled or fairly levelled field due to better seed placement, germination, and uniform distribution of irrigation water and plant nutrients. Zero tillage allows timely sowing of wheat, enables uniform drilling of seed, improves fertilizer use efficiency, saves water, and increases yield up to 20%. Similarly, the importance of the no till system in India is quite evident in terms of greenhouse gas emission and carbon sequestration (Venkatesh et al., 2013) as for each liter of diesel fuel consumed, 2.6 kg of CO_2 is released to the atmosphere. Assuming that 150 liters of fuel are used per hectare per annum for use of tractor and irrigation in conventional system, it would amount to nearly 400 kg CO_2 being emitted per annum per hectare. Thus, the role of no tillage/conservation agriculture in economic growth can't be undermined.

In FIRB planting systems, the crop is sown on ridges or beds of 15–20 cm height and 40–70 cm width depending on the crops to enhance crop productivity and save the irrigation water. Potential agronomic advantages of beds include improved soil structure due to reduced compaction through controlled trafficking, and reduced water logging and timelier machinery operations due to better surface drainage. Typical irrigation savings range from 18% to 30%–50%. Trials by farmer/researcher in IGP suggest irrigation water savings of 12% to 60% was accrued for direct seeded (DSRB) and transplanted (TRB) rice on beds, with similar or lower yields for TRB compared with puddled flooded transplanted (PTR) rice. Similarly, raised bed planting out-yielded flat planting by 18.8% and also enhanced both water use and WUE in chickpea (Ali and Kumar, 2005; Ali, 2009).

Drop in soil organic matter (SOM) due to limited/reduced return of organic biomass has been identified as one of the key factors for unsustainability of the system. Improper crop residue management (burning) due to inadequate *in-situ* recycling not only leads to loss of considerable amount of N, P, K, and S but also contributes to the global NO_2 and CO_2 budget and destruction of beneficial micro-flora of the soil as a substantial quantum (80.12 m t per annum) of crop residues is available for recycling in the rice-wheat system. Similarly, growing a cover crop/crop diversification improves the stability of the CA system and agro-ecosystem biodiversity since legume intercropping in cereals grown with wider row spacing reduces nitrate leaching. This is why CA systems will be the biggest thrust of future farming.

In this context, efficient management of water - a key input for sustained crop production through water-saving measures like need-based micro-irrigation - is the major consideration for pulses grown mostly under rainfed conditions. There is a need for use of precious water more judiciously, sensibly, and need based through modern technology when ever-increasing competing sinks like households water supply and industries consume their major share, even in water surplus areas like Indo-Gangetic Plains. One of the approaches for effective on-farm management of allocated precious water is the use of drip-fertigation, where both water and fertilizer are applied precisely at the root zone during pick crop demand, ensuring direct benefit to the plants. This supplementary irrigation, especially during a long dry spell after rainy months, could possibly alleviate moisture stress in the growing crop.

For example, in micro-irrigation techniques, precision technologies are used for efficient management of both water and nutrients precisely near the root zone of the crop plant with proven advantages of enhanced conveyance and water-use efficiency. In the era of supplementary irrigation, there is a greater need to apply both fertilizer and water through drip, especially at very critical stages to improve input productivity of the crop, water, and nutrients. A study also suggests that a single irrigation (20 mm in 5 splits) by drip fertigation with half of N+K fertilizers at branching produced significantly higher (20%) seed yields and economic return over rainfed pigeonpea (Praharaj et al., 2017; 2018). In chickpea, pre-plant irrigation + one irrigation at pre-podding stage increased seed yield by 77% over no irrigation.

Micro-irrigation techniques use precision technologies for efficient management of both water and nutrient precisely near the root zone of the crop plant. The major advantages in terms of water application include three factors that directly enhance both conveyance and water use efficiency, viz., water is applied directly to the root zone of plants and can be combined with other nutrient/agrochemicals/inputs; water is applied in frequent intervals in precise quantities as per the crop water requirement; and water is applied through a low-pressure pipe network comprising mains, sub mains, laterals, and emitting devices. Thus, there are perceptible advantages for these techniques, such as water is applied daily/alternate day at field capacity and near the root zone. Here, saline water up to 8–10 mmhos/cm can be used. Fertilizer can be combined with drip-water; thus, precision application of water results in fewer weeds and pests and greater pod retention. The likely benefits are substantial and include the followings:

- Uniform germination and optimum stand
- Reduced water use up to 55% (may be maximum)
- Elimination of wide fluctuation of water
- Control of weeds and reduced weeding cost
- Increase in efficiency of fertilizers
- Early and uniform maturity
- For early planting - prerequisite for IPM
- Allows summer crop (in pest-free environment)
- Opportunity for high-value crops
- Maintenance of soil health
- Increased/doubled yield
- In the case of the semi-arid, arid, and saline soil-water condition, drip has also been a boon to agriculture

As far as its application is concerned, it has wider application in respect to many considerations, such as the following:

- Possibility of a wide range of field crops, including all the pulses
- Rainwater can also be harvested and stored for supplemental irrigation through drip
- Possibility that more acreage can be irrigated though drip as there is considerable amount of water being saved by these techniques
- Additional benefit of fertigation helps in higher nutrient and water-use efficiency realized in many field crops
- For a rainfed crop, one or two irrigations to save crop from total collapse play a bigger role on productivity stability and sustainability through drip or micro-irrigation

- Thus, all these help in raising crop/water productivity by increasing yields and decreasing the amount of water used besides life-saving irrigation through drip

A peculiar characteristic of pigeonpea - a pulse - is that being a deep-rooted dicot, it is known to utilize sub-surface water more efficiently at the time of need/stress. The misconception in the farming community is that it does not require any irrigation. However, it has been scientifically proved that the crop can be profitably grown, even with a couple of life-saving irrigations applied as per crop demand during its critical stages for realizing the best achievable yield under a given set of conditions (Praharaj et al., 2016). Once the plant is established, it grows on its own, utilizing the resources available *in situ*. However, an initial boost is required to have a minimum threshold biomass to bear adequate reproductive flushes later in the season, along with a second one if required, at pod development for adequate and good pod/seed setting. Many a time, severe limitations in moisture at the root zone during its critical stages could also jeopardize its subsequent growth and productivity. Further restrictions imposed as a result of climatic aberrations in terms of deficiency in rainfall and its diminished frequency/distribution, especially at flower/pod development, is also not conducive for realization of its potential yield; and is going to be a harsh reality in the context of climate change (Praharaj et al., 2013).

Furthermore, in an experiment carried out during 2010–2012 involving precision irrigation through drip-fertigation, schedules revealed a potential seed yield of 3,708 kg/ha was realized under drip-fertigation at branching only (Praharaj et al., 2014). Although different planting patterns could not influence crop performance, a single irrigation (2 cm through 5 splits) through drip-fertigation with half of N+K fertilizer at branching (3,419 kg/ha) produced significantly higher (19.6%) seed yields over rainfed pigeonpea. In addition, drip-fertigation at both stages also out-yielded significantly over improved practice (furrow irrigation) during second year (9.4%) and in pooled data (6.3%). Yield attributes, such as pods/plant, 100-seed weight, and harvest index, showed a similar trend with that of seed yield. Lower water use, greater profile soil moisture content (Figure 11.1) and water-use efficiency (65.1 kg/ha-cm), higher plant NPK uptake with improved soil nutrient availability, and greater net return (INR 9,700/ha) were evident with drip-fertigation at both the stages (Table 11.4). Water-saving measures through micro-irrigation could possibly be extended to large areas, enabling efficient management of precious water through community sharing of irrigation infrastructures through village cooperatives and welfare schemes.

Our experience shows that drip-fertigation has a distinct advantage in long-duration pigeonpea crops on many counts. Drip irrigation at branching or at both branching and pod development was better as it produced, on an average, 18.4% higher yield over rainfed pigeonpea. Drip-fertigation at branching (3,708 kg/ha) and that at both branch and pod development (3,701 kg/ha) stages gave higher seed yield even over furrow irrigation. In a normal rainfall year, the effect of drip-fertigation applied only at branching was even more pronounced and evident. There was substantial saving of water and raising of water-use efficiency through drip irrigation. Similarly, sprinkler application helped in minimizing water

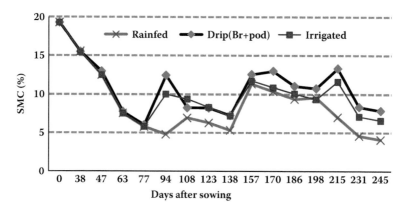

FIGURE 11.1   A typical periodic soil moisture content (SMC) in 0–60 cm soil profile.

TABLE 11.4

Effect of Drip-Fertigations on Economics, Efficiencies and Soil Organic Carbon+

Drip-Fertigation~	Seed yield (kg/ha)	Net return (₹000/ha)	WUE (kg/ ha-cm)	Agronomic efficiency (kg grain/kg NPK)	SOC (%)	
					0–15 cm	15–30
Rainfed	2,858	66.40	58.2	10.6	0.27	0.18
Drip[Br]	3,419	74.91	66.9	16.9	0.31	0.23
Drip[pod]	3,092	64.36	60.1	13.2	0.28	0.19
Drip[Br+pod]	3,468	76.05	65.1	17.4	0.32	0.25
Irrigation[Br+pod]	3,262	74.49	60.2	15.0	0.29	0.22
C.D. (0.05)	225	7.01	4.4	2.6	0.21*	0.17*

+pooled data, ~Treatments as described in material methods; WUE, water-use efficiency; SOC, soil organic carbon, * initial status of soil at the start of the trial, 1$= ₹56.59.

TABLE 11.5

On-Farm Demonstration of Drip-Fertigation at District-Level KVKs

Treatment	Chitrakoot		Chandauli	
	Seed yield (kg/ha)	Increase over rainfed (%)	Seed yield (kg/ha)	Increase over rainfed (%)
Rainfed (farmers' practice)	1710	–	1,370	–
Irrigation[Br+pod] (improved practice)	1980	15.8	1,645	20.1
Drip[Br+pod] (optimum practice)	2625	53.5	1,900	38.7
Remarks	32.6% increase over improved practice		15.5% increase over improved practice	

use by the crop in summer mungbean. When the same was accompanied with laser leveler, the result was remarkable in the context of water saving, higher water-use efficiency, and productivity.

To add further, a field demonstration was also undertaken at the farmer's field to study its impact both on the farmer's perspective (through feedback) and viability/sustainability (crop performance at on-farm trial). Therefore, to have a greater visibility of the technology, the trial on drip-fertigation in long-duration pigeonpea was carried out at district level involving two KVKs (Krishi Vigyan Kendra) at Chitrakoot and Chandauli (Table 11.5). These KVKs are regarded as the hub of all extension activities at the district level as the farmers have direct access to the technology because of its proximity to the villages and source of seed/other inputs/information. Thus, the KVK machineries were used with the fund support from ICAR (Indian Council of Agricultural Research) as the Government body (Praharaj et al., 2014; ICAR, 2014).

There was also an involvement of manufacturers of drip-fertigation tools for briefing the farmers about their benefits, application, maintenance, and above all, the monetary exemptions offered by the Government so as to facilitate procurement of these tools directly from the manufacturer. The need for farmers' cooperatives and association to use such a remunerative eco-friendly technology with saving of precious water is also arisen and well-conceived by farmers' themselves. This enables better management of precious water with community sharing approach through cooperatives and village welfare schemes. This sort of trial (*learning while doing*) at the district level involving farmers could be perceived as an eye opener to others for adoption of such technologies at bigger scale (district, state and country level).

In addition, use of anti-transpirant (HICO) gave significantly higher seed yield (33%) over control under rainfed conditions, although no such improvement was recorded in irrigated condition (Ali, 2009). As conservation efforts often concentrate on maximizing the efficiency of the existing system, improved back-up practices, such as chiselling compacted soils, creating furrow dikes to prevent runoff, and using soil moisture and rainfall sensors to optimize irrigation schedules, have their role to play.

Therefore, viable technologies are fast disseminated through knowledge sharing, adequate training/up scaling of skills, and of course more importantly, through both financial and logistic incentives. Problems cropping up out of adoption, if addressed properly and amicably, always scope for actual high adoption rate. Therefore, all the concerned stakeholders should share ideas on how to develop more effective policies to solve the already dwindling water crisis and its management in dry areas for food security, which are associated with intricate social issues like poverty, employment, and women empowerment. The development of such policies should definitely be based on an assessment of the current state of knowledge, the lessons learned from R & D programs in different countries, and a better understanding of the inter-relationships between water policies, food security, employment, and the environment.

CA poses a challenge both for the scientific community and the farmers to overcome the *past mindset* and *explore the opportunities* that CA offers for natural resources improvement. Successful adoption of CA systems will call for greatly accelerated effort in developing, standardizing and promoting quality machinery aimed at a range of crop and cropping sequences, permanent bed and furrow planting systems, harvesting operations to manage crop residues, etc. Managing CA systems will be highly demanding in terms of knowledge base as it calls for enhanced capacity building and partnerships with concerned stakeholders. CA also determines the whole system performance. For example surface maintained crop residues act as mulch and therefore reduce soil water losses through evaporation and maintain a moderate soil temperature regime. However, at the same time crop residues offer an easily decomposable source of organic matter and could harbor undesirable pest populations or alter the system ecology in some other way.

11.3.2 Promotion of Efficient Water Management Technologies

Application of certain viable technology, such as efficient management of water through optimum water-saving measures such as micro-irrigation for rainfed areas, has to be popularized at both the local and global level, keeping in view the consistent depletion of water resources and competing factors needing potable water. This has been more accentuated now-a-days because of the recent spurt in climate change and higher frequency of extreme climatic events. In addition, managing agro-inputs with the help of modern tools/techniques such as micro-irrigation is crucial so as to enhance agricultural productivity through improved input use efficiency. Further impetus in input use efficiency and productivity *per se* could also be increased through incorporation of suitable short duration intercrops/strip cropping during rainy season including cereals (jowar, bajra, maize, and other minor millets), pulses (mungbean and urdbean), oilseeds (sesamum, soybean and groundnut), and vegetables (for leaves or fruits) depending on demand and requirements of a commodity(ies) for the region. This is more important in the context of understanding agro-ecology of a region and socio-economic condition of the clientele (farmers) and applying sound agricultural principles then and there in order to achieve stability in agricultural production (and productivity) for a better future.

Thus, CA has emerged as a way for transition to the sustainability of intensive production systems over the past 2–3 decades globally. Since CA permits improved and efficient management of water and soils for agricultural production, it has assumed importance in view of the widespread natural resource degradation. This is attainable through effective and appropriate CA strategies aided RCT technologies. Attempts to promote CA globally are underway as reflected from developments worldwide, where the objective of bringing together farmers, scientists, private sector stakeholders, and decision makers to share information and experiences and to encourage interaction for future research and development efforts.

Water, fertilizer, energy (fuel), and other agrochemicals, including herbicides, are the necessary inputs in modern input-intensive cropping systems for enhancing productivity. Among all these inputs, water is the soul considered to be the Elixir of Life. There has been substantial increase in food demand as a result of population increase. In addition, increasing competition in demand for water for agriculture against those for industry and household sectors, ever diminishing agricultural land due to rapid urbanization and non-agricultural use, and mounting energy demand for maintaining a stable yet sustainable agricultural growth are more likely to be intensified further in the near future.

Water - a critical input for sustained crop production - is becoming limited depending on its availability, competing factors, allocation to priority crop(s), and the season of the year. It warrants all of us to use water more judiciously, sensibly and need-based in agriculture through modern technology, especially in the presence of diverse constraints. Various need-based and efficient approaches for effective on-farm management of allocated precious water include water conservation and its judicious allocation/ utilization at the time of need. This calls for use of water that could sustain productive potential of crop through alleviation of moisture stress, in synergy with conservation agriculture. A few efficient technological innovations could reinforce this through providing a sound backup for better water delivery and its usage. This includes precision water management, micro-irrigation, drip fertigation, precision land leveling, no-till systems, furrow-irrigated raised bed (FIRB) planting systems, crop diversification, and its residue management, which have shown incredible potential for lowering water use and/or increased water productivity and water-use efficiency. In the era of deficit rainfall/dry or dryland farming amalgamated further with rapid and visible climate change (many times accompanied with extreme climatic events), there is a greater need to apply the most critical input - water - at the point of interception (through micro-irrigation) to improve resource use efficiency (RUE) along with higher productivity of crop(s). Hence, precision in tactical water management could play the significant role in sustainable intensification of constrained food production systems (upland systems) in India.

Therefore, it is inferred from the above that improved agro-technologies in relation to water use have been a boon to profitable pulses cultivation. This includes various precision based technologies which have shown tremendous potential for higher water productivity and its use efficiency needed for sustainability. For optimum water management in pulses, normally 1-2 irrigation at critical stages, such as branching and/or pod development, prove highly productive in most of the season (non rainy) pulse crops on light/medium textured soils in comparison to other food crops. Incorporation or introduction of grain legumes could emerge as a transition toward sustainability in intensive agricultural production systems in India against a possible natural resource degradation/vagary of climate. We need to reorient not only the water management practices and techniques but also the policies that ensure better use of water for productive agriculture in New India.

11.3.3 Shifting of Pulses in Niche Areas

Six major states (Madhya Pradesh, Maharashtra, Rajasthan, Uttar Pradesh, Andhra Pradesh and Karnataka) where pulses are grown together contribute 79% of pulses area and 80% of pulses production across India. However, recently it's been witnessed that the area used for chickpea has shifted from north India to south and central India (2.2 m ha to 5.1 m ha between the 1970s and late 2000s), mainly due to the development of heat-tolerant varieties (e.g. JG11, K59, PG 186, JG 14) suitable for mechanical harvesting, which are also suitable for the vast rice fallow areas that remain available for cultivation after harvest of rice in central and south India (Singh et al., 2016). In addition, the area shares of *rabi* pulses (chickpea, lentil) and spring mungbean/urdbean has also been enhanced compared to *kharif* pulses (pigeonpea, *kharif* mungbean and urdbean). The major reason of this paradigm shift in area of pulses can be attributed to changes in climatic pattern in recent year.

11.3.4 Crop Improvement Strategies

11.3.4.1 Non-lodging, Input Responsive, Short-Duration Pulse Cultivars

In north India, crop diversification from a cereal-based to a pulses-based system is required for sustaining cropping system productivity with assured policy decisions like crop diversification with inclusion of pulses, improvement in seed replacement rate, and crop production techniques improvement. Developing chickpea varieties that are lodging resistant can be more profitable and competitive. It can be made by keeping plant height in check, preferably not more than 60–65 cm, responsive to high-input conditions, and early to extra-early maturity and terminal heat tolerance. An early maturing (115–120 days) heat-tolerant chickpea variety Sabour Chana-2 was recently released, and is expected to gain popularity in eastern India due to its high yield and suitability for its cultivation in rice fallow area. Development of super early thermo-sensitive (ICPL 20348, ICPL 20325, ICPL11255, ICPL 20326,) pigeonpea genotypes, lead it toward being a stable breeding line that may change the perception of growing pigeonpea only as a monocrop rather multiple cropping. These lines provide a number of opportunities like pigeonpea - wheat cropping system since pigeonpea matures within 100 days (super early), allowing time to prepare the land for wheat, which is not possible with traditional medium- and long-duration varieties. Extra-short duration pulses have a potential to be cultivated in new niches, like pigeonpea can be grown in diverse areas such as Uttarakhand, Rajasthan, Odisha, and Punjab. Short-duration pigeon pea variety ICPL 88039 has been very well adopted in the states of Rajasthan, Uttarakhand and Odisha, in addition to ICPL 88039, extra short-duration pigeonpea varieties ICPL 85010 and ICPL 84031 varieties were also released earlier in Himachal Pradesh and Andhra Pradesh, allowing farmers to grow pigeonpea in various cropping systems. Likewise, a substantial area of lentil is sown under the late-sown condition in rice-fallow fields of the Indo-Gangetic plains. Early maturing, resistance to wilt, rust, and stemphylium blight varieties possessing high biomass and tolerance to high temperature at the reproductive stage are required. There is also needed to reduce maturity duration of mungbean to fit these varieties in the wheat-rice dominated cropping system (Sultana et al., 2016).

11.3.4.2 Breeding Abiotic and Biotic Stress Tolerance Cultivars

Rabi Pulses, especially chickpea and lentil, are susceptible to various abiotic stresses, including terminal heat stress and drought, which are major problems for the places where rice is harvested late and farmers want to grow them as the next crop. Some traits like photosynthesis, chlorophyll content, transpiration, membrane stability, and canopy temperatures are influenced by rising temperatures (Rosyara et al., 2010). In northern India, heat stress is a major abiotic constraint for chickpea and lentil cultivation as it coincides with the fertilization period of plant growth, which affects grain yields drastically. As the receding residual soil moisture and increasing temperatures toward the end of the crop season impact the crop growth severely, early maturing cultivars that can escape the heat stress terminal stage are required to combat these stress conditions. A new chickpea variety (Pusa chickpea 10216) with enhanced drought tolerance has been developed (jointly by ICAR, state university and ICRISAT) through marker-assisted breeding by crossing Pusa 372 (recipient parent) x ICC4958 (donor parent). However, the unpredictable patterns of rainfall in India turn the country highly defenseless to abiotic stresses, especially for pigeonpea and urdbean (*kharif* crop). As pigeonpea is highly sensitive to waterlogging (Sultana et al., 2013; Chauhan et al., 1997; Perera et al., 2001; Khare et al., 2002), it has been found that drought and waterlogging in southern India, waterlogging and low temperature in eastern India, and salinity and waterlogging in the north, central, and western part of India are major threats for pigeonpea production and productivity. Around 30%–35% estimated area of pigeonpea is annually affected by waterlogging, which leads to 25%–30% yield losses. Breeding lines with enhanced drought and terminal heat tolerance have been developed through molecular breeding, which can be developed to combine stress tolerance in the case of chickpea. However, several pigeonpea lines, such as ICP 5028, ICPL 20092, and ICPL 84023, were screened and showed promise to waterlogging tolerance, which can be used in a breeding program to develop high-yielding tolerant cultivars. Low temperature (<10°C) during the early flowering phase leads to flower and pod drop in pigeonpea; the crop produces a second flush of flower, leading to delayed maturity and significant yield losses (Sultana et al., 2014). Most of the cultivars of pigeonpea are injured or killed by non-freezing low temperatures, and they exhibit various symptoms of chilling injury, such as chlorosis, necrosis, or growth retardation. Low temperature primarily affects the development and growth of flower buds and the opening of flowers (Choudhary et al., 2011; Sultana et al., 2014).

Likewise, *Fusarium* wilt and dry root rot (DRR) have appeared as highly devastating root diseases for chickpea and lentils in central and southern India. Although many wilt-resistant sources are available, there is still a great effort needed in this direction for identifying new sources of resistance to DRR in the germplasm of cultivated and wild species of chickpea and for combined resistance to DRR and wilt in the newly developed varieties for central and southern India. Again, pod borer (*Helicoverpa armigera*) remains a major threatening and challenging insect-pest for all the pulses, but it is more detrimental for chickpea and pigeonpea crops. Greater chances for development of pod borer resistant cultivars exist through application of transgenic technology. Hence, concerted efforts are needed for using different transgenes and promoter options for developing transgenic events and their evaluations for effectiveness and bio-safety. The second major threat for pigeonpea is wilt and sterility mosaic. It is estimated that the total cost of cultivation decreased with the increasing adoption of Integrated Pest

Management, along with the promotion of improved disease-resistant varieties of pigeonpea (Sultana et al., 2020).

11.3.4.3 Added Breeding Approaches

To cut short the long breeding cycles and time taken to develop and release a new variety, a new breeding technique, speed breeding, has been advocated. Speed breeding is a new breeding approach that advances the next breeding generation quickly by artificial manipulation of environmental conditions, where crops are grown with the aim to accelerate the reproductive period and seed set.

11.3.4.4 Inclusion of Speed Breeding

The development of new high-yielding varieties using conventional breeding approaches is resource-intensive and takes a very long time, at least 7–8 years. To overcome the time constraint and advance the generations quickly, some crop breeders opt for off-season nurseries. This approach has exploited in breeding early maturing pigeonpea and chickpea cultivars and is based on germinating immature seeds.

11.3.4.5 Pre-breeding

Most of the pulses are self-pollinated and lack sufficient genetic variability, which is prerequisite for its improvement. So, pre-breeding is another breeding approach to generate genetic variability in a self-pollinated crop, as the wild relatives of a cultivated species are a known reservoir of new genes. In crop improvement programs of various pulse crops, a number of genes, mined from wild species, have been used successfully for a resistance breeding program (Pratap et al., 2012).

11.3.4.6 Hybrid Breeding

Although most of the pulses are self-pollinated, pigeonpea is often cross-pollinated and possesses 10%–20% outcrossing. This offers pigeonpea a unique opportunity for breeding hybrid parents to break yield plateau. This is facilitated by cytoplasmic nuclear male sterility system (CMS System). It allowed the development of hybrids in early and medium maturity groups (Tikka et al., 1997; Saxena et al., 2014), such as ICPH 2671 and ICPH 2740. This was followed by the release of four pigeonpea hybrids (Saxena and Tikle, 2015). The unique three-parent hybrid breeding systems (A, B, and R lines) sometimes become fragile due to invasion of certain undesirable genetic factors associated with specific cytoplasm (Levings, 1993). In order to overcome such threats, efforts need to be made to breed female parents with a diverse cytoplasm base.

11.3.4.7 Genomics-Assisted Breeding

The annual rate of yield improvement in most of the pulses has remained stagnant over the past few decades. This is a great concern among the scientific fraternity working on this crop. Increasing yield with an ongoing conventional breeding program in order to meet the future demand for plant-based protein still remains a big challenge. Thus, new and multi-disciplinary approaches are needed to accelerate the crop breeding process to develop new high-yielding variety. Some of the DNA sequencing-based technologies that have revolutionized the crop breeding process and opened the "genomics era" for pulse improvement are required.

11.3.4.8 Genomic Resources

The narrow genetic diversity in self-pollinated pulses restricted the effective utilization of a conventional breeding approach as well as the development and utilization of genomic tools. To enable genomics-assisted breeding in pulses, the Indian Council of Agricultural Research (ICAR) and the

Government of India, under the umbrella of Indo-US Agricultural Knowledge Initiative (AKI), floated the Pigeonpea Genomics Initiative (PGI) in November 2006 (Varshney et al., 2010).

11.3.4.9 Candidate Genes and Trait Discovery

A large set of Simple Sequence Repeat markers (Bohra et al., 2011; Dutta et al., 2011; Mir et al., 2017), Diversity Array Technology markers (Yang et al., 2006, 2011), Single Feature Polymorphism (Saxena et al., 2011), and Single Nucleotide Polymorphism Genotyping platforms (Varshney et al., 2012) have been developed for generating low-, moderate-, and high-density genetic maps in pigeonpea. These molecular markers and genetic maps provide greater opportunity to discover genes/QTLs responsible for important targeted traits leading to genetic improvement of the crop. In addition to this, association mapping, marker-based QTL mapping, candidate gene-based association mapping, transcriptomics, and whole-genome sequencing have been used to identify markers and candidate genes responsible for traits like flowering time, fertility restoration, wilt and SMD resistance, determinacy (Mir et al., 2013), yield, as well as phenology in pigeonpea (Mir et al., 2017).

11.3.4.10 Virus-Induced Gene Silencing

Those plant species that are not acquiescent to tissue culture technology and transgenic development due to recalcitrance, have virus-induced gene silencing (VIGS) to play a great role for its improvement. Although VIGS uses RNA interference to silence the genes, it is transient gene function validation technology overcoming the use of stable transformants, which is often difficult in plants species (Senthil-Kumar and Mysore, 2011). VIGS has been widely used to silence genes (in fruits and vegetables, especially tomatoes) attached to plants. The phytoenedesaturase (Pds) gene is the most commonly used reporter gene, although not much is known about the changes that occur due to its silencing. However, it can be used in pulses for modification of genetic regions affecting the protein content and other nutritional factors.

11.3.4.11 CRISPR/Cas9 Induced Genome Editing

The most recent tool among these is CRISPR/Cas 9 systems. It edits the gene by precisely cutting DNA and letting natural DNA repair processes take over. The system consists of two parts, the Cas 9 enzyme and guide RNA. CRISPR/Cas in nature is part of the bacterial defense mechanism against phages and other invasive genetic elements. It can be used to introduce a variety of genomic modifications by one of two main DNA repair pathways - non-homologous end joining (NHEJ) and homology-directed repair (HDR) - and during this repair desired changes are incorporated or omitted into the genome. CRISPR/Cas is also involved in genome imaging and protein recruitment for sequence-based gene regulation. It also has the capability for engineering nucleotide substitutions at target sites. Similarly, studies related to pulses for protein and other nutritional factors can be taken, and CRISPR/Cas can be employed for its improvement.

11.4 Conclusion

India is the largest producer and consumer of food legumes. Pulses are the source of protein for the majority of vegetarian people in India, which increases the demand. To fulfill the demand and supply gap, productivity enhancement with the interventions of agronomic technologies, coupled with breeding improvement, while managing natural resources is the most important requirement. Addressing the productivity constraints requires identification of challenges and adoption of localized strategic solutions, including water productivity-enhancing approaches, resource use efficient agro-techniques, approaching niche-areas, growing input responsive cultivars, managing biotic and abiotic stresses, and using key measures.

REFERENCES

Ahlawat, I.P.S., B. Gangaiah, and I.P. Singh. 2005. Pigeonpea *(Cajanus cajan)* research in India-an overview. *Indian Journal of Agricultural Sciences* 75(6): 309–320.

Ali, M. 2009. *25 years of pulses research at IIPR*. Indian Institute of Pulses Research, Kanpur, p. 211.

Ali, M., and S. Kumar 2005. Chickpea (*Cicer arietinum*) research in India: accomplishments and future strategies. *Indian Journal of Agricultural Sciences* 75(3): 125–133.

Bahadur, A., and K.P. Singh. 2005. Optimization of spacing and drip irrigation scheduling in indeterminate tomato. *Indian Journal of Agricultural Sciences* 75(9): 563–565.

Bohra, A., A. Dubey, R.K. Saxena, R.V. Penmetsa, K.N. Poornima, N. Kumar, A.D. Farmer, G. Srivani, H.D. Upadhyaya, R. Gothalwal, and S. Ramesh. 2011. Analysis of BAC-end sequences (BESs) and development of BES-SSR markers for genetic mapping and hybrid purity assessment in pigeonpea (*Cajanus* spp.). *BMC Plant Biology* 11(1): 56.

Chauhan, Y.S., S.N. Silim, J.K. Rao, and C. Johansen. 1997. A pot technique to screen pigeonpea cultivars for resistance to waterlogging. *Journal of Agronomy and Crop Science* 178(3): 179–183.

Choudhary, A.K., R. Sultana, A. Pratap, N. Nadarajan, and U.C. Jha. 2011. Breeding for abiotic stresses in pigeonpea. *Journal of Food Legumes* 24(3): 165–174.

CSE 2021. India's pulses problem: we need real reform. Society for Environmental Communications, Centre for Science and Environment, Down to Earth, New Delhi, India. URL: https://www.downtoearth.org.in/blog/agriculture/india-s-pulses-problem-we-need-real-reform-78753. Accessed April 13, 2022.

DES 2021. Directorate of Economics and Statistics, Department of Agriculture, Cooperation & Farmers Welfare. URL: https://eands.dacnet.nic.in/APY_96_To_06.htm. Accessed February 13, 2022.

Dutta, S., G. Kumawat, B.P. Singh, D.K. Gupta, S. Singh, V. Dogra, K. Gaikwad, T.R. Sharma, R.S. Raje, T.K. Bandhopadhya, and S. Datta. 2011. Development of genic-SSR markers by deep transcriptome sequencing in pigeonpea [*Cajanus cajan* (L.) Millspaugh]. *BMC Plant Biology* 11(1): 17.

ICAR 2014. Indian Council of Agricultural Research, New Delhi. URL: https://icar.org.in/content/annual-report-2014-2015. Accessed November 11, 2021.

IIPR 2020. Annual report, ICAR-Indian Institute of Pulses Research, Kanpur, Uttar Pradesh. URL: https://iipr.icar.gov.in/pdf/IIPR%20AR-2020%20English.pdf. Accessed March 11, 2021.

Jat, M.L., R.K. Malik, Y.S. Saharawat, R. Gupta, B. Mal, and R. Paroda. 2012. Regional dialogue on conservation agricultural in South Asia. *Asia Pacific Association of Agricultural Research Institutions (APAARI), International Maize and Wheat Improvement Center (CIMMYT), Indian Council of Agricultural Research (ICAR), New Delhi, India*, 34.

Khare, D., S. Rao, J.P. Lakhani, and R.G. Satpute. 2002. Tolerance for flooding during germination in pigeonpea. *Seed Research* 30: 82–87.

Levings, C. 1993. Thoughts on cytoplasmic male sterility in CMS-T maize. *Cell Report* 5: 1285–1290.

Mir, R.R., I.A. Rather, M.A. Bhat, G.A. Parray, and R.K. Varshney. 2017. Molecular mapping of genes and QTLs in pigeonpea. In *The pigeonpea genome*. Springer, Cham, pp. 55–64.

Mir, R.R., R.K. Saxena, K.B. Saxena, H.D. Upadhyaya, A. Kilian, D.R. Cook, and R.K. Varshney. 2013. Whole-genome scanning for mapping determinacy in Pigeonpea (*Cajanus* spp.). *Plant Breeding* 132(5): 472–478.

Page, K.L., Y.P. Dang, and R.C. Dalal. 2020. The ability of conservation agriculture to conserve soil organic carbon and the subsequent impact on soil physical, chemical, and biological properties and yield. *Frontiers in Sustainable Food Systems* 4: 31. doi: 10.3389/fsufs.2020.00031

Palanisamy, K., and V. Palanisamy 2000. *Socio-economic aspect of drip irrigation*. Training manual published by water technology centre, Tamil Nadu Agricultural University, Coimbatore.

Perera, A.M., H.S. Pooni, and K.B. Saxena, 2001. Components of genetic variation in short-duration pigeonpea crosses under waterlogged conditions. *Journal of Genetics & Breeding* 55(1): 21–38.

Praharaj, C.S. 2013. Managing precious water through need based micro-irrigation in a long duration pigeonpea under Indian Plains. In International Conference on Policies for Water and Food Security, Cairo, Egypt June 24-26, 2013, ICARDA, FAO, IFAD, IDRC, CRDI and ARC. P.4 (Extended Abstract).

Praharaj, C.S., U. Singh, and K. Hazra. 2014. Technological interventions for strategic management of water for conserving natural resources. In Proceeding of 6th World Congress on Conservation Agriculture – Soil Health and Wallet wealth, Winnipeg, Manitoba, CANADA, June 22-26, 2014, pp. 4–6.

Praharaj, C.S., U. Singh, S.S. Singh, and N. Kumar. 2017. Micro-irrigation in rainfed pigeonpea-upscaling productivity under eastern gangetic plains with suitable land configuration, population management and supplementary fertigation at critical stages. *Current Science* 112(1): 95–107.

Praharaj, C.S., S. Ummed, S.S. Singh, and N. Kumar. 2018. Tactical water management in field crops: the key to resource. *Current Science* 115(7): 1262–1269.

Praharaj, C.S., S. Ummed, S.S. Singh, N.P. Singh, and Y.S. Shivay. 2016. Supplementary and life-saving irrigation for enhancing pulses production, productivity and water use efficiency in India. *Indian Journal of Agronomy* 61 (4th IAC Special issue): S249–S261

Pratap, A., D.S. Gupta, and N. Rajan. 2012. Mungbean. In Bharadwaj D. (ed.) *Breeding Indian field crops*. Agro-bios Publishers, New Delhi, pp. 208–227.

Ramamurthy, V., N.G. Patil, M.V. Venugopalan, and O. Challa. 2009. Effect of drip irrigation on productivity and water-use efficiency of hybrid cotton (*Gossypium hirsutum*) in *Typic Haplusterts*. *Indian Journal of Agricultural Sciences* 79(2): 118–121.

Rani, A., A. Kumari, and J. Kumar, 2020. Water resource and use efficiency under changing climate. In S. Kumar et al. (eds.) *Resources use efficiency in agriculture*. Springer Nature Singapore Pte Ltd., pp. 519–576. doi: 10.1007/978-981-15-6953-1_15

Rosyara, U.R., S. Subedi, E. Duveiller, and R.C. Sharma. 2010. The effect of spot blotch and heat stress on variation of canopy temperature depression, chlorophyll fluorescence and chlorophyll content of hexaploid wheat genotypes. *Euphytica* 174: 377–390.

Saxena, K.B., and A.N. Tikle. 2015. Believe it or not, hybrid technology is the only way to enhance pigeonpea yields. *International Journal of Scientific and Research* 5: 1–7.

Saxena, K.B., R.V. Kumar, and M. Bharathi. 2014. Studies on fertility restoration of A 4 cytoplasm in pigeonpea. *Euphytica* 198(1): 127–135.

Saxena, K.B., R. Sultana, R.K. Saxena, R.V. Kumar, J.S. Sandhu, A. Rathore, P.K. Kishor, and R.K. Varshney. 2011. Genetics of fertility restoration in A4 based, diverse maturing hybrids of pigeonpea [*Cajanus cajan* (L.) Millsp.]. *Crop Science* 51(2): 574–578.

Senthil-Kumar, M., and K.S. Mysore. 2011. New dimensions for VIGS in plant functional genomics. *Trends in Plant Science* 16(12): 656–665.

Singh, N.P., C.S. Praharaj, and J.S. Sandhu. 2016. Utilizing untapped potential of rice fallow of East and North-east India through pulse production. *Indian Journal of Genetics* 76(4): 388–398.

Sultana, R., A.K. Choudhary, A.K. Pal, K.B. Saxena, B.D. Prasad, and R. Singh. 2014. Abiotic stresses in major pulses: current status and strategies. In R.K. Gaur, and P. Sharma (eds.) *Approaches to plant stress and their management*. Springer India, New Delhi, pp. 173–190. doi: 10.1007/978-81-322-1620-9_9.

Sultana, R., K.B. Saxena, A. Ghatak, R.K. Sohane, A.K. Choudhary, S.K. Chaturvedi, Dharamsheela, R.R. Kumar, P.K. Singh, and J.B. Tomar. 2016. Can short duration pulses bring self sufficiency in Bihar: an overview of current status and the potential strategies for the way forward. In National Conference on Bringing Self-sufficiency in Pulses for Eastern India Organized Jointly by BAU, Sabour and ISPRD, Kanpur at BAU, Sabour, Bhagalpur on August 05-06, 2016; ISBN: 978-93-85516-73-3). Souvenir & Abstract, pp. 67–76.

Sultana, R., M.I. Vales, K.B. Saxena, A. Rathore, S. Rao, S.K. Rao, M.G. Mula, and R.V. Kumar. 2013. Waterlogging tolerance in pigeonpea (*Cajanus cajan* (L.) Millsp.): genotypic variability and identification of tolerant genotypes. *The Journal of Agricultural Science* 151(5): 659–671.

Tikka, S.B.S., L.D. Prmar, and R.M. Chauhan. 1997. First record of cytoplasmic-genic male-sterility system in pigeonpea (*Cajanus cajan* (L.) Millsp.) through wide hybridization. *Gujarat Agriculture University Research Journal* 22: 160–162.

TWB 2021. The World Bank. Water in Agriculture-World Bank Group. URL: https://www.worldbank.org/en/topic/water-in-agriculture#1. Accessed May 04, 2022.

Varshney, R.K., W. Chen, Y. Li, A.K. Bharti, R.K. Saxena, J.A. Schlueter, M.T. Donoghue, S. Azam, G. Fan, A.M. Whaley, and A.D. Farmer. 2012. Draft genome sequence of pigeonpea (*Cajanus cajan*), an orphan legume crop of resource-poor farmers. *Nature Biotechnology* 30(1): 83.

Varshney, R.K., R.V. Penmetsa, S. Dutta, P.L. Kulwal, R.K. Saxena, S. Datta, T.R. Sharma, B. Rosen, N. Carrasquilla-Garcia, A.D. Farmer, and A. Dubey. 2010. Pigeonpea genomics initiative (PGI): an international effort to improve crop productivity of pigeonpea (*Cajanus cajan* L.). *Molecular Breeding* 26(3): 393–408.

Venkatesh, M.S., K.K. Hazra, P.K. Ghosh, C.S. Praharaj, and N. Kumar. 2013. Long-term effect of pulses and nutrient management on soil carbon sequestration in Indo-Gangetic plains of India. *Canadian Journal of Soil Science* 93(1): 127–136.

Yang, S., W. Pang, G. Ash, J. Harper, J. Carling, P. Wenzl, E. Huttner, X. Zong, and A. Kilian. 2006. Low level of genetic diversity in cultivated pigeonpea compared to its wild relatives is revealed by diversity arrays technology. *Theoretical and Applied Genetics* 113(4): 585–595.

Yang, S.Y., R.K. Saxena, P.L. Kulwal, G.J. Ash, A. Dubey, J.D. Harper, H.D. Upadhyaya, R. Gothalwal, A. Kilian, and R.K. Varshney. 2011. The first genetic map of pigeon pea based on diversity arrays technology (DArT) markers. *Journal of Genetics* 90(1): 103–109.

12

Climate-Induced Droughts and Its Implications for Legume Crops

Md. Abul Kashem and Mohammad Zabed Hossain
Ecology and Environment Laboratory, Department of Botany, University of Dhaka, Dhaka, Bangladesh

CONTENTS

DOI: 10.1201/9781003214885-12

12.1 Introduction

12.1.1 Drought and Desertification

Drought is generally defined as an extended period of dry weather caused by a lack of rain or snow (Li et al., 2013; Fang et al., 2010). It occurs primarily due to insufficient precipitation or exceptionally high temperatures, evaporation, and low humidity. Drought causes a situation where there is a severe moisture deficit below expected levels, restricting some kinds of activity (Wilhite et al., 2007). Drought has also been defined as a complex insidious event (Wilhite et al., 2007; Hisdal and Tallaksen, 2003) that does not have clear entry, duration, and termination points compared to other natural phenomena, such as floods, fires, and storms.

Desertification, on the contrary, is defined as the process by which natural or human-induced causes reduce the biological productivity of drylands (arid and semi-arid lands) in the world (Smith et al., 2013; Mortimore, 2016). The direct causes of desertification mainly depend on land management and other factors such as deforestation, overgrazing of livestock, over-cultivation of crops, inappropriate irrigation, and natural fluctuations. Both natural variability in climate and global warming can also affect rainfall patterns around the world, which can contribute to desertification. Since rainfall has a cooling effect on the land surface, a decline in rainfall can allow soils to dry out in the heat and become more prone to erosion. On the other hand, heavy rainfall can erode the soil itself and cause waterlogging and subsidence. Consequences of drought are immense since it affects agricultural productivity and the livelihood of farmers, creating crisis in the socioeconomic condition of people across the globe.

12.1.2 Types of Drought

Drought is classified into two types: (1) conceptual, and (2) operational droughts. Conceptual definitions help to understand the meaning of drought and its effects. For instance, drought is a protracted period of deficient precipitation, which causes extensive damage to crops, resulting in loss of yield. Operational definitions of drought help to identify the beginning, end, and degree of severity. An operational definition for agriculture may compare daily precipitation to evapotranspiration to determine the rate of soil-moisture depletion, and express these relationships in terms of drought effects on plant behavior. The definitions also reflect differences in regions, needs, and disciplinary approaches. Wilhite and Glantz (1985) reported four types of droughts: meteorological drought, hydrological drought, agricultural drought, and socioeconomic drought. The first three approaches deal with ways to measure drought as a physical phenomenon, whereas the last one deals with drought in terms of supply and demand, tracking the effects of water shortfall as it ripples through socioeconomic systems.

12.1.2.1 Meteorological Drought

Meteorological drought is defined on the basis of the degree of dryness, in comparison to a normal or average amount, and the duration of the dry period (Golian et al., 2015). Definitions of meteorological drought must be region-specific, since the atmospheric conditions that result in deficiencies of precipitation are highly region-specific (Alborzi et al., 2018; Hisdal and Tallaksen, 2003). For example, some definitions of meteorological drought identify periods of drought on the basis of the number of days with precipitation less than some specified threshold. This measure is only appropriate for regions characterized by a year-round precipitation regime such as a tropical rainforest, humid subtropical climate, or humid mid-latitude climate.

12.1.2.2 Agricultural Drought

Agricultural drought links various characteristics of meteorological or hydrological drought to agricultural impacts, focusing on precipitation shortages, differences between actual and potential evapotranspiration, soil-water deficits, reduced groundwater or reservoir levels, and so forth (Golian et al.,

2015; Mekonnen and Gokcekus, 2020). Water demand of plants depends on the prevailing weather conditions, biological characteristics of the specific plant, its stage of growth, and the physical and biological properties of the soil. Deficient topsoil moisture at planting may hinder germination, leading to low plant populations per hectare and a reduction of final yield. Thus, impacts of drought on agriculture are of immense significance since it ultimately hampers food security of human beings.

12.1.2.3 Hydrological Drought

Hydrological drought refers to a persistently low discharge and/or volume of water in streams and reservoirs, lasting months or years (Tabari et al., 2013). This kind of drought is a natural phenomenon that may be exacerbated by human activities. The frequency and severity of hydrological drought is often defined on a watershed or river basin scale. Hydrological droughts are usually out of phase with or lag the occurrence of meteorological and agricultural droughts (Shobair, 2001). It takes a longer period of time for precipitation deficiencies to show up in components of the hydrological system, such as soil moisture, streamflow, and groundwater and reservoir levels. As a result, these impacts are out of phase with impacts in other economic sectors.

12.1.2.4 Socioeconomic Drought

Socioeconomic definitions of drought are linked with the supply and demand of some economic good with elements of meteorological, hydrological, and agricultural droughts (Tabari et al., 2013; Wilhite and Glantz, 1985). Occurrence of this kind of drought depends on time and space processes of supply and demand to identify or classify droughts. The supply of many economic goods, such as water, forage, food grains, fish, and hydroelectric power, depends on weather. Because of the natural variability of climate, water supply may be ample in some years and unable to meet human and environmental needs in other years. Socioeconomic droughts may occur when the demand for an economic good exceeds supply as a result of a weather-related shortfall in water supply (Tabari et al., 2013).

12.1.3 Links between Drought Severity and Climate Change

Understanding the relationship of drought with climate change urges the importance of distinction between weather and climate. Weather is a description of atmospheric conditions over a short period of time, whereas climate is how the atmosphere behaves over relatively long periods of time. Climate changes, thus, occur over longer periods and can be observed as changes in the patterns of weather events. As temperatures have warmed over the past century, the prevalence and duration of drought has increased (Thomas et al., 2009). Global climate change affects a variety of factors associated with drought. Increased temperatures will lead to more precipitation falling as rain rather than snow, earlier snow melt, and increased evaporation and transpiration (Konstatinos and Lettenmaier, 2006). Thus, the risk of hydrological and agricultural drought increases as temperatures rise. Declines in productivity may be the result of climate change, deforestation, overgrazing, poverty, unsustainable irrigation practices, or combinations of these factors. The concept does not refer to the physical expansion of existing deserts but rather to the various processes that threaten all dryland ecosystems, including deserts and grasslands (Seitz et al., 2011; Safriel and Adeel, 2008). Climate is the average weather in a given area over a longer period of time. A description of a climate includes information on average temperature in different seasons, rainfall, and sunshine over a long period of time (such as 50 or 100 years). A description of the (chance of) extremes is often included. Climate change is also defined as any systematic change in the long-term statistics of climate variables, such as temperature, precipitation, pressure, or wind, sustained over several decades or longer. Since 1901, researchers have found that the current droughts normally occur but got intensified by the rise in temperature worldwide. In spite of the fact that need of precipitation is still the essential driver of drought, anthropogenic warming has resulted in a significant trend toward drought and has expanded the likelihood of severe drought generally (Strelich, 2015).

12.1.4 Causes of Droughts

The major causes of drought on earth are natural and anthropogenic (Li et al., 2013). The natural causes include lack of rainfall or snowfall (i.e. precipitation) and evapotranspiration. No food reserves, high food prices in markets, overgrazing, and lack of knowledge about adaptive farming techniques are the most common anthropogenic causes of droughts throughout the world. Reduced rainfall compared with the usual average one causes depletion of soil moisture. If this situation continues for several weeks, months, or years, the flow of streams and rivers decreases, and water levels in lakes, reservoirs, and wells fall. Eventually, the unusual dry weather causes water supply issues, and the dry period becomes a drought.

12.1.4.1 Lack of Rainfall or Precipitation

The main reason for drought is low or lack of rainfall (Li et al., 2013; Fang et al., 2010). When a region goes for long periods without any rain, especially for more than a season, then the situation leads to dry conditions and water deficiency, which results into a drought event. Farmers plant crops in anticipation of rain, so when rain fails and irrigation systems are not in place, then droughts happen. But the quantity of water vapor in the atmosphere pretty much impacts the precipitation of an area. When a region has moist and low pressure systems, there is a huge probability that rain, hail, and snow will occur, and the opposite situation causes droughts (Wilhite et al., 2007).

12.1.4.2 Anthropogenic Causes

Human activities play a significant role in maintaining the water cycle. Human acts such as deforestation, construction, and agriculture negatively affect the water cycle (Alborzi et al., 2018). Trees and vegetation cover are essential for the water cycle as they help to limit evaporation and store water. Deforestation increases the evaporation rate and reduces the ability of soil to hold water, leading to increased susceptibility to desertification. Over-farming is another human activity contributing to drought incidence (Golian et al., 2015). Over-farming causes loss of soil, allowing erosion to take place (Golian et al., 2015), Soil erosion compromises the ability of soil to hold water.

12.1.4.3 Drying Out of Surface Water Flow

The primary suppliers of downstream surface water in various geographical regions are small lakes, rivers, and streams (Noori et al., 2019). In extremely hot seasons or because of certain human activities, these surface water flows dry out downstream, contributing to drought (Tabari et al., 2013). Another reason for the water shortage is the higher demand for water supply than the available water. Irrigation systems and hydro-electric dams are some of the human activities that can significantly diminish the amount of water flowing downstream to other areas (Tabari et al., 2013).

12.1.4.4 Climate Change and Global Warming

Excessive emission of greenhouse gases is leading to the increase in temperature and resulting in the continued rise of the global average temperature (Sayari et al., 2014). Consequently, evaporation and evapotranspiration levels have increased, and higher temperatures have led to wildfires and extended drought events (Tabari et al., 2013; Sayari et al., 2014). Thus, global warming adds up to drought. Global warming is accelerating desertification, and by 2050 a large part of the earth will have limited access to fresh water. Desertification will affect African and Asian countries most severely. Drought is, thus, caused by a brief water shortage and can be caused by a lack of precipitation, soil moisture, streamflow, or any combination of the three (Carrao et al., 2014). The frequency and severity of extreme weather events such as drought are growing dramatically as a result of climate change, which has devastating consequences for the fragile ecosystem and human society (Maliva and Missimer, 2012). Since the 1970s, the dry areas of the world have increased by 1.5 times (Guo et al., 2019). Drought calamities have claimed the lives of over 11 million people since the 1990s. China was similarly threatened by persistent droughts in the second part of the 20th century, which wreaked havoc on natural ecosystems and socioeconomic systems (Zargar et al., 2011). Every year, tens of millions of hectares of crops experience yield loss (Hao and Kouchak, 2013). Drought is expected to worsen as a result of climate change in many places of the world. In the Northern Hemisphere, particularly critical locations like Sierra Nevada of California, warmer winter temperatures are causing less precipitation to fall as snow. Even if the overall yearly precipitation remains constant, a decreased snowpack can be an issue. This is due to the fact that many water management systems rely on snowmelt in the spring. Because snow works as a reflective surface, reducing the amount of snow on the ground raises surface temperatures, intensifying the drought (Wilhite et al., 2007).

12.1.4.5 Inappropriate Farming Practices

Cultivation practices can largely influence the severity of drought. Dependence on a single crop can intensify effects of extreme weather events (Golian et al., 2015) because this can cause drying of water from the land and thus may change the climate around it. Human activities, lack of awareness, deforestation of trees, ancient ways of farming, and lack of new technology use can affect drought (Golian et al., 2015). For instance, the major constraints to applying agricultural adaptation strategies in Africa have been a general lack of knowledge, expertise and data on climate change issues, a lack of specific climate change institutions to take on climate change work, and the need for a better institutional framework in which to implement adaptation.

12.1.5 Major Drought Prone Areas of the World

There are two kinds of deserts occupying earth: the cold desert of the Arctic and the Antarctic and the hot desert of which the large stone is the Sahara Desert (Figure 12.1).

12.1.5.1 Drought Prone Areas in Africa

In Ethiopia, droughts have occurred quasi-periodically during the last several centuries. Destitute harvests and repetitive insecurity in a few locales of Ethiopia have led to food insecurity and falling food

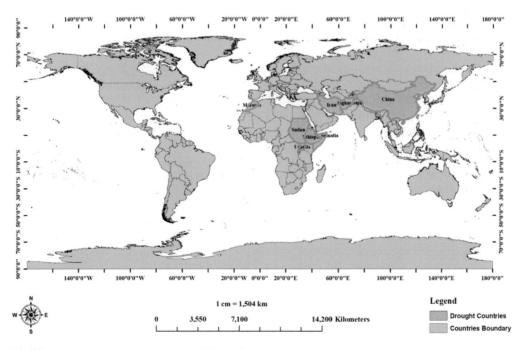

FIGURE 12.1 Severe drought-prone areas of the world.

reserves across the country (Mekonnen and Gokcekus, 2020). The causes of drought are either natural or manmade or both. Scientific investigations have revealed that the primary cause is the fluctuation of the general atmospheric circulation. As a consequence of such fluctuations, the rain-producing components for Ethiopia have been weakened or dislocated during drought years. Human interferences, such as deforestation, overgrazing, and overcultivation, enhance the severity and prolongation of drought recurrences. However, the rainfall analyses do not show distinct characteristics concerning trend or periodicity of drought occurrences in the country. Therefore, it is essential to evaluate the magnitude, severity, and possible periodicity of drought incidents in Ethiopia.

Sudan is another country in Africa that is severely affected by drought (Abdelrahman, 2008; May, 2008). Extreme impacts are felt in southern Sudan, and desert impact depends on the Nile River for water. Arable land is found along the banks of the river. The development of the amazing Ethiopian Renaissance Dam on the Blue Nile threatens to reduce the flow of water on the Nile, considerably raising the dry season in Sudan. Drought's impacts on crop production and livestock show remarkable decrease in yield of both food and cash crops. Degradation of grazing resources is one of the major livestock production problems as a result of drought coupled with other factors, namely overgrazing and the expansion of large-scale mechanized farming on marginal grazing lands (Abdelrahman, 2008).

Having only 1.75% arable land, Somalia has food security as a widespread concern (Majid and McDowell, 2012; Maxwell and Fitzpatrick, 2012). Somalia has 6 cubic kilometers of renewable water resources, with 97% used for livestock and agriculture. Three percent is for urban and domestic use. Consecutive years of poor rains and harvests have decimated crops in Somalia (Maxwell and Fitzpatrick, 2012).

Uganda is another drought-prone African country with about 71.89% agricultural land, 34.41% arable land, and 10.36% forest cover (Bamanyaki and Aogon, 2020). The Congo forest covers eastern Uganda, but the northern part bordering South Sudan is exposed to the encroaching Sahara desert. Drought has contributed to the vulnerability of rain-fed agriculture, dryland farming, and pastoralism, which comprise the backbone of the local communities' livelihoods and the country's economy (Twinomugisha, 2005). Drought events have been manifested as serious decline in livestock productivity and crop failures. The trend for the future is reflected in the high uncertainty of onset and cessation of rainfall seasons. High evaporation rates and increased frequency and intensity of droughts are likely to seasonally affect agricultural/livestock production, food security, and household incomes, particularly in northern Uganda (Twinomugisha, 2005).

Periodic drought is a key feature of Moroccan agriculture, and given that 90% of agricultural land is not irrigated, it poses the single greatest hazard (Skees, 2001; Swearingen and Bencherifa, 2000). The Sahara Desert covers a large part of Morocco, with 18.22% of the country's arable land under vegetation, 12.62% forest cover, and the rest desert. Since 1980, Morocco has experienced a 25% decrease in average rainfall, accompanied by an increase in the frequency and severity of droughts (Azzam and Sekkat, 2005; Barakat and Handoufe, 1998; Skees, 2001).

12.1.5.2 Drought Prone Areas in Asia

Among the Asian countries that are severely affected by droughts, the notable ones include China, Afghanistan, Pakistan, and Iran. Afghanistan is among the driest and most barren countries in the world. Severe drought has been reported recently in the northern and southwest parts of China. Crops wilt while farmers and herders are in desperate need of water for their farmlands and animals. About 3 million people in Shanxi Province in northern China are in dire need of water, whereas a third of the wheat crop in the area dries up due to lack of irrigation or rainwater (Li, 1994). The deserts of China are spreading at an annual average of 1,300 square miles a situation that has seen the deployment of soldiers by the government to plant trees (Li, 1994; Zhong et al., 2000).

Between 1998 and 2002, Pakistan experienced the most noticeably awful dry spell in 50 years (Anjum et al., 2012). The government states that a deficiency of food and water threatens nearly 3 million people (Anjum et al., 2012). The Thar Desert in the southern part of the country has been abandoned as thousands of people and millions of livestock migrate in search of humane conditions. It is expected that by 2025 Pakistan will face an absolute scarcity of water as the country's largest supplier of fresh water, the Indus River basin, continues to dry up (Shah et al., 2007).

A large part of Iran (73%) is considered desert land, leaving 27% as agricultural land (Maghrebi et al., 2020), indicating the magnitude of the drought severity in this country. About 6.5% of the land is under forest cover, whereas a mere 1.1% is considered permanent cropland (Maghrebi et al., 2020). Clearly, the changes in irrigated agricultural area and production in Iran did not follow the patterns of natural water availability across time and space. The continued increase in irrigated agricultural area and production despite the reduction in precipitation have not been feasible without extensive reservoir building for surface water storage (Madani, 2014), implementing inter-basin water transfer projects (Madani and Mariño, 2009) and overuse of groundwater (Mirzaei et al., 2019) that have created significant environmental and socioeconomic problems (Madani, 2014; Madani et al., 2016; Shahriar et al., 2018).

12.1.5.3 Drought Severity in Australia

Droughts have become a common occurrence in Australia throughout the years, having a considerable impact on agricultural output and productivity. Drought reduced crop production in Australia from 18% to 56% from 1990 to 2019. (Roy et al., 2021). Drought in Australia can be mitigated by lowering soil evaporation, choosing the proper crop and crop variety, and following effective crop management methods (Siddique et al., 2001). Many Australian farmers also mitigate the effects of drought to some extent by employing drought adaptation practices such as crop selection, irrigation management, and ploughing (Stone and Meinke, 2007). Developing and introducing drought-resistant crop varieties and promoting appropriate agricultural techniques appear to be very effective in overcoming the lack of irrigation systems near the Murray-Darling Basin in Australia (Jiang and Grafton, 2012).

12.1.5.4 Drought Severity in Europe

The drought in Europe at the beginning of the 21st century is generally considered to be extremely severe. These extreme events are mainly related to the temperature increase and record-breaking heat waves that have affected Europe since 2000, as well as the lack of rainfall in summer (Vicente-Serrano et al., 2014). The recent European hydrological droughts are the most extreme droughts. For instance, compared to 2003 and 2015 events, the area affected by the most extreme hydrological droughts and drought severity was larger by 40% and 55%, respectively (Laaha et al., 2017).

12.1.5.5 Drought Severity in South America

Impacts of El Niño have become prominent in the South American countries. The El Niño weather phenomenon has intensified the severity of droughts in Brazil, Colombia, Chile, and Venezuela.

In Brazil, drought is distinguished by its extensive spatial coverage and is most common in the Northeast region, mainly due to its water fragility. Brazil is experiencing its worst drought in 35 years, and heavily populated areas, particularly the country's southeast, rely on local reservoirs and aquifers that are not being replenished as a result of the drought (Gutiérrez et al., 2014). Considering the drought that has been affecting most of the Brazilian territory for the past, the federal government has requested information for the identification of the municipalities affected by the phenomenon with the main objective of supporting emergency impact mitigation measures (Cunha et al., 2019).

Drought severity in Venezuela has been prolonged over the recent decades. The effects of the drought have been compounded by the El Nino weather phenomenon, which is pushing back the start of the rainy season (Parra et al., 2018). In Peru, the agricultural sector has been impacted by drought, and several provinces, including Apurimac and Junin, have been declared emergencies. Water shortage in Peru has been a serious problem in recent history (Groves et al., 2019).

In Ecuador, drought conditions have had severe impacts on agriculture. It is foreseen that by spring 2016, production will drop in different crops (Vicente-Serrano et al., 2017). This will decrease the food security of vulnerable households as well as the local and national economy.

Colombia is experiencing the greatest drought and forest fires in its history because of the weather phenomena El Nino. The scenario is expected to worsen, according to meteorologists. Exceptionally hot and dry weather in Colombia led to drought and forest fires (Cerón et al., 2015). The most impacted departments in the country include La Guajira, Bolivar, and Magdalena in the north; Valle del Cauca on the Pacific coast; Boyaca and Cundinamarca in the middle; and Tolima and Quindio in the western central region (Cerón et al., 2015).

12.1.5.6 Drought Severity in North America

Impacts of drought on agriculture have been widespread across North America (Cook et al., 2007). Extreme weather events, such as lengthy droughts, are expected to rise steadily, according to UN Intergovernmental Panel on Climate Change forecasts, posing a threat to the region's energy supply. Droughts are more common in some parts of the United States than in others. Drought hit the Dakotas, New Mexico, Colorado, Wyoming, Iowa, Kansas, and parts of Missouri, Illinois, and Minnesota in the summer of 2020. In July 2021, after two more extremely dry winters, Lake Powell dropped to its lowest level since 1969, when the reservoir was first filling. Lake Mead fell to a level expected to trigger federally mandated cuts to Arizona and Nevada's water supplies for the first time in history. The long period of dry weather in central and southern South America has had widespread consequences. Many of the affected areas have faced unusually intense and widespread outbreaks of fire. Winter corn crops have suffered low yields, and the late arrival of spring rain has delayed new plantings of soy (Shannon and Motha, 2015).

The drought that swept across Canada from 1999 to 2005, causing significant agricultural, environmental, economic, and societal damage, is an example of a very severe drought (Bonsal et al., 2011). The extent of this drought was massive, reaching from British Columbia across Canada to the Atlantic Provinces and also farther northward than other major droughts. Saskatchewan and Alberta have the highest levels of intensity. Agricultural production losses in the Canadian Prairie Provinces due to drought during 2001–2002 was significant (Wheaton et al., 2008). There have also been reports of other more recent droughts. The catastrophic drought in British Columbia, Alberta, and Saskatchewan in 2015 has been linked to climate change (Szeto et al., 2016). Droughts can affect broad areas not only in Canada, but also across much of North America and elsewhere, and they can be very severe and endure for a long time (Wheaton et al., 2008).

Mexico has a lengthy history of severe, long-term droughts dating back to prehistory. Drought over Mexico is influenced by ocean-atmospheric fluctuation in the Atlantic and Pacific oceans, raising the prospect of long-range seasonal climate forecasting that may help mitigate the economic and social effects of future dry periods (Mendez and Magaña, 2010; Allen et al., 2012). Although the instrumental record of Mexican climate prior to 1920 is limited, tree-ring chronologies developed from old-growth forests in Mexico can provide an excellent proxy representation of the spatial pattern and intensity of past moisture regimes (Nicholas and Battisti, 2008).

12.1.6 Impacts of Drought on Agriculture

Drought affects all components of the environment. Drought effects can often be grouped as economic, environmental, and social impacts. All of these impacts must be considered in planning for and responding to drought conditions. Farmers face economic loss if a drought destroys their crops since they have to spend more money on irrigation or to drill new wells, if the water supply is too low. Ranchers may have to spend more money on feed and water for their animals. Businesses that depend on farming, like companies that make tractors and food, may lose business when drought damages crops or livestock. People who work in the timber industry may be affected when wildfires destroy stands of timber. Businesses that sell boats and fishing equipment may not be able to sell some of their goods because drought has dried up lakes and other water sources. Power companies that normally rely on hydroelectric power may have to spend more money on other fuel sources if drought dries up too much of the water supply. Water companies may have to spend money on new or additional water supplies. Barges and ships may have difficulty navigating streams, rivers, and canals because of low water levels, which would also affect businesses that depend on water transportation for receiving or sending goods and materials (Shahriar et al., 2018).

Drought also affects the biotic components of the environment, plants, and animals, through influencing the food supply and changing the habitat. Such environmental damages might be temporary or long lasting (Swearingen and Bencherifa, 2000). Drought can also cause increased stress on endangered species or even extinction and also migration of wildlife. Frequent wildfires and poor-quality soil are associated with droughts. Declining ecosystem productivity and increasing mortality are the general consequences of drought on both aquatic and terrestrial biodiversity. Competitive species that adapt to cold and humid conditions, as well as species with low reproductive rates and/or limited mobility, seem to be more affected. However, the species-specific impact is regulated by mechanisms that allow drought resistance. The short-term impact of drought on biodiversity depends on the ability of species to resist and recover after drought and the competitive interactions between species. Although the abundance of many species generally declines during droughts, the number of certain taxa may increase during or shortly after drought. The impact of repeated droughts must be evaluated in the broader context of global changes in climate and habitat (Archaux and Wolters, 2006).

Social impacts of drought are ways that drought affects people's health and safety (Shahriar et al., 2018). Social impacts include public safety, health, conflicts between people when there isn't enough water to go around, and changes in lifestyle. Examples of social impacts include: anxiety or depression about economic losses caused by drought, and health problems related to low water flow and poor water quality. Health problems are related to dust during the drought condition. Threats to the safety of the public are from an increased number of forest and range fires. People may have to face low income and migrate from place to place. Drought may also cause fewer recreational activities and loss of human life.

Crop failure and pasture losses are the principal direct economic effects of drought in the agriculture sector. Crop and livestock productivity suffers significantly when soil water availability is depleted. Furthermore, during a drought, surface and groundwater supplies may decline, reducing water availability and raising the cost of obtaining water for crop or forage irrigation and watering. With a return to normal precipitation, soil moisture often recovers long before surface and groundwater supplies are replenished. Drought combined with high temperatures has the potential to spread pests and illnesses that impact crops, forage, and livestock. Drought-prone specialty crops *viz.* fruits, vegetables, tree nuts, and some medicinal plants are more vulnerable to drought than field crops. As a result, if agricultural water demands exceed the water supply during a drought, there may be a higher risk of economic loss (Ziolkowska, 2016; Wang, 2005).

12.2 Legumes and Their Origin

Legumes, belonging to the family Fabaceae, are one of the largest and most important families of flowering plants and are also believed to be the earliest human domesticated plants. Among legumes, lentils were also the component of the cropping systems of ancient Egypt, and faba beans are mentioned in the Bible (Allen and Allen, 1981; Ahmed and Hasan, 2014). Carbonized seeds of pea and lentils have been found in fire places of the Neolithic age (7000 to 8000 years B.C.) in Turkey. In Switzerland, the lake inhabitants who lived between 4000 and 5000 B.C. cultivated peas and a dwarf field bean. In China, farmers began cultivating soybean between 2000 and 3000 B.C. Beans, soybean, and staple crops were domesticated in America and Asia, respectively, more than 3,000 years ago (Ahmed and Hasan, 2014). Romans used legumes in pastures and for soil improvement dating to 37 B.C. (Allen and Allen, 1981). Legumes are extremely nutritious grains that are rich in protein, minerals, and many other micronutrients.

Legumes can adapt to a wide range of environmental conditions. They can survive in harsh environments with poor nutrient conditions (Gowda et al., 2009). Therefore, these crops are cultivated in marginal lands. The origin of the legume species happened in different continents on earth. The origin and most cultivating countries are shown in Table 12.1.

The biggest producers of pulses (70% of world production) are positioned in areas that experience water scarcity, such as India, China, and many African countries (Gowda et al., 2009). These countries thus rely heavily on variable rainfall to support agriculture production, which, consequently, is highly

TABLE 12.1

The Center of Origins and Main Producing Countries of Legumes of the World

Legumes	Center of origin	Main producers	References
Mung bean (*Vigna radiata* L)	India and Pakistan	China, India, Brazil, Myanmar	Daryanto et al., 2015
Black gram (*Vigna mungo* L)	India and Pakistan	China, India, Brazil, Myanmar	Daryanto et al., 2015
Garden pea (*Pisum sativum* L)	Central Asia Center (India, Pakistan, Afghanistan, south Russia), Middle East Center (Iran, Iraq), Africa (Ethiopia)	Canada, France, Russia, China	Daryanto et al., 2015
Chickpea (*Cicer arietinum* L)	Central Asia Center (India, Pakistan, Afghanistan, south Russia), Middle East Center (Iran, Iraq)	India, Turkey, Pakistan, Australia, Iran	Ahmed and Hasan, 2014 Daryanto et al., 2015
Pigeon pea (*Cajanus cajan* L)	Indian Center (India, Pakistan)	India, Myanmar, Malawi, Tanzania, Kenya	Nedumaran et al., 2015 Daryanto et al., 2015
Lentil (*Lens culinaris* Medik.)	Central Asia Center (India, Pakistan, Afghanistan, south Russia), Middle East Center (Iran, Iraq).	India, Canada, Turkey, USA, Nepal	Daryanto et al., 2015 Nedumaran et al., 2015
Lablab bean (*Lablab purpureus* L)	Indian Center (India)	India, Australia, UK, Poland, Mozambique	Daryanto et al., 2015
Soybean (*Glycine max* L)	Chinese Center (north and central China)	USA, Brazil, Argentina, China	Nedumaran et al., 2015 Daryanto et al., 2015
Peanut (*Arachis hypogea* L)	Brazil and Paraguay Center	China, India, Nigeria, USA	Nedumaran et al., 2015 Daryanto et al., 2015
Common bean (*Phaseolus vulgaris* L)	Southern Mexican and Central American Center	China, India, Brazil, Myanmar	Daryanto et al., 2015

vulnerable to drought. It is also important to recognize that the effect of drought on crop yield can be variable, and therefore there is a need to consider legume crop and management factors (e.g. species selection, planting date) as these can determine crop response to water scarcity and in the long run yield loss (Kumar et al., 2016; Ahmad et al., 2015; Samarah et al., 2006; Shrestha et al., 2006).

12.2.1 Global Production of Legumes

As reported by Rawal and Navarro (2019), the annual global production of legumes was about 77 million tons in 2014, and out of this, the production of dry bean accounted for about 24 million tons, chickpea production for about 13 million tons, dry pea production for about 11 million tons, and cowpea production for about 7 million tons (Figure 12.2). The annual production of lentil was estimated to be 5 million tons, whereas that of pigeonpea and faba bean was about 4 million tons each. Since the 1970s, there have been two phases of high growth in the production of pulses. The first phase, over the 1980s, saw the annual production of pulses increase from about 36 million tons at the start of the decade to about 48 million tons by the end of the decade (Rawal and Navarro, 2019). In this period, the growth of pulses production was led by dry pea production. Increased dry pea production over the 1980s was a result of a simultaneous increase in yields and expansion of area. Globally, between 2001 and 2014, the annual production of dry bean increased by about 7 million tons. In the same period, the annual production of chickpea went up by about 5 million tonnes, that of cowpea by about 3.8 million tonnes and that of lentil by about 1.6 million tonnes (Rawal and Navarro, 2019). Daryanto et al. (2015) found that the quantity of water cut was positively associated to yield loss, although the magnitude of the effect differed depending on the legume species and the phenological stage of the drought. Legumes grown in

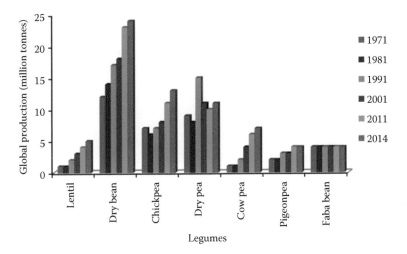

FIGURE 12.2 Global production (million tonnes) of legumes, trienniums ending 1971, 1981, 1991, 2001, 2011, and 2014.

medium texture soil likewise had lower yields than those produced in coarse or fine texture soil. Regions and their associated climatic conditions, on the other hand, had no effect on the lowering of legume yields (Daryanto et al., 2015).

In the triennium ending 1991, at about 2 tons per hectare, the average global yield of dry pea was higher than the average yield of all other legumes. The period of high growth of production in the 1980s was followed by a period of stagnation in the decade of the 1990s. The production of dry pea fell sharply over the 1990s, and the slow growth of dry bean, chickpea, and cowpea over the decade was barely enough to compensate for the decline in dry pea (Rawal and Navarro, 2019). Between 2001 and 2014, the last year for which data on legume production are available, the global production of legumes increased by over 20 million tons. This increase came about primarily on account of an increase in the production of common bean, chickpea, cowpea, and lentil. Although the largest increase in absolute levels of production was in the case of dry bean (Figure 12.2), the most striking yield growth over this period was seen in the case of lentil, cowpea, and chickpea (Figure 12.3). In the triennium ending 2014, among the major legumes, average yields were highest for faba bean (1,807 kilograms per hectare), followed by dry pea (1,616 kilograms per hectare), lentil (1,152 kilograms per hectare), and chickpea

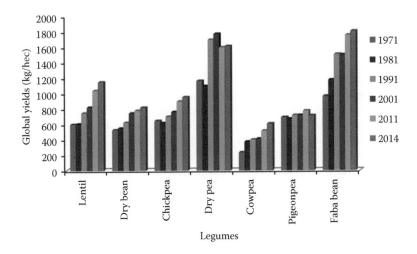

FIGURE 12.3 Global yields (kilograms per hectare) of legumes, trienniums ending 1971, 1981, 1991, 2001, 2011, and 2014.

(956 kilograms per hectare), but cowpea had a lower average yield (614 kilograms per hectare) than all others. Globally, between 2001 and 2014, the annual production of dry bean increased by about 7 million tons. Rawal and Navarro, 2019 showed in their study that, in the same period, the annual production of chickpea went up by about 5 million tons, that of cowpea by about 3.8 million tons, and that of lentil by about 1.6 million tons (Figure 12.3).

12.3 Drought Effects on Legume Crops

12.3.1 Seed Germination and Growth Reduction

Under water deficit conditions, legumes are unable to imbibe and germinate even if other conditions are favorable. Hence, the primary signs of drought at early crop growth stages are reduced seed germination and poor stand establishment (Nadeem et al., 2019). Many legumes have shown poor seed germination under drought stress. For instance, poor seed germination and stand establishment were recorded under water deficit conditions in peas (Farooq et al., 2016; Mittal et al., 2014). Under drought stress, the germination rate was significantly reduced in soybean (Heatherly, 1993). Awari and Mate (2015) noted a decrease in the germination rate in chickpea under a water deficit. Moreover, poor germination in alfalfa (*Medicago sativa*) was also recorded under drought stress conditions (Pushpavalli et al., 2015). Li et al. (2018) observed that drought stress commonly occurs at the seedling stage and significantly reduced yield in faba bean. Drought stress delays imbibition process and reduces germination rates and at last prompts decreased germination percent and seedling vigor (Liu et al., 2015). Desclaux et al. (2000) explained that germination and seedling establishment stages are most vulnerable to drought stress. A study conducted on five pea (*Pisum sativum* L.) cultivars proposed that water stress causes impeded germination and diminishes early seedling development in peas (Okcu et al., 2005). It seems to be clear that water deficit causes poor germination and reduced stand establishment in legumes. Therefore, adequate moisture supply is an absolute requirement for early growth of various crops. Thus, germination and reproductive stages are highly sensitive to water deficit.

12.3.2 Root Growth

Drought causes significant modifications in the root system in legumes. In most cases, the root growth under mild drought conditions is not severely affected. For example, the root growth in maize was not substantially affected under water deficit conditions (Sacks et al., 1997), but roots of chickpea are influenced significantly under terminal drought conditions (Kashiwagi et al., 2005). In general, drought stress increased the root-shoot ratio in different plant species (Wu and Cosgrove 2000, Hossain et al., 2016).

12.3.3 Leaf Traits

Drought stress causes significant reduction in leaf area of legumes among many other plant functional types. Leaf area is an important factor for photosynthesis and grain yield (Jaleel et al., 2009). Water deficit conditions affect leaf area by reducing leaf expansion and thus affect the process of photosynthesis (Rucker et al., 1995). Furthermore, the leaf area of soybean (Zhang et al., 2004) and many other field crops (Farooq et al., 2009) is significantly affected under limited water conditions. Plants grown under drought condition have a lower stomatal conductance in order to conserve water. As a result, CO_2 fixation and photosynthetic rate decline, resulting in lower assimilate generation for plant growth and yield. Drought stress causes a decrease in leaf chlorophyll concentration (Ommen et al., 1999). Drought stress resulted in a significant decrease in chlorophyll a, chlorophyll b, and total chlorophyll concentration in all sunflower cultivars studied (Manivannan et al., 2007a). Drought-induced chlorophyll loss is mostly due to damage to chloroplasts (Smirnoff, 1995). Plants can store osmolytes in order to defend themselves from mild drought stress. In drought-stressed plants, proline is one of the most prevalent suitable osmolytes. For example, when peas were subjected to drought, their proline content increased (Alexieva et al., 2001). Other stressors, such as salinity, can also cause proline buildup (Hossain et al., 2018). Proline buildup in plant tissues is also a strong indicator of environmental stress, particularly in drought-stressed plants. Proline buildup could possibly be a stress signal that affects adaptive responses (Maggio et al., 2002).

12.3.4 Plant Height

The internal plant factors that influence plant height are substantially affected by drought stress. A decline in plant height has been attributed to reduction in cell expansion, increase in leaf abscission under drought conditions (Manivannan et al., 2007b), and impaired mitosis (Hussain et al., 2008). Generally, lower cell enlargement and higher leaf senescence are the basis of reduction in plant height. Several studies reported that plant height in different legumes, such as peas (Kabay et al., 2007) and soybean (Specht et al., 2001), was decreased under drought stress.

12.4 Yield Reductions in Legumes

Drought stress generally causes grain yield reduction in all legumes. The yield reduction due to drought stress in different legume crops has been listed in Table 12.2.

The grain yield reduction mainly depends upon the time of the onset of drought and developmental stage of the legume crop. Similarly, drought stress reduced the grain yield in mung bean (Ahmad et al., 2015), common beans (Martinez et al., 2006), and cowpea (Ogbonnaya et al., 2003), which is shown in Table 12.2. Furthermore, drought stress reduced the total number of grains and grain yield in chickpea (Nayyar et al., 2006). Drought stress at heading and maturity stages reduced the total dry biomass and grain-filling percentage in soybean (Samarah et al., 2006). Drought significantly decreased the final yield in faba bean (Ghassemi-Golezani et al., 2009) and pigeon pea (Nam et al., 2001), as shown in Table 12.2. The effect of drought on final yield could be very complicated, and for the duration of the plant life cycle, flowering and reproductive stages are highly susceptible to water scarcity in lentil (Shrestha et al., 2006). A more recent study observed a significant decrease in seed yield (21%–54%) per plant in field pea under drought stress (Kumar et al., 2016).

12.5 Recommendations for Better Water Use

The emission of greenhouse gases should be stopped or reduced in order to curb global warming. Carbon (C) sequestration through plantation and adoption of climate-friendly agricultural practices can help reduce C emissions. Development of drought-resistant plant varieties can help ensure cultivation in the marginal lands to avoid water requirements. Use of an appropriate crop species can be considered to be used as a

TABLE 12.2

Yield Reduction (%) in Different Legumes Crops Under Drought Stress

Crop	Yield reduction (%)	References
Mung bean (*Vigna radiata* L)	31–57	Ahmad et al., 2015
Faba bean (*Vicia faba* L)	68	Ghassemi-Golezani et al., 2009
Lentil (*Lens culinaris* Medik.)	70	Shrestha et al., 2006
Soybean (*Glycine max* L.)	46–71	Samarah et al., 2006
Pigeon pea (*Cajanus cajan* L)	40–55	Nam et al., 2001
Cowpea (*Vigna unguiculata* L)	55–65	Ogbonnaya et al., 2003
Chickpea *Cicer arietinum* L.)	45–69	Nayyar et al., 2006
Common bean (*Phaseolus vulgaris* L)	58–87	Martinez et al., 2006
Field pea (*Pisum sativum* L)	21–54	Kumar et al., 2016

cover crop so that it can help retain moisture in the soil. Farmers should be aware of the importance of conservation approaches in agricultural practices. Water-use efficient crops should be developed through traditional and biotechnological approaches so that cultivation can be ensured in drought-prone areas. Waste of water can be minimized through improved techniques, such as drip irrigation. Climate-smart cultivation techniques should be developed and available to farmers in order to reduce dependency on water use in agriculture.

12.6 Conclusion

The increasing population and growing economies are creating demand for more water supply globally. Further, anticipated global warming is likely to reduce availability of water intensifying the drought-related problems in many parts of the world. Therefore, drought problems should be dealt globally taking appropriate adaptation and mitigation measures. Legumes are valued worldwide as a sustainable and inexpensive protein-rich diet as an alternative to animal protein that can reduce the risks of global climate change. Potentials of legumes in mitigating climate change should be explored and implemented to tackle this global environmental issue, which is unprecedented in the history of humankind. Sustainable water-management plans, clear monitoring, and management policies can help enhance legume production and ensure sustainable agriculture as well.

REFERENCES

Abdelrahman, M.E. 2008. The development of alternative and supplementary livelihood system to reduce pressure on land based resources in Sudan dry land; United Nation Environment Program (UNEP), 2007. Sudan Post–Conflict Environmental Assessment. - United Nation Environment Program.

Ahmad, A., M.M. Selim, A.A. Alderfasi, and M. Afzal. 2015. Effect of drought stress on mungbean (*Vigna radiata* L.) under arid climatic conditions of Saudi Arabia. *Ecosyst. Sustain. Dev.* 192:185–193.

Ahmed, S., and M.M. Hasan. 2014. Legumes: An overview. *J. Pharmacy Pharmaceutical Sci.* 2(1):34–38.

Alborzi, A., A. Mirchi, H. Moftakhari, I. Mallakpour, S. Alian, A. Nazemi. et al. 2018. Climate-informed environmental inflows to revive a drying lake facing meteorological and anthropogenic droughts. *Environ. Res. Lett.* 13:084010.

Alexieva, V., I. Sergiev, S. Mapelli, and E. Karanov. 2001. The effect of drought and ultraviolet radiation on growth and stress markers in pea and wheat. *Plant Cell Environ.* 24:1337–1344.

Allen J, A. Assaf, J. Small, and H. Riebeek. 2012. Drought causes Mexico food shortages. NASA earth observatory images, January 21, 2012.

Allen, O.N., and E.K. Allen. 1981. Inleguminosae. A source book of characteristics, uses and Nodulation. University of Wisconsin Press, USA.

Anjum, S.A., M.F. Saleem, M.A. Cheema, M.F. Bilal, and T. Khaliq. 2012. An assessment to vulnerability, extent, characteristics and severity of drought hazard in Pakistan. *Pakistan J. Sci.* 64(2):138–148.

Archaux, F., and Wolters V. 2006. Impact of summer drought on forest biodiversity: What do we know? *Ann. Forest Sci.* 63(6):645–652.

Awari, V.R., and S.N. Mate. 2015. Effect of drought stress on early seedling growth of chickpea (*Cicer arietinum* L.) genotypes. *Life Sci. Int. Res. J.* 2:356–361.

Azzam, A., and K. Sekkat. 2005. Measuring total-factor agricultural productivity under drought conditions: The case of Morocco. *J. North African Stud.* 10 (1):19–31.

Bamanyaki P., and G. Aogon. 2020. Reshaping the future: Gender-responsive climate smart agriculture options for northern Uganda. Unpublished report prepared for the GIZ Promotion of Climate Smart Agriculture Project.

Barakat, F., and A. Handoufe 1998. Approche agroclimatique de la sécheresse agricole au Maroc. *Sécheresse* 9:201–208.

Bonsal, B., E. Wheaton, A. Chipanshi, C. Lin, D. Sauchyn, and L. Wen. 2011. Drought research in Canada: A review. *Atmosphere-Ocean* 49(4):303–319.

Carrao, H., A. Singleton, G. Naumann, P. Barbosa, and J. Vogt. 2014. An optimized system for the classi-fication of meteorological drought intensity with applications in frequency analysis. *J. Appl. Meteor. Climatol.* 53:1943–1960.

Cerón, W.L., Y.C. Escobar, and O.L.B. Montoya. 2015. Índice estandarizado de precipitación (SPI) para la caracterización de sequías meteorológicas en la cuenca del río Dagua-Colombia. *Estud. Geogr.* 76:557–578.

Cook, E.R., R. Seager, M.A. Cane, and D.W. Stahle. 2007. North American drought: Reconstructions, causes, and consequences. *Earth-Sci. Rev.* 81(1–2):93–134.

Cunha, A.P.M.A., M. Zeri, K.D. Leal, L. Costa, L.A. Cuartas, J.A. Marengo et al. 2019. Extreme drought events over Brazil from 2011 to 2019. *Atmosphere (Basel)* 10:642.

Daryanto, S., L. Wang, and P.A. Jacinthe. 2015. Global synthesis of drought effects on food legume pro-duction. *PLoS ONE* 10(6):e0127401.

Desclaux D., T.T. Huynh, and P. Roumet. 2000. Identification of soybean plant characteristics that indicate the timing of drought stress. *Crop Sci.* 40(3):716–722.

Fang, X., N.C. Turner, G. Yan, F. Li, and K.H.M. Siddique. 2010. Flower numbers, pod production, pollen viability, and pistil function are reduced and flower and pod abortion increased in chickpea (*Cicer arietinum* L.) under terminal drought. *J. Exp. Bot.* 61:335–345.

Farooq, M., A. Wahid, N. Kobayashi, D. Fujita, and S.M.A. Basra. 2009. Plant drought stress: Effects, mechanisms and management. *Agron. Sustain. Dev.* 29:185–212.

Farooq, M., N. Gogoi, S. Barthakur, B. Baroowa, N. Bharadwaj, and S.S. Alghamdi. 2016. Drought stress in grain legumes during reproduction and grain filling. *J. Agron. Crop Sci.* 203:81–102.

Ghassemi-Golezani, K., and A. Hosseinzadeh-Mahootchy. 2009. Changes in seed vigour of faba bean (*Vicia faba* L.) cultivars during development and maturity. *Seed Sci. Technol.* 37:713–720.

Golian, S., O. Mazdiyasni, and A. AghaKouchak. 2015. Trends in meteorological and agricultural droughts in Iran. *Theoretical Appl. Climatol.* 119(3–4):679–688.

Gowda, C.L.L., R.P. Parthasarathy, and S. Bhagavatula. 2009. Global trends in production and trade of major grain legumes. In International Conference on Grain Legumes: Quality Improvement, Value Addition and Trade; February 14–16; Indian Institute of Pulses Research, Kanpur, India: Indian Society of Pulses Research and Development, pp. 282–301.

Groves, D.G., L. Bonzanigo, J. Syme, N.L. Engle, and C.I. Rodriguez. 2019. Preparing for Future Droughts in Lima, Peru: Enhancing Lima's Drought Management Plan to Meet Future Challenges. World Bank, Washington, DC.

Guo, Y., S. Huang, Q. Huang, H. Wang, W. Fang, Y. Yanga, and L. Wang 2019. Assessing socioeconomic drought based on an improved multivariate standardized reliability and resilience index. *J. Hydrol.* 568:904–918.

Gutiérrez, A.P.A., N.L., Engle, E.D. Nys, C. Molejón, and E.S. Martins. 2014. Drought preparedness in Brazil. *Weather Climate Extremes* 3:95–106.

Hao, Z., and A. Kouchak. 2013. A multivariate standardized drought index: Aparametric multi-index model. *Adv. Water Resour.* 57:12–18.

Heatherly, L.G. 1993. Drought stress and irrigation effects on germination of harvested soybean seed. *Crop Sci.* 33:777–781.

Hisdal, H., and L.M. Tallaksen. 2003. Estimation of regional meteorological and hydrological drought characteristics: A case study for Denmark. *J. Hydrology* 281:230–247.

Hossain, M.Z., I.U. Rasel, and R. Samad. 2016. Soil moisture effects on the growth of lentil (*Lens culinaris* Medik.) varieties in Bangladesh. *Mol.* 16:30–40.

Hossain, M.Z., M.M. Hasan, and M.A. Kashem. 2018. Intervarietal variation in salt tolerance of lentil (*Lens culinaris* Medik.) in pot experiments. *Bangladesh J. Botany* 47(3):405–412.

Hussain, M., M.A. Malik, M. Farooq, M.Y. Ashraf, and M.A. Cheema. 2008. Improving drought tolerance by exogenous application of glycinebetaine and salicylic acid in sunflower. *J. Agron. Crop Sci.* 194:193–199.

Jaleel, C.A., P.A. Manivannan, A. Wahid, M. Farooq, H.J.A. Juburi, R.A. Somasundaram, and R. Panneerselvam. 2009. Drought stress in plants: A review on morphological characteristics and pigments composition. *Int. J. Agric. Biol.* 11(1):100–105.

Jiang, Q., and R.Q. Grafton 2012. Economic effects of climate change in the Murray–Darling Basin, Australia. *Agricultural Syst.* 110:10–16.

Kabay, T., C. Erdinc, and S. Sensoy. 2007. Effects of drought stress on plant growth parameters, membrane damage index and nutrient content in common bean genotypes. *J. Anim. Plant Sci.* 27(3):940–952.

Kashiwagi, J., L. Krishnamurthy, H.D. Upadhyaya, H. Krishna, S. Chandra, V. Vadez, and R. Serraj. 2005. Genetic variability of drought avoidance root traits in the mini-core germplasm collection of chickpea (*Cicer arietinum* L.). *Euphytica* 146:213–222.

Konstatinos, M.A., and D.P. Lettenmaier. 2006. Trends in 20th century drought over the continental United States. *Geophys. Res. Lett.* 33:L10403.

Kumar, K., S. Solanki, S.N. Singh, and M.A. Khan. 2016. Abiotic constraints of pulse production in India. In Disease of Pulse Crops and Their Sustainable Management. Biotech Books, New Delhi, India, pp. 23–39.

Laaha, G., T. Gauster, L.M. Tallaksen, J.P. Vidal, K. Stahl, C. Prudhomme, B. Heudorfer. et al. 2017. The European 2015 drought from a hydrological perspective. *Hydrol. Earth Syst. Sci.* 21:3001–3024.

Li, D., H. Liu, Y. Qiao, Y. Wang, Z. Cai, B. Dong, C. Shi, Y. Liu, X. Li, and M. Liu. 2013. Effects of elevated CO_2 on the growth, seed yield, and water use efficiency of soybean (*Glycine max* L.) under drought stress. *Agric. Water Manag.* 129:105–112.

Li, P., Y. Zhang, X. Wu, and Y. Liu. 2018. Drought stress impact on leaf proteome variations of faba bean (*Vicia faba* L.) in the Qinghai–Tibet Plateau of China. *3 Biotech.* 8:110.

Li, Q. 1994. Study on urban drought and water shortage in Shanxi Province. *Shanxi Hydrotech.* 24:65–71.

Liu, M., M. Li, K. Liu, and N. Sui. 2015. Effects of drought stress on seed germination and seedling growth of different maize varieties. *J. Agricultural Sci.* 7(5):231–240.

Madani, K. 2014. Water management in Iran: What is causing the looming crisis? *J. Environ. Stud. Sci.* 4(4):315–328.

Madani, K., A. AghaKouchak, and A. Mirchi. 2016. Iran's socio-economic drought: Challenges of a water-bankrupt nation. *Iranian Stud.* 49(6):997–1016.

Madani, K., and M.A. Mariño. 2009. System dynamics analysis for managing Iran's Zayandeh-Rud river basin. *Water Resour. Manag.* 23(11):2163–2187.

Maggio, A., S. Miyazaki, P.Veronese, T. Fujita, J.I. Ibeas, B. Damsz, M.L. Narasimhan, P.M. Hasegawa, R.J. Joly, and R.A. Bressan. 2002. Does proline accumulation play an active role in stress-induced growth reduction. *Plant J.* 31:699–712.

Maghrebi, M., R. Noori, R. Bhattarai, Mundher, Y.Z.Q. Tang, and N. Al-Ansari. 2020. Iran's agriculture in the Anthropocene. *Earth's Future* 8:e2020EF001547.

Majid, N., and S. McDowell. 2012. Hidden dimensions of the somalia famine. *Global Food Security* 1(1):36–42.

Maliva, R., and T. Missimer 2012. Aridity and Drought. Arid Lands Water Evaluation and Management, Environmental Science and Engineering (Environmental Engineering). Springer, Berlin, Germany, pp. 21–39.

Manivannan, P., A.C. Jaleel, B. Sankar, A. Kishorekumar, R. Somasundaram, G.M.A. Lakshmanan, and R. Panneerselvam. 2007a. Growth, biochemical modifications and proline metabolism in *Helianthus annuus* L. as induced by drought stress. *Colloids Surfaces B: Biointerf.* 59:141–149.

Manivannan, P., C.A. Jaleel, A. Kishorekumar, B. Sankar, R. Somasundaram, R. Sridharan, and R. Panneerselvam. 2007b. Changes in antioxidant metabolism of *Vigna unguiculata* L. Walp. By propiconazole under water deficit stress. *Colloids Surf B: Biointerf.* 57:69–74.

Martinez, J.P., H. Silva, J.F. Ledent, and M. Pinto. 2006. Effect of drought stress on the osmotic adjustment, cell wall elasticity and cell volume of six cultivars of common beans (*Phaseolus vulgaris* L.). *Eur. J. Agron.* 26:30–38.

Maxwell, D., and M. Fitzpatrick. 2012. The 2011 Somalia Famine: Context, causes, and complications. *Global Food Security* 1(1):5–12.

May, B.H.H. 2008. Food Gaps in Drought Areas Affected in Sudan. The Administration of Food Security, Ministry of Agriculture and Irrigation.

Mekonnen YA, and H. Gokcekus. 2020. Causes and effects of drought in northern parts of Ethiopia. *Civil Environ. Res.* 12(3):29–38.

Mendez, M., and V. Magaña. 2010. Regional aspects of prolonged meteorological droughts over Mexico and Central America. *J. Climate* 23:1175–1188.

Mirzaei, A., B. Saghafian, A. Mirchi, and K. Madani. 2019. The groundwater–energy–food nexus in Iran's agricultural sector: Implications for water security. *Water* 11(9):1835.

Mittal, N., A. Mishra, R. Singh, and P. Kumar. 2014. Assessing future changes in seasonal climatic extremes in the Ganges river basin using an ensemble of regional climate models. *Clim. Change* 123:273–286.

Mortimore, M. 2016. Changing paradigms for people-centred development in the Sahel. In The End of Desertification? Disputing Environmental Change in the Drylands. Behnke, R and Mortimore, M. (eds.). Springer, Berlin, Germany, pp. 65–98.

Nadeem, M., J. Li, M. Yahya, M. Wang, A. Ali, A. Cheng, X. Wang, and C. Ma. 2019. Grain legumes and fear of salt stress: Focus on mechanisms and management strategies. *Int. J. Mol. Sci.* 20:799.

Nam, N.H., Y.S. Chauhan, and C. Johansen. 2001. Effect of timing of drought stress on growth and grain yield of extra-short-duration pigeonpea lines. *J. Agric. Sci.* 136:179–189.

Nayyar, H., S. Kaur, S. Singh, and H.D. Upadhyaya. 2006. Differential sensitivity of Desi (small-seeded) and Kabuli (large-seeded) chickpea genotypes to water stress during seed filling: Effects on accumulation of seed reserves and yield. *J. Sci. Food Agric.* 2082:2076–2082.

Nedumaran, S., P. Abinaya, P. Jyosthnaa, B. Shraavya, R. Parthasarathy, and B. Cynthia. 2015. Grain Legumes Production, Consumption and Trade Trends in Developing Countries. Working Paper Series No 60. ICRISAT Research Program, Markets, Institutions and Policies. Patancheru 502 324, Telangana, India: International Crops Research Institute for the Semi-Arid Tropics, p. 64.

Nicholas, R.E., and D.S. Battisti. 2008. Drought recurrence and seasonal rainfall prediction in the Rio Yaqui Basin, Mexico. *J. Appl. Meteorol. Climatol.* 47:991–1005.

Noori, R., N. Asadi, and Z. Deng. 2019. A simple model for simulation of reservoir stratification. *J. Hydraulic Res.* 57(4):561–572.

Ogbonnaya, C.I., B. Sarr, C. Brou, O. Diouf, N.N. Diop, and H. Roy-Macauley. 2003. Selection of cowpea genotypes in hydroponics, pots, and field for drought tolerance. *Crop Sci.* 43:1114–1120.

Okcu G., M.D. Kaya, and M. Atak 2005. Effects of salt and drought stresses on germination and seedling growth of pea (*Pisum sativum* L.). *Turkish J. Agriculture Forestry* 29(4):237–242.

Ommen, O.E., A. Donnelly, S. Vanhoutvin, M. van Oijen, and R. Manderscheid. 1999. Chlorophyll content of spring wheat flag leaves grown under elevated CO_2 concentrations and other environmental stresses within the ESPACE-wheat project. *Eur. J. Agron.* 10:197–203.

Parra, R.M., B.O. Olivares, A. Cortez, D. Lobo, J.C. Rey, and M.F. Rodriguez. 2018. Characteristics of drought weather (1980–2014) in two towns of Venezuelan Andes agricultural. *Revista de Investigacion* 42:38–55.

Pushpavalli, R., M. Zaman-allah, N.C. Turner, R. Baddam, M.V. Rao, and V. Vadez. 2015. Higher flower and seed number leads to higher yield under water stress conditions imposed during reproduction in chickpea. *Funct. Plant Biol.* 42:162–174.

Rawal, V., and D.K. Navarro. 2019. The Global Economy of Pulses. Food and Agriculture Organization of the United Nations, Rome, p. 3.

Roy, R.N., S. Kundu, and R.S. Kumar. 2021. The impacts and evidence of Australian droughts on agricultural crops and drought related policy issues. *Int. J. Agricultural Technol.* 17(3):1061–1076.

Rucker, K.S., C.K. Kvien, C.C. Holbrook, and J.E. Hook. 1995. Identification of peanut genotypes with improved drought avoidance traits. *Peanut Sci.* 24:14–18.

Sacks, M.M., W.K. Silk, and P Burman. 1997. Effect of water stress on cortical cell division rates within the apical meristem of primary roots of maize. *Plant Physiol.* 114:519–527.

Safriel, U., and Z. Adeel. 2008. Developments paths of drylands: Thresholds and sustainability. *Sustain.Sci.* 3:117–123.

Samarah, N.H., R.E. Mullen, S.R. Cianzio, and P. Scott. 2006. Dehydrin-like proteins in soybean seeds in response to drought stress during seed filling. *Crop Sci.* 46:2141–2150.

Sayari, N., M. Bannayan, A. Alizadeh, A. Farid, M.R.H. Kermani, and E. Eyshi Rezaei. 2014. Climate change impact on legumes' water production function in the northeast of Iran. *J. Water Climate Change* 6(2):374–385.

Seitz, D., M.K.B. Ludeke, and Walther. 2011. Categorisation of typical vulnerability patterns in global drylands. *Glob. Environ. Change* 21:431–440.

Shah, A.A., I. Kasawani, and J. Kamaruzaman. 2007. Degradation of Indus delta mangroves in Pakistan. *Int. J. Geol.* 3(1):27–34.

Shahriar, A., G.A. Mozaffari, and S. Poudineh. 2018. The impact of drought periods and wind erosion on the physical development of desert cities (case study: Zabol-Iran). *Desert* 23(2):199–209.

Shannon, H.D., and R.P. Motha. 2015. Managing weather and climate risks to agriculture in North America, Central America and the Caribbean. *Weather Climate Extremes.* 1(10):50–56.

Shobair, S.S. 2001. Current Drought Situation in Afghanistan, Drought Assessment and Mitigation in Southwest Asia. International Water Management Institute.

Shrestha, R.A., N.C.A. Turner, K.H.M.A. Siddique, D.W.B. Turner, and J.C.A. Speijers. 2006. Water deficit during pod development in lentils reduces flower and pod numbers but not seed size. *Aust. J. Agr. Res.* 57:427–438.

Siddique, K.H.M., K.L. Regan, D. Tennant, and B.D. Thomson. 2001. Water use and water use efficiency of cool season grain legumes in low rainfall Mediterranean-type environments. *Eur. J. Agronomy* 15:267–280.

Skees, J. et al. 2001. Developing Rainfall-Based index Insurance in Morocco. World Bank Policy Research Working Paper, p. 2577.

Smirnoff, N. 1995. Antioxidant systems and plant response to the environment. In Environment and Plant Metabolism: Flexibility and Acclimation. Smirnoff, V (ed.), BIOS Scientific Publishers, Oxford, UK.

Smith, P. et al. 2013. How much land based greenhouse gas mitigation can be achieved without compromising food security and environmental goals? *Glob. Chang. Biol.* 19:2285–2302.

Specht, J.E., K. Chase, M. Macrander, G.L. Graef, J. Chung, and J.P. Markwell. et al. 2001. Soybean response to water. *Crop Sci.* 41(2):493–509.

Stone, R.C. and H. Meinke. 2007. Contingency planning for drought – A case study in coping with agrometeorological risks and uncertainties. In Managing Weather and Climate Risks in Agriculture. Sivakumar, M.V.K. and Motha, R.P. (eds.). World Meteorological Organisation – India Meteorological Department, Springer, Berlin, pp. 415–433.

Strelich, L. 2015. Global warming intensifies drought conditions in California. Eos 96. 10.1029/2015EO034713

Swearingen, W.D., and A. Bencherifa. 2000. An Assessment of the Drought Hazard in Morocco. D. A. Wilhite (ed.). vol. 1. New York, Routledge, pp. 279–286.

Szeto, K., X. Zhang, R. White, and J. Brimelow. 2016. The 2015 extreme drought in Western Canada. In Herring S, Hoell A, Hoerling M, Kossin J, Schreck III C, Stott P. (Editors). Explaining extreme events of 2015 from a climate perspective. *Special Supplement to the Bulletin of the American Meteorological Society* 97(12):S42–S46.

Tabari, H., J. Nikbakht, and P.H. Talaee. 2013. Hydrological drought assessment in Northwestern Iran based on streamflow drought index (SDI). *Water Resour. Manag.* 27(1):137–151.

Thomas, G.A., R.C. Dalal, E.J. Weston, K.J. Lehane, A.J. King, D.N. Orange, C.J. Holmes, and G.B. Wildermuth. 2009. Pasture-crop rotations for sustainable production in a wheat and sheep-based farming system on a Vertosol in south-west Queensland, Australia. *Anim. Prod. Sci.* 49(8):682–695.

Twinomugisha, B. 2005. A Content Analysis Reports on Climate Change Impacts, Vulnerability and Adaptation in Uganda. CLACC-Fellow DENIVA-Uganda.

Vicente-Serrano, S.M., E. Aguilar, R. Martínez, N. Martín-Hernández, C. Azorin-Molina, A. Sanchez-Lorenzo. et al. 2017. The complex influence of ENSO on droughts in Ecuador. *Clim. Dyn.* 48:405–427.

Vicente-Serrano, S.M., J.I. Lopez-Moreno, S. Beguería, J. Lorenzo-Lacruz, A. Sanchez-Lorenzo, J.M. García-Ruiz. et al. 2014. Evidence of increasing drought severity caused by temperature rise in southern Europe. *Environ. Res. Lett.* 9:044001.

Wang, G. 2005. Agricultural drought in a future climate: Results from 15 global climate models participating in the IPCC 4th assessment. *Climate Dynamics* 25:739–753.

Wheaton. E., S. Kulshreshtha, V. Wittrock, and G. Koshida. 2008. Dry times: Hard lessons from the Canadian drought of 2001 and 2002. *Canadian Geographer* 52(2):242–262.

Wilhite, D.A., M.D. Svoboda, and M.J. Hayes. 2007. Understanding the complex impacts of drought: A key to enhancing drought mitigation and preparedness. *Water Resour. Manag.* 21:763–774.

Wilhite, D.A., and M.H. Glantz. 1985. Understanding the drought phenomenon: The role of definitions. *Water Int.* 10(3):111–120.

Wu, Y., and D.J. Cosgrove. 2000. Adaptation of roots to low water potentials by changes in cell wall extensibility and cell wall proteins. *J. Exp. Bot.* 51:1543–1553.

Zargar, A., R. Sadiq, B. Naser, and F.I. Khan. 2011. A review of drought indices. *Environ. Rev.* 19:333–349.

Zhang, M., L. Duan, Z. Zhai, J. Li, X. Tian, and B. Wang. et al. 2004. Effects of plant growth regulators on water deficit induced yield loss in soybean. In Proceedings of the 4th International Crop Science Congress, Brisbane, Australia, pp. 252–256.

Zhong, Z., J. Zhao, X. Yu, and H. Ju. 2000. Main dryland crops in northern China for water calculation and analysis. *China J. Agrometeorol.* 2:25–53.

Ziolkowska, J.R. 2016. Socio-economic implications of drought in the agricultural sector and the state of economy. *Economies* 4(19):1–11.

13

Implication of Climate Change on the Productivity of Legumes

PS Basu[1], Ummed Singh[2], Surendra K Meena[3], S Gurumurthy[4], Vaibhav Kumar[1], Kalpana Tewari[1], Krishnashis Das[1], Kusum Sharma[1], and SK Chaturvedi[5]
[1]ICAR-Indian Institute of Pulses Research, Kanpur, Uttar Pradesh, India
[2]Agriculture University, Jodhpur, Rajasthan, India
[3]ICAR-IIPR, Arid Pulses Research Centre, Bikaner, Rajasthan, India
[4]ICAR-National Institute of Abiotic stress Management, Pune, Maharashtra, India
[5]Rani Lakshmi Bai Central Agriculture University, Jhansi, Uttar Pradesh, India

CONTENTS

DOI: 10.1201/9781003214885-13

13.1 Introduction

In general, crop productivity is adversely affected by high temperature and drought (Barnabás et al., 2008). The rise in global mean temperature and drought have affected agricultural productivity worldwide (Awasthi et al., 2014). According to IPCC (2013), decreasing water availability and increasing temperature are posing a great threat to food security. Therefore, it is an urgent need to identify tolerant plant species for these stresses (Zandalinas et al., 2018). The pulses or food legumes are rainfed crops grown under diverse soil types and agro-ecosystems in low rainfall areas of semi-arid regions, including India, Pakistan, Bangladesh, Myanamar, and Nepal. The pulses have an extremely important place in the agricultural system as they require less chemical fertilizers and limited moisture. The legumes or pulses crops include chickpea (*Cicer arietinum* L.), pigeonpea (*Cajanus cajan* L.), greengram (*Vigna radiata* L.), blackgram (*Vigna mungo* L.), and lentil (*Lens cullinaris* L.), which are considered to be major pulse crops, and fieldpea (*Pisum sativum* L.), kidney bean or rajmash (*Phaseolus vulgaris* L.), lathyrus, cowpea, horsegram etc., which are considered to be minor pulses because of their lesser consumption by people. These pulses are broadly catagorized into cool-season legumes constituting chickpea, lentil, fieldpea, rajmash, and lathyrus, whereas warm season legumes include pigeonpea, greengram, blackgram, cowpea, and horsegram. Pulse seeds have high nutritive value with low glycemic index comprising approximately 18%–30% protein, which varies among legumes species. Besides being a rich source of protein, the pulses also supplement essential amino acids, resistant starches, complex oligosaccharides, fibers, minerals, vitamins, phenolics, tannins, phytic acids, antioxidants activity, and folic acids, which have enormous health benefits (Singh et al., 2016). In addition, pulses improve soil health by contributing soil nitrogen through fixing atmospheric nitrogen by symbiotic association of N_2 fixing *Rhizobium* in their root nodules. Pulses host a number of beneficial microbes in their rhizosphere, such as phosphate solubilizing bacteria (PSB) that add soluble phosphates in the soil. They are hardy crops thriving well with their vigorous root system and have a strong ability to proliferate their root system into the deep soil layers. These crops enrich soil fertility and help soil conditioning by breaking the hard pan of sub-soil, contributing organic matter in the soil, mitigating adverse effects of nitrous oxides in the air. Keeping in view of the growing demand, additional lands are required for expanding the areas of cultivation of pulses. The productivity of pulses has always been low as they are threatened by great challenges of climatic aberrations, such as inadequate rainfall, drought, and heat. Among several abiotic stresses, drought and heat are considered to be the major yield-limiting factor, followed by unprecedented high temperature during the reproductive phase (Daryanto et al., 2015; Fahad et al., 2017). High-temperature stress affects various physiological processes and alters the plant-water relationship (Summerfield et al., 1984). The rise in temperature beyond 35°C may cause irreversible damage to the growth and development of the plant (Wahid et al., 2007). Heat stress affects flower initiation, flowering duration, pollen formation, pollen viability, microsporogenesis, pollen development and germination, anther dehiscence and pollination, hypanthium elongation, fertilization and pod set/development, nodule growth, and nitrogen fixation in pulses (Prasad et al., 2001; Kakani et al., 2002). However, genetic variability for heat tolerance was reported in many food legumes (Sita et al., 2017). Pulses are particularly sensitive to heat stress at the bloom stage; only a few days of exposure to high temperatures (40°C–45°C) can cause heavy yield losses through flower drop or pod abortion (Siddique et al., 1999). Both heat and drought stresses are often superimposed on each other and reduce yield by more than 40% in pulses, depending upon the severity of the stresses. Pulses are becoming high demanding crops in terms of their high nutritional values and sustaining soil health and preservation of the ecosystem (FAO, 2017). It is, therefore, imperative to analyze critically the implications of climate change on pulses. There are several knowledge gaps in our understating toward low productivity of pulses, particularly when drought and heat are both imposed on crops (Morison et al., 2008). Efforts are needed to make pulses more climate-resilient and productive (Acevedo et al., 2020). Our current understanding is not sufficient to counter the challenges imposed by climate adversities (FAO, 2017). Therefore, systematic approaches should be taken to hit the primary targets of achieving higher productivity with limited resources and sustain our ecosystem, maintain soil health, and protect the environment, keeping in view the fact that pulses play a central role in sustaining our agro-ecosystem under the climate change scenario.

13.2 Consequence of High Temperature and CO_2

Climate change is primarily driven by rise in temperature, which affects the hydrological cycle, leading to erratic distribution or scanty rainfall in some pulse-growing regions of south Asian countries, where more than 70% of the world's total pulses are grown. In the south Asian countries in particular, pulse-growing agro-ecological zones are most vulnerable to climate change. Increasing carbon dioxide in the atmosphere is the main contributing factor toward the rise in global temperature. High temperature × CO_2 interaction studies revealed a negative impact on some legume crops. High temperatures often coincide with sensitive stages of reproductive development of pulses crops. High CO_2 increases photosynthesis and seed yield; however, CO_2 increase did not offset the negative effects of high temperatures on reproductive processes and yield (Prasad et al., 2002). The beneficial effects of CO_2 enrichment toward increase in yield in kidney bean (*Phaseolus vulgaris L.*) have been shown to be counteracted by increased temperature (> 34/24 °C) (Prasad et al., 2002). Earlier findings indicated formation of leaf starch at high CO_2, leading to poor assimilate export from source to sink, and grain filling is adversely affected. High carbon dioxide is, however, beneficial after setting of strong sinks i.e. developing grains with high sucrose synthase activity in redgram (Vanaja et al., 2010). The growth of soybean at elevated CO_2 stimulates photosynthesis, whereas decreasing *in vivo* Rubisco capacity in soybean (Bernacchi et al., 2005). In several C3 plants, downregulation of light-saturated net photosynthesis, P_{max} at elevated CO_2 has been reported, which could be associated with feedback inhibition due to excessive accumulation of photosynthates in chloroplasts or nitrogen limitation. Vanaja et al. (2007) reported increased growth, biomass, and pod number in blackgram under elevated conditions. At podding stage when sink demand is high, both photosynthesis and transpiration tremendously increased under elevated CO_2 conditions and without any water-limiting conditions. However, high CO_2 level during vegetative stage contributed toward increased water-use efficiency as compared to ambient CO_2 (300 ppm). High photosynthesis accompanied by increased transpiration and stomatal conductance under elevated CO_2 supported high sink demand during grain filling. In a study conducted under enriched carbon dioxide of about 500 ppm, seeds of mungbean showed high starch and low protein content as compared to ambient CO_2 condition (Lamichaney et al., 2021).

13.3 Pattern of Climate Change

Pulses have limited scope to diversify as cereals and commercially important crops are competitively pushing pulses toward more resource-poor conditions and climatically vulnerable agro-ecological zones. Unusually high or low temperatures, drought, flooding, and erratic rainfall during the crop season are some of the recurring climatic events observed during the past several years that adversely influenced food legume productivity and threatened global food security (Saina et al., 2013). When drought and high temperature are imposed together during crop season, their combined effects are more detrimental, particularly during the reproductive stages (Fahad et al., 2017). South Asia, the legume basket of the world, is most vulnerable to climate change (Venkatachalam et al., 2012). Major impacts of climate change will be on rainfed crops, including pulses, which account for nearly 60% of cropland area (Asha latha et al., 2012). Almost all cool-season winter legumes under northern plains of south Asia are gradually shifting toward "warm winter." This is primarily because of asymmetric pattern of warming, that is, night-time minimums increasing more rapidly than daytime maximums (Richardson et al., 2016). Among winter pulses, chickpea (*Cicer arietinum* L.), lentil, and fieldpea are covering more than 50% of rainfed area are now severely threatened by climatic changes that lead to recurrent incidence of less dew precipitation. This dew water is highly beneficial for winter pulses for biomass production before the onset of the reproductive phase (Basu et al., 2016). The winter and summer pulses often experience abnormally high temperature (>35°C) beyond their threshold level of tolerance during the reproductive phase (Figure 13.1 and Figure 13.2). Therefore, efforts need to be made to evolve crop varieties resilient to climatic conditions with multiple abiotic and biotic stress tolerance. At present, crop varieties having combined resistance for drought and heat are very rare. The physiological responses of combined stresses are difficult to study as several effects are common or sometimes adverse effects become aggravated. It is also important to investigate the performance of pulse germplasms under diverse climatic conditions for validating the stability of germplasms across different locations, intogression of traits into a given genotypes with high-yielding agronomic background, and further efforts to combine multiple stress tolerance to evolve climate smart crops. In the future, introducing suitable cropping systems, climate-friendly agrotechniques, and management and development of climate-resilient crops would be options to sustain agricultural productivity, particularly for rainfed crops. Pulses are cultivated under rainfed conditions, which means they need more attention as they are not grown under assured irrigation. For efficient crop, soil, and water management, development of stress-tolerant crops using modern breeding techniques can help to overcome the deleterious effects of anticipated climate change (Dar and Gowda, 2013).

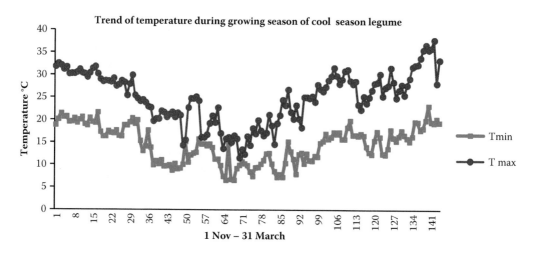

FIGURE 13.1 Daytime maximum reaches 30°C–35°C for cool season legumes chickpea, lentil, and fieldpea during the reproductive stages, including flowering and podding (February to March).

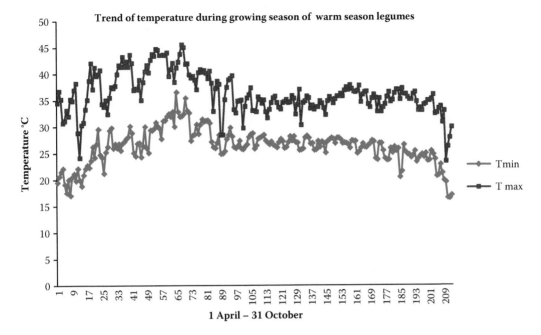

FIGURE 13.2 Daytime maximum reaches 40°C–45°C for summer legumes greengram and blackgram during the reproductive stages, including flowering and podding (April-June).

13.4 Yield Constraints in Major Grain Legumes

13.4.1 Photothermosensitivity

Sensitivity to photo- and thermoperiods is considered to be the other major factor responsible for yield instability in pulses (Razia et al., 2020). Therefore, development of photo- and thermoinsensitive genotypes is the primary requirement to address the climate risk. Due to high *Genotype × Environment (G×E)* interaction, the grain yield of pulses tends to vary across different environments. Photoperiod sensitivity is a major constraint destabilizing the yield of *Vigna* group to a considerable extent (Basu et al., 2019; Sengupta et al., 2021). Most genotypes show quantitative short-day responses, with flower initiation being delayed by photoperiods longer than 12–13 hours. To achieve high yields, the photoperiod should not exceed >12 hours. The interactive effects of photoperiod and temperature in greengram are inadequately understood, although both factors are crucial determinants of grain yield; therefore, photothermoinsensitivity is a major attribute in breeding strategy in the development of greengram varieties with higher stability across diverse climatic conditions. Generally, a higher mean temperature hastens flowering, or a lower mean temperature delays flowering in all photoperiods (Sharma et al., 2015). Lateef et al. (2018) reported temperature × flowering interactions in greengram with high mean temperatures (24°C to 28°C) and long photoperiods (15 to 16 h). The production is considerably influenced by changes in the photoperiod and temperature across the growing regions of greengram, extending from low to high latitudes. Because greengram is a quantitative short-day crop (Chauhan and Williams, 2018), short-day length at low latitude hastens flower initiation, and the plants rapidly reach the reproductive phase without adequate vegetative biomass production. By contrast, long photoperiod at high latitudes delays the onset of the reproductive phase, but the biomass is adequate and has a high leaf area index. Blackgram is a highly photothermo-sensitive crop. Therefore, its yield potential varies across locations due to variable daylength and thermal regimes (Sengupta et al., 2021). Thus, minimizing the genotype × environment interactions can help to achieve stable yield of blackgram. The high temperature stress above the threshold across the locations during the summer season could be the compounding effects of both heat and photosensitivity (Sengupta et al., 2021). One of the strategies for selecting photothermoinsensitive lines is to evaluate different genotypes at multi-locations having varying daylength and thermal regimes. As a result, genotypes having stable yield across the locations could be identified as putative photothermoinsensitive lines. This strategy should be made to screen thermo-tolerant lines from the panel of photothermoinsensitive lines so that widely adapted stable heat-tolerant lines could be identified that have less influence of photothermoperiods.

13.4.2 Drought

Yield reduction in pulses has been directly correlated with intensity of drought (Daryanto et al., 2015). Among rainfed pulses, *Vigna* species greengram and blackgram are warm season crops that require four irrigations until crop maturity. Sources of drought tolerance in *Vigna* crops are very rare, though greengram is relatively better adapted to warm climates. The highest yield reduction was observed during the reproductive stage of many pulses. However, yield reduction in pigeonpea under drought was lower than that of lentils, groundnut, cowpea, and greengram. In extra short duration pigeonpea, the impact of drought stress is evident at the vegetative, flowering, and pod-filling stages (Nam et al., 2001). The germination and seedling growth, seedling vigor, and hypocotyls length is adversely affected by drought stress in pigeonpea. Tolerance to drought in short-duration pigeonpea has been ascribed to the crop's ability to maintain total drymatter, a small pod size, few seeds in the pod, high seed mass, and low flowering synchronization (Lopez et al., 1996). The important mechanisms of drought tolerance in pigeonpea were included with high root resistance to water flow; slow shoot development; limited initial root development at depth; partitioning of assimilates into vegetative parts; leaflet movement during water stress; dehydration tolerance; and osmotic adjustment (Sayan, 1991). The lethal leaf water potential, i.e. the lowest water potential experienced by the last viable leaf, was a key measure of dehydration tolerance. The pigeonpea has more dehydration tolerance than others. The ability of cells to continue metabolism at low leaf water status is termed dehydration tolerance (Turner et al., 2001). Membrane disorder is often measured as leakage of solutes from the cell (Leopold et al., 1981). Water status parameter, like relative water content, may be a good indicator of drought tolerance in pigeonpea under semi-arid condition (Kimani et al., 1994). Accumulation of proline in cell in response to water deficit is another mechanism protecting protein structures as cell dehydrate, and as an organic nitrogen source. The relative drought tolerance in a range of pulses is based upon physiological traits such as osmotic adjustment, root system, and lethal leaf water potential. Thus, the order of drought tolerance in different pulses could be pigeonpea >chickpea>lentil> blackgram>greengram.

13.4.3 High Temperature

High temperature results in an overall reduction in plant growth, including roots, leaf area, and dry weight (Incrocci et al., 2000). Many studies on climate change have indicated that the average surface temperatures are expected to rise by 3°C–5°C, posing a major threat to crop production (including legumes) and agricultural systems worldwide, especially in the semi-arid tropics. Moreover, increase in temperature will have more adverse effects, especially on cool-season crops (e.g. chickpea and lentil) than the summer and rainy-season crops (Van Der Maesen, 1972). It has been predicted that an average 1°C increase will reduce yield by at least 3%–4% in many crops (Mishra, 2007). Heat stress causes considerable reduction in biomass production and grain yield in several crops (Giaveno and Ferrero, 2003). A rise in temperature may limit the development of various yield components (Boote et al., 2005). A temperature increase of 1°C–2°C above the threshold level is sufficient to reduce yield in many legume crops, such as cowpea (Hall, 1992), groundnut (Prasad et al., 1999), common bean (Rainey and Griffiths, 2005a), lentil (Barghi et al., 2012), and chickpea (Gaur et al., 2008; Devasirvatham et al., 2012).

The majority of the food legumes, including chickpea, lentil, pigeonpea, greengram, and blackgram, are grown by developing countries of south Asia under rainfed situations. They are often heavily influenced by climate variables. Crops grown at lower latitudes are often exposed to high temperatures above 40°C. Grain yield reduction in heat stress has been reported to be associated with a decrease in photosynthetic capacity because of altered membrane stability (Horváth et al., 2012; Rakavi and Sritharan, 2019) and enhanced maintenance respiration (Reynolds et al., 2007), along with a reduction

(a)   (b)

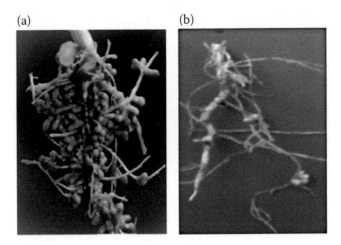

FIGURE 13.3 Effect of high temperature on in chickpea nodulation. A. Normal sown chickpea nodule (25/15°C max/min), B Late sown chickpea nodule (40/27°C max/min).

in radiation-use efficiency. Photosynthesis is the most sensitive physiological process impaired by heat stress (Wang et al., 2009), which could be due to structural and functional disruptions of chloroplasts, reduction of chlorophyll, inactivation of chloroplast enzymes (Langjun et al., 2006), or both stomatal and nonstomatal limitation (Wahid et al., 2007). High temperatures adversely affect starch and sucrose synthesis through a reduction in the activity of sucrose phosphate synthase and ADP-glucose pyrophosphorylase (Zhao, 2013). Crops exposed to high temperature are often subjected to oxidative stress-producing reactive oxygen species (ROS), which are highly toxic to cellular functions in plants because they damage nucleic acids and cause protein oxidation and lipid peroxidation; this oxidative damage eventually causes cell death (Suzuki et al., 2012; Meriga et al., 2004). ROS toxicity during various stresses is considered to be one of the major causes of low crop productivity worldwide (Vadez et al., 2012). An increase in the activity of antioxidant enzymes, such as guaiacol peroxidase (GPX) and catalase (CAT), plays a significant role in minimizing the toxic effects of stress-induced ROS production (Hassan and Mansoor, 2014). High temperatures adversely affect nitrogen fixation in chickpea (Rodrigues et al., 2006). Increased day temperatures ranging from 32°C to 35°C have shown reduction in nodule formation and nitrogen fixation in chickpea (Figure 13.3). It has been reported that high temperature delays nodulation, retards nitrogen fixation, and impairs nodule function and structure in chickpea (Kurdali, 1996; Minchin et al., 1980; Rawsthorne et al., 1985).

13.5 Effect of High Temperature on Reproductive and Seed Development in Pulses

The reproductive phase of major pulses is highly sensitive to temperature extremities (Hedhly et al., 2008). High temperature inhibits flower set and flower retention, impairs normal development of male and female gametophytes leading to ovule abortion, reduces pod settings, and impairs grain filling, which eventually results in significant yield loss. Several reports have indicated that heat stress caused reproductive failure due to impaired sucrose metabolism in the leaves and developing grains, and inhibition of sucrose transporters that results in decreased carbon source to the anthers and developing pollen grains (Kaushal et al., 2016). The heat stress results in drastic yield losses due to the decline of relative tissue water content (RWC) and leaf water potential LWP (Omae et al., 2005) pollen or ovule inactivity, flower abortion, and postfertilization impaired growth and development of embryo or seed in many pulses (Sita et al., 2017). Ultrastructural studies revealed that pollen sterility could be due to degenerated tapetum owing to heat stress (Suzuki et al., 2001). Temperature extremities have specifically detrimental effects on male gametophyte, causing disrupted meiosis, tapetal hypertrophy, stunted development of pollen grains, anther protein degradation, pollen sterility, and pollen tube deformation (Basu et al., 2019), whereas heat stress adversely affects female gametophyte, causing reduced size of style and ovary, disrupted meiosis, reduced stigma receptivity, callose deposits in style, damaged embryo sac components, and fertilization arrest. Flowering is either early or delayed. Flowers abscise and become distorted, and shedding occurs. The grain-filling process is impaired due to altered source-sink relations, which leads to seed abortion and yield loss. However, the relative heat sensitivity varies for different crops (Sung et al., 2003). High temperatures reduce yield and yield attributes, such as dry matter accumulation and partitioning (Omae et al., 2007), pod set, pod weight, and harvest index in snap beans (Omae and Kumar, 2006). Temperatures above 40°C resulted in reduced pod set, seed production, and yield in soybean (Board and Kahlon, 2011). The water scarcity in floral parts and leaves due to high-temperature driven increased transpiration causes heavy yield losses in snap bean (*Phaseolus vulgaris*) (Tsukaguchi et al., 2003).

High temperature also adversely affects pollen germination and pollen tube growth. In cool season legume lentils, pollen germination and pollen tube growth have been found to be retarded above 35°C (Barghi et al., 2013). Stressful temperature often leads to impaired microsporogenesis and megasporogenesis at the pre-fertilization stage in various legumes, such as chickpea (*Cicer arietinum*) (Kumar et al., 2010) and *Phaseolus vulgaris* (Porch and Jahn, 2001; Suzuki et al., 2001). Loss of pollen viability and pollen germination have been reported at high temperature in *Cicer arietinum* (Kumar et al., 2013), *Phaseolus vulgaris* (Porch and Jahn, 2001), and *Arachis hypogea* (Kakani et al., 2005). Loss of stigma receptivity, loss of ovule viability, and flower abscission have been reported in *Cicer arietinum* (Kumar et al., 2013) and *Phaseolus vulgaris* (Suzuki et al., 2001). Most of the pulse crops, such as chickpea and lentil, are sensitive to heat stress when day temperature exceeds above 35°C, resulting in reduced pollen germination (Figure 13.4), and decreased pod number and seed size (Figure 13.5). Arrest of fertilization and reduced embryogenesis have been reported at extreme temperatures in chickpea (Clarke and Siddique, 2004) and *Glycine max* (Ohnishi et al., 2010). The pigeonpea often experiences high temperature during the reproductive phase, which results in pollen sterility, slowed germination, and pollen load on stigma, reducing the pollen receptivity on stigma and length of pollen tubes (Kumar et al.,

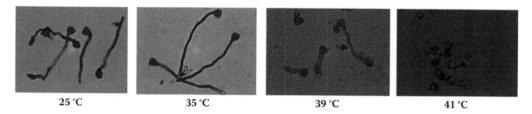

| 25 °C | 35 °C | 39 °C | 41 °C |

FIGURE 13.4   Pollen germination in response to high temperatures in chickpea. The length of pollen tube tends to reduce as temperature increases from 25°C to 41°C.

FIGURE 13.5   Failure to set pods in heat sensitive chickpea ICC 4567 while normal pod set in heat-tolerant chickpea ICC 15614 (Left). Reduced seed size in chickpea at high temperature (right).

2013). Consequently, heat stress has detrimental effects on both microsporogenesis and megasporogenesis, causing incomplete cell division and eventually loss of viability of pollens and ovules (Kaushal et al., 2016). Failure of anthesis would be a likely cause of flower abscission, and also discontinuity of sustained photoassimilate mobilization to the developing grains results in pod abortion (Pang et al., 2017). Identifying mechanisms of reproductive temperature tolerance in various legumes could be achieved through screening diversified germplasm available in gene banks. Warm season legumes, such as greengram, pigeonpea, blackgram, and cowpea, have a higher temperature tolerance limit, so they are also affected negatively, leading to a reduction in pod set in response to moderately-high night temperatures (Thiaw and Hall, 2004). Thus, various legumes are sensitive to temperature extremities to different degrees from the vegetative to reproductive stage, resulting in metabolic and reproductive dysfunction that finally results in low yields.

13.6 Effect of Combined Stresses of Drought and Heat

There is a need to identify the tolerance mechanism of pulses in response to simultaneously occurring heat and drought stress (Priya et al., 2019). It is considered that demand of water will proportionately increase with rise in temperature due to increase in soil-plant evapotranspiration water loss. To improve pulses for dual tolerance, traits that confer the tolerance to both heat and drought must be studied. Similarly, it is urgently needed to inherit combined tolerance in pulses also. When both high temperature and drought stresses are superimposed, their combined effects are more detrimental and negative. The combined effects could have deleterious additive effects on phenology, growth, chlorophyll content, photosynthesis, grain number, fertility, grain filling duration, and grain yield in several crops (Perdomo et al., 2017). For example, the combined drought and heat stress decreases leaf chlorophyll content by 49%, whereas drought or heat alone reduce it by 9% or 27%, respectively (Pradhan et al., 2012). Reproductive stages are more sensitive to combined heat and drought stresses than individual ones (Barnabás et al., 2008). However, in some ways, drought and heat stress are interlinked. Both the stresses significantly reduce photosynthetic efficiency, stomatal conductance, leaf area, and water-use efficiency in many crops e.g. wheat, rice, chickpea (Farooq et al., 2019). Heat stress increases evapotranspiration from soil and the plant canopy that leads to a disruption of water relations, and plants often succumb to drought stress driven by high temperatures (Lamaoui et al., 2018). Crops may respond to drought and heat stress individually or combined in a different manner (Rivero et al., 2014), which eventually leads to yield reduction. Pigeonpea, chickpea, lentil, and fieldpea are often exposed to drought and high temperatures simultaneously, particularly during the reproductive stage (Fahad et al., 2017).

The basic physiological mechanisms of tolerance to drought and heat may differ or be common with respect to some traits. For example, reduction of photosynthesis is a common phenomenon under drought and heat; however, photosynthetic inhibition due to drought is largely attributed by stomatal closure, reduced biomass production, and decreased leaf size. Drought limits gaseous exchange by triggering stomatal closure and in this way modifies plant-water relations, whereas heat stress inhibits photosynthetic electron transport and PS II activity, causes conformational changes in thylakoid proteins, causes distortion of membranes, alters Rubisco enzymes, and causes changes in the solubility of CO_2 and O_2 inside mesophyll cells. Heat stress has detrimental effects on reproductive parts, such as microsporogenesis and megasporogenesis of male and female gametophytes, loss of pollen viability and retards pollen germination and pollen tube growth, decreased stigma receptivity and pollen load on stigma, cell division, and accelerated rates of respiration and inhibition of carbohydrate metabolism in developing grains. However, there are common tolerance or avoidance mechanisms against both heat and drought stress, such as generation of harmful ROS, to counteract the deleterious effects of ROS. Both the stresses are induced to produce an antioxidative enzyme complex that enables scavenging of superoxide radicals being generated when plants are exposed to high temperature in combination with drought and heat. Several heat shock proteins (HSPs) are expressed in response to high temperatures, which helps to protect the membrane and vital molecules from denaturation and allows cellular machinery to operate normally. Both heat and drought stress adversely affect water relation characteristics of the plant, which include declines in leaf RWC, water potential, and osmotic and turgor potential.

13.7 Water-Use Efficiency, Canopy Temperature, and Transpiration under Drought and Heat

High water use or transpiration use efficiency, which is defined as more photosynthetic gain per unit loss of water through transpiration or transpiration efficiency, is a ratio between biomass and transpiration. The transpiration use efficiency could be one of the best strategies toward improved adaptation under the stress environment. Improving water-use efficiency is associated with stomatal density, efficiency of RuBisco, and other physiological parameters of mesophyll cells of leaves. Significant genotypic variation has been observed in chickpea and pigeonpea in water-use efficiency (Kashiwagi et al., 2006). A decrease in transpiration rate due to drought may result in an increase of leaf internal temperature due to decreased evaporative cooling of the leaf; therefore, drought-stressed plants show higher leaf or canopy temperatures than well-watered plant (Reynolds et al., 2009). Cool canopies are associated with better yield output as a result of higher transpiration and photosynthesis (Pinto and Reynolds, 2015). To maintain a cool canopy under drought and heat, plants should have a deeper root system to access water from the deep soil layer. Key physiological traits like osmotic adjustments and root architecture need to be modified to make the canopy cool under heat and drought stresses. Osmolyte accumulation also alters photoassimilate allocation between roots and shoots. Drought-induced osmolytes accumulation tends to allocate more photosynthates toward roots. As a result, plants are able to adapt under drought by extracting more water from soil.

13.8 Response of Major Food Legumes to Climate Change

13.8.1 Cool Season Legumes

13.8.1.1 Chickpea

Chickpea (*Cicer arietinum* L.) is the second largest grown food legume of the world after beans. India, Australia, Pakistan, Turkey, Myanmar, Ethiopia, Iran, Mexico, Canada, and USA are the major chickpea producing countries. Chickpea is a good source of protein (20%–22%) and rich in carbohydrates (~60%), dietary fiber, and minerals (Jukanti et al., 2012). The demand for chickpea is increasing, keeping in view its enormous health benefits, which include prevention of cardiovascular diseases, type 2 diabetes, digestive diseases, and even cancer (Ryan, 1977). Chickpea fixes atmospheric nitrogen through symbiotic nitrogen fixer rhizobium, resulting in less dependence on chemical fertilizer, and residual nitrogen left in the soil after harvest benefits the subsequent crop. Drought and heat are the major abiotic stresses and constraints limiting chickpea production globally, which together account for about 50% of the yield losses (Gaur et al., 2007). Chickpea is largely grown under rainfed on residual soil moisture after withdrawal of monsoon. The crop often experiences terminal drought if winter rain fails and the soil moisture starts receding and reaching below to a critical level at grain-filling stages, causing heavy yield losses primarily due to water limitation. Exposure to heat stress ($\geq 35°C$) at flowering and podding in chickpea results in drastic reductions in seed yields (Wang et al., 2006). High temperature adversely affects seed germination, photosynthesis, respiration, membrane stability, fertilization, fruit maturation, quality of seeds, nutrient absorption, protoplasmic movement, transport of materials, and also modulated level of hormones and primary and secondary metabolites (Fowden et al., 1993; Wahid et al., 2007). Summerfield et al. (1984) observed lower grain yields with greater exposure to hot days (30°C–35°C), during the reproductive period. Heat stress at the reproductive stage is thus increasingly becoming a serious constraint to chickpea production due to climate change. The optimal temperatures for chickpea growth range between 15°C and 30°C (Kalra et al., 2008).

13.8.1.2 Lentil

Lentil (*Lens culinaris* Medik) is another cool season food legume grown widely and consumed for edible purposes and intensifying the cereal-based cropping systems. Lentil often experiences high temperatures (>35°C) during the flowering and pod filling stage, which leads to forced maturity and consequently affects seed yield and quality (Delahunty et al., 2015). The delayed sowing of lentil coincides with terminal heat stress. Consequently, a large portion of cultivated areas (~11.7 million ha) remains fallow after late harvest of rice (Subbarao et al., 2001). In Australia, ~70% yield losses in lentil were observed due to a 6-day heat wave with a maximum temperature of 35°C or above (Delahunty et al., 2015). In recent years, heat stress as a result of global warming has become a major challenge to crop production and productivity in general (Kaur et al., 2015). Development of heat-tolerant lentil cultivars is required to sustain production and productivity of lentil for semi-arid regions. These issues could be addressed by distinguishing the heat tolerant and sensitive lentil genotypes at a critical temperature (Gaur et al., 2015). Thus, identification of key physiological traits that impart heat tolerance can help to facilitate a breeding program for developing heat-tolerant lentil cultivars, leading to a reduction the yield losses under a changing climate scenario (Scafaro et al., 2010). High and low temperature causes photo damage to PSII (Murata et al., 2007), which could be due to damage of proteins that are involved in photo damage–repair cycle (Allakhverdiev and Murata, 2004). However, cyclic electron transport around PSII constitutes an effective protective mechanism against photo-inhibitory damage (Allakhverdiev and Murata, 2004), and some phenolic compounds have been identified in this protection (Allakhverdiev et al., 1997). In lentil, pollen and leaf traits could also be helpful in identifying heat-tolerant genotypes (Sita et al., 2017).

13.8.2 Warm Season Legumes

13.8.2.1 Greengram or Mungbean

Greengram thrives most effectively at temperatures between 30°C and 40°C; however, significant flower shedding occurs at temperatures beyond 40°C (Sita et al., 2017). Rainey and Griffiths (2005b) reported that the abscission of reproductive organs is the primary determinant of yield under heat stress in several grain legumes, including mungbean. Greengram or mungbean is an important protein-rich food legume crop grown during summer or rainy season. This is a short-duration crop with a yield potential of about 1,200–1,500 kg per hectare. Among all food legumes, mungbean contains a high amount of easily digestible seed proteins ranging between 24%–28%, which is higher than chickpea, lentil ,and pigeonpea. Greengram (*Vigna radiata* L. Wilczek), also known as mungbean, is an important grain legume that contains a high quantity of proteins, amino acids, sugar, minerals, soluble dietary fiber, and vitamins. It is cultivated across seasons, in different environments, and in variable soil conditions in south and southeast Asia, Africa, South America, and Australia (Parihar et al., 2017). During the reproductive stage, high temperatures cause flower drop, induce male sterility, impair anthesis, and shorten the grain-filling period. The productivity and adaptability of mungbean is seriously affected by a range of abiotic stresses, including heat and drought. In mungbean, high temperature increases flower shedding (Sinha, 1977), pollen sterility, and dehiscence of anthers (Hall, 1992). Being a summer crop, it is often exposed to temperature exceeding 40°C, resulting in high turnover of sterile pollens, infertility, flower abortion, and adversely affected grain filling. High night temperature also affects grain filling. Further increase in the day maximum temperature to 44°C or above causes production of smaller and hard seeds. The pollen viability and germination were extremely sensitive to high temperature (>40°C) in mungbean, though a wide genotypic variation in the pollen germinability was observed. Seed size reduces, however, the majority of genotypes had reduced, shriveled, or deformed grains at high temperatures exceeding 40°C. The critical temperature range for damage of reproductive organs was found somewhere in between 40°C and 45°C; however, sensitivity varied among genotypes. Earlier reports suggest that brief exposure of plants to high temperatures during seed filling accelerate senescence, diminish seed set and seed weight, and reduce yield (Siddique et al., 1999). In mungbean, remobilization of pre-anthesis reserves carbohydrates and nitrogen in leaves, podwalls, and stems and contributed significantly toward grain filling. In the changing scenario of climate, sudden rise in the temperature beyond 35°C causes increase in the respiration rates and unusually high degradation of stored starch as major chloroplasts carbon source was observed. As a result, failure to set pods and reduced or incomplete grain development at high temperature could be partly due to inadequate supply of carbon and nitrogen from leaves or by decrease in the activity of sucrose synthase, the key enzyme playing a crucial role in grain development. Poor partitioning of carbon and nitrogen at high temperature leads to low harvest index and low productivity in mungbean. The productivity and adaptability of greengram are adversely affected by several abiotic stresses, including heat, drought, salinity, and waterlogging, which affect crop growth and development by altering physiological processes and the plant-water relationship (Landi et al., 2017). Several studies have reported a reduction in growth and development of legumes because of high-temperature stress (Bindumadhava et al., 2016).

13.8.2.2 Blackgram or Urdbean

Blackgram (*Vigna mungo* L. Hepper) is a popular food legume grown in many Asian countries, including India, Pakistan, Myanmar, Bangladesh, Thailand, and China. India is the largest producer and consumer of urdbean. It is a warm season food legume, which requires 25°C–35°C temperature along with high humidity for its normal growth and development. However, prevailing high temperature (>40°C) during flowering results in deformation of flower parts or flower drop, leading to negative impact on yield. Nutritionally, urdbean is dense with protein (21%–28%), dietary fiber (161–187 g/kg), iron (16–255 mg/kg), zinc (5–134 mg/kg), and other micronutrients like other pulses (Sengupta et al., 2020). Ur bean is grown in different ecological conditions and seasons across the growing regions. In India, it is grown mainly in the rainy season (July-October) and in the southern part it is also cultivated as a winter season crop (November to February). However, its cultivation is not wide in the summer season due to excessive heat stress and a lack of humidity in the atmosphere. Thus, availability of heat-tolerant cultivars can bring more areas under urdbean cultivation. Ur bean is a close relative of mungbean, which is extensively cultivated in identical ecological conditions. In this crop as well as in another *Vigna* pulse crop, e.g, cowpea, sources of heat tolerance have already been identified (Basu et al., 2019). Knowledge of genetics underlying key traits imparting heat tolerance helps the breeder to make genetic improvements more precisely. In recent years, molecular markers helped to decipher the genetics of complex key morpho-physiological traits imparting heat tolerance in several crops (Roy et al., 2011).

13.8.2.3 Pigeonpea

Pigeonpea (*Cajanus cajan* L.) Millsp is a major grain legume of the arid and semi-arid regions of the world (Nene and Sheila, 1990). Drought and high temperature during the reproductive stage are becoming a recurrent phenomenon in these regions, resulting in significant yield loss in pigeonpea. Among pulses, pigeonpea is the hardiest crop and an excellent source of dietary proteins. The pigeonpea is considered to be a climate-smart crop because it is well adapted to diverse climatic conditions, including semi-arid, arid, and marginalized regions. It is generally grown where the temperatures are in the range of 18–30°C, but this crop even tolerates a high temperature of 35°C if soil moisture is optimally available. Pigeonpea is primarily grown in areas with less than 600 mm rainfall and cultivated in a wide range of climatic conditions, from tropics to subtropics between 30 °N and 30 °S latitude, and is best grown in a wide range of soil textures, low fertility soils from sandy soils to heavy clays with a wide range of soil pH 5.0–7.0. It is predominantly grown in regions of south Asia and Africa and believed to be originated from Indian subcontinent. Among pulses, the pigeonpea is an inherently drought- and heat-tolerant crop to some extent (Upadhyaya et al., 2012). High temperature leads to excessive water loss from crop canopy and soil through increased evapotranspiration. The decrease in soil moisture below a certain threshold level and rise of temperature exceeding 35°C or more during the grain-filling stage often leads to poor yield in pigeonpea (Basu et al., 2016). The high temperature causes oxidative damage, affects cell division, and may cause severe damage to the membranes and proteins and their synthesis, along with inactivation of major enzymes (Smertenko et al., 1997). Even exposure to the high temperature for a shorter period during the seed filling can result in accelerated filling, and eventually it results in incomplete grain development, poor quality, and reduction in the yield. High temperature beyond 35°C often leads to flower shedding, pod abortion, and incomplete grain development, inhibiting photosynthesis (Song et al., 2014) with increased respiration, which cumulatively imbalances the source-sink relation (Fahad et al., 2016). Precision phenotyping for heat tolerance involving fluorescence and thermal imaging, membrane stability, gaseous exchange, pollen fertility, carbohydrate metabolism in developing grains, and assessment of oxidative stress could be employed to identify genotypes with heat tolerance in pigeonpea.

Drought tolerance in pigeonpea is due to its deep-rooting tap root reaching up to 6 feet (2 m) in depth that helps to improve water infiltration into the deep soil (Valenzuela and Smith, 2002). Inherent drought tolerance in pigeonpea could be associated with prolific root system with a higher number of thin lateral roots, higher hydraulic resistance to restrict flow of water or conserve available water more efficiently, and smaller but high stomatal density that regulates transpiration water loss at a minimum level but maintains photosynthesis with lower order but not completely inhibited. Among all legumes, drought-tolerance characteristics of pigeonpea also involve high osmotic adjustment and very low (more negative) lethal leaf water potential, indicating a higher degree of dehydration postponement and dehydration tolerance. Genes expressing HSPs, dehydration responsive element-binding DREB, and cyclophilin have been found to be responsive to combined stresses drought and heat in pigeonpea (Zhang et al., 2009; Sekhar et al., 2010). Signalling effects of abscisic acid and ROS, calcium, and calcium-regulated proteins have been well characterized for their role in signal transmission under stress (Mazars et al., 2010). Extensive efforts have been made to identify genes/QTLs in chickpea, pigeonpea, and other pulse crops (Kumar et al., 2019). Recently, genomics tools have been becoming an integral part of current conventional breeding, which could be applied for genetic improvement for climate-smart pulses (Kole et al., 2015). Genome sequences of major pulses, including pigeonpea, are now available (Varshney et al., 2011).

13.9 Climate Smart Food Legumes

Pigeonpea and chickpea are considered to be the most climate-resilient crop among all pulses (Valenzuela and Smith, 2002). The pigeonpea can survive and has better grain yield during severe drought (Flower and Ludlow, 1986) as compared to other legumes (Okiror, 1986). This crop has tremendous potential and flexibility to tolerate climate aberrations and has the ability to mitigate the adverse effects of the climate change, whereas the majority of other crops are adversely affected (Dar and Gowda, 2013). Its tremendous ability for nitrogen fixation improves soil health, The crop demonstrated a positive response to elevated CO_2 level (Vanaja et al., 2010). The pigeonpea exposed to high CO_2 levels resulted in higher growth, increased root nodule and biomass, and higher radiation use efficiency with increased seed yield (Saha et al., 2012). Experimental evidences proved that the pigeonpea sequesters a substantial amount of atmospheric CO_2, allowing water infiltration in the deep soil by its deep-rooted system and fulfills the nitrogen requirements of successive non-leguminous crops in rotation (Yadav, 2017); therefore, the crop is most important as climate-friendly legumes that have multiple benefits for animals as well as for the ecosystem. Pigeonpea recycles nutrients efficiently, stores moisture, and fixes more nitrogen per unit, requiring much less inorganic fertilizer than other legumes (Emefiene et al., 2013). Pigeonpea possesses high osmotic adjustments (Subbarao et al., 2000); therefore, it maintains better photosynthesis than other legumes under drought (Lopez et al., 1987). Few genotypes of pigeonpea, such as RVK275, JKM 189, AKT 9913, Bennur Local, VKS-11–24-2, ICP-8840, ICP 3451, ICP 348, BSMR-736, and JSA 59, showed a consistent increase in the osmolytes in the leaves under drought. The best performing genotypes with stable yield across different environments had high osmotic adjustment. Pigeonpea roots release piscidic acid that helps to increase solubilization and uptake of phosphorus. A deep understanding of pigeonpea's adaptation mechanisms in a changing climate might have enormous relevance toward improving yield of pigeonpea.

13.10 Phenotyping of Grain Legumes

Knowledge of key traits imparting heat and drought tolerance can help to improve the grain yield of food legumes (Scafaro et al., 2010). Therefore, understanding of physio-biochemical mechanisms associated with these key traits imparting tolerance is essential for large-scale phenotyping of pulse germplasms under both field and controlled conditions (Gaur et al., 2019). In several crops, various physiological and biochemical traits, such as accumulation of phenolic compounds, organic acids, photosynthetic activity, water-use efficiency, canopy temperature, rooting length, osmotic adjustment, membrane stability, and pollen viability (Asseng et al., 2015; Sita et al., 2017), have been used to identify heat- and drought-tolerant genotypes, and a significant genetic variability has been reported for key physiological traits under stress conditions (Challinor et al., 2007).

13.10.1 Thermal Imaging

Thermal imaging of irrigated and drought-stressed crop of chickpea revealed that irrigated crop had the cooler canopy as compared to drought-stressed crop (Figure 13.6). Several genotypes were grown under a drought plot, and a uniform moisture regime was created. The best adapted genotypes with high biomass, more green foliage, and lower canopy temperature under drought field were selected. Thus, field evaluation of germplasm can be done using thermal imaging based upon canopy temperature. The limited biomass growth under water stress is the main limiting factor determining the yield. Hence, initial faster biomass accumulation is a desirable trait for high yield in pigeonpea, followed by cooler canopy at reproductive stage. The genetic variation in the canopy temperature was evident based on the differential thermal imaging of canopy; hence, it could be one of the potential phenotyping tools for initial genotypic ability to perform at field condition.

13.10.2 Identification of Stable High-Yielding Genotypes

The genotypes with consistent stable yield and phenology based on multilocation trials for several years in diverse climatic conditions could be a potential mechanism to identify putatively photothermoinsensitive

FIGURE 13.6 Thermal images of chickpea crop under drought and irrigated rows showing differences in canopy temperature depicted through color code of thermal images. Middle and left row showed higher canopy temperature (blue) as compared to right row (pink). Thermal scale is shown just adjacent to top picture. Each row is of different chickpea cultivar.

genotypes. The next approach is to characterize stable high-yielding selected genotypes physiologically and morphologically for their tolerance to drought and heat based on precision phenotyping. Based upon multilocation field data using 116 greengram genotypes, 12 promising genotypes were identified in greengram (IPM 02–16, IPM 9901-10, IPM 409-4, IPM 02–3, PDM 139, IPM 02-1, IPM 2–14, IPM 9–43-K, PDM 288, EC 470096, IPM 2K14-9 and IPM 2K14-5) that have been confirmed to be tolerant to heat and drought (Basu et al., 2019). Based upon chlorophyll fluorescence, membrane stability index, antioxidant enzyme activities, sucrose synthase activity, and protein profiling, a few promising greengram (mungbean) were identified as heat tolerant that have been validated by repeated field trial across diverse agroclimatic zones prone to be affected by recurrent high-temperature stress. These genotypes were EC 398889, PDM 139 (Samrat), IPM-02-1, PDM 288, IPM-05-3-21, and ML-1257 as heat tolerant, whereas LGG 460 was identified as extremely heat sensitive.

13.10.3 Photosynthesis and Chlorophyll Fluorescence

Photosynthesis is the most thermosensChlorophyllitive plant function (Kim and Portis, 2005), which can occur optimally at wide temperature ranges between 15°C and 35°C, although is is adversely affected at temperatures ranging between 35°C and 40°C and above. The cultivars can be distinguished based on the photosynthetic performance under high temperatures. Inhibition of photosynthesis at high temperatures can be assessed through gaseous exchange or chlorophyll fluorescence imaging technique. The fluorescence imaging technique visualizes the activity or effects of stress on photosystem II (PSII), photosynthetic membrane system, and electron transport rates (ETR). The ETR in pretreated leaves (40°C) of heat-tolerant greengram EC 398889 was less affected at high irradiances, whereas heat-sensitive genotype LGG 460 with similar treatment showed complete reduction of photosynthetic ETR. Reduced electron transport and damaged photosystems caused by high temperature have been reported in poplar by Song et al. (2014). Chloroplast stroma and thylakoid membranes are damaged by high temperatures (Wang et al., 2010). PSII in the light reaction (Heckathorn et al., 2002) and Rubisco (ribulose1, 5-bisphosphate carboxylase/oxygenase) activase in the Calvin cycle (Crafts-Brandner and Salvucci, 2000) are both thermolabile. Heat stress thus impairs the electron transport chain and affects the activation and activity of the enzyme Rubisco (Ahmad et al., 2010). Although PSI and PSII are both adversely affected by high temperatures, PSII is more sensitive to heat stress than is PSI (Moustaka et al., 2018).

Chlorophyll fluorescence is a rapid and non-invasive, high-resolution technique to determine changes in photochemistry through monitoring the fluorescence emission of PSII *in situ* (Murchie and Lawson, 2013). High temperature affects membrane stability, cell viability, and the quantum efficiency of PSII, as measured by chlorophyll fluorescence (Mohammed and Tarpley, 2009). Chlorophyll fluorescence as affected by heat stress causes a decrease of Fv/Fm ratio in susceptible wheat compared with tolerant lines (Izanloo et al., 2008). The quantum yield is one of the powerful non-destructive parameter to differentiate tolerance levels of large number of genotypes with respect to particular abiotic stress. QTLs have been reported for chlorophyll fluorescence in drought- or heat-stressed wheat. The fluorescence parameters, such as minimal Fo, maximal fluorescence Fm, and variable fluorescence Fv, changes when plants are subjected to various abiotic stresses and eventually quantum yield of PSII (ratio of variable to maximum fluorescence, Fv/Fm) is affected. Using s large number of different fluorescence data, modifications of the photosynthetic process under stresses can be assessed precisely, which includes thylakoid membrane organization, electron transport, and carbon assimilation (Kalaji et al., 2018). The images captured for effective PSII quantum yield (YII) in high temperature-treated leaves under high irradiances would be able to distinguish heat-tolerant and susceptible genotypes. The numerical values of different fluorescence parameters, such as Fo, Fm, and Fv/Fm, were converted to image format to visualize the adverse effects of heat on photosynthetic machinery at the chloroplast level. The image transformation with specific color code is shown in the Figure 13.7. The intensity of the color depicts increase or decrease in the numerical values of fluorescence parameters. Similarly, the light response of ETR based on calculation using quantum yield (Fv/Fm) and PAR was also able to distinguish the genotypes based on their sensitivity to heat stress. Overall, this technique involving chlorophyll fluorescence imaging has proved to be an effective and precise phenotyping method for screening germplasm of pulses in a big way for stress tolerance. A number of crop species e.g. rice and wheat have been

(a) **Fluorescence images of Heat tolerant blackgram UPU 85-86**

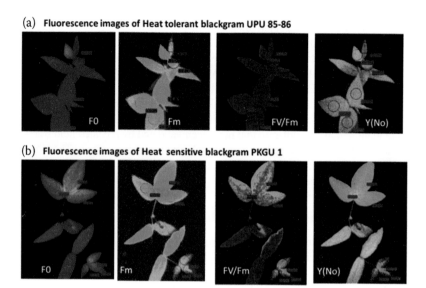

(b) **Fluorescence images of Heat sensitive blackgram PKGU 1**

FIGURE 13.7 Fluorescence images for heat-tolerant blackgram genotype, top row (**A**; UPU85–86) and heat-susceptible genotype, bottom row (**B**; PKGU-1). Heterogeneity of fluorescence images were clearly visible. The effect of high temperature treatment (43°C) on fluorescence parameters (Fo, Fm, Fv/Fm and Y (No)) of leaves was different in heat tolerant (UPU 85–86) and sensitive (PKGU-1) genotype as depicted by changes in the fluorescence color code. About 65% reduction in mean quantum yield (Fv/Fm) was observed in heat-sensitive line PKGU-1 (Fv/Fm; 0.24, Sky blue) as compared to heat-tolerant line UPU 85–86 (Fv/Fm;0.68, intense blue) when both were treated at 43°C for 1 h (Sengupta et al., 2021).

phenotyped using chlorophyll fluorescence (Pradhan et al., 2019) for stress tolerance. One of the mungbean line EC 398889 has been identified as highly heat tolerant based on chlorophyll fluorescence imaging and pollen fertility, and this line was used as one of the donor parents for developing a short-duration mungbean variety "Virat." Similarly, about 100 blackgram genotypes were tested at diverse climatic conditions differ in latitudes and putative stable genotypes were identified, which were further phenotyped for heat tolerance based on fluorescence imaging. This experiment could identify several heat-tolerant blackgram genotypes (e.g. UPU85–86, IPU94-2, IPU 98/36, NO- 5731, PGRU 95014, PGRU 95016, PLU-1, BGP-247) and sensitive genotypes (e.g. KGU-1, H-1, HPU-120, IC-21001, IC-10703, IPU90–321, IPU95-13, IPU 96-1, IPU 96-12, IPU 99–128) (Sengupta et al., 2021) (Figure 13.7). This phenotyping method has proved to be a successful strategy to develop climatically matching mungbean (greengram) development. The first distinct change in both structure and function of PSII was reported to occur at 40°C–50°C in barley (Lípová et al., 2010). The first temperature-induced transient changes were shown at 42°C–48°C, with a disruption of the PSII donor side and corresponding loss of oxygen evolution (Cramer et al., 1981) followed by changes in thylakoid membranes at about 60°C and loss of electron transport through PSII (Smith et al., 1989), representing a denaturation of the PSII reaction centers. At about 75°C, a denaturation of light-harvesting complex of PSII (LHCII) was observed (Smith et al., 1989).

The modification of chlorophyll florescence in response to heat stress has been reported in numerous crops, and heat tolerance of plant species can be quantified by measuring chlorophyll florescence (Willits and Peet, 2001). When leaves are exposed to high temperatures and high light intensity simultaneously, the combined effects are more detrimental to photosynthesis. The relative assessment of fluorescence images for quantum yield (Fv/Fm) in high temperature treated in several greengram genotypes revealed that light-adapted leaves of the heat-tolerant greengram genotype EC 398889 exhibited higher quantum yield than the heat-sensitive genotype, LGG 460. The photosynthetic system partially or completely collapsed in light-adapted leaves of LGG 460. The fluorescence images combined with the light curve of ETR strongly could precisely differentiate varying sensitivity of photosynthesis to heat stress in the two contrasting genotypes e.g. heat-tolerant greengram EC 398889 and sensitive ones LGG 460 (Basu et al., 2019). Differential degree of membrane thermostability may distinguish the genotypes toward different sensitivity to heat stress. Chen et al. (2018) reported that chloroplast-targeted AtFtsH11 protease plays critical roles for maintaining the thermostability and structural integrity of photosystems under high temperatures. Therefore, the photosynthetic efficiency may be modified under heat stress by improving FtsH11 protease in photosystems, hence, to improve plant productivity.

13.10.4 Membrane Stability

Under stress conditions, a sustained function of cellular membranes is considered crucial for maintaining cellular processes such as photosynthesis and respiration (Blum, 1998). The integrity and function of cell membranes are sensitive to high temperatures, as heat stress alters structures of membrane proteins, leading to increased permeability of membranes, resulting in increased loss of ions or solutes. The increased solute leakage is closely associated with cell membrane thermostability (Ilık et al., 2018), and various attempts have been made to use this method as an indirect measure of heat tolerance in diverse plant species, such as food legumes (Srinivasan et al., 1996), soybean (Scafaro et al., 2010), potato, cotton, tomato (Hu et al., 2010), and wheat (Blum et al., 2001). A study conducted using greengram germplasm for assessing the membrane stability index (MSI) and chlorophyll content or greenness index showed that both MSI and chlorophyll remained higher in heat-tolerant greengram line EC 398889 as compared to sensitive line LGG 460 when plants of these two contrasting genotypes were grown under high thermal regimes 42/28°C maximum/minimum temperature (Basu et al., 2019).

13.10.5 Acquired Thermotolerance

Acquired thermotolerance is a mechanism naturally occurring in plants and has been extensively used in thermotolerant line identification (Song et al., 2012). The germinating seeds of the selected greengram genotypes were exposed to heat shock in the range 37°C–52°C, and their recovery after heat shock was assessed at 30°C. The seedlings emerged from heat-tolerant greengram EC 398889, turned completely green, and rejuvenated after heat shock, whereas sensitive line LGG 460 failed to recover after heat shock (Figure 13.8). The genotype EC 398889 was characterized by high acquired thermotolerance (76.8%) as

| A. Viable leaf | B. Greening of seedlings | C. Rejuvenation of seedlings |

EC398889 (Heat tolerant) (after heat shock 52°C)

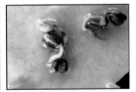

| C. Non-viable leaf | D. Non-green seedling | E. Loss of seedling viability |

LGG 460 (Heat sensitive (after heat shock 52°C)

FIGURE 13.8 Acquired thermotolerance in greengram involving slow increase in the growth temperature from normal 35°C to maximum 52°C with incremental increase of temperature by 2°C and then reverting back to normal temperature with the same sequence. If genotype gradually acquires thermotolerance, it will survive and turn green to attain a normal green plant under optimum conditions, as seen in heat-tolerant line EC 398889; however, sensitive line LGG did not show such revival ability.

compared with LGG 460 (34.5%). In addition, the heat-tolerant genotype had a unique attribute to start accumulating chlorophyll in cotyledonary leaves, followed by regeneration of new green leaves from the seedlings after severe heat shock (52°C), gradually revived after a series of heat episodes from 37°C to 52°C; however, readjustment of physiological processes toward normalization took a long time for recovery. The cell viability after heat shock was tested using 2% triphenyl tetrazolium chloride (TTC). Cells were considered viable if tissue turned purple color when treated with TTC; on the other hand, faint purple color or if tissue did not take stain was considered dead. Thus, the TTC test for tissue viability and chlorophyll accumulation after heat shock appeared to have some promise to identify thermotolerant genotypes with the ability to acquire thermotolerance. Heat-sensitive greengram genotype LGG 460 lost cell viability after heat shock and thus were identified as TTC negative. Thus, higher membrane thermostability and cell viability after heat stress could be monitored by the TTC test, and the technique has been widely used for assessment of heat tolerance (Gupta et al., 2010). The TTC reduction assay measures the level of mitochondrial respiration activity, which serves as an indicator of cell viability (Berridge et al., 2005). Variability was detected among the 56 greengram genotypes for acquired thermotolerance, ranging from 14.1% to 61.3%.

13.10.6 Expression of Heat Shock Protein

One HSP of molecular size of 101 KDa has been shown in the heat-tolerant greengram genotype EC 398889 grown under 45/30°C max/min temperature, which was absent in heat-sensitive genotype LGG 460 in SDS-PAGE (Figure 13.9). Expression of various HSPs is an adaptive strategy in heat tolerance (Yoshida et al., 2011). Some HSFs (Hsp101, HSA32, HSFA1, and HSFA3) are critical for thermotolerance and play a crucial role in stress signal transduction, protecting and repairing damaged proteins and membranes, protecting photosynthesis as well as regulating a cellular redox state (Chi et al., 2019). Hsp101 has been considered to be a molecular chaperon that imparts heat tolerance to plants (Suk and Elizabeth, 2001); furthermore, it has special significance in maintaining proper conformation of proteins and facilitates the survival of organisms in high-temperature stress. HSPs are induced by heat and strongly linked to heat tolerance (Yıldız and Terzioğlu, 2006). Different classes of HSPs play different roles in protection from stress; however, most HSPs serve as chaperons.

Stress-induced expression of HSPs are the chaperon proteins that protect the membrane and vital molecules from denaturation and other cellular machinery. Basu et al (2019) reported expression of one low molecular weight HSP approximately 100 KDa in greengram subjected to heat shock at 43°C. The molecular network of drought and heat-stress response was studied in model crops, which includes several drought stress responsive proteins or heat-stress transcription factors (DSF, HSF), and signal transduction proteins (Mittler et al., 2012). The genes identified have been found to be responsive to combined stresses drought and heat in durum wheat that include a chaperon homologous to a putative t-complex protein 1 theta chain (Rampino et al., 2012). Expression of heat shock factors, A6 and C2, have shown to enhance heat tolerance in transgenic wheat, overexpression of TaHsf in transgenics, upregulation of HSP genes in grain during grain filling under heat, and in leaves under drought stress

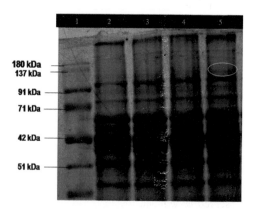

FIGURE 13.9 Expression of heat shock protein of approx. 100 KDa in heat-tolerant greengram genotype EC 398889 (Lane 5) (Basu et al., 2019).

(Hu et al., 2018). Expression of dehydration-responsive element-binding (DREB) proteins may also play a role in enhancing wheat tolerance to simultaneous heat and drought stress (Morran et al., 2011).

13.10.7 Specific Leaf Area (SLA), Chlorophyll, and Water-Use Efficiency (WUE)

SLA has been found positively correlated with delta carbon, indicating that lower values of delta carbon are associated with low SLA values. High radiation-use efficiency and high WUE are attributed to low SLA coupled with low delta carbon values, as exhibited by heat-tolerant greengram EC 398889. SLA has been reported to be associated with variation in photosynthetic capacity and chlorophyll density (Kalariya et al., 2015). High chlorophyll index measured through SPAD chlorophyll meter reading (SCMR) contributes to high photosynthesis and ultimately to increased yield. The low SLA indicates high chlorophyll content in leaves that contribute to high photosynthesis and yield (Arunyanark et al., 2009; Koolachart et al., 2013). The heat-tolerant greengram genotype EC 398889 had low SLA (leaf area g^{-1} leaf weight) with a high chlorophyll meter reading (SCMR), or greenness index, which suggested higher chlorophyll levels within a smaller leaf surface area, which enabled the plant to absorb more solar radiation per unit area of leaf in comparison with heat-sensitive greengram genotype LGG 460. More chlorophyll per unit of leaf area in EC 398889 was likely to enhance photosynthesis than in the genotypes having higher SLA and low SCMR, such as LGG 460.

13.10.8 Sucrose Synthase Activity

Sucrose synthesis in developing grains plays a crucial role in sink development and also determines the sink strength in several crops. It also acts as a signal molecule for promoting the conversion of transported sugar into starch. Sucrose synthase activity at different developmental stages differed among the pulses genotypes. In heat-tolerant chickpea genotype ICCV 92944, the sucrose synthase activity in developing seed was found to be 5 times higher than heat-sensitive genotype ICC 10685. Reduced sucrose metabolism under high temperatures has been attributed to the changes in sucrose synthase and invertase (Dai et al., 2015). The activity of sucrose synthase in developing grains of heat-sensitive greengram genotype LGG 460 remained low, whereas the tolerant genotype EC 398889, Samrat, and Virat showed a sharp increase in the activity of sucrose synthase after day 5 of pod setting with a concomitant increase in the sucrose content in developing grains. The early activation of sucrose synthase in the test genotypes EC 398889 appeared to be responsible for rapid grain filling and pod development and is likely to be associated with early pod maturity. In LGG 460, decrease in photosynthesis also limits sucrose transport to the sink, which might have influenced sink development at high temperatures. Thus, sink development is inhibited in heat-sensitive genotypes. The first step in the conversion of sucrose to starch is likely to be primarily catalyzed by sucrose synthase. These results also suggested that sucrose synthase activity could be considered a marker for sink strength. The enzymes responsible for metabolizing sucrose may regulate sucrose import into the sink. High activities of sucrose-metabolizing enzymes results in large amounts of sugar imported for metabolism and storage. Wang et al. (1993) emphasized the importance of sucrose synthase rather than acid invertase as the dominant enzyme in metabolizing imported sucrose in a growing sink. Sucrose synthase is responsible for the breakdown of sucrose, thus providing intermediates for the synthesis of starch and other polysaccharides.

13.10.9 Pollen Viability and Germination

Many legumes exhibit a high sensitivity to heat stress during flowering. One of the major yield determinants in food legumes is pollen fertility and flower shedding at high temperature. The pollen sap may be altered and becomes more viscous by progressive increase in the temperature beyond 37°C. The transformation of pollen sap into a dense and viscous fluid probably hinders the smooth movement of male gametes. A reduction in the pollen tube length was observed in the heat-tolerant chickpea ICCV 92944 and greengram genotype EC 398889 at 40°C and beyond. In contrast, multiple pollen abnormalities, including emergence of multiple tubes single or coiled forms and bursted pollen tubes, were observed in heat-sensitive greengram LGG 460 at high temperatures. Earlier reports on rice have also indicated that an increase in temperature could limit yield by affecting pollen germination and grain formation (Wassmann et al., 2009). The male gametophyte is particularly sensitive to high temperatures at all stages of development, whereas the pistil and the female gametophyte are considered to be more tolerant (Hedhly, 2011). The pollens are most sensitive to high temperature; the crop yield is affected when the temperature rises during pollen development (Ploeg Van der and Heuvelink, 2005). High temperature decreases pollen viability and leads to sterile pollens and decrease of pod set and yield (Hasanuzzaman et al., 2013). In legumes, heat stress during post-anthesis results in poor pollen germination on the stigma and reduced pollen tube growth in the style (Talwar, & Yanagahira, 1999). Under high temperatures (>30°C), flower sterility has been correlated with diminished anther dehiscence, poor shedding of pollens, and germination of pollens on stigma (Fahad et al., 2016). The reduction in photosynthesis under high temperature may also restrict the supply of photoassimilates such as sucrose, hexoses, and starch in the developing pollens, resulting in a decrease in pollen fertility (Basu et al., 2019). The role of sugars and invertase/sucrose synthase activity in anther development and pollen germination has been reported in several crops (García et al., 2013). Some of the thermotolerant food legumes flowered and set pods at high temperature. Therefore, assessment of pollen viability and *h* pollen germination at high temperature proved to be potential screening tools for heat tolerance.

13.11 Phenotyping for Drought and Heat Tolerance

Phenotyping for drought-tolerant traits involves traits such as early maturity (drought escape), large and deep root systems, high water-use efficiency, smaller leaflets, reduced canopy temperature, low carbon isotope discrimination, and high leaf chlorophyll content (drought avoidance) (Upadhyaya et al., 2012). High throughput phenotyping for drought and heat tolerance have been developed based on chlorophyll fluorescence imaging, gaseous exchange, thermal imaging, osmotic adjustment, thermal induction response (TIR), water-use efficiency, and pollen fertility (Tuberosa, 2012; Obidiegwu et al., 2015; Pratap et al., 2019; Murchie and Lawson, 2013; Reynolds et al., 2020). The genotypes screened for drought and heat tolerance were simultaneously subjected to multilocation hot spots across different climatic conditions and best lines selected. Precision phenotyping for heat tolerance in pigeonpea was done using variable fluorescence (Fv). Variable fluorescence decreases in leaves as test temperature increases beyond 35°C. In greengram, some cultivars are more drought tolerant due to enhanced ability to close the stomata in the leaves and reduce the rate of growth and leaf expansion during periods of severe water stress. Severe drought reduces vegetative growth, flower initiation, and pod set (Morton et al., 1982). There is variation in the root system in the cultivars of mungbean, which can be exploited in a breeding program to develop varieties with delayed dehydration. Greengram tend to lose more water by evapotranspiration and therefore have lower water-use efficiency, lower rates of photosynthesis, and lower rates of growth than chickpea, pigeonpea, and lentil. The crop produces less drymatter and tends to recover slowly after drought episodes. Drought-tolerance rating or sensitivity of pulses is as follows.

> Lathyrus>Horsegram>Cowpea>Pigeonpea>Chickpea>Lentil>Greengram>Blackgram>Fieldpea > Rajmash

The lethal water potential is defined as the water status of the leaf at the point where the plant cannot survive any longer. Comparative studies showed that turgor loss in pulses occurs at much lower leaf water potential than wheat and potato, indicating the high tolerance of pulses to drought. However, as compared to pigeonpea, mungbean has four times less dehydration tolerance, which needs to be improved further.

Drought and high temperature cause inhibition of photosynthesis, whereas drought is primarily responsible for stomatal closure, restricting the entry of CO_2 in the leaf and conserving cellular water by reducing transpiration (Farooq et al., 2019). High temperature adversely affects photosynthetic apparatus like PS II, thylakoid membrane, and electron transport, assimilating supply (Sharma et al., 2015) and causing oxidative stress damage due to the production of ROS in the chloroplasts and subsequent faster leaf senescence.

13.11.1 Oxidative Stress

Plants produce antioxidant enzyme systems as a defensive mechanism, which involves superoxide dismutase (SOD), catalase (CAT), and peroxidase (POX) for scavenging ROS under stressed conditions (Chen et al., 2012). Heat-sensitive genotypes of blackgram were induced to express more SOD and POX under heat treatment as a defensive mechanism of protection from ROS; however, heat-tolerant genotype is inherently tolerant to stress and therefore produces less ROS (Figure 13.10). During prolonged stress exposure, photosynthetic activity is further inhibited by excessive accumulation of ROS, causing damage to the membranes, proteins, and chlorophyll molecules of the photosynthetic apparatus (Redondo-Gómez, 2013; Awasthi et al., 2014). Plants use a complex antioxidant system to regulate ROS levels and avoid toxicity, but changes in redox status are also perceived by plants as a signature of a specific stress that will result in a corresponding acclimation response (Choudhury et al., 2017). ROS scavenging is commonly induced under drought and heat stress through enhancing antioxidant activities, and this is correlated with tolerance to stress (Suzuki et al., 2014). In some wheat genotypes, tolerance to drought or heat stress was associated with increased antioxidant capacity and reduced oxidative damage in some wheat genotypes. Under prolonged stress exposure, photosynthetic activity is further inhibited by excessive accumulation of ROS, causing damage to the membranes, proteins, and chlorophyll molecules of the photosynthetic apparatus (Redondo-Gómez, 2013).

13.11.2 Combined Effects of Drought and Heat

Combined stresses drastically decrease pigment contents due to extensive photo-inhibition and photo-destruction of pigments, protein complexes, and disruption of photosynthetic membrane (Kumari et al., 2018). Decreased chlorophyll content under drought is primarily due to either destruction of enzymes synthesizing chlorophyll or enhancing activity of enzymes that degrade chlorophyll content (Dias and Brüggemann, 2010), whereas in heat stress, reduction of chlorophyll could be due the damages of thylakoid membranes (Ristic et al., 2007). Water deficit in general alters photosynthesis, respiration, ion uptake, translocation, nutrient metabolism, carbohydrate assimilation, and growth promoters, resulting in damaged plant growth (Farooq et al., 2019). Plants under drought and heat stress tend to accumulate compatible solutes, such as soluble sugars, soluble proteins, and proline (Rivero et al., 2014). The increased accumulation of proline under drought and heat stress helps to stabilize membranes, subcellular structures, and cellular redox potential by destroying the free radicals (Kavi Kishore et al., 2005). Jin et al. (2016) reported the accumulation of certain amino acids (glutamine, ornithine, valine tryptophan, and tyrosine,) in purslane plants in response to combined drought and heat stress. Significant increase in soluble sugar contents was observed in plants subjected to drought and heat stress as compared to control

PKGU 1 (SOD) Heat sensitive   UPU 85-86 (POX) Heat tolerant   PKGU 1 (POX) Heat sensitive   UPU 85-86 (POX)Heat tolera

FIGURE 13.10 Antioxidant activity (SOD and POX) in blackgram. The SOD and POX were expressed more in heat-sensitive blackgram genotype.

(no stress). Soluble sugars and sucrose synthase activity increased with stress exposure; hence, soluble sucrose content was also increased (Asthir and Bhatia, 2014). Both drought or heat stress enhances the antioxidants' activities, such as catalase, peroxidase, superoxide dismutase, and ascorbate peroxidase (Thalmann and Santelia, 2017), which are helpful to scavenge destructive ROS, including superoxide radical (O), singlet oxygen (O), hydroxyl radical (OH), and hydrogen peroxide (H_2O_2) (Rivero et al., 2014). Drought-induced production of ROS accelerates production of abscisic acid, known to be a signal molecule under stressed conditions, and regulate the gene expressions that control the production of antioxidants, such as superoxide dismutase and catalase (Thalmann and Santelia, 2017).

13.11.3 Stem Remobilization and Respiration

Drought may reduce plant respiration due to reduction in carbon substrates available (Schauberger et al., 2017), whereas high temperature enhances respiration. The rate of grain filling from stem reserves is increased with increasing temperature, reducing grain-filling duration (Blum et al., 1994). Genetic variation for stem water-soluble carbohydrate content has been explored with known QTLs in drought or heat stress and in combined drought and heat stress. Zhang et al. (2014) explicitly investigated water-soluble carbohydrate QTLs under drought, heat, and combined drought and heat stress and were able to identify additive effects and combinations of favorable alleles for both content and remobilization, suggesting that the genetic mechanisms underlying tolerance will not depend purely on accumulation of stored carbohydrates. QTLs for respiration are now being studied in wheat for the first time under the International Wheat Yield Partnership umbrella.

13.11.4 Root Traits for Combined Tolerance to Heat and Drought

Pulses have a vigorous and extensive root system, which is essential trait for adaptation under low soil moisture conditions. Among pulses, pigeonpea and chickpea have a stronger root system as compared to lentil, rajmash, fieldpea, greengram, and blackgram. Root system of pigeonpea consists of a central tap root with numerous lateral and secondary branches. The length of the lateral roots differs with the variety; usually tall, upright varieties produce longer and more deeply penetrating roots, whereas spreading types produce shallower, more spreading, and deeper roots. Drought tolerance in pigeonpea is due to its deep-rooting taproot, reaching up to 6 feet (2 m) in depth that helps to improve water infiltration into the deep soil. Depending upon the severity of drought, the growth of the root system is stimulated and promoted to grow deeper in the soil in search of water. Among pulses, pigeonpea root characteristics have been well attributed as having the deepest roots system to adapt under a water-limiting environment and rated as the most drought-tolerant species, though genotypic variations have been reported in this crop. Pigeonpea has a prominent tap root system with considerable lateral branching (Singh and Jauhar, 2005). The lethal leaf water potential in pigeonpea is very low, suggesting that plants will not die, even under severe water stress. Pulses such as pigeonpea could be one of the most suitable crops under water-limited environments due to their special attribute of having unique root anatomical features that differentiate these crops from other species. Pigeonpea has a relatively thinner cortex than the other legumes. Xylem vessel size and the numbers are the most discriminating traits of legumes (Ramamoorthy et al., 2013). Pigeonpea conducts small quantities of water per unit time due to narrow xylem vessels that results in conservative early growth (Ramamoorthy et al., 2013). Difference in root anatomy between species revealed that pigeonpea had higher root resistance to water flow than other legumes (Sayan, 1991). Higher numbers of metaxylem facilitate water movement and also influence rapid growth. Increasing the number of metaxylem vessels would enhance the efficiency of water uptake in soybean (*Glycine max*) and decrease the yield gap in water-limited environments (Prince et al., 2017). The increases in metaxylem number has been considered as an adaptation to drought by improving root hydraulic conductivity, particularly relevant for faster growing crops under a water-limiting environment. On the contrary, narrow xylem vessels in pigeonpea increase hydraulic resistance, and in turn, passage of water is restricted, and water conductivity is finely regulated in pigeonpea through appropriate balancing of stomatal conductance so that water loss through transpiration should remain minimum. This allowed the maintenance of shoot physiological processes optimum and sustainable and longer time under water-limited conditions (Prince et al., 2017). This trait was found to be useful in enhancing grain yield under drought. The number and size of the xylem in legumes confer adaptation toward regulated water use and transpiration under limited soil moisture. Thus, pulses such as lentil, chickpea, and lathyrus can thrive well under rice fallow under zero-till conditions mainly because of greater root penetration capacity into the soil and breaking the hard middle layer soil crust along with increased hydraulic resistance of the roots due to smaller size of xylem imparting drought tolerance through restricted water-use till their maturity. Chickpea and cowpea showed moderate xylem passage per root, indicating that they are capable of absorbing water moderately and are well equipped for regular drought episodes. The extensive roots of pigeonpea act as natural ploughing of the hard deep soil, which enables infiltration of rainwater deep into the soil and thereby makes proper conditioning of the soil for subsequent crops. Pigeonpea tends to conserve water through limited root proliferation at depth and maintenance of leaf and root turgor through osmotic adjustment. With progressive decline in the soil moisture, root growth also decreases simultaneously, resulting in stomatal closure, and leaf movement becomes evident. Leaf movement in response to water stress was evident in both terminal and lateral leaflets in pigeonpea. Changes in relative water content (RWC), leaf water potential (ΨL), osmotic potential (πL), and turgor potential (PL) differed among species under drought stress. Symbiotic association of arbuscular mycorrhizae (AM) with pigeonpea had shown positive effects on the root system, plant height and stem diameter, higher chlorophyll content, photosynthetic rate, and stomatal conductance. The AM association with root in pigeonpea confers enhanced tolerance to drought through soluble sugar as osmotic solute (Qiao et al., 2011). A large intraspecific and varietal difference in a number of root traits has been reported by Mia Mel et al. (1996). Chickpea produces thick and long laterals roots while branching frequency of thinner laterals roots are high in groundnut and pigeonpea. The pigeonpea and groundnut are more efficient in the uptake of nutrients compared to chickpea, which could be related to the high proliferation of the thin lower order roots. Therefore, pigeonpea and groundnut, among the legumes, and sorghum and millet, among the cereals, had a relative advantage in the acquisition of low available nutrients due to the large proliferation of thin higher order lateral roots (Rao and Ito, 1998). The extensive root system of pigeonpea improves soil structure by breaking plow pans, and enhances water-holding capacity of the soil (Mallikarjuna et al., 2011). Its deep taproot is able to extract nutrients (like P) from the soil low layers, and bring them to upper layers, where they can benefit other crops (Valenzuela, 2011).

13.11.5 Relevance of Combined Tolerance to Heat and Drought in Pulses

Winter pulses, such as chickpea and lentils, and summer pulses, such as pigeonpea, are often exposed to drought and high temperatures simultaneously, particularly during the reproductive stage. The combined effects are more detrimental in terms of reducing grain number or weight, incomplete grain development, or reduced seed size. In several other crops such as wheat, genetic variation and underlying quantitative trait loci for either individual stress is known (Collins et al., 2008). The combination of the two stresses has rarely been investigated, and genetic loci controlling tolerance to the combined stress are likely to differ from those for drought or heat stress tolerance alone. A precise and fine control of water relations during the entire growth period could be beneficial for combined tolerance.

13.11.6 Strategies to Improve Yield under the Changing Scenario of Climate

13.11.6.1 Identification of Cultivars with Wider Adaptablity

Pigeonpea is highly sensitive to photo thermoperiods (Basu et al., 2016). The crop phenology and yield is highly influenced by changing the photothermal regimes. Acquiring photothermal insensitivity traits into the pigeonpea genotypes could be one of strongest breeding approaches toward stabilizing the grain yield across different environments (Yan and Hunt, 2010). The simplest way to ensure genetic stability in diverse pigeonpea genotypes is to evaluate them in diverse climatic conditions with varying temperature and daylength regimes. The yield and phenological stability have been worked out based on multilocation trials conducted for consecutive several years of testing. About 275 contrasting pigeonpea genotypes, including mini-core collection from ICRISAT, India, were evaluated under irrigated and rainfed conditions at five locations of India. Based on the multilocation data and morphological traits *viz.* days to flower initiation, days to 50% flowering, plant height, physiological maturity, pod bearing length, number of pods per plant, pod length, number of seeds per pod, 100-seed weight, and seed yield per plant, a few genotypes were identified, such as, RVK275, JKM 189, AKT 9913, Bennur Local, VKS-11–24-2, ICP-8840, ICP 3451, ICP 348, BSMR-736, and JSA 59, showing stable yield, which might have possessed photothermoinsensitive character.

Thus, in order to identify photothermoinsensitive pulse germplasms, the best way to grow a set of germplasms under diverse climatic conditions is to have different photothermoperiods. The genotypes showing little change in phenology, biomass, yield, and maturity across different environments were selected as stable genotypes with wider adaptability. Photoinsensitive and thermotolerant greengram genotypes setting pods at 43/25°C max/min temperature and 11 h and 16 h daylength were identified in greengram, such as IPM 02–3; MH 3–18: Ganga 8; TARM 1; ML 1257; Copergaon; HUM 1. Greengram accessions were evaluated and characterized based on 37 morpho-physiological traits across diverse climates. Two extra early greengram genotypes, IPM 409-4 (INGR 11044) and IPM 205-7 (INGR 11043), have been developed based on multilocation trial.

13.11.6.2 Osmotic Adjustment

When different pulses were evaluated for photosynthesis at high temperature (37°C) with increasing level of water stress, it was observed that maximum net photosynthetic rates (Pmax) at saturated light intensity declined to almost zero at moderate stress level ranging between −1.5 to −2.0 MPa in greengram and blackgram, whereas reduction of photosynthesis in pigeonpea and chickpea was observed at much higher level of stress (−2.5 MPa) and also combined drought and heat caused less inhibition of photosynthesis in pigeonpea and chickpea. The low reduction in the Pmax in chickpea and pigeonpea could be due to higher osmotic adjustment as compared to greengram and blackgram. The degree of osmotic adjustment (OA) has also been shown to be correlated with yield under dry land conditions in pulses. Among pulses, chickpea and pigeonpea are more drought tolerant by virtue of high osmotic adjustment and deep root system as compared to greengram and blackgram (Table 13.1). Genetic diversity of OA can be exploited to inherit strong drought-tolerant mungbean with fewer water requirements as water demand is proportionately less if OA increases. Moreover, OA increases only when drought is intensified. A large number of different food legumes were evaluated under drought environment based on OA. The best genotypes across different environments had high osmotic adjustment. Many crop species accumulate organic osmolytes during the process of cellular dehydration (Ingram and Bartels, 1996). The active accumulation of compatible solutes known as OA, such as proline, pinitol, mannitol, trehalose, and glycine betaine, are controlled by genes and have been considered as an adaptive role to protect subcellular structure. The increase in cellular osmolarity allows influx of water into cells and maintains the necessary turgor for cell expansion, maintains membrane

TABLE 13.1

Range of Osmotic Adjustment and Rooting Behavior of Some Pulses and Their Drought-Tolerance Characteristics

Species (Pulses)	Range osmotic adjustment (M Pa) in leaves	Degree of dehydration postpontment	Root system	Lethal water potential (M Pa)	Dehydration tolerance
Pigeonpea	0.1 to 1.4	High	Very high and deep	−7.0 to −8.2	Very high
Chickpea	0.0 to 1.3	High	High and deep	−3.0 to −5.0	High
Lentil	0.0 to 0.6	Moderate	Moderately high	−1.8 to −3.5	Moderately high
Greengram	0.3 to 0.4	Low	Moderate	−1.9	Low
Black gram	0.4 to 0.5	Low	Moderately high	−1.2 to −2.5	Moderate

integrity, prevents protein denaturation under adverse environmental conditions, such as drought or high or low temperatures (Crowe et al., 1992), and confers protection against oxidative damage (Rhodes and Hanson, 1993). The accumulation of mannitol in chloroplasts leads to increased resistance to oxidative stress in tobacco (Shen et al., 1997). The accumulation of osmolyte in response to drought has a critical role in the mitigation or avoiding/delaying the adverse effects of stress. The accumulation of osmo-regulatory solutes has been considered as a unique biochemical trait that could be manipulated by breeding or transformation technologies.

13.11.6.3 Modification of Crop Duration and Phenology with High Biomass

Identification and development of heat-tolerant genotypes is an important aspect of food legume breeding under climate change. Simple adaptations such as change in planting dates and development of crop varieties resilient to climate extremities could help in reducing impacts of climate change. In mungbean, extra early maturing genotypes (IPM 205-7and IPM 409-4) have been developed that mature in 46–48 days (Pratap et al., 2013). Improving reproductive-stage tolerance through selection and short duration varieties escaping terminal heat and drought should be the primary goal to develop climate-resilient pulses. Phenotypic plasticity i.e. adjusting flowering time (daylength and temperature) is one of the best strategies for adaptation of pulses in diverse climates. This needs to be properly exploited to develop many short-duration varieties.

13.12 Traits Intogression for Combined Tolerance

13.12.1 Use of Wild Accessions

The pulses have narrow genetic diversity to accept the challenges of global warming and associated changes in water availability (Rana et al., 2016). Therefore, it is necessary to exploit wild species and land races for extensive gene mining for useful adaptive traits/genes to incorporate into our present cultivars. The wild species are the rich sources of many useful genes (Choudhary et al., 2018) as they have evolved under natural selection to survive climatic extremes and can potentially provide further genetic gains (Maxted and Kell, 2009). Therefore, wild species need to be exploited in genetic improvement programs to alleviate the challenges of global warming and its related effects in pulses. Two wild accessions of *Vigna* were identified as photothermoinsensitive. These include one accession each of *V. glabrescens* (IC 251372) and *V. umbellata* (IC 251442) based upon viable pollen and normal pollen tube formation, podding, and seed set at high temperature up to 44°C and low temperature up to 4.4°C. Distant hybridization program for climate resilience in mungbean was initiated using this wild *Vigna* species.

Wild relatives of pigeonpea are known to have many useful traits for tolerance to various abiotic stresses (Choudhary et al., 2018). The wild species of pigeonpea, like *C. Sericious, C. Scarabaeoides,* and *C. Aquitifolius,* showed a high degree of osmotic adjustment, OA (−2.5 to −5.0 MPa), imparting drought and heat tolerance based on the chlorophyll fluorescence imaging and pollen fertility test. These wild species showed fertile pollens and pod setting under severe drought. The photothermoinsensitive accession of wild *C. scarabaeoides* ICP 15671 demonstrated high OA and normal pollen germination at temperatures as high as 47°C. The heat tolerant ICP 15671 showed normal pollen fertility and the ability to set pods even at 47°C (Figure 13.11, 13.12). The accumulation of osmolytes with higher order plays a major role as thermo and dessication protectant preventing damage of membrane and vital macromolecules. This wild species is photothermoinsensitive as well as heat and drought tolerant; therefore, this wild *Cajanas sps* (ICP 15671) appeared to be a potential reservoir of genes for multiple abiotic stress tolerance. Many wild derivatives developed from crosses *C. cajans cajan* × *C. scarabaeoides* (ICP 15671) showed significant genetic variation in the combined tolerance to both drought and heat stress. The pre-breeding line ICP 711 developed from a cross between cultivated vs wild chickpea *C. arietinum* × *C. judaicum* showed an increased number of primary branches, pods per plant, and green seeds for further use in the chickpea improvement program (Brumlop et al., 2013).

Under drought (44% podding)   Under Irrigated (55% podding)

FIGURE 13.11 Wild pigeonpea *Cajanas scarabaeoides* having combined tolerance to drought and heat.

(a)   (b)

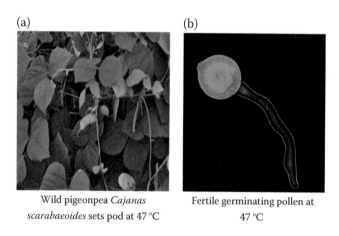

Wild pigeonpea *Cajanas*   Fertile germinating pollen at
scarabaeoides sets pod at 47 °C   47 °C

FIGURE 13.12 Wild accession ICP 15671 showing pod setting at 47°C.

13.12.2 Sources of Heat-Tolerant Genotypes in Pulses

The precise phenotyping demonstrated significant differences in the light-temperature response of photosynthesis, chlorophyll fluorescence imaging of quantum yield (Fv/Fm), electron transport rate (ETR), rooting behavior, water-use efficiency, membrane stability, acquired thermotolerance and pollen fertility, and sucrose synthase (SuSy) activity among diverse pulse germplasm. The pollen germination and SuSy activity were high at 40°C in heat-tolerant greengram EC 398889, and that enabled faster grain filling under high temperature. Molecular profiling of selected accessions showed polymorphism with 11 SSR markers, and the markers CEDG147, CEDG247, and CEDG044 distinguished tolerant (EC 398889) and sensitive groups (LGG 460) of accessions. Based on multilocation evaluation, a panel of 97 blackgram diverse genotypes was assessed for yield under stress and non-stress conditions with an aim to identify heat-tolerant genotypes. This study identified 8 highly heat-tolerant and 35 highly heat-sensitive genotypes based on heat susceptibility index. Further, based on physiological and biochemical characterization, a group of six highly heat-sensitive and seven highly heat-tolerant urdbean genotypes were identified showing variability in leaf nitrogen balance index (NBI), chlorophyll (SPAD), epidermal flavnols, chlorophyll fluorescence, anthocyanin contents, pollen fertility, and antioxidative enzymes activity when grown at 42/25°C max/min temperature. The most highly sensitive genotype PKGU-1 showed a decrease in different fluorescence parameters with a reduction in the quantum yield of PS II as compared to a tolerant genotype. Fluorescence kinetics showed the delayed quenching of maximal fluorescence, Fm, in highly heat sensitive (PKGU 1) and fast quenching in tolerant (UPU 85–86) genotypes, respectively. Moreover, tolerant genotype (UPU 85–86) had high antioxidant activities, explaining their role for scavenging superoxide radicals (ROS), protecting delicate membranes from oxidative damage. Molecular characterization further pinpointed genetic differences between heat-tolerant (UPU 85–86) and heat-sensitive genotypes (PKGU 1). Some of the pulse germplasms were identified for different abiotic stress tolerance, which are listed in Table 13.2.

13.12.3 Genomic and Transgenic Approaches

The development of candidate gene markers for crucial heat-tolerance genes may allow for the development of new cultivars with increased abiotic stress tolerance using marker-assisted selection (Jespersen et al., 2017). Molecular profiling of greengram accessions was done using 79 SSR markers, of which 11 were polymorphic. Among the polymorphic primers, three markers showed a clear differentiation between heat-tolerant and heat-susceptible genotypes. These markers exhibited a large amount of genetic variability among different accessions. The marker CEDG 147 distinguished tolerant and susceptible group of accessions and amplified at 300 bp in the heat-tolerant genotype EC 398889 and at 285 bp in sensitive genotype LGG 460 (Figure 13.13). Similarly, another marker CEDG 247 also distinguished heat-tolerant and heat-susceptible genotypes at 161 and 168 bp, respectively. Likewise, marker CEDG 044 distinguished between tolerant and sensitive genotypes at 192 and 162 bp, respectively.

Molecular marker analysis was done in 58 genotypes of *Vigna*, including 50 wild accessions and 4 standard check cultivars, each of mungbean and urdbean. These genotypes were subjected to SSR screening using already reported 87 primer pairs from *Phaseolus*, adzuki bean, mungbean, and urdbean background. Fifty-two (52) SSRs have been screened for diversity analysis in all 58 accessions, among which 40 were found polymorphic, whereas 12 were found monomorphic.

The linked QTLs for root and high yield (MAS) have been identified. Molecular markers will soon be available for major heat tolerance QTL in some legumes, which will further facilitate breeding for heat and drought tolerance. The induction of multiple signals leads to changes in specific gene expression. The expression of HSPs, ranging from 10kDa to 100 kDa in different species of plant, play significant role in heat adaptation. Other proteins are also synthesized, which function as molecular chaperons, helping in folding and unfolding of essential proteins under stress, and ensuring three-dimensional structure of proteins for sustained cellular functions and survival under heat stress (Wahid et al., 2007). Recently, molecular markers have been used to decipher the genetics underlying the heat tolerance and quantitative trait loci (QTL)/genes for key morpho-physiological traits contributing to heat tolerance, and they have been mapped in several crops (Paliwal et al., 2012). Several molecular markers, including simple sequence repeats (SSRs), genic SSRs, and single nucleotide polymorphisms (SNPs), are available for QTL mapping in lentil (Hamwieh et al., 2009; Kaur et al., 2014). Functional markers (FMs), such as intron spanning markers (ISMs), have also been developed in lentil (Gupta et al., 2018). Having complete linkage to the favorable alleles and located in or near candidate genes of interest (Andersen and Lübberstedt, 2003), these markers can be used in breeding programs for identifying individuals or lines carrying those particular genes (Kalendar et al., 2011). Markers developed from the gene sequences encoding the different HSPs have been used to characterize heat tolerant and sensitive genotypes in maize (Ristic et al., 1998). These markers have also been used to characterize heat-tolerant genotypes of lentil. Further, in the case of SSR marker data-based dendrogram, a highly heat-tolerant blackgram genotype (UPU 85–86) was distinctly clustered from the highly heat-sensitive genotype (PKGU-1).

13.12.4 Genes for Drought Tolerance in Pulses

In response to drought, different genes are expressed at the transcriptional level and play a vital role toward tolerance to drought. Stress proteins produced may play an important role in stress tolerance by hydration of cellular structure. The expression of stress-responsive genes may enhance yield under adverse conditions (Priyanka et al., 2010a). The genes expressed in pigeonpea are induced by water

TABLE 13.2

List of Some Promising Tolerant Pulses Lines Identified Based Upon Precision Phenotyping

Food legumes	Stable heat/drought-tolerant genotype	Heat-sensitive genotype	Source	Screening method	References
Chickpea	ICC 456, ICC 637, ICC 1205, ICC 3362, ICC 3761, ICC 4495, ICC 4958, ICC 4991, ICC 6279, ICC 6874, ICC 7441, ICC 8950, ICC 11944, ICC 12155, ICC 14402, ICC 14778, ICC 14815, ICC 14346, ICC 5597, ICC 5829, ICC 6121, ICC 7410, ICC 11916, ICC 13124, ICC 14284, ICC 14368, ICC 14653, ICCV 92944, ICC 98902, ICC 15614, ICC 11944, ICC 12155	ICC 4567, ICC 10685, ICC 10755, ICC 16374	ICRISAT, India reference set	Heat tolerance index (HTI), phenology and yield attributes at high temperature	Krishnamurthy et al., 2011; Gaur et al., 2015
				Membrane stability index, chlorophyll fluorescence, pollen fertility at high temperature	Devashirvatham et al., 2012
Pigeonpea	RVK-275, JKM 189, AKT-9913, ICP-3451, ICP-12654, ICP-348, BENNUR LOCAL, ICP-8840, ICP-13304, JKM-7, ICP 6049, BSMR-736, VKS-11–24-2, JSA-59, JKM-7, ICP-14832, Bahar. Wild accession of *Cajanus Scarabaeoides* (Acc 15671), *C. aaquitifolius, C. sericious*	CPL-8863 AL-1809 ICPL-332 AK-101 ICP-15685	Landraces, local collection, ICRISAT released varieties	Osmotic adjustment, chlorophyll fluorescence, pollen germination	
Lentil	IG 3330, IG 2507, IG 4258, IG 3546, IG 3327, ILL 10712	DPL 15, IG 3973, IG 3364, IG3575, IG 3568	ICARDA, USDA, PAU Ludhiana, India, IIPR, Kanpur, India	Pollen viability, chlorophyll fluorescence, membrane stability, molecular characterization	Kumar et al., 2017
Blackgram	UPU 85–86, IPU 94-2, IPU 98/36, NO 5731, PGRU 95016, PLU 1, PLU 1, BGP 247	IPU 99–200, IC 21001, Shekhar 2, PU19, H-1, PKGU 1	Germplasm collection from different origins, released cultivars	Heat susceptibility index (HSI), chlrophyll fluorescence, antioxidant enzyme expression, membrane stability index	Sengupta et al., 2021
Greengram	Ganga 8, HUM-12, China mung 1, IPM 02–14, IPM 99–125, PDM-262, EC-520011, EC 398889, PDM-87, IPM-02-3(red), Sona Yellow, HUM-16, UPM-02-17, IPM-02-1, TARAM 2, GM-9911, ML-1256	MH 2–15, Pusa 672, ML-5, EC-581523, NSB 007, CO4 KM-2241, SML-191 Kopergaon, LGG 460, Vamban 3	Germplasm collection, released cultivars	Pollen germination, chlrophyll fluorescence, antioxidant enzyme expression, membrane stability index, molecular characterization	Basu et al., 2019

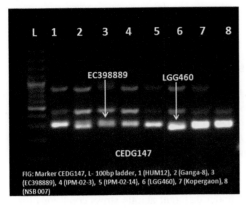

FIG: Marker CEDG147, L- 100bp ladder, 1 (HUM12), 2 (Ganga-8), 3 (EC398889), 4 (IPM-02-3), 5 (IPM-02-14), 6 (LGG460), 7 (Kopergaon), 8 (NSB 007)

FIGURE 13.13 Differentiation of heat-tolerant (EC 398889) and sensitive greengram (LG 460) genotypes based upon molecular marker CEDG147.

stress with diverse functional groups such as transporter genes, osmotic stress genes, signal transduction, and transcriptional regulator genes and biological (metabolism, structural organization, DNA and RNA processing) process genes etc. (Priya et al., 2010). They can recognize a large number of stress-related proteins that confer adaption to drought. Suppression subtractive hybridization (SSH) technique and differentially expressed ESTs (expressed sequenced tags) identified from root tissues of pigeonpea were able to identify candidate targets potentially associated with drought tolerance (Priyanka et al., 2010b). The expression of selected drought-induced genes upregulate ornithine aminotransferase, peroxidase, DREB, and cyclophilin in pigeonpea (Choudhary et al., 2017). Over-expression of *Cajanus cajan* CYP (CcCYP) gene in Arabidopsis plants has shown marked tolerance against major abiotic stresses, suggesting this gene plays a major role in abiotic stress tolerance in pigeonpea (Sekhar et al., 2010). Earlier reports indicated that increased osmotic tolerance in transgenic tobacco plants accumulating proline (Kavi Kishor et al.,1995), fructans (Pilon-Smits et al., 1995), and mannitol (Tarczynski et al., 1993) led to increased root-shoot ratios. It is also required to identify QTLs for canopy temperature depression in pigeonpea and other pulses. Several QTLs have been identified for canopy temperature depression under drought in wheat (Pinto and Reynolds, 2015). Cooler canopy genotypes are able to extract more water at depths under water stress due to a greater proportion of deeper roots (Pinto and Reynolds, 2015).

13.12.5 Transgenic Approach

Drought-specific genes, Dreb 1A, Dreb 1B, and Osmotin, are being used for developing drought-tolerant chickpea, mungbean, and pigeonpea. Transgenic chickpea lines carrying transcription factor, dehydration responsive element- binding protein 1A from *Arabidopsis thaliana* (AtDREB1A gene) driven by stress-inducible promoter rd29a, have been developed, with an aim of enhancing drought tolerance in chickpea (Das et al., 2021). The transgenic line showed 10% increase in yield, photo-synthesis and water-use efficiency with enhanced tolerance under water-deficit conditions. Based on non-invasive chlorophyll fluorescence imaging, carbon isotope discrimination, osmotic adjustment, and membrane stability index, it indicated that AtDREB1A transgenic chickpea lines are physiologically better adapted to water-deficit conditions.

13.12.6 Signaling and Drought Stress Tolerance

Plants have different mechanisms to detect drought or heat stress through various signaling effects (Zhu, 2016). Among these chemical signals that involve ROS, calcium, calcium-regulated proteins, and Mitogen-activated protein kinase cascades and cross-talk between different transcription factors (Zhang et al., 2016), mitogen-activated protein kinase plays an important role in signal transmission and connecting the perception of external stimuli to cellular responses (Sinha et al., 2011). It has been reported that osmotic adjustment, abscisic acid, and induction of dehydrins are the vital players, providing drought tolerance by preserving high tissue water potential in cells. Drought-specific signal molecules ABA and their role in drought tolerance have been characterized. Among many signalling effects, the role of Ca^{++} is considered to be important.

13.12.7 Molecular Markers for Adaptive Traits

Genes controlling traits for wider adaptability appear to be important for developing abiotic stress-tolerant pulses. Efforts have been made to identify genes/QTLs in chickpea, pigeonpea, and other pulse crops. Identification of QTLs/genes for pods per plant (qPD4.1) and flowering (qFL4.1 and qFL5.1) in pigeonpea (Kumawat et al., 2012), QTLs (*HQTL-1* and *HQTL-2*) for pollen viability in azuki bean, and thermotolerance (Thudi et al., 2014) in chickpea and lentil may be helpful to construct new plant types for stress environments (Kumar et al., 2017). Paul et al. (2018a) identified QTLs associated with heat tolerance comprising 25 putative candidate genes in chickpea from recombinant inbred lines (RILs) of a mapping population. Diaz et al. (2018) evaluated RILs under different abiotic stress conditions for a number of traits and identified molecular markers linked with QTLs for abiotic stress tolerance. Genetic variation for stem water-soluble carbohydrate content has been explored with known QTLs in drought or heat stress and in combined drought and heat stress. Zhang et al. (2014) investigated water-soluble carbohydrate QTLs under drought, heat, and combined drought and heat stress and identified additive effects and combinations of favorable alleles for remobilization. QTLs for respiration are now being studied in wheat under the International Wheat Yield Partnership umbrella.

13.12.8 Genomics Approaches for Stress Tolerance

Genomics tools are becoming an integral part of current conventional breeding, which could be applied for genetic improvement for climate-smart pulses. Genome sequences of major pulses, including pigeonpea, are now available in the public domain (Varshney et al., 2019). Development of next-generation sequencing (NGS)-based genomics tools led to the identification of the functional and regulatory genes controlling abiotic stress tolerance in many pulses (Abdelrahman et al., 2018). These NGS tools have helped to develop SNP and INDEL markers (Doddamani et al., 2014) and expression atlases (Kudapa et al., 2018) to understand the signaling pathways for tolerance to various abiotic stresses in different pulses (Abdelrahman et al., 2018).

13.12.9 Conventional and Omics-Based Breeding for Stress Tolerance

Tailoring suitable plant types with improved adaptability in diverse climatic conditions is now required. An ideal plant type of pigeonpea has been conceptualized comprising early flowering, a deep-rooted system, fast seedling emergence with early vigor; indeterminate growth; spreading or semispreading branches; a large number of secondary and tertiary branches with profuse flowering bunches; long podding branches etc (Saxena et al., 2018). Earliness, has been considered as an escape mechanism from drought and terminal heat stresses, and incorporations of earliness in pulses has been quite a successful strategy in all breeding programs (Kashiwagi et al., 2015). In chickpea, significant progress has been made toward developing early maturing varieties (Kumar et al., 1996). The extra or super-early variety has been developed in chickpea (Kumar and van Rheenen, 2000) and pigeonpea (Vales et al., 2012) by International Crops Research Institute for the SemiArid Tropics (ICRISAT). Different—omics fields, such as genomics, transcriptomics, epigenomics, proteomics, metabolomics, and phenomics, have emerged recently that have enabled speeding up of breeding programs more precisely for the major food crops (Parry and Hawkesford, 2012). Similarly, omics-based strategies can also be used to develop climate-smart pulses.

13.13 Conclusions

Pulses such as chickpea, pigeonpea, lathyrus, cowpea, horsegram, and lentil are inherently drought tolerant as compared to other food legumes, such as greengram, blackgram, fieldpea, and kidney beans.

In spite of inherent drought tolerance, pulses are often subjected to drought and heat stress at the terminal reproductive phase if the severity of these stresses is intensified, resulting in significant yield loss. Early flower and plant vigor, faster canopy development, vigorous root system, and osmotic adjustment are the common traits toward escaping terminal heat and drought stress in pulses. Targeting traits toward improving water relation characteristics should be the primary focus. Both heat and drought stress inhibit photosynthesis and reduce biomass and plant growth by altering the plant's water relation characteristics. The reproductive stage is very sensitive to drought and heat. There are ample opportunities for genetic enhancement of osmotic adjustment, water-use efficiency, root characteristics for early and efficient water mining, modifying size of the stomatal aperture, and density for conserving moisture. Gene mining for tolerance to abiotic stresses, restructuring plant types, changing cropping pattern, and efficient nutrient and water management are some of the better options to address climate change. To improve pulses for combined tolerance, the germplasm must acquire photothermo-insensitivity, having been least influenced by different climatic conditions. For combined stress, water relations characteristics should be much stronger to cope with both stresses. Useful traits are likely to be attributed by finely regulated transpiration through small, dense stomata; maintenance of optimal hydraulic conductance in different tissues; a fast-growing deep root system; the ability to retain water in essential organs to avoid tissue dehydration; and efficient HSPs to protect enzymes and membranes against high temperature with efficient ROS scavenging system. Adequate genetic resources are available that could be utilized and characterized for combined tolerance. Some of important traits, such as deep and higher root length density, osmotic adjustment, stable photosynthetic system, higher water-use efficiency, and thermoresistant rhizobium strains for nodulation, may play a critical role in imparting combined tolerance to drought and heat. The rationale for identifying and deploying alleles for combined drought and heat tolerance in pulse breeding is essential. Precision phenotyping of physiological traits conferring tolerance to drought and heat and genomic information have been made available. A large genetic variation in morphophysiological traits have been identified, and using precision phenotyping, the tolerance level of genotypes can be quantified. This precision phenotyping, which includes chlrophyll fluorescence imaging, thermal imaging, NDVI and SCMR values, membrane stability, acquired thermotolerance, antioxidants activity, osmotic adjustment, pollen fertility, specific leaf area and chlorophyll, carbon isotope discrimination, and expression of HSPs, has been well established. Several pulse germplasms have been identified using these phenotyping methods and are being heavily utilized as donors for developing climate-resilient varieties under breeding programs. Genomics, transcriptomics, epigenomics, proteomics, metabolomics, and phenomics tools have enabled speeding up of breeding programs more precisely.

REFERENCES

Abdelrahman, M., S. Jogaiah, D.J. Burritt, and L.S.P. Tran. 2018. Legume genetic resources and transcriptome dynamics under abiotic stress conditions. *Plant Cell Environment* 41:1972–1983.

Acevedo, M., K. Pixley, N. Zinyengere, S. Meng, H. Tufan, K. KarenCichy, L. Bizikova, K. Isaacs, K. Ghezzi-Kopel, and J. Porciello. 2020. A scoping review of adoption of climate-resilient crops by small-scale producers in low-and middle-income countries. *Nature Plants* 6:1231–1241. doi: 10.1038/s41477-020-00783-z

Ahmad, A., H. Diwan, and Y.P. Abrol. 2010. Global climate change, stress and plant productivity. In A. Pareek, S.K. Sopory, H.J. Bohnert, and Govindjee (Eds.), *Abiotic stress adaptation in plants: Physiological, molecular and genome foundation by* (pp. 503–521). Dordrecht: Springer Science Business Media BV. doi: 10.1007/978-90-481-3112-9_23

Allakhverdiev, S.I., V.V. Klimov, and R. Carpentier. 1997. Evidence for 55 the involvement of cyclic electron transport in the protection of photosystem II against photoinhibition: Influence of a new phenolic compound. *Biochemistry* 36:4149–4154. doi: 10.1021/bi962170

Allakhverdiev, S.I., and N. Murata. 2004. Environmental stress inhibits the synthesis de novo of proteins involved in the photodamage–repair cycle of Photosystem II in Synechocystis sp. PCC 6803. *Biochimica et Biophysica Acta (BBA) - Bioenergetics* 1657:23–32. doi: 10.1016/j.bbabio.2004.03.003

Andersen, J.R., and T. Lübberstedt. 2003. Functional markers in plants. *Trends in Plant Science* 8: 554–560. doi: 10.1016/j.tplants.2003.09.010

Arunyanark, A., S. Jogloy, N. Vorasoot, C. Akkasaeng, T. Kesmala, and A. Patanothai. 2009. Stability of relationship between chlorophyll density and soil plant analysis development chlorophyll meter readings in peanut across different drought stress conditions. *Asian Journal of Plant Science* 8:102–110. doi: 10.3923/ajps.2009.102.110

Asha latha, K.V., G. Munisamy, and A.R.S. Bhat. 2012. Impact of climate change on rainfed agriculture in India: A case study of Dharwad. *International Journal of Environmental Science and Development* 3:368–371.

Asseng, S., F. Ewert, P. Martre, R.P. Rötter, D.B. Lobell, D. Cammarano, B.A. Kimball, M.J. Ottman, G.W. Wall, J.W. White, et al. 2015. Rising temperatures reduce global wheat production. *Nature Climate Change* 5:143–147. doi: 10.1038/nclimate2470

Asthir, B., and S. Bhatia. 2014. In vivo studies on artificial induction of thermo-tolerance to detached panicles of wheat (Triticum aestivum L) cultivars under heat stress. *Journal Food Science and Technology* 51:118–123.

Awasthi, R., N. Kaushal, V. Vadez, N.C. Turner, J. Berger, K.H.M. Siddique, and H. Nayyar. 2014. Individual and combined effects of transient drought and heat stress on carbon assimilation and seed filling in chickpea. *Functional Plant Biology* 41:1148–1167.

Barghi, S.S., H. Mostafaii, F. Peighami, and R.A. Zakaria. 2012. Path analysis of yield and its components in lentil under end season heat condition. *International Journal of Agriculture Research Review* 2:969–974.

Barghi, S.S., H. Mostafaii, F. Peighami, R.A. Zakaria, and R.F. Nejhad. 2013. Response of in vitro pollen germination and cell membrane thermostability of lentil genotypes to high temperature. *International Journal of Agriculture Research Review* 3:13–20.

Barnabás, B., K. Jager, and A. Feher. 2008. The effect of drought and heat stress on reproductive processes in cereals. *Plant Cell and Environment* 31:11–38.

Basu, P.S., A. Pratap, S. Gupta, K. Sharma, R. Tomar, and N.P. Singh. 2019. Physiological traits for shortening crop duration and improving productivity of greengram (Vigna radiata L. Wilczek) under high temperature. *Frontiers in Plant Science* 10:1508. doi: 10.3389/fpls.2019.01508

Basu, P.S., U. Singh, A. Kumar, C.S. Praharaj, and R.K. Shivran. 2016. Climate change and its mitigation strategies in pulses production. *Indian Journal of Agronomy* 61:S71–S82.

Bernacchi, C., P. Morgan, D. Ort, and S., Long. 2005. The growth of soybean under free air [CO_2] enrichment (FACE) stimulates photosynthesis while decreasing in vivo Rubisco capacity. *Planta* 220:434–446. doi: 10.1007/s00425-004-1320-8

Berridge, M., P. Herst, and A. Tan. 2005. Tetrazolium dyes as tools in cell biology: New insights into their cellular reduction. *Biotechnology Annual Review* 11:127–152. doi: 10.1016/S1387-2656(05)11004-7

Bindumadhava, H.R., R.M. Nair, and H. Nayyar. 2016. Salinity and high temperature tolerance in mungbean [Vigna radiata (L.) Wilczek] from a physiological perspective. *Frontiers in Plant Science* 7:957. doi: 10.3389/fpls.2016.00957

Blum, A., B. Sinmena, J. Mayer, G. Golan, and L. Shpiler. 1994. Stem reserve mobilisation supports wheat-grain filling under heat stress. *Functional Plant Biology* 21:771–781.

Blum, A. 1998. Drought resistance, water-use efficiency, and yield potential—are they compatible, dissonant, or mutually exclusive? *Australian Journal of Agricultural Research* 56:1159–1168. doi: 10.1071/AR05069

Blum, A., N. Klueva, and H.T. Nguyen. 2001. Wheat cellular thermotolerance is related to yield under heat stress. *Euphytica* 117:117–123. doi: 10.1023/A:1004083305905

Board, J.E. and C.S. Kahlon. 2011. Soybean yield formation: What controls it and how it can be improved? In H.A. ElShemy (Ed.), *Soybean physiology and biochemistry* (pp. 1–36). Rijeka: InTech Open Access.

Boote, K.J., L.H. Allen, P.V.V. Prasad, J.T. Baker, R.W. Gesch, A.M. Snyder, D. Pan, and J.M.G. Thomas. 2005. Elevated temperature and CO_2 impacts on pollination, reproductive growth, and yield of several globally important crops. *Journal of Agricultural Meteorology* 60:469–474.

Brumplop, S., Reichenbecher W., Tappeser B., and M.R. Finckh. 2013. What is the SMARTest way to breed plants and increase agrobiodi-versity? *Euphytica* 194:53–66.

Challinor, A., T. Wheeler, C. Garforth, P. Craufurd, and A. Kassam. 2007. Assessing the vulnerability of food crop systems in Africa to climate change. *Climate Change* 83:381–399. doi: 10.1007/s10584-007-9249-0

Chauhan, Y.S., and R. Williams. 2018. Physiological and agronomic strategies to increase Mungbean yield in climatically variable environments of Northern Australia. *Agronomy* 8:83. doi: 10.3390/agronomy8060083

Chen, J., W. Xu, J. Velten, Z. Xin, and J., Stout. 2012. Characterization of maize inbred lines for drought and heat tolerance. *Journal of Soil and Water Conservation* 67:354–364.

Chen, J., J.J. Burke, and Z. Xin. 2018. Chlorophyll fluorescence analysis revealed essential roles of FtsH11 protease in regulation of the adaptive responses of photosynthetic systems to high temperature. *BMC Plant Biology* 18:11. doi: 10.1186/s12870-018-1228-2

Chi, Y.H., S.S. Koo, H.T. Oh, F.S. Lee, J.H. Park, K.A. Thi Phan, et al. 2019. The physiological functions of universal stress proteins and their molecular mechanism to protect plants from environmental stresses. *Frontiers in Plant Science* 10:750. doi: 10.3389/fpls.2019.00750

Choudhary, A.K., R. Sultana, M.I. Vales, K.B. Saxena, R.R. Kumar, and P. Ratnakumar. 2018. Integrated physiological and molecular approaches to improvement of abiotic stress tolerance in two pulse crops of the semi-arid tropics. *Crop Journal* 6:99–114.

Choudhury, F.K., R.M. Rivero, E. Blumwald, and R. Mittler. 2017. Reactive oxygen species, abiotic stress and stress combination. *The Plant Journal* 90:856–867.

Clarke, H.J. and K.H.M. Siddique. 2004. Response of chickpea genotypes to low temperature stress during reproductive development. *Field Crops Research* 90:323–334. ISSN 0378-4290 10.101 6/j.fcr.2004.04.001

Collins, N.C., F. Tardieu, and R. Tuberosa. 2008. Quantitative trait loci and crop performance under abiotic stress: Where do we stand? *Plant Physiology* 147:469–486. doi: 10.1104/pp.108.118117

Crafts-Brandner, S.J., and M.E. Salvucci. 2000. Rubisco activase constrains the photosynthetic potential of leaves at high temperature and CO_2. *Proceedings of the National Academy of Sciences* 97:13430–13435. doi: 10.1073/pnas.230451497

Cramer, W.A., J. Whitmarsh, and P.S. Low. 1981. Differential scanning calorimetry of chloroplast membranes: Identification of endothermic transition associated with the water-splitting complex of photosystem II. *Biochemistry* 20:157–162. doi: 10.1021/bi00504a026

Crowe, J.H., F.A. Hoekstra and L.M. Crowe. 1992. Anhydrobiosis. *Annual Review of Physiology* 54:579–599.

Dai, Y., B.B. Chen, Y. Meng, W. Zhao, Z. Zhou, M.O. Derrick, et al. 2015. Effects of elevated temperature on sucrose metabolism and cellulose synthesis in cotton fibre during secondary cell wall development. *Functional. Plant Biology* 42:909–919. doi: 10.1071/FP14361

Dar, W.D., and C.L.L. Gowda. 2013. Declining agricultural productivity and global food security. *Journal of Crop Improvement* 27:242–254. ISSN 1542- …

Daryanto, S., L. Wang, and P.A. Jacinthe. 2015. Global synthesis of drought effects on food legume production. *PLoS One* 10:e0127401. doi: 10.1371/journal.pone.0127401

Das, A., P.S. Basu, M. Kumar, J. Ansari, A Shukla, S. Thakur, P Singh, S. Datta, S.K. Chaturvedi, M.S Sheshshayee, K.C. Bansal, and N.P. Singh. 2021. Transgenic chickpea (Cicer arietinum L.) harbouring AtDREB1a are physiologically better adapted to water deficit. *BMC Plant Biology* 21:39. doi: 10.1186/s12870-020-02815-4

Delahunty, A., J. Nuttall, M. Nicolas, and J. Brand. 2015. Genotypic heat tolerance in lentil. In Proceedings of the 17th ASA Conference (Hobart), 20–24.

Devasirvatham, V., P.M. Gaur, N. Mllikarjuna, R.N. Tokachichu, R.M. Trethowan, and D.K.Y. Tan. 2012. Effect of high temperature on reproductive development of chickpea genotypes under controlled environments. *Functional Plant Biology* 39:1009–1018. doi: 10.1071/FP12033

Devasirvatham, V., Tan, D., Gaur, P.M., Raju, T., and R. Trethowan. 2012. High temperature tolerance in chickpea and its implications for plant improvement. *Crop and Pasture Science* 63:419–428. doi: 10.1071/CP11218

Dias, M.C., and W. Brüggemann. 2010. Limitations of photosynthesis in Phaseolus vulgaris under drought stress: Gas exchange, chlorophyll fluorescence and Calvin cycle enzymes. *Photosynthetica* 48:96–102.

Diaz, L.M., J. Ricaurte, E. Tovar, C. Cajiao, H. Terán, M. Grajales, J. Polanía, I. Rao, S. Beebe, and B. Raatz. 2018. QTL analyses for tolerance to abiotic stresses in a common bean (Phaseolus vulgaris L.) population. *PLoS ONE* 13:e0202342.

Doddamani, D., M. Katta, A. Khan, G. Agarwal, T. Shah, and R. Varshney. 2014. CicArMiSatDB: The chickpea microsatellite database. *BMC Bioinformatics* 15:212. doi: 10.1186/1471-2105-15-212

Emefiene, M.E., A.B. Salaudeen, and Y. Yusuf. 2013. The use of pigeon pea (Cajanus Cajan) for drought mitigation in Nigeria. *Academic Journal of Interdisciplinary Studies* 1:6–16. 10.5901/ajis.2013.v2n12p29

Fahad, S., A.A. Bajwa, U. Nazir, S.A. Anjum, A. Farooq, A. Zohaib, S. Sadia, W. Nasim, S. Adkins, S. Saud, M.Z. Ihsan, H. Alharby, C. Wu, D. Wang, and J. Huang. 2017. Crop production under drought and heat stress: Plant responses and management options. *Frontiers in Plant Science* 8:1147. doi: 10.3389/fpls.2017.01147

Fahad, S., S. Hussain, S. Saud, F. Khan, S. Hassan, and Amanullah. 2016. Exogenously applied plant growth regulators affect heat-stressed rice pollens. *Journal of Agronomy and Crop Science* 202:139–150. doi: 10.3389/fpls.2017.01147

FAO. 2017. The future of food and agriculture – Trends and challenges. Rome.

Farooq, M., M. Hussain, S. Ul-Allah, and K.H.M. Siddique. 2019. Physiological and agronomic approaches for improving water-use efficiency in crop plants. *Agricultural Water Management* 219:95–108.

Flower, D.J., and M.M. Ludlow. 1986. Contribution of osmotic adjustment to the dehydration tolerance of water-stressed pigeonpea (Cajanus cajan (L.) millsp.) leaves. *Plant Cell Environment* 9:33–40.

Fowden, I., T. Manstield, and J. Stoddart. 1993. Plant adaptation to environmental stress. Landan, pp. 109–132.

García, C.C., M. Guarnieri, and E. Pacini. 2013. Inter-conversion of carbohydrate reserves from pollen maturation to rehydration in a chili pepper. *American Journal of Plant Science* 4:1181–1186. doi: 10.4236/ajps.2013.46146

Gaur, P., S. Saminen, L. Krishnamurthy, S. Kumar, M. Ghane, S. Beebe, I. Rao, S K. Chaturvedi, P.S. Basu, H. Nayyar, V. Jayalakshmi, A. Babbar, and R. Varshney. 2015. High temperature tolerance in grain legumes. *Legume Perspectives* 7:23–24.

Gaur, P.M., C.L.L. Gowda, E.J. Knights, T.D. Warkentin, N. Acikgoj, S.S. Yadav, and J. Kumar. 2007. *Breeding acheivements, in chickpea Breeding and management* (Eds., SS Yadav and B. Redden, W. Chen and B. Sharma), CABI, Wallingford, pp. 391–416.

Gaur, P.M., J. Kumar, C.L.L. Gowda, S. Pande, K.H.M. Siddique, T.N. Khan, T.D. Warkentin, S.K. Chaturvedi, A.M. Than, and D. Ketema. 2008. Breeding chickpea for early phenology: Perspectives, progress and prospects. In Kharkwal MC (Ed.), *Food legumes for nutritional security and sustainable agriculture*, Vol. 2, (pp. 39–48). New Delhi, India: Indian Society of Genetics and Plant Breeding.

Gaur, P.M., Samineni, S., Thudi, M., Tripathi, S., Sajja, S., Jayalakshmi, V., Mannur, D.M., Vijayakumar, A.G., Ganga Rao, N.V.P.R., Ojiewo, C.O., Fikre, A., Kimurto, P., Kileo, R.O., Girma, N., Chaturvedi, S.K., Varshney, R.K., Dixit, G.P., and W. Link. 2019. Integrated breeding approaches for improving drought and heat adaptation in chickpea (Cicer arietinum L.). *Plant Breed* 138:389–400.

Giaveno, C., and J. Ferrero. 2003. Introduction of tropical maize genotypes to increase silage production in the central area of Santa Fe, Argentina. *Crop Breeding and Applied Biotechnology* 3:89–94.

Gupta, D.S., J. Kumar, S. Gupta, S. Dubey, P. Gupta, N.P. Singh, and G. Sablok. 2018. Identification, development and application of cross-species intron spanning markers in lentil (Lens culinaris Medik.). *The Crop Journal* 6: 299–305, ISSN 2214-5141. doi: 10.1016/j.cj.2017.09.004

Gupta, S., S. Kaur, S. Sehgal, A. Sharma, P. Chhuneja, and N.S. Bains. 2010. Genotypic variation for cellular thermotolerance in Aegilops tauschii Coss., the D genome progenitor of wheat. *Euphytica* 175:373–381. doi: 10.1007/s10681-010-0185-0

Hall, A.E. 1992. Breeding for heat tolerance. *Plant Breeding Review* 10:129–168.

Hamwieh, A., S.M. Udupa, A. Sarkar, C. Jung, and M. Baum. 2009. Development of new microsatellite markers and their application in the analysis of genetic diversity in lentils. *Breeding Science* 59:77–86. doi: 10.1270/jsbbs.59.77

Hasanuzzaman, M., K. Nahar, M.M. Alam, R. Roychowdhury, and M. Fujita. 2013. Physiological, bio-chemical, and molecular mechanisms of heat stress tolerance in plants. *International Journal of Molecular Science* 14:9643–9684. doi: 10.3390/ijms14059643

Hassan, M., and S. Mansoor. 2014. Oxidative stress and antioxidant defense mechanism in mung bean seedlings after lead and cadmium treatments.© TÜBİTAK. *Turkish Journal of Agriculture and Forestry* 38:55–61. doi: 10.3906/tar-1212-4

Heckathorn, S.A., S.A. Ryan, J.A. Baylis, D. Wang, E.W. Hamilton, and L. Cundiff. 2002. In vivo evidence from an Agrostis stolonifera selection genotype that chloroplast small heat-shock proteins can protect photosystem II during heat stress. *Functional Plant Biology* 29:935–946. doi: 10.1071/PP01191

Hedhly, A., J.I. Hormaza, and M. Herrero. 2008. Global warming and plant sexual reproduction. *Trends Plant Science* 14:30–36.

Hedhly, A. 2011. Sensitivity of flowering plant gametophytes to temperature fluctuations. *Environmental and Experimental Botany* 74:9–16. doi: 10.1016/j.envexpbot.2011.03.016

Horváth, I., A. Glatz, H. Nakamoto, M.L. Mishkind, T. Munnik, and Y. Saidi. 2012. Heat shock response in photosynthetic organisms: Membrane and lipid connections. *Progress in Lipid Research* 51:208–220. doi: 10.1016/j.plipres.2012.02.002. https: //doi.org/10.1071/FP17211

Hu, Z., R. Wang, M. Zheng, X. Liu, F. Meng, H. Wu, Y. Yao, M. Xin, H. Peng, Z. Ni, and Q. Sun. 2018. TaWRKY51 promotes lateral root formation through negative regulation of ethylene biosynthesis in wheat (Triticum aestivum L). *The Plant Journal* 96:372–388.

Hu, X., Y. Li, C. Li, H. Yang, W. Wang, and M. Lu. 2010. Characterization of small heat shock proteins associated with maize tolerance to combined drought and heat stress. *Journal of. Plant Growth Regulation* 29:455–464. doi: 10.1007/s00344-010-9157-9

Ilik P., Spundova M., Sicner M., Melkovicova H., Kucerova Z., P. Krchnak, et al. 2018. Methods Estimating heat tolerance of plants by ion leakage: a new method based on gradual heating. *New Phytologist* 218:1278–1287. doi: 10.1111/nph.15097

Incrocci, L., A. Pardossi, P. Vernieri, F. Tognoni, and Serra. 2000. Effects of heat stress and hypoxia on growth, water relations and ABA levels in bean (Phaseolus vulgaris L.) seedlings. *Acta Horticulturae* 516:31–39. doi: 10.17660/ActaHortic.2000.516.3

Ingram, J., and D. Bartels. 1996. The molecular basis of dehydration tolerance in plants. *Annual Review of Plant Physiology and Plant Molecular Biology* 47:377–403.

IPCC. 2013. Climate Change 2013: The Physical Science Basis. Contribution of Working Group I to the Fifth Assessment Report of the Intergovernmental Panel on Climate Change [Stocker, T.F., D. Qin, G.-K. Plattner, M. Tignor, S.K. Allen, J. Boschung, A. Nauels, Y. Xia, V. Bex and P.M. Midgley j (Eds.)]. Cambridge University Press, Cambridge, United Kingdom and New York, NY, USA, p. 1535.

Izanloo, A., A.G. Condon, P. Langridge, M. Tester, and T. Schnurbusch. 2008. Different mechanisms of adaptation to cyclic water stress in two South Australian bread wheat cultivars. *Journal of Experimental Botany* 59:3327–3346.

Jespersen, D., F. Belanger, and B. Huang. 2017. Candidate genes and molecular markers associated with heat tolerance in colonial Bentgrass. *Plos One* 12:e0171183. doi: 10.1371/journal.pone.0171183

Jin, R., Y. Wang, R. Liu, J. Gou, and Z. Chan. 2016. Physiological and metabolic changes of purslane (Portulaca oleracea L) in response to drought, heat, and combined stresses. *Frontiers in Plant Sciences* 6:1123.

Jukanti, A., P.M. Gaur, C.L.L. Gowda, and R. Chibbar. 2012. Nutritional quality and health benefits of chickpea (Cicer Arietinum L.): A review. *The British Journal of Nutrition* 108(Suppl 1):S11–S26. doi: 10.1017/S0007114512000797

Kakani, V.G., Prasad, P.V.V., Craufurd, P.Q. , and T.R. Wheeler. 2002. Resp onse of in vitro pollen germination and pollen tube growth of groundnut (Arachis hypogaea L.) genotypes to temperature. *Plant, Cell & Environment* 25:1651–1661. 10.1046/j.1365-3040.2002.00943.x

Kakani, V.G., K.R. Reddy, S. Koti, T.P. Wallace, P.V.V. Prasad, V.R. Reddy, and D. Zhao. 2005. Differences in in vitro pollen germination and pollen tube growth of cotton cultivars in response to high temperature. *Annals of Botany* 96:59–67. doi: 10.1093/aob/mci149

Kalaji, H.M., A. Rastogi, M. Živčák, A. Brestic, A. Daszkowska-Golec, K. Sitko, K.Y. Alsharafa, R. Lotfi, P. Stypiński, I.A. Samborska, and M.D. Cetner. 2018. Prompt chlorophyll fluorescence as a tool for crop phenotyping: An example of barley landraces exposed to various abiotic stress factors. *Photosynthetica* 56:953–961. doi: 10.1007/s11099-018-0766-z

Kalariya, K.A., A.L. Singh, N. Goswami, D. Mehta, M.K. Mahatma, B.C. Ajay, et al. 2015. Photosynthetic characteristics of peanut genotypes under excess and deficit irrigation during summer. *Physiology and Molecular Biology of Plants* 21:317–327. doi: 10.1007/s12298-015-0300-8

Kalendar, R., A.J. Flavell, T.H.N. Ellis, T. Sjakste, C. Moisy, and A.H. Schulman. 2011. Analysis of plant diversity with retrotransposon-based molecular markers. *Heredity* 106:520–530. doi: 10.1038/hdy.2010.93

Kalra, N., D. Chakraborty, A. Sharma, H.K. Rai, M. Jolly, S. Cher, K.P. Ramesh, S. Bhadraray, D. Barman, R.B. Mittal, M. Lal, and M. Sehgal. 2008. Effect of increasing temperature on yield of some winter crops in northwest India. *Current Science* 94:82–88.

Kashiwagi, J., L. Krishnamurthy, J.H. Crouch, and R. Serraj. 2006. Variability of root length density and its contributions to seed yield in chickpea (Cicer arietinum L.) under terminal drought stress. *Field Crops Research* 95:171–181.

Kashiwagi, J., L. Krishnamurthy, R. Purushothaman, H.D. Upadhyaya, P.M. Gaur, C.L.l. Gowda, O. Ito, and R.K. Varshney. 2015. Scope for improvement of yield under drought through the root traits in chickpea (Cicer arietinum L.). *Field Crops Research* 170:47–54.

Kaur, S., N.I. Cogan, A. Stephens, D. Noy, M. Butsch, J. Forster, et al. 2014. EST-SNP discovery and dense genetic mapping in lentil (Lens culinaris Medik.) enable candidate gene selection for boron tolerance. *Theoretical and Applied Genetics* 127:703–713. doi: 10.1007/s00122-013-2252-0

Kaur, R., T.S. Bains, H. Bindumadhava, and H. Nayyar. 2015. Responses of mungbean (Vigna radiata L.) genotypes to heat stress. Effects on reproductive biology, leaf function and yield traits. *Scientia Horticulturae* 197:527–541. doi: 10.1016/j.scienta.2015.10.015

Kaushal, N., K. Bhandari, K.H.M. Siddique, and H. Nayyar. 2016. Food crops face rising temperatures: An overview of responses, adaptive mechanisms, and approaches to improve heat tolerance. *Cogent Food and Agriculture* 2:1134380. doi: 10.1080/23311932.2015.1134380

Kavi Kishor, P.B., Z. Hong, G.H. Miao, C.A.A. Hu and D.P.S. Verma. 1995. Overexpression of Δ1-pyrroline-5-carboxylate synthetase increases proline production and confers osmotolerance in transgenic plants. *Plant Physiology* 108:1387–1394.

Kavi Kishore, P.B., S. Sangam, R.N. Amrutha, P.S. Laxmi, K.R. Naidu, K.R.S.S. Rao, et al. 2005. Regulation of proline biosynthesis, degradation, uptake and transport in higher plants: Its implications in plant growth and abiotic stress tolerance. *Current Science* 88:424–438.

Kimani, P.M., A. Benzioni, and M. Ventura. 1994. Genetic variation in pigeon pea (Cajanus cajan (L.) Mill sp.) in response to successive cycles of water stress. *Plant Soil* 158:193–201. doi: 10.1007/BF00009494

Kim, K. and A.R. Portis. 2005. Temperature dependence of photosynthesis in Arabid opsis plants with modifications in Rubisco activase and membrane fluidity. *Plant Cell Physiology* 46:522–530.

Kole, C., M. Muthamilarasan, R. Henry, D. Edwards, R. Sharma, M. Abberton, J. Batley, A. Bentley, M. Blakeney, J. Bryant, H. Cai, M. Cakir, L. Cseke, J. Cockram, A. Oliveira, C. Pace, H. Dempewolf, S. Ellison, P. Gepts, A. Greenland, A. Hall, K. Hori, S. Hughes, M. Humphreys, M. Iorizzo, A. Ismail, A. Marshall, S. Mayes, H. Nguyen, F. Ogbonnaya, R. Ortiz, A. Paterson, P. Simon, J. Tohme, R. Tuberosa, B. Valliyodan, R. Varshney, S. Wullschleger, M. Yano, and M. Prasad. 2015. Application of genomics-assisted breeding for generation of climate resilient crops: Progress and prospects. *Frontiers in Plant Science* 6. URL https://www.frontiersin.org/article/10.3389/fpls.2015.00563. doi: 10.3389/fpls.2015.00563

Koolachart, R., B. Suriharn, S. Jogloy, N. Vorasoot, S. Wongkaew, C.C. Holbrook, etal. 2013. Relationships between physiological traits and yield components of peanut genotypes with different levels of terminal drought resistance. *SABRAO Journal of Breeding and Genetics* 45:422–446. doi: 10.1016/j.fcr.2013.05.024

Krishnamurthy, L., Gaur, P.M., Basu, P.S., Chaturvedi, S.K., Tripathi, S., Vadez, V., Rathore, A., Varshaney, R.K., and C. Gowda. 2011. Large genetic variation for heat tolerance in the reference collection of chickpea (Cicer arietinum L.) germplasm. *Plant Genetic Resources: Characterization and Utilization* 9:59–69.

Kudapa, H., V. Garg, A. Chitikineni, and R.K. Varshney. 2018. The RNA-Seq-based high resolution gene expression atlas of chickpea (Cicer arietinum L.) reveals dynamic spatio-temporal changes associated with growth and development. *Plant Cell Environment* 41, 2209–2225.

Kumar, J., and H.A. Van Rheenen. 2000. A major gene for time of flowering in chickpea. *Journal of Heredity* 91:67–68.

Kumar, J., Basu, P.S., Gupta, S., Dubey, S., Sen Gupta, D., and S.N. Pratap. 2017. Physiological and molecular characterisation for high temperature stress in Lens culinar is. *Functional Plant Biology* 45:474–487.

Kumar, J., S.C. Sethi, C. Johansen, T.G. Kelly, M.M. Rehman, and H.A. van Rheenen. 1996. Potential of short-duration chickpea varieties. *Journal of Dryland Agriculture Research and Development* 11:28–32.

Kumar, J., A. Choudhary, D.S. Gupta, and S. Kumar. 2019. Towards exploitation of adaptive traits for climate-resilient smart pulses. *International Journal of Molecular Sciences* 20. doi: 10.3390/ijms20122971

Kumar, U., A.K. Joshi, M. Kumari, R. Paliwal, S. Kumar, and M.S. Roder. 2010. Identification of QTLs for stay green trait in wheat (Triticum aestivum L.) in the _Chirya 3' 9 _Sonalika' population. *Euphytica* 174:437–445. doi: 10.1007/s10681-010-0155-6

Kumar, S., P. Thakur, N. Kaushal, J.A. Malik, P.M. Gaur, and H. Nayyar. 2013. Effect of varying high temperatures during reproductive growth on reproductive function, oxidative stress and seed yield in chickpea genotypes differing in heat sensitivity. *k* 59:823–843. doi: 10.1080/03650340.2012.683424

Kumari, A., R. Kaur, and R. Kaur. 2018. An insight into drought stress and signal transduction of abscisic acid. *Plant Science Today* 5:72–80.

Kumawat, G., R.S. Raje, S. Bhutani, J.K. Pal, A.S. Mithra, K. Gaikwad, T.R. Sharma, and N.K. Singh. 2012. Molecular mapping of QTLs for plant type and earliness traits in pigeonpea (Cajanus cajan L. Millsp.). *BMC Genetics* 13:84.

Kurdali, F. 1996. Nitrogen and phosphorus assimilation, mobilization and partitioning in rainfed chickpea (Cicer arietinum L.). *Field Crops Research* 47:81–92.

Lamaoui, M., M. Jemo, R. Datla, and F. Bekkaoui. 2018. Heat and drought stresses in crops and approaches for their mitigation. *Frontiers in Chemistry*, 6:26–30.

Lamichaney, A., K. Tewari, P.S. Basu, P.K. Katiyar, and N.P. Singh. 2021. Effect of elevated carbon-dioxide on plant growth, physiology, yield and seed quality of chickpea (Cicer arietinum L.) in Indo-Gangetic plains. *Physiology and Molecular Biology of Plants* 27:251–263. doi: 10.1007/s12298-021-00928-0. Epub 2021 Feb 13. PMID: 33707867; PMCID: PMC7907398.

Landi, S., J.F. Hausman, G. Guerriero, and S. Esposito. 2017. Poaceae vs. abiotic stress: Focus on drought and salt stress, recent insights and perspectives. *Frontiers in Plant Science* 8:1214. doi: 10.3389/fpls.2017. 01214

Langjun, C., L. Jianlong, F. Yamin, X. Sheng, and Z. Zhen. 2006. High temperature effects on photosynthesis, PSII functionality and antioxidant activity of two Festuca arundinacea cultivars with different heat susceptibility. *Botanical Studies* 47, 61–69.

Lateef, E., M. Abdel, M. Abdel-Salam, M. Selim, M. Tawfik, A. El-Kramany, et al. 2018. Effect of climate change on mungbean growth and productivity under Egyptian conditions. *International Journal of Agriculture Forestry and Life Sciences* 2:16–23.

Leopold, A.C., M.E. Musgrave, and K.M. Williams. 1981. Solute leakage resulting from leaf desiccation. *Plant Physiology* 68:1222–1225.

Lípová, L., P. Krchňák, K.J. Josef, and P. Ilík. 2010. Heat-induced disassembly and degradation of chlorophyll-containing protein complexes in vivo. *Biochimica et Biophysica Acta* 1797:63–70. doi: 10.1016/j.bbabio. 2009.08.001

Lopez, F.B., C. Johansen, and Y.S. Chauhan. 1996. Effects of timing of drought stress on phenology, yield and yield components of short duration pigeonpea. *Journal of Agronomy and Crop Science* 177:311–320.

Lopez, F.B., T.M. Setter, and C.R. McDavid. 1987. Carbon dioxide and light response of photosynthesis in cowpea and pigeonpea during water deficit and recovery. *Plant Physiology* 85:990–995. doi: 10.1104/pp.85.4.990

Lu, F., M.C. Romay, J.C. Glaubitz, et al. 2015. High-resolution genetic mapping of maize pan-genome sequence anchors. *Nature Communications* 6:6914.

Lu, B., X.B. Chen, Y.C. Hong, H. Zhu, Q.J. He, B. Yang, et al. 2019. Identification of PRDX6 as a regulator of ferroptosis. *Acta Pharmacologica Sinica* 40: 1334–1342. doi: 10.1038/s41401-019-0233-9

Mallikarjuna, N., K.B. Saxena, and D.R. Jadhav. 2011. Cajanus. In Chittaranjan Kole (Ed.), *Wild crop relatives: Genomic and breeding resources - legume crops and forages.* Springer-Verlag Berlin Heidelberg.

Maxted, N., and S.P. Kell. 2009. *Establishment of a global network for the in situ conservation of crop wild relatives: Status and needs.* FAO Commission on Genetic Resources for Food & Agriculture, Roman, Italy.

Mazars, C., P. Thuleau, O. Lamotte, and S. Bourque. 2010. Cross-talk between ROS and calcium in regulation of nuclear activities. *Molecular Plant* 3:706–718.

Meriga, B., B. Krishna Reddy, K. Rajender Rao, L. Ananda Reddy, and P.B. Kavi Kishor. 2004. Aluminium-induced production of oxygen radicals, lipid peroxidation and DNA damage in seedlings of rice (Oryza sativa). *Journal of Plant Physiology* 161:63–68. doi: 10.1078/0176-1617-01156

Mia Mel, W., A. Yamauchi, and Y. Kono. 1996. Root system structure of six food legume species: Inter and intraspecific variations. *Japanese Journal of Crop Science* 65:131–140.

Minchin, F.R., Summerfield, R.J. , and M.C.P. Neves. 1980. Carbon metabolism, nitrogen assimilation and seed yield of cowpea [Vigna unguiculata (L.) Walp.] grown in an adverse temperature regime. *Journal of Experimental Botany* 31:1327–1345.

Mishra, B. 2007. Challenges and preparendness for increasing wheat production in India. *Journal of Wheat Research* I(1 and 2):1–12.

Mishra, S., R.K. Singh, A. Kalia, and S.R. Panigrahy. 2017. Impact of climate change on pigeon pea. *Economic Affairs* 62:455–457. doi: 10.5958/0976-4666.2017.00057.2

Mittler, R., A. Finka, and P. Goloubinoff. 2012. How do plants feel the heat? *Trends in Biochemical Sciences* 37:118–125.

Mohammed, A.-R., and L. Tarpley. 2009. Impact of high night time temperature on respiration, membrane stability, antioxidant capacity, and yield of rice plants. *Crop Science* 49:313–322.

Morison, J.I., N.R. Baker, P.M. Mullineaux, and W.J. Davies. 2008. Improving water use in crop production. *Philosophical Transactions of the Royal Society of London. Series B, Biological Sciences* 363:639–658. doi: 10.1098/rstb.2007.2175

Morran, S., O. Eini, T. Pyvovarenko, B. Parent, R. Singh, A. Ismagul, S. Eliby, N. Shirley, P. Langridge, and S. Lopato. 2011. Improvement of stress tolerance of wheat and barley by modulation of expression of DREB/CBF factors. *Plant Biotechnology Journal* 9:230–249.

Morton, F., R.E. Smith, and J.M. Poehlman. 1982. *The mungbean*. Department of Agronomy and Soils, University of Puerto Rico, Puerto Rico.

Moustaka, J., G. Ouzounidou, I. Sperdouli, and M. Moustakas. 2018. Photosystem II is more sensitive than photosystem I to Al3+induced phytotoxicity. *Materials* 11:1772. doi: 10.3390/ma11091772

Murata, N., S. Takahashi, Y. Nishiyama, and S.I. Allakhverdiev. 2007. Photoinhibition of photosystem II under environmental stress. *Biochimica et Biophysica Acta(BBA)–Bioenergetics* 1767:414–421. doi: 10.1016/j.bbabio.2006.11.019

Murchie, E.H., and T. Lawson. 2013. Chlorophyll fluorescence analysis: A guide to good practice and understanding some new applications. *Journal of Experimental Botany* 64:3983–3998. doi: 10.1093/jxb/ert208

Nam, N.H., Y.S. Chauhan, and C. Johansen. 2001. Effect of timing of drought stress on growth and grain yield of extra-short duration pigeonpea lines. *Journal of Agricultural Science* 136:179–189. doi: 10.1017/S0021859601008607

Nene, Y.L., and V.K. Sheila. 1990. Geography and importance. In Y.L. Nene, S.D. Hall, and V.K. Sheila (Eds.), *Pigeonpea* (pp. 1–14). Wallingford, UK: CAB Intl.

Obidiegwu J., G. Bryan, H. Jones, and A. Prashar. 2015. Coping with drought: Stress and adaptive responses in potato and perspectives for improvement. *Frontiers in Plant Science* 6:542. URL: https: //www.frontiersin.org/article/10.3389/fpls.2015.00542. doi: 10.3389/fpls.2015.00542; ISSN=1664-462X

Ohnishi, S., T. Miyoshi, and S. Shirai. 2010. Low temperature stress at different flower developmental stages affects pollen development, pollination, and pod set in soybean. *Environment and Experimental Botany* 69:56–62.

Okiror, M.A. 1986. Breeding for resistance to fusarium wilt of pigeon pea (Cajanus cajan L./MILLSP) in Kenya (Ph.D.thesis). University of Nairobi, Kenya.

Omae, H., Kumar, A., Egawa, Y., Kashiwaba, K. , and M. Shono. 2005. Genotypic differences in plant water status and relationship with reproductive responses in snap bean (Phaseolus vulgaris L.) during water stress. *Japanese Journal of Tropical Agriculture* 49:1–7.

Omae, H., A. Kumar, K. Kashiwaba, and M. Shono. 2006. Influence of high temperature on morphological characters, biomass allocation, and yield components in snap bean (Phaseolus vulgaris L.). *Plant Production Science* 9:200–205. doi: 10.1626/pps.9.200

Omae, H., A. Kumar, K. Kashiwaba, and M. Shono. 2007. Influence of temperature shift after flowering on dry matter partitioning in two cultivars of snap bean (Phaseolus vulgaris) that differ in heat tolerance. *Plant Production Science* 10:14–19.

Paliwal, R., M.S. Röder, U. Kumar, J.P. Srivastava, and A.K. Joshi. 2012. QTL mapping of terminal heat tolerance in hexaploid wheat (Triticum aestivum L.). *Theoretical and Applied Genetics* 125:561–575. doi: 10.1007/s00122-012-1853-3

Pang, J., N.C. Turner, T. Khan, Y.L. Du, J.L. Xiong, T.D. Colmer, R. Devilla, K. Stefanova, and K.H.M. Siddique. 2017. Response of chickpea (Cicer arietinum L.) to terminal drought: Leaf stomatal conductance, pod abscisic acid concentration, and seed set. *Journal of Experimental Botany* 68:1973–1985. doi: 10.1093/jxb/erw153

Parihar, A.K., A.K. Basandrai, A. Sirari, D. Dinakaran, D. Singh, K. Kannan, et al. 2017. Assessment of mungbean genotypes for durable resistance to yellow mosaic disease: Genotype × environment interactions. *Plant Breeding* 36:94–100. doi: 10.1111/pbr.12446

Parry, M.A., and M.J. Hawkesford. 2012. An integrated approach to crop genetic improvement. *Journal of Integrative Plant Biology* 54:250–259. doi: 10.1111/j.1744-7909.2012.01109.x. PMID: 22348899.

Paul, P.J., S. Samineni, M. Thudi, S.B. Sajja, A. Rathore, and R.R. Das. 2018a. Molecular mapping of QTLs for heat tolerance in chickpea. *International Journal of Molecular Science* 19:2166. doi: 10.3390/ijms19082166

Paul, P.J., S. Samineni, S.B. Sajja, A. Rathore, R.R. Das, A.W. Khan, et al. 2018b. Capturing genetic variability and selection of traits for heat tolerance in a chickpea recombinant inbred line (RIL) population under field conditions. *Euphytica* 214:27. doi: 10.1007/s10681-018-2112-8

Perdomo, J.A., S. Capó-Bauçà, E. Carmo-Silva, and J. Galmés. 2017. Rubisco and Rubisco activase play an important role in the biochemical limitations of photosynthesis in rice, wheat, and maize under high temperature and water deficit. *Frontiers in Plant Science* 8:490.

Pilon-Smits, E.A.H., J.M.E. Michel, J.P. Matthew, J.W.J. Marieke, J.W. Peter, and C.M.S. Sjef. 1995. Improved performance of transgenic fructan-accumulating tobacco under drought stress'. *Plant Physiology* 107:125–130.

Pinto, R.S., and M.P. Reynolds. 2015. Common genetic basis for canopy temperature depression under heat and drought stress associated with optimized root distribution in bread wheat. *Theoretical and Applied Genetics* 128:575–585. doi: 10.1007/s00122-015-2453-9

Ploeg Van der, A., and E. Heuvelink. 2005. Influence of sub-optimal temperature on tomato growth and yield: A review. *The Journal of Horticultural Science and Biotechnology* 80:652–659. doi: 10.1080/14620316.2005.11511994

Porch, T.G., and M. Jahn. 2001. Effects of high-temperature stress on microsporogenesis in heat-sensitive and heat-tolerant genotypes of Phaseolus vulgaris. *Plant Cell Environment* 24:723–731. doi: 10.1046/j.1365-3040.2001.00716.x

Pradhan, G.P., P.V.V. Prasad, A.K. Fritz, M.B. Kirkham, and B.S. Gill. 2012. Effects of drought and high temperature stress on synthetic hexaploid wheat. *Functional Plant Biology* 39:190–198.

Pradhan, B., K. Chakraborty, N. Prusty, D. Shakyawar, A. Mukherjee, K. Chattopadhyay, et al. 2019. Distinction and characterization of rice genotypes tolerant to combined stresses of salinity and partial submergence, proved by high resolution chlorophyll fluorescence imaging system. *Functional Plant Biology* 46, 248–261. doi: 10.1071/FP18157

Prasad, P.V.V., P.Q. Craufurd, V.G. Kakani, T.R. Wheeler, and K.J. Boote. 2001. Influence of high temperature during pre- and post-anthesis stages of floral development on fruit-set and pollen germination in peanut. *Australian Journal of Plant Physiology* 28:233–240.

Prasad, P.V.V., P.Q. Craufurd, and R.J. Summerfield. 1999. Fruit number in relation to pollen production and viability in groundnut exposed to short episodes of heat stress. *Annals of Botany* 84:381–386. doi: 10.1006/anbo.1999.0926

Prasad, P.V.V., K. Boote, L. Allen, and J., Thomas. 2002. Effects of elevated temperature and carbon dioxide on seed-set and yield of kidney bean (Phaseolus vulgaris L.). *Global Change Biology* 8:710–721. doi: 10.1046/j.1365-2486.2002.00508.x

Pratap, A., D.S. Gupta, B.B. Singh, and S. Kumar. 2013. Development of super early genotypes in greengram [Vigna radiata (L.)Wilczek]. *Legume Research* 36:105–110.

Pratap, A., S. Gupta, R.M. Nair, S.K. Gupta, R. Schafleitner, P.S. Basu, et al. 2019. Using plant phenomics to exploit the gains of genomics. *Agronomy* 9:126. doi: 10.3390/agronomy9030126

Prince, S.J., M. Murphy, R.N. Mutava, L.A. Durnell, B. Valliyodan, J.G. Shannon, and H.T. Nguyen. 2017. Root xylem plasticity to improve water use and yield in water-stressed soybean. *Journal of Experimental Botany* 68:2027–2036. doi: 10.1093/jxb/erw472

Priya M., O.P. Dhanker, K.H.M. Siddique, B. Hanumantha Rao, R.M. Nair, S. Pandey, S. Singh, R.K. Varshney, P.V.V. Prasad, and H. Nayyar. 2010. Drought and heat stress-related proteins: An update about their functional relevance in imparting stress tolerance in agricultural crops. *Theoretical and Applied Genetics* 132:1607–1638. doi: 10.1007/s00122-019-03331-2

Priya, M., O.P. Dhanker, K.H.M. Siddique, H. Bindumadhava, R. Nair, S. Pandey, S. Singh, R.K. Varshney, P.V.V. Prasad, and H. Nayyar. 2019. Drought and heat stress-related proteins: An update about their functional relevance in imparting stress tolerance in agricultural crops. *Theoretical and Applied Genetics* 132:1607–1638. doi: 10.1007/s00122-019-03331-2

Priyanka, B., K. Sekhar, V.D. Reddy, and K.V. Rao. 2010a. Expression of pigeonpea hybrid-proline-rich protein encoding gene (CcHyPRP) in yeast and arabidopsis affords multiple abiotic stress tolerance. *Plant Biotechnology Journal* 8:76–87.

Priyanka, B., K. Sekhar, T. Sunita, V.D. Reddy, and K.V. Rao. 2010b. Characterization of expressed sequence tags (ESTs) of pigeonpea (Cajanus cajanL.) and functional validation of selected genes for abiotic stress tolerance in arabidopsis thaliana. *Molecular Genetics and Genomics* 283:273–287.

Qiao, G., X.P. Wen, L.F. Yu, and X.B. Ji. 2011. The enhancement of drought tolerance for pigeon pea inoculated by arbuscular mycorrhizae fungi. *Plant Soil Environment* 57:541–546.

Rainey, K.M., and P.D. Griffiths. 2005a. Inheritance of heat tolerance during reproductive development in snap bean (Phaseolus vulgaris L.). *Journal of American Society of Horticultural Science* 130:700–706. doi: 10.21273/JASHS.130.5.700

Rainey, K., and P.D. Griffiths. 2005b. Evaluation of Phaseolus acutifolius A. Gray plant introductions under high temperatures in a controlled environment. *Genetic Resource and Crop Evolution* 52:117–120. doi: 10.1007/s10722-004-1811-2

Rakavi, B., and N. Sritharan. 2019. Physiological response of greengram under heat stress. *Journal of Pharmacognosy and Phytochemistry* SP1:181–185.

Ramamoorthy, P., Z. Mainassara, M. Nalini, P. Rajaram, L. Krishnamurthy, and C.L.L. Gowda. 2013. Root anatomical traits and their possible contribution to drought tolerance in grain legumes. *Plant Production Science* 16:1–8. doi: 10.1626/pps.16.1

Rampino, P., G. Mita, P. Fasano, G.M. Borrelli, A. Aprile, et al. 2012. Novel durum wheat genes up-regulated in response to a combination of heat and drought stress. *Plant Physiology and Biochemistry* 56:72–78. doi: 10.1016/j.plaphy.2012.04.006

Rana, J.C., N.K. Gautam, M.S. Gayacharan, R. Yadav, K. Tripathi, S.K. Yadav, N.S. Panwar, and R. Bhardwaj. 2016. Genetic resources of pulse crops in India: An overview. *Indian Journal of. Genetics and Plant Breeding* 76:420–436.

Rao, T.P., and O. Ito. 1998. Differences in root system morphology and root respiration in relation to nitrogen uptake among six crop species. *Japan Agricultural Research Quarterly: JARQ* 32:97–103.

Rawsthorne, S., P. Hadley, E.H. Roberts, and R.J. Summerfield. 1985. Effects of supplemental nitrate and thermal regime on the nitrogen nutrition of chickpea (Cicer arietinum L.) II: Symbiotic development and nitrogen assimilation. *Plant and Soil* 83:279–293.

Razia, G., A.B. Tauseef, A.S. Tahir, A.W. Owais, F. Suhail, N. Aijaz, A.A.. Saad, J. Seerat, N. Insha, and Rifat-un-Nisah. 2020. Climate change impact on pulse in India-A review. *Journal of Pharmacognosy and Phytochemistry* 9:3159–3166.

Redondo-Gómez, S. 2013. Abiotic and biotic stress tolerance in plants. In G.R. Rout, A.B. Das (Eds.), *Molecular stress physiology of plants* (pp. 1–20). New Delhi: Springer India.

Reynolds, M., S. Chapman, L.C. Herrera, G. Molero, S. Mondal, N.L. PequenoDiego, F. Pinto, F.J.P. Chavez, J. Poland, C.R. Amado, C.P. Saint, and S. Sukumaran. 2020. Breeder friendly phenotyping. *Plant Science* 295:110396.

Reynolds, M.P., C.S. Pierre, A.S.I. Saad, M. Vargas, and A.G. Condon. 2007. Evaluating potential genetic gains in wheat associated with stress-adaptive trait expression in elite genetic resources under drought and heat stress. *Crop Science* 47:S-172–S-189. doi: 10.2135/cropsci2007.10.0022IPBS

Reynolds, M.P., Y. Manes, A. Izanloo, and P. Langridge. 2009. Phenotyping for physiological breeding and gene discovery in wheat. *The Annals of Applied Biology* 155:309–320.

Rhodes, D., and A.D. Hanson. 1993. Quaternary ammonium and tertiary sulfonium compounds in higher plants. *Annual Review of Plant Physiology and Plant Molecular Biology* 44:357–384.

Richardson, M., K. Cowtan, E. Hawkins, and M.B. Stolpe. 2016. Reconciled climate response estimates from climate models and the energy budget of Earth. *Nature Climate Change* 6:931–935.

Ristic, Z., U. Bukovnik, and P.V. Prasad. 2007. Correlation between heat stability of thylakoid membranes and loss of chlorophyll in winter wheat under heat stress. *Crop Science* 47:2067–2073.

Ristic, Z., G. Yang, B. Martin, and S. Fullerton. 1998. Evidence of association between specific heat-shock protein(s) and the drought and heat tolerance phenotype in maize. *Journal of Plant Physiology* 153:497–505. doi: 10.1016/S0176-1617(98)80180-6

Rivero, R.M., T.C. Mestre, R. Mittler, F. Rubio, F. Garcia-Sanchez, and V. Martinez. 2014. The combined effect of salinity and heat reveals a specific physiological, biochemical and molecular response in tomato plants. *Plant Cell and Environment* 37:1059–1073.

Rodrigues, C.S., M. Laranjo, and S. Oliveira. 2006. Effect of heat and pH stress in the growth of chickpea Mesorhizobia. *Current Microbiology* 53:1–7.

Roy, S.J., E.J. Tucker, and M. Tester. 2011. Genetic analysis of abiotic stress tolerance in crops. *Current Opinion in Plant Biology* 14:232–239. doi: 10.1016/j.pbi.2011.03.002

Ryan, J.G. 1977. A global perspective on pigeonpea and chickpea sustainable production systems: Present status and future potential. In A.N. Asthana, and M. Ali (Eds.), *Recent advances in pulses research* (pp. 1–31). Kanpur: Indian Institute of Pulses Research.

Saha, S., V. Sehgal, S. Nagarajan, and M. Singh. 2012. Impact of elevated atmospheric CO_2 on radiation utilization and related plant biophysical properties in pigeon pea (Cajanus cajan L.). *Agricultural and Forest Meteorology* 158:63–70. doi: 10.1016/j.agrformet.2012.02.003

Saina, C.K., D.K. Murgor, and F. Murgor. 2013. Climate change and food security. In S. Silvern, and S. Young (Eds.), *Environmental change and sustainability*. IntechOpen. doi: 10.5772/55206

Saxena, K.B., A.K. Choudhary, R.K. Saxena, and R.K. Varshney. 2018. Breeding pigeonpea cultivars for intercropping: Synthesis and strategies. *Breeding Science* 68:159–167.

Sayan, S. 1991. Adaptive mechanisms of Blackgram (*Vigna mungo* (L.) Hepper) and pigeonpea (*Cajanus cajan* (L.) Millsp.) to water stress at different growth states. PhD Thesis, School of Land, Crop and Food Sciences, TheUniversity of Queensland. doi: 10.14264/uql.2017.579

Scafaro, A.P., P.A. Haynes, and B.J. Atwell. 2010. Physiological and molecular changes in Oryza meridionalis Ng., a heat-tolerant species of wild rice. *Journal of Experimental Botany* 61:191–202. doi: 10.1093/jxb/erp294

Schauberger, B., S. Archontoulis, A. Arneth, et al. 2017. Consistent negative response of US crops to high temperatures in observations and crop models. *Nature Communications* 8:13931.

Sekhar, K., B. Priyanka, V.D. Reddy, and K.V. Rao. 2010. Isolation and characterization of a pigeonpea cyclophilin (CcCYP) gene, and its over-expression in Arabidopsis confers multiple abiotic stress tolerance. *Plant, Cell and Environment* 33:1324–1338. doi: 10.1111/j.1365-3040.2010.02151.x

SenGupta, D., P.S. Basu, J. Souframanien, J. Kumar, P. Dhanasekar, S. Gupta, M. Pandiyan, S. Geetha, P. Shanthi, V. Kumar, and N.P. Singh. 2021. Morpho-physiological traits and functional markers based molecular dissection of heat-tolerance in urdbean. *Frontiers in Plant Science* 12:719381. doi: 10.3389/fpls.2021.719381

Sen Gupta, D., U. Singh, J. Kumar, Y.S. Shivay, A. Dutta, V.S. Sharanagat, et al. 2020. Estimation and multivariate analysis of iron and zinc concentration in a diverse panel of urdbean (Vigna mungo L. Hepper) genotypes grown under differing soil conditions. *Journal of Food Composition and Analysis* 93:103605. doi: 10.1016/j.jfca.2020.103605

Sharma, D.K., S.B. Andersen, C.O. Ottosen, and E. Rosenqvist. 2015. Wheat cultivars selected for high Fv/Fm under heat stress maintain high photosynthesis, total chlorophyll, stomatal conductance, transpiration and dry matter. *Physiologia Plantarum* 153:284–298. pmid:24962705.

Shen, B., R.G. Jensen, and H.J. Bohnert. 1997. Increased resistance to oxidative stress in transgenic plants by targeting mannitol biosynthesis to chloroplasts. *Plant Physiology* 113:1177–1183.

Siddique, K.H.M., S.P. Loss, K.L. Regan, and R.L. Jettner. 1999. Adaptation and seed yield of cool season grain legumes in Mediterranean environments of 5 south-western Australia. *Australian Journal of Agricultural Research* 50:375–387. doi: 10.1071/A98096

Singh, J., R. Kanaujia, and N.P. Singh. 2016. Pulse phytonutrients: Nutritional and medicinal importance. *Journal of Pharmacy and Nutrition Sciences* 6:160-160. doi: 10.6000/1927-5951.2016.06.04.5

Singh, R., and P. Jauhar (Eds.). 2005. *Genetic resources, chromosome engineering, and crop improvement.* CRC Press, Boca Raton. doi: 10.1201/9780203489284

Sinha, S.K. 1977. Food legumes: Distribution adaptability and biology of yield. In *Food and Agriculture Organisation of the United Nations, Plant Production and Protection Paper No. 3*, p. 124, FAO, Rome.

Sinha, A.K., M. Jaggi, B. Raghuram, and N. Tuteja. 2011. Mitogen-activated protein kinase signaling in plants under abiotic stress. *Plant Signaling & Behavior* 6:196–203. doi: 10.4161/psb.6.2.14701

Sita, K., A. Sehgal, H.R. Bindumadhava, R.M. Nair, P.V.V. Prasad, S. Kumar, P.M. Gaur, M. Farooq, K.H.M. Siddique, R.K. Varshney, and H. Nayyar. 2017. Food legumes and rising temperatures: Effects, adaptive functional mechanisms specific to reproductive growth stage and strategies to improve heat tolerance. *Frontiers in Plant Science* 8:1658. https://www.frontiersin.org/article/10.3389/fpls.2017.01658. doi: 10.3389/fpls.2017.01658

Smertenko, A., P. Draber, V. Viklicky, and Z. Opatrny. 1997. Heat stress affectsthe organization of microtubules and cell division in Nicotiana tabacumcells. *Plant Cell Environment* 20:1534–1542. doi: 10.1046/j.1365-3040.1997.d01-44.x

Smith, K.A., B.K. Ardelt, N.P.A. Huner, M. Krol, E. Myscich, and P.S. Low. 1989. Identification and partial characterization of the denaturation transition of the light harvesting complex II of spinach chloroplast membranes. *Plant Physiology* 90:492–499.

Song, L., Y. Jiang, H. Zhao, and M. Hou. 2012. Acquired thermotolerance in plants. *Plant Cell, Tissue and Organ Culture (PCTOC)*. 111. doi: 10.1007/s11240-012-0198-6

Song, Y., Q. Chen, D. Ci, X. Shao, and D. Zhang. 2014. Effects of high temperature on photosynthesis and related gene expression in poplar. *BMC Plant Biology* 14:111. doi: 10.1186/1471-2229-14-111

Srinivasan, A., H. Takeda, and T. Senboku. 1996. Heat tolerance in food legumes as evaluated by cell membrane thermostability and chlorophyll fluorescence techniques. *Euphytica* 88:35–45. doi: 10.1007/BF00029263

Subbarao, G.V., Y.S. Chauhan, and C. Johansen. 2000. Patterns of osmotic adjustment in pigeonpea-its importance as a mechanism of drought resistance. *European Journal of Agronomy* 12:239–249.

Subbarao, G.V., J.V.D.K. KumarRao, J. Kumar, C. Johansen, U.K. Deb, I. Ahmed, M.V. Krishna Rao, L. Venkataratnam, K.R. Hebbar, M.V.S.R. Sai, and D. Harris. 2001. *Spatial distribution and quantification of rice-fallows in South Asia-potential for legumes*. ICRISAT, Patancheru, India.

Suk, W.H., and V. Elizabeth. 2001. Hsp101 is necessary for heat tolerance but dispensable for development and germination in the absence of stress. *Plant Journal* 27:25–35. doi: 10.1046/j.1365-313x.2001.01066.x

Summerfield, R.J., R. Hadley, E.H. Minchin, and F.R.S. Awsthorne. 1984. Sensitivity of chickpea (Cicer arietinum) to hot temperatures during the reproductive period. *Experimental Agriculture* 20:77–93.

Sung, D.-Y., F. Kaplan, K.-J. Lee, and C.L. Guy. 2003. Acquired tolerance to temperature extremes. *Trends in Plant Science* 8:179–187.

Suzuki, K., H. Takeda, T. Tsukaguchi, and Y. Egawa. 2001. Ultrastructural study on degeneration of tapetum in anther of snap bean (Phaseolus vulgaris L.) under heat stress. *Sex Plant Reproduction* 13:293–299. doi: 10.1007/s004970100071

Suzuki, N., S. Koussevitzky, R. Mittler, and G. Miller. 2012. ROS and redox signalling in the response of plants to abiotic stress. *Plant Cell Environment* 35:259–270. doi: 10.1111/j.1365-3040.2011.02336.x

Suzuki, N., R.M. Rivero, V. Shulaev, E. Blumwald, and R. Mittler. 2014. Abiotic and biotic stress combinations. *New Phytology* 203:32–43. doi: 10.1111/nph.12797

Talwar, H.S., and S. Yanagahira. 1999. Physiological basis of heat tolerance during flowering and pod setting stages in groundnut arachis hypogaea L. JIRCAS Working Report, No. 14, pp. 47– 65. JJRCAS, Tsubuka, Japan.

Tarczynski, M.C., R.G. Jensen, and H.J. Bohnert. 1993. Stress protection of transgenic tobacco by production of the osmolyte mannitol. *Science* 259:508–510.

Thalmann, M., and D. Santelia. 2017. Starch as a determinant of plant fitness under abiotic stress. *New Phytology* 214:943–951.

Thiaw, S., and A.E. Hall. 2004. Comparison of selection for either leaf-electrolyte leakage or pod set in enhancing heat tolerance and grain yield of cowpea. *Field Crops Research* 86:239–253. doi: 10.1016/j.fcr.2003.08.011

Thudi, M., H.D. Upadhyaya, A. Rathore, P.M. Gaur, L. Krishnamurthy, M. Roorkiwal, S.N. Nayak, S.K. Chaturvedi, P.S. Basu, N.V. Gangarao, F. Asnake, K. Paul, P.C. Sharma, M.S. Sheshashayee, T. Satoshi, J. Kashiwagi, O. Ito, K. Andrzej, and R.K. Varshney. 2014. Genetic dissection of drought and heat tolerance in chickpea through genome-wide and candidate gene-based association mapping approaches. *PLoS ONE* 12:e0175609.

Tsukaguchi, T., Y. Kawamitsu, H. Takeda, K. Suzuki, and Y. Egawa. 2003. Water status of flower buds and leaves as affected by high temperature in heat tolerant and heat sensitive cultivars of snap bean (Phaseolus vulgaris L.). *Plant Production Science* 6:4–27.

Tuberosa, R. 2012. Phenotyping for drought tolerance of crops in the genomics era. *Frontiers in Physiology* 3:347. doi: 10.3389/fphys.2012.00347

Turner, N.C., G. Wright, and K.H.M. Siddique. 2001. Adaptation of grain legumes (pulses) to water-limited environments. *Advances in Agronomy* 71:193–231. doi: 10.1016/S0065-2113(01)71015-2

Upadhyaya, H.D., J. Kashiwagi, R. Varshney, P.M. Gaur, K. Saxena, L. Krishnamurthy, C. Laxmipathi Gowda, R. Pundir, S.K. Chaturvedi, P.S. Basu, and I.P. Singh. 2012. Phenotyping chickpeas and pigeonpeas for adaptation to drought. *Frontiers in Physiology* 3:179. doi: 10.3389/fphys.2012.00179

Vadez, V., A. Soltani, L. Krishnamurthy, and T.R. Sinclair. 2012. Modelling possible benefit of root related traits to enhance terminal drought adaption of chickpea. *Field Crops Research* 137:108–115. doi: 10.1016/j.fcr.2012.07.022

Valenzuela, H., and J. Smith 2002. Pigeonpea: Sustainable Agriculture Green Manure Crops Aug. 2002, SA-GM-8 Cooperative State Research, Education, and Extension Service, U.S. Department of Agriculture, and the Agricultural Experiment Station, Utah State University, under Cooperative Agreement 98-ESAG-1-0340. Portions of this text were adapted from the USDA Natural Resources Conservation Service Hawaii Field.

Valenzuela, H. 2011. *Pigeon peas: A multipurpose crop for Hawaii. Hanai'Ai/The Food Provider, CTAHR Sust. Agr. Newsl.* March-April-May edition, pp. 1–8. Univ. Hawaii Coop. Ext. Serv.

Vales, M.I., R.K. Srivastava, R. Sultana, S. Singh, I. Singh, G. Singh, S.B. Patil, and K.B. Saxena. 2012. Breeding for earliness in pigeonpea: Development of new determinate and nondeterminate lines. *Crop Science* 52:2507–2516.

Van Der Maesen, L.J.G. 1972. Cicer L.: A monograph of the genus, with special reference to the chickpea (Cicer arietinum L.) its ecology and cultivation / Mededelingen Landbouwhogeschool Wageningen.

Vanaja, M., P.R.R. Reddy, N.J. Lakshmi, S.K.A. Razak, P. Vagheera, G. Archana, S.K. Yadav, M. Maheshwari, and B. Venkateswarlu. 2010. Response of seed yield and its components of red gram (Cajanus cajan L. Millsp.) to elevated CO_2. *Plant Soil Environment* 56:458–462.

Vanaja, M., J. Narayana, M. Mandapaka, P. Vagheera, R. Pasala, M. Jyothi, S. Yadav, and B. Venkateswarlu. 2007. Effect of elevated atmospheric CO_2 concentration on growth and yield of balckgram (Vigna mungo L. Hepper) a rainfed pulse crop. *Plant Soil and Environment* 53:81–88.

Varshney, R., W. Chen, Y. Li, A. Bharti, R. Saxena, J. Schlueter, M. Donoghue, S. Azam, G. Fan, A. Whaley, A. Farmer, J. Sheridan, Aiko Iwata-O, Reetu Tuteja, R. Penmetsa, Wu, H.D. Upadhyaya, Shiaw-Pyng Yang, T. Shah, and S. Jackson. 2011. Draft genome sequence of pigeonpea (Cajanus cajan), an orphan legume crop of resource-poor farmers. *Nature Biotechnology* 30:83–89. doi: 10.1038/nbt.2022

Varshney, R.K., M.K. Pandey, A. Bohra, V.K. Singh, M. Thudi, and R.K. Saxena. 2019. Toward the sequence-based breeding in legumes in the post-genome sequencing era. *Theoretical and Applied Genetics* 132:797–816.

Venkatachalam, A., B. Meinhard, P. Selvarajah, and V. R. Reddy. 2012. *Climate change in Asia and the pacific how can countries adapt?* (Eds). Published by Vivek Mehra for SAGE Publications India Pvt Ltd, New Delhi. ISBN: 978-81-321-0894-8 (HB).

Wahid, A., S. Gelani, M. Ashraf, and M.R. Foolad. 2007. Heat tolerance in plants: An overview. *Environment and Experimental Botany* 61:199–223. doi: 10.1016/j.envexpbot.2007.05.011

Wang, J.Z., Cui, L.J., Wang, Y., J.L. Li . 2009. Growth, lipid peroxidation and photosynthesis in two tall fescue cultivars differing in heat tolerance. *Plant Biology* 53:247–242.

Wang, G.P., X.Y. Zhang, F. Li, Y. Luo, and W. Wang. 2010. Overaccumulation of glycine betaine enhances tolerance to drought and heat stress in wheat leaves in the protection of photosynthesis. *Photosynthetica* 48:117–126. doi: 10.1007/s11099-010-0016-5

Wang, F., A.G. Smith, and M.L. Brenner. 1993. Isolation and sequencing of tomato fruit sucrose synthase cDNA. *Plant Physiology* 103:1463–1464.

Wang, J., Y.T. Gan, F. Clarke, and C.L. McDonald. 2006. Response of chickpea yield to high temperature stress during reproductive development. *Crop Science* 46:2171–2178. doi: 10.2135/cropsci2006.02.0092

Wassmann, R., Jagadish, S., Sumfleth, K., Pathak, H., Howell, G., and A., Ismail. 2009. Regional vulnerability of climate change impacts on Asian rice production and scope for adaptation. *Advances in Agronomy* 102:91–133. doi:10.1016/S0065-2113(09)01003-7

Willits, D.H., and M.M. Peet. 2001.Measurement of chlorophyll fluorescence as a heat stress indicator in tomato: Laboratory and greenhouse comparisons. *Journal of American Society of Horticultural Science* 126:188–194. doi: 10.21273/JASHS.126.2.188

Yadav, R.C. 2017. Cropping practice and makeup shortfall of pulse production with reduced emission of green house gas nitrous oxide. *Archives in Chemical Research* 1:2.

Yan, W., and L. Hunt. 2010. Genotype by environment interaction and crop yield. *In book: Ch 4 Plant Breeding Reviews* 16:135–178. doi: 10.1002/9780470650110

Yıldız, M., and S. Terzioğlu. 2006. Heat shock of cultivated and wild wheat during early seedling stage: Growth, cell viability and heat shock proteins. *Acta Biologica Hungarica* 57:231–246. doi: 10.1556/ABiol.57.2006.2.10

Yoshida, T., N. Ohama, J. Nakajima, S. Kidokoro, J. Mizoi, and K. Nakashima. 2011. Arabidopsis HsfA1 transcription factors function as the main positive regulators in heat shock-responsive gene expression. *Molecular Genetics and Genomics* 286:321–332. doi: 10.1007/s00438-011-0647-7

Zandalinas, S.I., R. Mittler, D. Balfagon, V. Arbona, and A. Gomez-Cadenaz. 2018. Plant adaptations to the combination of drought and high temperatures. *Physiolgia Plantarum* 162:2–12.

Zhang, B., W. Li, X. Chang, R. Li, and R. Jing. 2014. Effects of favorable alleles for water-soluble carbohydrates at grain filling on grain weight under drought and heat stresses in wheat. *PLoS One* 9:e102917.

Zhang, L., Li, F.G., Liu, C.L. Zhang, C.J., and X.Y. Zhang. 2009. Construction and analysis of cotton (Gossypium arboreum L.) water-related cDNA library. *BMC Research Note* 2:120.

Zhang, X., X. Xu, Y. Yu, C. Chen, J. Wang, C. Cai, et al. 2016. Integration analysis of MKK and MAPK family members highlights potential MAPK signaling modules in cotton. *Scientific Reports* 6:29781. doi: 10.1038/srep29781

Zhao, F.C. 2013. Effects of heat stress during grain filling on sugar accumulation and enzyme activity associated with sucrose metabolism in sweet corn. *Acta Agronomica Sinica* 39:1644–1651. doi: 10.3724/SP.J.1006. 2013.01644

Zhu, J.K. 2016. Abiotic stress signaling and responses in plants. *Cell* 167:313–324. doi: 10.1016/j.cell. 2016.08.029

Index

For Product Safety Concerns and Information please contact our
EU representative GPSR@taylorandfrancis.com Taylor & Francis
Verlag GmbH, Kaufingerstraße 24, 80331 München, Germany